Work in France

Work in France

REPRESENTATIONS, MEANING, ORGANIZATION, AND PRACTICE

EDITED BY

Steven Laurence Kaplan

and Cynthia J. Koepp

Cornell University Press

ITHACA AND LONDON

First published 1986 by Cornell University Press.

International Standard Book Number 0–8014–1697–3
Library of Congress Catalog Card Number 85–22352
Printed in the United States of America
*Librarians: Library of Congress cataloging information
appears on the last page of the book.*

*The paper in this book is acid-free and meets the guidelines for
permanence and durability of the Committee on Production Guidelines
for Book Longevity of the Council on Library Resources.*

307394

To the workers of Vins de Postillon,
Ivry-sur-Seine, 1962

CONTENTS

Contents

PREFACE

Most of the essays collected in this book were first presented at Cornell University on 28–30 April 1983 as part of a conference entitled Representations of Work in France. By "representations" we intended not only language, iconography, and ideas about work, but also those activities that are called work (that represent work to members of a given society) as well as representations of those who practice (or avoid practicing) such activities. The conference demonstrated that "representations" could not be abstracted or separated from the whole tissue of the work experience: thus the four-part subtitle of this book.

Only in recent years has work received significant scholarly attention. Perhaps this is not surprising. Work seems to be such a common and pervasive fact of life that we often do not recognize that "what work is" is not self-evident. In the past twenty years or so, however, historians have begun to entertain a whole series of questions about the activity of work—some of which have rarely been addressed before. They are investigating work practices: the relation of the worker to his tools or machines, to other workers in the shop or factory, to supervisors, to customers, to the products he or she makes, to innovations in the production process. They are also considering the ways work has been organized and shaped from the outside: by police, by legislation, by definitions of work time, and by other external constraints. More general questions are finally being raised as well: What are the meanings of work? What is the (normative or legal) place of work in a society? What about hierarchies or dichotomies of work such as manual/intellectual, urban/rural, men's/women's? How does the organization of work relate to the larger organization of economic, social, and political institutions? And some historians have decided that "work on work" can benefit from new approaches like those of cultural anthropology; new theoretical undertakings, more often than not still oriented by positive or negative reference to Marxism, but in some cases leading to wholly new forms of social analysis; and new combinations of methodologies proper to intellectual, political, economic, and social history.

The purpose of our conference, then, was twofold: first, to serve as a forum for some of this recent scholarship on work, and second, to provide a moment for discussion that might stimulate further reflection and investigation. Like the conference itself, this book shares those two goals.

The chief sponsor of the conference was the Western Societies Program at Cornell University, which has acquired an international reputation for its promotion of research on European subjects. Precious support was also provided by the Ecole des Hautes Etudes en Sciences Sociales, the Maison des Sciences de l'Homme, and the Council for European Studies, and by the following institutions at Cornell: Society for the Humanities, Department of History, College of Arts and Sciences, University Lectures Committee, Department of Romance Studies, and School of Labor and Industrial Relations. In myriad ways John Weiss, director of the Western Societies Program, has helped us move from conference to publication.

For enriching the debate at the conference we are indebted to Stuart Blumin and John Weiss of Cornell's Department of History, to John Merriman of Yale's Department of History, to Maurice Garden of the University of Lyons II, and to Jeffry Kaplow of the University of Paris VIII.

We are grateful to Lawrence Malley and John Ackerman for their "book" wisdom and to Shirley Rice and Kathy Whigham for typing parts of the manuscript.

S. L. K.
C. J. K.

Ithaca, New York
Iowa City, Iowa

Work in France

France: Some cities and towns mentioned in this book

—1—

Introduction

CYNTHIA J. KOEPP and

STEVEN LAURENCE KAPLAN

Near the end of *Candide* the Turk, while describing his family's life on their twenty acres, remarks that "work protects us from three great evils: boredom, vice, and poverty." Pangloss, not one to miss the similarities between this exotic and idyllic plot of land and Eden, agrees that "man was not born to repose." Martin adds that "to work without thinking is the only way to make life endurable." And Candide himself, after reflecting upon his own misadventures and perhaps with the Turk's bountiful success in mind, concludes that all their talk is well and good but "il faut cultiver notre jardin." Thus Candide and his companions end their journeys and settle down to work their land.

How they arrived at cultivating their garden has less to do with work than with stuffing their pockets with the diamonds of El Dorado. No, in *Candide* there are few clues that labor has anything to do with acquiring property or wealth. Indeed the dominant structure of the text occludes this insight. Yet work is nevertheless offered as a solution to problems in other areas. As philosopher and social theorist, Voltaire posits work as an agency of social control, the antidote to vice, ennui, and want; as storyteller, he uses work as a device to solve the problem of narrative closure. At precisely the moment Candide and his friends begin to labor in their garden, the narrative stops. Eating pistachios and candied fruit from the Turk's harvest is one thing, but actually plowing the fields, planting the seeds, weeding the plants, and pruning the trees in the blistering sun do not make for a good story. Narration and work are antithetical activities.

Although the Turk may say that work helps us avoid boredom, by not showing us any work Voltaire seems to imply that work itself is uninteresting, or at least that reading and writing about it are. Whether or not he is right, no scholar can ignore the challenge. Certainly we should not be surprised that *Candide* ends when work begins, for the things that labor ostensibly guards against—idleness, crime, and poverty—are the very elements that often generate our plots.

A few scholars have perceived that *Candide* is somehow a book about work, indeed the work ethic, and have taken the final passage at face value: that tending one's garden is Candide's answer to evil in the world. Yet the movement of the novel as a whole, and the bitter irony throughout, seems to belie that very understanding. Even the Turk's simple pronouncement on the virtue of work—in a story whose subtitle is "or Optimism"—has a negative or "pessimistic" quality that should not be overlooked. There is virtually no sense of work as philosophically positive, as aesthetically creative, or as enhancing one's moral worth. The virtue of work is extolled only at the end of the story, and even then primarily in terms of prophylactic or privative utility. It is true that after the violence, cruelty, and vertiginous irony of the earlier passages the garden scene comes as no little relief. But Adam's curse—to toil in the fields—has finally caught up with Candide and his friends, and the tedious business of survival in their Eden has, ironically, just begun.

Although it would be a mistake to read *Candide* as the universal metaphor for the meaning of work in eighteenth-century France, it does provide a seminal example of the complex baggage bound up with the concept. What is especially interesting for historians of work is the way echoes of pejorative attitudes toward work inherited from classical and religious sources undermine newer, more positive notions of work current in eighteenth–century economic theory. Take, for example, the way the narrator mystifies the connection between labor and wealth. What allows the characters to travel from place to place? What enables them to ransom their companions from bondage? Or, if you prefer, what force drives the narrative forward? Consorting with the rich and powerful or finding diamonds in the streets!

Only for one fleeting moment, when Candide and Cacambo meet a black slave who describes his life in a sugar mill, do we find an unsettling scene of recognition of what work really means to both eighteenth-century Europeans and Africans.[1] The black man tells of the punishments meted out by his Dutch owner: a hand cut off for tasting the

---

[1]This chapter, unlike others in its lucidity about the connections between labor and wealth, did not appear in the earlier drafts of *Candide* but apparently was added shortly after Voltaire read a passage on slavery in *De l'esprit* by Helvetius in the fall of 1758. To compare the remarkably similar language, see the introduction to the critical edition of *Candide*, edited by René Pomeau, *Candide, ou l'Optimisme* (Paris, 1979), pp. 38–39.

sugar, a leg cut off for attempting to escape. No mild platitudes about the virtue of work here. Work is cruel, debased, inhuman, an activity performed by slaves. Only here is a flickering, tacit admission that labor power produces wealth, but it is wealth produced by slaves, only to be confiscated by the master. And at what cost? As the black man laconically comments, referring to his severed limbs, "This is the price of the sugar you eat in Europe." In *Candide*, then, work is signified as an absence: the black man's missing hand and leg. Thus work represents the precise conjuncture where the adventures must stop.

Now, insofar as Voltaire's narrator emphasizes the negative aspects of work and obscures the relation between labor and wealth, he is further from his near contemporaries across the channel[2] and closer to the writers of classical antiquity, who rarely recognized labor as a positive source of wealth. Indeed, the ancients associated labor with poverty, observing self-prophetically that only the needy had to work. They perceived wealth not as a product of labor, but rather as something derived from inheritance or conquest, or perhaps, as in Candide's case, dumb luck. Similarly, the Turk's comment that work helps us avoid evil reformulates the Christian tenet that "idleness is the mother of all vice"— an axiom endlessly intoned by moralists and administrators throughout the eighteenth century. Insofar as it opposes *oisiveté*, work helps keep one out of trouble. In Old Regime France, work functioned as a means of social classification and social control. One's place in the hierarchy of work defined one's behavior in the complex nexus of social, political, and economic relations and thus gave at least the illusion of a stable and predictable social order. And work contributed to public order too, since it kept people occupied, their actions accountable to their immediate superiors and to the police. The nervousness of the police on holidays when workers were "free" to roam, drink, and disrupt neighborhoods stands as further evidence of the utility of work. In this sense *Candide* refers to the mischief, evil, and disasters that follow when people are not tied to a workplace. But Christian theology rationalized work in moral terms: as duty to one's fellowman, as a means of charity for the needy, as activity increasing individual self-discipline, self-reliance, and moral fortitude. Working in Candide's garden, on the other hand, diminishes moral responsibility, for at the end Candide and his companions purchase their own peace of mind at the cost of any concern either with others or with the recognized evils of a world so demonstrably in need of remedy.

---

[2] Adam Smith's *Wealth of Nations* (1776), a treatise asserting that labor was the source of all wealth, was still two decades away. However John Locke, in the *Second Treatise of Government* (1690), had argued persuasively that labor was the true source of property, and Voltaire was a great student of Locke.

It is in the light of this profound ethical problematic that one genuinely new notion of work (one first expounded in the late seventeenth century and early eighteenth century, especially by the philosophes) appears in *Candide* in its full irony. It is the belief that work helps one avoid boredom. Obviously the relevance of this observation is confined to a limited spectrum of society. The great majority of workers in eighteenth–century France had no luxury of choosing "interesting" work. And in contrast to the philosophes' speculations, most people expressed (in story, song, or myth) the desire to be released from their labors, not their ennui. Yet that some theorists perceived boredom as a problem in the first place and, further, offered work as its cure indicates that the evaluation of work and leisure was at some level undergoing a conceptual and social shift.

From Greek myths through peasant folktales, paradise had often been conceived of as a place where no one had to work. Even in most conceptions of Eden, Adam somehow tended the garden without effort and certainly without pain. Yet myths and fairy tales are also populated with deformed workers silently bearing witness to the sheer physical cost of manual labor. Weavers are made nearly blind from their toils at the loom, and spinners' hands and feet are misshapen after years of working the thread. The ultimate prize won in these folktales is, if anything, some vague happiness guaranteed by material comforts, ensuring that tedious and painful labor will no longer be required for survival. And there is the El Dorado of *Candide*, where people do not pray to God, but merely thank him for providing for their every need. El Dorado is a society with no prisons, no pain, no poverty. But compare Candide's response. He gets tired of El Dorado after one month and leaves, preferring to trade this utopia for what he knows to be an evil and unhappy world. Like Samuel Johnson's Prince Rasselas of Abyssinia, one simply becomes bored with "Happy Valley" because work is not necessary there, and one needs *something* to do.

In the social structure of *Candide*, then, as in Samuel Johnson's short essay, work is a source of unhappiness both for those who do work and for those who don't. These stories, as well as the myths, religious allegories, and folktales circulating in France during the eighteenth century, reveal a deep confusion in the understanding of the meaning of work, one riddled with contradictory variants. Work is demeaning, yet work is a source of dignity. Paradise is the place where no one has to work, yet paradise without work is tiresome. Work encourages good morals, yet work diminishes moral responsibility. Work keeps one out of trouble, yet workers are inherently troublesome and disruptive. Work is Adam's curse, yet work is the very source of wealth, felicity, and culture.

Voltaire's *Candide* represents these multiple and seemingly incompatible notions of work in a single text. Written in 1759, *Candide* was symptomatic both in its revealing and its repressing of our topic. In mid-eighteenth-century France, many of the most hotly contested social debates implicitly (or explicitly) advanced ostensibly new positive (or negative) valorizations of work while at the same time retaining remnants of attitudes more or less consciously inherited from the classical and Christian traditions. Abstract discussions about slavery or noble status or guild organizations were (whether their participants knew it or not) in fact about contemporary and concrete social structures and hierarchies and the role that work and the economy played in maintaining and challenging those distinctions. Just as *Candide* ends when work in the garden begins, and just as subsequent historians and scholars avoided addressing the role of work and workers until the late nineteenth century, many of the eighteenth-century debates obscured and denigrated the value of manual (especially artisanal) work even as they stressed its utility in keeping order and guarding morals and the body politic.[3]

One such contested topic was the relatively new political economy. And discussion of it was initially dominated by the physiocrats. Guided by François Quesnay, the physiocrats constructed an abstract theoretical model of a market economy that sharply differentiated urban work from rural, artisan from farmer. For Quesnay the only authentically productive work was agricultural. Only nature—admittedly with the help of human labor—could produce a genuine surplus, and thus it was the true source of wealth. The physiocrats further believed that cultivating the land encouraged moral development, for the closer one was to nature, the more likely it was that one would divine the natural laws that govern the physical and moral order of the universe. By contrast, commerce and manufacturing were "sterile," nonproductive, and (not surprisingly) morally corrupting and profane. Incapable of yielding a "real" surplus, they served primarily to circulate necessary commodities throughout society. Although we do not want to underestimate the numerous continuities that persisted from mercantile theory and practice to physiocracy (and even to capitalism), physiocrats nevertheless made a substantial break with mercantilists, who located wealth in money and precious metals, favored luxury trades, and urged diverting investment from agriculture to industry. Despite all their rhetoric in praise of the moral and economic benefits of farming, the physiocrats were ambiguous when it came to the respect and esteem owed agricultural work and workers. In general, they ignored the large number of small peasant proprietors already tilling the land and instead encouraged a new group of entre-

---

[3]The analysis of *Candide* and following discussion of physiocracy, nobles, the church, beggars, guild organization, and the *Encyclopédie* are part of a larger project by Cynthia Koepp investigating notions and attitudes toward work in eighteenth-century France.

preneurial farmers whose large-scale operations would attract wealth and investment. But did work on the soil ennoble the farmer? The physiocrats were unwilling to address this question frankly. Further, some of these same theorists advocated barely subsistence "ironclad" wages, believing that the laboring classes must be kept poor lest they become unindustrious—hardly an argument to "elevate" attitudes toward work, especially given the low place afforded commerce and industry in physiocratic doctrine.

Also at midcentury the Abbé Coyer published *La noblesse commerçante* (1756). This essay, urging that the nobility be encouraged to participate in commerce, touched off a great debate between those who sided with the Abbé and those who believed that the nobility would be compromised by engaging in commercial ventures and trade.[4] But when Coyer questioned the utility of the traditional practice dictating that to preserve one's noble rank one had to be "oisif," he also implicitly challenged the underlying system of social classification and representation based on distinction and privilege, conferred and conveyed by one's activity in society (whether work or something else). The issue was never that rank was defined by whether one worked or was idle, but whether one was *supposed* to work or be idle, according to the normative schema inherent in the ideal of the three estates. For some nobles the idea of participating in commerce was synonymous with taxonomical self-mutilation. Their traditional distinctions, they argued, were necessary for society's "equilibrium." Others disagreed. Moralists and churchmen observed that idleness led to vice and debauchery, even among elites, and political economists measured noble "oisiveté" in terms of a net loss of potential revenues. For decades the monarchy had quietly proposed its own incentives to encourage commerce and industry, offering to ennoble a few very successful merchants while at the same time eliminating the penalty of *dérogeance* for nobles who engaged in large-scale trade.

Indeed, by the eighteenth century, a certain confusion had crept into practice and language. To live "*bourgeoisement*" meant living off annuities and other noncommercial investments, essentially the same as "*vivant noblement.*" To reach that *état*, however, a person (most often a merchant) was in the paradoxical position of having to work all the more assiduously to create a successful business that could later be sold in exchange for an estate and the chance to live "like a noble." One earned the right to

---

[4]Voltaire participated in—indeed almost initiated—this debate in 1750 when he wrote *Anglomanie*, an essay in which he took a stand in favor of a commercial nobility, like that existing in England. The Marquis de Lassay condemned Voltaire for his position in a 1754 issue of the *Mercure*. But Coyer's essay proved to be the catalyst that began the controversy in earnest. See Leonard Adams, "Coyer and the Enlightenment," *Studies on Voltaire and the Eighteenth Century* 123 (1974): 11–197.

be idle through hard work. Ironically, this striving for noble status was going on at a time when reformers (like Coyer) were challenging the value and validity of the second estate and (when it served its purposes) even the monarchy was making sporadic attempts to raise the esteem of work. In any case, the controversy over Coyer's essay provided a crucial forum for those who felt that an end to dérogeance would benefit both nobles and the nation, and for its critics, who charged that noble honor (and thus the category of nobility itself) was at stake, thereby resurrecting all the old prejudices against work held by the traditional aristocracy and its defenders.

Another common topic of discussion concerned those who did not work: the beggars and vagabonds. In theory the church had always been tolerant of the humble, unfortunate beggar to whom others might give alms and thus earn salvation. By the early eighteenth century or even earlier, however, the problem of beggary had become so widespread and immense that both church and civil authorities began to advocate harsher treatment, sometimes even ignoring the long-recognized distinctions between able-bodied "professional" beggars and genuine victims of circumstance, the *pauvres honteux* who begged only as a last resort and indeed were ashamed to do so. In countless tracts, treatises, and edicts devoted to the issue of eradicating begging in France, authors warned that mendicancy, a source of moral decay, could lead to great disorder in society. Like prostitutes and criminals, beggars were considered outside the institutions that normally limited and prescribed social behavior. As people who refused to work, and indeed who often could beg as much in a day as a laborer could earn (and enjoy a kind of personal autonomy as well), beggars represented one segment of the population that could not easily be "incorporated" into the social structure (though in some places they were taxed!). Furthermore, there was always the fear that the beggar's life of idleness would appeal to others and, like a contagion, would spread and contaminate the whole. Those who faced seasonal unemployment or unexpected *chomage* (voluntary or unwelcome) could find through begging entry into a netherworld of professional beggars, vagabonds, prostitutes, and other *gens sans condition*, a floating population that continually confounded the police and authorities. We should not be surprised, then, that the most commonly proposed solution for mendicancy in the eighteenth century was *work* itself, often forced labor, which it was hoped would put an end to the beggar's pernicious idleness and threatening geographical mobility and instead would encourage discipline, good morals, and maybe even profit.

During the eighteenth century, debate also arose among churchmen horrified by the encroaching values of the new economic order. To a church accustomed to setting the limits on what was permitted and what was not, the new political economy posed a real threat: it had its own rules, its own internal logic, and seemingly no limits. There was no room for fraternity in the marketplace and none for charity either. As a steward of social theory (and at the same time social practice), the church taught that divine providence determined each individual's immutable place within the Great Chain of Being. Priests sermonized to those born rich and born poor but did not seem to admit that a person born into modest beginnings could, by the end of life, have amassed a sizable fortune. In addition, part of the value of work in Catholic theology was its harsh and painful aspects, which presumably aided in weaning man's affection away from "this-worldly" concerns towards thoughts of salvation. But what could it say to this (somewhat) new creature, the relatively mobile bourgeois, who related to God in terms of his profession, by working in the world? For him there was no sense that an ultimately inscrutable God had solely determined his station in life. Through his self-confidence, his ambition, and a belief in his ability to manage his own affairs, the self-made man put the guardians of Catholic theology on the defensive.[5] And to turn the tables even further, by the latter half of the eighteenth century even the clergy were being criticized, like beggars and nobles, for being idle and unproductive members of society.

One seminal publishing event also posed the crucial question of work. In 1751 the first volume of Diderot's *Encyclopédie* appeared. According to its editors' lengthy introduction, this monumental project was committed to gaining "respect" for the long-neglected arts and sciences. Consequently, in the various articles of the *Encyclopédie*, the editors described in great detail the techniques and practices of the manual arts, in hopes of raising the esteem of "the lowly artisan to whom all society was in debt." Their efforts were not unambiguous, however, for the entries in the *Encyclopédie* emphasized work processes and technological advances, usually with significantly more praise for the tools and machines themselves than for those who operated them.

A last topic of controversy concerns the attack on the guilds that began to gather steam at midcentury. From physiocrats arguing for "liberté" in all aspects of the economy to Diderot's fears that work techniques kept secret would obstruct progress in the mechanical arts and to philosophes complaining of corrupt and unfair corporate practices, the crit-

[5]For a rich discussion of the disputes between neo-Augustinian Jansenists who refused to compromise their doctrine with new bourgeois sensibilities and the Jesuits who—to some extent—did, see Bernard Groethuysen, *The Bourgeois: Catholicism vs. Capitalism in Eighteenth-Century France*, trans. Mary Ilford (New York, 1968), especially pp. 78–101, 155–90. Groethuysen shows the ways Jansenist and Jesuit teachings were and were not compatible with bourgeois values and further claims that the lengthy debate between these rival persuasions helped to generate disbelief among an increasing number of the "Enlightenment" bourgeoisie.

icism against the guild system, like that leveled against the idle nobility, was a direct threat to the traditional organization of society, based (at all levels) on a corporate model. Those in favor of abolition recognized that the processes of the arts and crafts were not static but changing, or at least could change if enlightened knowledge were to participate in their progress and reorganization. Others saw this same potential for transformation as worrisome. For them the end of the guilds would mean the end of a clearly defined network of relationships, attitudes, and expectations among masters, journeymen, and apprentices, on the one hand, and buyers and sellers, on the other. Without the safeguard of the corporations, they wondered, how would workers' insubordination be kept under control? How would the standards of the arts and crafts be maintained?

By the time *Candide* appeared, then, moralists and theorists, monarchs and reformers, public officials and prelates, encyclopedists and physiocrats had begun to recognize—implicitly, when not explicitly—the importance of work both as a concept of political economy and as an economic and social necessity. For centuries theologians and philosophers, from Plato to Pascal, had speculated on the social and moral significance of work. But *Candide* is symptomatic of the fact that by the mid-eighteenth century a confused legacy of attitudes toward work inherited from classical and feudal times and from religion clashed head-on with newer social, economic, and psychological realities. One way to conceptualize this confrontation (although historians are sometimes hesitant to do so) is to invoke the changing dynamics of early capitalism. Even if we cannot define capitalism per se, we can at least speculate about capitalist ideology. We have learned that it is not inappropriate to discuss changes in attitudes, in modes of production, and in corporate relations in the context of eighteenth-century France. Indeed it is important that we do so, for all the transformations associated with early capitalism are crucial for our understanding of what work means in the eighteenth century and thereafter. The physiocrats' emphasis on huge enterprise and investment, the echoes of managerial interests in the *Encyclopédie*, the attacks on nobles, mendicants, and clergy for being idle and nonproductive, the desire for free trade, the crystallization of sharper notions of property, the articulation of a theory of social individualism, the abolition of the guilds, the fear of workers' insubordination, and the search for new labor and capital markets are all inextricably linked to the social triumph of capitalistic forms and relations.

Toward the end of the eighteenth century many of these very tendencies accelerated their pace. And though we do not want to reduce the aftermath of 1789 to a simple victory of the dynamics of capital—it is obvious that the Revolution in many ways retarded the triumph of capitalism even as it created the conditions of its possibility—the French Revolution nevertheless makes visible many of the mutations that will later coalesce into full-blown capitalism. For example, anxieties about workers' potential for violence and a belief in their great insubordination throughout the eighteenth century indicate a recognition of the political, psychological, and economic threat workers posed for a society dependent upon the goods they produced and the services they performed. In 1791 the revolutionaries defused that potential power by enacting legislation that radically fragmented the corporate world of work as it sought to ensure freedom of commerce and the liberty of each citizen—in this case, the right of an individual to practice any craft or profession without the restrictions (or privileges) incumbent in the guild system. The first law, d'Allarde's, which completely abolished the corporations, was probably more disquieting to the masters than to the journeymen, for it deprived them of their social identity and privileges in addition to dismantling the *police des métiers*, leaving them disarmed vis-à-vis their workers. To make matters worse, for a short time the journeymen's brotherhoods (such as compagnonnage) remained untouched by the laws, which meant that workers could organize in opposition to masters who could not. The Le Chapelier law two months later reassured the masters and reinforced their position somewhat, since it forbade workers the right to assemble or to join in work-related associations of any type. With the corporations dissolved and workers' coalitions outlawed, society from now on would be composed of "equal," atomized individuals, free to pursue their own self-interest and negotiate their own contracts without appeal to a collective entity.

From the point of view of the workers, then, the French Revolution was a great equivocation. It gave them something they wanted: an *état politique*. Yet their nascent class consciousness was conveniently diverted into a civic consciousness, and soon after emancipation came frustration, not to mention conscription into the citizens' army. The workers were incorporated in the new nation, but not into the new society. And "incorporation" was now a strictly bureaucratic affair.

Here we might mention the phenomenon of the *sans-culottes* as a complex symbol of the confusion about work and workers both in the new order and in work historiography. Recently historians have begun to question the standard interpretation of the sans-culottes, which assumes that relations between masters and journeymen in the workplace before the French Revolution determined their political relations and activities during the Revolution—specifically, for example, that by (allegedly) living under the master's roof, eating at his table, and seeing the world through his eyes the journeyman came to adopt a similar petty bourgeois mentality. Granted the relationship between masters and journeymen is a central issue throughout the eighteenth century; but the thesis at hand tends to reason backward by inferring the reality of earlier workshop relations from the later revolutionary discourse of and about the sans-culottes. In fact we still know very little about how masters and journeymen got along, how they lived together day to day in the Old Regime. And we have yet to consider the extent to which other factors (corporate ideology or the political and institutional aspects of guild membership, for example) also helped prepare the future sans-culottes for the revolutionary activities they eventually pursued. In any case, what we do know of the sans-culottes—their complex ideology of radical democracy and their obsession with national unity, their intense fraternal loyalty and their vehement hatred of the *idle* rich, their bringing together the unlikely combination of master and journeyman, petty proprietor and wage earner—continues to challenge historians to rethink those relationships, as it also demonstrates the tensions between liberty and equality and the difficulty of accommodating a collective public will with individual interest. Even if the problematic of the sans-culottes does not speak to all the ambiguities of the French Revolution, it reminds us that the Revolution was far from a simple resolution of the full complexity of the question of work, and much more a failure to reconcile capitalist ambitions with the goals of a fraternal society. Other attempts at resolution would follow.

Even during the Revolution, Gracchus Babeuf perceived some of the contradictions inherent in the new order and was one of the first to form a coherent alternative ideology. Going beyond the Jacobins and sans-culottes, Babeuf recognized the inability of a society committed to private property and economic liberty to guarantee basic human needs to all its members. Thus Babeuf's Conspiracy of Equals urged communal management of property and stressed distribution of commodities. Each person would be required to work, and each would share equally the basic necessities of life. Although Babeuf was ultimately defeated and was executed in 1797, his ideas proved the inspiration for a number of nineteenth- and twentieth-century socialists and communists.

After the Revolution and Napoleon's demise, the legacy for work was still an ambiguous one as theorists—provoked by a complex amalgam of material conditions, the rhetoric of 1789, and Christian or humanitarian principles—tried to formulate new ways of organizing work and society that would foster social as well as civil justice. In the new society the phrase, "Liberty, Equality, Fraternity" referred exclusively to political and civil values, but many thought it should extend to social and economic realities as well. Thus, at just the time when new groups in society—petty bourgeois and proletariat—were demanding political recognition and expressing their own economic and social needs, socialist activists began to reread, reenact, and reproduce 1789 in their programs, in their ideologies, and on the streets. Charles Fourier devised a plan of self-contained, self-sufficient utopian communities; the Catholic Abbé Lamennais proposed Christian socialism; the layman Philippe Buchez urged the church to sponsor workingmen's associations that would own the means of production and distribution. Saint-Simon, in an effort to end ruthless competition and slave wages, and convinced that advanced technology and industrialism would lead to prosperity for all, envisioned a state advised by technocrats and engineers who would determine appropriate production and distribution for everyone. In his *Organisation du travail* (1840), Louis Blanc advocated state intervention in the economy, with worker control of all aspects of industry and public and collective ownership gradually replacing private business.

Although these various socialist programs found some adherents, in general they were ineffective in bringing about the kinds of changes they desired in the organization of work and the economy. In some cases their focus on agrarian and artisanal rejuvenation blinded them to the realities of an industrial revolution already under way; in others it was a misreading of attitudes and aspirations of the very people they wanted to help. Even Louis Blanc, who understood well the plight of the petty bourgeoisie and proletariat, never really had a well-organized or effective party attached to his cause. Yet in the eighty years that followed the French Revolution, especially in 1848 and 1870, socialist movements inspired political action and opposition that eventually brought the demise of monarchy and empire in France.

Obviously, one of those who inspired socialist activities in the latter half of the nineteenth century was Karl Marx. Although this is not the place to enter the immense "Marx industry," historians of work must acknowledge his paramount importance as historian, philosopher, critic, social theorist, and activist for a radical economic reorganization of society. Marx may not have been the first to explore the relation between work and wealth and between work and social relations, but he certainly was the most powerful and influential. After Marx it has become impossible for both working-class leaders and historians of work to think without his insights.

In addition to the enormous ideological and political upheavals that continued from 1789 throughout the nineteenth century, a great revolution in industry and technology began to create a new "anatomy" of work throughout Western Europe. Capitalist ideology informed practice as entrepreneurs and investors pressed their values of efficiency, profit, uniformity, speed, and mass production upon a formerly artisanal and peasant work force. In France large numbers of laborers were recruited from the countryside to operate machinery in cotton and woolen mills, in silk-weaving factories, and in chemical and mining enterprises. Not only were the organizations and practices of work transformed, but the meanings of work had changed as well. New equations linking labor directly to wealth and virtue overshadowed earlier notions of work as penance and punishment. The triumph of capital had drastically altered the historical landscape.

As the bourgeoisie became increasingly prominent socially and politically, the lived history of the workers' experience moved to center stage. Workers were the actors, as they began to perceive themselves as a distinct group; lines were drawn as they identified capitalist bourgeois entrepreneurs as their exploiters. The themes of the nineteenth century would be dominated by issues of class, class formation, and class struggle: bosses versus workers, workers' demands versus governments' responses, masters versus journeymen, artisans trying to maintain their place in a new industrial order, and a proletariat just trying to survive. But it would be reductive and counterproductive to polarize capital and labor. Neither was a homogeneous monolith. There were many kinds of labor, many kinds of capital, and a number of alternatives. Take the new corporate efforts of Agricol Perdiguier: Were they merely nostalgia or did they hold new promise for a historic reconciliation, an equal and fraternal association of all trades? And there were the socialist alternatives advocating associations that would own the means of production and distribution and thus ensure social and civil justice.

By midcentury, with the bourgeoisie well placed and the workers demanding their rights, the precise links between labor and wealth became more explicit. Then and only then did historians begin to take seriously and to analyze this previously neglected base of society: *les classes ouvrières*. In 1859 when Emile Levasseur published his first extensive study of the working classes in France, he could still begin with the following remark: "The history of the working classes has never been written. That should not surprise us. The royalty, the church, the nobles, masters of our former society, for a long time have had scholars to sift through their archives, historians to tell of their exploits. It is not much more than a half-century since the bourgeoisie took its place in our new society and became our most considerable order: its history is yet to be written."[6] We should not fail to notice a certain irony in this passage. Whether or

---

[6]Emile Levasseur, *Histoire des classes ouvrières en France depuis la conquête de Jules Cesar jusqu'a la Revolution*, 2 vols. (Paris, 1859), vol. 1, p. i. For a mine of provocative insights on the meaning of work, though lodged in a different time and place, see Aaron J. Gourevitch, *Les catégories de la culture médiévale*, trans. Hélène Courtin and Nina Godneff (Paris, 1983).

not historians had recognized it, the third estate had always been the principal foundation and sustaining force of society. Without the labor of the working classes supporting them, the royalty and the church would have accomplished very little worth reporting.

Within a few years countless historians followed Levasseur's lead without necessarily confronting the paradox contained in his remarks, and certainly by 1900 there was a veritable explosion of research on workers and workers' organizations in France, from the era of Julius Caesar to modern times. Although this is not the place to rehearse in detail this lengthy historiography, it seems worthwhile to ask why there was such great interest in workers at just this time. In part, no doubt, it sprang from the excitement and challenge of a great uncharted field, records untouched for centuries, stories of workers' exploits "lying peacefully in the archives waiting to be told." But more important is the Whiggish side of this burgeoning research on workers of the past. It was as if only by disrupting society and trying to claim their rights in their present could hitherto silent workers begin to take their rightful place in a past that had for so long repressed them. Indeed, most of the early histories of work, in their prefaces or conclusions, refer to the moment of their own composition, indicating one way the concerns and events of their respective "presents" weighed upon their authors' perceptions of the past, whether workers' strikes, failed revolutions, socialist tracts, the syndicalist movement, war, or, later, Bolshevism.

Insofar as the early historians of work were embarking on relatively unexplored territory, their immediate task was to classify workers and workers' organizations and to provide taxonomies for the myriad terms previously left silent or ill defined, namely concepts such as *jurande, corporation, compagnonnage,* and *confrèrie.* They painstakingly documented the regulations governing each *métier*: rights and privileges of masters, number of years of apprenticeship, restrictions on buying and selling, corporate hierarchies, and rules of competition. They gave detailed accounts of royal and municipal legislation, and they enumerated the technological advances that gradually changed the face and state of industry in France forever. But beyond these catalogs of rules, laws, and work practices, one of the most pressing ideological concerns of these early historians was "la question sociale": to describe the "condition" of the workers and to interpret the consequences of that condition.

What they meant by "condition" was subsistence: specifically the workers' standard of living, the rapport between wages and prices, and the long- and short-term effects of inflation, recession, unemployment, strikes, and bad harvests. In the late nineteenth century, historians and economists were only beginning to plot meticulous curves of economic growth and decline over the previous centuries, trying to determine the causes of these fluctuations and their effects upon the working population. But efforts to understand the effects of social conditions on workers were predominantly defined in terms of political and institutional considerations and indeed were subsumed under the most privileged issue in work historiography: the problem of worker self-consciousness, or "la question ouvrière."

When historians attempting to understand class consciousness began to study workers during the time of the French Revolution and the emerging proletariat of the early nineteenth century, their concerns fell within the sphere of what we now call labor history. These historians wanted to know who made up the working classes. Exactly when and how did they become conscious of themselves as members of a class with particular interests? From what groups in society (rural peasantry or urban poor, for example) were they recruited? Which trades were the most progressively militant, and which were the most successful? What political parties and movements did workers form? In what ways did they express their demands? How did authorities respond?

Together these two central issues, the "social question" and the "worker question," provided the dominant discursive and ideological terms of debate and a kind of dialectic of explanation for historians of the working classes and the laboring poor. From the first perspective, historians emphasized the workers as consumers; from the second, as producers. Some studied the perceptions of workers as potentially volatile and powerful from the point of view of, say, the police, administrators, or theorists, while others tried to untangle the processes whereby workers themselves came to realize their potential as a distinct social class. Sometimes the two questions collapsed into each other, as when historians attributed growing working-class consciousness and revolt less to work activities than to low standards of living and the general consequences of misery. Debates ensued over when in French society, at what moment during the French Revolution, or at what point in the development of industrial capitalism it became possible and even necessary for workers to gain class consciousness. Such discussions from the mid-nineteenth century on drew in most of the major social and economic historians of France, and by the early 1900s they had established the basic parameters and generated most of the issues that have dominated "work on work" to the present day. The consequences of that institutional and political focus have been that historians specifically interested in workers largely ignored much of the ancien régime and instead turned their attention toward what might be called "great moments" in French history: the French Revolution, 1830, 1848, and 1870. It is not surprising that "great events" (and more recently, smaller "events" such as, say, the 1834 silk workers' strike in Lyons or worker sabotage at a modern Renault plant) have received the most notice and study, not only because they are important and visible, but because in them there is a story to tell.

Through these events labor historians have charted the transformation and mobilization of workers and have undoubtedly made great strides toward increasing our understanding of the political roles of work in nineteenth- and twentieth-century France. Yet only in the past two decades have historians begun to look more seriously at many basic questions about work and workers that have never before been asked. Indeed, we might go so far as to suggest that for decades historians have followed the route of *Candide*, telling of the adventures and battles of kings and world travelers while remaining silent on the essential foundation of society: work and workers. And even when, in the late nineteenth century, historians finally turned their attentions toward this base, they did so within the domain of rather narrowly conceived political and institutional concerns.

This book, we think, attempts to widen that focus by investigating some basic questions: to return to the workplace itself, to consider work as it is actually lived, to determine its meaning for specific groups and individuals at a given time in a given society. It has meant investigating the ideological and hegemonic conceptions of work as well the way the organization of work relates to larger social organization and classification. Historians are now beginning to look at the iconography of work and at the rhythms of work, the dynamics of "morte saison," the harvest year, factory time, the assembly line, and the time clock. And they are taking notice of the popular culture of work: the workers' jargons, their jokes, their songs, their stories, their rites, rituals, and myths. In short, we are beginning to analyze all the representations of work. Like *Candide*, we begin in mid-eighteenth-century France, but we do not end there. And like Candide, whose odyssey took him from Westphalia to El Dorado and beyond, only to end on a plot of land in need of cultivation, many of us have shared an adventure to Paris and the provinces, to libraries and archives, and finally to that blank page where "real" work begins. But unlike Candide whose narrative stopped when the work began, historians are just now beginning to narrate those virtually unspeakable practices, structures, and meanings of "cultivating" the place that never was and certainly is not now a "garden."

In the first essay in this volume, Daniel Roche introduces us to Jacques-Louis Ménétra, a master glazier from Paris who left a rare legacy: an autobiographical document that covers most of the stages in the eighteenth-century trajectory of work (or, more precisely, what would later be called skilled work). It is debatable whether Ménétra is in any sense typical of the world of work, but there is no doubt that he is engaging and intriguing. Roche looks closely at this experience of work and reflects on how Ménétra represented that experience to himself and to others. Like Carlo Poni, Roche suggests that we must think in terms of work as culture and as a culture.[7] Through Ménétra, Roche explores the phases of journeyman and master socialization and hints at the tensions that play constantly between these two very different but deeply imbricated levels of work. He also underlines the ambivalence in Ménétra's attitude and behavior vis-à-vis economic integration (or petty bourgeois "success").

Roche compares the Parisian work experience with the provincial one. In Ménétra's case, the latter conforms more nearly to the stereotype of employer/employee harmony fostered by Albert Soboul and his followers. In the capital, however, "family type" work relations and the "paternalistic ideal" are gravely disjointed. Following the vehement complaints of masters about the increasing insubordination of their employees, a few recent historians of work in the Old Regime have tried to intuit changes in workers' attitudes. Ménétra proposes that we look in the other direction—at the "nouvelles modes" in the way masters practiced their craft and their overlordship. These new modes amounted to a betrayal of conventions that had a quasi-contractual aspect and thus provoked conflict.

We need to know more about the labor market, and the fight to control it, and about the workplace itself. The rhythm and character of Ménétra's work are different from those of many of his contemporaries in other trades. "Every man had to know how to do everything" in the glazier's craft, whereas in many professions there was an extraordinarily refined division of labor that generated highly complex work relations. Ménétra's own itinerary, from militant journeyman (leader in the clandestine journeymen's association called the Compagnonnage of the Devoir) to somewhat rebellious master invites inquiry into the connections between the two experiences. Did Ménétra's "liberalism" flow in part from his insubordinate past? Did his criticism of the guild oligarchy stem in part from his expectation that mastership meant the end of hierarchy? Or did Ménétra's narrative of his own "worker" past suffer the same sort of filtering and refracting (remember that it was written in retrospect) that characterized, in Roche's own terms, elite accounts of the people? In any event, Roche masterfully sets the agenda for many of the questions that define the world of work for the eighteenth and nineteenth centuries.

Curiously, much of what has come to stand as the history of the eighteenth-century workplace has been extrapolated backward from the republican rhetoric of the sans-culottes. In the next chapter Michael

[7]See the research project "Work and Family in Pre-Industrial Europe," directed by Carlo Poni and Stuart Woolf at the European University Institute, Florence.

Introduction

Sonenscher contends that it would be more fruitful and compelling to do it the other way round: to study the workplace and see how the experience of work and work relations may have shaped the recruitment, organization, and attitudes of the sansculottes. This is the broadest and boldest lesson to be drawn from this study. On a more pragmatic plane, Sonenscher's research also moves in a revisionist direction. He asks: How does one reconcile the image of workshop intimacy so powerfully embroidered by Soboul with the striking instability of workshop life?

Sonenscher argues that there was nothing in the respective positions of masters and journeymen that automatically or inexorably led to durable relations of cooperation. He focuses on the circumstances of workshop production to which historians have not paid sufficient attention (for example, the intricate division of labor in tailoring). These circumstances, far more than putative ideological concord, forged mutually profitable relationships between masters who needed workers over whom they felt little effective control and highly mobile workers who needed jobs but would not work without certain assurances of satisfactory treatment. The workshop invited both actors to subscribe to a "fiction" of intimacy—itself a form of work—that created flexibility to help reconcile the vagaries of journeyman behavior with the rhythms of workshop production. Rouen's journeymen were extremely mobile (time itself could not have engendered intimacy and familiarity), yet their mobility was not haphazard. It was "highly structured," in the end, less by the placement bureaus instituted by the guilds expressly to confiscate control of job recruitment than by the journeymen's residential network—the *logis* where they slept, ate, drank, obtained credit, exchanged information, planned common actions, and learned of job opportunities.

The inn was also Ménétra's base of operations on the Tour de France. Though Ménétra seems to have had to work less hard to achieve intimacy than most men (and not just at the workplace), one can nevertheless detect parallels between the démarches of the journeymen tailors of Rouen and the behavior of the glazier: the extracorporate circuits of placement; the stigmatization of shops operated by abusive masters; and the symbolic exchanges between masters (and their families) and journeymen.

Sonenscher points to the labor market as a critical arena of political, social, and cultural interaction between masters and journeymen. The circumstances of production shaped the labor market as much as the labor market fashioned work practices. And the circumstances of both accounted for the degree of collective association among workers and perhaps also for the policy orientations of the guilds.

Sonenscher concedes that patterns of employment among tailors were in many ways distinctive, but he believes that there were similar structures of relations in other trades and in other places. By "denaturalizing" the social relations of production in the workplace and in the interstices of work, Sonenscher has made them more believable albeit more difficult to get at. Masters and journeymen "produced" relationships that ensured that work would get done. What are the implications of this labor of transformation, asks Sonenscher, for our understanding of the history of the First French Republic—and beyond?

Edward Shephard's point of departure is the well-founded lament that guild studies have yet to be drawn into the mainstream of French social history. Our knowledge of the guilds is largely institutional (and even here the picture is startlingly abstract and remote). The operation of the guild as a social and economic system, Shephard maintains, is largely a "matter of conjecture" owing to the lack of probing research. He makes an important contribution toward remedying this deficiency by looking closely at the city of Dijon. The issue Shephard has chosen to join is one of the most controversial and significant questions in the history of the Old Regime: Were the guilds closed castes of masters jealously restricting entry to their sons and sons-in-law? This stereotype sets the tone for the standard indictment of the guilds as reactionary, swaggering obstructionist forces, a view articulated most effectively by a group of economically oriented philosophes called physiocrats and uncritically internalized by most modern historians who are pleased to take the side of the Enlightenment and Progress.

Shephard contests the stereotype, but only in the context of a Dijonnais model of development. In other places, where capitalist and other socioeconomic pressure was acute, he allows that guilds might have been forced to become narrow and exclusivist in order to forestall deterioration of their status. But in towns like Dijon, which enjoyed moderate demographic growth and moderate but sustained prosperity, the guild system "provided for, satisfied, and corresponded to social and economic needs and realities."

Even as impermanence is the leitmotif of Sonenscher's essay, so stability is the refrain of Shephard's. And in Dijon, if stability informs ideology and shapes a sort of global consensus, it is not a fiction. Old Regime Dijon never experienced modernization like the Mediterranean and Atlantic boom centers. Its economy, like its social structure, rested upon its institutional apparatus—the overlapping and mutually reinforcing institutions of administration, judiciary, and church. The working population remained stable through the whole century; the reception of new masters kept the guilds at about the same levels. Yet the guilds were remarkably accessible to non-Dijonnais: over half of new masters were immigrants. And still more striking, the guilds were open to outsiders from the beginning of the century and became even more open as the century progressed, so that in the last decades of the Old Regime only 9 percent of new masters were following in the footsteps of their fathers. Thus Dijonnais stability afforded and was protected by a very high level of mobility and opportunity.

At the end of his essay Shephard speculates on the reasons the Dijon corporate system "worked." His focus remains ecological—that is, he does not look inside the guilds to social and political relations or inside the workplace to relations of production, though these perspectives are on his future research itinerary. Beyond the preindustrial, backwater character of Dijon, Shephard is most impressed with the city's remarkable ability to absorb new blood at apparently no social cost. He believes the mobility of journeymen was even greater than that of masters. And he attributes the integrating capacity of the guilds (and the fact that they never had to defend an embattled position) in large part to the opportunities that sons of masters had to rise on the socioprofessional ladder beyond the world of work. Finally, foreshadowing Cynthia Truant's functionalist thesis, Shephard hints that the unruly compagnonnages might have contributed powerfully to the stability of Dijon's system (even as the logis organization mitigated "impermanence" in Rouen) by helping to keep the labor market fluid and efficient.

Cynthia Truant's point of departure is the late eighteenth-century perception of apocalypse in the labor market and the workplace: the conviction that worker insubordination had been gaining dangerous momentum. She shows that sharp labor conflict had a deep, quasi-structural history dating back at least to the mid-seventeenth century in the cities of Nantes and Lyons. Like Sonenscher, Truant is interested in the coexistence of chaos and cooperation in the workplace. She proposes a functionalist conception of strife between masters and journeymen in which the clashes are shown to have a constructive side. The forms that conflict took—like Sonenscher's fiction of intimacy—ensured that the work would be completed. Truant, too, focuses on the labor market as the privileged arena of master/worker tension.

Like Shephard, Truant contends that the greatest destabilizing force in the world of work was capitalism, especially in its "emergent entrepreneurial" form and stage. Nantes and Lyons were anti-Dijons. In both places the traditional artisanal system was threatened, at least in a number of important trades, by the new capitalist methods of organization and production deployed by merchant-manufacturers. Truant claims that the critical hierarchical distinction emerging in the eighteenth-century world of work was between large-scale manufacturers and all other artisanal producers rather than between masters and journeymen. The small masters were threatened by the new forces of capitalism and at the same time suffered the more traditional yet ever growing encroach-

"false workers," experienced journeymen established illicitly in
hops (*chambrelans*) and itinerant or country producers (*forains*).[8]
son, Truant suggests, the small masters reacted with burgeoning
worker insubordination in the eighteenth century was that their
nding was deteriorating, their world crumbling. In the short run
man insubordination led to negotiated forms of cooperation on
on model adumbrated by Shephard. But the journeymen of Nantes
ons had no intimation of the longer-term consequences of their
ousness. They did not fathom their masters' problems and did not
ve them as "potentially their own." Thus they attempted to exploit
masters' difficulties for their own immediate advantage.

ant's journeymen were fundamentally different from Shephard's
ise most of them had no chance of reaching mastership (though
eed more precise evidence on this point). Most of them, Truant
ates, were aware of this and therefore had different (working)
dviews and strategies than their future masters. Many of them were
nbers of associations—especially compagnonnages—that shaped their
tudes and actions toward their masters. Perhaps even more impor-
t, these associations, and the struggles they waged against the masters,
conditioned the way the journeymen saw and represented themselves.
Truant discusses the organizational sources of the compagnonnage (her
suggestion on the church's role as *mère* and not merely as model is
especially stimulating) and their strengths (the blend of suppleness and
bureaucratic formalism). She argues that internecine rivalries did not
undercut the ability of the journeymen to win favorable settlements,
notwithstanding the postrevolutionary (Perdiguier) stereotype to the
contrary. She treats their tactics, especially in the placement theater, and
their striking resilience in overcoming countless official suppressions,
formal recantations, decapitations.

The patterns of conflict in Lyons and Nantes were very similar. One
finds in both cities a strong correlation between worker association and
conflict and, no less interesting, between the strength of the corporate
system and the incidence and intensity of conflict. These correlations point
to the need for a comparison with conflict outside the strictly corporate
sector, in the world of relatively large-scale production typified by the
big merchant-manufacturer or the royal manufacturer, and for a comparison between Truant's hard-core journeymen—really *alloués*—and
"factory" workers.

The journeymen won many concrete victories, but Truant concludes
they were not interested only in money and *pâtés*. Through their asso-

[8]See Steven L. Kaplan, "Les faux-ouvriers à Paris pendant le dix-huitième siècle," in *La France d'ancien régime: Etudes réunies en l'honneur de Pierre Goubert*, ed. Alain Croix, Jean Jacquart, and Francois Lebrun (Toulouse, 1984).

ciationist engagement, they acquired a new identity and a new self conception—a keen sense of their worth and of their rights. They wer not to be seen or treated as merely dependents and subordinates. Tha was the significance of the battles over registration: a struggle for dignit as well as for control over the labor market.[9]

Steven L. Kaplan is another among the historians in this volume en gaged in rethinking and reevaluating stereotypical and generally unex amined depictions of the corporations as corrupt and decrepit institutions. In this instance he investigates the way guild structures defined socia identity and behavior in late eighteenth-century France by focusing o a brief moment of their absence: the turbulent aftermath following Tu got's 1776 edict abolishing the guilds, an act that—as the subtitle "Tu got's Carnival" intimates—turned the world of work on its head.

As for the question whether the guilds were worth preserving, Kapl does not yet wish to take sides. What he does want, however, is a fu hearing of the masters' (self) defense of the corporations in the face o attack—more to gain an understanding of how the masters represented the social, political, and economic world to themselves than to judge its relation to "reality."

Much of Kaplan's essay, then, rehearses the actual response to Turgot's edict among various sectors of society. From the masters' perspective the guilds were not the corrupt, archaic, sterile, and oppressive insti tutions their contemporary critics (and later historians) claimed, but rather played vital and multiple roles in maintaining order—in several senses of the word. From the guildsmen's point of view, social relations pre ceded and to a considerable extent dictated economic relations: master ship constituted a system of social classification and representation before it denoted a system of production, distribution, and consumption. The obligation of journeymen to obey—no issue had worried the masters more during the eighteenth century than the question of worker disci pline, in Paris as well as Nantes, Lyons, and the rest of the kingdom— flowed not from their market relation as employees but from their socially prescribed subordination. In a curious way, masters and journeymen were dependent on each other for their social identities.

According to Kaplan, Turgot spoke for a world in which social rela tions were embedded in and largely determined by economic or market relations. For the masters this meant "confusion," "anarchy," "chaos," "the primal state of nature." Liberty and equality were synonymous: together they corroded the traditional taxonomy and undermined social peace and security. By destroying the bonds that riveted society together,

[9]On the friction over registration, see Steven L. Kaplan, "Réflexions sur la police du monde du travail, 1700–1815," *Revue Historique* 261 (December 1979): 21–25, 43–65, and idem, "The Luxury Guilds in Paris in the Eighteenth Century," *Francia* 9 (1982): 288–97.

they unleashed the antisocial, selfish, and narrow-minded spirit of "gnawing individualism" that celebrated all the wrong values (and that threatened to return the masters to the moral and psychological level of workers without état, for they would no longer have any collective rampart from which to resist the tide). Abolition dismantled the apparatus of control that ("gently") ensured worker submission. Naturally mutinous, workers would become permanent fugitives from classification yet would soon discover that the strictures of the unregulated marketplace were far harsher than the guild codes. In the meantime the public would be betrayed and cheated by the proliferation of "false" work, false keys, false gold, "ragoûts pernicieux." The guilds linked abolition squarely with "Modern Philosophy"—the all-azimuth campaign against tradition. They warned, too, of the grave political risks inherent in abolition, for the guilds were "political bodies" legitimized by the "constitution," part of a great chain of social being that led directly to the throne. Kaplan shows that the magistrates of the Paris Parlement espoused the corporate cause because they clearly understood the connection between social distinctions (institutionalized in the *corvée* as well as the guilds) and social order.

In Kaplan's account the journeymen's initial gleeful response to their "liberation" was exactly what the masters had feared: abandonment of the workplace in favor of the taverns and the streets, a bacchanal of revenge and ambition spawned by the belief that at last they would become their own masters. Jolted by these disorders and badly prepared for the new regime that it had just declared, within a matter of weeks the government imposed controls and restrictions to replace the corporations and their police, thus shattering the journeymen's hope of independence. Turgot's inability to effect a smooth transition to laissez-faire was one of the many causes of his disgrace in May 1776.

In August the guild system was reestablished. Kaplan discusses the ambiguity of the "restoration." On the one hand it was a reaffirmation of the traditional model of social classification and representation. On the other, it was a serious measure of reform: streamlining, simplifying, housecleaning. Many masters were uncomfortable with the rules of reestablishment, in large part because of its (extremely traditional) fiscal onus, but also because of the unequivocal assimilation of the "new masters" of carnivalesque vintage. The rebirth of the guilds did not result in the spontaneous regeneration of worker obedience. The stern disciplinary codes of the reestablished guilds did not succeed in domesticating the workers, who may have been more willing than ever before to contest corporate authority. Kaplan concludes with a series of reflections on the immense significance of the stakes in 1776, the struggle for control of the labor market, the various strategies the guilds employed to foster their ambitions, and the various strategies historians used to make sense of the corporations.

Cynthia Koepp shares Kaplan's preoccupation with classification and representation but from a different vantage point. She begins by showing that some of the most critical changes we associate with the Enlightenment had to do with the introduction of new ways of ordering. She then directs her attention to the *Encyclopédie*, the great symbol of eighteenth-century progress, which, she suggests, was both more and less than it is ordinarily made out to be. The *Encyclopédie* proposed two very different types of ordering: a philosophically justified hierarchical one and a conventional alphabetical one. Koepp's theme is that the latter undermined the former.

Work, it turns out, is granted much more importance in the alphabetical unfolding of the *Encyclopédie* than its lowly place in the epistemological tree promised—and more importance than many nobler entries. Yet the upshot is not to confirm the commonplace that the *Encyclopédie* bestowed new dignity on the trades, but to contest it and add substantial nuance. Diderot exalted work's utility as a social means; he had more praise for the machine than for its operator. The *Encyclopédie* portrayed manual labor in unflattering terms. The worker was a mindless automaton who depended on instinct rather than intellect, who bespoke body rather than mind (especially in the case of the workers who administered to the body's elementary needs: butchers, bakers, sausage makers). The *Encyclopédie* accorded work a major place less in order to rehabilitate it than to take possession of it for higher purposes than workers themselves could imagine.

The first step was to describe in probing detail each kind of work, not a task easily discharged by visiting the shops. Workers themselves were characteristically not conscious of how they worked: thus the stultifying technological lethargy in which they languished, according to Diderot. Moreover, they kept much of what they knew secret. Finally, even when they opened up, it was not easy to make sense of their discourse, itself a barrier against intrusion and a guarantee of cultural autonomy. Work resisted orderly classification even as the journeymen resisted registration at the guild office: both were forms of domestication and expropriation.

In Koepp's view, the *Encyclopédie* was an effort to take the knowledge and language of work out of the workers' hands, to decode it, to distill its fundamental principles, to devise a new language of mechanical arts available to the whole society. It was unimportant to Diderot that the worker would probably not comprehend the scientific version of his craft. The alphabetic ideology of the *Encyclopédie* called for the asphyxiation of the old oral, practical, physical culture by the new written, scientific, and literary culture. The culture of alphabetization had no genuine sympathy for the culture of work, for its mission was to equip the bourgeoisie with the language and tools for capitalist development in the market society composed of individuals.[10] The *Encyclopédie* would enable the entrepreneurs—the sorts of capitalists who were transforming the economies of Lyons and Nantes—not only to master the métier but to control the dispossessed worker as well. While acknowledging the significance of the progressive, optimistic, and rational side of the *Encyclopédie*, Koepp concludes that it is equally critical to look at its more repressive aspects.

William Sewell also pays heed to representations of work and workers, but addresses pictorial rather than discursive representations. Visual images should not be viewed, Sewell argues, merely as "illustrations" of verbal documentation: they have a dynamic and a language of their own.

Sewell begins his study with plates from the sixteenth and seventeenth centuries. These prints are characterized by an emphasis on the unity of the trade: "Whether by common subordination to a higher purpose, by a circular presentation of work process, by a device of inclining figures at the same angle, or by summing up the entire trade in one fantastic person, each mechanical art is presented to the viewer as a harmonic, unified whole."

The plates of the *Encyclopédie* break sharply with this apprehension of the world of work, echoing the ideological rupture between the philosophes and the custodians of Old Regime traditions. The plates are dominated not by working people but by tools and equipment. There is no compelling sense of the flow of the productive process. The large workrooms are strikingly barren. The human figures are small and their faces are blank, anonymous, abstract. Nor is there any communication between these isolated "generic" worker types. This representation betrays Diderot's ambivalence about work: the mechanical arts were not a base undertaking, yet they desperately needed to be perfected and to be transformed as social and economic instruments. The secretive, work-as-patrimony, *de-père-en-fils*, rule-of-thumb world had to yield to the rational, scientific future, even as the archaic corporate mentality had to give way to the ethos of the highly individualistic liberal bourgeoisie.

Sewell's reading parallels Koepp's, though what she characterizes as a contestatory discursive order he prefers to call an "early capitalist utopian vision." This repudiation of the more human, cluttered, and communal world represented in the sixteenth- and seventeenth- century prints demonstrates that the Enlightenment already had a clear notion of work as fully alienated, abstract labor power. For a long time it was

---

[10] See Steven L. Kaplan, *Provisioning Paris: Merchants and Millers in the Grain and Flour Trade during the Eighteenth Century* (Ithaca, 1984), chap. 11.

believed that such a vision was not conceivable before the profound technological changes of the nineteenth century. Sewell's argument is part of a larger revision of our understanding of the relations between capitalism, factory development, technological change, and proletarianization. "The plates of the *Encyclopédie* argue for a cultural construction of the capitalist mode of production well in advance of its practical realization."

By the mid-1830s, Sewell detects a new representation of work, closer to the early modern depiction than to that of the *Encyclopédie*. Laissez-faire failed to produce—right away—the docile, individualized work force that Diderot anticipated. Workers remained committed to the communal values of the corporate world and bitterly resented economic liberalism. The prints of the 1830s reveal workshop clutter and vivacity, and underscore human skill, personality, and communication. The "profoundly social character of work" displaces the "utopian illusion" of a scientifically ordered world of work. Reflecting the disappearance of old-style social relations, Sewell's final plates from the 1860s are a conservative and nostalgic evocation of the world the artisan had lost.

The Cornell conference provoked Maurice Garden to reflect on modes of both social analysis and representation. He begins by looking at the changing meaning of the "world of work," divorced from the countryside, assimilated to the city, identified especially with artisanal trades. He then turns to the extraordinarily rich Dijonnais sources used by Edward Shephard—sources that permit for the first time a global evaluation of artisanal population across a century during the Old Regime. Dominated by five categories of work distributed in twenty-two trades, the Dijonnais world of work suggests at least one sort of symbolic hierarchy, based on the relative openness of mastership recruitment to outsiders—candidates who were not sons of masters. Garden points out, however, that one must adduce other elements in order to reconstruct a convincing hierarchy: wealth, political as well as economic power, and geographical and social mobility.

Insufficiently scrutinized by historians of work, especially during the period before 1850, the problem of mobility is of particular interest to Garden. It must be examined in the context of the experience of urbanization peculiar to the city in question, ranging from the quasi-stagnation of cities such as Dijon and Rouen to the far more dynamic ones such as Lyons and Bordeaux. Using techniques of family reconstitution and drawing upon notarial records, one must try to discern the different groups in the world of work. Such a study would also enable one to test hypotheses such as Jacques Rancière's on the relation between the social and technical prestige of a trade and the political/ideological orientation of its practitioners. The crucial condition is to look across several generations, spanning the eighteenth and nineteenth centuries, with genealogical precision. To illustrate the possibilities of such an investigation, Garden cites the evolution and mutation of the butcher trade in Lyons, much less profoundly jarred by the Revolution than by the demographic surge after 1820 and its concomitant transformations. One of the most fruitful avenues of culture research, Garden concludes, lies in the study of the role of the family in the formation of a "culture proper to each métier." This culture has a social and moral as well as a professional and domestic dimension. The familial perspective could frame a long-run social and ethnohistory of the world of work from the halcyon days of corporatism to the resurgence of the artisanal milieu in our own time.

Michelle Perrot launches our section on the nineteenth century with the study of a worker's autobiography, but her subject is in most respects sharply different from Daniel Roche's. Norbert Truquin was illiterate until late in life. Perhaps it was his tardy acquisition of writing and reading skills that made him believe so passionately in the power of the written word. He urged workers to hasten the "social revolution" by telling the world about themselves.

Born in 1833 in Picardy, Truquin was the son of a ruined entrepreneur. Save for a long sojourn in Lyons where he was a silk weaver, his life was an odyssey that took him first to Algeria and later to Argentina and Paraguay, where he nourished the dream of conquering new land according to socialist principles. His conviction that the rootedness of the working class was the source of its misfortune was reinforced if not inspired by his own experience. From early childhood he wandered. Unlike Ménétra, he had no family trade and no corporate linkages to provide sociability, technical education, and employment. His apprenticeship to a wool carder consisted of getting beaten and reciting prayers, equally detestable moments for him. The work he did in his youth had no clear professional identity: it was stopgap drudgery. His was the work of the body, Perrot observes, like that performed by women and others bereft of tools. Often it amounted to a sort of personal domesticity; or it was the opportunism of the paltry street trades; or it was scavenging.

Given his lack of training and trade roots, Truquin led a work life of extreme geographical mobility and professional formlessness. Work meant the search for subsistence, and its rhythms were fluid; there was great insecurity, but also a certain freedom. "Economic determinism and existential choice combined in this perpetual activity," notes Perrot. Getting a job was not easy. Perrot shows that work was considered not a right but rather a reward for honorability and virtue, very much as it had been construed during the Old Regime. As in Ménétra's time, if one failed to adhere to the employer's disciplinary code, one suffered dismissal and received a "bad certificate" that made it difficult to find a

new position. For Truquin work was not the object of personal investment, but an abstract act of exchanging one's labor power for a wage.
Still, earning money became the inexorable basis for emancipation. Truquin's ambition, not unlike Ménétra's, was to set up his own business
and thus to achieve independence and autonomy. Marriage, one of the
classical vectors of establishment, led Truquin to become a silk weaver
at Lyons. Struck by the ease with which Truquin learned the craft, Perrot
invites inquiry into the meaning of skill and its relations both to social
status and to learning (a question that Jacques Rancière addresses in his
chapter). Crisis in the structures of the Lyonnais silk industry and the
experience of the Commune and its repression impelled Truquin to
strike out for virgin land abroad.

Truquin's agrarian community vision was hardly unique in a century
replete with utopian projects. What distinguished his plan was, first, that
he carried it out, and second, his choice of Latin America. A remnant
of physiocracy infused Truquin's conception: commerce was robbery
and waste; cities were bastions of sterility and corrupting luxury; the
land, an inexhaustible bounty, was the only source of true wealth. Perrot
elicits Truquin's ideal worker: self-reliant (dependent neither on God
nor on charity nor on the state) and austere (one less thing needed, one
more strength gained). From afar, Truquin looked pessimistically upon
the proletarianization and concentration of power engendered by industrial civilization. He believed that the worker could arrest and reverse
this tendency if he was willing to take risks and renounce old habits. But
he feared that the worker's longing for social protection would induce
him to accept the leviathan state's exorbitant growth.

Jacques Rancière challenges the historical representation of the artisan
as a category in nineteenth-century social history. He begins by questioning the connection between skill and militancy, a veritable dogma in
labor historiography. According to this view, the labor/socialist movement developed as an expression of working-class culture, based on the
words and gestures of the most highly skilled. Rancière contends that
this representation was in fact born of "political necessities": certain
segments of the labor movement used it to parry competing forces. The
tradition of "authentic" worker socialism thus formed was largely fanciful.

Rancière argues that the leading forces in the worker movement, the
shoemakers and the tailors, were not propelled by a consciousness of
their professional identity. Historians have nourished an illusion of eli-
tism by projecting onto artisanal practice certain bourgeois images. A
double error resulted: a misapprehension of the reality of working conditions and of the subjective value that workers assigned to their own
activities. Rancière describes shoemaking as the last of all trades, stigmatized "professionally and ideologically." If the shoemakers were ac-

tivists, it was not because of pride in craft but because they derived so little material and symbolic compensation from their work and because they had so much forced leisure. Less contemptible, tailoring was a similarly mediocre profession with a weak corporate tradition and little collective consciousness. Both shoemaking and tailoring were easy and erratic trades that made few intellectual demands on the workers, thus according them a wide range of "intellectual freedom" as well as a sort of psychological availability. Rancière believes that militant action is probably inversely proportional to the organic cohesion of a trade, its organizational strength, and its group ideology.

Maintaining that militant worker ideology was marked by a repudiation of the notion of "love of work," Rancière wonders about the meaning of the term artisan. When one looks at the trajectories of many nineteenth-century artisans, one discovers workers for whom work was a very "unartisanal" and "abstract" undertaking. These "artisans" remind us of the rocky, desultory lives of today's "marginal" workers. An examination of the case of Agricol Perdiguier, artisanal hero and apologist, leads Rancière to propose a second theorem of inverse proportionality: those who sang the praises of work loudest were those who most intensely experienced work as "degeneration." But what Rancière emphasizes is precisely the ambiguity and complexity rather than a triumphant reversal of interpretation: hatred of work, like love of work, was an equivocal notion containing self-contestatory elements.

These contradictory representations and practices, says Rancière, should encourage us to be "systematically cautious" whenever we wish to establish links between professional situations, militant activities, and ideological statements. Yet historians frequently fail to use critical discretion and discernment in making connections between very different kinds of data in order to fashion a picture of workers. One such example is the distorted image that emerges from a perfunctory reading of the *Statistique de l'industrie*, the subject of Joan Scott's essay. The same sort of distortion arises when one shifts from bourgeois statistics to workers' discourse. While the former glorified the world of the artisan, the latter spuriously assumed that worker "spokesmen" spoke transparently for workers. Behind the facade of collective discourse, warns Rancière, there often looms a hidden but decisive political ambition.

Rancière then raises a number of methodological issues regarding our interpretation of the culture of "others." First there is the problem of the relations between the labor movement per se and "outside" political and ideological influences. Rancière asserts that we attach too much importance to the collectivity/unity of workers and not enough to their cleavages; that we look too intently at work culture and not enough at its encounters with other cultures. We seek to locate the origin of the words of workers within the context of their trades, and we presume that their representations are solidly rooted within the collectivity they represent. But in so doing, Rancière claims, we avoid "one form of intellectual racism only to fall into another—one that consists of over-stressing the difference of identities." Thus we fail to see the spokesmen, a marginal group at the frontier of encounters with the bourgeoisie, as primordially a "particular category of intellectuals." By confining our-selves ethnographically to the professional experience of workers, we presume that they are concerned with nothing besides their work. But a carpenter does not "turn his sentences as he turns wood." How far we are from Diderot's sullen, nonverbal workers.

Rancière concludes by reaffirming his methodological and ideological admonition: there are immense complexities in any definition of the workingman and his values. He emphasizes the rupture constituted by the worker's entry into the domain of writing. He cautions against the culturalist models that posit the homogeneity of cultural practices: "this undifferentiated sense of culture is likely to miss the originality of the representations in or at play in workers' discourse and politics."

Joan Scott is interested in two different levels of representation. One concerns the way certain segments of French society viewed work and workers at the time of the revolution of 1848. Another deals with the way historians work: how they represent to themselves (and to their readers) the descriptions (or representations) of work and workers in the mid-nineteenth century. These two concerns merge in the scrutiny of a document (Scott would have us say a text) produced by the chamber of commerce of Paris. This document, the *Statistique de l'industrie*, because it is a series of statistics, enjoys a double dose of prestige and kind of immunosanctity. The first dose was administered by nineteenth-century social investigators imbued with the conviction that they had penetrated the laws of nature that found their most cogent expression in the rigor of numbers. Since their method was scientific, the statistics it generated constituted an objective and precise measure of reality. The second dose was more recently applied by certain historians of quantitative bent for whom numbers afford a privileged *entrée* into reality and who brandish a scientific standard that is often daunting.

Scott argues for a demystification of the document: not for its dis-qualification as a legitimate source, but for a fuller "conceptualization" and "problematization" of it that will lead to richer and more probing use. The *Statistique* must be "read," not merely transcribed. The positivist illusion that it simply and innocently recorded facts must be aban-doned—the *Statistique* constructed reality. To understand how it did so, one must look at its own construction: its categories, its assumptions, its exclusions. It is not only a question of subjecting the document to critical regard; in dealing with the *Statistique*, the historian must reflect on the large issue of the nature of the relation between representation and reality.

Scott explores the genesis of the *Statistique* (its political origins and mission), the process of data collection/selection, the form and rhetorical structure of the document, and its rubrics and content. Rather than being an "objective scientific" enterprise, the making of the *Statistique* was political combat. Its aim was to contest the "reality" depicted by the "new barbarians" (the workers and their allies) and to substitute a truer reality grounded on moral verities and consecrated and guaranteed by a scientific cachet (Say's political economy). It decentered the worker by subordinating him to the economy, by concentrating on "industry" instead of labor. It employed categories that shifted the focus from relations of production to the simple fact of productive activity. In this way it exorcised conflict. Preoccupied with the morality of workers, the *Statistique* used the family as a metaphor and model for organizing work and regulating behavior. The more closely the structure of work resembled a family, the more enmeshed workers were in the family, the better behaved the work force.

The *Statistique* invited the state, in the name of moral science, to strengthen the family's role. Within the family nexus, women served a sort of barometric function, metaphorically demarcating the extremes of worker comportment. The married woman represented the good worker—subordinated, faithful, under relentless surveillance and control. The woman living alone, outside fixed categories, loomed as a threat to the moral order—the mutinous, inconstant, and elusive worker.

The purpose of the *Statistique*, concludes Scott, was to reaffirm a vision of economic and social organization that had been strenuously challenged. Historians, she warns, must not allow themselves to be unwitting accomplices of this campaign of ideological and political reconquest.

William Reddy also writes about conflicting representations of workers' lives in the mid-nineteenth century. At issue was not the depiction of the physical conditions in which most of the laboring poor lived. It was generally agreed that they lived miserably. The divergence stemmed from a radically different appreciation of the moral consequences of that trying physical existence. For many social commentators, physicians as well as political economists, there was a deplorable but necessary symmetry between the physical and the moral: physical deprivation equaled moral degradation, dirt on the floor meant dirty lives, one bed for the whole family produced incest.

Reddy points out that there is very little evidence to sustain this view, largely the fruit of class prejudice and erroneous theoretical presumptions. The workers saw themselves differently. Although Reddy cautions against extrapolating "conditions" from their own representations of their lives, he believes that the cultural fabric from which these representations were cut utterly belies the idea of moral decay.

What can dialect songs and poems, composed for the most part by illiterate and semiliterate textile-mill workers of Lille, reveal about the laboring community's moral orientation toward its own grinding poverty? After positing a number of methodological caveats, Reddy reflects on the functions of the songs in the workers' lives, their subjects, the underlying principles that governed the choice of subjects, the literary conventions in which they were couched. To determine how the workers looked at their world, Reddy contends, one must examine the instruments they used.

By scrutinizing poems such as *Casse-Bras*, the story of an old man laid off from his factory job because of his age, who had to retire to a charitable institution because he could no longer support himself, Reddy uncovers the theme that runs throughout the whole dialect corpus. Casse-Bras has moral fiber. His poverty neither degrades nor embitters him. He and his entourage inspire admiration for their resistance and courage. Farce is one of the chief tools of their resistance. Reddy construes farce, or light irony, as a conscious moral response to hardship. The stories reveal the ugliest features of the working-class landscape, but the authors rehearse their woes in satire. The laboring poor, Reddy admits, are sorely tried by dirt, cold, and vermin, but their souls are not besmirched. For Reddy, this discursive material shows that the pervasive tone of irony was more than a literary convention, for ritual farce was celebrated in public as an integral part of the community ethos. Thus *Casse-Bras* is not just dialect poetry, but a key to the very structure of working-class culture. Encoded in the farcical ritual was a profoundly moral response to lives of deprivation. The workers refused to allow hardship itself to fashion their self-image. As Reddy concludes, they struggled to deny the representation of themselves as demoralized proletarians.

Most accounts of capitalist industrialization characteristically focus on the process of dispossession of the means of production (proletarianization). This process is said to be marked by the rapid disappearance of allegedly static, traditional forms of production—small-scale household and handicraft workshops—in favor of more modern forms of capitalist industry. Ronald Aminzade challenges this view. Small-scale artisan production, he argues, showed considerable vitality through much of the nineteenth century. Many artisans retained ownership of their shops, and their journeymen kept their tools. Proletarianization was not the only means by which labor became subordinated to capital during the industrial development of the nineteenth century. To understand how capitalist industrialization transformed class relations, one must study other strategies of capitalist accumulation (i.e., control over raw materials, credit, the labor market, work organization, and product markets). Concentrating first on household production in Saint-Etienne and then on handicraft production in Toulouse (both nonmechanized), Aminzade demonstrates that these forms were not remnants of precapitalism but were connected in new ways to an emergent capitalist system.

Silk-ribbon production, located in urban households and organized around the family, employed over half of Saint-Etienne's labor force. Master weavers owned their looms but depended on merchant capitalists for raw materials and marketing of finished goods. Power shifted increasingly from the artisans to the merchants in the course of the century as a result of the growing indebtedness of the weavers (obliged to buy more expensive and more productive looms in order to remain competitive) and as a consequence of the increasing control the merchants exercised over preparatory and finishing stages of production. The new strategies of capitalist accumulation were especially effective during crisis periods, when the workers were most vulnerable.

Handicraft production dominated Toulouse. Over two-thirds of the industrial labor force consisted of artisans with relatively small amounts of fixed capital, who were employed mainly in the production of food, clothing, and housing. The master artisans exercised control over the use of raw materials, the budgeting of time, and the recruitment and training of workers, but they were generally constrained by their workers to abide by traditional work regulations. These traditional regulations governing handicraft production were challenged about midcentury by three tendencies: (1) the growth of relatively small, nonmechanized factories; (2) the penetration of merchant capital into the garment, shoe, and construction industries, which entailed a more intensified division of labor, the entry of women and children into household production, and the introduction of subcontracting; and (3) the internal transformation of handicraft production by which the artisan, under sharp competitive pressure, became a capitalist practitioner in order to increase the pace and scale of production without regard to traditional regulations.

Aminzade concludes that industrialization in both Saint-Etienne and Toulouse altered class relations within the household as well as the handicraft spheres as producers were increasingly subordinated to merchant capitalists or capitalist masters. This subordination did not primarily result from dispossession of the means of production. Changes in legal ownership proved much less significant than changes in effective control over persons and productive forces. Only a broad view of capitalist development, Aminzade insists, can account for the diverse strategies of accumulation and mechanisms of subordination. Theories of economic development that rely on historical conceptual dichotomies to contrast the past and present typically emphasize the rapid eclipse of "precapitalist" or traditional forms by capitalist or modern forms of industry. Aminzade's research suggests that such theories fail to appreciate the "reconstitution of older forms of industry in the process of socioeconomic change." Historians as well as sociologists have overlooked this process of reconstitution, in part because it left intact the outward forms of production—household and workshop—while transforming class relations internally. To understand capitalist development, Aminzade calls for more historical case studies of the diverse local patterns of capitalist accumulation that marked off different phases of the process of industrialization.

Michael Hanagan is less interested in the genesis of proletarianization than in its consequences and its internal dynamics. He argues vigorously that the history of work cannot be written apart from the history of the family. Specifically, he is interested in the relation between large proletarian protest movements on the one side and changes in family structure and ideology, family employment patterns, and fertility strategies on the other. Family issues, he reminds us, were not the appanage of labor militancy. They were capable of reconciling capitalists with workers even as they were capable of generating conflict between them. Since capitalists themselves as well as other segments of society outside direct capitalist domination, including the church, believed in the sanctity of the family, family issues had considerable legitimacy in the political and social arena.

One way to measure the importance of the family nexus in industrial proletarian lives is to focus on what Hanagan calls the "family subsistence wage." This term represents income sufficient to support a worker's family at a "respectable" level in ordinary times and to permit them to survive the dislocations of crisis times. When the family subsistence wage fell too low, the family faced dissolution or degradation. Without the leverage afforded artisans by their control over labor recruitment and thus over work organization, industrial proletarians, far more completely "subordinated" than artisans, had to try to negotiate a family subsistence wage with employers by using the threat of strike or had to attempt to wrench it from the state as a political concession. The former course of action was much more common than the latter, in part because certain industries had incentives to deal realistically with workers' needs and in part because the working class had so little political weight.

Hanagan examines in detail the family/work dialectic in the Stéphanois coal-mining region in the period between the 1840s and the 1880s. The two spatial poles of his study are Rive-de-Gier, a coal mining town in the east that declined after midcentury as a result of convergent local and national factors, and Le Chambon, a town in the west that developed much later. In both places, family concerns more often stimulated worker protest than inhibited it, though in different contexts. In 1844, after a series of wage reductions and without many opportunities for female employment or other secondary revenue, workers feared they would not be able to support their families. The workers struck, and their families participated passionately in the protest movement.

Later in the century, as Rive-de-Gier became quiescent, militancy shifted to Le Chambon, where families were growing rapidly, in part as a result of female job opportunities and sanguine collective expectations. By the 1870s these opportunities contracted, and the families of Chambonnaire miners became increasingly dependent on the wages of the household head. Meanwhile, as a result of competition from northern producers and the reorganization of production in the Stéphanois region, mine income became increasingly unstable. In addition to wage fluctuations, accidents (more and more common as a consequence of reorganization) also threatened the stability of the family wage. Led by a workers' insurance mutual, the coal miners struck in 1869. Again, families were intensely involved in strike actions because the family as a whole was so deeply implicated in the genesis of the protest movement.

Hanagan insists on the complexity of the family issue. It was not only a matter of wages: family attitude and comportment also depended on family and household size and on female employment opportunities. Hanagan concludes that the affirmation of family values and goals was one of the critical responses to, and ways of resisting, the ravages of proletarianization.

In the next chapter Yves Lequin offers a revisionist reading of the crisis of apprenticeship in nineteenth-century France. To be sure, the striking decrease in the number of apprentices and the deterioration of legal, economic, and moral conditions within formal apprenticeship caused justifiable alarm. Apprenticeship appeared to be reduced to ordinary industrial labor when it was not experienced as a demeaning domesticity. Yet what precisely was lost in the metamorphosis of the nineteenth-century workplace? Lequin suggests that a certain nostalgia and mythicization have clouded our view of worker "custom" and practice.

There was an institutional as well as a literary/ideological resistance to the erosion of apprenticeship. Schools of apprenticeship, often run by religious organizations whose aims had less to do with the social problems of work than with the imperatives of moralization, sprang up in many places. Municipalities, Paris in the lead, founded schools and prizes and stimulated apprenticeship in other ways. Yet the achievements were slender, partly as a result of "bad masters," unable or unwilling to transmit knowledge, who cared only for immediate material gain, and partly as a result of the indifference or hostility of would-be apprentices, deterred by the high cost of apprenticeship, by the constrictive atmosphere of the workshop (Lequin insists on the "greater liberty" that prevailed in most factories), and by the perception that it made no sense to spend a long time learning when one could earn attractive wages for the simplest industrial routines. Apprenticeship seemed increasingly anachronistic in the new industrial landscape. At the same time a notion of general education was accorded priority over a concept of professional or technical education.

In Lequin's opinion, the "crisis" of apprenticeship was fundamentally less a matter of technical education than of the obsolescence of the traditional system of social reproduction based on the Old Regime model of gradual progression from employee to boss. He contends that the factory saved apprenticeship even as it destroyed the old social model from which it emerged and which justified it. But this was the nineteenth-century factory, not the integrated establishment of the twentieth century. The big industrial operation of the nineteenth century was characteristically a congeries of workshops on the old scale. Their spatial contiguity imposed certain changes in production and relations of production, but their internal organization, their distribution of work, and the circulation of craft knowledge within them followed surprisingly traditional patterns. The persistent centrality of certain kinds of "artisanal" skill no more implied technological stagnation than mechanization automatically resulted in deskilling. Work was not yet splintered in the big factories. Worker "polyvalence" was still necessary and prized. In this environment, young workers learned by watching the veterans, by emulating them, by suffering correction. The factory was a school of apprenticeship in which the tyros gradually acquired what used to be called the "secrets of the métier."

Apprenticeship, concludes Lequin, was displaced, not asphyxiated, by the factory and the machine. Apprenticeship itself changed less than the world of work in which it took place. If apprenticeship signifies the continuity of "real practices," it also and perhaps primordially marks an "initiation" into a *condition* and a way of life. The astonishing thing, in Lequin's mind, is that apprenticeship remained essentially what it had always been: entry into a community.

In the next essay Anson Rabinbach shows how the European science of work transformed the very basis for representing work and construing its significance. It broke sharply with earlier modes of perceiving labor founded on doctrines of moral and political economy by focusing on the body of the worker. The new model was medical, and it sprung from the "human machine" vision of the seventeenth and eighteenth centuries.

By the middle of the nineteenth century the metaphor shifted to the motor as the creator of energy: no longer were the forces powering the machine external to it. The dualism of matter and motion gave way to a unified vision of energy as the highest principle of nature. The new science of labor, predicated on the efficient expenditure of energy in the body, turned to the search for precise laws of muscles, nerves, and the deployment of energy within the human organism.

The new science, Rabinbach notes, made the classical preoccupations with work seem utterly obsolescent. "Social Helmholtzianism," named after a German pioneer in the science of work, offered the perspective of a labor force that did not have to be inculcated with eternal truths about the centrality of will, the sin of idleness, or the value of work. The old moral exhortations were replaced by a scientific and medicalized discourse on labor, even as the old forms of industrial discipline (paternalism, familialism, surveillance) gave way to questions of wages and hours and to the discipline of production itself. Since time and motion replaced will as the critical variables, it became possible to envision a purely technical solution to the crisis of discipline.

Helmholtzian physics not only provided a way of investigating the precise economics of labor power, it also identified fatigue, rather than the moral scourge of idleness, as the central mode of the body's resistance to work. The tradition of labor edification had been nourished by the idealization of the artisan, a discourse Jacques Rancière questioned in his essay. With the artisan's social decline, reasons Rabinbach, the image of idleness lost its capacity to conjure moral nightmares. The science of work posited a body undermined by excessive, irregular, and poorly organized work. The Italian physiologist Mosso proved that fatigue was an objective phenomenon, governed by laws analogous to the laws of energy. In his Parisian laboratory, Marey elaborated a new way to represent work through his invention of chronophotography, which enabled him to read motion as time. One of his collaborators juxtaposed the new representation, which reduced work to pure, quantitative performance, to the flawed representations in Diderot's plates, where the "movements are false."

After 1900 the science of work became increasingly entangled in politics, in part because of the controversial character of the issues it addressed (the length of the workday, working conditions, accidents on the job) and in part because of its conception of the state as the necessary arbiter of social conflict. For Rabinbach, "the greatest weakness of the science of labor lay in its most compelling assumption: that scientific objectivity and productivism were socially neutral discourses." Its partisans believed their science could provide an objective solution to the labor question that could mitigate if not foreclose the struggle between capital and labor. Initially, both capital and labor regarded the science of work with skepticism and mistrust.

Rabinbach argues that the introduction of Taylorism in Europe shortly before World War I provoked a serious crisis for the science of work. There were major differences between Taylorism and the science of work as well as a few similarities. The science of work emerged from the laboratory, not the shop floor; it enjoyed its greatest resonance among scientists, physicians, and social reformers, not engineers and managers; it aimed to mediate the social conflict by transforming work in the interests of both labor and management, whereas Taylorism was devoted exclusively to the interests of management by ensuring labor passivity and higher productivity. Both schools began by reducing labor to a series of abstract relations. For both, the body circumscribed the critical arena of labor power, not the social relations of work.

Proponents of the science of labor regarded Taylorism as a total regression to prescientific attitudes toward work, given its one-sided devotion to output and profits. Taylorism, Rabinbach contends, "threatened to eclipse" the paramount preoccupations of the science of labor: the rational determination of the point of maximum efficiency for both labor and capital, the regulation of the expenditure of energy, and the ascertainment of the laws of fatigue. The science of labor had to concede to Taylorism "its most essential point": that workers could become much more productive than they originally had been and that there was no hard-and-fast relation between work of any kind and fatigue. After the war, Rabinbach concludes, there was a growing recognition in both camps that the two methods were not irreconcilable and that a rapprochement would enhance the efforts of both.

In his essay Patrick Fridenson surveys the French industrial landscape during the period when the auto industry adopted American-style techniques. He explores the introduction, expansion and crisis of "Fordism à la française" in the period 1914–83. He detects fundamental changes in worker attitudes that betray not merely a reaction to "further dispossession of autonomy" but rather the elaboration of new strategies and a new kind of struggle.

How did workers deal with the advent of mass production? asks Fridenson. Their solace was wages, which were relatively high. Workers, especially women, felt "emancipated" in the factory. Autoworkers prized the security of the big factory "where everything is taken care of." Yet workers were unevenly and incompletely integrated into their firms. There were important differences between "stable" (skilled) and "mobile" (unskilled or semiskilled) workers. The nature of one's task shaped one's worldview. There was considerable maneuvering for more comfortable work. Semiskilled or unskilled workers complained of boredom and fatigue and resented the strictures against moving about or talking at work, whereas skilled workers retained considerable latitude and even leverage, in part because of the premium placed on quality of work.

One of Fridenson's key points is that workers' activities were characterized less by collective organization than by individual strategies. He attributes this individualism to the splitting of the labor force and its growth and constant renewal, to the complexity of the auto industry, and to the relatively high level of pay. Union vitality withered after World War I as a result of strike failures and strike repression and as a consequence of the scission of the national unions and the suppression of shop stewards. Individual strategies ranged from absenteeism and voluntary departure to on-the-job efforts to combat or alleviate Fordist constraints. Workers transmitted practices of resistance orally outside the workshop—in the locker rooms and at the bus stops. They violated disciplinary codes by sitting down and talking. Or they carried their resistance to the labor process itself by slowing up, limiting production, or using their technical knowledge to devise ploys that upset the schedule or changed the rhythm. Far from annihilating "the workers' spirit of mutual understanding," argues Fridenson, Fordism gave rise to a new kind of control over productive norms. Workers slowed down together and blacklisted or physically assaulted workers who did not join what eighteenth-century bosses would have called the "cabal." Finally, if workers resorted to individual resistance methods, "more or less concerted," it was partly because opposition to Fordism by unions and parties had waned or become ambiguous.

Fridenson ascribes the increasing tensions of the 1930s, which erupted into open conflict, partly to external factors (Nazism, the Popular Front) and partly to internal factors (rebellion against rationalization policies and low wages, the "unstable" combination of a minority of skilled and a majority of semiskilled workers). He discerns signs that workers were rejecting Fordism, especially the semiskilled, for whom the credo of productivism offered little allure. The government and the employers concluded that more coercion would be needed to make workers adapt to the exigencies of modern industry. World War II triggered another phase of insubordination, which now had the aura of patriotism—though worker resistance to the intensified rationalization of wartime production was as much anti-Ford as anti-Hitler.

Fridenson characterizes the period 1945–70 as the "general mechanization of work." The unions helped revive the "productivist consensus," yet the postwar strikes proved that workers saw no salvation in Stakhanovism. They criticized the increased pace of production articulated by machinery. The semiskilled majority resented arbitrary job assignment and deskilling. Through the "technical integration of production" and American-inspired "job evaluation," both of which enhanced management control, and through the decentralization of production, the automakers changed the very relation of workers to their work. They tried to stifle resistance by dismissing leaders, harassing unions, creating house unions, bludgeoning workers with propaganda, and offering higher real wages and job security in exchange for docility. Fridenson stresses the deeply ambivalent attitude toward their work of an increasingly heterogeneous semiskilled work force (heavily recruited from among peasants and immigrant workers)—an ambivalence that found violent expression in the strikes of May–June 1968 contesting mechanization and "reorganized" work.

Automakers further "remade" work by introducing automation in the 1970s. In an atmosphere of world economic crisis and burgeoning unemployment, they scored major successes. Yet Fridenson shows that worker "autonomy" survived as a result of the persistence of a "technological culture" of know-how and of innovative responses to new situations. Automation frequently broke down as Fordism revealed its structural limits. The auto companies had to call upon workers to move into the breaches. And workers used tricks and dodges to subvert or domesticate automation (even as peasants had used them to temper seigneurial tutelage). Though semiskilled workers have not completely lost command of the tempo of work, Fridenson concludes that they remain today deeply anxious about job security in a world of robots.

Unable to attend the conference that spawned this volume, Christopher Johnson agreed to write an Afterword. We asked him to reflect on the collection within a framework of his own design. Predictably, he crafted a vigorous, critical essay.

Johnson focuses on capitalist development and the reactions to it, which he sees as one of the chief unifying themes of this book. First he considers the current debate in the social sciences over work and its ramifications. He sharply castigates the "culturalists" for their reductionistic (mis)reading of Marxism as a sort of vulgar economism. At the same time he chides exponents of a "narrowly conceived Marxism." He suggests the need to recast the theoretical perspective in terms of a "historical dynamic" that connects "social relations" and "exogenous forces."

"There is perhaps no more fascinating area for examining changing social relations of production than the long and convoluted history of industrial capitalism's emergence against and within the household and artisanal mode of production" that is the subject of most of the essays, Johnson writes. In some of them he detects an unfortunate but probably unintended "idealist bias," the product of an overdrawn culturalist allergy to economism. Yet he himself may exaggerate the penetration of capitalist "rationalization" and the extent to which an apparently common "capitalist" ambition gave the legion of entrepreneurs a unity of purpose and practice. It may also turn out that the corporate milieu was less inimical, institutionally and culturally, to capitalism (allowing for all the ambiguities that coexist in this label) than we generally suppose. Johnson points to the need to look more closely at the relation between economic mutation and worker insurgency. He is sympathetic with the argument made in several essays that there was nothing inherently harmonious about "precapitalist" social relations of production—an argument that implies the need for a serious revision of the Soboulean portrayal of the sans-culottes, their origin, and their discourse.

Johnson regrets the lack of attention paid to the Revolution, which quickened the "fracturing and transformation of artisan industry." Drawing on his own research on the Causse family, he emphasizes the need to learn more about the "entrepreneurial" pathway of industrial capitalism taken by artisans of all stripes. Small-scale handicraft industry remained a major component of "the industrial mix" well into the nineteenth century, yet the increasingly intense pressure of competition "that only economies of scale could meet" issued in a heightening of class tension and conflict. On the one hand there were artisans deeply disappointed by capitalism's failure to fulfill its lush promises, and on the other hand some artisans were embittered by the cruelties of proletarianization. One important lesson Johnson draws from the essays is how significantly the meaning of work varies from one group of workers to another. To understand workers, however, he insists on the need to look at them not simply at work but in the context of their everyday "conditions of life." Ultimately he wonders whether an "excessive preoccupation with work" does not "lead us away inadvertently from the study of that [working-class] life in all its complexity." The essays deal with the politics of class relations, with capitalist hegemony, and with worker resistance on multiple levels. Yet Johnson suggests, as a result of a culturalist and structuralist bent, the "actual fights are rarely glimpsed."

As we begin to read the essays that follow, we would do well to recall the final words in *Candide* spoken by Martin, the self-proclaimed last Manichee on earth. "Let's work without speculating [*Travaillons sans raisonner*]," he says, "it's the only way to make life bearable." If there is any one lesson to be learned from our work on work, perhaps it is that historians cannot tolerate Martin's sectarianism. Rewriting Kant's famous dictum of enlightenment, we respond: Speculation without work is empty, work without speculation is blind.

Work, Fellowship, and Some Economic Realities of Eighteenth-Century France

Daniel Roche

For centuries, under the *ancien régime* in France, the lower classes were silent. Our only knowledge of these urban or rural people is furnished by the more or less sincere—or distorted—accounts written by members of the educated elite: men of the church, members of the administration, nobility, or police, and doctors or technicians. One theme runs through all of them: the desire to control and reform an unpredictable populace, made up of more or less uncouth and immoral people who lived in a world of superstition and pagan beliefs, and to lead them to Christian salvation by the straight and narrow path of church doctrine. The members of the clergy, the philosophers of the Enlightenment, the tax collectors, and the forces of law and order who wrote about the poor all insist upon the importance of understanding the masses in order to "socialize" them, but their own knowledge is filtered through their moral judgments. Thus our vision of the lower classes is relative to the observers' consciousness of the differences between them and the people they are describing.

Ménétra: Man, Genre

There are, nevertheless, a few more direct accounts that permit us to understand, at least to some degree, these working-class people's feelings

This article is an abridged version of Daniel Roche's introduction to *Journal de ma vie: Jacques-Louis Ménétra, compagnon vitrier au 18e siècle* (Paris, 1982).

Translator's note: French words and expressions in italics are those of Ménétra; those in quotation marks are those of Daniel Roche.

about their everyday occupations and their way of thinking. The auto-biography of Jacques-Louis Ménétra, journeyman glazier, is one example. Written between 1764 and 1800, it is a unique text but not an isolated one in that it presents traits common to three types of literary endeavor: the literary autobiography, the writing of memoirs and keeping of household accounts, and finally, working-class narratives of daily life.

As a literary genre, autobiography makes its appearance on the horizon of European culture just at the time when Ménétra is writing. The examples of Jamerey Duval and especially Rousseau are well known. But there is a difference between the narratives of these men of letters and that of Jacques-Louis Ménétra in that this simple worker has no ambition to demonstrate the success of his liberating enterprise by exploiting the social and personal advantages of a new identity. A man of the people, he is simply himself, faithful to his social origins and to his own character.

The tradition of autobiography is relatively restricted among the lower classes, but it would not be out of place here to recall the example of Pierre Ignace Chavatte, who kept a daily chronicle of his family life in Lille during the seventeenth century. Alternating between intimate details and accounts of memorable events, whether limited to his neighborhood or concerning the city at large, his text is both the history of a collectivity and the history of an individual. Ménétra, on the other hand, is not a chronicler concerned with posterity. He simply wants to talk about his own life, creating an individual identity rather than a collective one. This latter type of expression flourished for the most part during the nineteenth century, when urbanization and the Industrial Revolution were tearing traditional society apart. The militants of the corporate system, Perdiguier and Guillhanmou, were struggling then to save a tradition as much as to describe it. If Jacques-Louis Ménétra bears witness to his condition in a certain way, he certainly is not a militant; his account is one of a real life, written in the first person and subject to an occasional lack of modesty. He invents a new way of writing, expressing himself in a way deliberately different from a man of letters. By its presentation alone, his is a document that hints at another culture: searching for something new, his style is unformed and independent, with no regard for accepted spelling (nothing remarkable at the time), forming his words phonetically—which is more specific to him—with not one sign of punctuation for more than three hundred pages.

In deciphering this text, so rich and authentic, one cannot help wondering how men of little means conceived of themselves and organized their actions, socially and politically, and in what measure they were capable of analyzing these actions. Evidence of this type of analysis is to be found not only in Ménétra's ability to assimilate ideas gleaned from reading the works of others, but also in his obvious attempt to find new answers to problems as he was writing. To the autobiography per se are affixed a multitude of other productions: work songs, marches, poems (love poems, licentious poems, poems expressing tenderness to friends), picturesque or philosophical letters (one of which was addressed to Rousseau, whom he had met), patriotic, philosophic, and religious writings. This writer of the people is one whose work is a patchwork made of elements gathered from a literary culture poorly documented elsewhere and difficult to reconstruct, but whose obvious importance is reflected in his innumerable allusions to it. To this is added his observation of on-the-road experiences, chance meetings in convents, châteaus, inns, and the homes of parish priests. In this account of one life, we see the gradual development of one individual's behavior, an evaluation of others' behavior, and the logic behind both.

Ménétra provides us with a genuine account of the way people of the lower classes perceived social horizons, confronted authority, and defined a way of being. The situation of the workingman is defined by a code of behavior taught and learned at an early age and based not only on certain economic and legal realities, but also on the individual's reactions to them through his social relations; the collective fancy finds an echo in Ménétra's interpretation of these things. His personal position is nevertheless clearly stated: he is a commoner, without noteworthy ancestors, at the bottom of the social order. He is above all a citizen of Paris (*citoyen de Paris*), conscious of belonging to that intermediate group composed of artisans; son of an artisan, nephew of an artisan, he draws strength from a culture transmitted by trade and by family, dictated by work and its requirements. But he is also an individualist, born of his own work, a man of the future who needs no roots to make him every man's equal. He lives in a real way the period of transition between a society of orders and a society of classes.

Artisanal Family

In the years 1750–55, Jacques-Louis Ménétra's future is decided once and for all: he will be a master glazier like his father. During 1780–90 his son will follow him, smoothly and without contest. Young Parisians pass from childhood to adolescence with ease, at least if they are lucky enough to be born into a family of artisans or small shopkeepers. The control of capital, even a tiny sum, holding power over employees, the possibility or at least the hope of a certain social mobility, all separate the master craftsmen from those who are salaried in the strict sense of the word, even if these differences do not exclude a certain degree of political and professional cooperation and even if, in the area of mores and mentality, a clear boundary is difficult to establish. Ménétra's account is to be placed in the context of the former stratification of social and economic groups and communities. In his portrayal of lives covering three generations, there is ample material for reflection on traditional working methods.

Like his father before him, Ménétra sees in his son the impatience of his own childhood, fidgeting around the paternal workshop, showing off the new techniques he has just learned through the timeworn method of "show and tell" with an air of self-satisfaction and independence, up to the time when he begins to work as a journeyman, going from shop to shop (*courir les maîtres*). Although he has not yet finished his apprenticeship, he already aspires, like any fourteen- to-twenty-year-old, to the financial independence acquired by being able to make money. No, the master glazier of the rue du Petit Lion-Saint-Sauveur has no doubt that his son will succeed him, just as he succeeded his father—not by replacing him in his shop on the rue des Prêtres Saint-Germain l'Auxerrois, but by following in his footsteps in the profession. This was something that the corporate stability of the trade guilds permitted, but that the events and legislation of the Revolution would in large part undermine.

The old fox would not see his grandsons secure and established—history would decide otherwise. Everyone's future then was guaranteed by the paths traced by the trade guilds and the *compagnonnages*; the former would not survive the Revolution, but the latter would meet if not their hour of glory, their greatest moment of publicity during the struggles and changes opposing the working class to the transformations brought about by the Industrial Revolution. Ménétra's narrative is placed just at that strategic moment when the old trade associations are being battered by economists, reformers are preoccupied by the principles of utility and efficiency, and when working-class values that managed to survive the French Revolution are being affirmed. The text throws light on daily working conditions, contrasting aspects of the trade guild fraternity, the ways of doing things, and the profits of artisanal work.

The Glazier's Guild

Glaziers in Paris during the reign of Louis XV belonged to the society of glass cutters and stained-glass artists, a solid institution with precise statutes elaborated by Louis XI in 1467 and modified only slightly by Louis XIV in 1666. In the French capital it was not a prestigious group, ranking far behind the six corporations of influence, or "Six Corps."

The royal edict of 1691, which called for the reorganization of the *jur-ljandes*, placed the glaziers at the bottom of the third class. The edict of August 1776 reorganizing the guild system put the glaziers in nineteenth place. So we are talking about a small trade, both in prestige and in number (Savary records 300 master glaziers about 1730, and the *Almanach du commerce* for the year 1769 accounts for only 260 shops). The mastership code situates glaziery in the middle range: one must pay one thousand *livres* to acquire the title of master glazier, half as much as a haberdasher, only a fifth as much as an apothecary (placed at the very top of the economic rating of the guild masterships), but twice as much as a purveyor (this brings to mind the father of Sebastien Mercier, who was a gunsmith on the Quai de la Ferraille) and five times as much as a teaseler, a seamstress, a gardener, or a poor basketmaker, all of whom are at the very bottom of the trade scale. In the glaziers' guild, journeymen are held to six years' work as "compagnons" unless the worker decides after four years of obligatory apprenticeship to take to the road and ply his trade in the best towns of the kingdom, each of which issues him a certificate. This is what Ménétra decides to do: apprenticed from 1753 to 1757, he becomes a traveling journeyman from 1757 to 1764.

Ménétra's Itinerary to Mastership

In relation to the statutes, Ménétra's history is unclear. In the first place, only the son of a guild administrator (*juré*) had the right to be apprenticed to his own father; and yet Jacques-Louis Ménétra was never elected by the jurande to oversee the rules and regulations of the guild in the annual elections to that effect, even though he had been a master glazier for ten years and was foreman of the Brotherhood of Saint Mark, a sister corporation in the religious community. So Jacques-Louis's apprenticeship is invalid unless one counts the years spent working under various other foremen, or perhaps under his various uncles. One of them, in fact, Marseau Ile-St.-Louis, was elected juré sometime during the 1760s. In this case it seems that family connections worked hand in hand with corporate legislation.

In the second place, Ménétra did not acquire his classification of master craftsman by the usual route: he produced no masterpiece (one would imagine that, given his character, he would not have hidden this important event from his readers). No, Ménétra was a "master of letters" (*maître de lettres*). In other words, he crossed the first barrier a trade worker faces on the road to becoming a master by an indirect means: he bought letters of office, paid for by his grandmother as an advance against his inheritance. This was not a favor accorded by the glaziers' wardenship to master craftsmen's sons; while it is true that they sometimes accorded certain advantages to sons-in-law or guild members marrying widows, they awarded the title of master glazier to only two journeymen each year. Otherwise one had to wait for the retirement or death of an old master, in order to take his place. Thus we see the advantage of being a master without title (*maître sans qualité*). Ménétra was able to benefit from one of eight letters of mastership imposed by the government on each of the trade guilds in 1722, bought back by the Parisian wardenships and resold in order to deal with liquidity problems.

In a word, then, even within his own profession Ménétra is a special case. Although he is the son of a master craftsman, he does not profit from the advantages accorded to people in his position but follows the rules governing apprenticeship practices, refusing to wait for his father to step aside. He makes no masterpiece, closing the door to the usual road toward mastership, but because of his letters of office he can establish himself in any city of the kingdom where there are sworn glaziers. His future, like the future of any other journeyman, depends on how he fits into the establishment: he must be able to buy a shop, and therefore must have access to at least a small amount of capital. This he will find when he marries. In any case, he will always play a marginal role within the corporation, because a master without title is not permitted to be named as a juré before the age of sixty and has no right to sit in on decisions taken by the corporation.

We can now understand the conflicts between him and the Parisian jurés during the 1770s: Ménétra's journal clearly illustrates how the corporation works in its most intimate details, based as it is on a profound sense of hierarchy and discipline, guaranteed if need be with the help of the police. In this way, the corporate system keeps a delicate balance between equality and inequality, ensuring the privileged—whether master craftsmen or journeymen, albeit in differing degrees—a certain degree of social integration and economic independence, based on a monopoly of work possibilities and founded on a command of the everyday work skills, the masterpiece being simply the demonstration of ability to carry out the basic requirements of the trade. It also sets down as statutes the tenets of a contractual situation in which the act of working bears above all a social message that guarantees, institutionalizes, and fixes an economic mechanism the jurés are unable to control. The desire for control and a desire for freedom thus come to grips in dealings between journeymen and master craftsmen. Although the master mentality is rooted in the attitudes of the journeyman, both groups think somewhat differently than a fully established master tradesman invested with the duties of a juré. Ménétra's situation reveals itself to be exceptional in allowing us to grasp the nuances of a multifaceted system with imprecise boundaries.

Concerning the working conditions in the Parisian trade guilds and those of the traveling journeymen on the *Tour de France*, the differences are considerable. The Parisian journeyman arrives in the provinces with a technical reputation to defend, even if he decided to finish his apprenticeship in this way in order to learn the different procedures and tricks of the trade as they are practiced in the various regions of France. There is a chronic shortage of labor in the provinces, and the mobility of the journeymen permits the local *bourgeois* to draw upon a ready labor reserve in the network of compagnonnage inns. The employer/employee relationship seems a balanced one under Ménétra's pen, even if the ideals of independence play a role here as elsewhere. Ménétra's bourgeois and his *veuves*, widows who enjoy all the rights and privileges of their deceased husbands, are for the most part good employers; they are not too demanding about the way he works so long as the work is well done, they share their tables and houses with him, and above all, they are always ready to join him in a drink and to pay for it out of their own pockets. The best masters fight to win over the best unemployed journeymen; they ensure their security, protect them in their flight after a scandal, and bring them good food if they get caught and thrown in prison. In the end, through Ménétra's account of his wandering years, we see how a certain working and social community operates, in which conflicts arise but are settled either by negotiation (as was the case in Nantes) or by flight—always a tangible possibility. Even if the journeymanship system does not ensure upward social mobility for everyone, there is room for hope, and the marriage market it opens up, which seconds the work market in terms of economic possibilities, promotes these same hopes and illusions.

In Paris, on the other hand, there is no shortage of labor; with one or two journeymen in each workshop, there is a total of some six hundred glaziers available. The need for them becomes more pressing as the city expands—houses need windows—and the corporation keeps a close watch on the hiring of new journeymen, distributed by the jurés to the various masters. Little by little, the freedom of the workers becomes limited: they cannot leave the workshop without a fortnight's notice (*sans donner quinzaine*), and they are sometimes obliged to work a long time for a master they do not get along with because they cannot obtain authorization to leave. They are classed and identified by the work system, provoking conflicts that Ménétra describes in his journal. The paternalistic ideal and family-type situation that functions in the provincial cities become disjointed in Paris, owing to the conflict of interest between the small shopkeepers and the workers. The latter manage to make the best of their situation by acts of provocation: Ménétra, for instance, convinces some journeymen to leave their bad boss, Elophe; he flaunts his independence with bravado, insolence, and insult. Things take a bad turn, however—the police exile him to Versailles to equip the chateau and stables with windows, under the surveillance of the constables and glaziers of the king. He is branded a troublemaker, an agitator. But in the confrontations between Ménétra and his employers, it is almost always a question of his behavior rather than a conflict over wages or working hours.

For the journeyman, the freedom to work implies a fundamental feeling of independence, a refusal of constraint and immobility. When on the Tour de France, he quite literally does not stay in one place, leaving one construction site for another, moving from city to city. In Paris, before setting up his own shop, he works for several employers; in Ménétra's case, for six different ones in the course of two years. Ménétra moves from his brother-in-law's shop to that of old man Vilmont, from Vilmont to Elophe with Vilmont's permission, from Elophe to Jérôme, from Jérôme to Elophe, from Elophe to Langlois without Elophe's assent, from Langlois to Bellé, from Bellé to Jérôme, and from Jérôme to Vilmont. True, each time he attempts to better his condition, but above all he wants to escape the tutelage of the established teachers and masters while they do their best to tie him down, either by force or by sentiment—in the latter case using the presence of a pretty daughter, niece, or young widow in an attempt to still the wanderlust of the journeyman. A song written by Ménétra illustrates these clashes, at the same time idealizing the life of the journeyman under the old system (*ancienne méthode*). The boss should be neither proud nor cruel and should be polite to his men; authority should stem from his abilities and not be the result of money or pretense; the good master is a good worker with taste (*goût*), skill (*science*), and talent; he eats with his journeymen, serves only the best (*toujours du bon*) on unbroken plates with metal tableware, and he provides butter and salt. If we are to believe our journeyman, the "new style of today's masters" (*nouvelle mode des maîtres d'aujourd'hui*) makes a mockery of the old-fashioned system of values and creates conflict between the master and his workers.

Ménétra as Master

Once he becomes a master craftsman, Ménétra nevertheless does not forget his days as a journeyman; the hostile feelings he had toward his masters become directed, in a rather juvenile manner, toward the glaziers' jurande, far too meddlesome in his mind. He quarrels with the jurés over not having paid his inspection rights—even unestablished master craftsmen are obliged to pay them; he finds fault with the elections, he polemicizes against the head office over the belatedly declared hiring of a worker. In 1776 he commends the decision to abolish the distribution of masterships. In his professional life we see how certain conflicts, mitigated in the provinces but exacerbated in Paris, begin to divide the "hard-up small shopkeepers, completely separated from the proletariat by the barrier erected by property ownership (during social crises they always side with property's defenders), yet still very close to their lower-class origins as reflected in both their behavior and their tastes."[1] The insubordination of the workers, condemned by both the jurés and the police, is a symptom of the slow deterioration both of the economic situation and of social and personal relationships. Insubordinate as a journeyman, Ménétra becomes a rebellious master, manifesting the very spirit of revolt so feared and so vigorously denounced by Mercier and Rétif in the years just before the Revolution. Ménétra shares with the moralists of the time the idea that "in the old days" mores and social relationships were different and more harmonious. Undoubtedly this was one of the guiding principles learned on the Tour de France.

Journeymen's Associations: Work and Fraternity

The eighteenth century compagnonnages bring journeymen together in associations that are, at least in theory, clandestine, albeit tolerated by both employers and police, who keep a close eye on their meetings and goings-on in general: Ménétra and his friends are arrested on vague suspicions and flimsy evidence in Poitiers, and he is questioned again in the Cévennes. From the sixteenth century onward, the organization of the compagnonnages had become increasingly complex and effective, dividing the journeymen into professional chapters or callings (*la vacation*) and providing them with protection and help whenever needed. Their strength is less the result of myths and secrets (which have long fascinated the historians of esoterism in the working classes) than of their ability to answer the needs inherent in the itinerant life of the Tour and to incorporate themselves into the deep-rooted practices of youthful fraternities and religious societies connected to the various crafts. The symbolic customs and gestures, the strength of mythical ideas drawn

[1] Alain Faure, introduction to Agricol Perdiguier, *Mémoires d'um compagnon* (Paris, 1980), p. 12.

from any number of sources, reflect a general attitude toward the work ethic and toward the world in general that unifies traditional forms of sociability and facilitates the mobilization of these young men. The quarrels that oppose the different compagnonnages can thus be explained by the desire to impose, ultima ratio, the individualistic superiority of their ideals. The guild fraternity, as experienced by Ménétra, works on three levels: it defends the common interest, proclaims through its rites and ceremonies the value of Duty (*le Devoir*) and the excellence of each calling, and defines the sphere of social relations of the twenty- to twenty-five-year-old age group in terms of opposing forces, those of exchange and competition.

Ménétra is a compagnon of Devoir; he was initiated in the chapter (*cayenne*) in Tours, most likely in 1758. This tradition of Devoir is that of the children of Maître Jacques (*les enfants de maître Jacques*), also known as *les compagnons passants ou dévorants*, held to combat the children of Solomon (*les enfants de Salomon*) or *Gavots*, as well as those associated with father Soubise and called the good fellows (*les Bons Drilles*). These three traditions of journeymanship should on no account be confused with modern trade associations; they were movements made up of people united by the practice of a given trade. Theoretically, each association or sect corresponds to a specific craft, but depending on the time and the city in question, any number of different callings can in fact be incorporated. Finally, and above all, it may have been the initial clandestineness of these societies that was responsible, in the end, for the particular form of organization they maintained even after they were officially recognized as institutions. In such circumstances, precautionary and defensive measures become signs of distinction and a means of affirming differences in culture. Thus the code of discipline, the secrets, the nicknames that served not only to confound the police but also to unify the group, the close surveillance of strangers, the sponsorship of new members, and the pursuit of spies and traitors all had their *raison d'être*. Although Ménétra's journal does not paint the daily life of the compagnonnages with the precision of similar nineteenth-century accounts, we nevertheless see clearly three main themes: the control of working conditions, the force of solidarity raised almost to the level of an institution, and the functioning of a system based on hierarchy and discipline.

Ménétra benefits from all the protection the compagnonnages provide to their traveling members. Even before his initiation, upon his departure from Versailles, he is part of a network in which masters—often former traveling journeymen themselves—and guild representatives work together in a common action geared to consolidating the recruitment of workers. His itinerary therefore follows the offers transmitted from city to city, taking him from Montreuil-Bellay to Nantes, from Narbonne to Montpellier, from Lyons to Pont-de-Veyle. In each place people are waiting for him, ready to put him up and care for him; he is rarely unemployed, even temporarily, though we find one instance of this in Bayonne. The duration of the work expected of him is arranged in advance, and when it comes to term, he is free to leave the construction site or the workshop at will. Out of thirty work situations, the only disagreement of terms he encounters is in Carpentras.

Never inactive, on two occasions he fights to defend the jobs of fellow workers and protest the working conditions of the traveling journeymen. In the first instance, in Nantes, the city is boycotted (*défendue*) by the journeymen glaziers as a protest against working conditions. Ménétra and two other workers who stay behind for the cause drive the masters mad, taking it upon themselves to negotiate new terms with the local jurés. In Bordeaux the situation is more complex. Under Ménétra's pen it takes on a completely different dimension, aimed at building up his own role and the importance of the unity of action of workers of different trades. It is one of a series of conflicts that oppose the compagnonnages to the city jurés and masters over the issue of hiring policies, complicated by the general hostility of the working world to the military obligations decreed in 1758–59 during the war against England. The journeymen flee the city to avoid the draft and the militia, playing on local conflicts of interest in a way that shows real political know-how: they pit the local authorities, the intendent (Monsieur de Tourny fils), the municipality, the parlement, and the governor (Monsieur le Duc de Richelieu) against each other. The *damnation* or boycott of a city, large gatherings, even riots are common currency in these troubled times. If Ménétra exaggerates the number of workers concerned—he cites four thousand itinerant journeymen when the total artisanal population of Bordeaux numbers no more than six to seven thousand—if he ritualizes the actions and political positions, he nevertheless portrays in an effective way the real organizational capacity of the compagnonnages and their efficacy in defending their members. Here we see them confronting the native population of employers and city authorities in such a way that the local order and economy are disrupted.

This solidarity finds an echo in every domain, helping those wanted by the police to flee, instigating spectacular escapes, finding hiding places in outlying inns, as was the case in Lyons after a duel that took a bad turn. On a more daily level, it permits the Parisian journeyman to feel at home wherever he goes: if thrown in prison he is helped financially— five *sous* a day in corporation cases; he is taken to the hospital and visited, all with the understanding that he will render the same in due course. Thus the secular corporate organizations of the eighteenth century pre-

serve certain principles of Christian charity held by the religious brotherhoods from which they issued, though less conformist than their forebears. Even so, it is up to the association's officials to see that the rules
are followed and to act as arbiters in confrontations between their members and the bourgeoisie. In Ménétra's journal, the officials' power is
portrayed in a rather gentle light, in terms of both the way it functions
and the way difficult situations are dealt with.

Ménétra, initiated in 1758 after a few months as a candidate in Tours,
becomes a finished associate ("compagnon fini") a short time afterward
and head fellow ("premier compagnon") in Rochefort in 1759. He is
reelected to this office in Bordeaux, and in 1762 or 1763 in Lyons. As
capitaine, elected for one year (in theory, but the term can vary in practice)
he is responsible for everything concerning his craft or calling; he is
helped in his duties by a few of the other members like the registrar
(*rôleur*) in Lyons, who takes care of the distribution and payment of the
workers and former members of the Tour. Because of the number of
associates and the volume of business—this includes keeping up correspondence with the cities of the Tour de France, rendering justice, organizing ceremonies and festivals, taking care of society affairs, and
monitoring the members' conduct—Ménétra finds his time taken up to
the point that he cannot ply his trade. Not surprisingly, it is especially
in the large cities that these organizational duties are the most pressing:
in Nantes, where there are about one hundred glaziers; in Bordeaux,
where the glaziers' jurande covers some thirty master craftsmen and
more than a hundred local and traveling journeymen; in Lyons, where
Ménétra directs sixty-two journeymen himself and where there are some
fifty workshops representing twice that number of established workmen.
In the smaller cities like Angers with eight master craftsmen, Poitiers
with four or five, Mâcon with two or three, the fellowship members find
it unnecessary to establish such a complex organization, since professional and civil relationships are dealt with one to one. For much the
same reason, it is in the large cities that the rituals and ceremonies take
on special importance and major incidents occur.

Ritual and Sociability

The journal is extremely revealing about the ritualization of the workers' daily life. Every activity takes place against a background of ceremony
and meetings where the myths and ideology of the compagnonnage are
propagated and the reproduction of social roles is carried out, creating
a type of sociability that is in itself a sort of subculture. Ménétra recalls
two aspects of his initiation: the society members make him copy out the

corporation register (*rôle*)—the act of writing it is in itself a sort of initiation, at least when it concerns copying down the rules, the statutes, and the list of new members that was also probably included in it; and he is rebaptized. This changing of names plays both a useful and a symbolic role. We know that at that time these ceremonial baptisms included teachings that were essentially religious in nature but pedagogical in import. The themes of Christian baptism, the Passion of Christ, and the partaking of water, bread, and wine form only part of the initiation rite; in addition are the recitation of the society myths, the legends and torments of Maître Jacques, which reinforce the feeling of solidarity among the initiates and exalt the value of manual work in a society that demeans it, in a code of highly spiritualized moral values. The society baptism is a rite of passage, the definitive incorporation into adulthood and a trade, which at the same time inculcates the ideology of the fraternity—more or less democratic in the brotherhood of the children of Maître Jacques, more or less elitist in that of the Gavots. This same duality of purpose pervades all of the society's actions.

The ceremony of departure (*conduite*) is a good example of this. Ménétra clearly shows us its utility—sixty hardy companions offer real protection against the attacks of rival societies—but the symbolic function is evident; often no one really leaves the city at all. Then what counts are the music, the violins, the oboes, and the gestures (unfortunately undescribed) by which the moment of separation and the mission itself are acted out. The form of these enactments changes depending on the place and the quality of the traveler, but their purpose is always to anchor and make concrete memories too easily forgotten in an unstable society. The same duality is present in the corporation assemblies (*chambres du Devoir*): aspiring members or candidates are welcomed, affiliated members are initiated, the associates are finished—Ménétra becomes a finished associate in Tours—ceremonies, burials, and festivals are prepared, conflicts are settled. But above all, what counts is the sacred atmosphere and strict observance of hierarchy in the ceremonies. All the members are present, ranked according to their order of seniority, and bareheaded with the exception of the head fellow, who presides over the meeting with his head covered, a book and paper before him. The candidate, who affects a humble demeanor, is made aware of the new air he will breathe and the treasures he is to receive so that, in due time, he can share them with others. In the allusions he makes and the extreme discretion of his style, Ménétra reveals himself to be an uncompromising member of the fellowship and defender of its honor through the somewhat silly secrets that ensure the unity and strength of the society: ordeals, acknowledgments, greetings. He participates in a ritual meeting for the last time in 1764 in Châteauvieux, near Orléans. An era ends with the Tour de France, and the tone of the journal changes. Through Ménétra's account we come to understand a way of life, the meaning of fellowship for members of a certain age group, and the real significance of the Tour de France.

Everything centers on a kind of sociability that has its own particular localities and meeting places. Ménétra generally finds lodging and meals in suburban inns, less closely watched than those in the cities proper. Chapters are installed there and assemble the different callings. The "old ladies" (*mères*) and their husbands the "old men" (*pères*) run these places, keep the journeymen up to date on the latest news, offer work, lend them money, or offer credit that is covered by the common pool. Oran, one of the glaziers, will never be forgiven for robbing the old lady. Everyone meets in the tavern to eat, drink, sing, and relax. They sleep several to a room, or in dormitories. Everyone knows what everyone else is doing, and this little subsociety runs its everyday life in a constant exchange of oral customs (stories, songs) and written ones (letters, the rules, and the company register).

Scuffles and festivals play a double role in this system: they reinforce the feeling of solidarity in a spectacular way, and they proclaim the cult of youth and strength. In the stories, what counts is not so much the plausibility of the details as the overall meaning. In the accounts of Bordeaux and Angers, Ménétra's tendency to exaggerate the importance of events is evident, but considerable brawls in the world of the compagnonnages do exist; I could give several examples. These incessant skirmishes (Ménétra recounts at least ten) are the collective and ritualistic means of resolving discord among the excitable younger generation, as well as conflicts between rival societies, whether stemming from a desire to control the work force or from a deep-seated ideological antagonism. The fratricidal battles encountered on the Tour furnish provocative affirmation of the existence of a counterculture at odds with the official order. The "bourgeois" and militia simply turn their backs, the mounted police hotly pursue the fleeing conquerors and the conquered, the priests bury the dead when they find them, and fellow members do their best to save the wounded or hide the corpses of the slain. In his account of these major events, Ménétra demonstrates a certain preoccupation with a system of organization, more imaginary than real in all likelihood, that lays bare a certain ideal: to control and direct, in a military fashion, the violence of enemies by means of gigantic rows and fistfights, canings, stone throwing, and other such exercises that proclaim the group's physical superiority and the honor of the fellowship, all in eliminating the rival competition.

The festivals of the compagnonnages are the peaceful manifestation of the same creed. Anything can be the occasion for a party: Sunday's day off work (*la débauche du dimanche*), any number of religious and civil holidays, a Te Deum, the celebration of Epiphany in Nantes and Mâcon; each is an excuse to hold banquets, balls, or processions with music and songs. Even a burial becomes a time of enjoyment through the elaborate ceremony and banquet held in honor of the deceased. The festivals of each craft or calling—the feast of Saint Anne held on the twentieth of July in 1761, or the feast of Saint Luke—reunite the carpenters and the glaziers in the triumph of Devoir. For Ménétra, the feast of Saint Luke in Lyons is a personal triumph as well. He distributes roles to everyone: the head fellow, the former members of the Tour de France, the old ladies and old men, the finished associates, the affiliated members, the aspiring members, those just coming to the end of the Tour as well as those still on it, the "bourgeois" and their families. And he arranges everything with the authorities. The progression of the festival unifies time and appropriates space; it lasts nearly a week, night and day, acting out the taking of the city (going from shop to shop in a floral and bacchic ceremony), including a solemn procession, a demonstration of strength and honor, a High Mass with an offering, a ball, and four or five Gargantuan banquets, one after the other. If one were to give an overall interpretation of this ceremony, one could suggest that it embodies the reconciliation of order and disorder, calms the violence of the young, maintains appearances in spite of particularly generous libation, and reunites all the trades and the city, all the callings in the name of Devoir, and finally, the old and the young.

Because of all its symbolic meanings, the festival becomes the expression of a creed of the value of wealth, the fundamental nature of a wasteful economy coinciding with the duration of the Tour de France. Ménétra's narrative makes this quite clear: what is valued above all else, even strength, is generosity, the capacity for giving. All the activities of the fellowship are founded on turning over individual wealth to the common good, which is why Ménétra despises thieves and misers, who represent the ultimate expression of individual gain over the circulation and redistribution of wealth to the collectivity. Everything should be superb and ostentatious, the harvest of savings. A penny earned is a penny spent, the gift received from a "bourgeois" the pretext of social exchange and drinking in good company. Departure ceremonies, get-togethers in the local taverns after work, to say nothing of holidays, are so many godsends, permitting the symbolic manifestation of the acts of receiving and of giving, flaunting the principles of a liberating consumerism and, in so doing, condemning tightfistedness.

In Tours, five hundred days' salary goes up in smoke at the occasion of a Te Deum and the drinking parties that follow it. In Lyons the head fellow contributes one hundred days' salary to the festivities, to be added to more than two hundred days' worth other participants have put in the kitty (*mettent au coffre*), covering themselves with debts, which makes a total of more than three hundred livres, not counting the round of banquets and the gifts of their employers. Ménétra receives twelve livres from his employer and immediately uses it to hold a supper for his "calling"; he gives an afternoon tea, paying for violins and all the rest—in an instant the loan has disappeared into thin air.

Refusing the principle of saving, these young traveling journeymen (all from twenty to twenty-five years old) set up a system of loan and exchange, a perpetual fraternal potlatch that reinforces the common feeling of solidarity and covers not only their material life but their intimate personal life as well, including sexual exchanges along with the festivals and carnival celebrations. This economy of giving structures both the forms of conflict that arise, whether social or generational (the boss is both bourgeois and of an older generation), and the collective behavior of the members of the fellowship. It is easy to see why this economy of seduction and dissipation would worry the church, the police, the authorities, and with time, the economists. The fellowship rites put off settling down—it is impossible to save money: evidence of the refusal to accept the rules of a merchant society and individual commitment at the very moment of their historical foundation.

The Profession of Glazier

The passing from youth to the age of responsibility is also a time of economic conversion. But the bond created by community in work and an ideology based on merit bridge these two moments in a man's life. For most of the workers, the journeymanship system represents not the creation of an artisanal elite, but rather the transmission from generation to generation of certain traditional ways of working. "It was a mold in which a certain number of trades were preparing for a changing of the guard."[2] At the time, the Tour de France was the only trade school. To us, glaziery appears to be an unimaginative art demanding no great specialization, but we forget that the acquisition of windows played a fundamental role in changing social customs by completely changing one of the functions of urban and rural accommodation: the regulation of light and heat. We also forget the importance of the stained-glass window and the artistic and pedagogical role played by the glaziers and stained-glass artists in the postmedieval period. Ménétra paints a two-sided picture of the profession, on the one side sure of itself and of its

[2]Ibid., p. 9.

traditions, on the other side subject to the encroachment of changes and modifications in spite of the rules and regulations. Here, to be sure, is the dilemma of the entire artisanal economic structure, and one of the major problems encountered during the eighteenth-century take-off.

Ménétra also teaches us what being a glazier means, describing the techniques and procedures of the trade. The workshop (*boutique*) is where the basic tasks are carried out toward preparing the piece that will be taken to the work site. The glazier works dressed in a jerkin, leather breeches, and an apron—Ménétra's uniform until the police recognize our rakish journeyman with his bulging pockets full of loose change, nails, and glazier's hammer. On the road the apron is rolled and slung across the shoulder like a bandolier, and the hammer can serve as a light weapon. The hammer and nails represent the essential tools of the glassman, fixing the glass in the wooden frame prepared by the carpenter with nails that either hold a band of paper in place or reinforce the lute (*lut*), a kind of putty made with a mixture of heavy oil and chalk. Also indispensable are the glass-cutter's diamonds, either *à queue*, affixed to a little wooden handle, or *à rabot*, used without a handle to cut large sheets of plate glass. One of the primary worries of the traveling glazier is that his diamond will be stolen. Among the other tools in the workshop are the furnaces, stoves, and braziers used for annealing large pieces of glass or melting lead or resin; a large table whitened with chalk and called the *patron*; and the shelves upon which are arranged rulers, compasses, various molds, and lead-working instruments (*lingotières, moules à lien, tire-plomb*), pincers, putty knives, T squares, knives, brushes—in short, all the miscellany of the profession. Leaning against the walls or put away in the storeroom are the mounting frames, which, after forming molten lead, occasionally have to be taken outside and cooled with bucketfuls of water.

Glaziery necessarily groups together a multiplicity of tasks, implying a certain unstructured division of labor in which every man must know how to do everything. It is uninteresting work for the most part: taking measures, setting a pane of glass, gluing paper, painting part of a wall or a window. Ménétra carries out these tasks under the eyes of Rousseau in his lodgings in the rue Plâtrière; innumerable clients of modest means—merchants, neighbors, prostitutes, innkeepers—ask his services. The glazier is their handyman. But he becomes a skilled professional when he works on houses with carpenters or architects, or above all when he repairs, maintains, and sets the windows or stained glass of abbeys, convents, châteaus, the greenhouses of the aristocracy, the king's stables, or the halls of Versailles. He then becomes a first-class specialist who must know how to color glass, set it in lead (*mettre en plomb*), make decorative borders, and cut plate glass and mirrors with unerring dexterity. It is by this technical prowess that the glazier becomes an *artiste*, and though he is neither a glassmaker nor a glassblower, he claims this quality by right of the old system as opposed to the style of the day (*l'ouvrage à la mode*). The glazier's art demands quickness of hand and eye, skill and agility, when glazing churches, refectories, and monasteries.

On the Tour de France, Ménétra proves his talent. He leaves behind him veritable jewels of his art: a glass writing table, a chest, the bishop's coat of arms on the stained glass window of the hospital in Carpentras. In Montereau, to the detriment of his bourgeois, he wins a bet by installing eighty large glass panels in two weeks. He marvels at the stained-glass windows in the cathedral of Auch, with their biblical teachings and stories, and he keeps a sketchbook like a connoisseur of any art, goes from shop to shop to glean new ideas, lends his book to friends to share his discoveries, and sorely regrets losing his sketchbooks later. Here we see how the love of doing beautiful work comes into being and is passed on. We also see how, in its way, a simple profession is capable of passing on the fruits of a more modern material culture. Ménétra is heir to the Parisian artisans who built Versailles and who contributed to innumerable projects, both ordinary and prestigious. In the southern provinces he shares his know-how and habits. Country priests and gentlemen, magnificent abbeys or humble convents all contribute in their way to the progression and expansion of modern glasswork.

In the countryside and small cities, Ménétra spreads the new techniques of the trade as well as the new economy and management of windows; plate glass permits large glass panels in sizes we still use today; and the principles of making it were first laid out by Savot, followed by Félibien and Blondel, and reiterated in Diderot's *Encyclopédie* in 1750. For them at least, the only good glass is from France, more precisely from Paris, and the only good glaziers are Parisian. The movement that transforms customs all over the country (from Paris in the seventeenth century to the other large cities like Lyons by the beginning of the eighteenth, doing away with windows of cloth and oiled paper and replacing small panes of glass with large ones) spreads to the small provincial cities and towns from the workshops in the large centers like Toulouse or by means of the traveling journeymen from Paris. It is, to be sure, a slow technical transformation. The building maintenance records from Lyons prove that in the middle of the eighteenth century every conceivable form of door or window can be found in the local buildings, but living habits slowly begin to change. Little by little people grow used to better light and new visibility, to better protection against the cold. Ménétra is one of the instigators of this silent revolution.

From this point of view Ménétra reveals himself to be definitely on the side of progress, as much because it permits him to earn more money (glass cages for birds and white mice, frames for prints and engravings, statues of Henri IV) as because he defends his profession against the establishment of new rules and regulations. On his Tour de France, he rubs elbows with those in the high places of colonial and commercial capitalism while profits take off and climb throughout the century. In Nantes, La Rochelle, Rochefort, Bordeaux, Nîmes, and Lyons he sees how the fever of exchange and commerce mobilizes the most enterprising artisans into fitting the king's ships with windows, shipping glass panels to the islands, repairing and equipping the arsenals, hospitals, and aristocrats' greenhouses. Ménétra discovers the meaning of business sense when he helps the brazier, Rigandier, install lanterns in Montpellier: Ménétra defends him against unemployed journeymen and hesitant master craftsmen who lacked the audacity to bid on this city project. Around 1765 he takes part in a similar venture in Paris with old man Vilmont; here and there he collaborates with other artisans to better the quality and installation of city lighting.

Once he is established on his own he is an excellent businessman, "lively and pleasant," and his wife is an excellent business manager. He tries to introduce Alsatian glass—Baccarat—to the Parisian market, but this innovation is in conflict with the rules of the corporation, a problem he had already come up against when he authorized the activities of an unapproved master craftsman from the faubourg Saint-Antoine. To win his case, he is obliged to defy the statutes that establish the working regulations of the glass market, awarding a monopoly to the glassmakers of Normandy and fixing the prices and quantities of the wholesale market. His quarrel with the *gros jurés*, put into song in 1773 and 1774, criticizes the meddlesome side of the regulations, the way the oligarchy transmits and controls economic power through undemocratic elections, and the financial direction of the corporation.

Ideology

In 1776, exulting, he writes: "You, the ancient bachelors [this is a term given to former masters, ex-jurés, and syndics] of glass / Thémis has seen your wicked ways / And unfair workings of your monopolies / Your just deserts will come to pass / And bring you crashing to your knees" (Vous anciens bacheliers du verre / Thémis reconnaît vos travers / Vos monopoles injustement exercés / à bon droit eux et vous vont tomber / et dans la même secousse être cassés). Here, our enterprising artisan applauds the liberal initiative of Turgot. He is favorable to competition, free enterprise, and profit; in spite of the prohibitions issued, he opens a second shop on the rue Pavée, since he needs more space to produce what he calls his little works of glass (*petits ouvrages de verre*). He, his wife, and his journeymen have a lot of work. In the artisanal adventure of Jacques-Louis Ménétra we see, on a small scale, the importance of the stakes in the changing economic game of the time: the permanent battle between innovation, which ensures greater profits, and the technical and commercial stagnation that characterized the corporate system and ensured its existence. The glaziers' leadership does not feel hampered by this stagnation of its practices. On the contrary, their constancy is felt to be a guarantee of their continuation and the means through which the fellowship attains moral fortitude: it is by self-restraint and economy that one is enriched, not by expanding one's business. Ménétra's personal drama reproduces, in a curious way, the dichotomy in the society at large. His wife, Marie-Elisabeth Hénin, represents the day-by-day "a penny saved is a penny earned" philosophy of the jurés and parsimonious "rentiers." Jacques-Louis, on the other hand, stands for enterprise, an agent of the circulation of money and of initiative, a defender of public liberty.

As a journeyman on the Tour de France or in the Parisian workshops, Ménétra works to live and have a good time; he does not live to work. When he sets up shop with the dowry of Marie-Elisabeth, he takes his place among those who contribute to unblocking the frozen economy. He gives us an extraordinary account of the intertwining economic attitudes to be found in the world of the working class and small shopkeepers. For the journeyman, the dream of realizing a profit is synonymous with ostentatious spending, waste, and conviviality; he doesn't know how to count (*il ne sait pas compter*). The master craftsman works to increase his gains, through cunning and business expansion, but his attitudes still reflect the way of life and irresponsibility of his youth, a desire to earn in order to spend. He is a timid capitalist; he does not want to know how to count. His wife, who throws her whole life and small capital into the future of her glazier, is a good manager essential to the success of the shop, for it is she who runs it. Her imagination and horizons are as narrow as those of the jurés and rentiers; she counts too much. In this confrontation of generations and roles, in this personal biography, all the problems of an urban economy during the Enlightenment come into play.

Translated by Mary Hyman

–3–

Journeymen's Migrations and Workshop Organization in Eighteenth-Century France

MICHAEL SONENSCHER

Introduction

Two scenes come readily to mind as evocations of the world of artisanal production in eighteenth-century France. The first is an interior: a master artisan, his journeymen, and his apprentices are at work together in a workshop. In an adjoining room is a table with food and wine at which they and the master's wife and children will eat. Above the workshop is a room or rooms where the apprentices, and perhaps the journeymen, will sleep.[1]

The second scene is outdoors: at the gates of a city or the beginning of a winding road. A group of journeymen, members of a *compagnonnage*, are assembled for the *conduite* (departure) of one of their number. The

I would like to express my thanks to the British Social Science Research Council for financial support in enabling me to collect the material used in this essay. The computations, and the resulting figures and tables could not have been done without the work of Robyn Smits, formerly of the Middlesex Polytechnic Computer Centre, and Alison Shepherd of the Geography School of the Middlesex Polytechnic. I am most grateful to them for their help and kindness.

Further discussion of the questions raised here can be found in M. Sonenscher, "The Sans-Culottes of the Year II: Rethinking the Language of Labour in Revolutionary France," *Social History* 9 (1984): 301–28; and idem, "Les sans-culottes de l'An II," *Annales E.S.C.* 40 (September/October 1985).

[1]The image will be familiar to readers of Retif de la Bretonne's *Monsieur Nicolas*. There is a need to bring together engravings and paintings of the eighteenth-century boutique, as Arlette Farge and Daniel Roche have done for other areas of everyday social life in *Vivre dans la rue à Paris au XVIIIe siècle* (Paris, 1979), and *Le peuple de Paris au XVIIIe siècle* (Paris, 1981), respectively. See, however, the essay by William Sewell in this volume (chap. 8).

ceremony is an elaborate one. There are bouquets and music. The most recent arrival in town carries the cane and sack of the departing journeyman. Those remaining line up in order—from the *capitaine* or *premier compagnon* to the newest arrival (*dernier en ville*)—to make their farewells. Toasts are drunk and promises made. Everything is designed to ease the transition from the familiar intimacy of the *boutique* to the hazards and uncertainties of the *Tour de France*.[2]

Both images have their place in the historiography of artisanal production in eighteenth-century France. The first can be found most frequently in the work of historians of the popular movement of the Year II of the First French Republic. "Living and working beside his journeymen," writes Albert Soboul, "often a former journeyman himself, the small workshop master had a decisive ideological influence upon his journeymen...Even if they were in conflict with their master, journeymen of the small trades, formed in the school of the master, often living under their roof and eating at their table, had the same conceptions of the great problems of the time: the artisanal petty bourgeoisie fashioned the workers' mentality."[3]

The bonds created in the workshop were reinforced by a common suspicion of large merchants, contractors, and monopolists, so that the shared fear of dearth overrode potential conflicts over wages and working conditions.[4] In the context of 1793, hostility toward *accapareurs* (monopolists), counterrevolution, and foreign invasion ensured that the egalitarianism of the boutique acquired a public political presence in the figure of the *sans-culotte*. As William Sewell has put it, "during this entire period, journeymen and masters alike were swept up in the sans-culotte movement."[5]

The second image has its place, of course, in the history of the compagnonnages.[6] Ever since the great discovery of these semiclandestine associations in the years preceeding the revolution of 1848, the historiography of the compagnonnages has tended to reproduce a certain timeless image of the associations formed by journeymen in preindustrial France. Their identity, ritual, and structure appear to have been the same in 1650 as in 1750, endowing them with an aura of continuity that a closer examination of changes in the forms and geographical distribution of artisanal production may perhaps dispel.[7] Recently the impres-

[2]There is a good description of a conduite in Archives communales de Nantes, I² carton 3, d.4, 19 September 1810. More generally, until the publication of Cynthia Truant's study of the compagnonnages, see Emile Coornaert, *Les compagnonnages en France* (Paris, 1966).
[3]Albert Soboul, *Les sans-culottes parisiens en l'an II* (La Roche sur Yonne, 1958), p. 452.
[4]George Rudé, *The Crowd in the French Revolution* (London, 1959), pp. 21–22.
[5]William Sewell, *Work and Revolution in France* (New York and London, 1980), p. 101.
[6]See the works cited in note 2 above.
[7]See D. Garrioch and M. Sonenscher, "*Compagnonnages*, Confraternities and Associations of Journeymen in Eighteenth-Century Paris," forthcoming, *European History Quarterly;* M.

sion of impermanence, instability, and incessant perigrination associated
with the ceremonial of the Tour de France has been shown to have had
considerable importance in the organization of artisanal production itself. Rychner and Darnton, in their studies of the printing trades of
Neuchâtel and Paris (trades that were not, of course, associated with the
compagnonnages), have highlighted the scale of turnover of compositors
and pressmen in eighteenth-century printing shops and emphasized its
relationship both to the erratic nature of the rhythm of production and
to fluctuations in the level of journeymen's incomes.[8] As Darnton concludes after summarizing his analysis of one of the wage books of the
Société typographique de Neuchâtel, "the graph of manpower and productivity is extraordinarily jagged; it soars and plunges dramatically from
week to week, suggesting that labour management was a balancing act,
performed at a heavy cost, both economic and human."[9]

This essay will explore the apparent paradox implied by these contrasting scenes of intimacy and impermanence and respond to Darnton's
suggestion that "labor management" in eighteenth-century workshops
was "a balancing act, performed at heavy cost, both economic and human." The logic informing this balancing act was, I will suggest, one
that made it possible to translate impermanence into intimacy and intimacy into impermanence in order to maintain the continuity of the
workshop itself. This occurred because nothing in the respective positions of master artisans and their compagnons led automatically to a
stable relationship of cooperation. Cooperation was an artifice rather
than a natural consequence of sharing the same table and the same roof.
The circumstances of workshop production meant that master artisans
were called upon to command relatively substantial numbers of journeymen without having much effective power over either the pattern of their
movements or the rhythm of their work. Workshop organization thus required an elaborate series of fictions that made it possible to create the
flexibility needed to reconcile the possible vagaries of journeymen's behavior with the variety of different time schedules that were intrinsic to artisanal production. Of these, the fiction of intimacy—of a familial and
patriarchal sort—was one of the most powerful and adaptable resources
available to the workshop master. My contention is that it may be possible

---

Sonenscher, "Mythical Work: The *Compagnonnages* of Eighteenth-Century France," in *The
Historical Meaning of Work*, ed. Patrick Joyce (forthcoming, Cambridge University Press).

[8]See Robert C. Darnton, *The Business of the Enlightenment* (Cambridge, Mass., 1979), chap.
5, passim; idem, *The Great Cat Massacre* (New York, 1984). Jacques Rychner, "A l'ombre
des lumières...," *Studies on Voltaire and the Eighteenth Century*, 155 (1976): 1925–55; idem,
"Running a Printing House in Eighteenth-Century Switzerland," *Library* 6th ser., 1, no. 1
(1979): 1–24; idem, *Genève et ses typographes vus de Neuchâtel, 1770–80* (Geneva, 1984).

[9]Robert C. Darnton, *The Literary Underground of the Old Regime* (Cambridge, Mass., 1982),
p. 157.

to reexamine relations between masters and journeymen in the light of the temporal constraints, varying production schedules, and, to use Pierre Bourdieu's phrase, symbolic exchanges that endowed workshop production in the eighteenth century with its internal life, its drama, and its everyday stability.[10]

The Registration of Journeymen

It is well known that the migration of journeymen from place to place and job to job was a perennial problem for master artisans in eighteenth-century France.[11] Their corporate statutes, ratified by *arrêt* of the Royal Council or one of the parlements, usually contained a clause forbidding journeymen to leave their masters without due notice and prohibiting masters from engaging a compagnon unable to produce a certificate signed by his previous employer attesting to the satisfactory completion of his work.[12] The stipulation formed two of the three provisions of the first piece of general legislation regulating those employed in the *fabriques* (textile works) and manufactories of the kingdom in January 1749.[13] Over the following decades the provisions of the Royal Letters Patent were frequently invoked by master artisans in many different trades and localities. Often this was accompanied by a revision of their statutes to provide for a more formal system of control of journeymen's movements. In Paris and in the more substantial trades of the major cities of provincial France this took the form of the establishment of permanent employment offices or *bureaux de placement*, staffed full time by members of the corporation who were paid a fee by both journeymen (usually five *sous*) and masters (ten sous) for finding employment for the former and a supply of labor for the latter. These developments, which frequently encountered fierce resistance from journeymen (often with the support of a substantial minority of master artisans), meant that a relatively extensive network of corporate bureaux de placement was in existence by the last years of the Old Regime.[14]

The records of these bureaus do not appear to have survived in large

[10]Pierre Bourdieu, *Esquisse d'une théorie de la pratique* (Geneva, 1972); idem, *Le sens pratique* (Paris, 1981).

[11]Steven L. Kaplan, "Réflexions sur la police du monde du travail, 1700–1815" *Revue historique* 261 (December 1979): 17–77.

[12]Ibid., esp. pp. 56–57.

[13]Michael Sonenscher, "Journeymen and the French Trades 1781–90," in *Labor and the Law*, ed. C. D. Hay (forthcoming).

[14]There is much evidence of coordination between members of the same trades in different towns in the establishment of bureaux de placement. See, for example, H. Hauser, *Le compagnonnage des arts et Métiers a Dijon* (Paris, 1907), pp. 174–83.

numbers and appear only infrequently among the papers of the corporations transferred to the revolutionary authorities in 1791. Where they do survive, however, they provide an unparalleled opportunity to study the movement of journeymen in particular trades.[15] The information that was compiled when journeymen registered to find work makes it possible not only to reconstruct trade-specific patterns of migration but also to follow the movement of journeymen from boutique to boutique during the period of their residence in a particular town. Despite the opposition with which the establishment of formal systems of placement was usually met, it is likely that, at least in the years immediately following their creation, a considerable number of journeymen and masters, either because of the vigilance of the *jurés* (officials) of the corporation or the (usually temporary) destruction of alternative networks formed by the compagnonnages, made full use of the bureaus.[16] In an episodic way, therefore, the papers of the bureaux de placement provide a brief insight into the temporal and geographical patterns of journeymen's migrations in late eighteenth-century France.

Patterns of Migration

For the purposes of this essay, an analysis has been made of one of the registers of the employment office established by the master tailors of Rouen in 1778. Its creation followed a protracted series of conflicts between the master tailors and their journeymen over a number of related issues. Early in 1777 there were repeated complaints by various masters "that the maneuver and license of their journeymen and workers have resulted in ever more serious abuses every day. They have established associations attached to their "houses of call," with their own rules and fines to enforce them. They combine together continually to place one another in employment . . . and have gone to the length of demanding contributions from employers and a higher wage rate than has been customary."[17]

Accordingly, the corporation decided to reestablish a formal system of placement (there had, it appears, been previous attempts to do so in 1763 and 1766 that had not been successful).[18] Disputes in the tailoring

---

[15]There is unfortunately nothing to rival the details of autobiography for reconstructing journeymen's migrations. See Daniel Roche, ed., *Journal de ma vie: Jacques-Louis Ménétra, compagnon vitrier au 18e siècle* (Paris, 1982), pp. 55–127.

[16] Nor, as will be shown below, did the bureaus necessarily replace already established networks of placement.

[17]Archives départementales *Seine-Maritime* (hereafter ADSM), IBP 15 224, arrêt du parlement, 8 August 1777.

[18]The arrêt of 8 August 1777 refers to two others of 13 June 1763 and 14 August 1766 ordering the establishment of a bureau d'embauche.

trade in the major cities of eighteenth-century France were not uncommon (except, it seems, in Paris),[19] and as tended to occur elsewhere, the decision to establish a bureau de placement was resisted not only by the journeymen but by a small number of masters as well. Legal proceedings ensued, and during the winter of 1777 the Parlement of Rouen made a number of rulings that finally confirmed the decision of the majority of the corporation to create a bureau.[20] It eventually began its work on 13 July 1778. During the next twenty-two months, until 6 May 1780 when the register ends, it recorded the names of 2,342 journeymen tailors.[21] The register not only lists their names, places of birth, and previous places of work, either in Rouen or elsewhere, but also indicates where they were lodging in the city and records the names and addresses of the masters (or widows) for whom they went to work (see Appendix). It does not, unfortunately, record their ages. Nonetheless, the information it contains makes it possible to discover patterns of geographical mobility and follow the movement of journeymen tailors from boutique to boutique during the time they spent working in Rouen.

The procedure has certain difficulties. In the absence of any list of all the journeymen tailors in Rouen in July 1778, it is impossible to know how large a proportion of journeymen registered with the bureau. Second, since only journeymen arriving in Rouen or moving from one boutique to another would have used the bureau, anyone employed by one master for two years or more would not necessarily appear on the register. It is possible too that a number of journeymen would have left Rouen to find work elsewhere once the bureau was established because of their hostility to the new system. It is thus impossible to know how representative the substantial number of journeymen who did register with the bureau actually was and whether any extrapolations from the figures that can be constructed from the information contained in the register have a wider meaning.

It is probable that they do, however, because it is likely that the jour-

[19]This at any rate seems to be the case in light of a fairly extensive examination of the papers of the chambre de police and the minutes of the commissaires of the châtelet in the Archives nationales.

[20]ADSM, IBP 15 227, arrêt du parlement, 20 November 1777. The register of the bureau also refers to arrêts on 20 December 1777 and 3 March 1779. Neither of them can be found among the series of arrêts of the Parlement of Normandy. For reasons that are not clear, most of the arrêts of the parlement pertaining to the affairs of the corporations of Rouen have disappeared from the (otherwise very full) series of arrêts contained in the series IBP. Were they to be rediscovered, it might be easier to understand what was at issue between the supporters and opponents of the establishment of the bureau. The information the register contains about the six masters who appear to have opposed its establishment does not yield any significant differences between this minority and the majority who decided to create a bureau.

[21]ADSM 5E 709. Unless otherwise stated, all the figures that follow have been calculated from this source.

neymen who registered with the bureau made up a substantial majority of all those employed between summer 1778 and spring 1780. The corporation of tailors of Rouen was a large one, with a total membership of 271 or 274 masters in 1775, the year preceding the brief abolition and subsequent merger of the corporation with the *fripiers, chasubliers,* and *brodeurs.*[22] The register contains the names of 251 masters who either had employed or were about to employ journeymen, or some 91.6 percent of a total that the normal incidence of mortality, retirement, and bankruptcy renders somewhat notional.[23] Moreover, the six master tailors whose names are mentioned in an arrêt of the Parlement of Normandy as having been opposed to the establishment of the bureau appear as employers of journeymen with no less frequency than do the names of those who supported its creation.[24] There is thus every likelihood that once the bureau was established it was used widely and regularly by masters to engage the *garçons* (journeymen) they needed.

It is also probable that journeymen registered in large numbers. It is possible, of course, that those opposed to the system simply left Rouen. The register lists five individuals who refused to pay the fee required of them and were refused a boutique, and there may have been others. Yet finding work may not have been an easy matter. In thirty cases, mainly in autumn 1778, journeymen registered for work but were listed as being currently "sans boutique." Nor did masters automatically accept the journeymen supplied by the bureau. Journeymen were rejected on thirty-one occasions, for reasons that were not recorded. In both cases, however, they were later able to find work. The registration of journeymen was carried out retrospectively on a further ten occasions, indicating that the corporate officials in the course of their inspections had brought pressure to bear upon either them or their masters to comply with the ruling of the parlement. Finally, the fact that journeymen tended to change boutiques very frequently makes it unlikely that very many would have remained with one master from July 1778 to May 1780.

For these reasons, it is likely that the information disclosed by the register of the bureau de placement is substantial enough to allow some more general conclusions. With somewhat greater reservations, it is possible that some of these conclusions have a wider bearing upon the

[22]Marc Bouloiseau, *Cahiers de doléances du tiers état du bailliage de Rouen,* 1 (1957): 194. *Tableau de Rouen...année 1775* (s.v. "tailleurs").

[23]The annual turnover of master artisans in any of the trades of eighteenth-century France is a mystery. Some thoughts on the question can be found in Jean-Claude Perrot, *Genèse d'une ville moderne: Caen au XVIIIe siècle* (Paris, 1975), 1: 327–42.

[24]These six employed 17, 30, 20, 11, 11, and 47 journeymen between July 1778 and May 1780. The numbers do not differ from those of many supporters of the establishment of the bureau.

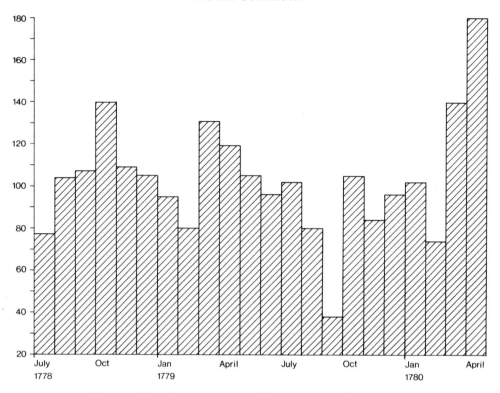

Fig. 3.1. Monthly registration of journeymen tailors—Rouen
(July 1778–April 1780)

structure of workshop organization as a whole. The final section of this
essay will deal with these more general considerations and with the
possible implications the patterns of mobility of journeymen tailors in
Rouen might have for understanding the nature of workshop production both before and after the abolition of the corporations in 1791.

Patterns of Employment

The most striking fact revealed by the register is the sheer volume of
movement. During the twenty-two months between the middle of July
1778 and the first week of May 1780, the bureau recorded 2,342 names—
an average of 106 a month or 9.3 per master. Many of the names of
course were the same, because journeymen moved from master to master
more than once. Of those who registered or reregistered, 1,463 or 62
percent were already domiciled in Rouen or had been working there.
The remaining 38 percent were new arrivals to the town. The movement

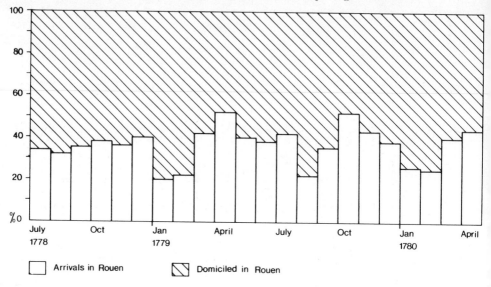

Fig. 3.2. Seasonal rhythms of migration of journeymen tailors

of the monthly aggregate of registrations and the rhythm of new arrivals recorded by the bureau are very similar (see figs. 3.1 and 3.2). March, April, and October, or the spring and early autumn, were the periods in which both movement from boutique to boutique and arrivals from other localities were most frequent. In these periods, about half of the monthly total of journeymen registering for work were new arrivals to Rouen. In the winter months, as one would expect, the proportion fell to about a fifth of the total, which in its turn fell from peaks of 140 and 180 a month in October 1778, March 1779, and April 1779 to between 80 and 100 a month in December, January, and February. For the moment, the substantial fall in the number of registrations in September 1779 remains a mystery.

The names of many journeymen were recorded more than once during the period covered by the register. Only 488 (21.6 percent) journeymen registered once. Reregistration was therefore frequent: one individual, Nicolas Vauquelin, from Caen, registered on sixteen occasions. A total of 304 journeymen registered on two or three occasions, and a further 197 individuals were recorded between four and sixteen times (see fig. 3.3). Thus the aggregate of 2,342 names represents, in fact, those of some 989 individuals.[25] Only 53 of them, or 5.3 percent,

[25]The figure has a rather spurious air of precision. Identifying the same journeymen in different entries is difficult. The orthography of the *buraliste* is often phonetic, so the same name may be spelled in several different ways, as may the names of towns or

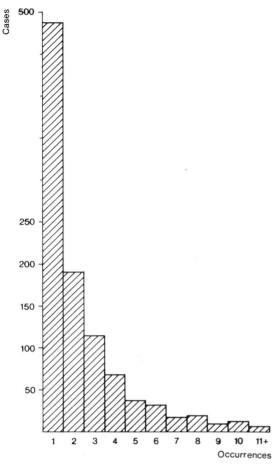

Fig. 3.3. Frequency of registration of journeymen tailors

were natives of Rouen (see fig. 3.4). By contrast, about 50 percent of the men married in Rouen at this time were natives of the city. Migration, in other words, was the normal experience of the great majority of journeymen. Most movement was, however, over relatively short distances and reflected the broader pattern of migration to the city.[26] A further 192 journeymen (19.4 percent) had been born in localities within

provinces. I have linked only those journeymen with the same name, the same place of origin, the same previous master, and the same new master. Thus the figure of 989 certainly contains three or four individuals (certainly a statistically insignificant number) with the same name, same place of origin, and often the same address in Rouen who left the city to work elsewhere and then returned a few months later. Accuracy in the fullest sense would only strengthen the proportions and figures presented here.

[26]Jean-Pierre Bardet, *Rouen aux XVIIIe siècles: Les mutations d'un espace social* (Paris, 1983), 2: 110, for the geographic origins of immigrants to Rouen.

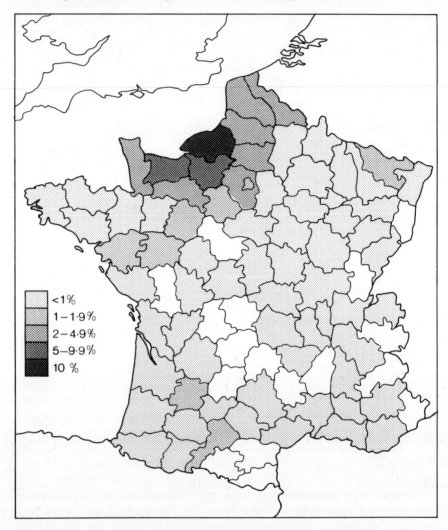

Fig. 3.4. Geographic origins of journeymen tailors

the area of the present-day department of the Seine-Maritime. In addition, natives of the adjoining departments of the Eure (7.9 percent) and the Calvados (6.8 percent) made up the two largest contingents of the journeymen born outside the Seine-Maritime. A substantial minority of the journeymen working in Rouen thus migrated from the small towns of the Cauche region, came from the Perche, or were natives of the Norman towns of Caen, Falaise, Dieppe, Lisieux, Avranches, Evreux, or Fécamp.

The broadly southerly direction of the journeymen's migrations is apparent from the relatively large number of men born in the area of the Pas de Calais (4.7 percent), Nord (2.9 percent), Oise (2.7 percent), and Somme (2.3 percent), and the larger number of natives of the Low Countries (8.1 percent). Here natives of Brussels (2 percent), Antwerp (1.7 percent) and Ghent (1.5 percent) were most numerous, forming, together with those originally from Paris (3.9 percent) or the Paris region (mainly Versailles and Saint-Germain en Laye, 2.6 percent), a group whose apprenticeship had been served in the major northern centers of the tailoring trade. The final third of the 989 individuals who worked in Rouen were natives of sixty departments, mainly in the northeast of France or in the west and southwest of the kingdom. Only one journeyman had been born in Lyons, and none at all were from Marseilles. The southeast had its own circuits of migration, whose northern limit was probably Paris.

The relatively wide geographical distribution of the places of birth of those who registered with the bureau becomes very much more limited if we examine the places where journeymen had been previously employed (see fig. 3.5). Obviously most registrations concerned those who had already worked in Rouen (1,463; 62 percent). Of the 879 journeymen who were new arrivals to the city, the greatest number by far had been working previously in Paris (288 or 32.8 percent of all new arrivals). After the capital came a cluster of Norman towns: Caen (39 arrivals), Dieppe (29), Le Havre (29), Elbeuf (24), and Yvetot (21). Versailles (32 arrivals) and the cities of Beauvais (25), Amiens (10), and Nantes (15) were the other main channels to Rouen. It is clear that journeymen followed two overlapping circuits of migration: one running between the Norman towns in the vicinity of Rouen, the other involving more extensive perigrinations centered mainly upon Paris, but also the major cities of the Picard plain or, to the south, Nantes. The distinction between the two is, however, more apparent than real. Journeymen tailors moved from town to town rather than from village to town, and the number of relatively substantial Norman towns meant that the major axis between Rouen and Paris merged with a multitude of microcircuits of smaller dimensions. The pattern indicates that it would be wrong to consider journeymen's migrations as a series of substantial journeys between major cities. Five individuals did arrive directly from Antwerp, and seven others from Ghent. Two had traveled from Montpellier and from Bordeaux and four from Brest. Three more exotic travelers arrived directly from "l'Amérique," London, and Madrid. Such long voyages were exceptional. The more usual pattern is likely to have had the form of a spiral, as journeymen worked for a period in one locality, moved a short distance away, returned, moved away again, and then proceeded to another major center.

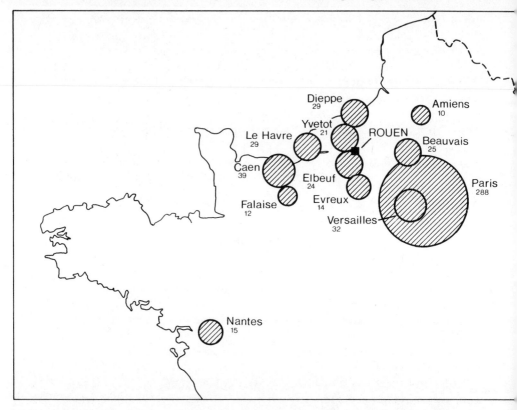

Fig. 3.5. Places of previous employment of journeymen arriving in Rouen
(ten or more occurrences)

The scale of movement was substantial. In some twenty two months 989 journeymen registered on 2,342 occasions, or an average of 2.4 times each. In this instance the average is even more misleading than usual because it is improbable that all of the 488 journeymen who registered only once had only one master during the time they spent working in Rouen. The sequence of registration minimizes the number about to leave the city when the bureau was established and the number who had recently arrived when the register ends in May 1780. The 501 journeymen who registered more than once did so 1,836 times. By following a journeyman listing the same name and place of birth from previous master to new master, it is possible to link the records of registration and calculate how long he spent working for a particular master. Links of this sort could be made on 1,164 occasions and the period of employment (Sundays and holidays included) calculated. Overall, the av-

Table 3.1. Measurable periods of employment of journeymen tailors

	Days					
	1–14	15–28	29–56	57–84	85–112	> 113
Number of occurrences	509	248	198	88	50	71
Percentage	43.7	21.4	17.0	7.6	4.3	6.0

Table 3.2. Total number of journeymen employed by master tailors of Rouen (July 1778–May 1780)

	Number						
	1	2–4	5–9	10–19	20–49	50–99	100 +
Number of masters	106	83	31	31	30	6	1
Percentage	36.8	28.8	10.8	10.8	10.4	2.1	0.3

erage number of days each journeyman worked for a master was 35 (table 3.1). Here too the average is misleading. Almost half (509 or 43.7 percent) of the periods of employment were for intervals of from one to fourteen days. A further 248 (21.3 percent) were for periods of fifteen to twenty-eight days. Thus nearly two-thirds of the 1,164 measurable periods of employment lasted no more than a month.

There were, on the other hand, a very much smaller but significant number of occasions (121 or 10.4 percent) in which journeymen were employed longer than three months, though in only one instance was the period longer than a year. This smaller group of journeymen employed for relatively long periods was distributed very widely among master tailors. At least sixty-four different masters employed at least one journeyman for three months or more. It is clear, therefore, that a typical workshop was likely to have had one or two journeymen working for relatively long periods, together with a more substantial number of men taken on for extremely short periods. The relatively stable core was surrounded by a constantly changing population of highly peripatetic journeymen tailors, occasionally employed as assistants (*aides*) for only a day or two.

Over the course of the period covered by the register of the bureau de placement, some masters employed a substantial number of journeymen, though the number working together at any one time was, of course, very much lower (see table 3.2). One master tailor, Pierre Vandercruysse on the rue Encrière, employed no fewer than 113 journeymen at one time or another between July 1778 and May 1780. Six masters (Bertrand, Brackmans, Couche, Deforge, Duport, and Zaly) each employed between 50 and 100 journeymen over this period as a whole. A further thirty employed between 20 and 49 journeymen, and thirty-one others between 10 and 19. The 12.8 percent of master tailors who employed twenty or more journeymen between 1778 and 1780 were responsible for 58.4 percent of all the registrations. Most masters, however (106), employed only a single journeyman tailor during the entire period. At any one time, of course, the number of journeymen employed by any master tailor is unlikely to have been more than half a dozen. The average number of registrations per master over the period as a whole is 9.3, a figure biased in favor of those who employed large numbers of journeymen for very short periods. The figures do not, of course, indicate anything about the wealth or scale of affairs of any of the master tailors in question. Arrangements for subcontracting work and divisions between production and retailing may mean that the largest employers of journeymen were not necessarily the wealthiest masters. They were, however, the largest wage payers, and in some cases their annual wage bills were comparable to the annual expenditure of those notionally very much higher up the social scale. If it were possible to compare monetary flows rather than capital assets, then the distance between the world of the boutique and that of the professions might not have been very great.[27]

Local Circuits of Employment

The sheer number of journeymen employed by some of the master tailors of Rouen, and the brief periods most spent in any one boutique, do little to suggest that intimacy or familiarity between journeymen and their masters was engendered simply by the passage of time. Mere figures, moreover, do little to reveal the internal organization of the trade and the relative amounts of time allocated to sale or production and the different tasks of cutting, stitching, embroidering, and finishing clothes for men or women. The need to coordinate a relatively intricate division of labor makes it unlikely that a master artisan spent much time working alongside his journeymen. It is tempting to characterize the tailoring trade, from the figures alone, as more similar to the modern "dispersed" factory than to the traditional workshop.

Yet the parallel would be somewhat misplaced. The journeymen tailors of late-eighteenth-century Rouen were very mobile, but their mobility was clearly highly structured. Although it is not possible to discern any

[27]The relationship between cash, paper, and other forms of credit in eighteenth-century France calls for further investigation. Some thoughts on the question as it bears upon the silk industry can be found in Michael Sonenscher, "Royalists and Patriots: Nîmes and Its Hinterland in the 18th Century" (Ph.D. diss., Warwick University, 1978).

significant correlation between the regional origin or place of previous employment of the 989 journeymen and the masters for whom they worked, some less global patterns are apparent. Journeymen did not move from boutique to boutique in a random way. Occasionally they returned to work for the same master on more than one occasion. More frequently they were employed by a relatively limited circle of master tailors, so that the previous masters of a group of journeymen working for one large employer can be distinguished fairly clearly from those of another group. The names of 24 masters appear among the previous employers of the 113 journeymen taken on by Vandercruysse. Only 9 of these masters appear among the previous masters of the 78 journeymen engaged by the master tailor Duport, on the rue des Bons Enfants. Thus what might appear to have been an anonymous labor market was, in fact, made up of scores of smaller circuits, each overlapping and intersecting with several others, so that it is impossible to distinguish the one from the other with any finality.

It is much easier to identify the link connecting journeymen of very different geographic origins or previous places of employment to the masters by whom they were employed. This link was formed by the inns or *logis* in which journeymen tailors lodged. It is clear that many master tailors turned to a particular inn or lodging house when they required additional journeymen and that the establishment of the bureau de placement did nothing to change this pattern. A majority, though not a large one (57.7 percent), of the journeymen who registered or reregistered with the bureau gave the name and address of their lodgings. The remainder (42.3 percent) did not and can be assumed to have lodged either with their masters or, if they were natives of Rouen, with relatives. Most of those in lodgings stayed in one of seven different lodgings. There is a very clear and varied pattern in the relationship between certain master tailors and certain inns (see table 3.3). A small number of masters housed all the journeymen they employed themselves. Others engaged journeymen who lodged in a number of different inns. The four establishments run by Baudouin, Bottey—"Au Chat Qui Dort," Pottier—"Aux Trois Images," and Lemeur supplied a relatively small number of journeymen to a wide variety of masters. The much larger number of journeymen lodging in the three other inns—chez Belliard, Deforge (a master tailor himself), and Naudin (a master upholsterer)— were usually employed by masters who recruited all their journeymen from the same source. Thus 34 of the 60 journeymen employed by Brackmans, on the rue Grand Pont, lodged chez Belliard, rue des Bons Enfants. All the others lodged with him. Vandercruysse housed 21 of the 113 journeymen he employed at one time or another. All 82 others lodged chez Naudin, rue Saint Lô.

Table 3-3. Lodgings and the pattern of journeymen's employment (sample of twenty-five masters)

Master	Lodging							Lodged with master	Other
	Baudouin	Belliard	Bottey	Deforge	Lemeur	Pottier	Naudin		
Alléaume		2	1			1		8	8
Aubert	1		2		4	7		2	8
Bataille					2	1		10	5
Benard	1						12	11	1
Bertrand							56	2	
Blanchant				14	1			3	
Bonsergent		36				1		16	
Brackmans								28	
Bréant			1			1		24	
Couche		29	2		2	2	1	29	1
Dartus		5	1	25	1	2		5	
Deforge		2	3	45	1			4	5
Delamare	2				1	1		31	1
Dumont	2							25	
Dupont		1	1		1	1	4	22	
Duport		33	1	3	1	1	29	9	
Fercy		3			2		4	45	
Glasson			1				35	6	
Lecomte		1		33		1		9	
Marais								25	
Najac		1		39	1	1	29	5	
Pimont			1					3	
Sauvé	1			23		1		4	
Segers	1						21	7	
Vandercruysse							92	21	

The close relationship between the logis where journeymen stayed (which have considerable similarities to the English journeymen tailors' houses of call)[28] and the masters they worked for, goes a long way toward explaining the tailors' complaints about the associations formed by their journeymen "sous le nom de logis." It is clear that the bureau de placement was designed to destroy these networks and equally clear that it failed to do so.

It is not clear, however, why journeymen lodging in certain logis worked only for certain masters. There is no evident correlation between particular lodging houses and the geographical origins or previous places of employment of the journeymen staying there. As one would expect, none of the journeymen who had been born in Rouen stayed in lodgings. The remainder, whether natives of localities in the immediate vicinity of Rouen or of cities as far afield as Dresden, Aix-en-Provence, Venice, or Antwerp appear to have lodged indiscriminately with any one of the seven individuals whose names appear most frequently on the register. Nor is there any indication that journeymen who were employed for brief periods and changed boutiques frequently stayed in lodgings whereas those employed for longer periods lodged with their masters. It is possible, but unlikely, that journeymen in particular lodgings specialized in a particular branch of the trade. The number of *garçons* who passed through the establishments managed by Deforge, Belliard, and Naudin, the three largest lodgings, suggests that this was not the case.

All this points to the likelihood that the link between the logis and certain masters was formed by the journeymen in the lodging houses themselves. The segmented pattern of journeymen's movements among a limited range of master tailors cannot be explained in terms of preexistent affinities of geographic origin or previous employment. It is probable that it owed most to the affinities created in some, but not all, of the places where the journeymen lodged. The fact goes a long way to explain why so much of the ritual of the compagnonnages was centered upon the inns where journeymen stayed rather than the places where they worked.[29] In many trades an inn was the nodal point linking journeymen dispersed among scores of different boutiques, forming a strategic zone in which the collective relationship between masters and journeymen was most amenable to general consideration.

Associations formed by journeymen tailors appear to have existed in most of the larger cities of provincial France: in Lyons, Marseilles, Bordeaux, and Nantes as well as Rouen.[30] It is possible that cities of this size were localities in which a relatively small number of masters (some thirty

[28]See most recently, C. R. Dobson, *Masters and Journeymen* (London, 1980), chap. 3.
[29]See the documents published in Coornaert, *Compagnonnages*, appendix.
[30]Ibid.

or forty at the most) employed relatively large numbers of journeymen, while Paris, with its vast corporation of master tailors and highly developed division of labor, was simply too large for any association of journeymen to be able to exercise effective control over the supply of labor in the eighteenth century. Significantly, journeymen in the Parisian tailoring trade were among the first group of workers whose associations were prohibited in the mid-seventeenth century.[31] Yet it has not been possible to find any trace of an association in the eighteenth century.[32] In the light of what it has been possible to establish about the number and the level of turnover of journeymen in late eighteenth-century Rouen, it may be that such associations tended to form when the internal structure of the trade reached a certain level of differentiation. Collective association may have been most frequent when the trade was poised between a form of organization centered upon the workshop and one that was more dispersed, where many journeymen worked either at home as *chambrelans* or in relatively large halls (*chambrées*), as was the case in eighteenth-century Paris. The English distinction between the "honorable" and "dishonorable" ends of the trade may have some relevance for an understanding of both the geographical and the temporal distribution of the compagnonnages, an idiom rather than an organization, whose resemblance to similar associations created by journeymen elsewhere in Europe has not been given sufficient emphasis.[33]

Conclusion

In a relatively large trade, like the tailoring trade of Rouen, most of the journeymen who registered to find work were temporary inhabitants of the city. The rhythms and patterns of their movements make it possible to suggest a number of ways of understanding the apparent paradox between the aura of intimacy associated with workshop production and the effectively impermanent and transient relationship of so many journeymen with their masters. Intimacies of a sort undoubtedly existed. They can be deduced from the segmented pattern of journeymen's movements and the limited range of masters for whom they worked and frequently returned to work. It is clear, however, that such intimacies were not the natural result of preexisting regional loyalties or the familiarity induced by the passage of time spent in the same workshop. They were created, and probably created very rapidly. At one level they

[31] The condemnation is well known. See Coornaert, *Companonnages*.
[32] See note 19 above.
[33] See, for example, Andreas Griessinger, *Das symbolische Kapital der Ehre* (Frankfurt, 1981).

were created within the inns where journeymen lodged, in the ceremonial of their associations, and in the relationship between particular
keepers of lodging houses and certain master tailors. At another level
it is likely that they were created in the interstices of work itself: in the
variety of procedures master artisans followed to ensure that their workshops were endowed with the reputation of being good places or *bonnes
boutiques*, where journeymen were fairly paid, well fed, and properly
treated.[34] At a third level they were created by the transactions between
journeymen and their masters on Sundays and trade holidays: in the
symbolic exchanges arising from eating and drinking together and dancing with wives and daughters.[35] In a sense, the creation of intimacy was
also work. Intimacy was an artifice, expressed too in a material sense by
a variety of different forms of wage payment—by the piece, by the
journée, by the *grande-journée*, and by the month—and different kinds of
rights: rights to cut, rights to keep, rights to sell.[36] If most journeymen
worked for most masters for a month or less, this did not imply that
they would work for any master. Intimacies were created and ensured
that a tailor's working career followed a relatively predictable itinerary.

There was thus a close relation between the creation of intimacy and
the erratic rhythms of workshop production. Journeymen were taken
on as and when they were needed, and most of them were expected to
leave and find work elsewhere after a very brief time. Sixty of the 113
journeymen employed by Vandercruysse completed their periods of
work before May 1780. They were engaged for periods ranging from
2 to 242 days. Only 20 of them worked longer than a month. Yet masters
required some assurance that they would obtain journeymen when the
need arose, that competent individuals would return, and that the frequently changing group of journeymen they employed would work together reliably. Only *in extremis*, or where a more general attempt was
made to overturn customary arrangements, would masters have recourse
to the statutes of the corporation and the panoply of legal provisions
regulating relations in the trade. In normal circumstances, the erratic
schedules of workshop production were negotiated in ways that made
it possible to establish affinities and loyalties between men of different
ages, origins, and experience.

It is very likely that the pattern of employment of journeymen in the
tailoring trade was distinctive and that other patterns existed in the

[34]These remarks arise from a general study of work and wage systems in eighteenth-
century France that is in progress.
[35]The autobiography of Jacques-Louis Ménétra (see above, note 15) is a rich source of
information on this matter.
[36]On such rights, see Michael Sonenscher, "Work and Wages in Eighteenth Century
Paris," in *Manufacture in Town and Country before the Factory*, ed. Maxine Berg et al. (London,
1983).

building, furnishing, or decorating trades.[37] The very high level of turn-over from boutique to boutique in the tailoring trade may have been unusual, but it is likely that the migration of journeymen itself was as extensive in other trades. Its frequency should be emphasized. Although the journeymen who worked in the tailoring trade in Rouen were mainly natives of regions that supplied the city with most of its immigrants, they were, to a much greater degree than the rest of the population, men who had not been born in the city and who would not settle there. About 50 percent of the men who married in Rouen during the eighteenth century were natives of the city; only 5 percent of the journeymen tailors who registered for work between 1778 and 1780 were native Rouennais. Furthermore, not one of the 989 journeymen appears to have been employed by a master tailor who was also his father. Doubtless other kinds of overlap between kinship and employment did occur: nephews were clearly taken on by their uncles, although it is not possible to as-certain the proportion with any precision. Yet the registers of marriages show that there was a high level of continuity in the same trade from one generation to the next in Rouen.[38] If very few natives of the city registered for work, but a much higher proportion entered the trade as masters, this indicates that migration was a much more usual occurrence in the lives of working people than is implied by figures derived from hospital records or parish registers. It is likely that some usually limited kind of migration was a normal corollary to the period between the completion of an apprenticeship on the one hand and marriage and the acquisition of a *maîtrise* (mastership) on the other.

The journeymen who worked in Rouen were not, therefore, neces-sarily expecting to settle there. But they were expecting to settle some-where, just as their Rouennais counterparts, working in other towns, were expecting to return, perhaps with a wife, to inherit or acquire a maîtrise. This, one suspects, may be one reason the journeymen tailors who registered for work in Rouen did not move from boutique to bou-tique in a random way. Their movements were structured, in part by the kind of relationship they were able to establish with particular masters and their families.

They were structured too, and in a more visible way, by the choice of the logis where journeymen stayed during their time in Rouen. The establishment of a corporate bureau de placement did not destroy in-

---

[37]Journeymen locksmiths in Rouen, for example, appear to have been employed for considerably longer periods. Journeymen shoemakers in Lyons were, it seems, as likely to change boutiques as the tailors of Rouen. A fuller discussion of journeymen's migrations will be presented in a projected study entitled "Work and Wages in Eighteenth Century France."

[38]Bardet, *Rouen*, 1: 211–13, 235–37.

formal networks of finding work. Journeymen lodging in one of the three largest inns that masters used to obtain their garçons followed a distinct and segmented series of patterns of employment. Journeymen lodging chez Naudin, rue Saint Lô, worked mainly for one group of masters; those staying on the rue des Bons Enfants, chez Belliard, worked for another; those lodging chez Deforge were employed by a third and equally distinct group. The places where journeymen lived, rather than the places where they worked, were the strategic points around which collective association was established and secured.

There was, then, as the establishment of a bureau de placement itself indicates, a certain distance and difference in the respective situations of masters and journeymen. My contention here has been that these were the usual conditions in the trade and that the "natural" relationship between journeymen and their masters was an impermanent one, characterized by brief periods of employment and a very high level of labor turnover. At the same time, however, journeymen did not move from master to master in a random way. This fact suggests that the "natural" anonymity of the relationship between journeymen and their masters was transformed into something else, and that impermanence was translated, if not into intimacy, then into something that ensured that durable circuits of employment could be maintained. At the least, it is clear from this one limited case that the everyday world of workshop production was more mobile and more highly structured and contained more complex kinds of division than was apparent from the characterization of that world presented in the introduction to this essay. In light of this, it may be worth considering how far the language of republican solidarity of the Year II—itself presented by its historians as predicated upon a more intimate characterization of workshop production—carried with it some of the injunctions and invitations that master artisans had drawn upon, in other ways and other contexts, to transform the impermanence of journeymen's effective presence in a town into the intimacy of the workshop. If, as Adam Smith put it, work consists of the production of "vendible commodities," it may also have consisted of the production of that aura of familiar intimacy associated with artisanal production. It is unlikely that that kind of work came to an end after the proclamation of the First French Republic.

Appendix 3.1.
An Example of the Registration of a Journeyman Tailor

Du 14 juillet 1778
S'est presenté le Sr Henry Frederick natif de Franquefort en Allemagne

sortant de chez Mad[e] la veuve Quettier suivant son billet de congé, logé chez M. Belliard rue des Bons Enfans, lequel a été envoyé chez M. Brackmans rue Grand Pont. (*Source*: Archives départementales Seine-Maritime 5E 709 fol. 2.)

4

Social and Geographic Mobility of the Eighteenth-Century Guild Artisan: An Analysis of Guild Receptions in Dijon, 1700–90

Edward J. Shephard, Jr.

In 1708 the town council of Dijon received a petition from a distraught journeyman, Nicolas Girardot. Girardot, aged fifty, a native of Chamerois in the diocese of Langres, had worked for twenty years as a journeyman cooper (*tonnelier*) under various masters in Dijon. He was prevented from earning a decent living for his wife and four children, so he claimed, by the refusal of the master coopers to accept him into their guild. For seven years his wife had been afflicted with "a terrible madness." She had three times tried to jump into the river and once into a well. Girardot threw himself on the mercy of the city magistrates to get himself received into the coopers' guild. The mayor and the town councillors were apparently moved by Girardot's unhappy situation, because they not only ordered his reception into the guild but also remitted the usual fees a new master had to pay for the right of residency (*droit d'habitantage*) and the right to open a shop (*droit d'ouverture de boutique*). Even the town syndic refused the customary fee "out of charity." The guild syndics, not surprisingly, *did* receive their ten *sous* honorarium.[1]

This is the time-honored picture conjured up of the urban trade guild at the end of the Old Regime—a closed caste of master craftsmen jealously restricting entry to the guild to their own sons and sons-in-law while their apprentices and journeymen were left with no hope of ever

[1] Archives municipales de la ville de Dijon (hereafter AMD), series G (Arts et métiers), liasse 110.

attaining status as independent tradesmen, at least in any town where the guild maintained its stranglehold over the trade. Is this an accurate picture of the urban guild community during the eighteenth century? Eighty years after Nicolas Girardot's desperate plea for municipal intervention in his behalf, another young cooper, Nicolas Gigot from Salmaise, came to Dijon from the countryside to seek his fortune.[2] At age twenty-eight could he too look forward only to twenty years or more as a journeyman worker in another master's shop?

The Corporate System and Its Historiography

The aim of this chapter is to assess the accuracy of this traditional view of French guilds and to explore neglected issues in guild history by examining several aspects of the socioeconomic structure and evolution of the guild community of Dijon during the eighteenth century. Historians of the corporate communities have concentrated on delineating the institutional character of the guilds. The guilds were one of many corporate bodies that constituted the society of estates in Old Regime France. They were one element in the complex web of power and authority that characterized early modern urban society. The evolution of French guilds has most often been presented in terms of their eventual subordination to and co-optation by the monarchy as one of many arms by which royal authority was enforced and extended throughout the fabric of French society. The monarchy used the guilds as agents of its encroachment upon and destruction of local municipal liberties. Guilds, along with other corporate bodies in Old Regime society, were subjected to the fiscal pressures and exactions of the monarchy in its never-ending search for revenue. Economic historians have focused on the emergence of new modes of production and labor organization that accompanied the growth of commercial and industrial capitalism. Their emphasis has been on the restructuring of production, the reorganization and redeployment of the labor force, and the realignment of social relations that occurred as a result of these changes. These studies tend to throw into relief the pressures that came to bear on existing social relations within a changing socioeconomic framework. Given the perspective of a relentless and triumphant capitalist evolution, guilds appear as anachronistic and backward-looking institutions that fought to retain an outmoded system of production and social relations.

The corporate regime evolved as a means of ensuring the smooth functioning of the artisanal mode of production as both an economic

[2]AMD, series G, liasse 183.

and a social system. As with all socioeconomic structures, its purpose was to achieve social and economic cohesion and stability. The guild was a means of economic and social integration, with its own mechanisms for maintaining an equilibrium of supply and demand in both production and labor. These mechanisms were diverted from their intended function in order to limit and restrict the effects of structural change in the economy and in society. Channels of integration were closed up in an attempt to stave off a deterioration in the guilds' economic and social position. The jealous guarding and retrenchment of privilege and monopoly by the guilds were reactionary defenses against economic and social change and have emerged as the salient, dominant features of Old Regime guild historiography. Workers were caught in a double bind. On the one hand, the independence of the skilled artisan and the control he maintained over his labor were threatened by the development of commercial and industrial capitalism. On the other hand, the institutional framework of the guild community no longer operated as a mechanism of integration but had become a means of exclusion in an attempt to defend a deteriorating position. While it is undeniable that the guild system became restrictive and reactionary where it was subjected to these pressures, it is also true that not all towns in France were undergoing these pressures for change. In some towns the guild community still provided for, satisfied, and corresponded to social and economic needs and realities. In these circumstances, how successful was the guild regime as a socioeconomic system? This chapter will take a first step toward answering this question.

The integration of guild studies into the mainstream of French social history has not proceeded much beyond examining the institutional character of the guild communities and their place in the institutional framework of Old Regime society. The operation of the guild as an economic and social system remains, for the most part, a matter of conjecture because of a lack of studies of individual guild communities. Little research has been undertaken into the demographic and social characteristics of the guild communities because of the scarcity of source materials. Urban historians have not been able to explore in any great detail the artisanal population of French towns. The survival of such records for Dijon offers the opportunity to make a detailed analysis of the social structure and dynamics of an Old Regime guild community.

The working population of Dijon existed on three levels. First, it was an aggregate labor force that altered in size and composition during the eighteenth century in response to the changing needs and requirements of the urban society for which it provided both goods and services. Second, it was a constellation of distinct but interrelated trades, each with a dynamic and characteristics of its own. Third, it was made up of a multitude of families and individuals who pursued their own personal goals and interests within the framework of the entire urban economy and society. The first part of this essay will deal with the working population of Dijon on the first level of analysis. It will situate the artisanal community within the general outlines of urban demographic change and development across the eighteenth century. The second part will focus on the individuals who made up the elite of the working community—the guild masters. Through a detailed analysis of all new guild masters in Dijon from 1700 to 1790, a social profile will emerge that will add significantly to our knowledge of this segment of French society. The second level—that of the trades that made up the town economy—will be integrated into the discussion in both sections as an organizational scheme appropriate both for subdividing the global working population and for grouping together individual guild masters.

Sources

The archives of Dijon are an unusually rich mine of material for the study of guild history in the eighteenth century. This chapter makes use of two major sources. The first of these is the *taille* registers for the seven parishes of Dijon. These tax rolls for the years 1700 and 1790 present a detailed census of the working population of Dijon at the beginning of the eighteenth century and at the end of the Old Regime. They offer the opportunity to assess changes in the community across the century.[3] The second source is the series of guild master receptions (*lettres de maîtrise*) contained in series G (Arts et métiers), liasses 83–185, of the municipal archives of the city of Dijon. This series extends from the beginning of the seventeenth century through the middle of 1790. It contains over 10,000 pieces, of which more than 7,500 date from the eighteenth century. The lettre de maîtrise was the written record of registration made by a new guild master before the municipal authorities of Dijon—the Chambre de conseil et de police. The candidate was presented by officers of the guild to the municipal council. This normally occurred within a few days of his reception by the guild. Information about the new master was taken down, and the guild syndics swore to the candidate's professional ability and to his upright

[3]Taille register for 1700—AMD, series L (Impositions), liasse 262; taille register for 1790—Archives départementales de la Côte-d'Or (hereafter ADC), series C, liasses 5909, 5910. The taille role for the Saint-Philibert parish is missing from the 1790 register. In its place the 1789 role has been used (ADC, series C, liasse 5908).

character. In an order and formula that never varied, the following details were recorded: the new master's name, his place of birth, his age, his father's name and profession (usually), and the guild he was joining (represented by the guild syndics). Other facts were sometimes noted down as well, such as the candidate's membership in another guild or his status as an army veteran or militiaman. Rarely would he be specifically identified as a compagnon, but in some instances he was so designated on the lettre de maîtrise. If the aspirant were a married woman, the information would normally include her husband's name and his profession plus the fact that his consent had been obtained. If she were a widow her late husband's name and trade were invariably mentioned.

Besides the honoraria paid to the guild syndics and to the municipal officers, the new master was required to pay two fees. The first was a residence tax, the droit d'habitantage. This was not required if the new master was a native of Dijon or had already paid the twelve livres fee in the past as a new resident. The second tax was the droit d'ouverture de boutique. This was, in effect, a license to open a shop. If the new master was already a master in another guild and had already paid this fee, he did not have to pay a second time unless he were opening a second shop. These fees were sometimes waived by the municipal council because of some service to the city or because of the candidate's extreme poverty or some other special situation (e.g., twelve children, which also exempted him from the taille). Profession of the Catholic faith was also required. Normally the new master's oath and signature were sufficient to satisfy the council. Occasionally, as with foreigners, some further proof was requested by the authorities, such as a certificate of confession from a local priest.[4]

Where possible, the completeness of the lettres de maîtrise series was checked against surviving guild registers from the E series in the Archives départementales de la Côte-d'Or. Registers do not survive for all the guilds of Dijon, and those that do still exist do not all contain records of reception of new masters. Lists of annual assessments or of payment of *confrérie* dues were another means of checking for completeness of the lettres de maîtrise. Such checks as were possible turned up a very small number of additional individuals, with sketchy biographical data. It was usually possible, however, to deduce whether they were native to Dijon or were sons of masters from the amount of their reception fee. The lettres de maîtrise series seems to be a virtually complete record of guild receptions in Dijon during the eighteenth century.

---

[4]The lettres de maîtrise are in manuscript until 1733. In that year printed forms were introduced that left blank spaces for filling in the appropriate information.

Urban Economy and Demography

Dijon was a prosperous provincial capital during the eighteenth century. Its prosperity did not approach that of the great boom centers of the century—Nantes, Bordeaux, Marseilles—but the 1700s ushered in the most flourishing period for the Burgundian capital since the time of the great Valois dukes. This prosperity, however, was not the result of an expanding and dynamic economy in the full throes of commercial or industrial development. Dijon participated in neither the commercial activity of the great port centers nor the transformations that were slowly being accomplished in the industrial structure of the economy. Its geographic position was not greatly favored by land or water. Dijon was on the major north-south axis running from Paris to Lyons and Marseilles, but the city was not much more than one of several prominent staging points on this highway. It was not on even a minor waterway, and although the construction of the Canal de Bourgogne in the 1780s offered the promise of increased commercial activity in the future, Dijon was not to become the hub of a wide regional network of production and distribution until the coming of the railway in the nineteenth century.

Dijon, like other Old Regime provincial capitals, derived its prosperity from the concentration within its wall of administrative, fiscal, judicial, and ecclesiastical institutions of the monarchy. It was the seat of the provincial estates of Burgundy and of a powerful parlement. The intendant and his subdelegates were the representatives and executors of the royal will in the province and also kept a close watch on the surviving municipal administration. Burgundy was a province with a long history of powerful patron/client relationships among the nobility. At the head of the second estate was the Condé family, princes of the blood who were hereditary governors of the province. These persons and the positions they occupied represented only the highest levels of competing and cooperating hierarchies of power and authority, with the lower levels extending down through the entire range of administrative, fiscal, and judicial offices of the Old Regime. Religious houses were numerous and powerful both within the city and throughout the province. Among these were branches of Clairvaux and Cîteaux, the Sainte-Chapelle, founded in 1172 by the Capetian dukes, and the powerful Benedictine abbey of Saint-Bénigne. In 1731 Dijon was separated from the diocese of Langres and was elevated to the rank of bishopric. In addition, Dijon was the seat of a university, founded in 1722, and of an academy, founded in 1736. The people who occupied these high levels in the social hierarchy and their immediate dependents constituted an enormous nonproductive group, estimated at approximately 25 percent of the total urban population. This large host of provincial nobility, royal officers and functionaries, administrative and judicial officeholders and personnel, secular and regular clergy, plus their families and dependents, created a stimulating demand for goods and services on which the modest economic prosperity of Dijon was based, one of whose manifestations can still be witnessed in the abundant eighteenth-century architectural splendors of the city. This demand fed a local economy that included the entire spectrum of common and luxury trades and that lacked other factors and stimuli to economic development.

Dijon's economic prosperity supported, and in turn stimulated, a moderate and continuous demographic expansion throughout the eighteenth century. There are no reasonably accurate or reliable population estimates for Dijon before the last decade of the Old Regime. Contemporary estimates of the size of the urban population are numerous, but they vary wildly and are based on no systematic method of calculation. Georges Bouchard critically examined all contemporary population estimates and compared them with results obtained from applying modern evaluative techniques to surviving demographic data.[5] He conclusively dismissed the repeated claims of contemporaries throughout the century that Dijon's population was steadily, if not precipitously, falling. One need not look far to find strong fiscal incentives for presenting the grimmest of demographic pictures as a buffer against the insatiable voracity of the royal fisc. Contrary to the hemorrhage reported by the members of the town council and of the parlement in 1763 and 1764, according to whom the population of the city declined from over 30,000 in the 1740s to under 15,000 at the end of the Seven Years' War, Dijon's demographic curve continued steadily upward throughout the century. The first reasonably accurate censuses were conducted independent of each other in 1784 and 1786 by the mayor and the intendant.[6] Both investigations arrived at a population of between 22,000 and 23,000. An examination of the detailed breakdowns of these figures by social/occupational categories indicates an underrepresentation of both extremes of wealth and poverty, and Bouchard considers that the actual population was closer to 24,000. Several methods of demographic reconstitution including the most reliable, that of using the number of hearths (*feux*) in the taille rolls, verify the accuracy of this rough figure. Applying these techniques to the beginning of the century, Bouchard considers

---

[5]Georges Bouchard, "Dijon au XVIIIe siècle: Les dénombrements d'habitants," *Annales de Bourgogne* 97 (1953): 30–65.

[6]*Extrait du dénombrement des citoyens de la ville de Dijon, fait par les officiers municipaux de ladite ville, pendant les six premiers mois de l'année 1784.* (Paris, 1786); *Dénombrement du duché de Bourgogne et pays adjacents rédigé en 1786 par la soin de Mr Amelot, lors intendant de la province* (Paris, 1790).

the figure of 18,000 to 20,000 a close approximation for Dijon's population in 1700. From this level the population rose by about 30 percent to 24,000 in 1790, representing a modest growth rate of approximately 3 percent per decade. Dijon was not a demographic "black hole" that continuously absorbed immigrants from the countryside without being able to maintain a stable population. The absence of intense economic development precluded a phenomenal population explosion, but Dijon's socioeconomic balance of supply and demand sustained a moderate economic prosperity and demographic expansion.

The city of Dijon was divided into seven parishes: Saint-Médard, Notre-Dame, Saint-Jean, Saint-Michel, Saint-Nicolas, Saint-Pierre, and Saint-Philibert. Saint-Médard, whose parish church in the eighteenth century was the abbey church of Saint-Etienne (later the first cathedral), coincided with the limits of the Gallo-Roman "castrum" and included both the Palais des Ducs and the parlement buildings. The château erected by Louis XI in 1479, more to dominate the city than to defend the surrounding territory, commanded the Porte-Guillaume, one of the four gates in the city walls. The houses and lands of the numerous religious orders covered approximately one-third of the surface area of the city. The parish of Saint-Philibert was the home of the ancient and powerful abbey of Saint-Bénigne where the kings of France, successors to the dukes of Burgundy, had come to swear to maintain the privileges of the province and the city, Henri III being the last to appear in person. But Saint-Philibert was also the parish of Dijon's vine dressers (*vignerons*). In fact, each parish had its own familiar aspect in popular tradition:

> Messieurs de Notre-Dame,
> Riches de Saint-Jean,
> Pélerins de Saint-Michel,
> Pauvres de Saint-Médard,
> Grands de Saint-Nicolas,
> Oiseaux de Saint-Pierre,
> Culs-bleus de Saint-Philibert.

To a large extent, the characterization of each parish in popular tradition was still accurate in the eighteenth century. The parish boundaries extended beyond the city walls, and the faubourgs Saint-Michel, Saint-Pierre, Saint-Nicolas, and d'Ouche (Saint-Philibert) were administratively attached to the city proper. The suburbs, in fact, were areas of considerable urban expansion. The area within the city walls enclosed practically no undeveloped terrain in the eighteenth century. The large area covered by public edifices, homes of religious orders, and the great hôtels of the nobility limited the space available for intramural expansion. As a result, urban expansion occurred mostly in the faubourgs, particularly the faubourg d'Ouche, through which ran the main highways in and out of Dijon.

The enumeration of hearths in the taille registers is the most reliable and accurate yardstick by which to measure the growth of the population of Dijon. It offers the opportunity to study changes on several levels of analysis. A comparison of the tax rolls for 1700 and 1790 shows that the demographic increase was unevenly distributed throughout the city (see table 4.1). The total number of hearths increased from 4,502 in 1700 to 5,837 in 1790, an increase of 27 percent. The "intra muros" increase, however, was only 18 percent whereas the population of the faubourgs grew 177 percent. In absolute figures, the town absorbed almost 800 new hearths and the faubourgs almost 600. The most populous sections of Dijon were and remained the large parishes of Notre-Dame, Saint-Jean, and Saint-Philibert, which made up the western half of the city. Rates of growth among the seven parishes did not follow this division, however. The populations of Notre-Dame, Saint-Michel, and Saint-Nicolas grew by only 2 percent to 6 percent each, while the others, including Saint-Médard, which had the least residential space available, grew by 25 percent to 106 percent. These different rates of growth did not result in a significant shift in population distribution throughout the city. Certain parishes remained virtually unchanged in the percentage of the total population they represented: Saint-Médard, 6 percent in 1700 versus 7 percent in 1790; Saint-Nicolas, 12 percent versus 13 percent; Saint-Jean, 19 percent versus 18 percent; Saint-Philibert, 18 percent versus 20 percent. The others changed by only 4 percent to 5 percent each, still a statistically small amount: Notre-Dame, 19 percent versus 14 percent; Saint-Michel, 19 percent versus 15 percent; Saint-Pierre, 7 percent versus 11 percent. In the faubourgs there was a marked difference between the faubourg Saint-Michel, which remained quite small, and the others that grew substantially.

The Working Population

The working population of Dijon experienced similar patterns of demographic change during the eighteenth century but also exhibited trends that varied slightly from those of the general population. The taille entries included the occupational designation or social station of each person enumerated on the registers. For the purposes of analysis I have used the following criteria in establishing the parameters of a discrete socioeconomic subpopulation that I refer to as the working population. All manual trades and professions are included, as well as merchants

Table 4.1. Summary of demographic changes for the city of Dijon, 1700–90

Parish	Total number on taille role[a]			Total number of workers[a]			Workers as percentage of parish population	
	1700	1790	Percent change	1700	1790	Percent change	1700	1790
Notre-Dame	856 (19)	873 (14)	+ 2	528 (24)	499 (21)	− 6	61	57
Saint-Jean	858 (19)	1,076 (18)	+25	523 (24)	570 (24)	+ 9	61	53
Saint-Médard	270 (6)	423 (7)	+57	99 (4.5)	111 (4)	—	37	24
Saint-Michel	860 (19)	904 (15)	+ 3.5	362 (16)	315 (13)	−13	44	36
Saint-Nicolas	539 (12)	758 (13)	+ 6	249 (11.5)	263 (11)	+ 6	60	60
Saint-Pierre	297 (7)	620 (11)	+106	67 (3)	107 (4.5)	+60	33	37
Saint-Philibert	822 (18)	1,183 (20)	+32	368 (14)	553 (23)	+32	49	56
City	4,185	4,952	+18	2,196	2,418	+10	53	49
City and faubourgs	4,502	5,837	+27	2,341	2,809	+20	52	47

[a]Figures in parentheses are parish as percentage of total city

and the few *négociants*. Over 250 trades are named in the taille roles. They cover the entire range of artisanal industries and services. Related occupations have been grouped into seven broad occupational categories: food trades, woodworking trades, construction trades, leather trades, metal trades, textile and clothing trades, and transport trades. Many occupations, however, do not fall neatly and conveniently into one of these categories. These include cabaret and tavern keepers, musicians and musical craftsmen, printers and booksellers, apothecaries, doctors, surgeons and dentists, billiard and tennis court keepers, schoolteachers, copyists, mathematicians, surveyors, and dancing masters. All other liberal professions have been excluded, as have domestic servants, members and employees of the various administrative, judicial, and fiscal institutions, military personnel, and agricultural workers. The occupational designations *ouvrier, journalier, manouvrier*, and their feminine equivalents offer a particular problem. Most of these people were probably unskilled laborers and odd jobs men in town, but it is also likely that a large number of them were agricultural workers who worked in the fields and vineyards surrounding the city. They are included in the figures for the urban working population even though there is no way positively to identify the actual nature of their occupations. Indeed, a great many of them were probably part of the large floating labor force that moved between the rural and urban economies according to the rhythm of the seasons and the employment opportunities offered at the particular moment. Widows' entries were usually accompanied by their late husbands' occupations or social categories. I have included them in the statistics for the aggregate working population. It is not always clear whether they continued their husbands' businesses. Therefore, when dealing with the active population of specific trades, I have included only those who were listed with the feminine form of a trade name (e.g., *mercière, rôtisseuse, fayancière, blanchisseuse*).

The growth of the working population of Dijon did not quite keep pace with the global demographic increase of the city. Whereas the total number of entries on the taille registers rose from 4,502 to 5,837, an increase of 27 percent, the number of workers, as defined above, rose from 2,341 to 2,804 from 1700 to 1790, an increase of only 20 percent. Since there is no indication of a dramatic increase in the size of the indigent and vagrant population of the city, it seems that the most rapidly increasing sectors of the urban population were the administrative, judicial, aristocratic, and ecclesiastical elements of society. To supply the increased demand for goods and services produced by these groups, the relatively shrinking labor force was required either to increase productivity or to import more of these goods and services, assuming that levels of consumption remained constant or rose. In either case, the result of this for the working population was a sustained level of moderate prosperity and opportunity throughout the century in a relatively stable economic environment.

The differences between rates of growth among Dijon's parishes noted above are even more striking when one considers the working population alone. In the faubourgs the labor force increase more nearly kept pace with that of the general population. The faubourgs d'Ouche, Saint-Pierre, and Saint-Nicolas were the most dynamic areas of expansion. Within the city itself major differences are apparent in the evolution of the work force in each parish. The total number of workers inscribed on the rolls of Notre-Dame and Saint-Michel parishes actually fell by 6 percent and 13 percent respectively from 1700 to 1790. The parishes of Saint-Médard, Saint-Jean, and Saint-Nicolas witnessed increases of between 6 percent and 12 percent in the absolute size of their work forces. The two parishes of Saint-Pierre and Saint-Philibert experienced tremendous increases of 60 percent and 50 percent in absolute figures. When the numbers are examined as proportions of the total number of hearths, the demographic patterns show that the distribution of the working population within Dijon was shifting. The parishes of Saint-Pierre and Saint-Philibert, which witnessed the largest increases in the size of their working populations, also witnessed increases in work force as a proportion of parish population. All other parishes except for Saint-Nicolas, which remained stable at 60 percent, experienced decreases in the working proportion of their populations. These changes affected the distribution of the working population among the seven parishes of the city. Again, Saint-Pierre and Saint-Philibert experienced increases at the expense of Notre-Dame and Saint-Michel, while the other parishes maintained the same proportion of the city's working population. None of these changes were of drastic proportion, but the trends are all in the same direction. The parishes of Notre-Dame and Saint-Michel witnessed a declining worker presence; Saint-Pierre and Saint-Philibert saw an increasing one; the others remained stable.

The occupational designations on the taille registers afford the opportunity to make a more detailed analysis of the occupational structure of the Dijon economy at the beginning of the eighteenth century and at the end of the Old Regime. On a first level of categorization the working population is divided into two major groups, those who are named in the tax rolls with a specific trade and those who are not. The latter fall under the designation ouvrier, journalier, or manouvrier. The total number of workers registered with a specific trade name declined by 14 percent for the entire city (by only 7 percent if the faubourgs are included). The same variations among parishes as were noted above are apparent among this subgroup of the working population, but to a greater extreme. Only the parishes of Saint-Pierre and Saint-Philibert registered an increase in the number of trade-designated workers. The other five parishes all registered a decrease, with Notre-Dame and Saint-Michel experiencing the greatest declines. Over the same period the number of non-trade-designated workers more than tripled. This opposite trend significantly altered the proportions of trade-designated and non-trade-designated workers. In 1700 the proportions were 90 percent and 10 percent; by 1790 they had changed to 70 percent and 30 percent, a significant difference. I hesitate to use the terms "skilled" and "unskilled" in this context, because equating trade-designated workers with skilled workers and non-trade-designated workers with unskilled laborers may obscure other operative factors. There seems to have been no significant change either in the types of trades and industries that made up the economy of Dijon or in the modes of production used in these trades. At the same time, different levels of skill and expertise were required in all trades at various points in the production process. Semantic changes in vocabulary and in expressing the nature of skill and production could also have led to a change in the perception of a reality that itself did not change. A shift in the definition of skill or of craftsmanship as it pertained to the process of artisanal work and production, restricting its application to the highest levels of the productive process, may have left those on the lower rungs of the ladder with no other normative tags available than ouvrier even though this change in nomenclature did not really signify any change in the type of work they performed. It is also unclear who was responsible for creating and applying the normative values used in the tax registers—the workers themselves or the administrators who drew up the registers.

The Dijon economy was oriented toward producing goods and services for local consumption. There were few industries geared to producing for an expanding market in any sector. The guild structure was the dominant mode of production, and capital accumulation and investment were not far advanced. There seem to have been no stimuli or pressures, economic or otherwise, to alter the existing preindustrial, artisanal structure of the economy. Little change occurred in the trades and industries of the town economy or in the distribution of the work force among them between 1700 and 1790 (see table 4.2). The largest part of the working population was engaged in the textile and clothing trades. Thirty percent of the work force was employed in the manufacture of fabrics, the confection of clothing and related products, or the sale of these items. The manufacture of cloth was still an urban occupation in Dijon. In both 1700 and 1790 more than 150 persons were listed as carders, combers, spinners, weavers, fullers, dyers, and such. The total number of workers in these trades must have been substantially larger since the

Table 4.2. Working population of Dijon divided by trade category

Trade category	1700		1790	
	Number of persons engaged in trades	Percentage of total	Number of persons engaged in trades	Percentage of total
Food	295	15.0	314	15.0
Wood	164	8.0	177	8.5
Leather	69	3.5	47	2.0
Construction	262	13.0	291	14.0
Metal	154	7.5	115	5.5
Textiles/ clothing	597	30.0	658	31.0
Transport	135	7.0	93	4.5
Others (including cabaret owners and innkeepers)	297 (92)	15.0	406 (144)	19.0
Total	1,973		2,101	

Note: Percentages have been rounded to nearest 0.5 percent.

dependents of these workers were without a doubt also involved in the production process. The food trades continued to represent 15 percent of the work force throughout the century. The constant demand for public and private construction in Dijon during the eighteenth century supported 13 percent to 14 percent of the work force in the building trades, including many luxury trades that decorated the hôtels of the sword and robe nobility. The woodworking, metal, and leather trades each occupied under 10 percent of the labor force, as did trades providing transportation and cartage of goods and persons. Between 15 percent and 19 percent of the occupations listed on the tax rolls cannot easily be put into one of these categories. They include myriad small trades that provided a host of goods and services to the urban population. The single largest of these was cabaret or tavern keeper, which alone accounted for approximately 4 percent of the total labor force. Others include the printing and book trades, teachers, copyists, apothecaries, doctors, surgeons and dentists (there were two in 1790), billiard and tennis hall keepers, artists, musicians, and a vast array of artisans who produced a varied assortment of household and consumer goods.[7]

[7]For comparison, see Michel Vovelle, Ville et campagne au XVIIIe siècle: Chartres et la Beauce (Paris, 1980), p. 35; Mohamed El Kardi, Bayeux aux XVIIe et XVIIIe siècles: Contribution à l'histoire urbaine de la France (Paris, 1970), p. 67; and T. LeGoff, Vannes and Its Region: A Study of Town and Country in Eighteenth Century France (Oxford, 1981), pp. 33–34.

Edward J. Shephard, Jr.

The Organization of the Guild and the Recruitment of Masters

Having delineated certain trends in the demographic evolution of the working population of Dijon during the eighteenth century, I will now examine one important historical problem concerning one subgroup of the entire labor force—the question of access to the guild mastership. The artisanal economy of Dijon was a network of integrated industries and trades. More than 250 occupations can be identified in the tax rolls— practically the entire spectrum of manufacturing and commercial activity. The taille rolls afford a bewilderingly detailed and complex picture of the occupational matrix of the economy. They do not, however, allow us to penetrate the organization and structure of economic relationships within the economy. The most important of these structures was the guild. The organization of production into small units of master, journeymen, and apprentices was predominant in all sectors of the economy. The series of lettres de maîtrise offers the opportunity to analyze the guild structure of the economy insofar as it relates to workers' access to the independent status of master. This necessarily reduces the scope of the inquiry to only the highest level of the guild community—the masters, who alone possessed the right to manufacture and market their products within the jurisdiction of the municipality. The other members of the guild community—apprentices, compagnons, and *alloués* (workers who were neither apprentices nor compagnons)—do not enter directly into the analysis because of the limitations of the sources. Nevertheless, this aspect of the guild system is central to the dynamics of social and economic change and opportunity at the end of the Old Regime.

The guild system itself continued to evolve during the eighteenth century and never reached a point of stasis. The lettres de maîtrise series includes only trades that were institutionalized; that is, that had a corporate identity and status as guilds. For fifty-four guilds, many of which were composed of several different but related trades, the series covers the entire period 1700 to 1790. These guilds are distributed among all sectors of the economy and include trades with both large and small memberships. The shoemakers, joiners, drapers, and pork butchers normally registered five to ten new masters every year. Others such as the printers, furriers, and gunsmiths received new masters much less frequently. By the end of the Old Regime over eighty guilds were in existence in Dijon. Trades were continually integrated into the corporate institutional structure. Guilds constantly revised their statutes and presented them for official approval. This was solicited up the ladder of administrative sanction from the Chambre de conseil et de police of

Dijon through the intendant and the parlement to the Conseil du roi. The guilds often had to revise the financial provisions of their statutes in order to pay for the redemption of newly created offices, to buy up royal *brevets de maîtrise*,[8] to pay taxes, and to pay for other strategems the royal fisc used to extract revenue from the guilds. Usually the guilds resorted to a combination of borrowing, raising the reception fees of new masters (permanently or temporarily), and levying assessments on the masters of the guild.

Guilds also tried to protect their privileges and monopolies from the encroachments of unincorporated *chambrelans* and other guilds, or even from abuse by their own members, by strengthening the policing provisions of their statutes or by seeking ordonnances from municipal and royal authorities to redress their grievances. Many trades that had long existed with only informal or unofficial organization and recognition sought, or were made to seek, official sanction as incorporated trades (*métiers jurés*). The impetus for these moves came both from the royal administration and from within the trades themselves. Motives were usually economic or fiscal on both sides. The guilds attempted to use the royal administration to protect their monopoly on manufacture and commerce. The use of corporate institutions by the royal fisc as sources of revenue and, conversely, by guild members as a buffer against these same demands had a long tradition, and each side pursued its own policies and interests as best it could. The relative prosperity of the Dijon economy seems to have allowed the guilds there to adjust to the exactions and manipulations of the royal government, but not without the burden of increasing indebtedness and self-taxation. The 1730s in particular seem to have been a decade when the urban trades experienced renewed pressure and control from the central administration. Sixteen new guilds, which comprised over twenty trades, were incorporated and began to show up in the lettres de maîtrise series during this decade.[9] This development was one aspect of the tightening of royal control over the economy during the ministry of the controller general Orry. The central government continued a policy of strict control and use of the guild regime throughout the rest of the Old Regime, except for the abortive reforms under Turgot.

The number of new masters received into the Dijon guilds remained

[8] Also called lettres de maîtrise, these were granted or sold by the king upon special occasions or as a revenue-producing strategem. They exempted their holders from entry requirements of the guild and were valid in all cities of the kingdom except Paris.

[9] The following trades appear in the lettres de maîtrise series beginning in the 1730s: pork butchers, oil makers, wine merchants, fish sellers, builders/architects, painters/sculptors, tinsmiths/lead workers, ironmongers, secondhand-clothes dealers, card makers/papermakers, starch makers, tennis court/billiard hall/gaming house keepers, innkeepers/cabaret owners.

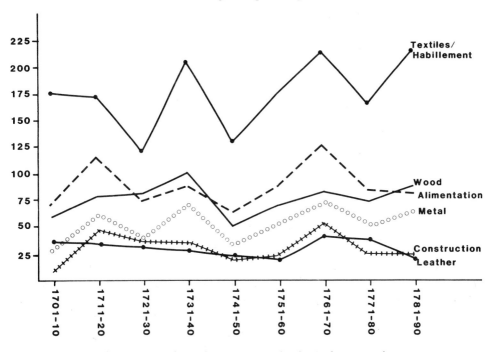

Fig. 4.1. Number of new masters in six trade categories

fairly constant during the eighteenth century. The annual totals of lettres de maîtrise rose continually from 1700 to 1790, but this was primarily because new guilds were being created, especially during the 1730s. The actual changes in the rate of reception of new masters must be measured against a constant base. Figure 4.1 charts the number of receptions in fifty-four guilds spanning the period 1700 to 1790. Only six of the seven occupational categories established above are included. The transport trades were among the latest to be institutionalized, and most did not become guilds until later in the century. The graph shows that master receptions did not change greatly between 1700 and 1790. In fact, the six occupational categories all followed basically the same up-and-down variations across the century. An increase in receptions during the first decade of the eighteenth century was followed by thirty years of reasonably constant levels of reception. A slight drop-off occurred during the 1740s, after which renewed increase brought the levels back up to those of the 1710s or slightly higher. The last two decades of the Old Regime showed a mixed movement among the occupational categories, but the general trend seems to have been a slight downswing. No dramatic change occurred in the reception rates in any category. Nor did their positions relative to one another change, although the number of masters received did not always correspond to the proportionate size of that trade category in the total work force (see pp. 109–10 above). The construction trades, which normally had a lower proportion of masters to workmen than many other trades, are at the bottom of the graph, but they were the third largest occupational category in the work force.

The number of masters in each trade guild remained fairly constant throughout the century. Most guilds made annual assessments on their members to pay the expenses of the confrérie, to finance interest payments on guild debts, or to pay taxes such as the vingtièmes d'industrie. Unfortunately, few of the guild registers that survive contain records dating back before midcentury. Thus it is difficult to follow guild membership across the century. For most guilds only the register in current use at the time of their suppression in 1791 has survived. For a handful of guilds, records of membership exist earlier than 1750, either because the last register went back that far or because earlier registers have survived. The following is a complete list of guilds for which an accurate record of membership can be traced earlier than 1750. The first figure is the membership of the guild at the earliest recorded date. The second figure is the last recorded membership figure.[10]

Glassmakers (E3474,3475)	15 (1700)	16 (1787)
Saddlers (E3362,3364)	15 (1701)	8 (1790)
Butchers (E3359)	23 (1703)	20 (1782)
Leather dressers (E3368)	13 (1708)	11 (1771)
Tapestry workers/upholsterers (E3458,3459)	14 (1727)	19 (1789)
Gunsmiths/cutlers/spur makers (E3392)	10 (1734)	9 (1790)
Painters/sculptors/gilders (E3392)	33 (1747)	32 (1789)
Clockmakers (E3407)	7 (1748)	7 (1788)
Hatters (E3370)	8 (1749)	8 (1781)

These figures show that the number of guild masters did not change much, reinforcing the picture of a stable working population as seen from our examination of the taille registers. The reception of new members kept the guild mastership at the same level or slightly above. Given the small increase in the total size of the work force during the same time period, the result was a very stable ratio between masters and workers within the guild community. The economy of Dijon remained one based on small workshop production.

It was not uncommon in Dijon for a person to be a member of more than one guild. Of the more than 7,500 masters who appear in the lettres de maîtrise series, almost 500 were already members of other guilds.

[10] ADC, series E.

The overwhelmingly predominant second occupation was that of cabaret/tavern keeper—370 of the 500 dual masterships. The vast majority of these were not real tavern keepers, but tended on the side small houses for eating and drinking. Thus, of the 910 entrants into the cabaret/tavern keepers guild, over one-third pursued another profession. Of the total 370 dual masterships involving cabaret owners, 300 members belonged to another guild first and subsequently became cabaret owners. Seventy were initially received as cabaret owners and later became masters in other guilds. Most of the women who ran cabarets were *"femmes authorisées"* of tradesmen husbands. This number could probably be added to the list of dual masterships (which does not include them), because it is highly likely that in both types of two-profession households the husband carried on his own trade while his wife tended to what served as a cabaret. The second occupation of these cabaret owners varied among forty-three different trades. However, 243 of the 370 belonged to one of the following trades: baker, pastrymaker, pork butcher, caterer/roast meat seller, vinegar maker, or wine merchant. A side business as a cabaret owner was most often associated with a primary occupation in another food trade.

The closely related nature of the trades involved was characteristic of the incidence of multiple professions. All eleven of the new master curriers who belonged to another guild at the time of their reception into the curriers' guild were already master tanners. Of 157 wine merchants, 63 were members of another guild, including 16 vinegar makers, 14 coopers, and 18 tavern keepers, all professions closely linked to the wine trade. In other trades, such as that of pork butcher or draper, members with two masterships were not concentrated in any particular second occupation but covered a wide range of professions. It is not likely, in any case, that most of the multiple masters continued fully in both trades at the same time. Unfortunately, it is impossible to know exactly how these multiple occupations were exercised.

In trades where there was a significant overlapping of production and materials, the inevitable and interminable disputes that arose between guilds over monopoly and jurisdiction could be avoided or resolved by multiple guild memberships. A master in one guild who was charged by another guild with infringement on their privileges could usually avoid protracted legal action by joining the other guild. Such a situation seems to have existed among the metal trades, where a relatively large proportion of masters belonged to more than one guild. For example, of the forty-eight master edge-tool makers, four were already master drill-bit makers, two were master wheelwrights, three were master shoeing-smiths, four were master farriers, and three were master toolgrinders. This practice seems to go against the fundamental nature of the guild system, which was based on protecting the livelihood of members by maintaining control over production and the marketplace. And yet the evidently widespread incidence of multiple guild memberships raises the question why the guilds would allow this to occur. There is no evidence of attempts by either the guilds or the government to put a stop to this practice. In fact the policy of the monarchy, which favored the consolidation of related trades into one body, especially in the aftermath of the Turgot reforms, was in the opposite direction. Some guilds that contained several related trades were organized along lines that kept the trades very separate within the single guild corporation. This was the case with the painters/sculptors/gilders, who constituted a single guild but whose members were received under only one professional capacity and could not exercise the other two. It was possible to maintain this type of arrangement in guilds where the trades were easily distinguishable; in others it was impossible. In addition, there were fiscal advantages for the monarchy, the municipality, and the guild in allowing multiple guild memberships. The crown and the municipality both derived revenues from new masters: reception fees, registration fees, syndics fees, and so forth. The guilds likewise had an interest in having a large assessment base in order to finance their sizable debt burdens. Financial and economic interests seem to have been stronger than corporate ideology in the realities of the guild community.

Geographic Mobility

The lettres de maîtrise are a rich source for the study of geographic mobility of craftsmen in the Old Regime. The *information sur les vie et moeurs* that was required of all new masters provides basic biographical data. In most cases the master's birthplace is specified by town or by province. The transcribing clerk usually added the province when the locality was outside Burgundy, except in the case of large and well-known towns. In approximately 2,000 instances the birthplace of the new master either was not given or was impossible to identify with reasonable certainty. The remaining 5,500 cases offer the opportunity to analyze patterns of migration among workers during the eighteenth century. The lettres de maîtrise do not tell how long the new immigrants had been resident in Dijon at the time of their reception, however. Therefore it is not possible, using this source alone, to determine the length of time it took for a newly arrived compagnon to rise to the status of master in Dijon. Nor can we study the incidence of emigration from Dijon.

Four distance parameters were chosen for this analysis: Dijon; the department of the Côte-d'Or; adjacent departments; and all others. A

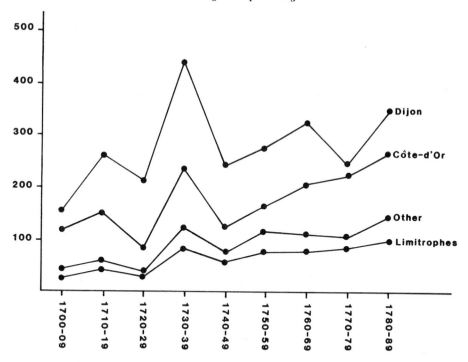

Fig. 4.2. Geographic origins of recipients of lettres de maîtrise

departmental rather than a provincial plotting was chosen solely to provide a more precise and detailed mapping of geographic origins. Inevitably, a few persons whose birthplaces were named only by province are not included, but the total number of these is low and their importance is small compared with the increase in precision using departments rather than provinces. The first parameter is the city of Dijon itself. Native inhabitants did not have to pay the twelve livres "droit d'habitantage." The second distance parameter is the area that later became the department of the Côte-d'Or. The third is the group of adjacent departments including the Aube, the Haute-Marne, the Yonne, the Nièvre, the Saône-et-Loire, and the three departments of the Franche-Comté: the Haute-Saône, the Doubs, and the Jura. This area falls within an approximate radius of 150 kilometers from Dijon. The fourth category includes all places outside this range.

During the eighteenth century the guilds of Dijon were remarkably open to non-Dijonnais. Figure 4.2 plots the geographic origin of new masters over ten-year intervals according to the four distance parameters I have set up. Figure 4.3 indicates the percentages for each parameter

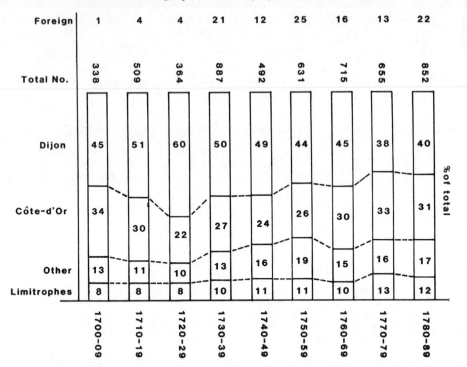

Fig. 4.3. Geographic origins of recipients of lettres de maîtrise, 1700–89

for each decade, with totals listed above each bar. At the very top of the bar graph are the numbers of new masters of foreign birth, which are not included in the totals. The inflated total for the 1730s represents the many new guilds created during that decade. All active members of these trades were required to register with the town council. A large number of these lettres de maîtrise from the 1730s, therefore, represent new masters only in an institutional and legal sense, not in the stricter context of new master craftsmen setting up their own shops.

Most new guild masters in Dijon were immigrants, as can be clearly seen from the figures. Over half of them were born outside Dijon. At the beginning of the century only 45 percent of new masters were native Dijonnais. This percentage rose slightly during the next several decades. During the 1720s there was a substantial drop in the total number of new guild masters received. Immigrant masters accounted for the greatest share of this decrease, while the number of Dijon-born masters remained the same. Consequently, the proportion of Dijon-born masters rose to 60 percent. After the 1730s the number of immigrant masters increased steadily until the proportion of immigrant to native masters reached three to two by the end of the Old Regime.[11]

The highest proportion of immigrants came from the area close by Dijon. One third of all new masters were from the region of the future Côte-d'Or. Their relative proportion fell to about one-quarter during the middle part of the century, then returned to one-third. Practically every village in the area contributed at least one new master to the Dijon guild community. Three important towns in the area each accounted for more than twenty-five new masters—Beaune (29), Langres (30), and Vitteaux (31). The small villages within five kilometers of Dijon—Talant, Ahuy, Saint-Apollinaire, Chenôve—were not overrepresented in the Dijon guilds. The number of masters from these villages did not exceed one every ten to twenty years. Within the region of the Côte-d'Or certain areas emerge as poles of heavier immigration. Three axes seem to radiate out from Dijon toward Beaune, Langres, and Vitteaux. The route north to Langres was an important highway to Champagne, Flanders, and the Rhine valley. Several villages along that road were the hometowns of sixteen to twenty-five Dijon guild masters. Many other tradesmen came to Dijon up the "route de Beaune" from small, but nowadays by no means unknown, villages—Meursault, Pommard, Aloxe-Corton, Nuits-Saint-Georges, Vosne-Romanée, Vougeot, Chambolles, Musigny, Morey-Saint-Denis, Gevrey-Chambertin. The heaviest concentration of immigration, however, was from the west through the upper valley of the Ouche River, Auxois plateau, and north through Vitteaux, Semur-en-Auxois, and Montbard. Fourteen towns along this route each accounted for ten or more new masters. This was the main highway from Paris during the eighteenth century, as it still is today.

While the proportion of new masters from Dijon declined and of those from the Côte-d'Or remained constant, the proportion of new masters from a greater distance rose from about 20 percent in 1700/1709 to about 30 percent in 1780/1789. The distribution of new masters by department of origin is shown on the map in figure 4.4. The departments adjacent to the Côte-d'Or accounted for two-thirds of "long-distance" immigration. The departments of the Haute-Marne and the Saône-et-Loire led the list with over 120 each, or about four persons every three years. The Franche-Comté was the region of next highest incidence of

[11]Compare these figures with those of Caen, where in 1666 54 percent of *salariés* and 43 percent of *chefs d'entreprises* were immigrants, and where in the year VI the figures were 51.5 percent and 52.8 percent respectively; Jean-Claude Perrot, *Genèse d'une ville moderne: Caen au XVIIIe siècle* (Paris, 1975). In Chartres, during the last decade of the Old Regime, 65 percent of *conjoints* among the *artisanat* and the *salariat* were from the city, 20 percent were from the Chartres region, and 15 percent were from the rest of France. See Vovelle, *Ville et campagne*, pp. 120–21.

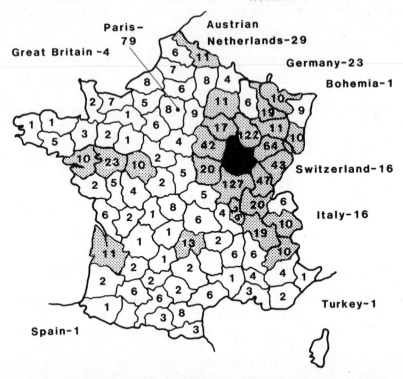

Fig. 4.4. Distribution of immigrant masters by department

immigration, whereas the less populous and less accessible regions to the west—the Nivernais and the Morvan—contributed relatively fewer new masters. Immigration was predominantly from eastern France. To the north and east immigration remained strong from Champagne on into Flanders and from Alsace-Lorraine on into Germany. To the south immigration patterns followed the Saône River south to Lyons, then moved southeast through Dauphiné and Savoie. Outside eastern France only a few regions provided a significantly large number of new masters to the Dijon guild community. One of these was the lower Loire valley— Touraine, Anjou, and the Nantes region. Another was Auvergne. Indeed, the less populous and more remote regions of the Massif Central— Auvergne, La Marche, Limousin, Bourbonnais—accounted for more immigrants than other more populous provinces such as Normandie, Picardie, Provence, and Languedoc.

The incidence of immigration from the major cities of the country was not high. Nearly all the large towns were represented, but few accounted for more than a couple of masters. Sixteen new masters came from Besançon; fifteen of twenty-six from the department of the Rhône came from Lyons; all eleven Girondins were from Bordeaux. Paris not only was a magnet that drew people from the provinces, it also sent out its own natives to the rest of France. Seventy-nine Parisians became guild masters in Dijon between 1700 and 1790. The vast majority of new masters, however, came from rural villages and small towns, few of which had guilds themselves.

A substantial number of foreigners became guild masters in Dijon during the eighteenth century. The largest numbers of them came from the Austrian Netherlands and from Savoie (29 each), followed by Germany (23), Switzerland (16), and Italy (8). Foreign-born masters followed many different occupations, including twenty-one shoemakers, sixteen tailors, seven edge-tool makers (all from Savoie), seven cabinetmaker/joiners, and four clockmakers (two Swiss). Four natives of Great Britain became guild masters in Dijon. Three were born in London, one in Edinburgh. The Londoners were François Perinot, age thirty-four (one can only guess the English form of his name), who became a master cabinetmaker/joiner in 1737;[12] Louis Olivier Bezançon, age twenty-eight, who joined the same guild in 1788;[13] and Jemima Gillet, the widow of Jean-Baptiste Martel, a paper merchant of Dijon, who herself became a member of the painters/sculptors/gilders guild in 1787.[14] The lone Scotsman was Charles Kiers, age forty-five, who became a master roofer in 1770.[15] Another much-traveled foreigner was Chrétien Zahn, age twenty-nine, from Scheiba in Bohemia (probably the city of Cheb, on the border today between Czechoslovakia and West Germany). Zahn was the son of a glass cutter and himself entered the Dijon glass cutters' guild in 1755.[16] By far the most exotic personnage to settle in Dijon from abroad was one Jérémie Hassan, a café keeper from Constantinople. He was received by the Chambre de conseil et de police in 1700. The town magistrates apparently thought it advisable to assure themselves of Hassan's Catholic faith, for they requested a certificate attesting to it from the curé of Saint-Médard parish and deposited it with Hassan's lettre de maîtrise.[17]

Immigrant masters were evenly distributed among all trades. Some guilds had a membership that was predominantly Dijonnais by birth. In others the masters born outside Dijon were in the majority. Most guilds, however, had a fairly even fifty-fifty split between the two groups. Only

[12]AMD, series G, liasse 130.
[13]AMD, series G, liasse 183.
[14]AMD, series G, liasse 182.
[15]AMD, series G, liasse 165.
[16]AMD, series G, liasse 148.
[17]AMD, series G, liasse 107.

in the metal trades does there seem to have been a noticeable imbalance between native Dijonnais and immigrant masters. Eight metal trade guilds either were evenly balanced between Dijonnais and non-Dijonnais (pin makers, casters/engravers, locksmiths) or had a high proportion of masters born outside Dijon (coppersmiths, drill-bit makers, knife makers/ spur makers, tool grinders, edge-tool makers). Only three metal guilds tipped the scales in favor of Dijon-born masters (pewterers, tinsmiths/ lead workers, ironsmiths). No guilds, no matter how small, were composed exclusively of Dijon-born masters. The majority of Dijon-born masters in any guild was rarely more than two-thirds. Only the fish sellers (85 percent), the heel makers/last makers (83 percent), and the tinsmiths/ lead workers (78 percent) had significantly higher rations of Dijon-born masters.

Several patterns of immigration emerge within certain trade groups. Among the bakers and weavers the vast majority of masters born outside Dijon came from the region of the Côte-d'Or. In the other trades with over two hundred new masters between 1700 and 1790 (shoemakers, cobblers, pork butchers, drapers/haberdashers) the proportion of non-Dijonnais from the Côte-d'Or varied between 40 percent and 60 percent. For the bakers and weavers this ratio was above 80 percent for both. These trades were all common professions requiring no great skill or extended period of training. Each employed large numbers of workers in all cities and towns. It is not surprising that recruitment for them was highly regional. Yet just the opposite was true for the tailors, another common and populous profession. Only 23 percent of non-Dijonnais tailors were from the Côte-d'Or region. Other trades had a high concentration of masters from specific geographic areas. Sixteen of twenty-eight clockmakers were born outside the Côte-d'Or. Twelve of them came from eastern France and bordering countries—Champagne, Lorraine, Switzerland, Savoie, and Italy. Of fifteen master whitewashers/plasterers from outside the Côte-d'Or, nine were natives of Languedoc, including three from Bézières, two from Auch, and two from Montpellier. Fifteen of twenty-one non-Dijonnais roofers came from the lower Loire valley, nine from Anjou alone. All eight master tool grinders received into the Dijon guild were from outside the region (there were no Dijon-born masters)—five Auvergnats and three Savoyards. The Auvergne also accounted for a large number of masters in other metal trades. Twelve of twenty-one master coppersmiths born outside the Côte-d'Or were from Auvergne. Four became masters on the same day in 1754.[18] They were all master drill-bit makers beforehand—two were from Tidernac, and the other two

[18]AMD, series G, liasse 147.

Table 4.3. Proportion of sons following their fathers' professions

Years	Total number of "lettres"	Percentage Dijonnais sons of masters	Percentage non-Dijonnais sons of masters
1693–1730	1,822	22.6 (413)[a]	8 (141)[a]
1731–60	2,379	12.6 (303)	5 (110)
1761–90	3,661	9.0 (326)	3 (119)

[a]Numbers of sons of masters in parentheses.

were brothers from Bouchey. Thirteen of thirty-five non-Côte-d'Or master drill-bit makers were Auvergnats, including those just mentioned. In all, six Auvergnats belonged to both the coppersmiths' and the drill-bit makers' guilds in Dijon.

Closed or Open Corporations?

One of the charges usually leveled against the guilds is that the mastership was restricted to the sons of masters and that it became nearly impossible for anyone other than a master's son or son-in-law to rise to this status. The lettres de maîtrise series of the Dijon guilds indicate that only a minority of guild masters in Dijon were themselves sons of masters, and that instead of increasing during the eighteenth century, their number actually decreased (see table 4.3). Not all guild masters who followed their fathers' professions were the sons of masters. Guilds did not exist in all trades in all towns of France. The small villages from which most Dijon masters came did not, as a rule, have organized guild communities. During the first thirty years of the eighteenth century only 30 percent of new guild masters in Dijon followed their fathers' professions. This in itself is initially a surprisingly low percentage. Of these 30 percent, 22 percent were natives of Dijon and 8 percent were not. The figures dropped to 12.6 percent and 5 percent respectively for the period 1731–60. During the last thirty years of the Old Regime the percentages dropped even lower, to 9 percent and 3 percent—a total of only 12 percent of sons following their fathers into the artisanal trades among guild masters. This represents a very high level of occupational mobility and of economic opportunity within a group that has traditionally been presented as a closed caste of families. The percentage of Dijon-born masters following their fathers' trades was much higher, but this figure, too, declined significantly, from 66 percent to 35 percent. Guilds that had a

higher proportion of native-born masters naturally had a higher proportion of masters' sons in their ranks than guilds with larger non-
Dijonnais membership.[19]

There were only a handful of guilds in which the number of masters
following their fathers' professions reached 50 percent or higher. These
include the whitewashers/plasterers (47 of 94), the carpenters (42 of 74),
the knife makers/spur makers/gunsmiths (13 of 24), the roofers (40 of
75), the casters/gilders/engravers (14 of 28), the furriers (10 of 12), the
pewterers/sword cutlers (12 of 22), the dyers (17 of 35), and the weavers
(125 of 236). All of these guilds fall into one of three occupational
categories—the building trades, the metal trades, or the textile/clothing
trades. Trades in which the highest degrees of skill and instruction were
required did not have a high incidence of continuity of profession from
father to son—three of ten apothecaries, one of ten printers, and none
of ten watchmakers.

A large number of guild craftsmen came from agricultural backgrounds. A total of 634 new masters identified their fathers as *laboureurs*.
These farmers' sons entered many different trades. A large number of
them became shoemakers (43 shoemakers, 37 cobblers), bakers (92), or
pork butchers (77). No farmer's son became a master in any of the
following guilds: apothecaries, button makers, drill-bit makers, gunsmiths, spur makers, tinsmiths, ironmongers, printers/booksellers, furriers, pewterers/sword cutlers, and dyers. Once again, the number of
metal trades in this list is noticeable.

Family connections were one channel of opportunity for non-Dijonnais workers to enter the Dijon guild community. Ninety-four instances
of non-Dijonnais relatives' entering the same guild occur in the lettres
de maîtrise series. The most common occurrence was that of two brothers, though there were cases of three brothers from Mandelot becoming
bakers[20] and three brothers from Morey-Saint-Denis becoming potters.[21]
In some guilds the incidence of non-Dijonnais brothers was high—bakers
(15 cases), weavers (9), drapers (6), vinegar makers (6), pork butchers
(5), butchers (5). It is not possible to tell whether the relatives came to
Dijon at the same time. Nor is it possible to determine how long they
had been in Dijon before becoming masters. Sometimes only a few years
separated the receptions of two brothers. In other instances ten or twenty
years elapsed between their entries into the guild. Many younger sons

---

[19]In Caen, the number of masters' sons entering the guilds declined from 52.6 percent
in 1730–39 to 32.8 percent in 1780–89; see Perrot, *Genèse d'une ville*, pp. 339–40. Also
compare with Chartres, 1791-year VIII, where 42 percent of the artisans were sons of
artisan fathers; Vovelle, *Ville et campagne*, p. 32.

[20]AMD, series G, liasses 108, 115, 116.

[21]AMD, series G, liasses 122, 130, 155.

probably became apprentices and compagnons in the shops of their older brothers before becoming masters themselves. There is one instance when a non-Dijonnais father and son became masters in the same guild. In 1768 Antoine Chevalier, a master tinsmith from Auvergne, entered the drill-bit makers'/tinsmiths' guild in Dijon. The next year his father, Jean Chevalier, also a master tinsmith, was received into the same guild. There is no indication where they had previously been received as master tinsmiths. Jean Chevalier had been in Dijon for at least ten years because he had been received as a master pork butcher in 1759. Apparently not one to let opportunity slip by, he also became a master coppersmith in 1771.[22] This is perhaps an extreme example of the cumulation of masterships in several related trades, and although it is unlikely that Jean Chevalier exercised all three trades concurrently, his case highlights the openness and fluidity of the Dijon economy and guild community.

There were two occurrences where brother and sister joined the same guild in Dijon. The first was that of Denise and Claude Chouard, children of a merchant of Vitteaux. Denise, apparently unmarried at age thirty-eight, became a maîtresse in the drapers' guild in 1748.[23] In 1760 her brother, twenty years her junior, joined the same guild.[24] The second instance also involved the drapers' guild, and again the sister preceded her brother into the guild. In 1755 Elizabeth Thomas, age twenty-six, an unmarried daughter of a merchant of Chagney, entered the drapers' guild.[25] She was followed by her younger brother Jean-Baptiste in 1759.[26] In both instances it is tempting to speculate that family arrangements were made whereby the younger brother was to inherit the business of an unmarried sister.

It is clear that a great deal of occupational mobility existed within the preindustrial guild economy. This was true both within the urban community and between the rural and urban contexts. The opportunity to become a guild master remained open in Dijon during the eighteenth century, and the status of master did not become the privileged reserve of masters' sons to the exclusion of all others. Indeed, it seems that relatively few masters' sons followed their fathers' professions. In Dijon the number of masters' sons continued to decline throughout the century while the guilds remained the same size or grew slightly. Unless one adopts the highly unlikely possibility that guild masters did not father enough sons to take their places within the guild comminity, one is left with the conclusion that within the relatively stable economic conditions

[22]AMD, series G, liasses 152, 163, 164, 166.
[23]AMD, series G, liasse 141.
[24]AMD, series G, liasse 153.
[25]AMD, series G, liasse 148.
[26]AMD, series G, liasse 152.

Table 4.4. Age distribution of guild masters at time of reception

Age	Dijonnais			Non-Dijonnais			Total, 1693–1790
	1693–1730	1731–60	1761–90	1693–1730	1731–60	1761–90	
Under 20	10%	10%	9.0%	1.0%	1.0%	1%	4.7%
20–29	66	50	50.0	48.0	45.5	40	49.8
30–39	20	26	27.5	40.0	40.0	40	32.4
40–49	3	10	8.0	8.5	12.0	14	9.5
50+	1	4	5.5	3.0	2.5	5	3.5
Total number	781	758	857	741	791	1,071	4,999

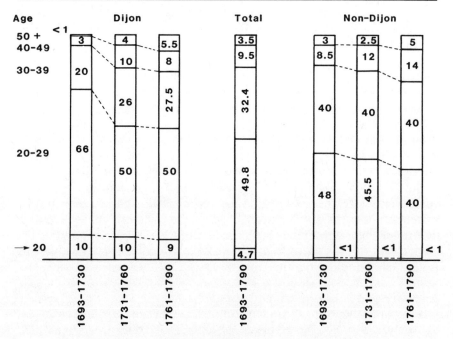

Fig. 4.5. Age distribution of guild masters at time of reception
(percentages)

of eighteenth-century Dijon, guild masters' sons were leaving their socioeconomic stratum, thus opening the opportunity for economic and social mobility and advancement to compagnons who were not the sons of masters.

The age structure of newly received guild masters is shown in table 4.4 and figure 4.5. The figures include only first-time receptions. They do not include the active members of trades, who were required to register when their trades were incorporated as métiers jurés. It is immediately apparent that Dijonnais masters entered guilds at an earlier age than those who were born elsewhere. The total incidence of new masters under the age of twenty is low, under 5 percent. Few of the under-twenty age group were non-Dijonnais. Those who were came mostly from the immediate vicinity (Plombières, Saint-Sauveur, Ahuy, Sennecey, Morey-Saint-Denis, Sainte-Reine), although there were two young Auvergnats and a thirteen-year-old joiner/cabinetmaker from La Plessié-en-Brie. Almost all the guilds received at least a few masters at an extremely young age. Among those that did not were trades that required highly developed skills and long periods of training (apothecaries, schoolteachers, copyists, clockmakers, printers, casters/gilders/engravers, painters/sculptors). Sons of masters who were received at a very early age usually stayed associated with their fathers and did not set up their own establishments. It was not at all uncommon for a son to remain associated with his father well into his adult years. These young masters enjoyed the rights and privileges of master status, but they did not represent an independent unit of production in the economy. Some guilds levied assessments to finance their debts or taxes only on masters with their own shops—that is, on each shop as a productive unit—rather than on each master individually.

The average age of masters at the time of their reception rose noticeably over the course of the century. This was not simply the result of the increasing proportion of non-Dijonnais masters, who on the average were older at the time of their reception, because the age shift is evident among this group as well. Nor was it caused by changes in the statutes of the guilds. There was no alteration either in age limits or in the length of terms of apprenticeship or compagnonnage in the Dijon guilds. Whatever the reasons for this change, it meant that, voluntarily or not, workers remained dependent longer and took more time to set themselves up as independent craftsmen.

Concluding Reflections

Eighteenth-century Dijon presents the surprising example of a guild regime that seems to have worked. The foregoing analysis has shown that the socioeconomic structure of Dijon was dominated by a pervasive and powerful guild system that regulated productive and social relationships within the working community but that nevertheless remained highly open and accessible to "new blood." Dijon did not experience the early industrialization that transformed the artisanal nature of other urban economies. To a large extent, the city remained unaffected by the evolution of a highly developed market economy, the accumulation and investment of commercial and industrial capital, and the consequent restructuring of production and labor. And yet the stability of Dijon's economy and of its social structure was due to more than just the absence of factors that were producing changes elsewhere. It was also the result of a unique set of economic and social factors that maintained its stable socioeconomic balance, the artisanal mode of production, an open and flexible guild system, and the prosperity the city enjoyed during the eighteenth century.

Of primary importance was the demographic evolution of Dijon's population. The city's population registered a decennial growth rate of 3 percent across the eighteenth century, which ensured a constant and increasing demand for goods and services. This modest growth rate was accompanied by no significant alteration in the social structure of the urban population. The social pyramid in Dijon remained very top-heavy, with a concentration of nobility, clergy, royal and provincial administrators, and judicial and financial elites that made up one-quarter of the citizenry. These wealthy, consumption-oriented groups fueled a prosperous urban economy. Yet these demographic pressures did not result in the transformation of the artisanal mode of production. Dijon lacked a mass-market outlet, either internal or external, that would have stimulated mass production and a restructuring of the nature of manufacturing. The relatively stable size of the lower end of the social spectrum provided no urban mass market, and Dijon developed no regional network of commercial distribution. Furthermore, the consumption demands generated by the wealthy elites of Dijon's population were for goods that were still highly artisanal in nature and not in the forefront of technological change or industrial transformation, including luxury goods and the building and decorating trades. These factors provided a stable socioeconomic environment in which neither the structural framework of urban society nor the network of productive relations underwent significant alteration or pressure for change.

These factors, however, only partly explain the apparent "success" of the guild regime in Dijon. They may explain the prosperity of the working population and the stability of the urban economic structure, but they do not account for its openness and the ease with which it absorbed a large influx of immigrant workers, perhaps the most crucial factor in the success of the Dijon guild community. The working population of Dijon, and the guild community in particular, remained virtually unchanged in size during the eighteenth century, despite the general population growth. Given this fact, the immigrant rate for new guild masters of over 50 percent, already a startling figure, becomes even more amazing. The prosperity of Dijon was an obvious attraction for itinerant compagnons from all over France, who settled there and became integrated members of the guild community, traditionally a closed caste of tightly knit families who jealously guarded their monopoly of production and market access. Yet while urban guilds elsewhere were forced to erect numerous defensive barriers to protect their privileged position and to wage a continuous war against infringements on their monopoly with the aid of royal and municipal police, the Dijon guilds seem to have been able to integrate a vast number of immigrants and at the same time to maintain the size of the productive force. Over 50 percent of all guild masters were from outside Dijon, and by the end of the Old Regime only 9 percent of new masters were following their fathers into the guilds. It is not possible to study the population of apprentices and compagnons with the same precision as for the masters, but it is likely that the rates of mobility and the openness of the lower levels of the corporate hierarchy were as high as or higher than for those at the top of the guild ladder. The Dijon working community was an evolving and changing population that was continually renewed by a major migration of labor, predominantly from the countryside.

Given the stability of its size and the influx of "new blood" into the mastership, there must have been an equally large movement of persons out of the guild community. The guild records on which this study is based do not allow us to follow this outward movement, but the social structure of an Old Regime provincial capital provides a likely explanation for it. The numerous administrative, judicial, financial, and ecclesiastical institutions that existed in Dijon afforded a multitude of possibilities for upward mobility to the sons of prosperous guild masters. The worlds of the parlement, the provincial estates, and the intendancy, to name only a few, offered many opportunities to take the first steps on the ladder out of the *roturier* class and to cleanse oneself of the meanness of manual labor. These channels of mobility out of the guild system satisfied the social ambitions of the successful master and also made room for newcomers in the working community. The experience of Dijon in the eighteenth century combined two heretofore seemingly contradictory developments. The corporate regime expanded to include more and more of the economic fabric of the town. At the same time, access to the mastership remained open and continued to increase as the century progressed. In Dijon, however, these trends were not contradictory. Guild expansion was not a reaction against deteriorating economic conditions, against the pressures of market and production growth and transformation, or against an overabundance of labor and competition. The guilds did not need to defend an embattled social position. Their status and their place in the socioeconomic nexus were not eroding, and opportunities for upward social mobility were not closed to them. No rearguard closing-off of access from below was necessary.

Other explanatory factors and mechanisms for the stability and "success" of the Dijon guild structure may exist and will need further exploration and study. Kinship ties that could be used to exclude and restrict access to the mastership worked as wide-ranging channels of mobility and integration into the Dijon guild community. However, other less apparent kinship relations may mask certain mechanisms. The incidence of marriage of compagnons to widows and daughters of masters needs to be analyzed before a truly definitive statement can be made on how "new" the "new blood" actually was. Nor have we been able to see those who failed to gain entry to the mastership or those unrecognized but tolerated bastards of the corporate work force, the alloués. Perhaps the most significant outside mechanism for the stability of the guilds in Dijon may in fact be the compagnonnages themselves. One aim of both guild and compagnonnage, over which there was much contention, was control of the labor market. We have seen that the working community of Dijon remained stable during the eighteenth century and was one factor contributing to the "success" of the guild system there. One of the explanations offered for this was the accessibility of the mastership to new people. In simple supply/demand terms, the demand for masters remained elastic and constant. However, there might also be a supply side that needs to be examined. The compagnonnages were strong and effective in Dijon, as evidenced in the 1763 blacklisting and quarantine of the entire city by the compagnons of the tour de France. With such a high degree of control over the labor supply, the compagnonnages might also have been an important factor in maintaining the stability of the guild regime in Dijon by regulating the flow of permanent and itinerant labor into the city.

The corporate regime in Dijon continued to provide an adequate and functioning framework for regulating productive and social relationships in the city until the end of the Old Regime. The mechanisms for balance that were built into the guild system were not taxed to the point where they became mechanisms for exclusion rather than integration, as they were elsewhere. Of course Dijon was not without its troubles between masters and compagnons, nor was the community of masters always a harmonious and unified group. These conflicts, however, were not structural. They do not indicate a dysfunctioning of the corporate regime. The stability of the Dijon guild community is one, albeit perhaps rare, example in Old Regime society where structural stability had not hardened into structural rigidity.

5

Independent and Insolent: Journeymen and Their "Rites" in the Old Regime Workplace

Cynthia M. Truant

When Old Regime literary figures and social critics such as Restif de la Bretonne, Louis-Sébastien Mercier, and Siméon Hardy bemoaned the chaos they believed was commonplace in the world of work at the end of the eighteenth century, they contrasted the actions of "volatile" and "hostile" workers with their own evocations of a pleasant time, not long past in their minds, when master and journeyman (*maître* and *compagnon*) lived and worked in hierarchy and harmony.[1] Present-day scholars of the French *corps des métiers*, or guilds, might well be skeptical of those who wrote with such self-assurance either of a golden age of harmony in the guilds or of a widespread disintegration of master/worker cooperation in the eighteenth century. Even more problematic would be the suggestion that chaos in the workplace, so frequently referred to in these authors' writings, reflected or caused a decline in the guild system itself. Yet were these writers' thoughts on conflict and chaos so mistaken?

That journeymen often thwarted their masters' best-laid plans for production, hiring, and disciplined workshop routine can be amply documented, but such activities were not peculiar to the late eighteenth-century workshop. Troublesome and demanding journeymen, frequently organized in associations of *compagnonnage*, regularly disrupted

---

Research for this paper was made possible in part by summer grants from the American Council for Learned Societies (1979) and the National Endowment for the Humanities (1980).

[1]See, for example, the statements and attitudes of these men, and others, cited by Steven Kaplan in "Réflexions sur la police du monde du travail, 1700–1815," *Revue historique* 261 (December 1979): 17–77, esp. pp. 28–29 and 70–72.

work routine and defied authority from at least the mid-seventeenth century.[2] Master artisans confronted journeymen whose behavior they labeled "independent," "insubordinate," and "insolent."[3] In a major criminal case against journeymen locksmiths in Lyons in 1661, for example, the masters vividly recounted their woes. The journeyman Marinet ("the Guepin") called his master a whore, and the journeyman Germain told guild officials that they would "get theirs."[4] Forty journeymen gathered in front of the shop of the guild official Maillard shouting threats and throwing stones. The range of charges in this case was great: journeymen insulted masters and made fools of them; they attacked masters' property, boycotted and walked out of workshops; most seriously, they held a complete monopoly over the job placement of all workers newly arrived in town.[5] Masters were deprived of all workers if they or incoming workers challenged the organized journeymen's claims to control worker placement.[6] Control of placement gave journeymen a powerful hold over their masters and thus some say in their working conditions. Masters and authorities expressed anger and frustration at their inability to put an end to workers' seriously illegal behavior or their less serious but equally vexing insolence.

Yet despite complaints, quarrels, and major conflicts, workers were hired, work got done, some masters sided with workers, and some workers sided with masters. How does one explain both the chaos and the cooperation that were an integral part of workshop life? The solution lies in an analysis of the particular forms of organization and conflict found in this period. These forms, drawing on models provided by existing institutions, generated by custom and reinforced by popular conceptions of justice, ensured that work would be completed and that some degree of cooperation would reign in the workplace. Workingmen's voluntary associations expressed their grievances and mediated the tensions and contradictions inherent in the workshop. The conflict these associations produced had creative and destructive faces; it could foster change and maintain stability; it encouraged defiance as well as accord. The contrast between rebellion and carnival, grave assault and the "rough music" of the charivari, insult and teasing is instructive here.

[2] See, for example, in Lyons: Archives municipales, Lyons (hereafter AML), locksmiths, HH 184, no. 5, twelve articles regulating the behavior of journeymen, 2 June 1634. For an even earlier case, in Dijon, see Paul Labal, "Notes sur les compagnons migrateurs et les sociétés de compagnons à Dijon à la fin du XVe siècle et au debut de XVIe," *Annales de Bourgogne* 22 (1950): 187–93, esp. p. 192.

[3] Kaplan, "Réflexions," pp. 17–22, 28–29, and 70–72. There are isolated cases of such behavior in the fifteenth and sixteenth centuries, but they become more common only by the mid-seventeenth century. I have thus limited the study roughly to 1650–1789.

[4] AML, locksmiths, HH 183, no. 16, "Extrait de sentence," 16 September 1661.

[5] Ibid.

[6] Ibid.

Conflict in the Old Regime workshop could be used, somewhat like carnival, to alter (even if temporarily) a highly structured, hierarchical situation.[7] In this context, workers' "carnivalesque" behavior—their "tricks," their strong language, their gatherings for drink, play, and the celebration of feast days—their turning the world "upside down," is as meaningful as their more direct attacks on the masters—boycotts, walkouts, and monopolies on placement. From sociability to protest, workers employed a range of behavior that could be, like carnival, a primary source of "liberation, destruction, or renewal."[8] Nantes and Lyons, two cities that underwent the growing pains of economic and social change in the seventeenth and eighteenth centuries, provide the setting for my analysis of this wide range of labor conflict and labor organization.

Nantes and Lyons: The Socioeconomic Background

A critical variable in the socioeconomic structure of seventeenth-and eighteenth-century Nantes and Lyons was the emergence of capitalism or, more precisely, entrepreneurial capitalism. This genre of capitalism was marked by a growing concentration and division of labor, the use of unskilled or semiskilled workers, and the establishment of wide networks of distribution for goods produced. The use of any of these techniques was well beyond the capacity of the ordinary artisanal master. Despite the existence of important capitalist ventures in both Nantes and Lyons, the guild system in each city, and particularly in Nantes, remained vigorous and firmly entrenched. The number of male artisans engaged in the traditionally organized sector held steady at about 20 to 25 percent of the total population in both cities in the prerevolutionary period. Gaston Martin, in his well-documented history of Nantes, estimates the number of master artisans in that city at between 2,000 and 2,500, or about 10 percent of adult male population in 1720.[9] From Martin's figures it is possible to approximate the total number of artisanal workers at roughly 10,000, that is, about 40 percent of the adult male population

---

[7]Cf. Natalie Z. Davis's discussion of carnival in "The Reasons of Misrule," in *Society and Culture in Early Modern France* (Stanford, 1975), p. 103. Davis cites and agrees with Victor Turner and Mikhail Bahktin on the ways "topsy-turvy play or rite" can, at least partially, transform rigorously ordered societies. Such "play," then, is not merely a safety valve for these societies but has creative and destructive potential as well. The transforming power of such activities, Bahktin argues (and Davis tends to agree), seems strongest in the pre-industrial world.

[8]Ibid.

[9]Gaston Martin, *Capital et travail à Nantes au cours du XVIIIᵉ siècle* (Nantes, 1932), p. 6. He bases his estimate on the fairly reliable capitation roll of 1720. From other indicators, the percentage of artisanal workers in Nantes does not appear to change significantly before 1789.

of Nantes and about 20 percent of the total population.[10] Maurice Garden, in his masterful and exhaustive work on Lyons, calculates that there were 36,685 adult male workers—roughly 25 percent of the total Lyonnais population in the late eighteenth century.[11]

The traditional master usually controlled all aspects of production, from the buying of raw materials to the sale and distribution of the finished product. For the most part the master worked on every stage of production alongside his journeymen (on the average two or three, rarely more than five or six) and one or two apprentices; his wife, children, and any servants of the household also played an important role in production.[12] The workshop usually doubled as living quarters and as a retail outlet. The apprentices, and often the journeymen, lived in the household and took at least some of their meals there. The degree to which the journeymen actually became part of the household varied a great deal by the eighteenth century and itself was a source of master/worker conflict.

Although the large-scale industries did not usurp the demographic and economic predominance of artisanal production (and would not do so until well into the nineteenth century), they made their presence felt in a variety of important ways. In Nantes, large-scale production that related to shipping—in food provisionment (e.g., biscuit making), in textiles, and in rope and cord making—led to the decline or virtual disappearance of artisanal production in these areas.[13] In the Lyonnais silk industry, for example, the traditional organization of work changed little, but masters of small workshops became increasingly dependent on the financial and marketing control of the merchant-manufacturers or wealthy middlemen.[14] In trades where production was more fundamentally altered, the small master could even be eliminated. Important examples of this in Lyons are found in the trades of hatting and dyeing.[15] The increased capital and productivity involved in large-scale manufacturing began to reorient the economy and society in the areas it touched.

In both Nantes and Lyons the horizons, the wealth, and the numbers of those who directed these new ventures, the merchant-manufacturers,

[10]Ibid. Martin estimates an average of three to four journeymen and/or apprentices per master.

[11]Maurice Garden, *Lyon et les Lyonnais au XVIIIe siècle* (Paris, 1970), pp. 34, 318.

[12]See, for example, Michael Sonenscher's cogent discussion of this mode of production in "Work and Wages in Paris in the Eighteenth Century," in *Manufacture in Town and Country before the Factory*, ed. M. Berg, P. Hudson, and M. Sonenscher (Cambridge, 1983), pp. 147–72.

[13]Martin, *Capital et travail*, pp. 86–88.

[14]Maurice Garden, "Ouvriers et artisans au XVIIIe siècle: L'example Lyonnais et les problèmes de classification," *Revue d'histoire èconomique et sociale* 4 (1970): 29–54, esp. pp. 50–51.

[15]Ibid. p. 46.

were expanded. Merchant-manufacturers or large-scale masters were masters in the sense that they were (generally) guild members and had a working knowledge of their trades. Increasingly, however, they did not actively participate in production, for example, acting as middlemen who provided work without working in the trade themselves.[16] These masters were particularly set apart from the ordinary guild masters by the large amounts of capital they invested in their businesses. The merchant-manufacturers lowered the cost of goods while maintaining the standards demanded by their respective trade guilds. Although the cheaper goods thus produced were not always in direct competition with traditionally produced goods, many were, and they posed a clear threat to the older system. The very existence of large-scale production, moreover, with its use of new financing techniques and new organization of labor and production, presented a general challenge to artisanal production.[17]

Competition from capital-and labor-intensive ventures was only part of the picture affecting the traditional trades. Competition from goods produced by rural outworkers, by *forains* (itinerant merchants granted some rights to make goods outside the city and sell them within city limits), and by *chambrelans* (illegal producers within the city) undercut the ability of masters to control the market and set prices.[18] Rural migration into the city placed additional strain on the guilds. Masters often fought to keep those who were not city natives out of the corporation altogether. Apprenticeship fees, years served as a journeyman, and fees paid for the mastership (at least in Lyons) were almost invariably greater for men coming from outside the city than for natives.[19] Even within the ranks of the guild masters all was not harmonious. Divisions between masters in terms of wealth, age, and economic orientation were increasingly the source of friction and disputes.

The competitive pressure placed on small masters by merchant-manufacturers, by illegal or quasi-legal workers, and by dissident masters

[16]See Garden's description of the "marchand–fabricant," *Lyon et les Lyonnais*, p. 283, especially n. 15.

[17]The development of large-scale manufacturing could have resulted in a rise in demand for artisanal goods owing to a type of "multiplier effect" of the investment in the capitalist sector. It appears from the evidence gathered thus far that any gain was very unevenly distributed among master artisans. Research remains to be done on this quesion.

[18]Some pertinent examples for Lyons: joiners, regulations against "forains," AML, HH 109, nos. 3 (1678) and 7 (1701); tailors, similar regulations, AML, SM 181, printed pamphlet, "Règlements," 1728. For Nantes: Martin, *Capital et travail*, pp. 11–12.

[19]See, for example, for Lyons: joiners—Lyonnais apprentices paid 75 livres in 1701 on becoming masters and 120 livres in 1711; non-natives or those not apprenticed in Lyons paid 100 livres in 1701 and 200 livres in 1711 (AML, HH 109, nos. 7 and 11). Tailoring shows a similar pattern: in 1728 Lyonnais apprentices paid 187 livres, 10 sous for the mastership; in 1728 non-Lyonnais apprentices paid 250 livres (AML, SM 181, printed pamphlet, "Règlements," 1728).

was encouraged by a trend, especially marked in Nantes, for the consumer rather than the guild to dictate standards of production. Consumers influenced the market by patronizing illegal or cheaper producers who, unlike the highly regulated guild producers, could vary production time, design, and quality of goods to suit their customers. The result of this wide variety of competitive forces faced by small masters was the crumbling of their socioeconomic standing. Great fortunes, even moderate ones, had never been made by master artisans, barring a few in the luxury trades. Their position, however, had been respectable and more or less secure. The intrusion of merchant-manufacturers and illegal producers into the economic and social arena threw the traditional hierarchy of the world of work into disarray.

The widening gap between the small master and the merchant-manufacturer can be estimated by comparing the income of these two groups in Nantes and Lyons. Although the data available for assessing wealth in the two cities vary (the poll tax records in Nantes; marriage contract data in Lyons), a rough comparison can be established. In Nantes the poll tax (*capitation*) rolls of 1720 grouped taxpayers into twenty-two categories based on estimated income. Out of a total of 2,781 individuals in the category "artisans and shopkeepers," 2,360, or 84.9 percent, paid 1 to 5 *livres* in tax.[20] Only 20 individuals, or 0.7 percent, in this category paid over 30 livres in tax.[21] By contrast, among the 204 individuals classified as "merchants, wholesalers, or industrialists," no one paid a tax lower than 5.1 livres; 42, or 20.6 percent, paid between 5.1 and 15 livres; and the majority, 118 or 57.8 percent, paid a tax of more than 30 livres a year.[22] The disparity in estimated taxable income between merchant and artisan categories is dramatic—more than 50 percent of the merchants were taxed at least six times as much as more than 80 percent of the artisans. Overall, about 80 percent of the merchants paid at least double the tax paid by more than 80 percent of the artisans.

For Lyons, Garden estimated the fortunes of various categories of masters and workers in the eighteenth century on the basis of marriage contracts listing goods to be exchanged at the time of marriage. Garden calculates the average goods held at the time of marriage for masters in several artisanal trades as follows: master shoemakers, about 720 livres; master tailors, about 1,000 livres; master joiners and carpenters, between 1,600 and 1,800 livres; and master bakers, the highest-ranking group

[20]Gaston Martin, *Nantes au XVIIIe siècle: l'adminstration de Gérard Mellier (1709–1720–1729)*, 2 vols. (Nantes, 1928), 1:241.

[21]Ibid. Eighteen paid between 30.1 and 50 livres and 2 paid between 50.1 and 100 livres.

[22]Ibid. Forty-four paid between 15.1 and 30 livres, 53 paid between 30.1 and 50 livres, 32 paid between 50.1 and 100 livres, and 33 paid over 100 livres.

among the traditionally organized trades, about 3,000 livres.[23] By contrast, merchant-manufacturers in the dyeing trades had an average fortune of about 5,500 livres; in hatting, these masters' goods averaged about 5,800 livres.[24] Thus, except for the wealthier bakers, artisanal masters in these cases had an average wealth between one-third and one-sixth that of merchant-manufacturers. Even the bakers had an average wealth only slightly more than half that of merchant-manufacturers.

Even more striking is Garden's comparison of the value of goods recorded in the contracts of journeymen (in traditional and large-scale production), small masters, and merchant-manufacturers. In shoemaking, tailoring, carpentry and joining, baking, and butchering, the goods owned by masters were generally worth about twice those of their journeymen.[25] While this is a significant gap, Garden sees it as minimal when compared with the vast difference found between the fortunes of merchant-manufacturers and *their* journeymen. Merchant hatters' goods at marriage were worth eleven times those of their journeymen; merchant dyers' goods were six times those of their journeymen.[26] In his data for the *Grande Fabrique* (the Lyonnais silk industry), Garden finds that 87 percent of the journeymen and 75 percent of the masters had goods at marriage with a value less than 1,000 livres. Only 4 percent of the merchant-manufacturers fell into this low category. The overwhelming majority of merchant-manufacturers, 86 percent, left a record of goods valued at over 2,000 livres. Only 10 percent of the small masters were in this category, and even 3 percent of the journeymen could claim a fortune of 2,000 livres.[27] Moreover, the average value of the goods of the 86 percent of merchant-manufacturers over the 2,000 livres mark was 12,000 livres, sixteen times that of the average value of the goods of all other silk workers.[28]

Given such data, it is evident that the most significant hierarchical distinction in the eighteenth-century world of work was between large-scale manufacturers and all other artisanal producers rather than between masters and journeymen. This is not to say that journeymen were prosperous. Their fortunes did not keep pace with those of their masters. Garden notes a slight increase in the distance between masters' and workers' fortunes in the course of the eighteenth century, based on his marriage contract data. The gap between the average fortunes of tra-

[23]Garden, "Ouvriers et artisans," pp. 45–46.
[24]Ibid., p. 46.
[25]Ibid.
[26]Ibid., pp. 45–46.
[27]Ibid., pp. 50–51.
[28]Ibid., p. 51.

ditional masters and all their workers (not just journeymen) increased from 2.4 percent to 3.3 percent between 1730 and 1786.[29] The main consequence of this differential, according to Garden, was the increased difficulty journeymen experienced in their pursuit of the *maîtrise* (mastership). However, most of the rapid and steep increases in fees for masterships in Lyons, sometimes double or triple the original fees, had occurred in the seventeenth century or very early eighteenth century. Almost all workers not related to a master had thus already been effectively barred from becoming masters.[30] Given the very real probability that the mastership would never materialize, most eighteenth-century journeymen were likely to work harder to defend what rights they had or, more critically, to establish new prerogatives for themselves based on a revised understanding of their futures. With the goal of mastership no longer a viable ideal, they worked together to create a domain of their own based on the skills they had to offer the hard-pressed masters. The frequent struggles between journeymen and masters over conditions of work and pay make sense both in the context of the working-man's declining economic situation and in terms of such workers' decisions to behave as if they had little or no hope of advancement in their trade guilds.

This picture of the economic gulf between various types of masters and between masters and journeymen is supplemented by data on the grave financial difficulties facing the guild organizations of many Old Regime trades. The guilds of trades such as shoemaking and tailoring often found themselves unable to pay their corporate debts, to fulfill their tax duties, to buy raw materials at reasonable rates, and to produce competitively priced goods. For example, a meeting of the *corporation* of joiners, a relatively prosperous guild, was held in Nantes on 17 March 1724 to discuss remedies for a series of unfavorable economic circumstances. The masters noted a serious rise in the cost of wood: from 2 *sous*, 3 *deniers* per foot to 4 sous per foot for oak in the course of 1723,

[29]Garden, *Lyon et les Lyonnais*, p. 339.

[30]The example of the joiners is relevant: for those apprenticed in Lyons, fees rose by about 50 percent between 1678 (45 livres) and 1701 (75 livres), increased by about 40 percent between 1701 and 1711 (to 120 livres), only increased 20 percent in 1733 (150 livres), and thereafter remained stable at 150 livres. With a fee of 120 livres in 1711, the mastership would already have been closed to anyone but a son or son-in-law of a master. The fees in such cases were far lower than for the ordinary journeymen (AML, HH 109, nos. 3, 7, and 11; and AML, Bibl. 304.331). For masons, the fee for native apprentices was 150 livres in 1709 and apparently did not change thereafter; for tailors the fee rose from 40 livres to 100 livres in 1702 (AML, masons, impr. 4.003, pp. 52–53; tailors, HH 185, no. 9). When the fee for tailors rose again in 1728 to 187 livres, 10 sous (and thereafter remained stable), it probably changed the journeymen's possibilities of becoming masters very little (AML, tailors, SM 181, "Règlements," 1728). See also Grace M. Jaffé's discussion of this question in her work, *Le mouvement ouvrier à Paris pendant la révolution française (1789–1791)* (Paris, 1924), pp. 33–36.

and from 420 livres a shipment in 1715–16 to 450–60 livres a shipment for walnut in 1724. Increases had occurred in rents and articles of consumption, notably bread and wine, while the prices of goods had fallen— armoires that had sold at 200 livres were now selling for 150 livres. The masters also complained of the excessive taxes being levied by the government. Worse yet, according to the masters, was the added financial burden of feeding their journeymen four times a day while these same journeymen, united in an association called the *Devoir* (duty), continually plotted to augment their pay and to withhold workers from masters who refused wage increases.[31]

Unable to resolve the problems raised by the economic conjuncture and the exigencies of royal taxation, the master joiners tried to reduce labor costs. This approach generally met with failure as organized journeymen joiners kept fighting for better wages and working conditions throughout most of the eighteenth century.[32] The guilds of other trades coped with their financial liabilities in much the same way as had the joiners' guild, by raising loans, increasing mastership fees, and combating illegal producers.[33] Again, these techniques had no great success. Masters' complaints against journeymen's "independence" and their power over placement frequently figured in documents concerning the guilds' financial troubles.[34]

Labor problems were often compounded by the overt or de facto economic and labor policies of the royal government. Even though the concept of strict guild monopolies was encouraged in the reign of Louis XIV, particularly under Colbert, guild regulations were constantly evaded by the opposing interests of large-scale business, illegal producers, and a public that wanted cheaper and more varied goods. The royal government, even in the seventeenth century, was largely unwilling or simply unable to assist the guilds or "communities" (an evocative contemporary term for guild) in ridding themselves of their opponents.

After 1750 opposition to the economic rights enjoyed by the guilds (as well as by other privileged groups) had grown and was particularly evident among the physiocratic circle surrounding Louis XVI's controller general, Turgot. As the failure of most of Turgot's reforms dem-

[31]Archives municipales, Nantes (hereafter AMN): joiners, HH 59, general commerce: report in response to a letter from the controller general of finances to M. Debron, intendant of Brittany.

[32]See appendix 5.1.

[33]See above, note 30.

[34]Again, the joiners' case is an excellent example (AMN, HH 59, general commerce, 17 March 1724). See also for Nantes: AMN, diverse trades, II 147 s.d. (1790–91), "Corps des arts et métiers à l'assemblée nationale"; and shoemakers, HH 127, 14 February 1772. For Lyons see: AML, saddlers, HH 181, no. 10, s.d. (early eighteenth century); and locksmiths, impr. 702.492, 1674.

onstrates, however, the groups most affected by Turgot's measures were still powerful enough to defend their traditional rights. Turgot's most noted attack on these rights, the Six Edicts, included an attempt to suppress the guild system. These measures provoked heated debate in the royal council in January 1776.[35] Debate ended in outright defiance when the edicts were presented to the Parlement of Paris for registration on 7 February. The parlementaires refused to register "a project stemming from an inadmissible system of equality, the first effect of which is to throw all the orders of the State into confusion."[36] Turgot convinced the king to override the parlementary veto, and the Six Edicts were registered on 22 February 1776. Nevertheless, continuing opposition to the decrees, in addition to ministerial intrigue, led to Turgot's forced resignation on 12 May 1776. The revocation of the Six Edicts followed in August of that same year.

Debate on the Six Edicts had not been limited to Paris or to high government circles. In both Nantes and Lyons, Turgot's reforms (or what was rumored of them) were favorably regarded by important segments of the population. In Nantes Martin asserts that "the state of public opinion (*d'esprit public*) had sapped the principle of the corporations even before the law would authorize their demise."[37] Among the large-scale masters and *négotiants* (wholesale merchants) and among part of the artisanal work force, the measure was welcomed.[38] Nantais merchants deeply regretted the demise of the Six Edicts. In a letter addressed to the municipality of Metz in 1781, a group of them publicly expressed their disappointment over the plan's failure.[39] Small masters and retailers, on the other hand, just as strongly favored maintaining the corporate system.

In Nantes the small masters' opposition to any weakening of guild regulations is illustrated by the events surrounding a police decree of 27 January 1776. Long-standing disagreements between masters and workers in the shoemakers' guild worsened in December 1775 and January 1776. Three major points of contention emerged. First, workers were unofficially assuming the status of masters. Second, journeymen were unequally distributed among masters and often quit their jobs without giving notice. Finally, the masters objected to the journeymen's demands for "liberty of placement."[40] The masters' original demand for police action, made in December 1775, stated that the guilds of other

[35]Keith Michael Baker, *Condorcet* (Chicago, 1975), p. 72.
[36]Jules Flammeront, ed., *Remontrances du parlement de Paris au XVIIIe siècle*, 3 vols. (Paris, 1888–98), 3:279, as cited by Baker, *Condorcet*, p. 72.
[37]Martin, *Capital et travail*, p. 88.
[38]Ibid., pp. 35–37 and 82.
[39]Ibid., p. 82.
[40]AMN, FF 92, "Arrêt de police," 27 January 1776.

trades had had or were continuing to have the same difficulties with their workers.[41] To most of these masters, and to many local authorities as well, it seemed obvious that decreased production and greater license among workers would prevail if the guilds were abolished.[42] Loss of control over the work force is the underyling fear expressed in the masters' petitions.

The masters' fears had a basis in reality. Even when the short-lived Six Edicts had been abrogated, some workers continued to act as if they were still in effect. On 17 December 1776, the police reported that four sons of master joiners in Nantes, believing in a "rumor that there were no longer any masterships," set themselves up as masters without paying any fees to the community.[43] When informed by guild officials that they were acting illegally, the four men refused to acknowledge the guild's authority.[44] Thus, even sons of masters, traditionally privileged in access to mastership, might have found it difficult, irksome or merely unnecessary to follow the community's dictates. Several other cases of individuals who opened shops without first having been received as masters were recorded on the same date.[45]

Lyons was reputedly a "city of free trades" where certain freedoms from guild control were guaranteed.[46] Yet, as in Nantes, Turgot's measure met with stiff opposition from small producers. The most reasonable hope for the success of Turgot's reforms lay in the fact that, in Lyons as in Nantes, the communities of arts and crafts were internally divided: opposition to reform tended to concentrate among the masters who were older, wealthier, and more ensconced in positions of authority.[47] In 1780 the officials of the community of locksmiths recalled that "several years ago rumors were being spread about rather publicly that led to the belief that the communities of arts and crafts of this city had been abolished as they actually had been in the capital at the beginning of 1776."[48] These masters linked the illegal and insubordinate behavior of dissenting masters and journeymen to such "rumors." The irony, of course, is that the guilds had been supressed in Lyons. The counterrumor (or misinformation) that they had not been was maintained by the masters. To

[41]Ibid.
[42]Cf. Kaplan, "Réflexions," pp. 26–30, for evidence on this point.
[43]AMN, joiners, HH 150, "Procès-verbal, commissaire de police," 17 December 1776.
[44]Ibid.
[45]Ibid., various trades. There are also numerous cases in this dossier of cabinetmakers' illegally doing the work of joiners and of illegal work done by joiners who were forains. I do not know how much the maîtrise in joining cost at this time in Nantes; in Lyons the mastership in this trade cost 150 livres, up from 45 livres in 1678 (AML, Bibl. 304.331 and HH 109, no. 3).
[46]Garden, *Lyon et les Lyonnais*, p. 558.
[47]Ibid., p. 557.
[48]AML, HH 184, no. 19, "Maîtres gardes serruriers au prévôt," 14 June 1780.

curb "abuses" by workers, these masters argued, the guild and its policing functions must be reestablished; they claimed that enforcement of regulations had been lax ever since 1776.[49] Indeed, control of the work force remained problematic; workers still chafed at guild regulations and harassed masters whenever and however they could.

Journeymen's Associations: General Characteristics

The journeymen tailors in this city designated [*se sont fait*] a Master Journeyman [and] some assistants [and drew up] certain articles, in the form of Regulations which established Rights [Droits] called Welcome, Nightcap, Initiation [Réception], Godparenthood and [levied] fines of five sous and two sous, six deniers. The first fine was for those journeymen who missed the Sunday assembly . . . the second fine was for those who worked before or after the assigned hours.[50]

This glimpse into the inner workings of an association of journeymen tailors in Lyons in 1688 clearly illustrates that it had grasped some of the most essential principles of effective labor organization in any age: strong leadership, solidarity, sociability, regular meetings, and control of the hours of labor. Journeymen who united in similar associations, the best known of which is compagnonnage, proved that they had the tools for persistent and concerted labor activity in the Old Regime. In creating labor associations, journeymen borrowed structures, principles, and rituals from a wide variety of existing institutions—the corps des métiers, the confraternities, the family, and the church—and adapted these borrowings to their own purposes. In this process of transformation, journeymen imparted some of the force, familiarity, and legitimacy of the established institutions to their own organizations without sacrificing their own originality and independence of action.

As early as the fifteenth century, when data on journeymen's conflicts with masters begin to be found, certain organizational terms or concepts appear and remain an integral part of these workers' associational life.[51] Chief among these is the devoir, or duty, a term first used in the corps des métiers to refer to the trade itself or to workers' duties. Journeymen

[49]Ibid.

[50]AML, SM 181, Petition of the master tailors to the Consulat, 3 October 1688, p. 32. I have translated the term réception as initiation. In compagnonnage and some related journeymen's organizations, the réception was a ceremony, based on Christian baptism, that officially received or initiated the new member into the association with all rights and duties.

[51]Labal, "Notes," p. 192.

took the word devoir and made it synonymous with their own associations. It came to signify the reciprocal obligations that existed between the journeyman and his association. In the Old Regime it was much more common for the term devoir to appear in documents on journeymen's associations than a term such as compagnonnage (which became common only in the nineteenth century). To be part of the devoir, which usually involved taking an oath, meant that a journeyman could expect protection, hospitality, aid in finding a job, and (ideally) friendship from members of the association while on his *Tour de France*. The Tour was a three-or-more-year journey to the various towns and cities of France that journeymen made in pursuit of masterships. In a society that regarded transients and outsiders with disfavor if not outright hostility, the devoir played a vital role for journeymen, rapidly integrating them into a new town. In return for these benefits, the journeyman had to support the devoir by obeying all its rules.

Journeymen received much of the devoir's protection and hospitality through the institution of the *mère* (mother) or less frequently, the *père* (father). The mère, one of the oldest traditions linked to journeymen's associations, referred both to the person who ran a boardinghouse for journeymen and to the house itself.[52] The "mother" not only extended the hospitality of her inn to her "sons," even allowing them credit when necessary, but also frequently demonstrated great loyalty to her journeymen. She might, for example, lie to the police to defend the journeymen's interests.[53] All innkeepers who lodged journeymen, even if not called "mothers" or "fathers," were thus regarded suspiciously by masters and officials as people willing to aid and abet illegal activities. If the family served as a model for the journeymen's innkeepers, other "parents" could be borrowed from the model of the church in the form of reverend fathers. Evidence of journeymen's regularly holding meetings in monasteries under the aegis of the clergy indicates that the church, at least in the eighteenth century, provided another recourse for journeymen who wished to associate. Although this link to the church existed, it did not mean that journeymen felt obligated to conform to church policy and practice.

In fact, in the seventeenth century journeymen's associations had been condemned by the church on the grounds that their practices were a blasphemous travesty of Catholic rituals.[54] The initiation ritual used by

---

[52] Ibid.

[53] AMN, I²137, no. 3, police pursuits against journeymen and their mères, various trades, 23 November 1791, and ironsmiths, June–July 1792.

[54] The Sorbonne condemned the devoir found in the trades of tailoring, saddlery, hatting, and shoemaking in 1655 (*Résolution des docteurs de la faculté de Paris, touchant les pratiques impies . . . pour passer compagnons, qu'ils appellent du devoir . . .*," Paris, 14 March 1655).

journeymen members of the devoir was based directly on the Catholic rituals of baptism and communion, reinforced with imagery from the Last Supper.[55] To the journeymen, their rituals were not travesties but rather renewals and affirmations of the ties of solidarity and loyalty generated in the workplace. Ritual oaths, gestures, and performances were used to bind members to their new brotherhood and to ensure fidelity to it.[56] The degree of secrecy that surrounded these associations attests to the efficacy of such procedures.

Religious organizations, especially lay religious organization, also provided a training ground for the journeymen's impressive grasp of bureaucratic method. Even more than the church, however, the guild itself served as an organizational model. The devoir's account books, or *rôles*, were used to keep track of vital information: members' dues, fines against members, and most important, the placement of members in workshops. Though not all journeymen's associations kept equally elaborate records, all seemed to have understood the importance of such record keeping. Structure and flexibility worked together in associations like compagnonnage. Instrumental in integrating these two aspects of associational life was the master journeyman, also called the *premier compagnon* (the first journeyman), the captain, or the head. All of these titles are obvious indications of the devoir's continued regard for hierarchy. Master journeymen were "chosen," "designated," "given the place of leader" by other journeymen in the devoir, although the means of selection (e.g., election, acclamation, seniority, literacy, cronyism) is not usually specified, at least in the eighteenth century.[57] Beyond generally defending and promoting the devoir's aims, the master journeymen kept the membership records and led the association's ceremonies.

In the Old Regime the other important leader of the devoir was the *rôleur* (roll keeper, chosen "by turn of the roll"), the journeyman in charge of the placement of his fellow workers. Because the rôleur was

[55]Cynthia M. Truant, "Compagnonnage: Symbolic Action and the Defense of Workers' Rights in France, 1700–1848" (Ph.D. diss., University of Chicago, 1978), pp. 116 and 119–30. Evidence of the use of rituals or ceremonies in journeymen's organizations is found in both Nantes and Lyons. In Nantes there are reports of journeymen joiners' holding "cérémonies du devoir" (AMN, HH 147, 27 January 1758). In Lyons the terms "réception, parrainage" are used by journeymen tailors (AML, SM 181, 3 October 1688, pp. 32–33).

[56]Truant, "Compagnonnage," and idem, "Solidarity and Symbolism among Journeymen Artisans: The Case of *Compagnonnage*," *Comparative Studies in Society and History* 21 (1979): 214–26.

[57]For example, journeymen tailors in Lyons "designated" or "made" (*se sont fait*) a master journeyman (AML, SM 181, 3 October 1688, p. 32). In Nantes journeymen joiners "make *(font entre eux)* chiefs whom they call captains" (AMN, HH 59, 17 March 1724). Jacques-Louis Ménétra, an eighteenth-century journeyman glazier du devoir who left a rare autobiography, tells us only that "he was given the place of premier compagnon" in Lyons (about 1762). He adds, however, that he remained in office with the assent of "the masters and the journeymen" (Ménétra, *Journal de ma vie*, ed. Daniel Roche [Paris, 1982], p. 123).

highly visible and because he interfered with the masters' control of placement, he aroused a great deal of antipathy among the guild officials. The position of rôleur was one that each member could hope to fill. While the existence of the journeymen's officers reveals a hierarchical structure in their associations and a mimicking of the structure of guild hierarchy, it would be misleading to see either the "head" or the rôleur as absolutely essential to the association's survival. Attempts to arrest the rôleur, even if successful, rarely stopped the journeymen's "liberty" of placement. Journeymen also managed to circumvent this "decapitation." The post of rôleur, for example, might change hands weekly, thus making it difficult for police to arrest a key individual. In other cases another journeyman would simply take over when the rôleur was arrested or fled town.[58] The primary labor strategy used by these artisans was control of hiring, but work stoppages, direct threats, and selective violence— against recalcitrant masters or unassociated journeymen—all had their role as well. Thus, leadership was important but the daily adherence of the rank and file was indispensable.

Although journeymen could be grouped into rival sects or rites of the devoir, such rivalries did not seriously undermine their ability to establish favorable working conditions or enforce minimum pay, at least for the prerevolutionary period. Workers accepting lower wages were frequently threatened, told to "hit the road," "beat it," or be beaten up. Such tactics led officials to state that these associations held sway over their members by "force or by friendship." It might best be said they held power by friendship if possible, by force when necessary. The result of such tactics was that journeymen's associations had a virtual monopoly over placement. It was the masters who often found it difficult to work together. Masters found themselves competing for workers against one another and sometimes against the larger manufacturers. Organized journeymen could pressure masters to increase their wages or benefits by offering their labor to those masters willing to grant the most favorable working conditions. Such maneuvers would be facilitated by the existence of a mère in each city, able to provide temporary aid to the journeymen. Further, there is evidence of interurban correspondence between journeymen that could inform them of uncooperative masters, available work, and other affairs of the devoir.[59]

[58]Three of the most obvious examples of incidents where organizations of journeymen continued after the departures, expulsion, or arrest of their rôleurs or master journeymen can be identified in Nantes: among the saddlers in 1738 (AMN, HH 162, 4 June 1738, renewed activity reported 12 November 1738); among joiners in 1751 (AMN, FF 246, 26 July 1751, active again at least by 1758); and among the tailors in 1762 (AMN, HH 170, 7 September 1762, renewed activity reported on 13 October 1762).

[59]See, for example, the certificates of the journeymen wigmakers, which reveal a wide interurban network (AMN, HH 102, 12 January 1787), and Ménétra's autobiography,

In short, in the Old Regime, when the need for skilled journeymen was not as limited as it was to be thereafter, compagnonnage and related associations were still in a creative and formative stage, developing rules, regulations, and codes of behavior as the circumstances demanded. Inherited or borrowed traditions of hierarchy and authority were mediated by the journeymen's own ideals and practice of liberty, equality, and brotherhood. The success and permanence of journeymen's associations were largely a result of their members' ability to adapt tactics to any given situation. The evidence from Nantes and Lyons bears this out and reveals a strong correlation between association and conflict.

Association and Conflict in Nantes and Lyons

In Nantes I examined the extant papers of twenty-seven corps des métiers, as well as available police commissioners' reports and other relevant papers for the late seventeenth and eighteenth centuries (see appendix 5.1). Among the twenty-seven guilds studied, seven left no apparent record of serious conflict between masters and journeymen. This group included drapers, printers, roofers, spur makers, pastry makers, preparers of roasted meats (*rôtisseurs*) and restaurateurs and caterers (*traiteurs*). Although printers were usually strongly organized (independent of compagnonnage) and active in labor disputes, journeymen in the other guilds named had no significant history of labor organization. Journeymen in two of these guilds, draping and roofing, became associated with compagnonnage but only after the Revolution. Among the other twenty corps des métiers, six—edge-tool makers (*taillandiers*), farriers, joiners, locksmiths, tailors, and wigmakers—show more than half a dozen incidents of conflict: walkouts, boycotts of shops, wage demands, demands for control of placement by journeymen, continued association and organization among journeymen.[60] Three other corps— carpenters, ironsmiths, and plasterers—witnessed major labor disputes provoked by organized journeymen between 1789 and 1791. All of these "active" trades in Nantes were ones that had associations of compagnonnage in the Old Regime in other French cities. The remaining eleven corps—basket making, cutlery, nail making, rope making, rug making, saddlery, shoemaking, stonecutting, tinsmithing, turning, and weaving—

---

which frequently mentions correspondence between journeymen informing them of work opportunities as well as of directives of the devoir (*Journal de ma vie*, especially pp. 62 and 82).

[60] AMN; the sources are: edge-tool makers, HH 166 and FF 258; farriers, HH 145; locksmiths, HH 164 and II 147; tailors FF 68 and HH 168, 170; wigmakers, HH 93–95, 101–2, and 104; and joiners, HH 59, 147, 149, 150, FF 67, 69, 256, II 147, and I² 137.

show fewer incidents of journeymen's organizations or labor disputes, but all of the events recorded in these eleven guilds are significant ones. They led to work stoppages, caused masters to set up official placement bureaus, or resulted in the promulgation of edicts against any type of association among journeymen.

In all twenty guilds where illegal activities were reported, supporting evidence indicates that official intervention was taken only after journeymen had disrupted the normal order of production over a long period. A typical example of this is found among the journeymen edge-tool makers. Despite a prohibition against journeymen's labor activities, issued as far back as 1732, minutes of the guild officials' meeting of 27 August 1764 reveal that journeymen's "disorders" had persisted.[61] Edicts were repromulgated, again without great success, in 1768, 1775, 1776, and 1782 to forbid journeymen from placing workers, controlling the composition of the work force, and making demands regarding changes in wages and working conditions. These edicts also emphatically denied that the journeymen had any right to meddle in such issues, contrary to the journeymen's own claims.[62]

In two corporations where only one formal charge against journeymen is recorded a similar pattern emerges. In shoemaking, the police took action against the journeymen's "so-called liberty" only after masters complained that they had had continual problems keeping the journeymen in order.[63] The date of this incident, 27 January 1776, is of special interest. Discussion of the abolition of the guilds may have reached the local level and encouraged the journeymen shoemakers to defy their masters. In turning, the other trade where only one incident of conflict is reported, masters wished to establish a placement office. The date of this request was 1783, but the masters claimed their workers had "for some time now perpetuated themselves in the devoir of compagnonnage."[64]

In Lyons I examined material similar to that seen in Nantes, this time in sixteen guilds (see appendix 5.2). All the guilds investigated in Lyons exhibited some form of master/worker conflict. Six of them—masonry and stonecutting, joining, locksmithing, saddlery, tailoring, and wigmaking—show continued patterns of activity over long periods. Joiners, locksmiths, tailors, and wigmakers had all begun their history of association and opposition to the masters in the seventeenth century. There is a similar permanence of labor activity and protest among journeymen hatters. I have not, however, examined the hatters in depth because

[61]AMN, HH 164.
[62]AMN, HH 166.
[63]AMN, FF 92, 27 January 1776.
[64]AMN, HH 177, 20 August 1783.

large-scale production techniques had already significantly altered this trade's organization. Among the other nine trades examined—baking, cabinetmaking, carpentry, currying and harness making, cutlery, shoe-making, turning, weaving, and wheel making and repairing—all record at least some incidence of conflict in the eighteenth century. The bakers had also been active in the 1680s and 1690s but seem to appear on the record again only in the 1770s, when they openly petitioned for official recognition of their "Mère." It is quite likely that further research on the subject of master/worker conflict, using the documents of the *Séné-chausée/Criminel* in both Nantes and Lyons will yield further cases for examination.

Detailed analysis of a selection of relevant examples from Nantes and Lyons demonstrates the way association encouraged independence and sparked demands for improved labor conditions among journeymen. I will focus on four guilds whose journeymen had a roughly equivalent history of association and labor conflict in Nantes and Lyons: locksmiths (and the related corps of the edge-tool makers in Nantes), joiners, tailors, and wigmakers. Each set of cases demonstrates the way "major" and "minor" incidents of conflict played an important part in defining the master/worker relationship and in establishing the power of associated workers.

Locksmiths

Journeymen locksmiths were the most "active" trade in Lyons. Their activities and organization were first recorded in 1634; their last conflict was reported in 1780. Throughout this long period, journeymen lock-smiths were frequently labeled seditious. In 1634 an edict was promulgated that prohibited journeymen from holding assemblies, maintaining a *boîte* (a savings chest), demanding money from new journeymen in town, or placing any journeymen in workshops.[65] This ordinance also noted the struggle between masters over journeymen and ruled that masters must not *débauche* (steal) another master's journeymen, nor must they attempt to lure journeymen by advancing them more than thirty sous. This last point sharply reveals how much masters may have needed to use the advance payment to win journeymen. The edict originally allowed masters to advance a sum of only 16 sous to journeymen. This figure was crossed out and replaced by the figure of 30 sous. Masters could still get around this limit if the advance were for "clothing and other necessities" and if the guild officials were informed.[66] It seems

[65] AML, HH 184, no. 5.
[66] Ibid.

clear that journeymen would easily prefer the more generous masters. Such masters might well have made deals with the journeymen's rôleur to send more workers their way. The 1634 ordinance, with some variation, was reissued in 1642, 1661, and 1662. Even the harsh edict of 1661, placing disobedient journeymen under "pain of exemplary punishment," was ineffective in halting the "monopoly" held by the journeymen.

A brief summary of the tactics used in the 1661 case is instructive. On 20 June the journeymen locksmiths walked out of their masters' shops and organized thirty to forty workers to appear in front of the shops of masters who would not acquiesce to their demands. The primary demand was that the masters tolerate the journeymen's control of placement.[67] The assembled workers shouted insults, threatened violence, and prohibited workers' entry into these blacklisted shops.[68] The journeymen's ultimate aim, according to the court record, was to usurp the masters' authority over the hiring of workers. This purpose was clear in mid-July when two new workers, Laroze (called Parisian) and Gervais Le Roux (called Breton), tried to work chez Maillard, one of the officials of the locksmiths' community who most opposed the journeymen's organization. A journeyman named Germain, acting for the "monopoly," demanded a gold piece (a *louis d'or*, worth twenty francs) from Laroze and, taking him by the arm, tried to direct him to another shop. When Maillard attempted to intervene, Germain threatened to mistreat both him and Laroze, if Laroze did not go with Germain. Germain finally left without Laroze, calling him and Maillard *bougres* (blackguards) and telling them they would "pay for it." Germain then joined about fifteen other journeymen at a cabaret, the "Logis de la Pucelle." Although Germain was not successful this time, the masters stated that he and his fellow journeymen generally did succeed in controlling the incoming journeymen.[69] Moreover, the court decision in favor of the masters did not end such problems.[70]

Incidents of a less serious or "secondary" nature connected with the 1661 case were no less bothersome to the masters. As Maurice Garden suggests, "secondary conflicts" may reveal important underlying antagonisms and problems in the eighteenth-century world of work.[71] Journeymen locksmiths, on numerous occasions, confronted masters and

[67]AML, HH 183, no. 16, "Extrait de sentence," 16 September 1661.
[68]Ibid.
[69]Ibid.
[70]In 1662 a new edict appeared that condemned journeymen locksmiths for the same activities reported in 1661 (Archives départementales de la Rhône [hereafter ADR] BP 3622, June 1662).
[71]Garden, *Lyon et les Lyonnais*, p. 563.

insulted them with impunity.[72] When Ruissel Marinet, the "Guepin," went seeking employment, he told a prospective master that he wanted to leave his present "whore of a master." He then boldly demanded an advance of seven livres from the new master.[73] Journeymen sometimes used the masters' own ploys to mock, embarrass, and outwit their employers. As previously noted, masters commonly advanced money to workers as a lure and as insurance that valuable (and all too mobile) journeymen would remain at work until all debts were paid and all pending projects finished.[74] Along these lines a master locksmith of the Croix Rousse area of Lyons willingly advanced the sum of twenty sous to a journeyman presented to him for placement by another worker. Before commencing work, the journeyman asked for a brief leave so that he might finish some business in town. The unsuspecting master readily agreed and kept the worker's sack of belongings as security. The wily worker kept the 20 sous, never returned from his errands, and literally left his master holding the bag. When the master opened the sack he found nothing but a foul heap of garbage (*ordures*).[75] The journeymen probably thought this trick was great fun as well as a clever way of besting their masters. None of the plaintiffs in the case, however, were willing to regard such behavior merely as a boyish prank. Rather, this ruse was labeled a "mark of malice."[76] The journeymen's unity and organization enabled them both to tease their masters and to assert their "privileges" openly. They could pursue power rather than practice the deference their masters' so desired.

Although the law might temporarily thwart the plans of journeymen locksmiths, repeated bans on their organizations or arrests of the organizations' members never seriously cooled their ardor. In fact, journeymen's associations became more complex, and another sect of compagnonnage made its appearance. By 1764 journeymen locksmiths in Lyons were organized into rival associations: the "*compagnons du Devoir*" or "*dévorants*" (those of the devoir), and those "*non du Devoir*" (not of the devoir) or "*gavots*" (those of the gorges). New prohibitions, warnings, or requests for edicts directed against journeymen were issued in 1674, 1764, 1767, and 1780. A judgment of the criminal court (Sénéchausée/Criminel) of Lyons in 1767 prohibited gatherings and illegal meetings. It stated that journeymen met in inns, private residences, and

[72] AML, HH 183, no. 16, "Extrait de sentence," incidents mentioned for various dates in June and July 1661.
[73] Ibid. Incident reported for 21 June.
[74] Kaplan. "Réflexions," p. 49, gives examples of this in eighteenth-century Paris.
[75] AML, HH 183, no. 16, "Sentence," exact date not specified, but the event appears to have occurred shortly before June 1661.
[76] Ibid.

even religious communities "to plot the excesses that gave rise to this trial."[77] Such illegal behavior had not abated by 1780 when the officials of the locksmiths' guild petitioned the *prévôt* (provost) of Lyons to issue a new ordinance permitting the arrest of insubordinate workers. Such an edict, the masters claimed, would prevent abuses of the public security and assure the masters' tranquillity.[78] The ordinance recalled previous attempts "at various times" to bring the journeymen back within "the devoir" (obviously the devoir of the corporation) and prior bans of cabals and associations "under the denominations of confraternities, devoir, gavotage—or others."[79] Rather than the "fidelity and service" journeymen owed masters, wrote the guild officials, journeymen committed unending disruptions. The reason for this negligence of duty and for the continued existence of journeymen's "cabals," they explained, was the "independence and insurbordination with which the majority of journeymen and workers behave toward their masters."[80]

Evidence of the conflicts of journeymen locksmiths in Nantes appears only in 1733, almost one hundred years after the first recorded case of their fellow artisans in Lyons. Nantais journeymen, however, made up for lost time between 1733 and 1780. An ordinance of 12 September 1733 accused journeymen locksmiths of assembly "under the pretext of the Devoir."[81] These journeymen were said to control the hiring of newly arrived journeymen by meeting in cabarets and other places. The ordinance wished to "extinguish the Devoir." Evidently the devoir was too hardy for this judicial reprimand, which had to be reissued in 1737. In 1738 troubles continued. As journeymen of the "so-called Devoir" continued to control the placement of workers, three journeymen were arrested.[82] Protesting these arrests, other journeymen came to plead the cause of their fellow workers. The police court tabled the affair and put it off until the next session.[83] No follow-up of this case exists, but it is noteworthy that these journeymen were organized enough to issue a strong protest and to receive some consideration of their viewpoint. The years 1755, 1776, and 1780 witnessed a revival of journeymen locksmiths' labor activities under the auspices of the devoir. The incident of 19 July 1776 concerned an illegal assembly that ended in a brawl among a large

---

[77]For the denominations reported in 1764: AML, impr. 701.414, 6 September 1764; and Garden, *Lyon et les Lyonnais*, pp. 564–65 (citing ADR, series B, Sénéchaussée/Criminel, 3 November 1764). For the judgment of 1767: AML, HH 184, no. 20, 24 September 1767.
[78]AML, HH 184, no. 19, 14 June 1780.
[79]Ibid.
[80]Ibid.
[81]AMN, locksmiths, II 147, 12 September 1733.
[82]AMN, HH 164, "Procès-verbal, commissaire de police," 21 June 1738.
[83]Ibid.

number of journeymen—not only locksmiths, but joiners and saddlers as well.[84] No reason for the trouble is given, but earlier incidents of quarreling among journeymen that year had been reported. It may well be that the infamous rivalries and brawls among sects of journeymen had begun in earnest. A court decree of 1779 made note of the names "Devoir, Bondrilles ["good fellows"], Gavot, etc."[85] Despite the rivalries and brawls between sects or "rites" of journeymen, however, their associations remained powerful.

Like the locksmiths in Nantes, their fellow metalworkers, the edge-tool makers, were first labeled troublemakers in the early 1730s. Again like the locksmiths, the first case involving the edge-tool makers revealed that they had previously been associating in the devoir. In fact the trouble was over a brawl between edge-tool makers and wheelwrights concerning adherence to the devoir. Seven journeymen were sent to prison for three months and then expelled from Nantes because of the resulting violence.[86] By 1764 the "spirit of sedition" among journeymen edge-tool makers had reached a high pitch. The journeymen, so masters claimed, kept wages high by forcing workers who would accept lower pay to leave town.[87] Those workers who remained became journeymen of the devoir. Much of this disorder, according to the masters, was due to the journeymen's leader, the *Roulleur* (sic). To the master tool makers of Nantes the journeymen's rôleur was a threatening creature: he "disposed of journeymen at will"; he "could force journeymen to leave the city"; he "could decide what the journeymen would make the master do."[88] The rôleur clearly had a great deal of power, but the claims and fears of the msters, in their probable exaggeration, are revealing. The masters' perception of what their workers might do, under the leadership of the fearsome rôleur, may best be interpreted as a reflection of the tensions and hostilities at work within this trade.

The latest demand of these journeymen was that the masters enter the journeymen's association and receive the *accolade* or fraternal salute as a type of initiation.[89] Despite the undoubted seriousness of this demand, the journeymen could not have failed to see its ironic side. They may well have reveled in their masters' consternation at a proposition so much at odds with the established hierarchy. The masters, finding themselves in such "disagreeable circumstances," urged that this association of devoir be destroyed. Laws were promulgated in Nantes to

[84]AMN, FF 92, 19 July 1776.
[85]AMN, HH 164, "Procès-verbal, commissaire de police," 28 November 1780, which refers to the court decree of 3 February 1779.
[86]AMN, FF 258, 13 November 1732.
[87]AMN, HH 166, "Sentence de police," 27 August 1764.
[88]Ibid.
[89]Ibid.

prohibit any type of compagnonnage and to set up an official placement office. Yet these efforts were in vain. According to an ordinance of 1782, the "dangerous independence of the journeymen edge-tool makers" had to be repressed, but masters doubted whether the "society of the journeymen du devoir" ever would be abolished.[90]

Joiners

Like journeymen locksmiths, journeymen joiners were among the best-organized workers in Nantes and Lyons. Master joiners of Lyons, in 1704, expressed anger at their inability to control their journeymen's "cabals" and "associations of devoir." Such groups had been in existence since at least 1699.[91] The masters were indignant that religious communities had accepted the journeymen's associations as legitimate and had given them the status of confraternities.[92] Journeymen joiners had drawn up statutes and kept "rolls" on which the names of members were inscribed; they had collected money from members to further the ends of their association. Like associations of compagnonnage found in other French cities, these journeymen had a mère who lodged them and permitted their assemblies to take place at her inn. The whereabouts of the mère of the joiners was quickly made known to journeymen newly arrived in town, and they were soon under the rule of the devoir. The force of the devoir was such that masters often claimed that its leaders could deprive them of workers unless masters willingly submitted to the journeymen's demands. These demands included the right to control the placement of all workers, to make new journeymen conform to the terms of the devoir, to assemble in the city or *faubourgs* as they pleased, and to "have their rolls and letters and to choose their Mère in order to hold their assemblies."[93] The demands and activities of such journeymen were a "pure vexation" for the masters, who requested that convicted journeymen receive harsh prison sentences and corporal punishment.[94] The masters' request was granted, but the edict that resulted was difficult to enforce. The journeymen joiners du devoir actively pursued their demands in Lyons until at least the 1760s.[95]

In eighteenth-century Nantes journeymen joiners made the same kinds of trouble for their masters. Journeymen, in the devoir since 1723, had "plotted" to "augment their pay" and "refuse journeymen to masters."[96]

[90]AMN, edge-tool makers, HH 166, 27 July 1782.
[91]AML, HH 109, no. 6, 29 January 1699.
[92]Ibid., and AML, HH 109, no. 8, 31 December 1704.
[93]AML, HH 109, no. 8, 31 December 1704.
[94]Ibid.
[95]AML, joiners, impr. 701.414, 23 May 1764.
[96]AMN, joiners, HH 59, minutes of the corporation, 17 May 1724.

Even though the lieutenant general of police had seized the roll and other papers of the journeymen in 1723, in the following year they continued to choose leaders called captains. On 16 May 1724 one of these captains was arrested in the chapel of Saint Gildas, where the association had previously received protection from the religious community.[97] The arrest of the captain, however, had little effect on the existence of the journeymen joiners' devoir. Even when extreme means of control were used, the journeymen's organizations survived. In the 1740s and 1750s master joiners, along with master tailors, wigmakers, and saddlers in Nantes, angry at the inability of edicts to put an end to journeymen's associations, hit upon the somewhat novel idea of making all their journeymen appear in front of the police magistrates and renounce their oaths to the devoir of compagnonnage. It is indicative of the power of compagnonnage that the masters assumed all of their journeymen were members of the devoir. This is the only plan of renunciation formulated by masters that I have found in my research on compagnonnage, although it is reminiscent of the condemnation of compagnonnage by the Sorbonne in the 1640s and 1650s.[98] Certainly not all journeymen were found and made to recant (if indeed they had even taken any oaths), but a determined effort was made to bring all journeymen in these trades in front of the police. Strenuous exertions were necessary, for, in at least a few cases, journeymen resisted the renunciations by refusing to respond to questions, by evading guild officials and by ignoring summonses to police headquarters. One such recalcitrant journeyman was finally arrested, imprisoned for eight days and then exiled from Nantes for six months. Generally, however, the police and masters were more successful, for they obtained the renunciations of 162 journeymen joiners, 62 journeymen tailors, and 22 journeymen saddlers.[99] The wigmakers seemed to have eluded both the police and the historian.

[97] Ibid. Apparently the captain was seeking sanctuary in this chapel.

[98] After the Sorbonne condemnations, Henri Buch and Baron Georges de Renty undertook a reform of journeymen shoemakers du devoir in Paris. They transformed the devoir into a lay religious organization that was sanctioned by the archbishop of Paris (Raoul Allier, *La cabale des devots, 1627–1666* [Paris, 1902], pp. 193–213). No such rehabilitation of the journeymen du devoir in eighteenth-century Nantes was proposed.

[99] For cases of journeymen who resisted recantation: AMN, HH 149 (joiners), "Procès-verbal, commissaire de police," 14 December 1744 and 14 July 1745, which reported cases occurring on 15 September 1744 and 5 May 1745. For the lists of renunciations: AMN, FF—"Audiences de police"—joiners (1743, 1745, 1750), saddlers (1750), and tailors (1743). This information helps substantiate a point made earlier about the masters' often critical need for journeymen, for it can be used to estimate the ratio of journeymen to masters. On the evidence available from lists of renunciations and from guild records, the probable ratio of journeymen to masters ranged from roughly 1.0 among the tailors to an average of 1.4 among the joiners. Such ratios would have been far lower than the average of three to four journeymen per master suggested by Martin for eighteenth-century Nantes (*Capital*

How so many journeymen could make these renunciations needs some explanation, for the oath to maintain the devoir was to be upheld to the death. At least in the nineteenth century, and probably before, it was taken under solemn ritual circumstances and was not supposed to be a pro forma act. Given the evidence thus far, however, it is clear that many journeymen in the Old Regime were not fully or formally initiated into the association; some of them may have even been forced to join the devoir. For members initiated in such ways, the force of the recantations may have been diminished, particularly because the denials seem to have been made en masse. More likely, I think, is the conclusion that most members of these illegal associations had learned to hide any overt signs of their adherence and would simply go along with the recantations for safety's sake. Given the journeymen's persistent flouting of police edicts, their very common denials of complicity in association even when the evidence proved otherwise, and their refusal to answer police interrogations, it seems probable that a renunciation of the devoir before the police did not carry a great deal of moral weight. The real significance of these renunciations lies in the fact that, whether journeymen recanted or not, the devoir in these trades did not perish.

Journeymen joiners continued their activities throughout the next decades. In 1781 they were meeting frequently, sometimes daily. At this time there was at least one other rival group of organized journeymen joiners in Nantes called gavots (or non du devoir). The journeymen of the gavot sect, like the journeymen joiners and locksmiths in Lyons and the journeymen locksmiths in Nantes, were protected by the church. It is not certain if they had been accepted as a confraternity, but it is known that many of the gavots' meetings in the late 1770s and early 1780s took place in rooms provided for them by clerics of the Jacobin and Cordelier monasteries. The topic of these meetings, according to the masters, concerned the journeymen's plans to prohibit or blacklist (*défendre*) the shops of certain masters. According to the journeymen, however, they were only meeting to discuss the offering of blessed bread for the next feast day.[100] Most likely the journeymen were there for both reasons. When the police arrived at the monastery, the reverend fathers refused to let them enter the room where they had spied (through the keyhole) the journeymen congregated around a table examining "a large quantity of papers."[101] The reasons for the clerics' protection of the journeymen are

---

et travail, p. 6). Some of the discrepancy might be accounted for by journeymen who escaped recantation. However, the difference is significant enough to suggest that journeymen in these trades might well be in demand and thereby find themselves in a strong position to act together against their masters.

[100]AMN, joiners, HH 150, 18 August 1781.

[101]Ibid. One Père Mory even told the police that "he would never allow them [the journeymen] to be arrested in the monastery."

not stated. Was the clergy trying to regain a lost spiritual and social ascendency over the urban workingman or trying to maintain their jurisdiction over the secular authority? The reasons for the journeymen's proposed blacklisting of shops, on the other hand, are very clear. These workers were adamantly opposed to a new corporate regulation requiring that all journeymen be placed in shops by a guild official. Contrary to any such corporate law, the journeymen declared that all hiring would take place only under the auspices of their own organization.[102]

Apparently these and other claims advanced by journeymen joiners were effectively carried out. In 1787 masters described a world of work turned upside down: "The journeymen's liberty has the most dangerous effects...[for it] puts the masters in a sort of dependence on the journeymen....The deadly association of Devoir holds the masters under their [the journeymen's] empire."[103] The journeymen's spirit was strong; whatever obstacles they encountered, they kept organizing and reorganizing. Through the years, the "dangerous effects" of the journeymen joiners' "liberty" and "empire" had included a continuing struggle to control the placement of workers, to force masters to advance them money, to be well fed, and generally, to socialize as they pleased. Masters saw a vicious link between labor demands and this sociability. According to this view, money "extorted" from the masters or other workers was merely squandered on drunkenness and debauchery that rendered workers unfit for work and ever more likely to threaten both the masters and their property.[104]

Tailors

As early as 1688 journeymen tailors of Lyons had a well-established organization. The goal of this association, complained the masters, was to cause daily disruptions in the workshop. Journeymen tailors worked only when they pleased and "demanded sums [payments] from their masters in excess of that set by the ordinance of police—seven sous per day in the dead season and eight sous per day in the active season, in addition to meals."[105] Wage demands were thus linked to living conditions as journeymen fought to maintain certain economic standards. The masters argued that the journeymen's "monopoly" gave them great power and demanded that the *Consulat* take harsh steps against these workers.

---

[102]Ibid.

[103]AMN, HH 147, 14 December 1787.

[104]AMN, HH 147, "Mémoire of the master joiners to the judges of the Siège royal de police," 12 September 1781. The mémoire refers to edicts banning all journeymen's societies under any denomination, e.g., "du devoir, bondrille, gavots."

[105]AML, SM 181, 3 October, p. 32.

Like the master joiners in Nantes, master tailors also angrily complained about their journeymen's social activities. Celebrations such as the welcome, "nightcap," initiation, and godparenthood found the journeymen eating and drinking together in the city or, more generally, in the faubourgs—farther from the master's watchful eye. Such celebrations were not only rites or rituals, structured in set patterns, but were also considered rights (droits) that journeymen insisted on upholding.[106] The masters, however, saw no good in what was, to them, simply an excess of revelry. Workers let themselves be "carried away all the more because the journeymen to whom their cabal gave the name of assistant masters [maîtres assistans] are usually idlers [fainéans] living off of these sorts of extortions, [their] only goal is to get drunk and debauched."[107]

Although the masters insisted that the journeymen's meetings and meals always ended in beatings, quarrels, and a large number of wounded, the journeymen's cabal remained united and powerful. Masters claimed that "the so-called Master Journeymen and assistants have made themselves so absolute in their cabal that a foreign journeyman who passes through this city to work and who neglects to pay the Rights they have established is obliged to leave the city."[108] Whether by choice or by coercion, then, no workers were allowed to stand outside the cabal of the journeymen tailors. Presumably this meant that no workers could undercut the "excessive sums" of pay journeymen demanded of masters. The journeymen tailors of Lyons continued to oppose the authority of the masters in this corporation until at least 1760.[109]

Journeymen tailors in Nantes first made their appearance in the police reports in 1743. It seems likely that an association had grown up among these journeymen that was very much like that of compagnonnage.[110] Perhaps hoping to nip any future trouble in the bud, masters in this trade acted together with masters in joining, wigmaking, and saddlery to force their journeymen to "renounce the devoir."[111] As we have seen, sixty-two tailors did duly appear before the police courts to forswear their oaths.[112] Yet troubles with these journeymen seem to have escalated in the 1760s. In June 1762 a police ordinance was promulgated prohibiting the activities of the journeymen du devoir, and once again the code of compagnonnage emerges. The members of the devoir carried canes, bâtons (staffs), and other arms. They placed themselves in workshops over

[106]Ibid.
[107]Ibid., p. 33.
[108]Ibid.
[109]AML, HH 185, Ordinance of the Consulat, 1 July 1760.
[110]AMN, FF 68, p. 5, September 1743.
[111]Ibid.
[112]Ibid.

the objections of their masters.[113] In September 1762 journeymen tailors, again linked to compagnonnage, were accused of the same infractions of placement regulations prohibited by the June ordinance. The four leaders of the cabal were imprisoned for fifteen days and then expelled from the city.[114] Such punishments did not put an end to the journeymen's associations. Indeed, organization seemed to be spreading to journeymen in other trades. In 1772 the municipal officials and the police in Nantes reported the existence of compagnonnage, "also known as the Société du devoir." They claimed that this organization had been "well known for some time" and had established itself among the journeymen of different trades. Wherever the society was found, it was an unending source of disruption in the workplace and the cause of riotous behavior.[115] Even royal edicts against these associations were powerless to destroy them. "Infallibly [they] reestablished themselves" as the "spirit of independence reasserted itself among journeymen."[116] There could be no clearer statement of the journeymen's own aims.

Wigmakers

Like many Old Regime trades, wigmaking was one that "overlapped" at its boundaries with a variety of other trades: coiffeuring, valeting, barbering. In fact, in both Nantes and Lyons, barbering and wigmaking were generally united into a single corps. Performance of the trade's skills, moreover, was not rigidly confined to the workshop. Perhaps for these reasons, journeymen wigmakers frequently escaped the strict control of their masters. They often proved to be independent, clever, and fairly literate. In Lyons a number of journeymen wigmakers were condemned in 1697 and 1700 for "working on their own," presumably in their lodgings (*en chambre*).[117] No mention of the devoir is made at this time; the relative ease with which the journeymen wigmakers set themselves up illegally may have precluded the need for organization. Problems with illegal workers seem to have diminished in the following decades, but in 1743 a new edict was issued condemning journeymen wigmakers who abandoned masters with shops in the Saint-Nizier quarter and began to work for those near the Fourrivière. Apparently the masters of the Fourrivière were luring the journeymen to their shops and learning the secrets of the Saint-Nizier masters. To prevent this rapid turnover, the Consulat decided that all journeymen must work for the Saint-Nizier

---

[113]AMN, HH 168, 8 June 1762. The ordinance was drafted on 15 April 1762.
[114]AMN, tailors, HH 170, 7 September 1762.
[115]AMN, HH 168, "Procès-verbal," 5 April 1772.
[116]Ibid.
[117]ADR, wigmakers, BP 3612, judgments of 29 November 1697 and January 1700.

masters for three months before working on the Fourrivière side.[118] In yet another example of a topsy-turvy world of work, journeymen were "instructing the masters in the practices of those they had left."[119]

By 1762 the relationship between masters and journeymen had definitely worsened. A parlementary edict was issued on 12 November 1762 establishing a placement bureau for journeymen wigmakers.[120] This edict was necessitated because journeymen wigmakers changed or left masters without notice. This practice was especially common on the eves of feast days and Sundays, but it frequently occurred even when jobs were in progress. The edict stated that the community's rules were breaking down as journeymen assembled daily at fixed meeting places. In these assemblies, journeymen made plots and conspiracies to "walk out on the masters" and "to stop newly arrived journeymen from presenting themselves at the community's bureau."[121] Claiming that the same disorders "reigned" in Paris, the edict depicts a group of journeymen who now found strength in association. An edict of 24 November 1762 ordered the arrest and imprisonment of anyone found in opposition to the edict of 12 November, but Parlement had to intervene with a new edict in 1766. Master wigmakers were enjoined to feed and lodge their journeymen in the hopes of monitoring their behavior and curbing their "bad habits." Journeymen were prohibited from "associating...with anyone but masters or privileged [individuals]."[122] The edict further urged that the community be closed to outsiders and to "ideas of independence." The source of much of the community's trouble was said to be the *chambrelans*, illegal producers who worked out of their lodgings. It was "the chambrelan who makes himself independent, scorns the masters and their status, leads a scandalous life, debauched and dissipated, followed by cabals, assemblies, brawls, and notorious disputes... leading to vice and prostitution."[123] In 1772 so many individuals were working illegally as wigmakers, barbers, coiffeurs, and the like that a number of letters patent were issued in an attempt to regularize the situation of some of these people. At the same time, however, a royal edict repeated the various prohibitions against the "irregular conduct of the journeymen wigmakers" and forbade their associations, assemblies, meetings, and activities. Henceforth a journeyman would need written leave from his master before being accepted for employment by a new master.[124]

[118]AML, barbers/wigmakers, HH 175, "Extrait des registres," 28 November 1743.
[119]Ibid.
[120]AML, HH 176, no. 30, "Arrêt de parlement."
[121]Ibid.
[122]AML, HH 176, no. 31, "Arrêt de parlement," 6 February 1766.
[123]Ibid.
[124]AML, HH 176, "Lettres patentes du roi," 12 December 1772.

In Nantes journeymen wigmakers had a long history of illegal association in the Old Regime—from at least 1695 to 1787. Unlike the journeymen wigmakers of Lyons, those in Nantes were identified as belonging to the "devoir of compagnonnage" from 1695 on.[125] The head of these journeymen wigmakers in 1695 was one Douzé, who had "awarded himself the status of syndic." His signature and this title were found on notes he had written and sent to other journeymen wigmakers. This correspondence is an important example of Old Regime journeymen's use of literacy: Douzé's communications informed journeymen of pending business and of upcoming meetings at the lodge of the "Bons Enfants" ("Good Fellows," a term associated with compagnonnage).[126]

Journeymen wigmakers participated in a number of illegal activities, including the placement of workers, assemblies, and convocations. An edict of 1695 prohibited all such practices and also banned the *conduite*. The conduite was a leave-taking ceremony made infamous by compagnonnage. Journeymen of the devoir would assemble on the outskirts of town with a departing journeyman to toast him farewell and wish him a good voyage as he ventured off to the next town on the Tour de France. Conduites were the scene of a great deal of drinking, merry making, and fraternal vaunting of the devoir, activities that often led to quarreling and brawling between the celebrants and any hapless passersby. Violence between those holding the conduite and any nearby journeymen of other sects was especially common. Conduites united the journeymen of the devoir, but they also "disturbed public tranquillity" and rendered many of the participants unfit for work the next day.

The 1695 edict did not end labor disputes between masters and journeymen. The minutes of a meeting of master barber/wigmakers in 1712 reveal that journeymen wigmakers were still being placed in workshops by their "so-called syndic," who "disposed of arriving journeymen as he thought fit."[127] The community decided to establish an official placement bureau, headed by an appointed clerk, to oversee the hiring of these new arrivals. The clerk was instructed to send journeymen to the masters with the fewest workers. As seems to be the pattern, however, placement of journeymen by journeymen continued. In 1733 the masters wanted all earlier police edicts reissued because their journeymen persisted in "illegal assemblies and cabals" with no regard for the law or public welfare (*bien publique*).[128] Goodly numbers of journeymen assembled not only on Sundays and holidays but also on workdays; they were simply "abandoning the workshops." This behavior was declared prejudicial to

[125]AMN, HH 102, 31 August 1695.
[126]Ibid.
[127]AMN, HH 93, "Registre," p. 13, 4 (?) June 1712.
[128]AMN, HH 94, "Registre," p. 10, 30 June and 3 July 1733.

the masters and to the public. Finally, in 1743 the master wigmakers ordered their journeymen to renounce the devoir.[129] Confirming the police ordinance of 5 September 1743, an edict of the court was issued condemning "all journeymen du devoir and masters who favored them."[130] Henceforth master wigmakers could give work only to those journeymen who had gone to the police and renounced their oath of devoir. As noted previously, no lists of journeymen wigmakers have been found in the police records even though it is evident that many of these journeymen were members of the devoir. The wigmakers—perhaps stronger in the devoir than the joiners, tailors, or saddlers—may have found a way to avoid the renunciations.

Finally, after a series of conflicts with their journeymen in 1754, 1764, 1772, and 1773, master wigmakers established a placement bureau that lasted for more than twelve years—from June 1773 to January 1786.[131] My preliminary study covers the register's first and last full years. In 1774–75 there were 435 cases: 74 percent were journeymen entering Nantes; 26 percent were those changing shops or leaving town (these two categories were conflated and may be incomplete for 1774–75). In 1785–86, 1144 names appear: 41 percent were new arrivals; 25 percent changed shops; and 33 percent left town (0.6 percent unidentified). Some names are repeated by workers changing shops or leaving and returning to Nantes in the same year. Closer analysis of the 1774–75 data shows that most journeymen came to Nantes from northern and north-western France (44 percent). The next most common areas of recruitment were western and south-western France (28 percent) and central France, including Paris (19 percent). Only a few cases came from the south-east; this area probably had its own, more regional placement networks. Some "exotic" cases, from America, were also reported. None of the cases were from the north-east, but this was not an active area for compagnonnage. These findings support those of Michael Sonenscher in the present volume: journeymen tended to work in and around a major regional center for certain periods of time before moving on to more distant areas.[132] As one might expect, most journeymen worked last in shops that were at best a two-to-four day walk from Nantes.

What accounts for the almost threefold increase in the placement bureau's activity from 1774–75 to 1785–86, or for its demise after January 23, 1786, remains among the objects of my proposed study of the

[129]AMN, HH 95, "Registre," pp. 66, 66 verso, 67.
[130]Ibid.
[131]AMN, HH 101, "Placement des garçons perruquiers, 1773–1786." The register's title page is dated 14 May 1773, but the records begin only on 13 June. For 1785–86 some pages may be missing, and part of this year is not dated by day and month.
[132]See Michael Sonenscher, "Journeymen's Migrations and Workshop Organization in Eighteenth-Century France," chap. 3 of this volume.

complete register. Even at this point, however, it is clear that a means for placing journeymen in workshops—whether official or clandestine—was essential. Significantly, new trouble with journeymen wigmakers cropped up one year after the end of the official bureau. In January 1787 some clever journeymen wigmakers were discovered to have forged sophisticated copies of the good conduct certificates required by the placement bureau. Journeymen had to present these certificates, duly signed by their masters, when they arrived in town or changed shops. The forgeries had evidently been in use for several years, allowing journeymen to leave their masters without giving notice.[133] A number of false certificates, including some purportedly from Metz, Marseilles, Lyons, Strasbourg, and Rennes, were found at the inn of Sieur David, the père of the journeymen wigmakers.[134] This père had come to Nantes as a journeyman from Caen; his name first figures in the official placement register in 1773.[135] Sheltered by Sieur David, the sly journeymen used their literacy to outwit their masters. Moreover, by forging certificates claiming to be from cities far outside the usual placement network of this trade, the journeymen may have prevented earlier detection of their ruse. The case demonstrates that whatever happened to the devoir of the journeymen wigmakers during the period of the placement bureau, by 1787 they were once again united, organized, and active in pursuit of their own interests.

A Comparative Perspective

The preceding evidence on the locksmiths, joiners, tailors, and wigmakers demonstrates that there is a strong correlation between association and labor conflict. The incidence, type, and chronology of conflict recorded for each of these trades in both Nantes and Lyons are also roughly equivalent. Finally, the link between organized journeymen, conflict, and compagnonnage is undeniable. These patterns are generally repeated in the full sample of trades examined in this study. An overwhelming resemblance between journeymen's associations in Nantes and Lyons thus emerges. Similarities in the structure, aim, and tactics of these associations outweigh the differences.

The differences that exist in the associational life of journeymen in Nantes and Lyons, while less striking than the similarities, indicate some noteworthy regional variations. A comparison of conflict and association by trades in Nantes and Lyons points to the existence of divergence

---

[133]AMN, HH 104, "Search at the Sieur David's, père of the journeymen wigmakers," 12 January 1787.
[134]Ibid.
[135]AMN, HH 101, "Placement des garçons."

primarily in three areas: the chronology of the appearance or "disappearance" of conflict; the frequency of conflict; and the degree of complexity or elaboration in organization. The earliest examples of labor conflict—for example, control of hiring, walkouts, disruptive behavior in the workshop, working independent of the corps des métiers—are found in Lyons. Serious and ongoing incidents of conflict among masters and workers in baking, joining, locksmithing, and tailoring appear in the seventeenth century. Several cases of a more minor nature are also recorded for the wigmakers in the late seventeenth century. By contrast, in Nantes, only the wigmakers are actively engaged in conflict in the seventeenth century, and then only at the end of that century. Among the other trades examined here no trade except that of baking in Lyons left a record of conflict dating from before the eighteenth century. If conflict left its record first in Lyonnais trades, it was last recorded in Nantes. Lyons, in the period after 1770, was relatively quiet—at least in the archival records. In Nantes no such period of calm ensued. Indeed, Nantes deserves special attention in light of the major labor disputes that occurred in a number of trades in the period after 1770 and even into the early revolutionary period.

Analysis of the frequency of conflict likewise reveals some interesting discrepancies between Nantes and Lyons. The greatest frequency of labor disputes did not take place in the same trades in the two cities. This conclusion is based on an examination of the number of complaints, incidents, trials, and edicts generated by each trade studied in both cities. In Lyons, journeymen locksmiths were most often engaged in conflict, while in Nantes journeymen joiners had that distinction. Journeymen in both trades in both cities, however, were very nearly equal in terms of organization and labor activity. In Nantes, moreover, journeymen edge-tool makers were as actively engaged in serious disputes with their masters as journeymen locksmiths. In the other trades examined that left records of conflict in both cities, a surprising degree of similarity exists in the incidence of disputes. Thus, in both cities, journeymen tailors and wigmakers were, after locksmiths and joiners, the workers who were most organized and most involved in labor disputes. Even the less active trades in both cities reveal an uncanny similarity in frequency of labor activity, although the dates of this activity may differ. Carpenters in Lyons had one major labor dispute in 1782; those in Nantes had one in 1791. Stonecutters in Lyons provoked two major disputes—one in 1769 and one in 1786; stonecutters in Nantes incited one major dispute in 1752. Shoemakers in Lyons led three major conflicts, in 1708, 1774, and 1776; shoemakers in Nantes led two, in 1772 and 1776. Differences are apparent in the trades of cutlery, saddlery, turning, and weaving: on the whole all these trades were more frequently involved in master/

worker conflict in Nantes than in Lyons. Moreover, though these trades were less active overall than many of the other trades examined, the disputes provoked by journeymen saddlers, turners and weavers in Nantes were significant ones.

In almost all of the trades where conflict appears, some degree of association is also reported. All of the four trades profiled in depth had high levels of master/worker conflict and of organization; for example, evidence of leadership, regular meetings, record keeping, means for the control of placement, and ability to plan for walkouts or boycotts. Yet some relevant differences in the nature and complexity of journeymen's organizations in each city can be found. In Lyons journeymen locksmiths, joiners, and tailors all had very old and very strong associations that closely followed the model of compagnonnage, although the most common terms of compagnonnage (devoir, mère) are rare or missing in the data until the mid-eighteenth century. Journeymen wigmakers in Lyons, moreover, though called independent and troublesome by their masters in the seventeenth century, were not very formally organized until 1762. In Nantes, on the other hand, associations among journeymen in these same four trades emerged later than they did in Lyons, but they emerged "full-blown" with written records—rolls, notebooks (*cahiers*), lists—and with the distinguishing linguistic markers of compagnonnage. Well before the mid-eighteenth century, then, the bureaucracy, leadership, tactics, and language of journeymen's associations in Nantes were well elaborated. The ritual and ceremonial aspects of journeymen's associations in these four trades—and in many of the other trades studied in Nantes—were also more in evidence than in Lyons. Does this mean that ritual played a smaller part in the Lyonnais journeymen's associations than it did in Nantes? Based on the data available, this seems to be true. Given the degree of secrecy that always surrounded (and surrounds) the subject of ritual in journeymen's associations, however, any conclusions on this point must remain tentative.

The most important difference found with regard to journeymen in Nantes and Lyons is the chronological variation in the start and end of their labor activity. Why does master/worker conflict apparently begin and end earlier in Lyons? Both economic and cultural factors seem to be at work in the earlier appearance of such labor activity and the associations that encouraged it. Lyons had been an urban and commercial center of long standing. It was a fertile crossroads between France and Italy, and between city and countryside, that yielded a strong tradition of popular culture. In Lyons the prerogatives and license of carnival were claimed by organized groups within the urban context, most notably by bands of urban youths, "the lords of misrule," who elected a king and enforced certain moral and social standards while "turning the world

upside down."[136] The combination of pranks, sociability, and social control practiced by such groups provided a rich storehouse of models that
young journeymen artisans in Lyons could adapt to their own purposes
in the world of work. Journeymen printers, moreover, had been especially active and well organized in Lyons in the early modern period,
providing yet another precedent of organization.[137] An even more direct
source for early Lyonnais journeymen's associations could have come
from relatively nearby Dijon, where the earliest records of journeymen's
organizations and their conflicts with masters appear. Adding to the likelihood of a Dijon–Lyons circuit is the fact that many of the early
interurban networks of compagnonnage were regional rather than national. Finally, local factors such as economic competition from rural
and illegal outworkers and from large-scale manufacturing occurred
earlier and more fully in Lyons than in Nantes, which in turn strained
the resources of the corps des métiers and created the potential for
master/worker conflict there.

The apparent or real decline in labor activity after 1770 in Lyons
poses a more perplexing problem. Maurice Garden suggests that the
abolition of the guilds in 1776, temporary though it was, dealt a severe
blow to the communities—a blow from which they never really recovered
in the last years before the Revolution. Garden thinks that the policing
of the guilds, including official record keeping and authorities' visits to
shops to enforce trade regulations, although reestablished, was not rigorously practiced after 1776.[138] Garden's supposition is supported by
evidence from the officials of the community of locksmiths in Lyons. In
1780 these guild officials petitioned the provost of Lyon to issue a decree
restoring some vigor to the community's regulations, which since 1776
had been ineffective.[139] Ironically, then, labor relations between masters
and workers may have worsened in this period in Lyons without leaving
a record. It is possible that master/worker conflict actually declined in
the 1770s and 1780s, though this seems unlikely given the extent of
labor activity before this time. If there were such a decrease, it might
be tied to an overall decline in the fortunes of the guilds. Yet journeymen's conflict did not often neatly coincide with times of economic prosperity or end with times of economic hardship. Journeymen locksmiths
and joiners seem to have been most active when their guild was prosperous, whereas journeymen tailors and wigmakers made heavy demands on masters when corporate records and other indicators point

[136]Davis, "Reasons of Misrule," pp. 114–23.
[137]Davis, "Strikes and Salvation at Lyon," in *Society and Culture in Early Modern France*
(Stanford, 1975), pp. 1–16.
[138]Maurice Garden, personnal communication, Cornell University, April 1983.
[139]AML, HH 184, no. 19, "Maîtres gardes serruriers au prévôt," 14 June 1780.

to economic decline and debt.[140] The question of labor conflict after 1770 in Lyons thus remains an open one.

The continued and vigorous labor activity in Nantes after 1770 might, by contrast, have resulted from the continuing strength of the guild system in that city. Activity among journeymen in the building trades, in particular, remained high or even began for the first time in certain trades in this period. The important boom in building projects in Nantes throughout the eighteenth century—but especially from midcentury on—helps to account for labor activity in this sector.[141] Another significant economic factor in eighteenth-century Nantes is the growth of the seaport and related industries, such as shipbuilding and outfitting, that ensured the continued strength of the artisanal sector.

Perhaps correlated with the persistence of conflict and association in Nantes and its relative decline in Lyons is the other noteworthy difference between the two cities: the complexity or degree of elaboration present in journeymen's organizations. It is not clear why ritual and the more formal signs of compagnonnage appear to be more prevalent in Nantes than in Lyons. Gaston Martin calls Nantes a "city that truly has the reputation for being a sort of school for compagnonnage."[142] The leaders of confraternities, the heads of the devoir, and the workers' *syndics*, he continues, "had a very precise and much respected authority that presupposed a real structure within the groups who submitted to their discipline."[143] Yet Martin gives no explanation for Nantes's reputation as a "school for compagnonnage." One possibility is that a link existed between the historically strong religious tradition of western France and Nantais journeymen's associations as the latter borrowed and transformed Catholic ritual and symbolism. Connections between the church and compagnonnage, noted at several points in this essay, were especially evident in Nantes and lend some credence to this theory. In Lyons two forces may have been at work in weakening journeymen's use of ritual and symbolism. First, Catholic tradition had been severely attacked during the period of the religious wars in the sixteenth century when Protestantism gained a major foothold in the Lyonnais region. Probably more important for the present case, however, is the fact that the Counter Reformation succeeded not only in largely eradicating Protestantism in the seventeenth and eighteenth centuries, but also in doing

[140]For Nantes: Martin, *Capital et travail*, pp. 5, 88. Also for Nantes: AMN, HH 59 (joiners); HH 164 (locksmiths); HH 168 (tailors); and HH 93, 101, and 102 (wigmakers). For Lyons: Garden, "Ouvriers et artisans," pp. 45–49. Also for Lyons: AML, HH 109 (joiners); HH 184 (locksmiths); HH 185 and SM 181 (tailors); and HH 176–77 (wigmakers).

[141]Jacques Depauw, "Illicit Sexual Activity and Society in Eighteenth-Century Nantes," in *Family and Society*, ed. R. Forster and O. Ranum (Baltimore, 1976), p. 167.

[142]Martin, *Capital et travail*, p. 87.

[143]Ibid.

away with many of the elements of popular religiosity prevalent before this period. Thus, the strong opposition to popular use (or "misuse") of religious symbols, rituals, and icons, found in both Protestantism and Counter Reformation Catholicism, may have been reflected in the somewhat less ceremonial orientation of Lyonnais journeymen's associations.[144] Such thoughts are clearly at the speculative stage at this point in our knowledge of the development and use of ritual and symbolism in journeymen's associations.

It would be misleading, in any event, to overemphasize the divergences in the behavior and organization of journeymen in Nantes and Lyons. To repeat my earlier findings: journeymen's associations and master/worker conflict in both cities are extremely similar. These similarities can be interpreted as the result of three interdependent sets of factors. First, given the ever-present and relatively uniform institutions of the church, the guilds, and the confraternities, a certain degree of conformity among journeymen's associations, which borrowed elements from these institutions, was inevitable. Next, similarities between journeymen's behavior and associations in Nantes and Lyons originated in the major and parallel economic changes occurring in those cities in the eighteenth century. Masters in the trade communities studied in each city were under common pressures, pressures that led journeymen in each of these cities to engage in labor struggles reflecting shared economic and social conditions. Finally, journeymen themselves transmitted and diffused their ideas and methods as they traveled on the Tour de France. The labor struggles and associations of journeymen artisans in Nantes and Lyons thus reveal a very consistent pattern of tactics and objectives.

General Conclusions

Restif de la Bretonne, Mercier, and Hardy were not mistaken when they talked about the insubordination and insolence of journeymen artisans in the Old Regime workplace. Yet no golden age of perfect master/worker harmony had given way to a late eighteenth-century era of hostility and conflict. Master/worker conflict in its many forms seems to have been an endemic part of the master/worker relationship throughout the Old Regime. Conflict ranged from minor verbal disagreements—part of

[144]On the success of the Counter Reformation in Lyons see Philip T. Hoffman, *Church and Community in the Diocese of Lyon, 1500–1789* (New Haven and London, 1984). Hoffman concludes that "both the Catholic and Protestant reformations sought to discipline the populace, to rob it of worldly diversions, joy and levity" (p. 170). Although the Protestants were obviously far more opposed to popular celebrations and rituals than were the Catholics, Hoffman maintains that both "waged war on popular culture" and tried to " 'disenchant' the world" (pp. 169–70).

the normal give-and-take in the face-to-face world of the workshop—to serious walkouts and placement disputes. Remembering their own Tour de France, many masters tolerated journeymen's less offensive remarks and pranks. Even journeymen's control of placement and demands for improved conditions were openly or tacitly agreed to by many masters. Journeymen's objections—big and small—to workshop life and routine became part of the mechanism of Old Regime production. However, when smaller masters increasingly came under economic and social attack in the eighteenth century while simultaneously demanding a more disciplined and docile work force, the range of conflicts generated by organized journeymen become both more threatening and more intolerable.

Journeymen had both economic and social objectives in the concerted use of their unity against the masters. Employing their primary tactic—control of placement, journeymen artisans could "negotiate" uniform wage rates and work conditions that were satisfactory to them. For example, in Nantes journeymen stonecutters formed a coalition in 1752 to keep workers newly entering town from "accepting lower wages"than the other workers. One of the leaders of the stonecutters, Blaise, called "La Liberté," was accused of having told these new workers that they "dishonored the other journeymen"and that they would be better off if they "left town."[145] Journeymen rope makers in Nantes established a new "law" against their masters in 1781. The journeymen wanted forty sous a day for their work; the masters were willing to pay thirty sous—already a small increase over the previously agreed upon wage.[146] The three leaders, nicknamed "Sans Chagrin" (Without Cares), "Sans Respect" (Without Respect), and "Le Divertissant" (the Diverting One), apparently fled town before they could be prosecuted. However, their goal had essentially been achieved: journeymen rope makers in Nantes gained a wage increase—even if the three leaders did not profit from it.[147] In Lyons in 1786 journeymen masons organized a walkout that began with a demand that their wages be paid promptly. The masons soon escalated their demands to include a new and higher price for the day's work. Masters complained, moreover, that these journeymen had continually been plotting and planning walkouts.[148]

Battles were also waged over what we might call living standards, for journeymen often demanded that masters provide them with certain quotas of food and drink. In 1781 a petition presented by the master joiners in Nantes to the head police magistrate of the city complained

[145]AMN, FF 259, "Audience de police," 13 May 1752.
[146]AMN, HH 122, 20 September 1781.
[147]Ibid.
[148]AML, printed ordinance, 703.991, "Extrait des registres," 27 July 1786.

of the heavy burden and expense occasioned by journeymen. According to the masters, journeymen not only received advance payment from masters and then neglected their work, but also insisted upon (and had been receiving) extra *pâtés* and suppers on their four offical feast days. Lasting from eight in the morning until late evening, such drinking and feasting was costly to masters both in their outlay of provisions and in work time lost—not only the feast day but the day after as well.[149] The corporation's officers wanted these meals suppressed, but some members of the community refused to approve this motion because they feared losing their workers.[150] In an era that saw a rapid inflation of food costs, workers were obviously not misguided in insisting on such standards. Gaston Martin thinks that salary was perhaps the least important aspect of workers' economic demands. It may well have been that extra benefits, particularly food and drink, determined whom a journeyman would work for and whether he would be favorably disposed to remain on the job.[151]

The existence of this kind of competition for journeymen among masters—encouraged and fostered by the journeymen themselves—is borne out by the fact that in every trade examined there are several— more often dozens—of complaints that masters are stealing journeymen from one another. Indeed, one of the aims of the official placement bureaus was to distribute workers more equally among masters. Without the community's enforcement of this equality many masters could not attract and keep sufficient numbers of journeymen. In many of the trades studied both in Nantes and Lyons, there were masters employing three to five journeymen while others had one or none—and could not fulfill the work orders they had.[152] It seems likely that masters who employed more than their fair share of workers agreed to the improved wages and working conditions (particularly the fringe benefits) de-manded by organized journeymen. The journeymen, having established these favorable conditions in some workshops, often acted to extend these benefits to all workshops in the trade.

The fact is, then, that organized groups of Old Regime journeymen were able to articulate their economic demands and, often, to have them

[149]AMN, HH 147, 12 September 1781.

[150]Ibid.

[151]Cf. Michael Sonenscher's convincing discussion of the crucial need to assess workers' nonmonetary remuneration when attempting to define the level of wages in eighteenth-century Paris ("Work and Wages in Paris," pp. 171–72).

[152]Evidence of this is particularly strong among the edge-tool makers. One report of 1775 indicates that in a community with twenty-nine masters there were forty-nine jour-neymen distributed as follows: one master had five journeymen; two masters had four journeymen each; four masters had three journeymen each; nine masters had two jour-neymen each; and thirteen masters had one journeyman each (AMN, FF 258, 4 July 1775).

met by masters. Moreover, journeymen artisans formed associations and "plotted and planned together" for more than economic motives—for even more than extra pâtés. Indeed, demands for pâtés and for money and time off for suppers, drinking, festival celebrations, and the like represent the intersection and interconnection of the journeymen's economic and social demands. These occasions for sociability encouraged solidarity and enabled journeymen to break through the boundaries of their regulated and hierarchical world of work not only at carnival time, as had been traditional, but almost continuously. With a "license" granted by associations like compagnonnage, the generally youthful journeymen were by turns playful and serious in their treatment of their masters and themselves. Masters were fair game for tricks, as were the authorities and even other journeymen. Pranks to enliven the tedium of the workweek were welcomed by journeymen, who baptized specialists in this art with nicknames like "the Diverting One" or "Without Cares." Like the journeymen wigmakers who forged false certificates of good conduct, those who thwarted their masters without getting caught showed their prowess and their cleverness. Yet far too often, from the masters' point of view, they crossed the line between playful joking and malicious intent. Were the journeymen edge-tool makers who demanded that the masters join *their* association and receive the fraternal accolade joking or in dead earnest? Even if they were serious, as seems likely from the evidence, they must have delighted in turning the tables on the masters.

Some journeymen's behavior and language was unambiguously defiant and lacking in deference. A journeyman joiner in Nantes, Jean le Fourreau ("the Scabbard") in a routine request for his papers, told the officials that "we [journeymen] do not have to give an account of ourselves." He also refused repeatedly to give his name, surname, and place of birth; he did so only after being locked up.[153] When faced with evidence of their illegal activities, journeymen often simply refused to answer or strongly denied all accusations, even if numerous witnesses contradicted them.[154] High-spirited nicknames (e.g., "the Girls' Pleasure") were matched by ones that loudly proclaimed a rejection of traditional expectations for journeymen: "Liberty," "Without Respect," "the Obstinate Dauphinois," and "Languedoc the Victorious."[155] In the range

[153]I have located at least twelve major incidents of a lack of verbal deference or respect in Lyons and Nantes: one incident in Lyons dates from the seventeenth century and the rest date from the eighteenth century.

[154]AMN, HH 149, 14 December 1744. The phrase "nous n'avons point de compte á nous rendre" also appears among journeymen joiners questioned in Nantes the following year (AMN, HH 149, 5 May 1745).

[155]For La Liberté: AMN, HH 259, stonecutters, 1752; for Sans Respect: AMN, HH 122, rope makers, 1781; for Dauphiné l'Obstiné and Languedoc la Victoire: ADR, Sénéchausée/Criminel, harness markers, 1764, cited by Garden, *Lyon et les Lyonnais*, p. 567.

of individual and collective actions seen in this essay, one theme remains dominant: journeymen demanded certain liberties and a type of independence in the world of work. This "liberty and independence" were enforced by the power of association. No longer wishing to be the dependent men in service that their journeymen's status dictated, they wished to turn things upside down—to "scorn the masters" and to "put the masters in a sort of dependence on the journeymen."[156]

Such journeymen claimed to be defending their rights. Particularly in regard to placement, journeymen on the Tour de France viewed their rights as absolute, inalienable, and utterly serious. They consistently opposed the placement offices proposed or established by masters as infringements on the worker's liberty of choice. This was certainly a liberty no law had ever granted the journeyman, and it thus reveals an undeniable assertion of independence by organized journeymen. This independence carried over to the individual level as well. One journeyman farrier in Nantes, called Angevin, when questioned about his refusal to register at the official placement office, replied: "If workers must have a placement card from the corporation official to be hired, [I] would much prefer to pass the city by without entering rather than submit to any such regulation."[157] This opposition, this refusal to submit, is a crucial aspect of the journeyman's identity.

When acting as unified groups pitted against the masters, journeymen were even better able to flout the legal sanctions against them. They did indeed cause chaos in the workplace. This situation led masters to the largely valid conclusion that disorder and change prevailed, that they were threatened, and that they could do little to arrest this course of events. The behavior and attitudes of journeymen in Nantes and Lyons, on the other hand, reveal a sense of power, strength, and defiance. It is the masters, not they, who can be made to cower. Even though journeymen could never change their economic conditions to the extent of countering severe inflation and changes in artisanal industry, they took important steps toward controlling their economic conditions by creating durable and beneficial voluntary associations. They understood and manipulated the weaknesses of the guilds. In the eighteenth-century world of the corporations, journeymen were perhaps freer than ever before to redefine the way the world would perceive them. With their labor in demand, journeymen might arguably see themselves as necessary and valuable collaborators rather than as unprivileged and dependent subordinates. They worked to keep all journeymen in town under the organization's control in order to set wage standards and working conditions

---

[156]For the first quotation: AML, wigmakers, HH 176, no. 31, 6 February 1766. For the second: AMN, joiners, HH 147, 14 December 1787.

[157]AMN, HH 145, "Procès-verbal, commissaire de police," 12 July 1763.

collectively. Not imagining their masters' troubles as potentially their own, journeymen used these difficulties to their immediate advantage.

Additionally, because journeymen tended to be younger, single men with fewer financial and family obligations and greater mobility than their masters, they might with less sacrifice withhold their labor by seeking work in a new town if conditions did not suit them. Employing such tactics meant that journeymen had to delay—perhaps indefinitely—settling down, marrying, beginning a family. Not enough of the demographic and population profile of this group is yet known for me to comment precisely on how this aspect of the economic situation determined or limited the journeyman's affective life. Perhaps journeymen desiring to settle in a city and unable to survive on a journeyman's wage began to work as illegal producers—the hounded chambrelans—or sought work in a trade not so severely limited by regulations. Many other journeymen simply kept moving on, probably leaving their partners and quite likely their illegitimate children behind.[158] Journeymen usually had little choice but to continue to be mobile and unattached. For them, however, the high degree of fraternity and sociability, the revelries, games, and tricks of the journeymen's associations, could substitute for or supplement more traditional family life.

Journeymen who rejected the economic and social roles assigned them by Old Regime society gained a certain power and freedom in their own world and built a foundation for a working-class consciousness. Gaston Martin, speculating on the well-established associations of journeymen in Nantes, even wonders if such associations played a role during the revolutionary period. There is evidence of some strike activity in Nantes before and for some months after the Le Chapelier law (14 June 1791) among organized carpenters, farriers, joiners, and plasterers.[159] Ironsmiths demonstrated their loyalty to compagnonnage (the term used in the police report) as late as June 1792.[160] These ironsmiths, on being told that their assembly was illegal, gave up their ribbons and emblems and stated that they were "ready to take on those of the nation."[161] Perhaps these workers were again recanting in public only to resume the ways of compagnonnage in private. On the other hand, it could be that, as Martin suggests, something remained of such workers' associations in the democratic clubs of 1792 and 1793.[162] The nature and type

[158]Cf. Depauw, "Illicit Sexual Activity," pp. 184–85 and 188–91.
[159]AMN, carpenters: I² 137, no. 3, 3 July 1791; farriers: I² 137, no. 3, 29 November 1791; joiners I² 137, no. 3, 9 August 1791; and plasterers: I² 137, no. 3, 12 March 1791.
[160]AMN, I² 137, no. 3, "Procès-verbal, commissaire de police," 25 June 1792.
[161]Ibid.
[162]Martin, *Capital et travail*, p. 87.

of activities begun among unified, defiant journeymen in a labor context are not incongruent with the political behavior of the "menu peuple."

Journeymen in the Old Regime, however, primarily sought liberty within the confines of the existing society and system of production. Much as was the case with Old Regime legislation, journeymen's associations "hedged liberty within a system of constraints, subordinating individual interests to the needs and values of the community."[163] Nonetheless, for journeymen artisans this liberty through association was a positive and compelling force because the association was now their own, not their masters'. Whether or not the "independent" artisans of the 1770s or 1780s became angry sansculottes, these workers, in their prerevolutionary attempts to level their masters' power, gained a mastery of their own. Journeymen could logically have heralded the final abolition of the guilds in March 1791 without expecting that the new regime would so quickly level their own associations as well. Journeymen did not accept this ban any more than they had accepted earlier ones. Their own brand of liberty, independence, and association reasserted itself once again on the other side of the Revolution.

---

[163]Keith M. Baker, "State, Society, and Subsistence in Eighteenth-Century France," *Journal of Modern History* 50 (December 1978): 701–11, esp. p. 703.

Appendix 5.1. Nantes: Summary of journeymen's labor activity in twenty-seven trades

Trade	Dates of activity	Types of activity
Basket makers	1775, 1778†	Placement disputes, assemblies, "excessive" wage demands
Carpenters	1791†	Assemblies, brawls, compagnonnage
Cutlers	1782–86	Placement disputes
Edge-tool makers	1732, 1764,† 1768, 1775,† 1776, 1782†	"Compagnons du devoir," placement disputes, sedition, work disruptions
Farriers	1763, 1774,† 1777, 1783†	Journeymen's abuses (lying, disobedience, sociability), subversion of guild economy
Ironsmiths	1792†	Assemblies, sedition
Joiners	1724, 1737, 1743,† 1745, 1750, 1751,† 1758, 1764, 1774, 1776, 1777, 1781,† 1787,† 1791†	Assemblies, attacks on masters and police, placement disputes, plots for higher wages, insubordination, society of devoir
Locksmiths	1733, 1737,† 1738,† 1775,† 1780†	"Compagnons du devoir," placement disputes, insubordination
Nail makers	1768†	"Revolt of journeymen," placement disputes, workers' "license"
Plasterers	1784, 1791†	Wage demands, placement disputes, society of devoir, walkouts
Rope makers	1781†	Wage demands, placement disputes
Rug makers	1791†	Brawls, blacklisting, coalition
Saddlers	1738,† 1750†	"Compagnons du devoir," ceremonies, destruction of the corps des métiers
Shoemakers	1772, 1776†	Illegal production, blacklisting masters' shops, placement disputes
Stonecutters	1752†	Coalitions, wage demands
Tailors	1743,† 1762, 1763, 1772†	Society of devoir, "unending" assemblies, work disruptions, independence
Tinsmiths	1783,† 1784, 1788	Society of devoir, daily assembly, control of placement
Turners	1783†	Society of devoir, workers "make their own laws," insubordination
Weavers	1786,† 1788	Society of devoir, gavots, cabals, placement disputes, walkouts, wage demands
Wigmakers	1695,† 1712, 1733,† 1743,† 1773,† 1787†	Assemblies, "syndics of journeymen," placement disputes, *society of devoir*, use of false certificates, insubordination

Source: Archives municipales, Nantes, HH, arts et métiers; FF, police; I², police.
Note: No cases of master/worker conflict were found among drapers, printers, roofers, spur makers, pastry makers, preparers of roasted meats, or restaurateurs/caterers.
†Major conflict.

Appendix 5.2. Lyons: Summary of journeymen's labor activity in sixteen trades

Trades	Dates of activity	Types of activity
Bakers	1680,† 1686,† 1699, 1776†	Lack of deference, coalitions, strike threats, insubordination, compagnonnage
Cabinetmakers	Sporadic activity, eighteenth century	Minor disputes over distribution of journeymen
Carpenters	1782†	Walkouts, illegal production
Curriers/harness makers	1763–66†	Assemblies, society of devoir, ceremonies, interurban network
Cutlers	1729	Minor dispute over placement
Hatters	1769–70,† 1778,† 1786†	Strikes, coalitions, brawls
Joiners	1699,† 1704,† 1707, 1764†	Assemblies, insubordination, control of placement, society of devoir (1764)
Locksmiths	1634, 1642, 1661,† 1662, 1764,† 1767, 1780†	Assemblies, control of placement, walkouts, insubordination, threats against masters and officials
Masons and stonecutters	1769,† 1786†	Coalitions, control of placement, walkouts, wage demands
Saddlers	1749,† 1758†	Assemblies, "compagnons du devoir," placement disputes, lack of deference
Shoemakers	1708,† 1774,† 1776†	Assemblies, illegal production, lack of deference, independence
Tailors	1688,† 1723, 1760†	Defiance, assemblies, association, placement disputes
Turners	Sporadic incidents, eighteenth century	Minor disputes over distribution of journeymen
Weavers	Sporadic incidents, eighteenth century	Minor disputes over distribution of journeymen
Wheelwrights	Sporadic incidents, eighteenth century	Minor disputes over distribution of journeymen
Wigmakers	1697,† 1700, 1743, 1762,† 1764, 1766,† 1772	Illegal production, plots, control of placement, boycotts

Source: Archives municipales, Lyons, HH, arts et métiers; FF, police; I², Police; and Archives départementales de la Rhône, BP 3613–23, Sénéchausée/Criminel.
†Major conflict.

–6–

Social Classification and Representation in the Corporate World of Eighteenth-Century France: Turgot's "Carnival"

Steven Laurence Kaplan

Enfin j'ons vu les édits
Du Roi Louis Seize
En les lisant à Paris
J'ons cru mourir d'aise
Voltaire's Correspondence, ed. T. Besterman (Geneva, 1953–65), letter no. 18903, 94: 6 (note 4).

Tout fut libre dans Paris. La carrière de tous les métiers et de tous les arts fut ouverte. On se réveillait tailleur, boulanger, serrurier, et tout ce qu'on vouloit. Quelques esprits étroits qui ne voient rien en grand trouvaient pourtant ce système monstrueux. Ils prétendirent que *tout est classe et corporation dans la nature.*
Jean-Louis Soulavie, *Mémoires historiques et politiques du règne de Louis XVI* (Paris, 1801), 3:123.

A dog suddenly appeared in the salon where the prince de Conti was serving tea:
[Il] fit ses ordures en présence de Son Altesse Serenissime, & sans aucun respect pour l'auguste compagnie. Un huissier vient le battre, le chasser à coups de baguette. "Arretez," lui dit le Prince, "liberté, liberté toute entière," persiflant ce mot favori des économistes, leur secte et leur système.
Louis Petit de Bachaumont, *Mémoires secrets pour servir à l'histoire de la republique des lettres* (London, 1780), 9:45 (18 February 1776).

Social organization implies social classification. Relations among members of a society are contingent upon the way they see themselves vis-à-vis others. The production and imposition of a social taxonomy is closely linked with the exercise of power. The tools of distinction used to forge the classification system are tools of social and political control. A ruling group uses a classification system (sometimes historicized or mythicized or sacralized or naturalized or rationalized) to legitimate and sustain its domination. This taxonomy must overcome and in some sense permanently disqualify rival systems, present and future. Through governmental as well as social institutions, the official taxonomy is inculcated. When members have internalized it—as they seem to have done during much of the Old Regime in France—it serves as a powerful integrating and stabilizing force. Yet at no moment is the official taxonomy transparent, a description of how the world is in some intrinsic sense; at no point is the official representation of the social world merely the mechanical reproduction of natural divisions, themselves the product of economic or technological inevitability.[1]

It is possible to argue that the fall of the Old Regime resulted in part from the breakdown of its social taxonomy—from its incoherence, its loss of credibility, its inability to prevent the crystallization of rival principles of classification or to accommodate pressing demands for the reassessment of boundaries. This question invites a debate, in both theoretical and substantive terms, far beyond the confines of this essay. For purposes of my discussion, let me suggest in general terms that the eighteenth century suffered from an acute identity crisis, and let me focus on one aspect of it. From many different levels and directions the official system of social classification came under attack. I want to look at one episode in the campaign against the traditional corporate form of social organization that underlines the way structure and classification were imbricated.

The struggle against the old system of classification was led by the philosophes and by members of the new elite, generated in part by the growth of capitalism. Excluded from power and denied the kinds of social gratification to which they felt entitled, these groups assailed the government and the taxonomic system through which it regulated society. The odd and interesting thing about the case I will examine is that the blow against the official system was struck from within the government in the mid-1770s by its leading minister, Anne-Robert-Jacques Turgot, scion of a noble family, experienced field administrator, and intimate friend of the "economic" philosophes called physiocrats.

---

[1]On tools of distinction, see Pierre Bourdieu, *La distinction* (Paris, 1979), and Luc Boltanski, *Les cadres: La formation d'un groupe social* (Paris, 1982).

In Turgot's view, French society was cankered and stagnant in large measure because it was badly (i.e., incorrectly) organized. The corporate model, inferred from the Great Chain of Being, contravened the laws of nature that were anterior to all forms of social organization and predicated a view of human nature that had little relation to man's true psychology. Among the steps Turgot took to reform society (in a quite literal sense) was the abolition of the guilds. These were the grass-roots corporations on which the whole social organization in some sense rested. At stake, as the most vehement defenders of the traditional order perfectly well understood, was not simply the organization of work (as important as it was), but the legitimacy and viability of the entire system of social representation. Turgot's edict was seen as a sort of carnivalization of social relations, an invitation to taxonomic chaos, social disarray, and political mutiny. I do not think that Turgot himself ever fully grasped the implications of his project, which, short-lived though it was, fixed the agenda for the revolutions of 1789, 1830, and 1848.

I am less concerned with Turgot's ideology and his reform ambitions than with the way his edict was received, especially in the world of work itself. The corporations had been subject to mounting criticism during the course of the century, not only from outside (the "liberal" critique of philosophes and officials), but also from within. A small but significant current of "masterly" dissidence belied the image of unity cultivated by the guild leaders. And discontent among the journeymen bespoke a deep alienation from the corporate system of classification. The masters relied upon the king-in-government to exercise social control by reinforcing the corporate hierarchy and the masters' "police." The masters of the guilds, like the magistrates of the parlements, regarded Turgot's law as a lethal blow.

The Liberal Recipe for Regeneration

In February 1776 Controller General Turgot, whose ministry embraced economic and social affairs, promulgated an edict abolishing the corporations, as the trade and craft guilds were called in France. This was one of a number of more or less radical measures inspired by Turgot's "liberal" analysis, which on most issues he shared with the school of political economy called physiocracy. Liberty was the watchword of these *économistes*; it bespoke a stringent critique of Old Regime institutions and practices and a sweeping program of economic and social reform. "After the freeing of the grain trade," Turgot told Louis XVI, he considered the abolition of the corporations and the removal of all obstacles [*gênes*] to the freedom of work as "one of the greatest steps that is to be taken . . . toward the regeneration of the realm."[2]

Over the course of the previous two decades, the guilds had come under increasingly strident attack. The bill of indictment changed little from the time of Clicquot de Blervache, a royal official dealing with commerce and industry who fired the first violent salvo against the corporate system in 1758, to the eve of abolition when one of Turgot's counselors published a diatribe written by the late Bigot de Sainte-Croix, a senior magistrate in the Parlement of Rouen.[3] The critics denounced the guilds for reducing apprentices and journeymen to an excessively long and arduous "serfdom"; for restricting membership to masters' sons, in part by raising fees to exorbitant levels; for imposing vexatious regulations that hampered exchange and impeded innovation; for indulging in ruinous quarreling and litigation with sister guilds; and for, as a result of these costly, exclusivist, and archaic policies, increasing public misery (higher prices, curtailed production, unemployment, and underemployment).

There are indications that some of the guilds liberalized their recruitment policies and simplified their regulatory apparatus in response to the liberal onslaught.[4] Yet it is equally clear that there was little sense of real urgency in these undertakings. Turgot's ascension worried corporate leaders; the heads of the most prestigious guilds, the Six Corps, rushed to point out the injustice and peril of Bigot's prescription for

[2]"Mémoires au roi," January 1776, in *Oeuvres de Turgot et documents le concernant*, ed. Gustave Schelle (Paris, 1913–23), 5:159. Cf. the riposte of the advocate general Séguier: "Le but qu'on a proposé à V. M. est d'étendre et de multiplier le commerce en le délivrant des *gênes*, des entraves, des prohibitions introduites, dit-on, par le régime réglementaire; nous osons, Sire, avancer à V. M. la proposition diamètralement contraire: ce sont ces *gênes*, ces entraves, ces prohibitions qui font la gloire, la sûreté, l'immensité du commerce de la France." Speech of 12 March 1776 in Jules Flammermont, ed., *Remontrances du Parlement de Paris au dix-huitième siècle* (Paris, 1898), 3:347.

[3]Simon Clicquot de Blervache, *Considérations sur le commerce, et en particulier sur les compagnies, sociétés et maîtrises* (Amsterdam, 1758); Bigot de Sainte-Croix, *Essai sur la liberté du commerce et de l'industrie*, ed. N. Baudeau (Amsterdam and Paris, 1775). The ministries preceding Turgot's seriously considered a number of projects geared to eliminate the abuses of the guilds rather than to abolish them. One such plan called for making entry easier by reducing admission fees, suppressing the masterpiece, and excusing particularly talented candidates from the standard apprenticeship. It also envisioned requiring the guilds to deposit their revenue with the royal government in order to curtail misuse by the jurés. Bibliothèque Nationale (hereafter BN), Collection Joly de Fleury (hereafter Coll. Joly) 1729, fol. 152.

[4]Steven L. Kaplan, *The Bakers of Paris and the Bread Question during the Eighteenth Century*, forthcoming, and idem, "The Luxury Guilds in Paris in the Eighteenth Century," *Francia* 9 (1982): 281–88. The guilds were aware of their abuses and were clearly willing to undergo reform—but not abolition. "These abuses," asked the hatters, "can they be corrected only by [our] destruction?" "Mémoire des couturières" and "Mémoire des fabriquants de chapeaux," BN, Coll. Joly 596, fols. 74 and 100.

dissolution.[5] But it was not until Albert, Turgot's lieutenant general of police, refused to accept the traditional New Year's gifts presented by the guilds in January 1776 ("to avoid engaging his gratitude") that a blow suddenly seemed imminent.[6] Even as they met in emergency session in early February, many guildsmen could not bring themselves to believe that the Parlement of Paris and their protectors at the royal court would allow them to perish. Incredulous yet terrified, the guild leaders launched a desperate drive to save their institution and their rank.[7] "Protector and apostle of liberty," Turgot could not tolerate the vehemence of the pro-corporate offensive. He obtained a royal order suppressing the *mémoires* in favor of the guilds—a gesture redolent of the authoritarian attitude that his supporter Voltaire reserved for his enemies.[8]

The Defense of the Corporations

Historians have paid little attention to corporate self-defense, largely because they subscribe to Turgot's indictment of the guilds as antiquated, artificial, oppressive, and corrupt. Their supposition is that the corporations had nothing loftier to agonize over than their narrow and venal self-interest. Even if the guildsmen were defending the indefensible, however, it is worthwhile to look at how they went about it. Moreover, it is perhaps even more important to look beyond the stereotypes and epithets to see just what the corporations believed they were fighting for in their appeals from death row. Faced with their imminent demise, how did they view themselves and their world?

One question that historians are loath to face because it is probably impossible to resolve is the extent to which official guild discourse represents rank-and-file, or constituent, opinion. The issue is particularly

[5]Louis Petit de Bachaumont, *Mémoires secrets pour servir à l'histoire de la république des lettres en France depuis 1762 jusqu'à nos jours* (London, 1780–86), 8:94 (28 June 1775). Cf. the prediction recorded several days earlier that "the project for liberation of the arts and crafts will be [shortly] realized." Ibid., 8:90 (25 June 1775).

[6]Siméon-Prosper Hardy's journal, BN, manuscrits français (hereafter MSS fr.) 6682, p. 165 (28 January 1776).

[7]Ibid., p. 172 (11 and 12 February 1776). On the patrons of the corporate world, including the prince de Conti and members of the king's immediate family, see ibid., p. 188 (12 March 1776), and Schelle, *Oeuvres de Turgot*, 4:53. Certain guildsmen consoled themselves with implausible, self-indulgent rumors, such as the news "that the king did not really believe in the new edict." Hardy's journal, BN, MSS fr. 6682, p. 176 (19 February 1776).

[8]Bachaumont, *Mémoires secrets*, 9:55 (1 March 1776); Hardy's journal, BN, MSS fr. 6682, p. 181 (1 March 1776); Turgot to Miromesnil, 21 February 1776, in Schelle, *Oeuvres de Turgot*, 5:256; François Métra, *Correspondance secrète, politique et littéraire, ou Mémoires pour servir à l'histoire des cours, des sociétés et de la littérature en France, depuis la mort de Louis XV* (London, 1787–90), 2:425 (16 March 1776).

delicate here because we know that the guilds were not the harmonious and cohesive institutions often portrayed by their adversaries as well as their advocates. Nor am I alluding to clashes between masters and their employees. In this context, corporate life means life among masters. This life in many, if not most, of the guilds was marked by serious friction, dissidence, and alienation, most of which was not directly a product of commercial rivalry. Thus it is reasonable to wonder whether many masters, like Daniel Roche's Ménétra, might not have been indifferent to the fate of their guilds, or at least deeply ambivalent about it.[9]

I believe that many masters felt uncomfortable about the vocation of the guilds and especially about their administration by the jurés or syndics. Yet I think that other concerns were probably more pressing and were capable of marshaling a consensus behind the official corporate position in 1776. The first addressed what we might call in an instrumental sense labor relations, though it is hard to wrench "labor" from the whole tissue of human, social, and cultural relations in the eighteenth century. Nothing troubled masters more than the problem of worker discipline. Virtually everyone who observed the world of work in the eighteenth century had the impression that "insubordination" was sharply on the rise. The abolition of the guilds threatened to transform a strained and potentially explosive situation into a nightmare of disarray. Whether or not a master felt good about his guild, the guild ethos and apparatus provided him with the indispensable means of governing his workers. Second, even for the masters who were disaffected, abolition pure and simple was too drastic a response to corporate difficulties. Where would it leave them? Malaise over the place they would occupy in a liberal tomorrow also mobilized masterly support for guild resistance to Turgot. On these grounds I contend that the official discourse, manifested in the many mémoires addressed to the royal government, represented the way most masters were likely to have represented themselves in 1776.[10]

Another "corporate" group of a different character joined forces with the guilds to combat Turgot's death decree. I am referring to the Parlement of Paris, which had criticized the liberal program (though not indiscriminately) since it first began to be implemented in the early 1760s. The Parlement, quite rightly in my view, perceived Turgot's edict as a

[9]Daniel Roche, ed., *Journal de ma vie: Jacques-Louis Ménétra, compagnon vitrier au dix-huitième siècle* (Paris, 1982); S. L. Kaplan, "The Character and Implications of Strife among Masters inside the Guilds of Eighteenth-Century Paris," forthcoming in *Journal of Social History*.

[10]Liberals and cynics pointed out the enormous stake that the lawyers who drafted (or signed) these mémoires had in the maintenance of the corporate system. The large sums that the guilds spent on litigation against each other filled the pockets of the lawyers. Yet it seems to me that the guilds had enough to worry about without requiring the prod of the bar to act.

direct threat to the kind of society and polity it prized. The magistrates articulated certain positions that the guilds had merely sketched, and they made crucial connections in a broader ideological framework. It is important to remember, despite the prevalent stereotypes, that the magistrates no more constituted a unified block of opinion on all the issues of the day than did the masters. There were significant differences of view within the Parlement (as there were among the various parlements) on how and what to reform or to preserve. For most magistrates, however, as for the bulk of the masters, Turgot's law was a kind of apocalypse.[11]

Corporate Social Identity

The abolition edict was a jolting blow to the economic interests of many of the masters, but I think that it was more intensely experienced as a violent assault on their social identity. Members of a corporation, the masters saw themselves as part of a social universe composed of interlocking corporate entities articulated in a hierarchy roughly analogous to the Great Chain of Being. One's place in the grand taxonomy determined virtually everything else. One's birth circumscribed one's corporate horizons. A noble, for example, faced different sorts of options than a commoner because certain honors and privileges inhered in his order. He enjoyed a sort of generic corporate status that was, with a few exceptions, unaffected by what he did in life. For the commoner, however, life was a struggle over classification. Clearly, wealth meant a great deal in one's quest for a corporate niche that would distinguish one from *most* of one's fellow commoners. Yet once one attained membership, say, in a guild, one tended to perceive the relationship between fortune and status in a more complicated way. One's critical capital was now one's social classification—one's *qualité* or *état* or *condition* in the sense *not* of birthright or of profession strictly speaking, but of rank and the value conventionally assigned to it. For a guild member, this capital and rank were his mastership. That status or distinction theoretically guaranteed him his living, as well as a host of other

[11] Hardy claimed that the Parlement was "absolutely unanimous" in requesting the withdrawal of the abolition edict (along with certain other reform measures, including the transformation of the corvée). Hardy's journal, BN, MSS fr. 6682, p. 175 (17 February 1776). Yet two days earlier Hardy cited the opinion of Rolland de Challeraye, a seventy-six-year-old magistrate, who characterized abolition as "the most beautiful gift" that a king could offer his subjects. Ibid., p. 173 (15 February 1776). Six years earlier the same Rolland had spearheaded parlementary resistance to the liberalization of the grain trade. Steven L. Kaplan, *Bread, Politics and Political Economy in the Reign of Louis XV* (The Hague, 1976), 2:516–17. Once again it is clear that in the variegated domain of liberty, *tout ne se tient point.*

less palpable perquisites. But first of all it conferred upon him his identity. In the words of one guild, mastership was "this sign that imprints upon the merchant, the artist, [or] the trader an indestructible social meaning." Or as the glovemakers put it, "one exists only through the corps of which one is a member."[12]

In this perspective mastership was a system of social classification and representation before it denoted a system of production, distribution, and consumption. Social relations, molded by the corporate code, were anterior to economic relations and in some ways determined or at least significantly shaped them. Economic relations were embedded in social relations—in social institutions and ideology. One's social place invested one not only with economic leverage but also with a kind of political power and responsibility. Individually and collectively, this power was exercised to safeguard rights and prerogatives that distinguished one's corporation from others (thus the internecine warfare among the corporations) and, even more important, to enforce masterly dominion in the labor market and discipline in the workplace. For here, too, social relations preceded and determined economic relations. The workplace relationship was first one between master and journeyman and only then, derivatively and accessorily, one between an employer and an employee. The employee owed certain obligations to the employer not so much because he worked for him but because he was his journeyman in a relationship of inferiority and subordination prescribed by the code that guaranteed the master his status. The journeyman had to obey—at least from the master's vantage point—because submission was his social role, and only incidentally because he needed to be paid regularly. The journeymen were not members of the guilds, but they constituted an integral part of the corporate system. Without (some of) them, the guilds could not reproduce themselves, and (most) masters could not do business. Equally telling, without the journeymen the masters could not fully enjoy the social distinction of mastership. The masters and the journeymen were dependent upon each other for the practice of their social identities.

Standing the World on Its Head

It is no wonder the guilds viewed Turgot's edict as a kind of carnivalization of the social order, standing the world on its head. "It is not my intention to mix conditions," asserted Louis XVI, but this is pre-

[12]"Réflexions des marchandes et maîtresses lingères," BN, Coll. Joly 596, fol. 101; "Observations des maîtres-gantiers," ibid., fol. 114.

cisely what abolition seemed to do. Either it meant the end of the notion of états or the attribution of an état to everyone—the corporations were not sure how liberty would work.[13] The outcome, however, would be the same. A "revolution," the hatters and the engravers called it.[14] "Anarchy" and "social confusion," warned the tailors and the pewterers, echoed by the magistrates of the parlement.[15] Order implied hierarchical categories described by vertical and horizontal lines that made clear-cut distinctions. "To annihilate the corps, the guilds," wrote a spokesman for the leading corporations, "is to draw nothing but an immense circle in which all individuals who sell and who work will be mixed and confused." This was to "take things back to primal disorder."[16] The hatters also saw the new regime as an atavism, a step backward from civilization. Far from being "the palladium of the state," Turgot's "unlimited liberty" belonged to the infancy of states, to a primitive and unsorted time.[17]

[13]"Observations des maîtres boutonniers," BN, Coll. Joly 462, fol. 108. On the question of état and Etats and more generally on the nature of social stratification in Old Regime France, see William H. Sewell, "Etat, Corps, and Ordre: Some Notes on the Social Vocabulary of the French Old Regime," in *Sozialgeschichte Heute: Festschrift für Hans Rosenberg zum 70. Geburtstag*, ed. Hans-Ulrich Wehler (Gottingen, 1974), pp. 49–68; François Olivier-Martin, *L'organisation corporative de la France d'ancien régime* (Paris, 1938); Roland Mousnier, *Les institutions de la France sous la monarchie absolue, 1598–1789*, vol. 1, *Société et état* (Paris, 1974); and Mousnier's much less successful foray into political sociology, *Les hiérarchies sociales de 1450 à nos jours* (Paris, 1969).
[14]"Mèmoire des fabriquants de chapeaux," 23 February 1776, BN, Coll. Joly 462, fol. 112, and "Mémoire des graveurs," ibid., fol. 122.
[15]"Réflexions des tailleurs," BN, Coll. Joly 462, fol. 174; potiers d'étain, "Déliberation du 17 février 1776," ibid., fol. 139; remonstrances, 2–4 March 1776, in Flammermont, *Remontrances du Parlement de Paris*, 3:312. Hardy echoed this fear of the "disorder and confusion" that would inescapably result from suppression. Hardy's journal, BN, MSS fr. 6682, p. 172 (11 February 1776). The author of "Observations sur la liberté générale" warned of "the trouble and the confusion that would supplant order, harmony, and the established distinctions." BN, Coll. Joly 1729, fol. 148.
[16]"Mémoire pour les Six Corps," BN, Coll. Joly 462, fol. 153. Cf. the remonstrances that advert to "this dangerous law that... would tend to substitute confusion for good order"; remonstrances, 2–4 March 1776, in Flammermont, *Remontrances du Parlement de Paris*, 3:318–19.
[17]"Mémoire des fabriquants de chapeaux," BN, Coll. Joly 462, fol. 112. Cf. the song cited by Métra:

> On verra tous les états
> Entr'eux se confondre
> Les pauvres sur leurs grabats
> Ne plus se morfondre
> Des biens on fera des lots
> Qui rendroit les gens égaux
> Le bel oeuf à pondre!
> Oh gué!

The song ends in an ironical celebration of "the perfect model" of "full liberty" that we owe to "Turgot et compagnons"; *Correspondance secrète*, 3:43–44 (April 1776). In a mock mémoire of protest against abolition, the sewer drainers worried that persons of all walks

The end of the traditional social taxonomy was terrifying because it reduced things to the state of a "tabula rasa."[18] Without rules and norms and boundaries the dyers foresaw only "the most horrible chaos."[19] Masters no longer knew how to survive in the social jungle. "Mixing" meant rubbing elbows with everyone else, pushing and shoving: they were unequipped for such turmoil. The tabula rasa inserted "what was arbitrary in the place of what was right." It put an end to the "stability" that was the guarantee of the masters' serenity and the most exalted corporate ideal. The tabula rasa expelled the masters from the promised land, consigning them "to wander in an immense void, confounded with a mob of intriguers, usurers, servile men without honor."[20]

What would happen in a world in which "anyone could meddle in any profession with impunity?"[21] The ultimate perversion, or rather inversion, the full symbolic measure of Turgot's carnival, was the ascension, or the trespass, of the Jews, "foreigners," the perfect outsiders and interlopers, "a proscribed nation whose conduct in every sort of activity authorizes us to despise it or fear it." The Jews would surge to the top, since "legitimacy" and "honor" and "patriotism" no longer mattered. Thus enshrining "the enemies of God," Turgot's measure was a gesture of blasphemy as well as an act of social vandalism.[22]

---

of life would be entitled "to mix themselves [se confondre] with us" in our night soil. Hardy's journal, BN, MSS fr. 6682, p. 175 (16 February 1776).

[18]The phrase is from a satire of Turgot's program called "Les mannequins," reported by Métra, *Correspondance secrète*, 3:94–95 (29 May 1776).

[19]"Mémoire des teinturiers," BN, Coll. Joly 462, fol. 178. On the anarchy/chaos theme as the leitmotif of Turgot's ministry, see the verses addressed anonymously to the procurator general of the Parlement of Paris:

> Turgot est l'ennemi de l'ordre
> Turgot n'aime que le désordre
> Turgot veut tout rompre et détordre
> Turgot enrage et veut tout mordre
>
> Turgot dans notre Monarchie
> Veut introduire l'Anarchie
> Turgot prend pour philosophie
> Son Audace et sa phantaisie

(BN, Coll. Joly 462, fol. 274).

[20]"Mémoire pour les Six Corps," BN, Coll. Joly 462, fol. 153. I suspect we owe the stereotype of the mob as *canaille* as much to the masters, who knew the workers more or less intimately, as to the upper classes, who knew them only vicariously, or across considerable distance or mediation.

[21]"Procès-verbal de la Chambre des comptes," 19 March 1776, BN, Coll. Joly 462, fol. 247.

[22]"Réflexions des Six Corps," BN, Coll. Joly 462, fol. 156; "Mémoire pour les Six Corps," ibid., fols. 152–53; "Observations des tapissiers," ibid., fol. 177. On the long-festering anxiety of the Six Corps regarding Jewish competition, see Emile Levasseur, *Histoire des classes ouvrières et de l'industrie en France avant 1789* (Paris, 1900–1901), 2:579, and anon.,

Equality and Liberty

It is revealing that where Turgot said liberty the masters read equality. From our post-Tocquevillean perspective, we are used to focusing on the tension between liberty and equality rather than on their linear relationship. Turgot himself had no interest in promoting equality. On the contrary, he knew that liberty would issue in inequality, but in what he regarded as a natural, tonic inequality, an impermanent and reversible inequality—the "wandering in the void." The inequality that was unacceptable to him was precisely the prescriptive and ascriptive inequality begotten and consolidated by the corporate social taxonomy. Turgot spoke for a world in which social relations were embedded in and largely determined by economic or market relations. This was the "revolution" that the guilds decried. Liberty was a law of nature that existed before any form of social organization. It was inviolable. It belonged to individuals rather than to groups. The business of the state—really its only legitimate business—was to ensure that "all subjects had the full and entire exercise of their rights." The first and most basic expression of the natural law of liberty was the right to dispose freely of one's property in oneself, that is, the right to work without being hampered in any way. The free exchange of property was to be mediated exclusively by what we now call the market.[23]

For the guilds, liberty meant equality because it corroded the institutional and legal arrangements that perpetuated a certain kind of inequality. The guilds linked order with inequality because both were based on "the submission of men to wise rules," that is, to a particular social taxonomy.[24] For the guilds, corporate social classification was neither arbitrary nor artificial. On the contrary, it emerged inexorably from "nature's order." Regardless of their immediate destiny, the buttonmakers confidently predicted that Turgot's "project will not be able to destroy the order that nature has placed between the men of each estate. Some must occupy the first ranks, while others are subordinated to them: to seek to put them all in the same rank is to confound that which must not be confounded, that which will always be distinguished and differentiated regardless of the efforts one makes to mix them together." "Even without mastership," concluded the button makers, "there will always be masters and workers, that is, the order of things traced by the hands of the Divinity himself."[25]

Lettre ou réflexions d'un milord à son correspondant à Paris au sujet de la requête des marchands des Six Corps contre l'admission des Juifs aux brevets (London, 1767).
[23]Edict of February 1776, BN, Coll. Joly 462, fol. 258.
[24]"Mémoire pour les Six Corps," BN, Coll. Joly 462, fol. 153.
[25]Boutonniers, "Observations sur le projet de supprimer les maîtrises," BN, Coll. Joly

Ironically, this was precisely the outcome that Turgot imagined. He had no doubt that liberty (i.e., the market) would engender a social structure of dominators and dominated, of entrepreneurs and workers, of haves and have-nots. It was his ambition not to destroy inequality, but to displace it and refound it on truly natural grounds instead of on social conventions. Because it ostensibly called for no barriers to entry, prescribed no rules of conduct save those dictated by self-interest, and allowed for endless shifting and adjusting, Turgot's project seemed incapable of producing (and reproducing) a stable society. The guilds could not imagine such a society freely emerging from the give-and-take—the collision— of countless individuals. They believed there would always be distinctions—masters and workers without incorporation— provided there was social life. In their eyes, Turgot's project threatened the very existence of social life as they understood it.

The journeymen also understood liberty to mean equality: the repudiation and dismantling of the social structure based on the corporate taxonomy. Even before the edict was officially promulgated, observers reported them to be "overjoyed" and "emboldened."[26] "They already see themselves as the equals of their masters," the bakers noted bitterly.[27] Songs and poems celebrated "equality among men" as it was seen by the journeymen. The millenarian refrain was that each person is now free to chart his own course:

> J'abolis les Brevets, bannis les exacteurs,
>   Plus de maîtrises à Cythère,
> Plus d'inconstans jurés, plus de jurés trompeurs;
> Tout ce que je fais, moi, chacun pourra le faire,
>   Sans gêne, sans contradicteurs
> Trompera qui voudra; liberté toute entière[28]

The alleged social mission of the corporate system was nothing more than bloated mystification devised to justify extortion and monopoly.

> Il ne tient qu'à nous demain,
> Avecque franchise

462, fol. 110. On the "chimerical" notion of equality and on the idea that the law could forge distinctions but not create equality, see "Réflexions des Six Corps," ibid., fol. 155. Cf. Jean-Louis Soulavie, *Mémoires historiques et politiques du regne de Louis XVI* (Paris, 1801), 3:123.

[26] Hardy's journal, BN, MSS fr. 6682, p. 191 (7 March 1776).

[27] "Mémoire des maîtres boulangers," BN, Coll. Joly 462, fol. 106. For the same outraged appraisal, see "Observations des boutonniers," ibid., fol. 109, and "Observations des tapissiers," ibid., fol. 177.

[28] "La réforme de l'amour, épitre à Zirphe," cited by Métra, *Correspondance secrète*, 3:116 (1 June 1776).

D'aller vendre bierre & vin,
 Tout à notre guise,
Chacun peut de son mètier
Vivre aujourd'hui sans payer
Juré ni mâitrise
 Oh gué,
Juré ni maître.[29]

A third song reminds us of the visceral side of the masters' reaction to "equality," which not only worried them but also "humiliated them." Leveling provoked shame as well as indignation—shame at losing distinction and honor and at being "mixed" and thus tainted.[30]

The System of Independence

Disorders were now unavoidable, for liberty trampled the social system that inculcated "the spirit of subordination" and engendered in its place "the love of independence"—an allergy to regimentation, subjection, and coerced deference.[31] According to the luxury cloth makers, the picture of work relations since the beginning of the century was "a tableau of uprisings by the journeymen." Revolt was built into the fabric of work relations. Only the constant prod of authority could prevent "sedition." The cloth makers had joined the debate with Turgot five months before the February edict when the controller general pushed through an arrêt suppressing fixed wages in the luxury cloth sector. The aim of the measure was expressly "to free the destiny of the workers" from "total dependence on the will of the masters." From the latter's vantage point, however, the arrêt announced the "ruin of subordination" and the triumphant resurgence of the "pernicious spirit of independence."[32]

[29]Ibid., 3:37 (April 1776).
[30]"Commencement du Saint-Evangile," cited by Métra, *Correspondance secrète*, 3:39 (13 April 1776).
[31]Speech of Séguier, 12 March 1776, in Flammermont, *Remontrances au Parlement de Paris*, 3:349. Cf. a similar assessment in "Remontrances sur le lit de justice du 12 mars 1776," 8–19 May 1776, in ibid., 3:373, and the speech of J.-B.-J. Le Marié d'Aubigny, avocat du roi de la Chambre des comptes, 19 March 1776, BN, Coll. Joly 462, fol. 243. On the "natural and legitimate subordination that journeymen owe masters," see also Archives Nationales (hereafter AN), Y 9534, 6 June 1776, and Steven L. Kaplan, "Réflexions sur la police du monde du travail, 1700–1815," *Revue historique* 261 (December 1979): 22–23.
[32]"Requête au roi," fall 1775, BN, Coll. Joly 596, fols. 81ff. Cf. an unusually frank memorandum denouncing the unfair subjugation of journeymen, who were not even allowed to "haggle over the price of their labor, their only property." "The slightest murmur" gave masters the pretext to have them arrested as "disturbers of the public order." "Mémoire sur les communautés," ca. 1772, BN, Coll. Joly 1729, fol. 139.

Masters predicted that "the system of independence" promoted by Turgot would impel the journeymen to seek immediate vengeance by abandoning their shops without regard to the work they left unfinished.[33] Curiously, the masters could not think in economic or market terms even in relation to the workplace itself. In the absence of sociojuridical constraints, they supposed the journeymen would not work. The need for a wage apparently would not move them. Presumably they would be able to find sustenance outside their shops.[34]

Very few of the guilds invoked the (vestigial) bonds of intimacy and reciprocity that might have linked masters and their journeymen—probably because they realized how little credibility such a claim would command. The dyers wailed that abolition would "undermine the good harmony that reigns in the guilds." Yet in the same breath they acknowledged that their journeymen would leap at the chance "to abandon their masters in order to become masters themselves." The ribbon makers also talked about "the happy correspondence" between masters and their workers. But they made a fine and crucial distinction that suggests that this correspondence was not all-embracing. It linked the masters with the future masters: the "good" workers known for talent and skill. "It has never happened," contended the ribbon makers, "that the good, well-behaved worker has not found the material means [to reach mastership], either as a result of help from individual guild members or through a marriage with a daughter or a relative of one of the masters." The wine merchants voiced a similar optimism about their journeymen's chances for upward mobility. The "good journeyman" saved enough to prepare and ensure his future. But in any event the masters were always ready to recognize "fidelity and intelligence in the journeymen who have served them" by helping them to get established. The wine merchants' guild was a sort of El Dorado: "It can be said that it costs nothing or almost nothing for a good subject to become a member of the corps." To judge by the actual results of recruitment during the eighteenth century, the vast majority of journeymen wine merchants must not have been able to qualify as good subjects.[35]

[33]"Observations des fabriquants de chapeaux," BN, Coll. Joly 462, fol. 112; "Mémoire des maîtres boulangers," ibid., fol. 106.

[34]"Réflexions des Six Corps," BN, Coll. Joly 462, fol. 155.

[35]"Mémoire pour les teinturiers," BN, Coll. Joly 462, fol. 178; "Réflexions sur l'édit concernant la suppression des jurandes par les maîtres et marchands tissutiers-rubanniers," 21 February 1776, BN, Coll. Joly 596, fols. 98–99; "Représentations du corps des marchands de vin," BN, Coll. Joly 596, fol. 105. Cf. the Parlement's perception of the world of work and the conditions for upward mobility: "There are two kinds of workers: hard-working, active, well-behaved on the one hand and dissipated, undependable, and badly behaved on the other. Sooner or later all the corporations opened their doors to the first group, because success always accompanies perseverance and good behavior." The Parlement added that abolition favored the undeserving second group (nasty but strong) over

The masters expected the worst. Nor did they try the familiar rhetorical ploy of distinguishing the mass of fundamentally loyal and docile workers from the handful of *boutefeux* and *meneurs*. The allure of independence was presumed to be irresistible; the *cabale* was universal this time. Some workers would run off to organize and plan their future in "tumultuous and seditious assemblies." Others would fall into debauchery. Still others would set up as "false workers" (*faux-ouvriers*) at the "very door of their [former] masters." Somehow they would manage to steal away their masters' clients, doubtless as a consequence of their wiles rather than their craftsmanship.[36] Even the widow's journeyman, without whom she could not survive, would become a "cruel usurper" now that the "regulations" no longer "contained" him. There were no golden age illusions about reciprocity on the eve of Armageddon. From the masters' point of view, good feeling in the workshop had never been spontaneous and genuine but had been induced or imposed and ritualized by the corporate model of subordination.[37] Nor was there an end in sight to this "internal war between the masters and the workers" so long as the system of independence prevailed, according to the parlementaires.[38]

The masters were not the only victims of journeymen's usurpation. The guildsmen took pains to show that what was dangerous for them was equally dangerous for the public, whose interests the corporations served, Turgot's caricatural strictures to the contrary notwithstanding. The guilds were the guarantors of morality. They served as a "filter" to siphon off the corrupting elements. The onset of liberty was "the triumph of usury and deception," of "bad faith," of "brigandage," of "imperfect workmanship," of "indifference and negligence." Without guild standards, guild pride ("esprit de corps"), and guild controls, the marketplace would be flooded with fraudulent goods and services. Cooks without experience or conscience would offer up "ragoûts pernicieux" that would introduce the same sort of "disorders in the human machine" that Turgot

---

the praiseworthy first group (good but somehow unequipped for unregulated competition). Remonstrances, 12 March 1776, BN, MSS fr. 10947, fol. 23.

[36]"Mémoire des potiers d'étain," BN, Coll. Joly 462, fol. 139; "Mémoire des marchands fabriquants d'étoffes d'or, d'argent et de soye," BN, Coll. Joly 596, fol. 112. The luxury cloth makers pointed out that even under the corporate regime, false workers pullulated. The "general confusion," warned an opponent of abolition, would cause "the overturning of fortunes." As a result of worker fraud and encroachment, masters would face failure (*faillite*). "Observations sur la liberté générale," BN, Coll. Joly 1729, fol. 148. Cf. the denunciation of this usurping subspecies of "gens sans consistance et sans aveu" in "Procès-verbal de la Chambre des comptes," 19 March 1776, BN, Coll. Joly 462, fol. 247.

[37]"Mémoire des tailleurs," BN, Coll. Joly 462, fol. 174.

[38]Remonstrances, 2–4 March 1776, in Flammermont, *Remontrances du Parlement de Paris*, 3:316. For a similar argument on the volatility and malevolence of journeymen made in 1789, see Didelot, *Le Furet, avant-coureur, journal étranger, politique, critique, littéraire et commerçant* (N.p., 1789), p. 7.

introduced into the social machine.[39] False workers would fashion "false keys" and "false gold," both of which symbolized the breakdown of security.[40] The hidden *chambre*, seat of the false worker, refuge of adulteration and dissipation, would replace the transparent workshop.[41] "All of Paris will become the faubourg Saint-Antoine," the privileged locus of libertinage and disorder, exempt from corporate inspection, where false workers conspired against their masters and the public.[42] Paris would lose its very integrity: it would literally become a *faux*-bourg, a false city—unsound, artificial, perfidious—gorged with *faux*-ouvriers producing false goods and services. It was no accident that Turgot specifically cited the faubourg Saint-Antoine in the February edict as living proof that workers in an environment of liberty "work no less well" than those in a corporate ambience.[43] For the guilds, the faubourg model meant the end of quality control and the concomitant loss of the capital's international reputation for craftsmanship, thus drying up one of the kingdom's chief sources of prosperity.[44]

Social Classification and Police

Integrity did not inhere in a man any more than submissiveness or skill. The worker was naturally turbulent, mutinous, inclined to evil.[45]

---

[39]"Observations sur l'édit concernant la suppression des jurandes par les maîtres queulx, cuisiniers, traiteurs," BN, Coll. Joly 462, fol. 180.

[40]"Mémoire des marchands de vin," BN, Coll. Joly 462, fol. 130; "Observations des fabriquants de chapeaux," ibid., fol. 112; "Mémoire des maîtres graveurs," ibid., fol. 122; remonstrances, 2–4 March 1776, in Flammermont, *Remontrances du Parlement de Paris*, 3:312, 318–19.

[41]"Mémoire des maîtresses lingères," BN, Coll. Joly 462, fol. 128.

[42]"Observations des boutonniers," BN, Coll. Joly 462, fol. 111.

[43]Edict of February 1776, BN, Coll. Joly 462, fol. 258.

[44]On the guilds as the only guarantors of the international renown of French products, see the "Mémoire des fabriquants d'étoffes d'or, d'argent et de soye," BN, Coll. Joly 596, fol. 110. See also Galiani's remarks on the "fatal blow to French manufactures"; Galiani to Madame d'Epinay, 13 April 1776, in *Lettres de l'Abbé Galiani à Mme d'Epinay*, ed. Eugene Asse (Paris, 1882), 2:222–23. Diderot rebutted Galiani's contention that the end of the guilds meant poor-quality craftsmanship; Diderot to Galiani, 10 May 1776, in *Diderot correspondance*, ed. Georges Roth and Jean Varloot (Paris, 1968), 14:191 (no. 864). Cf. an anonymous "lettre écrite de la Haye," which "predicts with confidence that if the guilds are suppressed today, they will necessarily be reestablished one day [soon]—they will be reestablished because of their utility and [the need to promote] the progress of the arts inside [France] and [France's] foreign trade"; 23 March 1776, BN, Coll. Joly 596. Although it ardently supports the corporatist position, this "Dutch correspondence" raises questions about the privileged connection, upon which the guildsmen and the magistrates insisted, between the political organization of France and its socioeconomic organization. For "the republic of Holland is nothing other than an ensemble of congregations of masters."

[45]Nicolas-T.-L. Des Essarts, *Dictionnaire universel de police* (Paris, 1789–90), 3:459–61 and 8:401; Nicolas Delamare, *Traité de la police* (Paris, 1705–38), 1:389 and 4:21, 84.

Workers without the état conferred by the corporate system were especially "volatile."[46] They were permanent fugitives, fleeing classification and thus control; they were socially unknown, strangers, and thus threats.[47] The parlements trembled at the thought of unyoking "these beings born to trouble the order of societies," men of "brute energy" and "untamed passions."[48] Only the "wise regulations" of the corporate system could prevent the journeymen from jeopardizing the public interest as well as the interests of the masters. Apprenticeship and compagnonnage probation endowed the journeyman with the moral values and the technical training he needed to perform responsibly and competently, but unless he was subject to relentless corporate surveillance (which penetrated even into "the details of his personal life"), he risked lapsing into his naturally wicked state.[49]

One of the paramount advantages of the corporate system was that it was a structure of regulation and control as well as a structure of ranks. Social distinctions implied police: "Today a severe hierarchy contains everyone and guarantees order: each shop is subordinated to a master who exercises a first rampart of police. The master answers to his guild whose officers are constantly at the call of the Lieutenant General Of Police."[50] The guilds provided the administration with "a sure means of governing without difficulty a mob of robust individuals . . . they cease being objects of dread once they march in distinct and coherent troops."[51] Internalized in the social structure, guild police spared the administration the need to intervene save in unusual circumstances (and spared the guilds from this meddling in their affairs). Though this police force was frequently harsh, peremptory, and intrusive, the guilds idealized it as a familial mode of regulation and contrasted it to the brutality of the outside police. "What police force could be gentler than that of the guilds?" asked the parlementaires.[52] Corporate police protected the guild and the public against wayward masters even as it protected the masters and the public against the workers. Corporate "honor" was the instru-

---

[46]"Mémoire des tailleurs," BN, Coll. Joly 462, fol. 173.

[47]"Mémoire des marchands de vins," BN, Coll. Joly 462, fol. 130. On the danger of the excessive mobility encouraged by liberty, which made reclassification virtually impossible, see remonstrances, 2–4 March 1776, in Flammermont, *Remontrances du Parlement de Paris*, 3:315.

[48]Remonstrances, 2–4 March 1776, in Flammermont, *Remontrances du Parlement de Paris*, 3:309.

[49]"Observations des boutonniers," BN, Coll. Joly 462, fol. 108; remonstrances, 2–4 March 1776, in Flammermont, *Remontrances du Parlement de Paris*, 3:309.

[50]"Réflexions des Six Corps," BN, Coll. Joly 462, fol. 155.

[51]"Mémoire des marchands lingères," BN, Coll. Joly 462, fol. 129.

[52]Remonstrances, 2–4 March 1776, in Flammermont, *Remontrances du Parlement de Paris*, 3:310.

ment of this police.[53] It was effective because it bespoke the commitment of all the members to the same code of values and conduct. Corporate honor was the expression of corporate consensus. It threatened violators with far more devastating sanctions than could a purely civil police force.

Having undermined the "domestic authority of the masters over their journeymen," Turgot substituted "a police of individuals for a police of corps." Turgot's police would necessarily be rough and repressive rather than paternalistic and preventive.[54] The irony of liberalism was that they would have to bludgeon people into enjoying their putative freedom responsibly. "Will society give lessons on liberty with whip in hand?" queried the Six Corps. "What will society have gained if instead of easy-going and humane jurés it needs archers, gallows, and executioners?"[55] Jail might prove to be more hospitable than the other forms of control that liberty reserved for the worker. For emancipation led directly to a new type of subjection, this time not to a master and a corporation, but to the impersonal and implacable arbitrage of the market. Turgot boasted that abolition would especially favor the unenfranchised worker. Yet very few of them would make it in the new environment, predicted the guild spokesmen, either because of character flaws or because the competition would be too vicious. For these workers liberty would be no less a "fatal gift" than it had been for the consumers when it was applied to the grain trade.[56]

Liberalism and Individualism

Liberty was perilous not only because it unleashed or abandoned the workers, or both, but because it also threatened to reduce or return the

[53]"Réflexions des tissutiers-rubanniers," BN, Coll. Joly 596, fol. 99.

[54]"Réflexions des Six Corps," BN, Coll. Joly 462, fol. 155; speech of first president, 12 March 1776, in Schelle, *Oeuvres de Turgot*, 5:178.

[55]"Réflexions des Six Corps," BN, Coll. Joly 462, fols. 155–56. Cf. the wine merchants' argument that a new police force would be required under liberty, that this outside, professional force would be far more costly, subject to corruption, and uninformed than the old corporate police. "Représentations du corps des marchands de vin," BN, Coll. Joly 596, fol. 106. For a similar argument, see "Observations pour la communauté des maîtres et marchands fourbisseurs," 26 February 1776, ibid., fol. 97.

[56]"Observations des boutonniers," BN, Coll. Joly 462, fols. 108–9; "Réflexions des Six Corps," ibid., fol. 156; remonstrances, 2–4 March 1776, in Flammermont, *Remontrances du Parlement de Paris*, 3:316. Cf. "Les mannequins": "Togur déploie grand étendard de la liberté, le peuple qui se croit assez libre pourvu qu'il ait du pain ne comprend rien à ce signal; mais malheureusement ce signal devient celui d'une disette, et ce même peuple alors prenant la liberté au pied de la lettre, se mutine et se soulève. Togur toujours passionné pour son système, mais un peu embarrassé des conséquences, prend le parti d'appuyer ses raisonnements par des soldats," Métra, *Correspondance secrète*, 3:98 (19 May 1776).

masters to the moral and psychological level of workers without état. This was a prospect that the masters themselves were reluctant to envision, for it reminded them of how much they shared with their journeymen. For the masters, too, were no better than their social organization and encadrement. They too had to be contained, or rather integrated, by the corporate bonds.[57] By destroying the corporate system, liberty uprooted the master, like the worker, and cast him into a terrible state of isolation. The social hell evoked by the guilds was precisely the kind of society that Turgot hoped to create (or restore to its natural destiny). For Turgot recognized only the existence of individuals in society. The "common interests of the members of particular constituted groups" were perforce inimical to the interests of the society at large.[58] The only proper way to "class" citizens was as individuals, not as bodies or groups. Yet at no price did the members of the corporate structure want to be treated as atoms. In their view, Turgot stripped away everything that socialized and civilized them. Their defense of corporate values became a searing indictment of Turgot's brave new world of liberalism and individualism.

The guilds believed that a society had to be greater than the sum of its parts. "General societies" resulted from combining many "particular societies that must have principles and regulations appropriate to maintain and conserve them so that they can be useful to the general society." Liberty, also known as "Modern Philosophy," destroyed general society by "dissolving all the knots that were formed to unite men." What happened when these "primal links that gather men together" were liquidated? "If these ties are relaxed, if the corps is annihilated, if the members of the community are disunited," wrote the ribbon makers, "then each *fabricant* will view himself as an isolated individual." "Isolated, holding on to nothing," the tailors commented, the former guild member will be "nothing more than a gnawing individual."

If he were deprived of his mastership, the tradesman would have merely a job and no social identity. His life would be devoid of meaning beyond earning a livelihood. His attachment to his état would be purely a function of his profit margin. Left to his own devices, the isolated individual had "only one consideration: his personal interest." This

---

[57]In a number of guilds, masters in fact played the role of journeyman more or less permanently. According to the tailors, half of their total contingent of two thousand masters "subsisted only as a result of work given them by their confrères." BN, Coll. Joly 462, fol. 174. The ribbon makers claimed that most guilds were dominated by a few rich merchants, for whom many masters served as workers (in a way reminiscent of the Lyons silk industry); ibid., fol. 147. It would be worthwhile to look into the psychological, institutional, and commercial implications of relations between "fallen" or dependent masters and their employers.

[58]Edict of February 1776, BN, Coll. Joly 462, fol. 258.

blinding and almost involuntary self-regard exposed the individual to be consumed either by "the thirst for profit" or by "a sterile libertinage."[59]

Unrestrained by either the corporate code or the corporate ethos, individuals would lapse into a sort of Hobbesian relation of belligerent, deceitful, and destructive competition. The specter of unlimited and unregulated competition horrified the guilds in moral and political as well as economic terms. By its nature, open competition was "perfidious" because it set individuals against each other without rules to structure and buffer the clash of their interests. This sort of game was "fatal" to a large number of the players. Competition would favor the dishonest and scheming players who cared only about winning. These villains, mostly former journeymen, would use the tainted money they amassed to drive out of business the honest tradesmen, mostly former masters. Skill would be "choked to death" by "avidity." Unfettered competition would force a massive realignment of production and distribution factors that would be experienced like an "earthquake." Mediated by the guilds, individualism had beneficial results for society; outside the guild, it turned against society and ultimately against the individual.[60]

Modern Philosophy

The fruit sellers leveled the most far-reaching critique of modern philosophy: "The more one reflects on our Modern Philosophy the more one is convinced that the first of all its principles is egotism. *Liberty, property*, these are its rallying cries. Society was introduced uniquely to guarantee the enjoyment of these rights. Each individual owes it nothing; he must attach himself exclusively to his personal interest." Before they could implement this "dangerous system," its partisans had to challenge the very foundations of the traditional social order: "Modern Philosophy had to attack everything: Religion, subordination, the essential differ-

---

[59]"Mémoire des tissutiers-rubanniers," BN, Coll. Joly 462, fol. 146; "Mémoire des tailleurs," ibid., fol. 174; "Mémoire des fruitiers-orangers," ibid., fols. 120–21; "Mémoire des cordonniers," ibid., fol. 113; remonstrances, 2–4 March 1776, in Flammermont, *Remontrances du Parlement de Paris*, 3:311, 319; speech of Séguier, 12 March 1776, ibid., 3:346. See the slightly different versions of the tissutiers-rubanniers and the fruitiers-orangers briefs in BN, Coll. Joly 596, fols. 99 and 104. Cf. the focus on making *individuals* happy, in part by dissolving "the social chains" forged by inequality in "Les mannequins," in Métra, *Correspondance secrète*, 3:94–95 (29 May 1776).

[60]"Réflexions des marchandes et maîtresses lingères de Paris sur le projet de détruire les jurandes," BN, Coll. Joly 596, fol. 101; "Observations des maîtres graveurs," ibid., fol. 109; "Observations pour la communauté des maîtres gantiers," ibid., fol. 114; "Réflexions des maîtres tissutiers-rubanniers," ibid., fol. 94. On the destructive character of untrammeled competition, see also the speech of J.-B.-J. Le Marié d'Aubigny, avocat du roi de la Chambre des comptes, 19 March 1776, BN, Coll. Joly 462, fols. 243 ff.

ences that characterize the estates; nothing was respected." The liberal doctrine taught that "men are equal, the barriers conceived to contain them, the very laws are so many injustices that prejudice liberty and property." The specter of this cruel, ruthless, atomized world horrified the fruit sellers. The uninhibited exercise of self-interest, founded on the inviolability of property, did not guarantee justice and order. "Man is truly free only to do good, he must be stopped when he wants to do evil, and he must not abuse his property right by using it to deprive his fellow citizens of objects absolutely indispensable to their existence."[61]

Focusing specifically on the danger of entrusting the survival of society—its subsistence—to the free play of self-interest, the fruit sellers shrewdly broadened the debate by vividly showing how the different parts of the liberal program were really all of a piece. Regulations against hoarding and monopoly, the fruit sellers suggested, were in a way violations of the rights of liberty and property (theft, the économistes contended), and yet they were decisively in the general interest.[62] The fruit sellers obviously knew that Turgot did not share this viewpoint, as he had made clear in September 1774 when he liberated the grain trade from controls and again in several of the edicts accompanying the abolition of the guilds. Turgot had denied grain social distinction in the same way that he denied it to the masters. Grain, despite its special vocation, was declared to be no different from any other commodity. All goods had to be treated equally—like all citizens of the world of work.

The fruit sellers were not the only defenders of tradition to make this sort of linkage (though it was very much resisted by many individuals and groups who stood to benefit from one part of the liberal program— say, higher grain prices and land rents—while they detested others— say, more equitable taxation policies or freedom of religion). Back in 1769, the Rouen Parlement had warned that liberty could not easily be applied "sectorially." Freeing the grain trade was a prelude to total lib-

---

[61]"Mémoire des fruitiers-orangers," BN, Coll. Joly 462, fols. 120–21. On the destructive character of modern philosophy, see Mathieu-François Pidansat de Mairobert, *L'espion anglais, ou Correspondance secrète entre milord All'eye et milord All'ear* (London, 1785), 3:303–4.

[62]Turgot could have turned this argument back against those guilds that staked their right to survive on the "sacred right of property." "Mémoire des tapissiers," BN, Coll. Joly 462, fol. 177; "Mémoire des fabriquants de chapeaux," ibid., fol. 112; "Mémoire des cordonniers," ibid., fol. 115; "Mémoire des potiers d'étain," ibid., fol. 139; "Mémoire des graveurs," ibid., fol. 122. Turgot did not consider the *maîtrise* to be legitimate property. The corporate leaders probably committed an error in making their status claims contingent (in part) on the purchase of a piece of property. Ready to countenance the violation of a grain trader's rights, the Parlement was not prepared to see the property rights of the masters disparaged or disqualified simply because their property was a "privilege." Speech of Séguier, 12 March 1776, in Flammermont, *Remontrances du Parlement de Paris*, 3:350.

erty. "When all regulations are suppressed, leaving an uncircumscribed liberty, then the ties of society are destroyed and the peoples are mixed."[63] It was hardly necessary for their Parisian counterparts to articulate the connection that Turgot himself emphasized by submitting his edict suppressing the corporations in the same bundle with edicts extending the freedom of the grain trade and transforming the corvée into a tax on all landowners.

The reaction of the magistrates to the conversion of the corvée was strikingly parallel to the way they treated the abolition of the corporations. At stake, here too, was the very system of social taxonomy on which the traditional structure of France rested. And the sinister leveling and mingling principle was the same. Even as the masters were humiliated by the plan of amalgamating them with their domestic servants, as many of them viewed their workers, so the nobility was mortified by the sight of "a system that made the lord and the vassal two equal proprietors, two jealous neighbors, two redoubtable enemies." Like the equality of Turgot's freedom to work, the equality of his corvée overturned civil society, "whose harmony is grounded uniquely on the gradation of powers, authorities, preeminences, and distinctions that keeps each man in his place and guarantees all estates against confusion."[64]

Political Chains

The corporate system, its exponents insisted, was as deeply rooted in "nature" as Turgot's rights of liberty and property. "From the first [corporations] of all, which are empires, to the last, which are families," the parlementaires intoned, "men have always united to protect themselves, commanded by superiors or watched over by parents who guarantee the general stability by ensuring the stability of their own groups." The "principle of incorporation" embraced all of France in "a chain" whose

[63]Remonstrances of 25 January 1769, registre Saint-Martin, Archives départementales Seine-Maritime. On the generic threat of "unlimited liberty that knows no other laws than its caprices, that admits of no other rules than those that it makes for itself," see Séguier's speech, 12 March 1776, in Flammermont, *Remontrances du Parlement de Paris*, 3:344.

[64]"Remontrances sur le lit de justice du 12 mars 1776," 8–19 May 1776, in Flammermont, *Remontrances du Parlement de Paris*, 3:378; R. R. Palmer, *The Age of the Democratic Revolution: A Political History of Europe and America, 1760–1800* (Princeton, 1959), 1:451. I think that Palmer fundamentally misapprehends the significance of both Turgot's edicts ("points of detail") and the Parlement's passionate reaction (incommensurate with such "small things"). Critics of liberalism such as the prince de Conti regarded the corvée "as a fundamental boundary that separates the last classes of the people from the superior classes...to suppress the corvée, to replace it with a general tax was to efface this line of demarcation, it was to abolish the distinction of ranks"; Pidansat de Mairobert, *L'espion anglais*, 3:168.

links led directly to the "authority of the throne."[65] The advocate general Séguier reminded the king of his stewardship of the corporate universe:

> All your subjects, Sire, are divided into as many different corps as there are different estates in the realm: the Clergy, the Nobility, the soverign courts, the lesser tribunals, the universities, the academies, the companies of finance, the companies of commerce...[all these] corps can be seen as links in a great chain, the first of which is in the hands of Your Majesty as chief and sovereign administrator of everything that constitutes the body of the Nation.[66]

The guilds formed "a portion of this indivisible whole," added Séguier. "The very notion of destroying this precious chain" he found "frightening."

Guildsmen and magistrates made the same political argument. The guilds were "political corps": they were established to give "a multitude of honest citizens a political existence," that is, a place and a stake in the scheme of social classification.[67] The guilds were "analogues to the constitution of the state." The ethos of "independence," born of liberty, equality, and egotism, "is a vice in the political constitution."[68] French society was built on distinctions that "derive from the constitution of the monarchy."[69] As another critic of abolition put it, in the absence of corporations "the Sovereign would not know, so to speak, to whom to make his will known."[70] The guilds were "one of the most precious motors of the Government."[71] The dissolution "of the union of all the corps" was an undertaking profoundly "incompatible with the principle of a Monarchy."[72] To the guilds, it seemed clear that the government jeopardized its own existence as well as the survival of traditional society

---

[65]Remonstrances, 2–4 March 1776, in Flammermont, *Remontrances du Parlement de Paris*, 3:309, 321.

[66]Speech of Séguier, 12 March 1776, ibid., 3:345. The advocate general also compared the guilds to "so many little republics exclusively concerned with the general interests of all the members that compose them." The lieutenant general of police, Lenoir (who had been dismissed by Turgot in 1775 as a result of disagreements over the handling of provisioning problems), and the philosophe L.-S. Mercier both used the chain image to criticize corrosive liberalism. Papiers Lenoir, Bibliothèque Municipale of Orléans, MS 1422; Louis-Sebastien Mercier, *Tableau de Paris* (Amsterdam, 1782–88), 10:322.

[67]"Mémoire des tailleurs," BN, Coll. Joly 462, fol. 173; "Observations des boutonniers," ibid., fol. 111.

[68]Speech of Séguier, 12 March 1776, in Flammermont, *Remontrances du Parlement de Paris*, 3:346, 351.

[69]Speech of first president, 12 March 1776, in Schelle, *Oeuvres de Turgot*, 5:278. Cf. "Remontrances sur le lit de justice du 12 mars 1776," 8–19 May 1776, in Flammermont, *Remontrances du Parlement de Paris*, 3:378.

[70]"Observations sur la liberté générale," BN, Coll. Joly 1729, fol. 149.

[71]"Mémoire des fabriquants de chapeaux," 28 February 1776, BN, Coll. Joly 596, fol. 100.

[72]"Réflexions des tissutiers-rubanniers," 21 February 1776, BN, Coll. Joly 596, fol. 94.

by tolerating the end of the corporate system in the realm of work: "In recent years there has been an apparently universal outcry against the corporations in general: One hears only of liberty; one breathes only independence; one abhors exclusive privileges; one appeals out loud for competition. It is not for merchants to say in what way this principle should be admitted or modified in a Monarchy."[73]

The Workers' Insolent Rapture

We know much more about the psychological and ideological disarray provoked by Turgot's edict than about its actual impact on social relations. The Abbé de Véri boasted that "all of Paris, with the exception of a small number of senior masters and corporate officials, rejoiced at the liberty accorded to commerce and industry."[74] As friend and counselor to Turgot, Véri can hardly have been inclined to take a negative point of view. Disputing the claim of the first president of the Parlement of Paris that the people of the capital were "deeply troubled" by abolition, another observer found everywhere "un vrai délire."[75] Hardy, the bookseller and diarist, who had grave reservations about the wisdom of abolition, remarked that the "little people" were possessed by a violent fever of "joy." Journeymen bakers and roofers lit bonfires and set off fireworks. Wall posters proclaimed "long live the king and liberty," without betraying any anxiety about the compatibility of the two. Yet Hardy sensed that the joy was·not universal even among the "lie du peuple," who instinctively feared serious disruption of familiar patterns of daily life. "Well now," he quoted a woman congratulating a ragpicker, "you must be real happy, for now you're a master!" "Me," he replied, "I would give ten écus of six livres for all of this not to have happened."[76]

To the masters, the rapture their workers manifested was nothing less than a provocation: signs of "insolence" and "disorder." The workers rejoiced precisely because the old criteria of submission and order were

---

[73]"Réflexions des Six Corps," BN, Coll. Joly 462, fol. 154. The rhetoric of a pamphlet deploring the abolition of the guilds in 1791 is strikingly redolent of the discourse of corporate resistance in 1776 (even as d'Allarde was inspired by Turgot). It laments "the confusion of all the états of society," the destruction of "all relations," the "isolation of men" from each other, the "ruin" of commerce. "First indefinite liberty was proclaimed," explained this writer, "and then in order to destroy the ranks and privileges an absolute liberty was added." "Abused," the liberty became "license," and equality became merely "the law of the strongest"; *Rétablissez les maîtrises et la France est sauvée* (Paris, year 5).

[74]*Journal de l'Abbé de Véri*, ed. B. J. de Witte (Paris, 1928), 1:423.

[75]Pidansat de Mairobert, *L'espion anglais*, 3:171–72. Soulavie seconded the contention that the edict was "popular"; *Mémoires historiques et politiques*, 3:130, 156.

[76]Hardy's journal, BN, MSS fr. 6682, p. 192 (18 March 1776).

no longer valid. The brawls that erupted between journeymen "drunk with their future liberty" and their masters were not always incited or orchestrated by the workers. Yet it is clear that many felt a need to act out their emancipation more or less violently, as if the brazen performance of (what used to be called) insubordination was the only true proof of their new status.[77]

Physical assault was not the only way the journeymen displayed their "independence." They taunted and insulted their masters in another sort of ritual inversion meant to register a profound change in relations. Even before the promulgation of the February edict officially confirmed the anticipated emancipation, the three journeymen of widow baker Gresel had begun to "do as they pleased, making the law over her" instead of deferring to her authority.[78] A worker returning in a coach from a *guinguette* to his room in the faubourg Saint-Antoine played out his personal carnival by baring his buttocks to passersby and shouting as loud as he could "long live liberty."[79]

Replete with symbolic significance, the most serious forms of insubordination also had grave and immediate practical consequences. Many journeymen read the edict as authorization to quit their masters regardless of their obligation. "The bars overflowed with workers who had abandoned their masters," reported the *Mémoires secrets*.[80] Emboldened as never before, journeymen bakers "refused to work [and] imagined that they could become masters, without capacity, without fortune, without means," complained the bakers' guild. Brandishing the "arrêt" that freed them from "the discipline of the corporation," the baker boys gathered in large numbers to celebrate in the taverns of the Porcherons and the grain ports.[81] In a cabaret in the Marais, a journeyman baker slapped a police agent who tried to force him to return to the master whom he had fled "as a show of independence."[82] Master cabinetmaker Jean Morysse lured journeymen to work with substantial cash advances but complained that they left without notice after only a few days despite their pledge to earn their wage—a situation that had not frequently occurred in the old days because the workers feared they would be blacklisted.[83] Two shoemakers, twenty-

---

[77]Ibid., pp. 191 (16 March 1776) and 194 (21 March 1776).
[78]AN, Y 14424, 21 February 1776.
[79]Hardy's journal, BN, MSS fr. 6682, p. 214 (7 May 1776).
[80]Bachaumont, *Mémoires secrets*, 9:70 (21 March 1776).
[81]"Mémoire des maîtres boulangers," BN, Coll. Joly 462, fols. 106–7.
[82]Hardy's journal, BN, MSS fr. 6682, p. 191 (16 March 1776). Like other hostile commentators, Hardy underlined the connection between the spirit of independence and the tavern where it was most warmly affirmed: the baker boy was "doubly intoxicated by the wine and by the hope of liberty."
[83]AN, Y 15978, 18 June 1776.

four-year-old Louis Degaine and his seventeen-year-old brother Jean, conspired to close down their master's shop by inducing his other employees to quit. They beat up those who refused to follow them.[84] Apprentices followed the lead of journeymen, expressing contempt for their contractual commitment or challenging its meaning.[85]

From Serenity to Constraint

Faced with gloomy predictions of social disorganization from the adversaries of liberty, Turgot's official line was that the transition from incorporation to laissez-faire was taking place in a climate of serenity. By mid-March, however, his trusted adviser, Lieutenant General of Police Albert, could no longer afford to avert his eyes from the streets. "I am informed," he wrote, "that some difficulties have arisen between the masters of the arts and métiers and their journeymen, some of whom believe they have the right to quit their masters immediately." Albert ordered his commissaires to disabuse these journeymen of their illusions. Liberty did not excuse them from giving their masters ample notice before they left. And though under the corporate regime the time required was settled individually by each guild, the new rule fixed two weeks as the standard. Among the journeymen arrested in Albert's crackdown against illegal departures were three shoemakers, two carpenters, a cabinetmaker, and a cloth maker.[86]

Even the journeyman who planned to set up on his own was not yet his master's equal, Albert reminded Parisians. This was doubly true, for the journeyman who wanted to open his own business had to declare his intention formally to the lieutenant general of police. Had relations in the world of work not seriously deteriorated, it is doubtful that Albert would have felt it necessary to reiterate the self-evident axiom that the "journeyman can in no case mistreat the master, his wife, his family nor even the other journeymen." The lieutenant general enjoined his commissaires not to hesitate to send all disobedient journeymen to jail.[87]

---

[84]AN, Y 9479, 28 August 1776.

[85]See, for instance, AN, Y 13128, 18 May 1776, and Y 14561, 14 March 1776.

[86]Albert to Gillet, 19 March 1776, AN, Y 13728; Livre d'écrou, Grand Châtelet, Archives de la préfecture de police, A B/223, fols. 69 (14 April 1776), 79 (30 May 1776), and 92 (30 July 1776); AN, Y 11707, 27 April 1776; AN, Y 9479, 28 August 1776.

[87]Albert to Sirebeau and other commissaires, 19 March 1776, AN, Y 15666 and Y 15853[A]. There were of course stories of exemplary journeymen such as Mathieu Nicolas, a blacksmith who postponed his "own establishment" in order to run his master's shop—until his master got out of jail. AN, Y 14995, 1 April 1776. And there were instances of overwrought masters, outraged and confused by abolition, who took it out on their journeymen. See, for example, master butcher Thion's brutal assault on his journeyman Bouquil. AN, Y 13820, 1 April 1776.

Hardy detected, with relief, a franker and more stringent government position on the disorders arising from abolition. He reported that "prohibitions" against worker waywardness were posted in various quarters of the city, and he echoed a rumor that the king had ordered the journeymen to remain with their preemancipation masters for a full year.[88] The police had to increase patrols, even during the day, and call upon the French Guards for help in quelling disturbances. The Parlement commented ironically on the "contradiction" in Turgot's policy, "which promotes liberty and deploys constraint."[89]

The Difficulties of Practicing Liberty

Turgot and Albert were no less unprepared for the bureaucratic consequences of abolition than for its sociopsychological impact. They apparently had not thought out the problem of integrating ex-workers into the mainstream of production and distribution. It is hard to believe that they imagined that the invisible hand would somehow do the job for them. In any event they were not ready.[90] The clerks in Albert's office were stunned by "the infinity of persons who came to enroll with the goal of opening a business." Albert tried to slow things down, in part in order to develop administrative structures to deal with the new conditions and in part to forestall the commercial dislocation that massive journeyman desertion and a surge of new establishments were likely to cause. The lieutenant general's staff "rebuffed a great many of the applicants" on various pretexts, including the need for further information, evidence that the prospective tradesmen had "sufficient capital to form a solid business," and proof that they were not "stained with some dishonorable mark." Hardy heard that the police rejected candidates unable to post five hundred livres' bond "to serve as surety and guarantee of their engagements."[91] Jewish applicants were turned

[88]Hardy's journal, BN, MSS fr. 6682, pp. 191 (16 March 1776) and 194 (21 March 1776).

[89]"Remontrances sur le lit de justice du 12 mars 1776," 8–19 May 1776, in Flammermont, *Remontrances du Parlement de Paris*, 3:373–74. The guard had been called into action as early as the first week of February, when "rumors of imminent liberty" had caused "the greatest disorders on the trading floor of the central markets." Only the presence of the soldiers was said to prevent wholesale pillage. "Mémoire des fruitiers-orangers," BN, Coll. Joly 596, fol. 104.

[90]Hardy was astonished at Albert's failure to anticipate "the labyrinth of disputes" that abolition would occasion. "So badly put together," this reform could not last longer than three to six months, he predicted. Hardy's journal, BN, MSS fr. 6682, p. 192 (8 March 1776).

[91]Ibid., pp. 194 (21 March 1776) and 195 (23 March 1776). In the preamble to the February edict, Turgot had confidently written: "Nous ne craindrons pas non plus que l'affluence subite d'une multitude d'ouvriers nouveaux ruine les anciens et occasionne au commerce une secousse dangereuse." BN, Coll. Joly 462, fol. 259.

away, at least provisionally. Albert's liberalism had limits—he would not touch this controversial issue until he received explicit orders from Turgot.[92]

Whatever sort of gradual social and economic adjustments Turgot really may have had in mind, there is no doubt that most contemporaries, and not just impatient journeymen, interpreted the February edict as nothing less than the "elevation of the journeymen and the workers to the rank of Master."[93] Or they viewed it from the opposite vantage point, with the same practical results. Take the case of the Bertons, uncle and nephew, natives of Picardy, who worked as journeymen joiners. On the morrow of the publication of Turgot's edict, the nephew—and perhaps also the uncle, though this is not clear—abruptly left the employ of their master, Brizard. The nephew apparently went to work somewhere in the faubourg Saint-Antoine, perhaps on his own, and subsequently disappeared from view. In response to Brizard's complaint, and in conformity with Albert's hard line on overly impetuous journeymen, Police Inspector Bourgoin found Berton the elder and instructed him to "return" his nephew to Brizard's shop and sway. Retorted the uncle: "Since the passage of the new law, there are no more masters; it will take another law to get him to go back."[94]

It is easy to imagine the perplexity, frustration, and sense of betrayal that many journeymen and workers must have felt. Instead of being congratulated on their liberty and encouraged to exercise it, they found themselves treated as quasi-delinquents and would-be insurgents, subjected to intimidation and to the threat of incarceration. Instead of being welcomed into the milieu of commerce, they encountered delays, harassment, and unexpected requirements that seemed like tricks devised to fool them and deny them satisfaction. To both masters and workers, Turgot's language of nature seemed anything but simple, direct, "evident." It was in fact never Turgot's intention to forgo entirely the regulation of the world of work, but he had not made this clear.[95] Indeed, Turgot later hinted that his own downfall may have been hastened by disregard of rules and the erosion of order. He referred explicitly to the easy accessibility of "false keys"—a by-product of the proliferation of false work, his critics charged—that had led to an increased incidence

[92]Hardy's journal, BN, MSS fr. 6682, p. 194 (21 March 1776). Cf. Hardy's hint that the government planned to make money from abolition by selling the right to an état to eager Jews and Protestants. Ibid., p. 189 (14 March 1776).

[93]Soulavie, *Mémoires historiques et politiques*, 3:86–87.

[94]AN, Y 11496, 16 April 1776 (kindly communicated by Professor Y.-M. Bercé). Berton referred incorrectly to "l'arrest du conseil." He meant of course the February edict.

[95]Cf. Keeper of the Seals Miromesnil's promise that "this happy liberty" would be "moderated by wise regulations." Of course Miromesnil was one of Turgot's leading critics in the ministry; "Lit de justice," 12 March 1776, in Schelle, *Oeuvres de Turgot*, 5:276.

of household burglaries, one of the signs of anarchy the guildsmen had pointed to.[96]

The number of workers who tried setting up shop or succeeded at it is not known. I have not found the registration books opened up by the lieutenant general of police. Discreet hints of change spring up fortuitously in the police archives. A thirty-five-year-old journeyman carpenter named Martin Fournier now "worked for himself in a rented room." Mayenne was a journeyman wine merchant "running his own cabaret on the rue de la Jassienne."[97] I suspect that many workers established themselves without formal permission, as much because the rules were articulated so vaguely and so inaudibly at first as because they turned out to be somewhat draconian. Then there were journeymen such as Pierre Doucet, a locksmith, who hired other journeymen to work for him. It is extremely likely that Doucet began this practice well before abolition. He was a subcontractor who toiled for various masters. Given the considerable division of labor in most crafts, it is probable that a substantial number of journeymen worked in this murky (and illegal) role.[98] In my view there were already a vast number of workers operating illicitly in the faubourg Saint-Antoine, in the other privileged places, and even in underground ateliers in the city proper. The validation that the February edict conferred may have been psychologically and socially of capital importance, but it probably

---

[96]Turgot to Dupont, 20 July 1776, in Schelle, *Oeuvres de Turgot*, 5:500. Turgot's tone suggests that he may have regarded this as part of an orchestrated effort to discredit abolition. This conspiratorial view is not surprising—the year before, Turgot had ascribed the Flour War to a series of plots. See Kaplan, *Bread, Politics and Political Economy*, 2:447. An ordinance promulgated by the lieutenant general of police on 10 July 1776 offered amnesty and compensation to workers who turned in counterfeit keys and warned them of grave consequences if they were found in possession of such keys. In execution of this measure, the police conducted periodic inspection raids on workshops dealing with metals of any sort. They confiscated scores of keys and arraigned their possessors. Hardy's journal, BN, MSS fr. 6682, p. 251 (18 July 1776); sentence of lieutenant general of police, 15 November 1776, BN, F 23717 (311); AN, Y 9479, 15 November 1776; AN, Y 15386, 19 May 1776; AN, Y 11707, 10 May 1776; Bibliothèque de l'Arsenal (hereafter Arsenal), MS Bastille 12248, pièce 213 (15 July 1776). There were a large number of condemnations for theft using "false" keys, though a few of the crimes in question seem to have been committed before the February edict. Two of the convicted thieves, a chimney sweep named Chaumont (who had "thirty-one keys fashioned and designed for evil purposes" at the time of his arrest) and a turner named Lanoise, were hanged on the Grève. Several of the others, before consignment to the galleys, had to stand on public display wearing a sign "voleur avec fausses clefs." Sentence of 9 August 1776, BN, F 23717 (304); arrêt du Parlement, 25 April 1776, BN, F 23675 (643); arrêt du Parlement, 14 May 1776, BN, F 23675 (650); arrêt du Parlement, 8 August 1776, BN, F 23675 (667); arrêt du Parlement, 7 December 1776, BN, F 23675 (691); arrêt du Parlement, 10 December 1776, BN, F 23675 (692); AN, Y 14561, 9 May 1776; Hardy's journal, BN, MSS fr. 6682, p. 307 (17 December 1776).

[97]AN, Y 11708, 31 August 1776; AN, Y 11707, 7 April 1776.

[98]AN, Y 13128, 23 July 1776.

did not affect the way they did business, at least not in the short run. It would be awkward to count these false workers among the newly established; at most they stepped out of the closet. Others, such as the journeyman hatter pushing a cart containing his utensils and materials, set up in the street, where the constraints were very different.[99] These itinerant artisans and peddlers are as elusive as their comrades in fixed locations. Nor can I estimate how many newly established men and women dropped out rapidly, before the restoration of the guild system at the end of the summer. Even if one could count all the "*agrégés*" who joined the guilds for the first time in their lives in the fall of 1776, one would not have a very satisfactory measure of the resonance of abolition/emancipation.

Workers who continued to function as journeymen evinced no more sympathy for liberty than did their masters—at least insofar as it affected their "horizontal" relations. The right to work might be natural and sacred, but the journeymen were determined to keep control of *their* labor market. For the roofers and the masons, that meant excluding non-Parisian journeymen from the search for work at the hiring exchange on the Grève.[100]

Building New Structures and Dismantling Old

Although Albert dragged his feet on the recruitment of new tradesmen, he moved vigorously to implement Turgot's plan for the spatial organization and administration of the world of work now that the guilds no longer provided the structure. The idea was to divide Paris into "arrondissements" of work/commerce, each composed of approximately three hundred artisans and merchants of all types. The sooner the new lines were drawn and the new institutions erected, Albert reasoned, the safer would be the February reforms. Thus he pressed each commissaire to draft rapidly "the plan and the distribution of the arrondissements of your quarter." Each arrondissement was to comprise two or three cantons, in which electoral assemblies would be held.[101] Each arrondissement would have leaders (syndics and adjoints) to serve

[99]Cf. Métra, *Correspondance secrète*, 3:48 (20 April 1776).

[100]AN, Y 14825, 19 June 1776.

[101]In a preliminary version of the Palais Royal plan, for example, the quarter was divided into two arrondissements of two cantons (Palais Royal and Quinze Vingt; Tuileries and Butte Saint-Roch) and one of three cantons (Place Vendôme, Place de Louis XV, and le Roule). Albert to Sirebeau, 18 March 1776, AN, Y 15853[A] and Y 15666; Albert to Machurin, 18 March 1776, AN, Y 12626; Albert to Sirebeau, 9, 16 April 1776, AN, Y 15666; Collot to Sirebeau, 24 April 1776, AN, Y 15666; Hardy's journal, BN, MSS fr. 6682, p. 204 (14 April 1776); Albert to Gillet, 6, 25 April 1776, AN, Y 13728.

as liaisons with the municipal and royal authorities. (Strictly speaking, they would not "represent" the "interests" of the collectivities, since "particular interests" of any group were considered inimical to the general interest.) There is some indication that Albert would have liked some of the old corporate jurés to serve as syndics in order to confer a certain grass-roots legitimacy on the new organization. In any case, he asked his commissaires to recruit "bourgeois notables," which meant fewer artisans and more merchants and manufacturers. Albert flattered himself that he could "name them without their agreement [because] they cannot refuse me," but he allowed that "nevertheless he would prefer those who seemed to desire to fill the position."[102]

Few of the new divisions were definitively traced before Turgot's disgrace. The gardes and jurés of the abolished guilds delayed the elaboration of the new institution by failing to provide the fiscal rolls that the commissaires requested. The (former) leaders of the powerful mercers actually proposed that they continue to collect the capitation tax more or less as if nothing had changed. And according to Hardy, "almost all" the tradesmen in the new arrondissements refused to stand for the position of syndic despite police pressure—an overt gesture of defiance that enraged Turgot, who considered punishing them by suppressing the consular jurisdiction, the business court run by the merchants and artisans themselves and dominated by veterans of the Six Corps.[103]

Even as Albert fashioned the new structures, he rushed to dismantle the old. Hardy was shocked that the lieutenant general of police began the "disagreeable" task of sequestering and sealing guild property only hours after the lit de justice by which the government compelled parlementary registration of the February edict.[104] Commissaires and their clerks labored round the clock to cover the vast corporate space of the world of work, their haste apparently prompted by fears that the guild leaders would attempt to remove or conceal financial documents and property. Until the day of the lit de justice, most of the guild leaders seemed not to have believed that the abolition would really come to pass—at least not so brusquely and so completely. Few of them appeared to have taken steps to protect their corporate patrimony against royal expropriation. This may explain why a number of them angrily resisted the commissaires' sudden intrusion. To get the fruit sellers to allow him

---

[102]Albert to Gillet, 30 April 1776 and Collot to Gillet, 14 May 1776, AN, Y 13728.

[103]Albert to Sirebeau, 17 April 1776, AN, Y 15666; Hardy's journal, BN, MSS fr. 6682, pp. 201 (6 April 1776) and 215 (7 May 1776). Cf. Albert to Duchesne, 12 March 1776, AN, Y 15284.

[104]Hardy's journal, BN, MSS fr. 6682, p. 188 (12, 13 March 1776).

access, one commissaire had to use "military force"—investment by squads of guet and robe courte.[105]

The "sealing" commissaire took stock of every item in corporate headquarters. Thus the offices of the roofers contained, in the main room, thirty-seven chairs, a big table, curtains, a large painting of Christ, and a bust of Louis XV in bronze; in a smaller room, four chairs and three tables; in a room on the third floor, some objects in porcelain and pewter, a wall safe boasting twenty-two livres in cash, and a closet that stored all manner of corporate records (minutes of assemblies, debt and *rente* obligations, engagement of apprentices, reception of new masters, confrérie affairs, accounts of income and expenditure, police sentences, and royal legislation).[106] The commissaires paid particular attention to the corporate papers, in which the government was confident it would find overwhelming evidence of the "abuses" Turgot so harshly denounced.

Hardy hinted that the commissaires were more interested in stripping the guilds of their wealth and their dignity. Indeed, Albert gave special instructions for the confiscation of cash, silver, and confraternal ritual goods that were known to be valuable.[107] "They carried things too far," reported Hardy: they removed from the church of the Cordeliers du Grand Couvent the ritual objects belonging to the confrérie of one of the smaller guilds.[108] The police found substantial caches of money, but not always where they expected it. The mercers, "who passed for the richest guild," had only 4,500 livres, while the shoemakers, one of the poorest, yielded 6,675 livres, and the fan makers, another marginal guild, hoarded 10,555 livres.[109] Rouillé de l'Estang, treasurer of police

[105]Ibid., p. 188 (13 March 1776).

[106]AN, Y 13686, 12 March 1776. The same commissaire also sealed the papers of the crieurs de vieux fer, imprimeurs, amidonniers, bouquetières, potiers de terre, and papetiers. See also Y 13969, 12 March 1776 (faïenciers, horlogers, évantaillistes, patenôtiers-bouchonniers, oiseleurs); Y 14825, 12 March 1776 (couteliers, tourneurs en bois, bourreliers); Y 15284, 12–13 March 1776 (pain d'épiciers, maîtres à danser, vidangeurs, rubanniers, jardiniers); Y 14995, 12 March 1776 (boulangers, rôtissiers, lapidaires, brassiers); Y 15666, 12 March 1776 (maréchaux, menuisiers, vanniers, maîtres en fait d'armes, luthiers); Y 11964, 12 March 1776 (parfumeurs, chaudronniers, plombiers, tablettiers); Y 12626, 12 March 1776 (cordiers, fruitiers-orangers, limonadiers); Y 13278, 12 March 1776 (cordonniers, corroyeurs); Y 11593[A], 12 March 1776 (vinaigriers, selliers, boursiers); Y 15385, 13 March 1776 (batteurs d'or, sondeurs, merciers, plumassiers).

[107]Albert to Sirebeau and other commissaires, 16 March 1776, AN, 7 15853[A] and Y 15666. Albert expected that the commissaires would find "an immense quantity of useless papers in the guild offices." These dossiers were to be carted off for temporary storage (and eventual destruction? It is not clear whether the post-1776 corporations reclaimed their old archives) at a convent. The commissaires were instructed to examine and describe only papers concerning property and finances; Albert to Gillet, 16 March, 6 April 1776, AN, Y 13728.

[108]Hardy's journal, BN, MSS fr. 6682, p. 189 (14 March 1776).

[109]Hardy's journal, BN, MSS fr. 6682, p. 194 (24 March 1776); AN, Y 13278, 12 March

funds, became the receiver of corporate goods and money. He verified the accounting of the commissaires, suggested ways to uncover hidden corporate wealth, and took charge of dealing with the guilds' creditors. He also arranged for the cancellation of the leases on the guild offices, providing indemnities for landlords who could not find new tenants rapidly.[110]

Nothing brought home the reality of abolition more brutally than these confiscations and the public auctions that followed. Hardy once again was scandalized by what he considered the precipitousness of the sales of guild furniture and effects. He also had doubts about their honesty and their utility, for he learned that items of great value were sold for piddling prices. The dressmakers complained bitterly that their effects were sold for "a miserable price," but they had nothing of truly great value. But why should the fruit sellers have allowed an old-clothes dealer to buy their funeral pall, worth 13,000 livres, for a mere 700 livres? Did they fail to bid for it (as individuals acting clandestinely in the collective name of their former guild) because they were in utter disarray, because they were excluded from the auction, or because they somehow expected that the whole nightmare would soon be undone and the topsy-turvy world set aright? As it turned out, the hopes of these guildsmen were only partially satisfied, for even after the disgrace of Turgot and the re-creation of the gilds, the confiscation was maintained and the auctions ("where things were not sold but given away") continued.[111]

The police assigned "sworn experts" to appraise the houses owned by the guilds and to offer them for public sale. Notices were posted describing the property, indicating the estimated price, and setting the time of auction. In most cases the bidding seems to have been brisk and the sale price equal to or above the valuation. A house owned by the tailors, for example, was estimated at 38,660 livres. The bidding opened at 25,000 livres, but the property ultimately commanded 52,052 livres.

1776, and Y 13969, 12 March 1776. Another reputedly rich guild, the clockmakers had 13,868 livres. AN, Y 13969, 12 March 1776. Turgot and Albert counted on the seized documents to show just how badly managed the guilds were, especially in financial terms. A number of guilds made a point of contesting the liberal ministry on precisely this issue. The dressmakers, for instance, boasted of their excellent financial situation. They possessed a house of unspecified value, rentes amounting to 63,500 livres in principal, silverware worth 5,000 livres, and 17,000 livres in cash. Since they had no debts, they contended that there was no justice in the confiscation of all their property. BN, Coll. Joly 596, fol. 87.

[110]Albert to Sirebeau, 6 April 1776, AN, Y 15853^A; Rouillé to Gillet, 2 April 1776, AN, Y 13728; arrêt du conseil, 16 March 1776, AD XI 11.

[111]Hardy's journal, BN, MSS fr. 6682, pp. 217–18 (10 May 1776), 221 (17 May 1776), 232 (11 June 1776), and 287 (22 October 1776). BN, Coll. Joly 596, fol. 87. Cf. Lenoir's order for the sale of the mercers' effects, well after the reestablishment of the guilds. AN, Y 15385, 16 October 1776. The reestablishment edict called for the continued sale of corporate goods, yet in ambiguous terms it authorized the guilds to keep buildings necessary for offices.

Appraised at 34,500 livres, a house belonging to the hosiers sold for 51,500 livres. The only counterpoint: the masons' house was purchased for about 8,000 livres beneath the estimated value of 76,500 livres—a very expensive property.[112]

Albert also used abolition as an opportunity to right some of the alleged wrongs that the guilds had committed. The government wanted to celebrate publicly the end of corporate tyranny and to mock the vestiges of corporate arrogance. The lieutenant general of police encouraged false workers of various kinds to petition for the restitution of merchandise seized from them by guild jurés as long ago as 1773. Still reeling from the seizure of eighty-seven fans in July 1773, the widow Letuve asked for and obtained from Albert the return of these items (or presumably their equivalent value). An illicit fine turner ("the harshness of the times not having enabled him to become master in this guild") won the return of twenty-two dozen tobacco boxes. Albert quashed a 1773 seizure by the glove makers on the grounds that "it was nothing other than a form of persecution meant to hurt the supplicant."[113] Albert also helped a number of semimasters to break their corporate contracts. These were journeymen who had apparently fulfilled the requirements for mastership but had not yet completed their payments for admission when abolition occurred. They petitioned the lieutenant general for the return not only of their cash down payments but also of their promissory notes to remit the balance. Albert was happy to collaborate in this retrospective (and institutionally but not symbolically gratuitous) thinning of the guilds.[114]

Restoration cum Reform

I suspect that the news of Turgot's dismissal in May provoked the same sort of "joy" and "delirium" among masters as abolition had among workers. On 11 June Hardy noted a rumor that the ministry had ordered suspension of implementation of the February edict. A week later he announced that the police had stopped restitution of guild confiscations

---

[112]Arrêt du conseil, 20 April 1776, AN, AD XI 11; AN, Y 9509. Some of the guild houses were not sold until the 1780s.

[113]Letter of Albert, 2 April 1776, AN, Y 13969; petition of Millerat, 22 March 1776, AN, Y 11964; dossiers Mension and Gaboreau, AN, Y 11964. Cf. the quashing of a seizure effected by the upholsterers/furniture makers. AN, Y 9479, 23 March 1776.

[114]Albert to Sirebeau, 20 March 1776, AN, Y 15666. In the past, ambitious journeymen would have used any pretext to lay a claim to mastership. Now they looked for pretexts to deny their masterly status. See the case of Moers, who claimed that he was technically not a master because he had never sworn before the royal procurator. Albert to Sirebeau, 24 April 1776, AN, Y 15666.

and had halted the appraisal of corporate real estate. The word circulated that the government had named a commission "to consider the means of reestablishing the corps and communities of the arts and métiers in some other form." Among the members were said to be Séguier, passionate defender of the corporate idea; Sartine, the former lieutenant general of police who by and large shared Séguier's vision; and Moreau, the royal procurator of the Châtelet and special magistrate for the guilds, who knew the system better than any other official and who had stood to lose much of his administrative power and revenue as a result of their suppression. By mid-July the new lieutenant general of police, Lenoir, who had been fired by Turgot in 1775 for his hostility to liberal policy, passed the word to the old jurés that the guilds would soon be restored. He authorized them to begin talking discreetly among the elders to prepare for the future.[115]

Louis XVI promulgated the edict reestablishing guilds in August, sooner than generally expected. Reestablishment signified the reaffirmation of the traditional model of social classification and representation. The preamble openly acknowledged that the law was in large measure a response to the mémoires of the guilds and the remonstrances of the Parlement. The chief purpose of the edict was to undo the "confusion des états" wrought by the law of abolition. Corporate classification and social stratification were coterminous, even as corporate order and public order were synonymous. Society was composed of stratified groups, not atomized individuals. Corporate organization gave meaning to social existence and at the same time served as a bulwark of the political system. The edict reflected Séguier's worldview, but it specifically addressed the anxieties of the masters. Even if the ideal of mastership was inescapably tarnished, the fundamental relationship with the rest of the working world that it implied was reconsecrated. This relationship was a sociopolitical one before it was an economic one, and it was only indirectly linked with the sort of market forces that Turgot counted upon to differentiate and rank individuals. Relegitimizing the old hierarchy, the August edict pledged to reimpose "the internal discipline" overturned by abolition. To preserve the traditional social taxonomy, the law of reestablishment guaranteed "the domestic authority of the masters over their workers." It vindicated the guildsmen's argument that the one could not survive without the other.[116]

[115]Hardy's journal, BN, MSS fr. 6682, pp. 232 (11 June 1776), 236 (18 June 1776) and 249 (12 July 1776). It is an interesting measure of the perceived density of corporate implantation that as well-informed an observer as Hardy referred to the 300 (formerly) existing guilds. In fact they had certainly numbered fewer than 150. According to Edme Béuillet, there were 124 guilds in 1767; *Description historique de Paris* (Paris, 1779).

[116]"Edit portant modification de l'édit de février 1776 sur la suppression des jurandes," August 1776, Bibliothèque Historique de la Ville de Paris (hereafter BHVP), fichier lég-

Though the vocation of the August edict was to reinstitute the old social system, it is revealing that the government chose not to emphasize this ideological commitment. Instead, the law stressed the reformist aspects of the new guild system. The ministry did not wish to be portrayed either as retrograde or as the captive of special interests. Nor were the rationalization and the modernization of the guild system incompatible with the government's conservatism. In this sense perhaps the physiocrat Dupont was right when he wrote subsequently that the new guild regime was infused with Turgot's spirit.[117] The preamble of the August edict announced the government's resolve "to eradicate the abuses" in the old guilds that "stood in the way of the progress of the arts." Toward this end, the edict reduced the number of guilds to fifty by combining communities that had "analogy" among them and by refusing to resuscitate others, thereby rendering those professions "free" or open; it opened virtually all professions to women, though they could not participate in the political life of the "men's" guilds; it authorized persons to exercise more than one profession; it eased the road to upward mobility in the corporate world by reducing entry fees to a "moderate" level; it assumed all corporate debts and laid the groundwork for healthy financial management; and it maintained Turgot's suppression of all interguild litigation and took steps to limit future bickering.

Malaise of the Old Masters

The masters did not greet the reestablishment bill with unvarnished enthusiasm—not because it vaunted "progressive" reforms that menaced their interests, but because it perpetuated a regressive and familiar royal practice that cast a dark shadow across the Old Regime. The edict envisioned a tripartite recruitment of masters—or rather of masters and those assimilated to them. First, individuals who had profited from the brief intermezzo of liberty to enroll with the police in order to set up in trade would be allowed to continue exercising their profession in return for paying the government each year one-tenth of the fee now demanded

---

islatif. See also the Parlement's registration, AN, X^{IA} 8568, fols. 335–36. Beyond the preamble, in concrete terms one article (40) renewed the traditional regulations governing job entry and departure meant to give the masters control of the labor market, while another (43) forbade the journeymen to form any sort of association.

[117] Pierre-Samuel Dupont de Nemours, *Mémoire sur la vie et les ouvrages de Mr. Turgot* (Philadelphia, 1782), 2:220–21. The stewards of reestablishment were reformers, but not liberals. Thus the market principle would not be allowed to decide the rest. For example, the practice of advertising and publicly competing for clients that had quickly proliferated during the abolition period was suppressed again. Nor could goods be freely hawked in the streets. Arrêt du conseil, 3 December 1776, AN, AD XI 11.

for admission to the guild of that profession. Or they could choose to stand for mastership according to procedures to be stipulated by the guilds themselves within the very nebulous guidelines of the edict, which aimed only at prohibiting graft and extortion. Second were the old masters, but they did not automatically recover their places in the corporate world. They had to pay "confirmation" fees (one-fifth admission charges) or "reunion" fees (one-quarter or one-third of admission charges). If they refused to satisfy these financial requirements, the old masters entered the third stream. Like the "agrégés" of the first group, they would have the right to exercise their profession, but they "could not be admitted as masters in the new guilds . . . or participate in their advantages or privileges."

The August edict was "revolting" to many masters because it was a "vrai travail de finances," a "véritable édit bursal." Once again, the government managed to contaminate a reform enterprise with a fiscal ingredient. The opportunity seemed irresistible from the government's perspective: the masters would surely pay for something they wanted so ardently. The parlementary leadership had grave misgivings about approving a "fiscal law" that would further burden the public. Hardy compared "murmurs" registered against the edict in the cafés and public places of the capital to the "sensation" and "ferment" that the news of the restoration of the corvée triggered in the countryside.[118]

The edict put the masters in an untenable position. They could refuse incorporation as a matter of principle, but only at the price of "seeing themselves ruled and governed by the young people and the newcomers," as the senior members of the united guild of stocking makers, fur makers, and hatters phrased it.[119] The goldsmiths had escaped abolition because the government had not dared to allow trade in gold to operate without surveillance. But the August edict amalgamated the wire drawers to the goldsmiths' guild, which meant that the old masters would have to pay the confirmation and reunion fees. The goldsmiths noted ironically that payment was not nearly "as free and voluntary" as the edict proclaimed, for if the old masters failed to pay, the new masters would take control of the corporation, which had a proud tradition of independence and large financial resources. The leaders were indignant that 150 of the 400 old master goldsmiths, including some of the "wisest and

[118]Hardy's journal, BN, MSS fr. 6682, pp. 260–61 (16 August 1776), 264 (26 August 1776), and 267 (29 August 1776). Cf. Métra's scathing comment on the fiscal wrenching: "Toujours de petits moyens chez nous, et jamais du grand, du bon, ni du vrai"; *Correspondance secrète* 3:268 (24 August 1776).

[119]Hardy's journal, BN, MSS fr. 6682, p. 297 (19 November 1776). For the argument that reestablishment satisfied no one, see Pierre Vidal and Leon Duru, *Histoire de la corporation des marchands merciers* (Paris, 1911).

most experienced" members, would not be able to participate in the new guild because they could not afford the fee. The spokesmen proposed that the guild pay the fee for all the old masters, who would reimburse it over a five-year period. They also objected to the stipulation that only the wealthiest members—those who paid the highest "industry" tax— would have full political rights. Wealth alone, they cautioned, did not guarantee talent, honesty, and leadership capability.[120]

As for the new masters, the goldsmith chiefs felt not only that they should not be allowed immediate political equality with the veterans, but that they should not be automatically admitted to the guild upon mere payment of the fee specified in the August legislation. The goldsmiths sought a filtering process that would prevent "the advent of ignorance and cupidity" in the profession. A new master should be required to present a certificate of sponsorship testifying to his capacity and character from an old master so favorably disposed that he was ready to stand surety for his protégé. This plan would surely favor sons or nephews of old masters, but they could not count exclusively on nepotism to obtain their admission, for they would still be required to complete a masterpiece, the traditional corporate litmus test of excellence that had been so mercilessly stigmatized by the critics of guild life. The goldsmiths wanted to salvage the whole system of recruitment via apprenticeship that the August edict seemed implicitly to suppress. Officially, the goldsmiths' demands were rejected. It may be, however, that at the level of practice the reestablished guild managed to implement some de facto mechanism of selection.[121]

Delay was the tactic of most masters in the vague hope that the ministry might change the conditions during the three-month grace period it allowed the masters to make up their minds. Lieutenant General of Police Lenoir vigorously pressed the former guildsmen to pay and reclaim their rightful places. Wild rumors circulated, perhaps planted by the police, warning that the government might decide to require fees from everyone at a higher rate or that the agrégés from the former master class would have their shops shut down if they did not pay up. At the end of November, Hardy declared somewhat cryptically that guild leaders had

---

[120]Deliberations of goldsmiths, 11 December 1776, AN, KK 1353, fol. 45. The goldsmiths also worried about how "territorial" disputes between them and their traditional rivals (mercers, precious-stone setters, etc.) would now be resolved. They felt that the old system of litigation, despite its costs, had guaranteed their freedom of action. Ibid., fols. 38–39 (11 April 1776) and 50–51 (8 January 1777).

[121]Deliberations of goldsmiths, 11 December 1776, AN, KK 1353, fols. 45–59. The formula used to admit members to the reestablished guilds did not contain the word *master*—as if not to devalue the venerable epithet. It read "prêter serment pour parvenir à son admission." See AN, Y 9393, October, November, and December 1776.

obtained "an indefinite delay or extension" on the deadline for payment of the incorporation charges.[122] In February 1777, in order to "accommodate the desire" of many old masters "not to be excluded" from guild civic life and in order to enable the guilds to profit from the "experience" of these masters, the government announced that it would accept payments of fees until 1 July 1777, though those who paid after 1 April would have to wait a year until they could exercise full membership rights.[123]

Even as many individual masters delayed, most of the guilds took rapid institutional form in their new juridical incarnation. Old leaders acted speedily to prevent the new guild from falling into the hands of the new masters; veteran guildsmen representing different trades now merged into one corporation negotiated draft agreements on new statutes in order to deny the royal administration a pretext for imposing a peace-making and cramping constitution. The August edict prescribed a system of governance that excluded the bulk of the masters from the decision-making process and that was meant to stifle internal political debate.[124] Depending on the size of the guild, twenty-four or thirty-six deputies were "to represent the entire community" and "to obligate everyone" by their deliberations. The gardes or jurés were to be chosen among those who paid the highest royal taxes.[125] The controller general appointed a distinguished panel of three councillors of state and three masters of requests to oversee the corporate renaissance.[126]

The Old Habits of the New Six Corps

The Six Corps adopted a two-tiered strategy. While the individual guilds protested solemnly against the "prejudicial" aspects of the August edict, the Six Corps as a collective institution rushed to reclaim the commanding status that it had traditionally enjoyed in the corporate structure. Lieutenant General of Police Lenoir ceremoniously installed the reformed (in fact, expanded) Six Corps, praised their service to the

[122]Hardy's journal, BN, MSS fr. 6682, pp. 275 (23 September 1776), 292 (6 November 1776), and 300 (28 November 1776). On the administrative aspects of the reestablishment, see BN, Coll. Joly 1729, fols. 188–95.

[123]Arrêt du conseil, 27 February 1777, AN, AD XI 11.

[124]On corporate governance and politics during the eighteenth century, see Kaplan, "Character and Implications of Strife among Masters."

[125]August edict, BHVP; BN, Coll. Joly 1729, fol. 193. On the choice of deputies in the goldsmiths' guild, see deliberations, 19 November 1776, AN, KK 1353, fol. 45. For an acrimonious quarrel that grew out of the implementation of the new governing procedures, see BN, Coll. Joly 1732, fols. 36 ff. (Twenty-five wine merchants aligned against the "tyrannical" and "despotic" governing clique.)

[126]BN, Coll. Joly 1729, fol. 188.

public as a sort of commercial and moral Argus, and appointed thirty-eight gardes from their ranks to govern the Corps. The gardes then began a round of visits—protocolary, but also political—to the royal ministers and the leading magistrates of the parlement. The Six Corps expressed their gratitude for their resurrection and elicited from the authorities an effusive celebration of the merits of the corporate principle in general and of the Parisian guild ethos in particular. Louis XVI himself received the gardes at his levée and promised his protection.[127]

The Six Corps sought to profit from this outpouring of goodwill by settling their score with the Jews who had intruded into their commerce under the cover of abolition. Back in 1767 several Jewish merchants had tried to enter the Six Corps. The rationale for their action was a royal measure aiming to stimulate commerce by allowing foreigners to enter the corporate system. The gardes of the Six Corps did everything in their power to keep the Jews out. Jews were not authentic foreigners, the gardes contended. They were men without a country, pariahs without honor or roots. They were usurers, well poisoners, rapacious wasps who "slit open the wombs" of helpless bees "to suck out their honey." To admit a single Jew was to open the floodgates to the whole nation, for it was well known that all Jews worked together to gain control by "oblique and shadowy means." The only way to guarantee the prosperity of the state was to expel the Jews definitively, concluded the gardes of the Six Corps.[128]

Rebuffed in 1767, a number of Jews returned in 1776 in response to Turgot's edict. Despite the obstacles Albert placed in their way, a few Jewish merchants apparently succeeded in setting up in business. They were among the first to seek to guarantee their status in the reborn corporate world by paying the assimilation fees stipulated in the August edict. Even more sure of themselves than they had been in 1767, the gardes of the new Six Corps sounded the "alarm" against "this dishonoring and dangerous" prospect and threatened to resign collectively unless the government banned the Jews. The ousting of the Jews, who represented precisely the sort of social perversion and confusion that the guildsmen associated with liberty, would provide them with a sort of symbolic closure to Turgot's carnival. Lenoir pledged to do all he could to prevent Jewish admission.[129] A royal arrêt ruled in favor of the Six Corps, denying Israel Salom and three other Jewish merchants the

[127]Deliberations of the Six Corps, 12, 22 September 1776, AN, KK 1343, fols. 2, 3, 6.
[128]"Requête des marchands et negociants de Paris contre l'admission des Juifs," 1767, BN, Coll. Joly 425, fols. 300ff.
[129]Deliberations of the Six Corps, 12 September 1776, AN, KK 1343, fol. 2. Symbolically, Jew lovers and liberty lovers became one. The Jewish question seems to have been the Six Corps' overriding concern on the morrow of reestablishment. They spent a good bit of energy arguing among themselves over precedence. See, for instance, ibid., fol. 7.

right to join the reestablished mercers but allowing them "exceptionally" to continue trading in Paris for two more years.[130]

Privileged Work and False Work

The edict of August proposed a fourth channel of legitimation expressly reserved for the inhabitants of the faubourg Saint-Antoine and the other privileged places. Portrayed as a gift, it was in many ways a trap, for it required the faubouriens and the others to renounce their special status, whose ambiguity protected them against a welter of burdens and intrusions. Article 47 allowed them three months to enroll with the police as artisans or merchants. They would be assimilated to the nonguild agrégés—free to exercise their profession anywhere in Paris but obliged to pay an annual fee indefinitely and to submit to the jurisdiction of the guilds. If they did not take advantage of this benevolence, they could no longer exercise any commerce or profession practiced by the members of the reestablished guilds, even on their home ground. Certain to be legally contested by their seigneurial patrons, these strictures infuriated the tradesmen of the privileged places. The police had to reinforce security in the faubourg Saint-Antoine, where "the populace grew angry" at the idea of being treated like other Parisians.[131]

The effort to domesticate the workers of the privileged places bespoke a deep-seated preoccupation with "false work" that marked yet another line of continuity between the old corporate world and the new. Unincorporated (and now nonagrégé) work was dangerous because it took place outside the structures of classification and control. False work—usurped, sub rosa, defective—was precisely what the abolition law had validated; it could not be allowed to flourish even within its traditional redoubts in the reformed and streamlined corporate world of the future. Thus, in addition to attempting to integrate the privileged places, the August edict prohibited masters and agrégés from renting out their franchises or lending their names to *gens sans qualité* and forbade them to employ journeymen to work outside their shops without special permission from their guilds. Another article sternly reminded workers that they were barred from exercising on their own any corporate profession regardless of the circumstances.

Just before Christmas the government published a royal declaration that took note of the anger of the faubouriens and of their protectress,

[130]Arrêt du conseil, 7 February 1777, AN, AD XI 11.
[131]Hardy's journal, BN, MSS fr. 6682, pp. 301–2 (3 December 1776).

the abbesse-prieure, and offered them "new marks of protection."[132] The declaration reminded them that even in the old days their liberty of enterprise had been "hampered by constraints"—above all by the prohibition against transporting goods fabricated or processed in Saint-Antoine into the city proper. All such merchandise was subject to seizure by the guilds, which zealously patrolled the frontier. The government now proposed a way to avoid this pitfall. Faubouriens would henceforth be allowed to join the guilds at a reduced price, the king renouncing 50 percent of the fees that legally accrued to him. Saint-Antoine tradesmen who recoiled at this idea of total assimilation would still be required to enroll with the police and pay an annual fee if they wanted to continue to operate. These registered tradesmen could later profit from a sort of discount integration: after ten years, they could join the guilds without paying any part of the king's fees (which represented three-fourths of the admission price). Those faubouriens who took advantage of these opportunities would escape harassment from both government and guilds, the declaration promised. But it hinted that the price of rejection would be an intensified border control centrally coordinated by the police and not dependent on the caprices of individual guilds. The most recent historian of the faubourg claims that a large number of citizens opted for mastership after reestablishment. Yet there had always been a stream of guild entries; it is not clear that the pattern changed significantly after August 1776. I suspect that a large number of faubouriens not only rebuffed the guilds but also ran all the risks involved in refusing the immunities conferred by agrégé status.[133]

The August edict allowed for a fifth channel of legitimation. Certain professions were declared "free"—the practice of the trade was to be unmediated by any formal corporate structure. Yet just as Turgot planned to organize the atomized world of work for administrative purposes, so his successors imposed a quasi-corporate apparatus on the free trades. Each was to have a syndic and an adjoint. In order to enjoy the right to exercise the trade in question, one had to register with the syndic and pay him three livres for his trouble. The "free" syndics, like their guild counterparts, were to collect taxes and to conduct inspections to check on quality of merchandise and fabrication. Masters of forgotten professions that were neither incorporated nor expressly labeled free were apparently required to "adopt" an established profession, presumably one close to their own, and to follow its guidelines.[134]

[132]Royal declaration, 19 December 1776, AN, AD XI 11.
[133]Raymonde Monnier, *Le faubourg St.-Antoine, 1789–1815* (Paris, 1981), pp. 69–70.
[134]Arrêts du conseil, 4 November and 19 December 1776 and 6 February 1777, AN, AD XI 11; déclaration du roi, 19 December 1776 in *Recueil des règlemens pour les corps et communautés* (Paris, 1779), BN, 4° Z Le Senne 975.

After Carnival: From Lackeys to Slaves?

The restoration of the corporate taxonomy—and the end of Turgot's carnival—did not mean the spontaneous regeneration of discipline and obedience in the field of work. This world was no longer structurally and officially topsy-turvy—but that implied only a return to the old *norms*; it guaranteed nothing about practice. For it is important to remember that worker insubordination had been the most serious problem confronting the guilds (from their point of view) well before Turgot's rise to power.[135] It remained an acute problem until the second and final abolition of the guilds in 1791. Relations between masters and workers appear to have been particularly strained in the period following reestablishment, though more research is needed to confirm this appreciation. Anxious to reassert their authority, a number of guilds may have acted ponderously and provocatively toward their journeymen. Prominent in all the new corporate statutes were stern prescriptions of discipline meant to subordinate the journeymen by denying them any real freedom of action in the labor market. These measures were not new, but whereas in the past there had been considerable variation from guild to guild, now there was something like a collectively shared code that covered the whole world of work. Certain masters seem to have blamed the aberration of liberty on the workers, most of whom in fact did not directly benefit from it, and treated them vindictively. Most masters probably acted as if nothing had happened—a fiction of short-term therapeutic value but an illusion that blinded them to the need to adapt to changing circumstances. It would be far too dramatic to affirm that, for the workers, nothing could ever be the same after the world had been stood on its head. Not only did most workers not profit from abolition, but it is likely that many were barely touched by it. Still, there are indications that thousands of workers were indeed mobilized by the experience. Surely they drew lessons from it—about the system, about their rights, about their relations with their masters, about their future.

The bakers give us a glimpse of the postreestablishment ambience. According to the masters, the journeymen refused to accept the return to the status quo ante: "insubordinate, the journeymen claimed that they were somehow exempt from the dispositions prescribed by the old regulations." To "halt such disorder and recall the journeymen to their duty," they called upon the lieutenant general of police to reiterate the traditional disciplinary measures and to make examples by

---

[135]Kaplan, "Réflexions sur la police du monde du travail," pp. 26–72.

imprisoning refractory workers.[136] In virtually all the trades, one encounters journeymen who rebelled against the idea that the particulars of their relations with their masters were predetermined by statute and thus not open to negotiation. Nicolas Civilly, called the Picard, was arrested for defying his master, a locksmith named Pelletier. Joachim Canot, a journeyman mason, landed in jail for trying to launch a strike in his master's shop. The police imprisoned another mason, Joseph Dantrey, for causing "an uprising" in his shop and trying to "make the law to his master."[137]

Tensions flared in the united guild of bookbinders and papermakers because the journeymen bookbinders refused to accept the sixteen-hour workday of the papermakers, two hours more than they were accustomed to. They struck, backed by a collective treasury to assist needy comrades and to finance the return trip of provincial journeymen called to the capital to replace them. Their "insulting parades" in front of their masters' shops came to an end only when the lieutenant general of police broke their spirit and organization by arresting six leaders.[138] The following year the journeymen printers were faced with a new disciplinary code that seriously limited their freedom of action in the labor market. According to Hardy, it "assimilated their future, so to speak, to that of the Negroes in America by making them real slaves."[139]

Did something analogous to the "aristocratic reaction" occur in the resuscitated corporate world in the wake of the nightmare of Turgot's carnival? Was there a tightening of the screws beyond the standards habitually practiced, for both compensatory and prophylactic reasons? From treating workers as lackeys to treating them as slaves? Hardy's metaphor was surely overdrawn. But there is no doubt that the horror of abolition haunted the corporate world until the very end.

Afterthoughts

What was at stake in 1776?[140] For Turgot it was a question of overcoming the deadening thralldom of the past. France was a stalemated

---

[136]Ordinance of police, 8 November 1776, BHVP, fichier des sentences de police. Cf. the arrest of seven journeymen bakers "sans ouvrage, suspects, et rodeurs de nuit"; AN, Y 10628, 7 December 1776.

[137]AN, Y 10628, 25 October and 28 November 1776; AN, Y 13627, 10 March 1777. Cf. similar "cabals" in Versailles. Amelot to Lenoir, 21 August 1776, Arsenal, MSS Bastille 12448, pièces 117–20.

[138]AN, Y 12826, October 1776, and Y 9479, 18 October 1776; Hardy's journal, BN, MSS fr. 6682, p. 281 (11 October 1776). The "guiding light of the plot," according to the police, was the innkeeper Lidy. Himself a former bookbinder, Lidy organized meetings in his inn, fed and counseled the journeymen, and promised them credit during the strike. In the eyes of the masters, the strike presaged "the end of all subordination."

[139]Hardy's journal, BN, MSS fr. 6682, p. 407 (3 October 1777), pp. 421 (28 November 1777), 429 (19 December 1777), and 431 (22 December 1777).

[140]I am deeply indebted to Claude Grignon for challenging me on many of the points

society because it was out of harmony with natural law. It had to be freed from the deeply flawed systems of regulation and classification that stifled economic development and paralyzed social life. Turgot envisioned a vast enterprise of liberation that would sweep away many of the basic institutions and policies that had (mis)governed France for centuries. Society would be regenerated by founding it anew on the self-evident principles of natural law: the imprescriptible rights of property and liberty, from which derived the right to work.

The word reform is too frail to capture the seismic energy of Turgot's vision: it was a radical assault upon the elementary structures of the Old Regime. Even as his laissez-faire provisioning policy was predicated upon the repudiation of the old social compact in favor of a wholly new relationship between state and society, so his abolition of the guilds implied a wholly new way to classify society and to articulate social relations. Nor were these the only spheres subject to the liberal cure: Turgot's objects included the promotion of capitalist agriculture, major changes in fiscal policy, the suppression of most forms of monopoly, the extension of free trade to virtually all types of commerce, untrammeled exportation, a more absolute definition of property and a sharper demarcation between public and private sectors of activity than ever previously imagined, and the introduction of rational forms of political representation.

Turgot rightly regarded the abolition of the guilds as one of his most daring and significant strokes—for what it did intrinsically and for the way it prefigured a more sweeping reordering of social relations. And the guilds understandably felt that they faced Armageddon in a carnivalized nightmare. Their reaction was not overdrawn; there was surprisingly little hyperbole in their discourse. If they framed their peculiar sense of peril in ecumenical terms, it was not merely to flatter themselves. It was because they could not see themselves apart from analogous corporate groups that together constituted society and because they genuinely felt that the destiny of the entire social order was jeopardized.

Certainly the guilds were right to identify "Modern Philosophy" as the enemy. Modern philosophy—what I have called liberalism—was indeed toxic to virtually all traditional institutions and practices. That was what it was supposed to do, after all: this view is not a self-centered reading on the part of the masters. The guilds said aloud what many others entrenched in the Old Regime were slow to understand: that one could not apply liberalism selectively (a myopic view of self-interest that ensnared many "privileged" Frenchmen who flirted with certain kinds of reform); that modern philosophy was a blueprint for a new world and

---

that I consider in these "Afterthoughts." I am also grateful to Maurice Aymard for his suggestions concerning labor markets.

that it was fundamentally incompatible with traditional ideas; and that Turgot was therefore a truly dangerous leader.

The critical point is not for us to decide whether the values that the guilds said they espoused were morally or socially superior to the values associated with the liberals (individualism, egotism, brawling competition, unbuffered market arbitrage). Rather, we must acknowledge the profound differences between these two constellations of values—the drastic breach that separated them. Nor is the point to execrate Turgot's naturalization of capitalist social relations by rehabilitating the guilds. Rather, it is to note how the guilds apprehended this ideological challenge (which is interesting, inter alia, because it preceded any real technological mutation that might have made it, or made it appear, more irresistible and less brutal).

The fruit sellers were shrewd to invoke the most mobilizing social issue in the Old Regime, the subsistence question, and to link grain liberalism to anticorporate liberalism. Turgot himself made the connection in theoretical and political terms. The guilds could point to the socially devastating results of the freeing of the grain trade—the "liberal" decade of 1765–75 was the most turbulent in the long reign of Louis XV. The guilds identified themselves with the consumers in the epic battle between what I have called the marketplace and the market principle.[141] More than a physical site, the marketplace was the *idée force* of regulatory ideology. Marketplace meant surveillance and control for the sake of public order. In the provisioning trade, marketplace implied the domestication and moralization of commerce. In the realm of social relations, the corporate system was the extension or expression of marketplace: it classified and ordered, it domesticated and moralized. The market principle was utterly corrosive of the marketplace as physical location and as regulatory apparatus. It meant laissez-faire: freedom from control and surveillance. It stemmed from natural laws that were said to be anterior to all forms of social organization. It frankly vaunted self-interest as its calculus, without regard to moral or political factors, and it postulated an underlying harmony of interests through infinite self-adjustment. Defined as a principle, the market was elusive, everywhere and nowhere at once, unclassifiable and mobile.

In the provisioning trade, the market principle implied total liberty through the dismantling of the regulatory structures. In the domain of social relations, it implied the end of officially imposed classification and stratification. In both cases the market principle recognized the individual as the only social actor and the market as the only social mediator

---

[141]See Kaplan, *Provisioning Paris: Merchants and Millers in the Grain and Flour Trade during the Eighteenth Century* (Ithaca, 1984), chap. 1.

(save for certain highly circumscribed functions assigned to a largely spectator government). The defenders of the guilds, like the proponents of the policing of grain, believed that social organization should not be submerged in the market principle (as it is in most modern "market" societies). Rather, the allocation of social identity, like the distribution of food, should be determined by collectively shared values that found expression in the traditional institutions. From the vantage point of marketplace ideology, freeing individuals from the corporate system would have the same calamitous consequences as freeing the grain trade from the police system.

Nothing preoccupied masters more than the control of the labor market. It was at the core of their struggle against the journeymen. Yet it is crucial to understand that this soi-disant labor market was conceived by the masters—and qualified by the law—as a (labor) marketplace in the sense that I have used the term. Labor relations, in the broadest sense, were determined and regulated by the classification system. The labor marketplace cast the worker in a relationship of subjection to the master. It kept him under constant surveillance: the *livret*, which gradually took form during the Old Regime, was only the most prominent tool of a control apparatus that had nothing less than panoptic ambitions. The purely economic relationship between employer and employee was secondary to the political and social one. Otherwise job placement would escape from the grip of the marketplace. Vis-à-vis the masters' marketplace the journeymen were instinctive combat liberals. (For the masters, journeymen's insubordination was the metaphor and the harbinger of Turgot's liberalism.) Along with many individual masters who were avid to enhance their competitive commercial position, they wanted the market principle to govern placement—at least insofar as it implied the end of guild tutelage. During the course of the eighteenth century, the bolder the journeyman cabals against the labor marketplace (and the more frequent and brazen the treachery of self-regarding masters), the more strident became the rhetoric of repression and the more formal and elaborate became the corporate methods of regulation. The more often the hiring process fled the marketplace, the bulkier and more tentacular the marketplace tried to become.

From this viewpoint, Turgot's edict responded directly to the ardent wishes of many journeymen and wrought what many guildsmen dreaded most: it disestablished and dismantled the (labor) marketplace entirely and projected the market principle in its place. Distinctions would no longer be conferred and guaranteed by the corporate taxonomy. Instead, the market (principle) would "distinguish" according to a very different set of techniques and values. The guilds warned that the new system would victimize rather than benefit the workers, but their admonitions were not credible. The workers themselves did not get a real taste of liberty, or at least not a serious and sustained one, for Turgot became frightened by the specter of disorder and erected barriers to stem the liberal current that he himself had unleashed. Turgot seemed to conclude that, at least in the short run, competition was a less reliable policing instrument than regulation. Nor would many of the journeymen have been content with Turgot's market principle, even had he been willing to apply it fully, for there were serious limits to their liberalism. They were adamantly against the official labor marketplace, yet they were not ready to renounce their own labor marketplace rooted in the compagnonnage/confrérie network of inns and *rôleurs*. The evidence suggests that the official labor marketplace was never fully reestablished after 1776, despite herculean efforts on the part of many guilds, in part owing to deep currents of (symbiotic) subversion on both sides.

The masters, like the consumers, should not be reproached for failing to recognize that history was on the side of the market principle rather than the marketplace. It was hard to see this from inside. The liberals were astonishingly farsighted, but they suffered the weaknesses of their strengths. They were unable to envision, prepare for, and deal with the short term—the volatile transition period from an old regime of regulation and ascription to a new regime of laissez-faire and *débrouillez-vous*. They had no clear plan for mitigating the shock of liberty to the provisioning system or to social relations in the world of work. Nor did they have any reckoning of the social and political costs. The liberals were buoyed by a resolute conviction that what they were doing was inscribed in nature, that it was inexorable, and that the sooner it took place the quicker France would be reborn. Among their adversaries, the consumers have a far more heroic stature than the guildsmen. Even the historian who takes the guilds seriously is hard pressed to find them sympathetic. There is very little that can be called lofty in what they stood for; there is a good deal more that is lofty in what they stood against (but this does not necessarily redeem their motives). Yet I do not think that the corporate attack on modern philosophy, despite its pathetic futility, should be dismissed as narrow-minded and vain obstructionism.

The guildsmen were not master sociologists who had a dazzlingly clear understanding of their society. They were master tradesmen who had a more or less coherent vision of the world as they construed it. That construction or representation has been, in part, the subject of this essay. In reconstituting the corporate representation of reality, I have sought to draw a picture not of how the world was, in some intrinsic sense, but of how I believe the corporations saw it and wanted it. I have suggested that corporate classification and social stratification were coterminous—

in the eyes of the guildsmen and their partisans. By stratification I mean the system of differentiation and evaluation—the reification of the taxonomy—not some underlying ("true") reality. For the actors, social classification *was* social organization. For historians or sociologists interested in reconstructing the past, social classification is only one aspect of social organization, what one might tremulously call a "subjective" rather than an "objective" aspect. Social organization can no more be reduced to a taxonomy than the struggle between social groups can be portrayed as simply a competition between rival systems of classification. Obviously there are other elements at play that I have not treated here.

Classification and its representation are meant to be descriptions of reality. I have treated them as one reality, an important reality frequently neglected or derided. Yet it is worth noting that before (and after) becoming a system of relations, classification was a strategy more or less consciously played out by the actors to improve their position in society. In the *beaux discours* of the guilds on social classification, ideology and interest were interlocked. By and large the function of this ideology was not to veil the corporate interests, but to broadcast them, connect and correlate them, and make them not only credible to outsiders but also intelligible to the actors themselves. Corporate ideology was a defense of corporate interests. These interests were not simply material benefits. They constituted the totality of the social aspirations of the guildsmen.[142] Ideology was the articulation and orchestration of these interests. It was founded on assumptions about human nature, the fragility of the social fabric, the relation of social stratification and political rule. To view the corporate representation of the world as mere rationalization—to stop here as so many historians have done—is a crudely reductionist and jaundiced step that flattens and distorts the picture and makes it impossible to fathom corporate mentality. Still, the emphasis on representation must not obscure the fact that the guilds constituted, indivisibly, both a system of production, distribution, and consumption and a system of social classification. If the masters were fighting in 1776 for the preservation of their identity and the principles it was based on, they were also struggling to conserve their privileges and advantages, material and symbolic. Among other things, representation was rationalization of relations of domination and exploitation. The different levels of corporate interest (and corporate ideology) were inextricably entangled. Corporate discourse was a compound of conscious and unconscious motives, of sincere and disingenuous claims, of coded and transparent idioms, of particu-

---

[142]On the eighteenth-century notion of interests, see Albert Hirschman, *The Passions and the Interests* (Princeton, 1977), pp. 32 ff.

laristic and universalistic anxieties, of self-serving calculations on the one hand and more complex and ambiguous social and political solidarities on the other.

I have contended that the sociopolitical character of the corporate system preceded and shaped its economic vocation. This view is partly a reaction against the gross and reductionistic line of what the French call *économisme primaire* (which, incidentally, is not the appanage of Marxism). But have I weighted the balance too far in the opposite direction? While I think not, I recognize that the question may remain open to debate. To determine precisely what was at stake economically in 1776 would require an exhaustive inquiry guild by guild—or at least type of trade by type of trade. Laissez-faire did not menace cobblers and goldsmiths and blacksmiths and grocers in the same way. The "liberal" perspectives of the mercer—a supermerchant who did a lot of embellishing but virtually no fabricating—were different from those of a baker or a cabinetmaker or a builder or a hatter. Technological factors had little incidence on the working lives of most guildsmen, but they were decisive for a few métiers, especially in textile manufacture. One would also have to take into account the effect of changing fashions and expectations, the competitive challenge from rural society, other towns, and foreign countries, the facilities of transportation and communication, and so on. Economic factors may have mattered more for individual masters than for whole guilds or trades. Most guilds (and trades) were less cohesive economically than they were ideologically. Guilds with great disparities of activity (kinds of activity, not merely magnitude) among masters or with a particularly intensive division of labor could be expected to betray more ambivalence or harbor a wider range of opinion than others. It is possible that the guildsmen accentuated the noneconomic or supra-economic aspects because they realized, from their own shop experience or from observing their peers, not that their economic argument was wrong, but that it was patently vulnerable.

What can be said about the political implications of abolition (beyond the disgrace of Turgot)?[143] Politically and symbolically, the edict suggested an alignment that had served the monarchy well in its historical effort to impose the royal will. By (ostensibly) siding with the journeymen against their masters, the king seemingly cast his lot as he had done before—with the people and against privilege, with the citizenry and against "local" rulers, with a vilified social group (e.g., the bourgeoisie) and against a prestigious social group (e.g., the nobility).[144] Was the edict

[143]On Turgot's fall, see the sprightly but uneven study of Edgar Faure, *La disgrâce de Turgot* (Paris, 1961).
[144]The liberal king in this scenario is much different from the liberal king who freed

perceived by anyone in this way? It is hard to know how significant the association of Louis XVI with the new law was in the minds of journeymen ("Long live the king and liberty"). Deeply scarred by the hatred that the people had reserved for his predecessor, the new monarch said over and over that he wanted above all "to be loved." By linking the edict to the king, the journeymen seemed to want to legitimize their "febrile joy." Against this hopeful background, how brutal must have been the disappointment that rapidly ensued! For it became manifest by mid-March that Turgot had no intention of freeing journeymen in the way they had desired. If something resembling a journeyman royalism flowered in February, like journeyman liberalism it had severe limits.

For the masters, liberty and monarchy were incongruous and irreconcilable (at least in the intransigent terms of Turgot's liberalism). For the guilds, and the Parlement of Paris, this was the tragedy and the irony of the edict. Turgot's critics posed a problem that had more than circumstantial polemical significance: What was to be the relationship between monarchy and market (as opposed to marketplace) society? With the repudiation of the traditional system of classification, what were the new tools of distinction through which the king could impose social and political control? Abolition, along with the other February edicts, broadened and deepened the coalition of groups hostile to and fearful of liberalism. Traditionally the guilds had entertained an ambivalent relation with the throne. The king was their protector, in a sense their creator; at the same time, he was their despoiler. Now the parlementary line—its conception of the meaning of fundamental law, of the sanctity of the established taxonomy, of the inviolability of conventional property such as mastership, of the dynamics of the social order, of the accountability of kingship—seemed to offer a more attractive and a more kindred political refuge. As I have argued elsewhere, the stakes for the Parlement of Paris went considerably beyond the king baiting for which historians usually castigate the magistrates. For the majority of the Parlement, liberalism was no less the world stood on its head than it was for the guilds.

What was to be the new social foundation on which liberal monarchy would rest? Journeymen and Jews, the guildsmen might have jeered. As ominous as a horizon of untethered journeymen was, I think that the most dangerous immediate threat to the guilds, on the morrow of abolition, came from their own Jews. By "their Jews" I mean the masters within the guild system whose attitudes were changed by the brief liberal experiment, including faithful guildsmen never before tempted by apos-

---

the grain trade, abandoning his paternal responsibilities and favoring the grain merchant masters in the social relations of provisioning. See Kaplan, *Bread, Politics and Political Economy*, chaps. 4, 5, 8–10.

tasy as well as masters like Ménétra who had, for various reasons—political, economic, social, cultural—long chafed against corporate strictures and tutelage.[145] (And one should remember that there were Ménétras in the parlements too.) These were the masters for whom the breath of liberal fresh air was tonic or even exhilarating. By dragging their feet in various ways, these were the masters who helped prevent the guilds from becoming as strong and coherent after reestablishment as they had been before abolition. These were the masters who in their everyday lives bypassed the marketplace in favor of the market (principle).

This (inferred) internal realignment underscores how astonishingly little we know about the guilds after 1776.[146] In a formal or institutional sense, it is clear what was and what was not restored or reformed or both. But we do not know how reestablishment was *thought* and how it was *lived* by the masters. Were there any masters who really believed that the clock could be turned back? (The "should" question is something else again.) Sharp confrontations with journeymen impelled many masters to reaffirm their "guildness" in both subtle and obvious ways. Yet other masters seem to have felt that a dialogue with their workers was possible—outside corporate space. The *apparently* tepid reaction of many (perhaps most) masters to the d'Allarde law of 1791 suggests not only that such a measure was hardly surprising after the liquidation of all the other bastions of the old social system, but perhaps also that the guilds no longer mattered (at least as they were then constituted and as they then functioned) to large numbers of masters. Perhaps by the eighties the guilds already were no longer seen (by many of their own members) as critical social institutions but were considered mere mediating institutions, officious government agencies. If the guilds remained of any real significance to masters by the time of the Revolution, I suspect that it was largely as engines of the police of work.

This speculation highlights the need for research and reassessment. It is time, in France, to put aside the terrible stigma of Vichy (itself an inviting subject for reflection) and (re)engage the history of the corporate experience from the Middle Ages through the present time (for our own world is rife with slightly *honteux* neocorporatism). It is time to venture a history of "corporate" work as historians have brilliantly treated the peasants, the land, certain cities, certain ideas. Outside France as well as within, it is time to abandon the Manichean reading of the eighteenth century—the self-indulgent dichotomy between good guys (the

[145]Ménétra, *Journal de ma vie*, p. 244 and passim.

[146]I do not mean to suggest that our knowledge of the guilds before 1776 is satisfactory. Far from it, for reasons that have only partly to do with the paucity of sources. See the opening remarks of Kaplan, "Character and Implications of Strife among Masters."

party of humanity-cum-modernization) and the bad (a long, black list of social groups and institutions that includes the guilds). At issue here is not value judgment, but method. It is perfectly unobjectionable to be on the side of the winners, but it is not justifiable to use their press releases as the epitaphs of the losers.

—7—

The Alphabetical Order:
Work in Diderot's Encyclopédie

CYNTHIA J. KOEPP

Introduction

There were a number of ways to order the cosmos in eighteenth-century France—perhaps too many. Although somewhat anachronistic, the ideal and ancient structure of the three estates provided one optic through which to view and organize society. This trinitarian scheme of clergy, noble, and third estate[1] (or, according to the classical mode, orator, bellator, laborator) predicated itself on function: the first estate prayed, the second estate waged war and provided protection, the third estate worked to support itself and the rest of society. In theory, these three categories were all complementary: together they formed a unity that was both hierarchical and organic, in which each was to serve the

---

[1] The tripartite division of society has been a subject of study for numerous scholars. Georges Dumézil, in *L'idéologie tripartite des Indo-Européens* (Brussels, 1958), was one of the first to trace the three-part division back to its Indo-European roots. Using ethnographic, sociological, and philosophical research and methods, he systematically laid out the tripartite ideology shaping social distinctions, theology, and mythology from India to Greece to Ireland. In *Les trois ordres ou l'imaginaire du féodalisme* (Paris, 1978), Georges Duby emphasized the ideological and idealized aspects of the tripartite system as he attempted to discover exactly when the structure was articulated in northern France and what conjuncture of economic, political, and cultural organization was present when it appeared. While recognizing the alleged universality of the three-part divisions throughout the world, Roland Mousnier, in his study of the three estates in France, concluded that canon law and the hierarchy of the Roman Catholic church greatly influenced the organization of orders and institutions in the Old Regime. See "Les concepts d'ordres, d'états, de fidelité et de monarchie absolu en France de la fin du XVe siècle a la fin du XVIIIe," *Revue historique* 247 (1972): 289–312.

needs of society and each other.[2] The ideal of the three orders stood as comprehensive; that is, it purported to account, in a general way, for all the groups and activities in society.

Numerous corresponding formal and informal institutions existed alongside the ideal of the three orders, giving specificity to the myriad facets of religious, social, political, and economic life. Medieval canon-law texts, for example, defined the ecclesiatical orders, describing with careful nuance the functions, duties, and dignities of the various ranks of churchmen and churchwomen. Large theological questions were "ordered," as was a morality—one predicated on the belief that appropriate moral behavior was not universal but depended upon one's precise place in society. Virtue should mean one thing to a nobleman, something else to a small shopkeeper.

The nobility itself, although constituting a single "état," was also divided by exact gradations of title from simple nobles to princes of the blood, each rank conferring specific rights and responsibilities, a code of conduct, and an elaborate system of social etiquette. At all levels of society, a complex understanding of expectations and a recognition of one's place mediated interaction and exchange.

The temporal order was similarly predictable and established. The daily church offices provided one clock, the rising and setting of the sun another. Religious feast days throughout the year were "high" or "low" depending upon the importance of the saint or event celebrated, while the growing season enforced its own rhythm of work schedules, family life, and festivities.

Corporate organizations of workers dictated the details of production, the workplace, and the workday and maintained rigid hierarchical distinctions among masters, journeymen, and apprentices. In addition, sometimes tacit, sometimes clearly articulated (though not always uncontested) notions of hierarchy among métiers insisted that all forms of manual work were not themselves of equal value. The status and privilege of a clockmaker, for example, put him well above, say, a *patissier*, while the day laborer would surely find himself at the bottom—except when compared to a lowly vagrant or criminal vagabond.[3]

---

[2]For a careful discussion of the various meanings and shades of meaning of "état," "ordre," and "corps," see William H. Sewell, "Etat, Corps and Ordre: Some Notes on the Social Vocabulary of the French Old Regime," in *Sozialgeschichte heute: Festschrift für Hans Rosenberg zum 70. Geburtstag*, ed. Hans-Ulrich Wehler (Göttingen, 1974), pp. 49–68.

[3]As William H. Sewell has noted, Charles Loyseau, a prominent seventeenth-century jurist, "attempted to arrange all the metiers or professions of the Third Estate into a hierarchy. But he was not sure of himself, and frequently hedged his statements with qualifiers:'à mon avis' [in my opinion],'quoi qu'il en soit' [be that as it may]. . . . The problem is that unlike the secular orders of the clergy or degrees of nobility, the various métiers of the Tiers Etat presented no indisputable criteria for ranking." Sewell, "Etat, Corps and Ordre," p. 63. Steven L. Kaplan explores guild rivalries within the luxury trades—for

During the eighteenth century another detailed expression of hier-archical society—the Great Chain of Being—resonated with traditional orders and the organization of church, work, politics, and society. Al-though ultimately undermining man's belief in his privileged position in the universe, the Great Chain of Being at the same time affirmed the idea of ascribed, inherited status. Every being had its own place on the continuum; man's duty consisted in fulfilling his responsibilities and staying put. To have ambitions or pretensions to higher levels, to strive for loftier social status, meant subverting the natural and divine order of the universe.[4]

These various schemes, concepts, and institutions, expressing a basi-cally static but highly articulated hierarchical vision of society, did not go unchallenged during the Old Regime. The ideal of the three orders was exactly that: an ideal. Actual society proved less easy to describe or control. Potentially crucial practical distinctions between the second and third estates, for example, were to some extent blurred and conflated. As early as the fifteenth century a very wealthy bourgeois could aspire to the ranks of the nobility—attesting to a certain fluidity between the two orders—although actually achieving noble status might take his family several generations. In addition, from the sixteenth century on, the nobility's claim to privilege by virtue of its military functions came in-creasingly into question as the nature of warfare and politics changed.[5]

In another realm, science as an ordering system described the physical universe in terms of laws, motions, and mathematics, beginning to pro-vide rational and logical explanations where religious and traditional beliefs had once sufficed. As a form of knowledge, science displaced metaphysical concerns about the nature of God by focusing attention on the external world. This new confidence in the orderliness of the physical universe extended beyond the initial purview of the natural sciences, so that methods of scientific inquiry and explanation were ap-plied to all branches of knowledge, in hopes that history, ethics, the economy, and politics could ultimately be reduced to a few simple, uni-form laws that any reasonable person could comprehend.[6]

Seeming to threaten the implicit social structure even more directly

---

example, the contempt of the goldsmith for the clockmaker. See "The Luxury Guilds in Paris in the Eighteenth Century," in *Sonderdruck aus Francia: Forschungen zur westeuropaischen Geschichte* 9 (1982): 257–98, esp. pp. 276–77.

[4]See Arthur O. Lovejoy, *The Great Chain of Being* (Cambridge, 1971), pp. 186–207.

[5]See Guy Richard, *Noblesse d'affairs au XVIIIe siècle* (Paris, 1974), and Davis Bitton, *The French Nobility in Crisis, 1560–1640* (Stanford, 1969).

[6]See Charles Coulston Gillispie, *The Edge of Objectivity* (Princeton, 1960), for an analysis of science before and during the Enlightenment. See also Keith Michael Baker, *Condorcet: From Natural Philosophy to Social Mathematics* (Chicago, 1975), especially chapter 4, for a discussion of the way the Newtonian model of science was applied to moral and political realms during the eighteenth century.

were emerging theories and practices of political economy. Mercantilism in the seventeenth century frightened some nobles, who saw it as wiping away their privileges and distinctions, destroying established morals, and promising increased political centralization.[7] Physiocracy, by advocating free-trade policies, the right to work, and the primacy of agriculture, challenged guild structures, which were perceived as corrupt and closed monopolies. And early capitalism, as it generated new forms of wealth, sharper notions of property, and a new theory of the social individual, further weakened traditional societal divisions.[8] Nobles, clergy—indeed all idle and nonproductive members of society—gradually began to lose legitimacy.

Thus alternative ways of "ordering" society, which stressed laws—whether of nature, the economy, or politics—disrupted, contradicted, and even began to displace traditional institutions and beliefs, many of them inherited from feudal times. As a result, a society of ascribed, inherited status seemed to be losing out to one in which individual effort and achievement could make a difference. For the first time, higher social status was worth striving for—indeed, worth *working* for.

Hierarchical and Alphabetical Orders

But by the eighteenth century another new way of ordering, and yet to our eyes perhaps one of the least obvious, had gained currency: a conception of nature and society structured by the alphabet and presented in its most ambitious form in the *Encyclopédie* of Diderot and d'Alembert. Alphabetical order, to a late twentieth-century reader, likely seems a commonplace and a given, not arbitrary or even consequential—

[7]See Lionel Rothkrug, *Opposition to Louis XIV: The Political and Social Origins of the French Enlightenment* (Princeton, 1965), pp. 110–16. See also Richard, *Noblesse d'affairs*, for information on the edicts and declarations issued periodically by the French monarchy from the early seventeenth century on, trying to lure the nobility into commerce and trade.

[8]Neither mercantilist theories nor physiocracy fully recognized what we would now call a labor theory of value. Mercantilist statesmen and writers believed that trade was the originator of economic activity and thus the mainspring of the accumulation of wealth. For them the basic object of foreign trade was to increase the "inflow" of precious metals, the result of an excess of exports over imports. Physiocrats discarded the mercantilists' emphasis on trade and instead searched for the surplus of goods produced over goods consumed. The surplus they regarded as a gift, attributable not to the productivity of labor, but rather to the productivity of nature. But insofar as mercantilists insisted upon importing cheap raw materials and exporting more expensive finished goods, they depended heavily upon labor to make this transformation. Physiocracy, too, required human labor to bring forth nature's bounty. In this sense the consequences of these economic theories (from the point of view of the worker or the state) were similar to those of capitalism, even if they did not explicitly conceive of labor as the real measure of exchange value for all commodities.

and certainly not revolutionary—just a convenient way to find a name in the telephone book or make up a class list. But we should not underestimate the alphabet as an organizing force, nor its potential for social change.[9]

To be sure, alphabetical order has no real connection with the information it catalogs; it is merely an arbitrary sequence existing only in language—and in a language that is more often printed (or at least written) than spoken. It is this "ordering" of knowledge, especially knowledge of the arts and crafts, that I intend to investigate here: the efforts of the encyclopedists to translate a more or less illiterate "world of work" into printed words, ordered by the alphabet.

The alphabet was not new in 1750 or even 1700, but it was being put to new purposes. Alphabetical dictionaries of a sort had existed for two centuries, but they were often merely bilingual word books, or catalogs of words, lists to aid spelling and vocabulary, sometimes without definitions. By the eighteenth century, however, with the progressive augmentation of their contents and the growing complexity of their techniques and ambitions, these catalogs had become full-fledged dictionaries of language as we know them, with definitions, grammars, etymologies, pronunciation keys, and historical examples.[10] Developing at the same time and out of the same sources as these *dictionnaires de mots* were *dictionnaires de choses*[11] or, more properly, encyclopedias—of

[9]Michel Foucault states that a passage in a short story by Borges describing the humorous and unexpected juxtapositions and orderings in an imaginary Chinese encyclopedia first gave him the idea of questioning the implications of the categories and orderings of language. See Michel Foucault, *The Order of Things* (New York, 1970), pp. xv–xxiv. Whether a link between alphabetical ordering and social change obtains in the East is another question. There have been many claims that the unwieldliness of Chinese characters and the lack of a manageable alphabet may partially explain why the very advanced Chinese civilization was slow to make the kinds of scientific and technological progress found in the West. However, recent scholarship shows that the Chinese did make substantial progress in science, but because it did not take the same form as the scientific revolution in the West, Western scholars did not recognize it. In addition, the last major encyclopedia was compiled by the Chinese near the time of Diderot's, and it is as rational in its internal organization and as easy to use as the French one. See Lionel Giles, *An Alphabetical Index to the Chinese Encyclopedia* (London, 1911), and N. Sivin, "Why the Scientific Revolution Did Not Take Place in China—Or Didn't It?" *Chinese Science* 5 (1982): 45–66. I am grateful to Nathan Sivin for the last two references. I should also acknowledge that Michel Foucault's work on "orders of discourse" first led me to explore the various ways of ordering knowledge and society (in eighteenth-century France) as social and discursive practices that allow certain kinds of questions to be raised while disallowing others.

[10]See B. Quemade, *Les dictionnaires du français moderne, 1539–1863*, (Paris, 1968), pp. 76–77.

[11]Ibid., p. 88. I should add that this gradual move to alphabetize information was not universally welcomed. In 1726, for example, numerous critics accused Philippe Le Cerf of having committed a "grave faute" for organizing his study of the history of the abbey of Saint-Maur according to alphabetical order instead of following the "more natural" chronological order. See J. Fr. Michaud, *Biographie universelle: Ancienne et moderne*, 45 vols. (Paris, 1854), 23:515.

morals, religion, and philosophy, commerce and politics, history and famous men, science and nature, and jurisprudence and police.

By our contemporary standards, the early encyclopedias seem arbitrary and exclusive, curious examples of intended but unachieved completeness. Often purporting to be comprehensive and systematic, they instead fascinate and frustrate the modern scholar by their omissions and lack of predictability. As historians, we need to develop ways of reading such sources that will enable us to uncover implicit notions of work in unexpected places. The Abbé Jacquin's dictionary of morals, *Des préjugés*, for example, expresses few attitudes toward work under such likely entries as "labeur" or "travail," but, surprisingly, we find indirect clues in the article "café" which reads: "Since the establishment of cafés, society has become more refined, the morals more decent, drunkenness less common. More people know how to think, to speak, and have good taste."[12] The Abbé thus implies that leisure is more conducive to good morals and polite society than is labor, offering an eighteenth-century version of the classical Greek notion of the necessary connection between leisure and virtue.[13] Desessarts, in his guide to keeping public order entitled *Dictionnaire universel de police*, discusses "aigrefin" (swindler) and refers the reader to other related terms including the entry "vagabond."[14] Unfortunately his last completed volume, number seven, ends with "police." Universality in this case excludes words beginning with the letters *q* through *z*. Savary des Bruslons's impressive *Dictionnaire universel de commerce, d'histoire naturelle, et des arts et métiers* of 1723, the first work of its kind to appear in Europe,[15] was criticized even during the eighteenth century for neglecting to develop general principles of economy and for ignoring such basic subjects as agriculture, luxury trades, manufacturing, and population.[16]

---

[12]L'Abbé Jacquin, *Des préjugés* (Paris, 1760), p. 89.

[13]In the classical texts of Plato, Aristotle, and Cicero, among others, virtue was dissociated from work, especially from manual labor. Leisure, not work, was thought necessary for the development of virtue, for it allowed the mind to be contemplative, without the distraction of physical activity or humble servitude. Both Plato and Aristotle excluded artisans from citizenship in their ideal commonwealths. In *The Laws* Plato states that citizens should be prevented from engaging in industry or trade, pursuing a craft, or promoting a business. Aristotle echoes the same sentiments in *The Politics*. Although this classical notion of virtue was not unchallenged in the Old Regime, a number of eighteenth-century authors defending traditional societal divisions made the same claims against work as the writers of antiquity.

[14]Desessarts (Nicolas-Toussaint Lemoyne), *Dictionnaire universel de police* (Paris, 1786–90).

[15]See Institut National d'Etudes Demographiques (INED), *Economie et population: Les doctrines françaises avant 1800*, cahier no. 28 (Paris, 1956), p. 587.

[16]The universal dictionary of Savary des Bruslons and his brother was criticized both by l'Abbé Morellet in his *Prospectus d'un nouveau dictionnaire de commerce* (Paris, 1769) and by Denis Diderot in his prospectus to the *Encyclopédie* (1750).

Going through these potentially rich texts, one begins to entertain fundamental questions about the organization and systematization of knowledge at this moment of Western culture, and about the consequences that specific organizations might engender. What are the effects, say, on morals, the economy, the arts and crafts, or whatever, of arranging a reference book by the conventional and arbitrary order of the alphabet? One historian, speaking of the first 150 years following the invention of the printing press, has recently remarked that "editorial decisions made by early printers with regard to layout and presentation probably helped to reorganize the thinking of readers." She continues: "The thoughts of readers are guided by the way the contents of a book are arranged and presented. Basic changes in format might well lead to changes in thought patterns."[17] One of the changes in format was, of course, a new reliance on alphabetical ordering, which so handily served the needs of the printers. But the alphabet, by the eighteenth century, was more than a conventional ordering device of the printer; it had begun to impose an order of its own.

Unlike the dictionnaires encyclopédiques mentioned above, which often restricted themselves to specific areas or aspects of society, the goal of the *Encyclopédie* was far more ambitious: to try to make what was known on every topic accessible to the educated Frenchman. As Diderot explains: "The objective of the Encyclopédie is to assemble all the knowledge scattered over the surface of the earth: to set forth its general system for those with whom we live and to transmit it to those who will come after us, so that the work of the past centuries will not have been useless for those who follow."[18] This aim put great demands upon the editors, for as Diderot notes, "one article left out of a common dictionary renders it only imperfect. In an encyclopedia such an omission breaks the chain, and damages both the form and the content."[19] But in addition to collecting as many facts (or links of the chain) as possible, the editors' second task was to arrange them "in the most natural order."[20] The order to which d'Alembert refers is not alphabetical, but rather is one adapted from Francis Bacon, based on hierarchical values. In 1750 Diderot's prospectus to the *Encyclopédie* appeared, outlining in great detail the goals and plans for the forthcoming volumes. Bacon's tree of knowl-

---

[17]Elizabeth Eisenstein, *The Printing Press as an Agent of Change: Communication and Cultural Transformation in Early Modern Europe* (Cambridge, 1979), pp. 88–89. See also Roger Chartier, "L'ancien régime typographique: Réflexions sur quelques travaux récents," *Annales E.S.C.* 36 (1981): 191–209.

[18]"Encyclopédie," in *Encyclopédie, ou Dictionnaire raisonné des sciences, des arts et des métiers,* 17 vol. (Paris, 1751–72), 5:635. All subsequent references to entries in the *Encyclopédie* come from the first edition.

[19]"Prospectus" to *Encyclopédie,* 1:xxxv.

[20]"Discours préliminaire" to *Encyclopédie,* l:vii.

edge, a systematic organization of all the "branches" of learning, would form the philosophical foundation and principle of the entire work.

One year later the first volume of the *Encyclopédie* was published. It opened with a lengthy "Preliminary Discourse" by d'Alembert, which incorporated much of Diderot's original prospectus. In addition to offering an apologia for the low status of the artisan, d'Alembert also reiterated Bacon's system, in which all human knowledge was classified and ranked according to the mental faculty brought into play by its pursuit—either memory, reason, or imagination. According to Bacon these three faculties were connected to three general divisions within human knowledge: history, philosophy, and poetry. Much of the "Preliminary Discourse" attempted to explain and to justify these divisions as well as the hierarchical arrangements within them.

Following the text of the "Preliminary Discourse," the editors inserted a visual representation (or adaptation) of Bacon's system, printed on a page that folded out to form a huge chart. This table, grandly entitled the "système figuré des connoissances humaines," spatially represented the relationships existing among the various branches of knowledge and human activities.[21] The editors formed three columns: under the category "History" they ranked all the forms of knowledge related to memory; under "Philosophy" all that they deemed manifestly dependent upon reason; and under "Poetry" all those things thought to be a product of the imagination. Everything was arranged hierarchically, depending upon its perceived importance. To say the least, such a visual document reveals many of the prejudices and values of its designers.

If one studies this chart and reads down the list of the three spheres of knowledge, under "Mémoire" (History) one eventually comes to "Arts. Métiers. Manufactures."[22] I say "eventually," for one must first get through sacred, ecclesiastical, and secular history, literary history, astronomy, the history of animals, vegetables, and minerals, and finally, nature's aberrations ("vegetaux monstreux," "animaux monstreux," and so on).[23] Only then follows a ranked listing of the various professions within the mechanical arts. Starting with the most honored, namely gold- and silver-smithing, it then moves down through the occupations that work with precious stones, iron, glass, leather, stone and plaster, silk, wool—while leaving a simple "etc." to indicate all the more lowly forms of employment. After the substantial "Preliminary Discourse" and the impressive

---

[21]"Système figuré," in *Encyclopédie*, 1:lii.

[22]Ibid.

[23]For a suggestive discussion on the possible significance of ranking the arts and métiers immediately after "nature's aberrations," see Jacques Proust, "L'article *Bas de Diderot," in *Langue et langages de Leibniz à l'Encyclopédie*, ed. Michele Duchet and Michele Jalley (Paris, 1977), pp. 245–72, esp. 269–71.

table laying out "all" the various levels of human activities and knowledge, the *Encyclopédie* proper finally begins. From then on alphabetical order takes over.

Indeed, after reading through the long opening statement and chart explaining Bacon's system of knowledge, a reader might have been surprised to find the rest of the *Encyclopédie* "disordered" by the alphabet, with no care given to grouping related articles together. The tree of knowledge looks more like a pile of leaves.

And there is much evidence to suggest that the editors themselves saw the discontinuity between theory and practice and were uncomfortable with it. In the more metadiscursive or self-referential articles we often find them trying to justify their decision to use alphabetical order. They do so first, of course, on the basis of convenience.[24] And second, as Diderot patiently points out in his article entitled "Encyclopédie,"[25] the *renvois* (cross-references) at the ends of the articles allow the readers to make for themselves the connections necessary to comprehend the organization of knowledge as a whole.[26]

The *Encyclopédie*, then, is organized by two very different types of ordering: a philosophically justified hierarchical one and a conventional alphabetical one. But how well do these two types of ordering fit together? Do they undermine or substantiate each other? And how are we to assess the place or picture of work they offer?

To compare the table of knowledge offered by d'Alembert with other great efforts at systematization—the ideal order of the three estates, for example—is to notice striking similarities. From the treatises of the sixteenth- and seventeenth-century jurists to the late eighteenth-century apologists for the tripartite ideal, certain patterns and attitudes repeat themselves, conforming to the list under "Mémoire" in d'Alembert's table.

In general, these apologists[27] begin by describing the clergy, and then

---

[24]Regarding alphabetical order, Diderot writes: "We believe we have had good reason to follow alphabetical order in this work. . . . If we had treated each science separately and followed it with a discussion conforming to the order of ideas, rather than that of words, then the form of this work would have been even less convenient for the majority of our readers, who would have been able to find nothing without difficulty." See "Prospectus" to *Encyclopédie*, 1:xxxvi.

[25]"Encyclopédie," in *Encyclopédie*, 5:642.

[26]For interesting commentaries on the system of cross-references (*renvois*), see James Creech, " 'Chasing after Advances': Diderot's Article 'Encyclopédie,' " *Yale French Studies* 63 (1982): 183–97, esp. 189–91. Also Christie V. MacDonald, "The Utopia of the Text: Diderot's *Encyclopédie*," *Eighteenth Century: Theory and Interpretation* 21, no. 2 (Spring 1980): 128–44, esp. 135–38.

[27]Charles Loyseau, *Traité des ordres et simples dignitez* (Chasteaudun, 1610), devotes ninety-four pages to the first and second estates, and a mere eleven to the third. Similarly, *Le cabinet du roy de France, dans lequel il y a trois perles precieuses d'inestimable valeur* (1581), by Nicolas Barnaud (under the pseudonym Nicolas de Crest), spends 523 pages discussing

the nobility, in astounding detail—carefully making all the distinctions from high ecclesiastics to lowly abbés, followed by long discussions on the privileges of the various ranks of nobles, the issue of *dérogeance*, the status of noble children, marriages between nobles and commoners, and so on and on—while insisting continually that their pronouncements reflect the "natural order." Finally, near the end of the volume, one usually finds a cursory description of the third estate that lacks detail and is sometimes even denigrating. The sheer number of pages devoted to describing the first two estates and the paucity of those left for the third, while reflecting the perceived importance of each respective group in the society, stands in inverse relation to their actual distribution, since laborers constituted over 95 percent of the population.

The order laid out in d'Alembert's "Discourse" seems compatible with these earlier treatises, both in its hierarchical arrangements and in its implicit values. "Etc." stands for all occupations more lowly than cloth making, just as only a few pages in a jurist's tract deal with all of the third estate involved in the manual arts.

But the *Encyclopédie*, insofar as it is alphabetical, imposes a very different order of its own on this same society. It is difficult to assess with precision what effect those differences might have had on readers.[28] Yet when one compares it to the traditional jurists' writings, or to the hierarchical system borrowed from Francis Bacon, one cannot ignore the fact, for instance, that in the *Encyclopédie* "mendiant" precedes "noblesse," and "chaircuitier" comes before "clerc." One can read more about the production of iron ore than about coats of arms. Twenty-three pages discuss "corderie," the art and process of rope making, while only a few describe that ancient noble privilege "la chasse." If one were to read the *Encyclopédie* entry after entry, volume after volume, would the picture of society—the relative importance of different groups, occupations, and activities—substantiate or undermine the hierarchical order standing at

---

the clergy and the nobles and barely 100 on the third estate. A similar distribution of attention can be found also in David du Rivault du Flurance, *Les estats, esquels il est discouru du prince du noble et du tiers estat, conformement à nostre temps* (Lyons, 1596). By way of contrast, one might consult *Les quatre etats de la France* (1789), attributed to Berenger, which reverses the traditional ordering by starting with chapter 1, "Le peuple," and devoting more or less equal space to the "people," the nobility, the magistrates, and the clergy.

[28]Since the *Encyclopédie* was published volume after volume from 1751 to 1772, it is unlikely that the work (at least in those earlier years) was read exclusively as we would use a large reference work today. Diderot himself was convinced that a number of people read the volumes cover to cover. Robert Darnton concurs. Referring especially to the quarto edition that enjoyed a wide readership in the late eighteenth century, Darnton asserts that contemporary readers considered it as much a synthesis of modern philosophy as a reference work and concludes that they "did not treat the *Encyclopédie* as modern encyclopedias are treated—that is, as a neutral compilation of everything from A to Z." Robert Darnton, *The Business of the Enlightenment: A Publishing History of the Encyclopédie, 1775–1800* (Cambridge, 1979), pp. 523–24.

the front of volume 1? Does manual work still belong at the bottom of the list in mid-eighteenth-century France? And if so, for what reasons? To try to answer these questions, to try to understand the order of work in the *Encyclopédie*, we must now turn to the articles themselves.

The Ambivalence of Utility

By now it is commonplace to say that the *Encyclopédie*, by so thoroughly describing and illustrating the mechanical arts, bestowed a new dignity on craft and technology in the eighteenth century.[29] But particular expressions of this view that trace the sources of this newfound esteem differ considerably among its proponents. Sometimes Diderot's primary goal is construed as simply to ensure that the mechanical arts be recognized as just as important as the liberal arts, to insist that "not only artisans but the whole of society had suffered from the invidious distinctions between the mechanical and liberal arts."[30] Other writers focus on Diderot's concern for the people hurt by "the prejudice which caused the manual trades to be regarded as unworthy"[31] and insist that his purpose was "to gain respect for those who traditionally had been disrespected," namely artisans and craftsmen.[32] Other explanations point to "utility," a growing praise and recognition of the useful, which came to include workers (when they were actually working),[33] while more general interpretations suggest that Enlightenment thinkers advanced the idea that "labor should be exalted as an essential foundation of human happiness rather than despised as a stigma of baseness and sin." Nowhere was this idea allegedly "more prominent than in the pages of the *Encyclopédie*."[34]

It is not difficult to find passages in this monumental text that substantiate these familiar interpretations, though perhaps not always without ambiguity. For example, how is one to interpret Diderot's ostensible

[29]Arthur M. Wilson offers an exemplary formulation of this thesis: "Diderot always respected craftsmanship, and although he sometimes spoke disdainfully or despairingly of 'the people' and employed the word in much the same sense that we now give to 'the masses,' he never spoke disparagingly of the artisan or his social usefulness. It was this attitude, faithfully reflected in a thousand places in the *Encyclopédie*, that made the work so revolutionary. New values were here being set forth and admired, the dignity of just plain work was being extolled." Wilson, *Diderot* (Oxford, 1972), pp. 136–37.

[30]William H. Sewell, *Work and Revolution in France: The Language of Labor from the Old Regime to 1848* (Cambridge, 1980), p. 65.

[31]F. G. Healy, "The Enlightenment View of 'Homo Faber,' " *Voltaire Studies* 25 (1963): 837–59, esp. 854–59.

[32]Clinio L. Duetti, "Work Noble and Ignoble: An Introduction to the History of the Modern Idea of Work" (Ph.D. diss., University of Wisconsin, 1954), p. 88.

[33]See Harry C. Payne, *The Philosophers and the People* (Princeton, 1976), esp. chap. 3.

[34]Sewell, *Work and Revolution*, pp. 64–65.

effort to gain esteem for the mechanical arts in his article "Art"? Here he writes:

> In examining the products of the arts, one perceives that some were more the work of the mind than of the hand, and that, in contrast, others were more the work of the hand than of the mind. Such is *in part* the origin of the preeminence that one accorded to certain arts over others, and of the divisions that one made between the liberal arts and the mechanical arts. This distinction, although well founded, has had an unfortunate effect of denigrating very estimable and very useful people.[35]

Diderot accepts, then, the fundamental dichotomy between liberal and mechanical arts (mind versus body) but not its *consequences*. He insists that these people are deserving of respect because of their usefulness to society—despite the fact that they work with their hands.[36] In the "Preliminary Discourse" d'Alembert also invokes utility in his defense of the manual arts: "Whatever advantage the liberal arts have over the mechanical arts, by the work that the former demands of the mind, and by the difficulty to excel in them, is sufficiently compensated for the most part by the much superior utility that the latter procures for us."[37]

Not only are the mechanical arts more useful than the liberal arts, but it is also the responsibility of the latter to raise the esteem of the manual arts to its rightful place. Diderot argues:

> Render finally to the artisans the justice that is owed them. . . . It is up to the liberal Arts to rescue the mechanical arts from the scorn where prejudice has held them for such a long time; the protection of kings must safeguard them from the indigence where they languish yet. The artisans believe themselves scornful because we scorn them; teach them to think better of themselves: it is the only means to obtain from them more perfect products.[38]

---

[35]"Art," in *Encyclopédie*, 1:714.

[36]To be fair, in the same passage Diderot condemns those who suggest that experiments and working with material objects are beneath the dignity of the human spirit, and he criticizes the "prideful reasoners, useless contemplators, and lazy, ignorant, and disdainful tyrants who abound in the cities and countryside." Yes, a more positive evaluation of work does exist in the *Encyclopédie*, but we must further explore its precise grounding. And we should not ignore the more critical, pejorative, and even repressive depictions of work and workers.

[37]"Discours préliminaire" to *Encyclopédie*, 1:xiii.

[38]"Art," in *Encyclopédie*, 1:714. For other entries expressing a concern to increase productivity see "Fêtes des Chrétiens," in which the author urges a reduction in the number of holidays in order to multiply the number of working days, for consequently "all the products of labor would increase in proportion" (*Encyclopédie*, 6:565). See also "Discours préliminaire," which urges a strict division of labor in order to ensure greater productivity (*Encyclopédie*, 1:xiii).

Although Diderot's aim here may be to elevate opinions toward the manual arts and increase workers' self-esteem, his text equivocates nonetheless. One might ask, for example, how the liberal arts could bring about these changes in attitude. Or why, if the mechanical arts are so important, they need justification and support from those who eschew manual labor. But these are minor considerations when we are faced with the last sentence, which is central to Diderot's project. *Why* do we need to have artisans think better of themselves? Because that is "the only means to obtain from them more perfect products." Thus his primary interest is not concern for unqualified respect for persons, nor the dignity of work itself, but plainly a desire to perfect products and enhance productivity.

Of course it is probably advantageous to the entire society, and not necessarily inimical to the interest of the workers themselves, that they produce more and better goods. And increasing one's productivity could help raise one's self-esteem. But something else is at stake. To put the stress on the workers' utility (and a utility based solely on productivity) is to conceive of workers as means merely, without ends of their own. Often Diderot finds more praise for machines and tools than for those who operate them. The entry "Bas" (stocking-weaving machine) is a case in point. Thus we must consider for a moment some further implications of Diderot's praise of the workers' utility.

Daniel Mornet has said that "Diderot sought to make more useful men, not more thoughtful ones,"[39] and eighteenth-century debates on popular education demonstrate that Diderot was not alone in this view. One historian, in a recent work, cites numerous writers who questioned the wisdom of extending education to the lower classes, fearing the consequences if workers were to recognize their miserable condition. The author suggests that Diderot's claim that universities should be open to all did not imply offering higher learning to the lower classes: "for this would have deprived society of the artisans and peasants upon which it depended."[40] Who would have remained to labor in the fields or the manufactories if there had been a genuine opportunity for higher education and a career afterward? Striking his own blow against social mobility, Diderot wrote that "nothing was more disastrous for society than this disdain of fathers for their occupation and these senseless emigrations from one condition [*état*] to another."[41] Despite the fact that

[39]Daniel Mornet, *Les origins intellectuelles de la révolution française* (Paris, 1933), p. 491.
[40]Harvey Chisick, *The Limits of Reform in the Enlightenment: Attitudes toward the Education of the Lower Classes in Eighteenth Century France* (Princeton, 1981), p. 147.
[41]Denis Diderot, "Plan d'une université pour le gouvernement de Russie," in *Oeuvres complètes de Diderot*, 20 vols., ed. J. Assezat (Paris, 1875–77), 3:527. Cited in Chisick, *Limits of Reform*, p. 148.

Diderot himself was the son of a modest provincial artisan, he "did not care to facilitate such 'emigrations' by encouraging the lower classes to study."[42] I would add that by their severe criticism of the church and the nobility, their praise of worker utility, and their desire to exclude the lower classes from anything more than the most rudimentary primary education, the encyclopedists advanced a new ideology of a social division of labor, one that moved far beyond the somewhat clumsy categories of the three orders inherited from feudal times. One might call it an "alphabetical order," for a new world in which sophisticated skills of literacy would be the key to progress, profit, and success. But it is an ideology riven with contradictions. To those workers who are "useful" but basically "analphabètes," the *Encyclopédie* (and hence the new hegemony) would be inaccessible, for to understand its discourse would require much more than simply knowing the order of the alphabet.

We are not surprised, then, that the description under the entry "Métier" (craft), while again appealing to the superior utility of the artisan, does not do so unambiguously. In their efforts to gain respect for the crafts, the editors at the same time tacitly remind us why manual labor is denigrated in the first place. The article "Métier" begins:

> One gives this name to any profession that demands the use of the arms and that is limited to a certain number of mechanical operations, aimed at creating one work, that the worker repeats without ceasing. I do not know why we have attached a vile scorn to this word; it is the crafts that give us all the things necessary for life.... I leave it to those who have some principle of fairness to judge if it is reason or prejudice that makes us regard with such a disdainful eye these men who are so essential. The poet, the philosopher, the orator, the minister, the warrior, the hero would be completely nude and lacking bread without this artisan, the object of his cruel scorn.[43]

[42]Chisick, *Limits of Reform*, p. 148.

[43]"Métier," in *Encyclopédie*, 10:483. What is really at stake in this passage is the issue of division of labor. This hypothesis becomes plausible when one compares this text with a remarkably similar moment in Adam Smith's *Wealth of Nations*, where, in chapter 2, "Of the Principle Which Gives Occasion to the Division of Labour," Smith argues as follows: "The difference between the most dissimilar characters, between a philosopher and a common street porter, for example, seems to arise not so much from nature as from habit, custom, and education. When they came into the world, and for the first six or eight years of their existence, they were perhaps very much alike.... About that age, or soon after, they came to be employed in very different occupations. The difference of talents comes then to be taken notice of, and widens by degrees, till at last the vanity of the philosopher is willing to acknowledge scarce any resemblance." Without man's disposition to exchange that led to division of labor, Smith concludes, each person would have had to procure all the necessities of life for himself and "had the same work to do, and there would have been no such difference of employment as could alone give occasion to any great difference of talents." Adam Smith, *The Wealth of Nations* (1776), ed. Andrew Skinner (New York, 1978), p. 120.

Here the author does seem to urge respect for the manual arts, again by virtue of their superior usefulness to all of us. But the place of work itself and that of the worker is less clear. The general description of the craftsman's routine makes him sound like a mindless automaton,[44] for his job requires the use of his hands and is limited to a certain number of mechanical operations that produce the same piece of work, made over and over again ad infinitum. Is this the activity deserving of "dignity" and "respect"? That the artisan builds and operates instruments of technology and produces the goods we all need saves the rest of society from these deadening, repetitive menial tasks—and allows it to pursue liberal, intellectual endeavors. At best it is not respect that is called for, but rather simple gratitude.

Further evidence of pejorative or cynical views of work and workers abound in the descriptions of particular métiers—of butchers, for example. Early in this article, after tracing a short history of murders and uprisings since the reign of Charles VI, in which butchers were the instigators, the author reflects:

> This is the guild, which holds between its hands the things necessary for the subsistence of the people, that is so very worrisome during the time of revolutions, especially if the guilds are rich, large, and composed of extended families. As it is impossible to be sure of their fidelity, it seems to me a good policy consists in dividing them: to this effect, they should be forbidden to form guilds, and it ought to be open to any individual to sell meat and bread from a butcher's stall.[45]

This passage attests to the perceived power of the butchers to disrupt a society dependent upon the subsistence they supply.[46] To lessen this potential threat, butchers should be denied participation in corporations or any groups that would increase their importance or would exclude outsiders from selling meat independently. The article continues by citing, among other things, the advantages of locating slaughterhouses outside the city proper, to avoid what it calls "a capital infected by filth and blood that pollute the air and make it unhealthy and disgusting."[47] The space for this kind of work belongs beyond the bounds of normal, polite society. Even more important, in the interest of public order and

---

[44] William H. Sewell makes a similar observation in *Work and Revolution*, pp. 68–69.

[45] "Boucher," in *Encyclopédie*, 2:351.

[46] Of course it is questionable how vital the subsistence supplied by the butcher was in a society that depended so heavily upon grain for the bulk of its calories. Yet it seems safe to say that meat undoubtedly found its way into the mouths of likely *Encyclopédie* readers vastly more often than into the mouths of members of their society in general. Diderot himself refers to the butchers as supplying "vital subsistance" and in the same article calls meat "the most common nourishment after bread."

[47] "Boucher," in *Encyclopédie*, 2:351.

safety, the butchershops should be scattered throughout neighborhoods rather than located all in one area: "Each butcher has at least four journeymen, many have six: they are all violent, uncontrollable men whose eyes and hands are accustomed to blood. Far from bringing together these sorts of people, it seems to me good order and salubrity would be served if they were dispersed one by one throughout the city like other merchants."[48]

After this warning—charged with both political ideology and folkloric anxieties—about the dangers of allowing butchers to remain in groups and their potential for violence, the entry, somewhat incidentally, spells out some of the rules governing the profession: restrictions on selling to be observed during Lent, for example, and guidelines for apprenticeships. Yet one finds no suggestions on how to establish a *boucherie*, no procedures for slaughtering an animal, and no methods of preparing and preserving meat for sale. Earlier in the same article, Diderot revealed his opposition to corporations and stated that "it ought to be open to any individual to sell meat and bread from a butcher's stall." But where is this motivated individual, isolated from professional groups and trade secrets, going to find the necessary technical information on butchering? Given Diderot's goal to make what was known on every topic available to any literate Frenchman, the "art of butchery" ought not to have been omitted. Even with the wealth of practical information contained in the *Encyclopédie*, its reader still needs an armed butcher to provide him with his favorite cut of meat.[49]

Other articles devoted to professions concerned with subsistence—

[48]Ibid. Roland Barthes has remarked on the unexpected violence of the plate "Tuerie" (slaughterhouse), which seems not to fit in with the other plates devoted to the food arts. See Barthes, "Image, raison, déraison," in *L'univers de l'Encyclopédie* (Paris, 1964). Like the engraving, the prose entry on the butchers stands out as an extreme example, perhaps because of its emphasis on the butchers' potential violence and the symbolic associations and anxieties traditionally surrounding blood, the slaughter of animals, and commerce in meat. I might also mention the richly ambivalent role of the butcher in the parodic rituals of carnival: as one who threatens dismemberment, violence, and rebellion and yet through slaughter provides the food necessary for growth, rebirth, and regeneration. For a fascinating discussion of the role of the culinary arts in carnival, especially that of the butcher, the carving knife, the charcutier, and minced meat for sausages and stuffings, see Mikhail Bakhtin, *Rabelais and His World*, trans. Hélène Iswolsky (Cambridge, Mass., 1968), esp. pp. 193–235.

[49]I hope eventually to work out explicitly the sorts of relations (and contradictions) that Diderot's liberalism implies in terms of training for a profession. In some instances the *Encyclopédie* suggests that to learn a craft a potential master craftsman need only consult the scientific canons and descriptions established by observers such as Diderot. In other cases there appears the supposition that the future master craftsman will be obliged, more or less informally, to take apprenticeship with current masters. Further, as Jacques Proust has pointed out in his monumental *Diderot et l'Encyclopédie* (Paris, 1962), it is unlikely that even the artisans who actually contributed to the *Encyclopédie* would have been able to afford a subscription to it; see Proust, *Diderot*, p. 61. This again raises questions. For whom does the *Encyclopédie* exist? Who are its intended readers? And how do they read it?

bakers and charcutiers, for example—depict these tradesmen too in a less than flattering light, though without the violent rhetoric aimed against the butchers. Nevertheless, these workers still emerge as untrustworthy and in need of strict surveillance. The "Boulanger" entry enumerates the professions incompatible with running a bakery, notably millers and grain merchants because of conflict of interest, and concludes by reminding the readers of the severe penalties inflicted upon bakers who "sell at false weights."[50] Similarly, the article "Chaircuitier" (pork butcher) dwells upon the deception and abuse found among practitioners and suggests that customers should beware of spoiled pork. The entry reads: "It is thus up to individuals to protect themselves against this fraud, by examining this merchandise, whose contamination is easily recognized by the presence of milletlike grains visible throughout the substance."[51] Throughout the discussion the charcutier receives no praise whatever for his skill; he gains no sense of pride from his delectable creations. Rather, he is to be scorned, distrusted, and reported to police if spoiled meat should leave his stall.[52]

True, the police kept a careful eye on all the arts and crafts, including the most prized professions. The encyclopedists, however, seemed to single out the more "lowly" crafts in their discussions of fraud and conflict of interest. We are warned of bakers who sell at false weights, charcutiers who offer bad meat, and wool producers who camouflage their improperly prepared fleeces. The police also watched, for example, goldsmiths, clockmakers, and mirror manufactures for fraud and poor workmanship, but the *Encyclopédie* articles stress instead the high quality of these products, guaranteed by the "cooperation" between these guilds and the government. Under "Horlogerie," for instance, there is no warning about clockmakers, who "deserve only praise," but rather an accusation against "unscrupulous merchants," "unqualified artisans," "domestics," and other "gens intrigans" who deceive the public.[53]

[50]"Boulanger," in *Encyclopédie*, 2:361–62.

[51]"Chaircuitier," in *Encyclopédie*, 3:12.

[52]Obviously, if no contaminated or underweight food is sold, all society is better served, those at the bottom as well as the top. The point is, rather, where is the careful description of the métier of "chaircuitier" that Diderot promised?

[53]"Horloger," in *Encyclopédie*, 8:302. See also "Miroitier," in *Encyclopédie*, 10:572, and "Orfèvrerie," in *Encyclopédie*, 11:627. The social historian must ask, then, When the *Encyclopédie* is critical (or praising) of workers, to whom does it refer? The definition under "Ouvrier" (written by the Chevalier de Jaucourt) offers little differentiation, for it reads: "any artisan who works at some craft whatever it may be," as well as "those who work at a manufactory" (*Encyclopédie*, 11:726). Further, as Georges Friedmann has suggested, "terms that today are almost contradictory appear to have been fully synonymous in the eighteenth century: terms such as 'artisan,' 'ouvrier,' 'manoeuvre,' specialiste,' and *a fortiori*, 'artiste.' " Friedmann, "L'Encyclopédie et le travail humaine," *Annales E.S.C.* 8, no. 1 (January 1953): 52–61. In many articles of the *Encyclopédie* enormous praise is lavished on the "artisan," but in countless others we find just the opposite. For example, in the article "Luxe" it is

Two articles that come soon after "chaircuitier" provide remarkable examples of another sort of ideology, one that stands out all the more thanks to the curious juxtapositions always possible in arrangements by alphabetical order. The first, "Chaise de poste," describes a small two-wheeled carriage as "an elegant vehicle, light and difficult to upset, in which one can quickly make long trips. . . . The post chaise, considered as a machine, is certainly one of the most useful and best designed that we have; the time and industry of workers have brought it to a degree of perfection upon which it is nearly impossible to improve."[54] The account ends by referring the reader to a detailed engraving of this outstanding carriage. The second article, "Chamois et chamoiseur," deserves attention too, for it fills four folio pages with extremely specific instructions on the art of preparing fine leather and concludes: "We have just described the art of leather curing and glove making to the last detail; one can use this discussion as a reference in complete confidence of its exactitude."[55] In this latter entry, the stated intentions of the encyclopedists indeed seem to be served: an enterprising person with this information could understand the processes necessary for the production of high-quality leather. Moreover, the glorification of the workers' skill and industry in the "chaise de poste" entry makes the earlier treatments of the food professions sound even more base and degrading.

But why this stark contrast between carriage makers, leather preparers, bread bakers, and sausage makers? Simple bourgeois sensibilities might prefer leather gloves and carriages to the vile (and violent) butchering of animals. Or the obvious improvements in carriages over the years might stand as tangible examples of progress and proof that man could indeed become master of his environment, whereas mundane sausages and bread would generate no such enthusiasm. One might point as well to the more complicated technology required to produce sophisticated modes of transportation and thereby justify the higher estimation. But it is more likely that this distinction among what are—after all—exclusively manual arts stems from remnants of a classical desire to be free from all sorts of physical bondage.[56] Butchers, bakers, and sau-

---

clear that by "artisan" the author intended the lowest level of worker. It is my contention that when the *Encyclopédie* offers negative depictions of workers, in general the editors mean the ones who shared the least (in terms of values, property, literacy) with the dominant, literate culture, and further, to the extent that workers/artisans/masters were actively literate, property owning, and so on, they were less likely to be criticized—as the references to the wealthy goldsmiths and clockmakers attest.

[54]"Chaise de poste," in *Encyclopédie*, 3:60.
[55]"Chamois et chamoiseur," in *Encyclopédie*, 3:74.
[56]The French word "besogne" in ancient ordonnances meant "travail penible" [painful work]. The modern word "besoin" traces its roots to "besogne," suggesting the close relation between work and need—namely that man works not for pleasure, but out of need and want.

sage makers all call attention to the baser necessity for daily subsistence: that the body is constrained by the continual need for nourishment and hence that man (like the animals) is not ultimately free. The stated purpose of the "chaise de poste" was to permit long and comfortable travel—in a sense serving the needs of the body too. But instead of constantly reminding man of his subservience to his physical self, this light and graceful carriage served his soul as well. It freed his mind and spirit as it led him outward to new places, different experiences, and loftier thoughts. And, we should not forget, it is the product of the workers' skill and industry—the carriage—and not labor itself that earns respect and admiration.

The faith in man's ability to progress in science and industry so simply expressed in the "chaise de poste" entry is thus characteristic of a kind of optimism found in many of the more technical or highly refined mechanical arts described in the *Encyclopédie*. Painstaking details on rope making, on locks, or on the production of iron ore can be and have been read as testimony to the editors' belief in humanity's ability to perfect itself. The aim of my argument has not been to document further this justification and praise of the manufacturing process (other historians I have cited have found much evidence of that), but rather to investigate the dissonances in the pronouncements on workers and their crafts that become visible when placed within the larger context of the encyclopedists' general goals and implicit ideology.

Translating the "World of Work"

The project itself, the conceiving of an encyclopedia that would attempt to classify, categorize, theorize, and describe all the world's knowledge, bespeaks a certain naïveté that while perhaps charming is grounded on a highly problematic theory of representation.[57] And it also suggests a faith in the capacity of words to describe physical processes and make sense of them in a way that the educated reader could comprehend. But when one begins translating the "world of work" into the "universe of the *Encyclopédie*," the shortcomings of language appear at every turn.

First, many of the technical processes and tools are difficult—if not impossible—to describe in a meaningful way in prose. In his prospectus Diderot suggests that people lacked sufficient practice. They had written and read so little on the mechanical arts that it rendered them "difficult

---

[57]For further discussions of the problem of representation in the *Encyclopédie*, see Foucault, *Order of Things*, esp. p. 206; Walter Moser, "Les discours dans le Discours préliminaire," *Romanic Review* 67 (1976): 102–16, esp. pp. 114–16; MacDonald, "The Utopia of the Text"; and Creech, " 'Chasing after Advances.' "

to explain in an intelligible manner."[58] However, since a picture has always allegedly been worth a thousand words, Diderot's remedy was to introduce the now famous engravings that would try to compensate for some of language's failings. After all, nothing is so "fruitless as to make great efforts at explaining extensively without drawings something that, with a very simple drawing, would need but a short explication."[59] Of course many of the illustrations in the *Encyclopédie* would be far from simple, for one should not underestimate the difficulties of illustrating technical crafts or of describing them in prose.

But as the editors soon discovered, often one can neither illustrate nor describe accurately in words the processes of a craft that one has not at least attempted to master oneself:

> There are crafts so unique, with operations so subtle, that without trying to work them oneself, without moving the machine with one's own hands, and without seeing the object form before one's own eyes, it is difficult to explain precisely the processes involved. Thus numerous times it was necessary to procure the machines, construct them, and try one's hand at the work; rendering oneself, so to speak, an apprentice and making an inferior product in order to learn how others make good ones.[60]

Here is a small acknowledgment that, at least in the realm of the mechanical arts, one learns by doing and not simply by reading books.

One aspect of the editors' task was to subject to critical scrutiny the everyday gestures and processes of the workers, whose lack of consciousness about their craft over the years had resulted, according to the editors, in a stultifying technological lethargy. This meant that a major source of information and expertise would be the "doer" himself, the individual craftsman. Indeed, Diderot, contrasting his encyclopedia with others he deemed less successful, describes with great pride how his writers went directly into the workshops for their information.

> We addressed ourselves to the most skillful artisans of Paris and the kingdom: we took the trouble to go into their workshops, to question them, to write under their dictation, to develop their thoughts, to draw from them the terms proper to their professions...and then (a precaution nearly indispensable) to rectify (with the help of those who had written treatises on the crafts) in long and frequent conversations what others had imperfectly, obscurely, and sometimes incorrectly explained.[61]

[58]"Prospectus" to *Encyclopédie*, 1:xxxix.
[59]Ibid., 1:xl.
[60]Ibid., 1:xxxix.
[61]Ibid.

The status of the artisan still suffers from a certain real ambivalence. Yes, the writers have gone to the workshops and talked with the crafts-people there, but afterward they have had to sort out with experts all the conflicting opinions, misinformation, and obscure terminology offered by these unreliable, yet indispensable, sources. Unfortunately, few artisans were "men of letters" whom one could count on for accurate information. In fact, most craftsmen seemed not up to the task of explaining their métier to outsiders, for they had never pondered the meaning of what they had always done. As Diderot says in the article "Charpentiers," "it would be nice if a few of these skillful masters would write about their crafts in a satisfying way."[62] Yet social reality dictates that most of the artisans will be inarticulate concerning their manual skills, for they "only take them up out of necessity, and act only out of instinct."[63]

Here other subtle traces of the classical notion of work surface: the shamefulness of being chained to labor by sheer necessity, of subservience to a body whose activities are instinctive rather than intellectual. The indictment continues, however, for among a thousand artisans one will find scarcely "a dozen in a state to express themselves with some clarity on the tools that they use and goods they produce."[64] It is not surprising, then, that for Diderot "in the atelier it is the moment that speaks, not the artisan."[65] And when he discusses the language of the craftsmen—their jargons, inaccuracies, and disputes—one gets the sense that Diderot may in fact prefer his artisans mute.

Throughout the "Preliminary Discourse" the editors insist upon an encyclopedia bound by order, hierarchy, theory, and empirical observation: a tree of knowledge without any missing branches. Everything is to be accounted for and put in its rightful and reserved place. Often in specific articles, however, the languages of the mechanical arts confound their aims by resisting simple, orderly classification. Like the workers themselves, who constantly posed the threat of insubordination and revolt, their jargons would not easily be domesticated. As Diderot describes it: "There are tools that have several different names, and others, in contrast, that have only a generic name, like engine or machine, without anything to specify it: sometimes the least little difference is

---

[62]"Charpentier," in *Encyclopédie*, 3:214.

[63]"Prospectus" to *Encyclopédie*, 1:xxxix. I spoke earlier of the editors' desire to translate an "illiterate world of work" into the *Encyclopédie*. In a moment I will talk of a conflict between the literate and official dominant culture on the one hand and a nonliterate popular/work culture on the other. I do not wish to imply that during the Old Regime workers are all "illiterate" or "nonliterate"; rather, in the world of work literacy does not play the same role that it does in the dominant elitist culture.

[64]"Prospectus" to *Encyclopédie*, 1:xxxix.

[65]Ibid.

enough to cause Artists to abandon a generic name and invent particular ones; other times a tool unique in both its form and its use has no name at all, or borrows one from another instrument with which it has nothing in common."[66] Thus Diderot bemoans the lack of order and system in the languages of the mechanical arts and advances a "rational" way to repair the situation. He hopes that "a talented Logician who knows the arts and crafts would create a grammar of the Arts." His first task would be to establish "the exact meanings for words such as *large, big, medium, thin, thick, weak, small, light, heavy,* and so on," and then to convince the artisans to adopt his recommendations. Language would become rational, uniform, and predictable. His second task would be to determine "the differences and the resemblances of the forms and usages between one instrument and another, and between one work process and another, to determine when they should keep the same names or be given different ones." Confusion would be eliminated, for there would be only one word for each unique process and each tool. Diderot concludes: "It is the lack of exact definitions, and the number, not the diversity, of movements in work processes that make it difficult to describe the Arts clearly."[67]

From the entry "Encyclopédie" we learn that Diderot hoped all the articles—not just those concerning the arts and crafts—would employ a clear, exact, constant terminology. He felt that "if we could define words according to unchanging nature, and not according to human conventions and prejudices that change continually," two benefits would follow. First, posterity would be able to understand the *Encyclopédie* fully, and second, "exact definitions would become the seeds for discoveries." In addition, Diderot urged the encyclopedists to develop a stable measure in order to determine the proper length of articles in relation to the exact importance their subject matter occupied in the larger scheme of things.[68]

Diderot's impatience with the language of the mechanical arts, however, stands as a further symptom of his distrust of artisans and his condemnation of the corporations. He ignores the corporation as a potential "ordering mechanism," one that could in theory further his desire for "true principles" and a uniform vocabulary, and instead vents his resentment against workers' secrecy and ignorance. His complaints about

[66]"Art," in *Encyclopédie*, 1:716.
[67]Ibid. Diderot's desire for a rational language shares much with Leibniz's well-known project for a universal language. See Leibniz, "Towards a Universal Characteristic" (1677).
[68]James Creech cites these references to Diderot's entry "Encyclopédie" and discusses in great detail Diderot's concern that the encyclopedists strive to establish a constant, unambiguous language and stable epistemology, so that future generations would be able to understand, improve upon, and eventually perfect the material amassed in its many volumes. See Creech, " 'Chasing after Advances,' " especially pp. 185–86.

their too many words, or too few, and about their inexact terminology and confusion reveal more than just a desire for a rational, precise, unchanging language of description. What seems to be happening is a tacit move, underneath the rhetoric, to prise the vocabulary of the manual arts away from the domain of the workers, to change it, to bring it under control, and finally, to create a new language of the mechanical arts available to "all." The irony, of course, is that it is quite likely that once a craft was defined by scientific canons and described in exact, theoretical prose, the artisans themselves would be unable to understand it. The "avertissement" to a 1781 edition of the *Encyclopédie*, explaining why its editors had not included the expensive plates, states than when an engraving of a Lyons silk weavers' workshop was taken back to the place that had served as its model, the workers did not even recognize it. Chances are they would not have identified or comprehended the prose article "scientifically" describing their activities either. In this case the "order" of the *Encyclopédie* would serve to defuse even the possibility of worker self-consciousness.

Just as the discourse of the *Encyclopédie* was accessible to one group while excluding another, so too the jargon and vocabulary of any specific craft functions as an ideological barrier. Its impenetrability defends its practitioners from the outside and not only makes it difficult for the uninitiated to classify or understand, but excludes them from participation as well. In groups like the corporations and compagnonnage, work secrets were maintained and protected in part by means of language comprehensible only to those on the inside.

Although Diderot earlier admitted that one learns by doing rather than by merely reading, he still refused to believe it. The language of the crafts developed over time, partly by accident no doubt, partly to serve the needs of the craftsman. In daily practice it made little difference whether artisans in the workshop referred to a specific tool as a "thingamajig" or a "two-hole punch" as long as all understood the message. To someone committed to the project of a rational organization of the mechanical arts, however, this sort of inexactitude meant only frustration, since it put up just one more obstacle to "progress," an obstacle perhaps more or less self-consciously imposed by guild members themselves.

The "avertissement" to volume 3 of the *Encyclopédie* reiterates both the optimism of the editors and the problems they faced in their efforts to rationalize the arts and crafts. Again, it depicts the artisan as little more than an automaton, working by instinct and blind practice, cut off from the light of reason in his cave, his skill in his hands but not in his mind. "The arts, these precious moments of human industry, will no longer have to fear being lost in oblivion: These facts will no longer be buried in the ateliers and the hands of the Artist; they will be unveiled by the Philosopher, and reflection will finally be able to illuminate and simplify blind practice."[69] A similar exhortation in the article "Art" invites craftsmen "to share with Savants the discoveries they make, and not allow them to perish. Those who keep useful techniques or information to themselves commit larceny against society."[70] Thus artisans who guard their work secrets (or perhaps are simply unable to articulate them satisfactorily) are little better than common criminals. The same concerns are expressed in slightly less pejorative tones in the entry "Botanique," which describes the informal ways agricultural knowledge gets passed on from generation to generation without the benefit of scientific methods or analysis. "The people of the countryside have a sort of tradition on this subject that they receive from their fathers and transmit to their children. Each one in his own canton supposes, without any precise knowledge, that such-and-such a terrain agrees or does not agree with such-and-such a plant. These prejudices, well or badly founded, pass without any examination."[71] The encyclopedists are concerned that as a result of this informal transmission of practice, not only will useful knowledge be forgotten, but mistaken beliefs might be preserved in its place. The *Encyclopédie*, then, offers itself as the antidote to the classical fear of literate cultures: that all knowledge not preserved in print is destined to be lost.

Conclusion

One view of the Enlightenment has described it as "an attempt to substitute empirical knowledge for traditional practice and belief,"[72] and

[69]"Avertissement" to volume 3, in *Encyclopédie*, 3:v–vi. One might well guess the problems that arise when philosophers go into the ateliers to rationalize the descriptions and theories of the arts and crafts. Steven L. Kaplan describes just this sort of encounter between a miller named Buquet and two scientists, Parmentier and Cadet de Vaux, who, armed with theory, chemistry, and scientific discourse, aimed to improve the practice of milling. Buquet, with years of experience, skill, and a certain critical knowledge of his own, bitterly resented the elites' arrogance toward practicing millers and their refusal to acknowledge the worth of his particular expertise and insights. See Kaplan, *Provisioning Paris: Merchants and Millers in the Grain and Flour Trade during the Eighteenth Century* (Ithaca, 1984), chap. 11.

[70]"Art," in *Encyclopédie*, 1:717. Cf. a similar observation made in a speech to the Academy of Besançon on 15 November 1757 at the occasion of the reception of a new member to the group: "All those who make valuable inventions or improve upon existing ones ought to diffuse them widely throughout the society; otherwise their work is in vain and they are not really Citizens." Fonds de l'Académie de Besançon, Bibliothèque municipal de Besançon, MS Vol. 6, fol. 146.

[71]"Botanique," in *Encyclopédie*, 2:343.

[72]Norman Hampson, *A Cultural History of the Enlightenment* (New York, 1968), p. 86.

the *Encyclopédie* furnishes ample support for this claim, although exactly how one is to interpret the motivations for substitution is still an open question. Much scholarship has emphasized the progressive, optimistic, rational sides of this effort, and yet its more repressive aspects should not be overlooked.

The attempt to "translate" the entire sphere of the mechanical arts into the *Encyclopédie* highlights the confrontation between an oral, practical, physical, and sometimes inefficient world of work and a dominant literate culture trying to make it rational and productive. There are a number of ways to discuss this confrontation. One might cite examples of the richness and color of the workers' language and discourse and contrast them to Diderot's goal of a clear, simple, prescriptive language for the manual arts. Work itself seems to have remained something of a bulwark of popular culture in the eighteenth century, through its trade secrets, its private languages, and the intricate hierarchies, rivalries, rites, rituals, symbols, and myths found among various occupational groups. Those who worked spent so much time at it, and so much of their lives even outside the workplace revolved around matters concerned with work, that we might speak of a popular culture of work in opposition to authority or society at large. For example, the article "Communautés" (guilds) seems to be setting up precisely this sort of confrontation:

> In effect these guilds have their own laws, which are nearly always opposed to the general good.... The first and most dangerous are the barriers to industry caused by the high costs and formalities of admission [to the craft]. In some guilds, where the number of members is restricted or where admission is reserved for sons of masters, one sees only a monopoly contrary to the laws of reason and the state, approaching a loss of conscience and religion.... [Even worse] many are indifferent to making progress in the Arts, even in the very ones they practice.[73]

This article suggests that some members of corporations are acting outside the bounds of conventional society, neither sharing in a commonwealth of ideals nor having an enlightened faith in human progress. Might we also speak of it as an instance of a popular or work culture's refusal to truckle to an official one?

I have found other evidence that literacy and language are a domain of conflict between the dominant, official culture and those who would challenge its "order." The arrest records of beggars in the Franche-Comté document a refusal of the *marginaux* to give in to literate authorities. The special preprinted forms used for the arrests of beggars had a series of set questions: name, address, age, and so on, as well as

[73]"Communautés," in *Encyclopédie*, 3:724.

questions that, if answered as the authorities intended, would be self-incriminating. On numerous occasions when a beggar was asked, for example, "How long have you begged?" he or she would reply: "I have never begged. I am a silkweaver, day laborer, or whatever." The beggar thus thwarted the rational printed form, for the clerk would be forced to scratch out the whole question and write in the margin: "So-and-so claims that s/he has never begged."[74]

The archives in Besançon containing the records of the Bon Pasteur (the house for repentent prostitutes) show the other side of the confrontation. A rule of silence was imposed throughout the house during the day and even at night in the dormitories. The inmates were never allowed to speak to each other, not even while working on their textile machines. In a sense their language, their "street talk," was taken away from them. In its place were taught very rudimentary reading skills, used only for reading the Bible. It was as if only by taking away their language would these women be delivered to virtue and pulled from their lives of disorder.[75] And one should not overlook the role work played in their rehabilitation.

There is thus a specific desire on the part of the dominant, elite culture to control language and discourse, whether it be municipal authorities domesticating prostitutes or, as in our main case, the editors of the *Encyclopédie* expropriating and transforming work techniques. By exposing and altering the secrets of the crafts, the editors sought to undermine the authority of the specialized worker. His formerly unique talents, knowledge, and abilities became dispensable, once the techniques were available in print to "all," that is, to anyone who could understand the discursive order of the *Encyclopédie*. Thanks to the careful description of any specific craft—"chamoiserie," for example—whatever esteem the artisan might have deserved as a result of his possessing particular knowledge no longer seems compelling, for "it is enough to have described exactly an art as it is practiced in one place, for it to be practiced everywhere."[76]

The "art"[77] of the crafts also seems to be losing out to a rational,

---

[74]Archives départementales du Doubs (Besançon), MS 1 C 531. My essay is part of a larger project analyzing the ideologies of work in eighteenth-century France. Going beyond the "alphabetical order," I examine the way work was "ordered" by institutions and the ways it was perceived as maintaining (or disrupting) the moral, social, and economic order in eighteenth-century France.

[75]Archives municipales de Besançon, MS G. G. 436, fol. 165.

[76]"Chamois et chamoiseur," in *Encyclopédie*, 3:74.

[77]See Sewell, *Work and Revolution*, pp. 21–25, for an interesting discussion of "art." If we accept William Sewell's argument that "art" in the eighteenth century meant rules, order, discipline, and proof of human skill and intelligence, then the rationalization of the manufacturing process may simply be its logical extension. While testifying to the

efficient means of organizing the manufacturing processes that demands a strict division of labor: "When a manufacturing process is complex, each operation requires a different person. One worker does and will do throughout his life only one single thing, another does something else: accordingly everyone works well and quickly, and the best-made products are also made for the cheapest costs."[78] This projection seems to ensure that workers will become almost robots, going through a few simple motions over and over again. Early in the "Preliminary Discourse" d'Alembert provides us with a comment on the sort of men who work in crafts and on the kind of work they do all day: "The mechanical arts depend upon manual operation and are enslaved, if I might permit myself this term, to a kind of routine. These arts have been abandoned to those men whom prejudice has placed in the most inferior classes."[79] One might reasonably expect the continuation of this statement (appearing as it does at the beginning of volume 1) to predict that when the mechanical arts finally get the respect they deserve, life at the bottom will not seem so lowly. But the insistence upon a strict division of labor in the passage cited above makes it likely that, in the interests of productivity and progress, the lowest classes of workers will continue to spend their workdays in blind practice and deadening routine.[80]

More optimistic views about the Enlightenment suggest that during the eighteenth century an awareness of society's dependence upon "*Homo faber*" led to a new respect and dignity for the mechanical arts and for those who performed them. There is little doubt that the editors of the *Encyclopédie* recognized the growing importance of work and suspected what a force industry and manufacturing could eventually become in France, as the many envious comparisons to England and Holland's successful commercial ventures indicate. And although we find ample lip service paid to fears of losing art and trade secrets "ensevelis dans les atteliers," it is more likely that the encyclopedists' real aim was to gain some powerful say over the uses to which those techniques and trade secrets were put. True, the incredibly detailed description of rope making[81] presents readers with the information necessary to make their own rope. But more important, it represents the work process in such a way as to encourage one to imagine how to control, dominate, and regulate rope manufacturing more efficiently.

Space allows but two further illustrations of what I see as the implicit

---

intelligence of its designer, however, a sophisticated machine may reinforce the mindlessness of those needed to operate it.

[78]"Art," in *Encyclopédie*, 1:717.

[79]"Discours préliminaire" to *Encyclopédie*, 1:xiii.

[80]And that may well be what the encyclopedists intended. See, for instance, my discussion above on the debates about education for the lower classes.

[81]"Corderie," in *Encyclopédie*, 4:215–38.

ideology of work in the *Encyclopédie*. First, in the entry "Forge" Diderot describes in over thirty folio pages how to establish a successful iron-works. He begins with advice to a future entrepreneur: one must have money to invest, good credit rating, good reputation, and managerial skills—resources beyond most artisans. Much of the article offers extensive details on hiring workers, where to locate mines, the importance of nearby forests for fuel, drilling procedures, scientific information on the composition of soils, and so on.[82] Second, there is the surprising eight-page entry "Livre," which reads: "Book, a term from commerce signifying the different registers in which merchants keep their accounts." What follows are comprehensive instructions on bookkeeping, with details for specific situations: current accounts, orders, commissions, expenses, accounts by the month, incoming and outgoing goods, and so forth. Even more striking, in the middle of pages 614–15 (volume 9) are printed two huge sample pages from two different types of account books, followed by explicit instructions. This entry (longer than the other article "Livre," which treats together "all" other kinds of books, including "lost," "ruined," "censored," "in parchment," "in leather," "spiritual," "profane," "useful," etc.) concludes by a discussion of the French monetary unit *livre*, and lists equivalent currencies from other countries.[83] These examples and others mentioned above suggest that the audience to whom these volumes are addressed is not the artisan himself who (expertly or instinctively) practices his métier, but rather the literate bourgeois reader of a particular type. He is the audience for whom the workers' language must be expropriated and rationalized—not so that he can learn to do the craft himself, but so that he can learn how to manage it, and simultaneously bring the workers under control as well.

What then is the place of work in the *Encyclopédie*? The care and attention devoted to the technical aspects of many of the mechanical arts indicate their great importance in eighteenth-century French society, and that careful treatment could be construed as implying a positive evaluation of the manual arts, as many scholars have suggested. But d'Alembert's hierarchical design put work at the bottom, reaffirming and perhaps reinforcing traditional prejudices that dictated that the third estate carry the burden of labor for the society as a whole. The messages in the individual alphabetically arranged articles are more equivocal. The length of many of the technical entries testifies to their

[82]"Forge," in *Encyclopédie*, 7:134–68.
[83]"Livre," in *Encyclopédie*, 9:611–18. For one more example see also the eight-page entry "Intérêt," which offers myriad complicated formulas on how to figure simple and compound interest on loans and investments. The article also includes a history of the uses of interest in world history, spells out carefully the laws regarding interest, and ends with a justification of setting interest at 5 percent. *Encyclopédie*, 8:819.

perceived importance, and positive views of the mechanical arts stress their complexities, their technology, their usefulness, and their role in human and material progress. Yet rather than any simple valorization of the manual arts, of labor, or of workers themselves, the articles are replete with traces of more classical (albeit sometimes veiled) notions of work: as vile, as thwarting attempts at virtue, as implying subservience to the body, to instincts, and to necessity. That some people build and operate technology in society saves everyone else from having to perform menial tasks and allows them to pursue liberal, intellectual endeavors. There is a residual attitude here, comprising both the positive and the negative utility of work. Work keeps people tied down; it is a kind of drudgery or even punishment. But by having a whole class of people engaged in manual labor, others are able to escape into a world of leisure, thought, philosophy, and art—not to mention wealth, privilege, and power.

"The alphabetical order" that names this essay thus does not simply refer to the convenient and familiar system of arrangement but, by drawing upon its French cognates, alludes as well to "les ordres alphabètes et analphabètes." Throughout the *Encyclopédie* one finds traces of a confrontation between a literate culture and a nonliterate one, a confrontation undertaken throughout the West and whenever ignorance and irregularity obstructed the coming of a new order, but a confrontation that the encyclopedists pursued with particular relish and to particular effect.

To the extent that workers were perceived as marginal and disruptive, their private languages, their corporate groups, their rites and rituals served to insulate them somewhat from the dominant official culture, to render them culturally self-sufficient, and to provide some small defense against the kinds of economic movements transforming industry in the eighteenth-century—in other words, to allow them a source of autonomous power. What we have in the *Encyclopédie* is a subtle and comprehensive expropriation of that nonliterate knowledge and hence power by the literate culture, an attempt, largely successful, to remove the inefficient and inarticulate world of work from the hands and mouths of the workers and to place it in printed form before the eyes of an enlightened "management" whose ordered purposes it would serve.

–8–

Visions of Labor: Illustrations of the Mechanical Arts before, in, and after Diderot's Encyclopédie

William H. Sewell, Jr.

In the summer of 1979, having completed the manuscript of *Work and Revolution in France*, it occurred to me that the book might be embellished by some illustrations.[1] Surely the changes in the conception and organization of labor that I had analyzed in my book must be reflected in pictorial representations of work and workers. I was, of course, already familiar with the plates of Diderot's *Encyclopédie* and had, in the course of my research, run across some interesting depictions of work dating from the nineteenth century. But at the very least I would have to supplement these with some images from the pre-Enlightenment era. With this thought in mind, I made a visit to the Cabinet des estampes in the Bibliothèque Nationale. There, to my astonishment, I found that some two thousand prints illustrating "métiers," dating from the Middle Ages to the twentieth century, had already been collected by the staff of the cabinet and arranged in alphabetical order in twenty-two folio volumes.

After spending a few days sorting through this remarkably rich col-

I thank Alan Bernstein, Tim Clark, Bonnie Grad, Steven Kaplan, Cynthia Koepp, Sarah Maza, and Timothy Riggs for their help and comments on this essay. A preliminary version was delivered as a lecture at Worcester Art Museum in connection with an exhibition entitled Visions of City and Country: Prints and Photographs of Nineteenth-Century France, in January 1983.
[1] William H. Sewell, Jr., *Work and Revolution in France: The Language of Labor from the Old Regime to 1848* (Cambridge, 1980).

lection, I reached a somewhat disconcerting conclusion. These prints clearly constituted a treasure-trove of information, both on the organization and techniques of production and on the way work and workers have been perceived by artists and by their public. Moreover, the changes in style and emphasis that could be traced out in the prints were consistent with and interpretable in terms of the developments I had analyzed in my book. But the visual images refused simply to "illustrate" my points. They had a dynamic and a language of their own that did not correspond in any direct way with the language or the dynamics of either intellectual discourse about labor or workers' organizational practices. Visual materials would either have to be introduced into the text on a par with other sources—that is, analyzed carefully in their own terms and integrated fully into the argument—or else left out. At that point the manuscript was too finished—and I was too exhausted—to make so major a revision of the text feasible. But I carried photographic copies of some of the prints back to the United States and filed them in a drawer, thinking I might yet be able to use them some day. The Cornell conference on work in France provided me with a perfect opportunity and inspired one more scholarly raid on the Cabinet des estampes in the summer of 1982.

The prints in the collection of the Cabinet des estampes include many types of illustrations of labor. There are pictures of individual workers representing the costume and physiognomy of those who ply some particular trade; pictures of workers in bizarre, exotic, or colorful trades (match sellers, ragpickers, water carriers, charcoal burners, smugglers, bootblacks, street singers); pictures of workers at rest from their labor; and so on. This essay will examine only a selected range of prints: those that attempt to represent not the styles and personalities of workers employed in a given trade, but the trade itself as a whole. All the images to be analyzed depict the actual process of production. They illustrate the division and the coordination of labor and reproduce the various tools, implements, and techniques employed in the trade. The best-known prints of this type are the plates of the *Encyclopédie*, and they will be examined at some length. But the prints from the Cabinet des estampes make it possible to situate the plates of the *Encyclopédie* historically within a broader genre of illustrations of mechanical arts. Seen in the context of illustrations dating from the late sixteenth century to the mid-nineteenth, the familiar images from the *Encyclopédie* take on a special meaning—and also come to look very odd.

One peculiarity of prints that depict mechanical arts as a whole is that they show male workers almost exclusively—even though it was and is well known that women actually worked in many of the trades in question. This itself tells us something important about contemporary conceptions of labor: whatever the reality of the situation, work was seen as essentially a male activity. There are in fact some representations of women who worked in strictly female trades—laundering, dressmaking, millinery, and so forth. But the female workers who are represented are virtually always young and pretty (or if not, then old and outrageously ugly) and are depicted alone, demurely (or occasionally saucily) looking up from their work. The work that women are doing is not very important in these images; it is hardly more than a pretext for depicting a pretty girl. Representations of women's work, in short, tell us a great deal about the artists' and the print-buying public's fantasies about working girls, but not much about women's work. This chapter will, consequently, be concerned essentially with images of men's work.

I should make it clear at the outset that I am not a professional art historian and that I consequently lack the art historian's depth of knowledge about iconography, stylistic conventions, conditions of production and consumption of art objects, and so on. I am acutely aware of these shortcomings. Moreover, I recognize that the collection of the Cabinet des estampes, though extensive, is far from an exhaustive collection of prints representing work from these centuries. A thorough search might well turn up pictures that modify or even contradict my interpretations. A genuine monographic study of the evolution of pictorial representations of work in France would necessarily be the work of many summers, not of a few weeks. It might well include a systematic quantitative enumeration of changing themes, subjects, iconographic items, and so on; it would certainly include a much more extensive comparison than I have been able to make between scenes depicting work and other artistic genres. Finally, it would have to determine in much greater detail who the artists were, who they were working for, and in what circumstances they produced prints about work. Such a monograph would be well worth someone's time to write. But in the absence of such a study, even a brief, highly tentative, and somewhat amateurish reconnaissance of the territory should be of some value.

Images of the Mechanical Arts in the Sixteenth and Seventeenth Centuries

When I began looking for sixteenth- and seventeenth-century representations of the mechanical arts, I expected to find a number of them more or less like the illustration of bread making by the late-sixteenth-century Flemish engraver Martin de Vos, which is reproduced as figure

Fig. 8.1. An illustration of bread making, by Martin de Vos. Courtesy of the Cabinet des estampes, Bibliothèque Nationale

8.1.[2] This print, I would argue, sets forth in visual form the duality of work in Old Regime culture that is signified in the term "mechanical art." In Old Regime culture, those occupations designated "mechanical arts" were at once *base*, because they were "mechanical" (that is, required manual labor), and *honorable*, because they embodied a certain "art" or skill. Although labor was intrinsically vile—the curse of Adam, a penance for original sin—art, which was defined as "a method for executing a thing well according to certain rules," was order giving and therefore

[2]Martin de Vos (1532–1603) worked in Antwerp. E. Bénézit, *Dictionnaire des peintres, sculpteurs, dessinateurs et graveurs*, new ed., 10 vols. (Paris, 1976), 10:574.

uplifting. Art was the means by which the spirit disciplined the flesh and imposed order in this vile and chaotic world.[3]

The institutional embodiment of art in the mechanical arts was the trade corporation. Trade corporations undertook to enforce the rules governing their particular trades—by restricting practice of a trade to those who were members of the corporation, by regulating apprenticeships, by enforcing certain standards of quality, and by requiring a masterpiece of anyone who wished to become a master. The corporation was a privileged community of men (or very occasionally of women) devoted to the practice and perfection of a given art. The practitioners of an art were united into a community not only by their common membership in the corporation and their common subjection to its rules, but by a whole set of mutual obligations. They contributed to a common fund to aid members in need, they provided corporate funerals to send departed brothers into the next world, and they were united in the veneration of the trade's patron saint and the joyous celebration of his annual feast day. They formed a spiritual as well as a practical whole, elevated above manual labor not only by their mastery of their art, but by the higher spiritual purpose symbolized by the patron saint.[4]

Martin de Vos's illustration of the baker's trade embodies much of this ennobling conception of mechanical art. The border of the engraving marks out the stages and techniques of the manufacture of bread. The production of grain is represented by the plow, the sheaf of wheat, and the scythes on the left. This is followed, moving clockwise, by milling, weighing the flour, kneading the dough, setting the loaves to rise on a table, baking them in an oven, and finally storing them on shelves ready to be sold. The extreme right-hand border illustrates the various tools of the trade: a spade and rake, a threshing flail and winnowing basket, a sack of grain, a rolling pin, and the baker's oven spade with two loaves of bread. But these representations of the tools and processes of production are not the center of interest of this print. They form only a kind of decorative and didactic border surrounding the far more edifying scene in the center. The caption to this central scene reads, "I have hungered, Ceres, and you have fed me." The chief figure is Ceres, the goddess of grain, who is seated at the right and who distributes loaves to the needy in the marketplace. (Soup is also being distributed, on the left.) In this print as a whole, then, the mundane activities of the art of bread making are subordinated pictorially to the goddess—and to the plenty and charity she represents. The emphasis, in other words, is not on the painful labor of baking, but on the lofty *ends* of the art—producing

[3]For an exposition of these ideas, see Sewell, *Work and Revolution*, pp. 21–25.
[4]On corporations, see ibid., pp. 25–39.

SACCHARVM.
Qua Saccharum paretur arte, plurimis *Pictura, quam vides, docebit te modis.*

Fig. 8.2. Sugar, by Jan van der Straet. Courtesy of the Cabinet des estampes, Bibliothèque Nationale

the staff of life, whose sacramental and metaphorical importance in Christian theology and in classical mythology hardly needs elaboration. The subordination of labor to higher spiritual purpose can be seen not only in the way labor is placed at the margins of this image, but in the contrasting artistic treatment of the mundane border and the ennobling central panel. The border is more roughly drawn and is static—even the toiling figures appear to be in suspended animation. The central panel, by contrast, is much more finely drawn and far more dynamic—with that sense of restless movement so familiar to us in the great painters of this period.

But de Vos's engraving is in fact quite unusual. To judge from my research, at least, such mixing of spiritual considerations into illustrations of the mechanical arts is rare. Far more typical is the print, illustrating the art of sugar making, that is reproduced as figure 8.2. This print is by Jan van der Straet (Latinized in the signature as Joan Stradamus), another Flemish engraver who was a contemporary of de Vos.[5] Van der Straet in fact illustrated a whole series of mechanical arts, including flour milling, distilling, printing, and oil pressing in addition to sugar manufacture. This print is explicitly didactic. The caption says, "this picture will show you how sugar is made." In the background we see the harvesting of cane and its transportation to the mill (both by land and by sea). The foreground and middle ground of the engraving depict the stages of manufacture in the sugar mill. The cane is first cut into pieces, then shoveled into baskets that are carried off and emptied into a water-powered grinding mill. The resulting pulp then enters a human-powered press. The sap runs out of the bottom of the press into a cistern in the floor, whence it is transferred in large buckets into boiling vats. There it is stirred until it reaches the right consistency, when it is ladled out into molds to dry. Finally, the sugar loaves are removed from the molds and stacked on a table.

This engraving is a remarkably lucid and concise depiction of the entire process of sugar production. It is realistic in its treatment of technical detail: the artist gives us accurate and easily comprehensible representations of tools and machinery. In other respects, however, the print is far from realistic. The perspective is distinctly peculiar. (Notice, for example, that the worker stacking sugar loaves at the rear of the table ought, according to normal rules of perspective, to be standing about as far back as the steps leading to the higher floor level. He should therefore be nearly as far from the viewer as the man carrying the basket of cut cane to the grinding mill. Yet he is twice as big—nearly as big as the men at the extreme front of the picture.) Moreover, the mill itself is an utterly implausible structure. (What is the function of the arched wall on the right? What happens to the three steps in the left middle ground when they disappear behind the table?) Finally, the arrangement of workers and equipment within the mill is highly artificial. (Notice, for example, that cane choppers and sugar-loaf stackers are crowded into the same space in the foreground in spite of the large empty area immediately to their rear. Also notice that the two workers turning the press at the rear will fall into the cistern with their next step.)

What the artist gives us is not a realistic reproduction, but a synoptic vision of sugar manufacture, with all stages of production open to our view at once—rather like medieval or early Renaissance depictions of saints' lives, where all the important stages of the saint's history are depicted in a unified space, as if they happened simultaneously. It is this purpose of representing the art of sugar making as a *whole* that explains

---

[5]Van der Straet (1523–1605) worked in Antwerp, Lyons, and Italy. Bénézit, *Dictionnaire,* 9:857.

William H. Sewell, Jr.

the artists' liberties with architecture and perspective and the unlikely arrangement of the workers. The artist also uses other devices to highlight the unity of the art. Notice that the flow of the labor process in the mill describes a complete circle, beginning and ending at the front of the picture. There is, moreover, a coordination in the movement of the figures, even between those engaged in completely disjointed activities. Notice how all the figures in the foreground have their heads and upper bodies inclined in just the same direction, creating a sense of bending to a common purpose. This common inclination is also echoed by the figures working in the rear of the mill and even by the steam emerging from the vats and the donkey hauling cane to the mill at the extreme right. If van der Straet's illustration of sugar making has none of the spiritually uplifting quality of de Vos's illustration of baking, it powerfully develops the theme of community or common purpose among the workers engaged in an art.

This same theme is also stated, though far less self-consciously, in a much more realistic engraving by Abraham Bosse, dating from the middle of the seventeenth century, which is reproduced as figure 8.3.[6] Once again this is a didactic work, accompanied by a lengthy text that begins, "this figure shows you how engravings are printed" and goes on to detail all the steps in the process. In this case the perspective is exact and the architecture of the building is perfectly plausible. The arrangement of the workers, however, is once again artificial. (Notice that if the worker on the right continues to turn the arms of the press so as to pass the printing table through the rollers, the table will eventually smash the worker at the extreme left up against the workbench. The worker on the left is placed there to give the composition a sense of balance, not out of respect for realism.) But most important, Bosse has made effective use of the device of inclining the workers' bodies at the same angle, an angle that is also reproduced by the arms of the press. By this means the three men and the machine are presented visually as being unified in a common task.

This concern with unity is taken to its logical conclusion in a late seventeenth-century engraving by Nicolas de Larmessin reproduced as figure 8.4.[7] This is one of a series of engravings by de Larmessin depicting the costumes of some fifteen to twenty trades, each more fantastic than the other. Like this image, all are personifications of the trade—with a vengeance. Here the various small tools of the trade form the clothing and bodily ornaments of the pastry maker, the oven is his chest, and his hat is composed of a sampling of the trade's wares. What does

[6]Bosse (1602–76) worked in Paris. Ibid., 2:196–97.
[7]De Larmessin (1638–94) worked in Paris. Ibid., 6:455.

Cette figure vous montre Comme on Imprime les planches de taille douce,

Lancre en est faite dhuille de noix, bruslée et de noir de lie de vin, dont le meilleur vient Dallemagne. Limprimeur prend de Cette ancre auec vn tampon de linge, on encre sa planche vn
chaude, lessuye apres legerem auec dautre linge, et acheue de la nettoyer auec la paume de sa main. Cela fait il met cette planche a lenuers sur la table de sa presse, aplique dessus vne feuille de papier
trempe et repose, et Couure cela dune foeuille dautre papier et dun ou deux Langes, puis en tirant les bras de sa presse il faut passer sa table auec sa planche entre deux rouleaux

faict a leau forte par *Bosse* a Paris en Lisle du palais lan 1642, auec priuilege

Fig. 8.3. An illustration of engraving, by Abraham Bosse. Courtesy of the Cabinet des estampes, Bibliothèque Nationale

this image signify, other than a fanciful sense of humor on the part of the artist? In my opinion it signifies the complete identification of the artisan with his trade. This print seems to be saying that not only are artisans unified in the practice of a common art, but their art makes them into a particular kind of person, with a single public personality, a single style of life, a single being. Louis XIV, who was king at the time this print was produced, was identified with the state in the famous phrase "L'état, c'est moi." The pastry maker represented in this engraving is no less completely identified with his trade. "Mon métier, c'est moi" might be an appropriate rendering of this print's message.

To summarize: Sixteenth- and seventeenth-century representations of the mechanical arts take a number of different forms, but nearly all of

Habit de Paticier

Fig. 8.4. Costume of the pastry maker, by Nicolas de Larmessin. Courtesy of the Cabinet des estampes, Bibliothèque Nationale

them emphasize, in one way or another, the unity of the trade. Whether by common subordination to a higher purpose, by a circular presentation of the work process, by the device of inclining figures at the same angle, or by summing up the entire trade in one fantastic person, each mechanical art is presented to the viewer as a harmonious, unified whole. A notable feature of these prints is their stylistic continuity with the art of the age. The pictorial conventions used by de Vos, van der Straet, Bosse, de Larmessin, and other artists who illustrated the mechanical arts were the same that they used in portrayals of the nobility, of religious scenes, of allegories, or of mythology and history. The composition of van der Straet's illustration of sugar making, for example, could easily be adapted to an adoration of the Magi or an Apollo attended by nymphs. This stylistic continuity mirrored the ideological continuity between ideas about labor and reigning conceptions of the cosmos and social order; depictions of labor, for these artists and their viewers, were mirrors of the grand providential scheme of life.

The *Encyclopédie*

The same Old Regime conventions for depicting the mechanical arts continued to flourish in the eighteenth century; any number of eighteenth-century prints reiterate the themes and devices found in sixteenth- and seventeenth-century works. But the plates of the *Encyclopédie*, which were produced in the 1750s and 1760s, marked a sharp break with tradition, a break that parallels the ideological rupture between the philosophes and surrounding Old Regime society. The divergence from preexisting conventions can be discerned in virtually any of the plates, for example, an illustration of pin making, reproduced as figure 8.5.[8] First, the picture surface is dominated not by human figures, who are limited to the upper third of the plate, but by the large-scale representations of tools and equipment that cover the lower two-thirds. Second, even in the upper panel the figures are small and inconsequential, usually dwarfed in a vast and bare room. The large bare room, which is a sharp contrast with the busy, cluttered spaces depicted by van der Straet and Bosse, was also far from a realistic depiction of the crowded workshops in which most eighteenth-century trades were carried on. Third, the illustration lacks the visual lucidity found, for example, in van der Straet's and Bosse's engravings. The tools and equipment are clearly drawn, and we can easily see how they are used, but we get no sense for the orga-

[8]"Epinglier," *Planches pour l'encyclopédie, ou Pour le dictionnaire raisonné des sciences, des arts liberaux, et des arts mécaniques, avec leur explication*, 2d ed., 11 vols. (Luques, 1765–73), vol. 4.

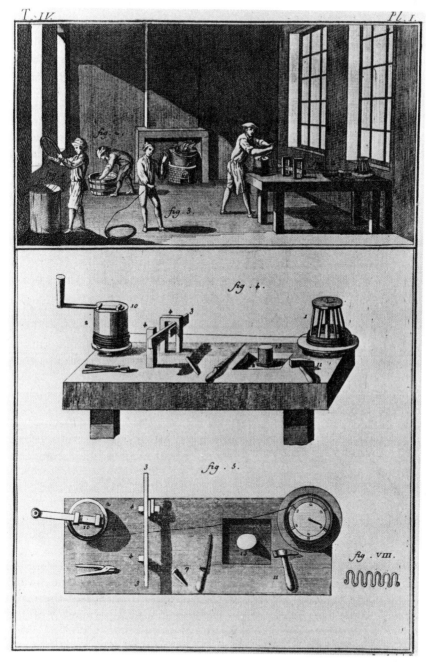

Fig. 8.5. Pin making, from the *Encyclopédie*. Courtesy of Special Collections, University of Arizona Library

nization or flow of the process of production. This fracturing of the flow of production was actually intensified by the encyclopedists' frequent practice of using more than one plate to illustrate a trade. The didactic function of the illustration is entirely dependent on the accompanying verbal explanations, which are provided on adjacent pages. Fourth, the human figures are anonymous. In sharp contrast to the vivid faces depicted by van der Straet or Bosse, the faces in this illustration are utterly unmemorable. The figures are quite without personality; they are purely *abstract* workmen, whereas van der Straet's or Bosse's workers appear to be real people with distinct physiognomies and personalities. Fifth, far from giving an impression of unity in a common task, the figures have no communication with one another. Each faces in a different direction; each is intent on his own work. The workers seem totally unaware of each other's presence.

Here it might be objected that the anonymity of the figures and their lack of communication are purely a function of the crudeness with which the plates were executed. The sixteenth- and seventeenth-century print-makers whose work has been discussed were all well-known artists, and their works are beautiful as works of art, quite aside from their illustrative function. The plates in the *Encyclopédie* are anonymous and were turned out in vast numbers in a brief space of time. Even the best of them cannot compare in quality with the sixteenth- and seventeenth-century prints examined above, and some, like the illustration of the pin makers, are very crude. But even the finer and more sophisticated of the *Encyclopédie*'s plates diverge from prior conventions in precisely the same ways that the crude ones do.

An example is the plate, illustrating the art of tanning, reproduced as figure 8.6.[9] It is certainly far more sophisticated and far better executed than the plate illustrating pin making. The figures are much less stiff; they seem actually to be moving in their work. Moreover, the composition is far more complex. The room is **L**-shaped, with windows on adjacent sides of the **L**. Through one window we can glimpse the neoclassical facade of a building across the street, and we can also look out one window and back into the shop through another, across the angle of the **L**. The arrangement of the figures is also much more complex and more balanced. The two men in the foreground are bent toward the center of the picture, drawing our attention inward to the three workers at the rear. These five workers form a neat pyramid, with the worker at the extreme rear of the room at its summit. At the same time, this formal symmetry is broken by the worker at the extreme left, whose attention is directed outward, to a hide against the left wall; by the worker

[9]"Corroyeur," ibid., vol. 3.

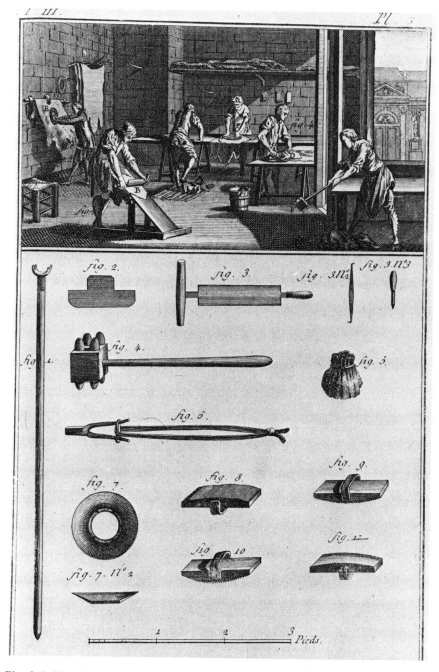

Fig. 8.6. Tanning, from the *Encyclopédie*. Courtesy of Special Collections, University of Arizona Library

bending over the table at the right, who seems to be gazing somewhat absently out the window; and by the intrusion of the L-shaped wall on the right. The result is a sophisticated mixture of symmetry and asymmetry, one that simultaneously suggests order and spontaneity. In brief, this illustration—in my opinion, one of the best in the *Encyclopédie*—is the work of an accomplished artist.

Yet even this plate shows the same traits pointed out in the much cruder plate on pin making. The room, though more crowded, is still remarkably bare for an eighteenth-century workshop. We get no sense of the flow or sequencing of the process of production. The figures also remain anonymous. The faces of four of the six workers either are turned away from the viewer, are completely in shadow, or are bent over at such an angle that their features cannot be made out clearly. And the remaining two faces, which can be seen in full light in profile, are once again blank and undistinctive—generic faces of anonymous workmen. Finally, even though the figures are carefully arranged to achieve an artistic balance, they still have absolutely no communication with one another. Each is isolated at his own particular task. In this artistically sophisticated plate, these characteristics *must* be understood as intentional; they cannot be explained by the artist's lack of skill.

This point can be confirmed by looking briefly at two more examples, both skilled compositions. Figure 8.7,[10] a plate illustrating the art of button making, reproduces all the features mentioned above. The room is bare, and there is no pictorial representation of the flow of production. The figures (with the partial exception of the man seated on the bench in the foreground) remain anonymous. Three have their faces in shadow, the face of another is blocked off by the saw, and the others have the usual bland, generic countenances. But what this plate shows with particular clarity is the lack of communication between figures. Here every worker is paired with one or more fellow workers in the operation of some tool or machine. Yet even in these circumstances they seem virtually unaware of one another's presence. Again, with the exception of the man at the bench in the foreground, all are either staring blankly into space or are totally absorbed in their own labor, seemingly taking no account of the co-worker at the other end of the saw or the drive wheel.

The final example is figure 8.8,[11] a plate illustrating scale making. Here the scene includes not only the worker, but a shop counter and a female customer out in the street. (Her by now familiarly blank face is half-hidden by the window frame.) One might expect the artisans to acknowledge her presence—attempting to sell her a scale or haggling

[10]"Boutonnier," ibid., vol. 4.
[11]"Balancier," ibid., vol. 2.

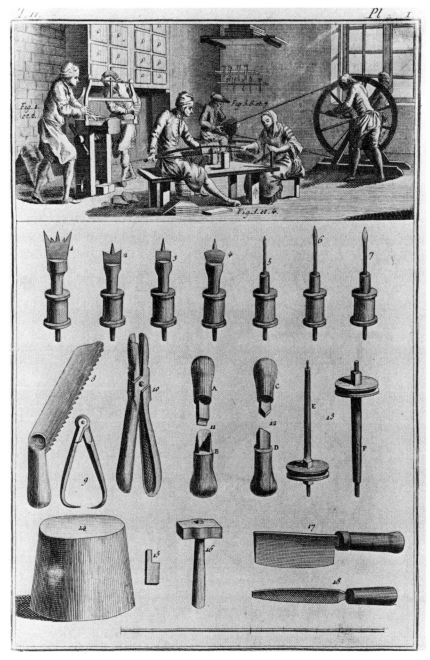

Fig. 8.7. Button making, from the *Encyclopédie.* Courtesy of Special Collections, University of Arizona Library

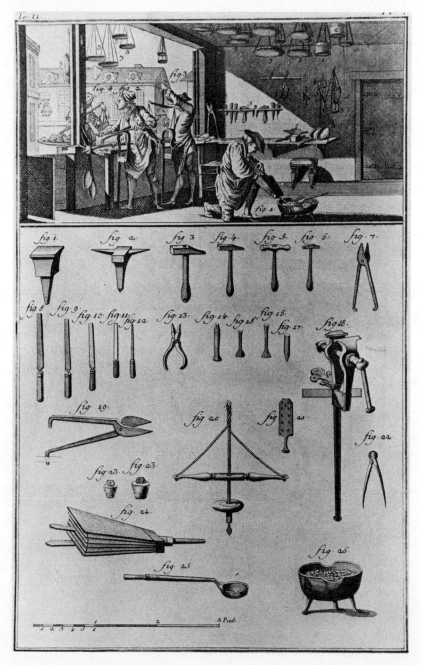

Fig. 8.8. Scale making, from the *Encyclopédie*. Courtesy of Special Collections, University of Arizona Library

over its price, for example. Yet two of the three workmen seem totally unaware of her presence, and the third, who is looking up at her from his work, gives the impression of being startled to find her there. He appears to regard her visit not as an expected event of the workday, or as a welcome opportunity for a sale or a conversation, but as an intrusion into his work. Once again this plate, otherwise sophisticated, shows an almost perverse unwillingness to acknowledge the necessity, let alone the joy, of human communication in the artisan's worklife.

One difference between the plates of the *Encyclopédie* and the six-teenth- and seventeenth-century prints may be the consequence of broader changes in artistic styles. It is certainly true that anonymous or generic faces were very much in vogue in mid-eighteenth century French art—the highly stylized baby-faced figures in the paintings of Fragonard or Boucher are an obvious example. The anonymity of the figures in the plates of the *Encyclopédie* may be at least partly explained as con-formity to contemporary artistic tastes. But the general drift of artistic style can hardly account for the other features of the plates—after all, Fragonard's and Boucher's pictures swirl with rococo clutter, and their figures are typically in rapt communication. The barrenness of the rooms, the lack of lucidity about sequences of production, or the odd isolation of the figures from one another—these characteristics are specific to the plates of the *Encyclopédie*. They can be understood only in the context of Enlightenment ideas about work—ideas expressed most cogently by Diderot himself in the text of the *Encyclopédie*.[12]

One of the major tasks that Diderot set for the *Encyclopédie* was to "raise the mechanical arts from the debasement where prejudice has held them for so long."[13] This program was in fact double-edged. On the one hand, Diderot wished to demonstrate to the educated public that the mechanical arts as they were currently practiced were complex and subtle achievements of human intelligence—and therefore that they should not be scorned as base. "In what systems of Physics or Meta-physics," Diderot asks, "does one find more of intelligence, wisdom, consequence, than in machines for spinning gold or making stockings ... ? What demonstration of Mathematics is more complicated than the mechanism of certain clocks?"[14] But at the same time, Diderot also be-lieved that the mechanical arts as currently practiced—and the artisans who practiced them—were in need of considerable improvement. Al-though the rules that governed the mechanical arts were complex and

---

[12]For a discussion of Diderot's ideas about the mechanical arts, see Sewell, *Work and Revolution in France*, pp. 65–72.

[13]"Art," in Diderot, *Encyclopédie, ou Dictionnaire raisonné des sciences, des arts et des métiers*, 17 vols. (Paris, 1751–72), 1:717.

[14]Ibid., 1:714.

subtle, the artisans who followed these rules generally understood them very imperfectly; they worked essentially by rote. Moreover, the organization of mechanical arts into corporations discouraged curiosity and initiative on the part of workmen, who were constrained to make products according to the tried-and-true methods sanctioned by the corporations. The *Encyclopédie*, through its articles and plates, intended to improve the mechanical arts by two means: first, by making public the best and most up-to-date techniques, and second, by setting forth the scientific principles on which these techniques were based.

Since, in Diderot's words, "the history of the arts and crafts is nothing but the history of nature put to use,"[15] the mechanical arts were really a kind of applied science. The transformations that natural objects underwent in the process of fabrication had by necessity to follow the laws of chemistry, physics, and biology. It therefore followed that knowledge of mechanical arts should be exact, rational, and publicly available, like other scientific knowledge. It should not, as was so often the case, be a mere collection of ill-understood rules of thumb, hedged by workmen's superstitions and guarded as the private secrets of the corporations. In the traditional scheme of things, the essence of a craft was the skills of the workmen, which were seen as the exclusive personal and collective possessions of the workers in a given trade. But in Diderot's vision, pride of place was taken by an anonymous and publicly available science. All of this implied an enormous change in the mechanical arts as institutions. Corporations, according to Diderot, should be suppressed, and individuals should be free to produce whatever goods they wished in whatever way they chose, subject only to the discipline of the market. The sense of solidarity, the technical conservatism, and the conformity of the corporate community should be replaced by a spirit of individualism, initiative, and widespread experimentation. The liberal mentality of the philosophes, in other words, should replace the archaic traditionalism of the corporate system.

It is in the context of this far-reaching Enlightenment program for the reform of mechanical arts that the peculiar features of the *Encyclopédie*'s plates begin to make sense. The large-scale renderings of tools and equipment that crowd the human figures into a small panel at the top mirror the primacy of science over human skill, as does the small size and anonymity of the human figures who are represented even on this upper panel. The barrenness and lifelessness of the workshops also represent a world ordered by scientific precision rather than by human skill. Diderot's "scientific" vision helps to explain the isolation of the workers from each other. Eighteenth-century scientific thought was pro-

[15]"Encyclopédie," in ibid., 5:647.

foundly analytical. To understand a phenomenon scientifically was to break it down into its elements. This is precisely what has happened to the workers in the plates. Each represents a discrete and separable step in the process of production, and the process as a whole consists of a simple adding up of these discrete steps—not, as in the sixteenth- and seventeenth-century prints, a unified whole that is clearly greater than the sum of its parts.[16] But this feature of the plates had a more directly social meaning as well. If the communication and common inclination of workmen in the sixteenth- and seventeenth-century prints was a visual invocation of the unity of the trade community, the odd isolation of workers in the *Encyclopédie*'s plates signified an opposition to the very notion of a trade community. The workers in the plates are in this sense highly individuated even though they are deprived of any personality. They are self-sufficient, bound to no larger community of workers.

In summary, the plates of the *Encyclopédie* represent a scientized, individualized, utopian projection of the world of work as imagined by the philosophes. It is not an attractive vision. It repudiated the more human, cluttered, and communal world represented in the sixteenth- and seventeenth-century prints. It is cold, analytical, and deadly serious. The robotic workers of the *Encyclopédie* lack the playfulness and wit we can discern in the faces portrayed by van der Straet or Bosse. Van der Straet's and Bosse's workers seem to have lives and personalities of their own, unconquered by the artist's pen; one can imagine them arguing about politics, playing a trick on the boss, or planning a strike. The workers in the plates of the *Encyclopédie* are docile automatons who carry out their scientifically determined tasks with the efficiency—and the joylessness—of machines.[17] Here, some decades before the beginnings of the first modern factories, workers are already portrayed as appendages

[16]This interpretation fits what is known about the provenance of the plates. Many were patterned on illustrations for a "Description des arts et métiers" originally undertaken by the Académie des sciences near the end of the seventeenth century. Illustrations were slowly accumulated until the mid-1750s, when Diderot procured the Académie's collection of drawings with the intention of using them as the basis of plates for the *Encyclopédie*. This effort roused the Académie, which rushed its own "Description" into publication, beginning in 1761, a year before the first volume of the *Encyclopédie*'s plates appeared. That the models for the plates of the *Encyclopédie* were originally prepared under the direction of the Académie makes evident their scientific inspiration. The Académie's collection was published under the title *Description des arts et métiers, faites at approuvés par Messieurs de l'Académie royale des sciences avec figures* (Paris, 1761–89). On the provenance of the plates of the *Encyclopédie*, see Jacques Proust, "La documentation technique de Diderot dans 'l'Encyclopédie,' " *Revue d'histoire litteraire de la France* 57 (1954): 340–47, and idem, *Diderot et l'Encyclopédie* (Paris, 1962), pp. 49–51, 54–57.

[17]This interpretation is in accord with the observations of Robert Darnton, *The Business of Enlightenment: A Publishing History of the Encyclopédie, 1755–1800* (Harvard, 1979), p. 242. It is fundamentally at odds with that of Roland Barthes, who sees the plates as "a sort of golden legend of the artisanate," in which men dominate machines. Roland Barthes, Robert Mazui, and Jean-Pierre Seguin, *L'univers de l'Encyclopédie* (Paris, 1964), p. 11.

to technology. In Marxist terminology, they are at once "free labor" and pure abstract "labor power." But they are at the same time deprived of the social being that makes resistance possible. For this reason, the plates of the *Encyclopédie* might reasonably be characterized as an early capitalist utopian vision.

It is worth dwelling for a moment on this point. Labor historians have traditionally been inclined to see the "mature" capitalist labor relationship as emerging only with the development of the factory, where the complex division of labor, the subjection of laborers to the rhythm of the machine, and the new opportunities for surveillance and discipline created a fully alienated and proletarianized labor force. Recent research on nineteenth-century labor has modified this notion in two ways. Work on artisans has demonstrated that division of labor, trivialization of tasks, and intensified discipline took place in many craft trades long before the introduction of significant new technology or factory production.[18] This work on the proletarianization of artisans continues to take the factory worker as the model proletarian, but it indicates that the process of proletarianization is not so directly linked to technological changes as had previously been assumed. Meanwhile, new research on factory workers undermines the assumed connection between mechanization and proletarianization from the other side. William Reddy demonstrates that large-scale mechanized production in the French textile industry did not automatically create a proletarianized labor force—in the first half of the nineteenth century, textile factory workers had a great deal of on-the-job autonomy, typically worked in self-disciplining family units, and long maintained essentially commercial rather than wage-labor relations with their employers. Reddy also shows that the pure, alienated proletarian was a standard figure of nineteenth-century discourse about textile workers long before such a figure made even the most halting appear-

[18]See Christopher H. Johnson, "Economic Change and Artisan Discontent: The Tailors' History, 1800–48," in *Revolution and Reaction: 1848 and the Second French Republic*, ed. Roger Price (London, 1975), pp. 87–114; *Utopian Communism in France: Cabet and the Icarians, 1839–1851* (Ithaca, 1974), esp. pp. 177–82; idem, "Communism and the Working Class before Marx: The Icarian Experience," *American Historical Review* 76 (June 1971): 657–67; Bernard H. Moss, *The Origins of the French Labor Movement: The Socialism of Skilled Workers, 1830–1914* (Berkeley, 1976), esp. chap. 1; Ronald Aminzade, "The Transformation of Social Solidarities in Nineteenth-Century Toulouse," in *Consciousness and Class Experience in Nineteenth-Century Europe*, ed. John M. Merriman (New York, 1979), pp. 85–105; idem, *Class, Politics and Early Industrial Capitalism: A Study of Mid-Nineteenth-Century Toulouse, France* (Albany, N.Y., 1981), chap. 2; Alain Cottereau's introduction to Denis Poulot, *Le sublime, ou Le travailleur comme il est en 1870, et ce qu'il peut être* (Paris, 1980), esp. pp. 63–81; and Alain Faure's introduction to Agricol Perdiguier, *Mémoires d'un compagnon* (Paris, 1980), pp. 21–22. The classic discussion of this problem is E. P. Thompson's analysis of London artisans in *The Making of the English Working Class* (London, 1963), chap. 8. On England, see also Raphael Samuel, "Workshop of the World: Steam Power and Hand Technology in Mid-Victorian Britain," *History Workshop* 3 (1967): 6–72.

ance on the factory floor.[19] The interpretation of the plates of the *Encyclopédie* made in this essay further contributes to this ongoing reassessment of the connection between technical development and the emergence of the capitalist labor relationship. It seems to indicate that a clear notion of labor as fully alienated abstract labor power was thinkable, and picturable, as early as the 1750s, decades before the development of the technology that supposedly made such a thing possible. The plates of the *Encyclopédie* argue for a cultural construction of the capitalist mode of production well in advance of its practical realization.

The Nineteenth Century

The *Encyclopédie* had enormous prestige in eighteenth-century France, and its plates, together with numerous virtually indistinguishable imitations, dominated the depiction of mechanical arts for decades. But by the 1830s new themes began to assert themselves. Much of the reform of the mechanical arts that Diderot had advocated was actually carried out in the French Revolution. The corporations were abolished, and all restrictions on economic enterprise were swept away. This reform, however, did not have quite the effects that Diderot and the philosophes had imagined. It is true that the pace of technical innovation increased and that science was now applied to industry more assiduously than it had been in the eighteenth century. But the destruction of the guilds and the generalization of laissez-faire did not succeed in producing a docile, individualized labor force. The workers, as I have tried to demonstrate in *Work and Revolution in France*, remained committed to the communal values of the corporations and bitterly resisted the economic liberalism of the new system—at first through their own clandestine corporate organizations and eventually through socialist movements.[20] By the 1830s or the 1840s, the beginnings of factory industry and the intensified working-class and socialist agitation produced a growing interest in the problem of labor among the educated public—an interest compounded of class fear, sympathy for the poor, pride in industrial progress, and sheer curiosity. The production of inexpensive prints depicting workers and their industries was one sign of this growing interest.

Many of these prints were devoted to the new factory industry that had grown up since 1820 or so. One example is figure 8.9, a print that dates from the 1840s and illustrates iron forging. This lithograph was one of a series of prints depicting work in factories entitled "Notions

[19]William R. Reddy, *The Rise of Market Culture: The Textile Trade and French Society, 1750–1900* (Cambridge, 1984).
[20]Sewell, *Work and Revolution in France*, chaps. 8–11.

Librairie de L. Hachette et Cie a Paris et à Alger   FORGES.   Lith. de P. Dinocteau, r des Maçons Sorbon

Fig. 8.9. Iron forging. Courtesy of Cabinet des estampes, Bibliothèque Nationale

industrielles." The contrasts between this print and the plates of the *Encyclopédie* are striking. First, though there is a good deal of emphasis on technical detail, the tools and machines are all shown in use, not in a segregated panel of the illustration. Second, the workshop is far from the barren, lifeless, rectangular rooms presented in most of the *Encyclopédie*'s plates. This metallurgical establishment appears to have been set up in some ancient, half-ruined stone building converted to industrial use—perhaps one of the abandoned convents or monasteries that so often met this fate in the postrevolutionary years. The interior space is complex, with arches, corners, and long, oddly shaped rooms. This space is filled with a jumble of workmen, machines, tools, steam, and bits of debris. Third, while certainly not up to the level of van der Straet, this illustration is a far more lucid depiction of the production process than most plates in the *Encyclopédie.* The various phases of iron making are represented: the forge is stoked, molten metal is poured out into pigs or into molds, the solidified but still red-hot iron is beaten by a huge mechanical hammer, and this wrought iron is then rolled out into a long, thin bar. The fourth contrast is the sense of communication between workers, which, while by no means as pronounced as in the sixteenth- and seventeenth-century prints, is much more notable than in the plates of the *Encyclopédie.* Here the main unifying device is the placement of the worker in the center foreground so that the rods held by the five workers behind him seem to radiate energy outward from his body. Fifth, the workmen are animated and highly individualized—almost to the point of caricature. Not only are their faces distinct and memorable, but each worker wears a different costume. The headgear is especially various. In part the artist may be making a point about this particular industry: metallurgy had the most cosmopolitan work force of any industry in the early Industrial Revolution. The Scottish tam-o'-shanter worn by the tall, bare-chested worker on the right is surely intended to make this point. But an "ethnographic" sense of the foreignness and quaintness of the workers is a feature of most nineteenth-century illustrations of labor. This should not be surprising, since the first half of the nineteenth century was the era of the first great studies of ethnography and folklore in France. These prints constitute another branch of the reconnaissance of French society undertaken by the early folklorists.

The same points can be made about the print depicting a soap factory that is reproduced as figure 8.10. The print was part of the same "Notions industrielles" series, but was by a different and rather less sophisticated artist. The workshop is once again cluttered and highly animated. The process of production is presented even more lucidly than in the illustration of iron forging. The raw materials are removed from barrels and shoveled into boiling vats. The liquid is next ladled out into buckets and transferred to a cooling trough, then pumped into molds, where it solidifies. Finally, the soap is cut into bars. Once again the faces, costumes, and personalities of the workers are distinctive, if less various and exotic than in the illustration of iron forging. And finally, the figures are strongly unified—largely by the now-familiar device of common inclination. All but the figure in the extreme right foreground are bending toward the right front of the picture, and this latter, by far the largest figure, balances them by directing his effort back toward them.

The same themes that appear in these illustrations of factory trades are also manifested in illustrations of old-fashioned artisan trades—the classical mechanical arts. Figure 8.11, which depicts shoemakers, is part of a parallel series to the "Notions industrielles" entitled "Arts et Métiers" (arts and crafts). This lithograph is signed by one Schultz, but I have

FABRIQUE DE SAVON.

Fig. 8.10. Soap factory. Courtesy of Cabinet des estampes, Bibliothèque Nationale

not been able to identify the artist further. In this print the tools and equipment are depicted in profuse detail—hammers, lasts, scissors, knives, needles and thread, glue pots—scattered over the floor and worktables and arrayed along the walls. The division of labor is clearly set forth. The worker at the left cuts out and hammers the soles. The rather distinguished-looking bespectacled worker at the right cuts out the leather for the uppers. (The "cutters" were always the aristocrats of the shoe-making industry.) The two workers in the center sew together the pieces the others have finished. The cluttered room fairly hums with life, and with ethnographic as well as technical detail. Besides the scraps of leather and the innumerable tools, there is a shopwindow filled with wares, four wine flagons (apparently empty), a songbird in a cage, and even a picture

LE CORDONNIER.

Fig. 8.11. The shoemaker, by Schultz. Courtesy of the Cabinet des estampes, Bibliothèque Nationale

of Napoleon on the wall. (This last is surely an allusion to the shoemakers' reputation for political radicalism.) The workers, who again sport colorful and various headgear, have vivid personalities and—in spite of the division of labor—seem to work in perfect communication. The worker at the left, who sports a fez and a cigar holder, seems to be telling a joke or a story, and the worker on the far right, while looking down at his work, also seems to be leaning forward to listen for the punch line. This illustration manages to provide a lucid and technically exact depiction of the craft and at the same time to present vividly the social relations that link the workers to each other.

To judge from the prints in these two series, at least, nineteenth-century illustrations of the mechanical arts are closer in their themes to the sixteenth- and seventeenth-century prints than to the eighteenth-century plates of the *Encyclopédie*. Human skill and personality are brought back with a vengeance; the workshops are cluttered and alive; the workers communicate on the job and appear to make up a harmonious community. The utopian illusion of a scientifically ordered world of work has been abandoned, even in representations of factories—themselves the greatest triumph of scientific industry. The experience of the post-revolutionary years, and especially the workers' assertion of their own human solidarity, has driven home a recognition of the profoundly social character of labor.

These tendencies in the depiction of labor can be seen even in prints that make a conscious effort to imitate the plates of the *Encyclopédie*. One example is figure 8.12, a print illustrating saddle making, which was produced in Alsace in the 1860s. Like the plates of the *Encyclopédie*, this print was explicitly didactic, intended, according to the caption, "for the instruction of youth." It even adopted the *Encyclopédie*'s convention of making large-scale representations of tools, separated off from a scene illustrating their use. Moreover, with the exception of the two workers making a buggy top on the right, each craftsman is intent on his own particular task; they do not seem to be communicating with one another. But in spite of all these resemblances, how different this print is from the plates of the *Encyclopédie*! The representation of the workmen is at the center of the picture surface rather than in a band at the top, and the tools are not arranged in orderly rows, but artfully crisscrossed and arrayed in a decorative border. Instead of dominating the human figures as in the *Encyclopédie*, the tools draw us inward to the human scene that is presented as the true core of the trade. And the complex central panel, in spite of the individual character of most of the work being performed, also negates the anonymous scientism of the *Encyclopédie*. The workshop is cluttered and vital, and the activity of the workmen appears to radiate outward from the workbench at the center. By the late 1860s, when this print was produced, even a conscious imitation of the *Encyclopédie* could not recapture its spirit and message. By then it was once again impossible, just as it had been in the sixteenth or the seventeenth century, not to recognize the social character of labor.

In one respect, however, this print differs significantly from the nineteenth-century prints examined so far. The prints in the "Notions industrielles" and "Arts et métiers" series are mildly ironic in tone and portray workers who definitely have wills of their own. The workers seem to be, if anything, even more capable of mischief toward the bosses or the authorities than the workers portrayed by van der Straet and

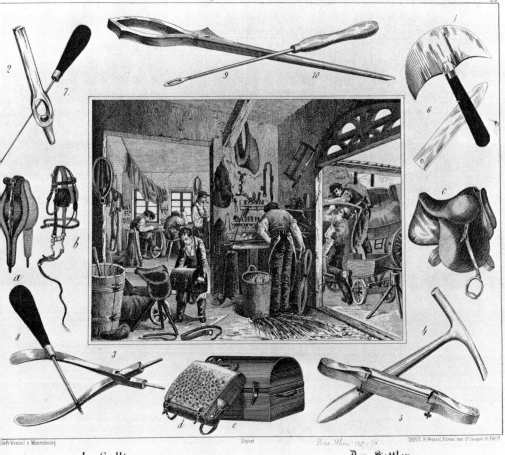

Tableaux d'après nature pour l'instruction de la jeunesse.   Bilder zum Anschauungs-Unterricht für die Jugend.

Le Sellier.   Der Sattler.

Fig. 8.12. The saddler. Courtesy of the Cabinet des estampes, Bibliothèque Nationale

Bosse. This illustration of saddling, on the contrary, is serious and sentimental, suffusing the trade in a kind of warm, nostalgic glow. These pious saddlers seem almost as unlikely to organize a strike as the willless robotic workers depicted in the *Encyclopédie*. If the plates of the *Encyclopédie* were a radical blueprint for the labor relationship of industrial capitalism several decades in advance of the factory system, this print is a conservative nostalgic invocation of the disappearing community of the preindustrial artisan, now, in the late 1860s, increasingly threatened with extinction by the spread of factories. As in the plates of the *Encyclopédie*, the ideological intent of the artist dominates the depiction, robbing the workers of their autonomous wills, constituting them as docile projections of the artist's wishes.

The illustration of saddling forms a fitting conclusion to this essay. It confirms the nineteenth-century artists' insistence on the social character of labor, but its nostalgia also hints that the old-style social relations of production were on the wane. Ironically, this was true even in the field of illustrating labor and technology, where engravings and lithographs were almost totally replaced by photography by the end of the nineteenth century. The artistic victory of social solidarity in nineteenth-century depictions of labor could not negate the real victory of industrial capitalism. The abstract robotic worker, the image of the worker as pure labor power, was excluded from artistic representations of labor, but it advanced triumphantly in other discourses, to achieve a kind of apothesis in the "scientific management" of Fredrick W. Taylor. The twentieth-century factory, with its assembly lines and time-and-motion studies, is the legitimate heir of the vision of labor elaborated in the *Encyclopédie*.

9

The Urban Trades:
Social Analysis and Representation

MAURICE GARDEN

Historians must continually open themselves to new paths and must never assume that a subject has received the "definitive treatment." Those of us who study the "*monde du travail*," for example, are far from having exhausted all the avenues of research, and one of our concerns must be to suggest areas that deserve further observation and reflection. The urban trades generally, and specifically the relation between social analysis and analysis of the ways the trades have been (heretofore) represented, provide an exemplary case in point.

Let us first avoid problems of definition and the traps of a chronology without limits. The expression "monde du travail" is replete with ambiguities and even appears a bit old-fashioned today. We must, within the rather strict limits of modern and contemporary history, establish the fundamental distinctions that are the consequences of the evolving systems of production and exchange. Today we no longer assume that a reference to the "monde du travail" or to "*travailleurs*" refers to individual workers in the sense of factory workers. Rather than rehearse the stereotypical discourse that speaks as much of agricultural work as intellectual, we must acknowledge that history has in fact privileged manual labor, especially that rooted in the burgeoning industrial sphere of the nineteenth century. But it would be a gross simplification to reduce the field to three great periods, or to three systems of work over time, for we must not forget the imbrications: the persistence of older structures in later times, and anticipations of the modern in earlier epochs.

We can find early descriptions of urban work that testify to its specificity in many medieval texts, not to mention the older Greek and By-

zantine models. The fourteenth-century *Livre des métiers* by Etienne Bo-
ileau and the first rules of urban crafts compiled by Alfred Franklin are
examples.[1] However, the long and continuous assumption that urban
work and the "monde du travail" are coterminous is not an insignificant
prejudice. How can we forget the very long and certainly quantitative
domination of the countryside in France at least until the beginning of
the twentieth century? Should we still accept the semantic evolutions that
have assimilated agricultural work to "labeur"—or to "labor" (from *la-
borare*)—when the terms designating agricultural worker—"*journalier*,"
"*brassier*," "*manouvrier*"—specifically call attention to the rhythm of work
(the day, *journée*) or to the absence of tools beyond the human motor,
namely the arms and hands (*bras* and *mains*)? For a long time we have
noticed, among the urban populations at the time of industrialization,
a rejection of journaliers and manoeuvres for their lack of specialization.
In the most recent research on the origins of large-scale industrialization
(and in all the descriptions and explanations of protoindustrialization in
Western Europe from 1700 to 1900) we find evidence of this evolution.
Little by little the functions that once were joined in the person of the
"weaver-peasant" or the "miner-peasant" (who worked for years in the
mines near Saint-Etienne, Montceau-les-Mines, or the Pas-de-Calais basin)
separated off. But it was a very long process. As late as the 1950s there
still existed "peasant-workers" in these old industrial regions who had
never yet totally rejected the older combinations of activities. In the
medieval and early modern periods the "city" term that was more or
less symmetrical with "laboureur" (a term that implied a different social
status from one province to another) and "journalier" was not "ouvrier,"
but rather "*artisan*," which implied not only maker but merchant.[2]

French social history at its origins, at least since Emile Levasseur, has
meticulously described the organization of artisanal work, a corporate
model that has been investigated numerous times, from case studies of
cities to monographs on particular crafts. The hierarchy of work was a
hierarchy inherited from the basic stages of life: apprentice, compagnon,
master. It was also a largely masculine organization: women's work was
considered inferior or even outside the corporate order. The world of
work was also a social hierarchy that granted the totality of rights to the
master alone—in particular, the management of the craft. Masters elected
from their own ranks representatives responsible for all aspects of corporate life: from enforcing the technical standards and regulations for
a particular craft (both commercial and ethical) to organizing and limiting competition, determining the conditions of access to the craft, and

[1] Alfred Franklin, *Dictionnaire historique des arts, métiers et professions exercés dans Paris depuis
le XIIIe siècle* (Paris, 1906).
[2] See Pierre Goubert and Daniel Roche, *Les Français et l'ancien régime*, 2 vols. (Paris, 1984).

deciding the methods of succession, rules of inheritance, and extent of openness to outsiders. At the end of a long line of historians, Emile Coornaert seemed to have definitively closed the book on corporations so that future local studies would serve only to embellish his work without ever challenging his findings.[3]

However, when there are rich and consistent sources that document the past over a long period, such as those E. J. Shephard, Jr., has inspected for Dijon in the eighteenth century, an analysis of artisanal activities can rise to another level. We know well the fissures that appeared in the corporate edifice during the course of the eighteenth century. While the general population of Dijon witnessed only slight growth, that segment composed of craftsmen exhibited a large variation: a lowering of their global proportion on the tax rolls, in spite of a growth in absolute numbers of 468 individuals; a relative decrease in the number of masters; and a large expansion in the number of workers (going from 226 to 796—that is, an augmentation higher than the growth in actual numbers of the group as a whole). This evolution in distribution among the ranks of artisans was happening at the same time as the general population was shifting its balance between the parishes of the old city and the faubourgs.

But for the first time, by combining several sources, it becomes possible to make a global evaluation of the artisanal population across a century. The major "urban" monographs for the early modern period—Amiens, Caen, Lyons, and more recently, Rouen and Bordeaux—have not offered such completeness, either because some of the records (specifically registers of apprenticeship and *lettres de maîtrise*) are missing, or because the sources furnish only a static picture at a given moment in time, from which historians can make only a (more or less justified) extrapolation.[4] The registers of access to the crafts collected by E. J. Shephard offer us a vision far more extended and total: about 2,000 artisans in this city of 20,000 inhabitants, with a total of 5,500 lettres de maîtrise granted between 1693 and 1789. Without a doubt, when interpreting these sources we must take into account the cycles of life in the Old Regime, the age of access to mastership (allowing the possibility of a significant time lag between the promotions of sons of masters and newcomers), and the average number of years an artisan would exercise his craft (a factor that recognizes the life expectancy for adults and the

[3]Emile Coornaert, *Les corporations en France avant 1789* (Paris, 1968).

[4]Pierre Deyon, *Amiens, capitale provinciale: Etude sur la société urbaine au 17e siècle* (Paris, 1967); Maurice Garden, *Lyon et les Lyonnais au XVIIIe siècle* (Paris, 1970); Jean-Claude Perrot, *Genèse d'une ville moderne: Caen au XVIIIe siècle* (Lille, 1974); Jean-Pierre Bardet, *Rouen aux XVIII siècle: Les mutations d'un espace social* (Paris, 1983); Jean-Pierre Poussou, *Bordeaux et le sud-ouest au XVIIIe siècle: Croissance économique et attraction urbaine* (Paris, 1983).

geographic mobility of the masters). About sixty receptions to mastership per year would imply an average life span of thirty-five years (surely excessive for the eighteenth century) and a total of about 2,000 masters. To put it otherwise, it is certain that the Dijonnais sources do not give us the total number of individuals who exercised a craft in the city, but only a very large proportion of them. Below is a list of those crafts that registered ninety or more receptions over this period (the minimum number is thirty, renewed three times in a century). The crafts are regrouped by general type of economic activity:

Food trades: butchers, bakers, pork butchers, grocers, pastry makers, caterers
Wine making and selling (local specialty): coopers, wine merchants, vinegar makers
Construction trades: plasterers, carpenters, sawyers, roofers, contractors, joiners, locksmiths
Clothing trades: shoemakers, cobblers, tailors, used-clothing dealers
Textiles: drapers, weavers

These five groups and twenty-two crafts together make up nearly 80 percent of the total number of receptions and from 60 to 70 percent of the total masterships granted between 1700 and 1790. With these data it is possible to construct a symbolic hierarchy of the crafts by studying, for example, the proportion of sons of masters who take up the work of their fathers. According to this criterion, we find wide variations, even among crafts classified under the same general rubric (see fig. 9.1).

In what is the oldest form of the textile industry, the weavers constitute a homogeneous group with a strong professional legacy: 60 percent of the receptions are sons of masters. This very stable Dijonnais craft also presents the highest rate of family ties and homogeneity. By contrast the drapers, often entrepreneurs and merchants, constricted their ranks while at the same time replacing old draper families with new: only 12 percent of the new drapers were sons of masters, even though the number of masters decreased substantially over the century and the children of that preceding generation alone could have supplied enough masters to replace their fathers. Other crafts show even more change. Wine merchants and pork butchers practically remade themselves anew each generation (with only 2 percent of the sons of masters receiving mastership among the former, 4 percent among the latter). Grocers, vinegar makers, and bakers also experienced a large number of new entries, with only about 20 percent of the sons of masters following in their fathers' footsteps. On the other end of the graph, among butchers about 40 percent of the new masters were sons of masters, while among the coopers, 50 percent were.

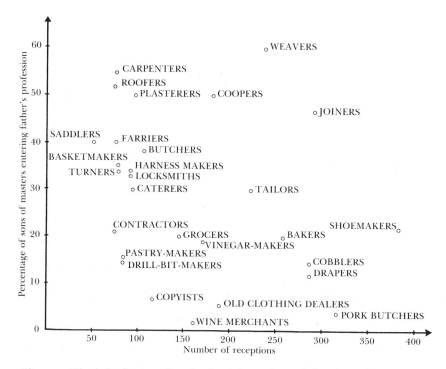

Fig. 9.1. The inheritance of trades in eighteenth-century Dijon: An ambiguous image of the hierarchies. Data from Edward J. Shephard, Jr., "Social and Geographic Mobility of the Eighteenth-Century Guild Artisan," chap. 4 of this book

With a quantitative analysis of the crafts in the city of Dijon before us, then, we can begin to question the homogeneity of this artisanal world of work, a world that continued to dominate urban production and consumption of both necessities and luxury goods even after the suppression of the corporations (that is, after the short-lived attempt of Turgot in 1776 and later, the Le Chapelier law). But is it possible to construct a symbolic hierarchy of the crafts from the data provided by Shephard? We would expect that those crafts highest on the scale would be those the most closed to outsiders, admitting the largest numbers of sons of masters, and accepting fewest newcomers with rural or peasant backgrounds. But there are other factors we must consider.

Throughout the Old Regime the old egalitarian notions of the corporations disappeared. Often a guild was in reality dominated by a "sanior et major pars" in which "sanior" signified the wealthiest members and "major" implied a small group with economic and political power. We must, then, find sources that contain economic information, not just concerning the various rights of access to a craft, but also concerning the success or failures of individuals practicing the craft. We might consult marriage contracts; after-death inventories; transfers of ownership of shops or residences or farms; wills and bequests; the assets and liabilities on commercial balance sheets; and probate division and distribution of property.

But the economic factor itself is only one component in a more complete and complex ensemble of indicators that describe the status of a given individual within his larger family or group. Although I cannot deny the difficulties of such an investigation, genealogical research is essential in any attempt at global analysis. Steven L. Kaplan has furnished one model in his work on the grain and flour trade and the fabrication and distribution of bread (principally by millers and bakers). I should also mention attempts on a broader scale such as that of Jean Le Yaouang on the retail trades in nineteenth-century Paris.[5] One of the greatest obstacles to this kind of study is the social and geographical mobility of tradespeople, much greater than we might expect for this milieu. Even today, in spite of their decreasing numbers, small retail shops play a stabilizing role in neighborhood life. But the stability of any given shop does not imply a similarly long tenure for the shopkeeper. In the 1970s in Paris, for example, butchers remained in one shop no more than seven years, though the actual closing of a shop was rare.

Beyond the food trades, which still employ a majority of artisans despite the double threat of industrialization and the increasing popularity of huge retail establishments, the decline has been even more rapid in other crafts where industrialization has taken over. Clothing and shoe salesmen, for example, have almost completely replaced tailors and shoemakers, but they do not play the same role in the urban social structure, nor have they preserved the technical skills of the traditional artisan.

Thus current researchers into the world of the French artisan ought to attempt to understand as precisely as possible these phenomena of mobility and change. Without a doubt, they do not take the same form in different epochs, in part because of changing professional qualifications as well as the larger influences of geographical migrations and population. (In France these changes took place without great demographical upheavals, unlike England and Germany, where there were large population explosions in the nineteenth century, or the United States, where

[5]Steven L. Kaplan, *Bread, Politics and Political Economy in the Reign of Louis XV*, 2 vols. (The Hague, 1976); idem, *Provisioning Paris: Merchants and Millers in the Grain and Flour Trade during the Eighteenth Century* (Ithaca, 1984); and idem, *The Bakers of Paris and the Bread Question during the Eighteenth Century* (forthcoming); Jean Le Yaouang, "La mobilité sociale dans le milieu boutiquier parisien au XIXe siècle," *Mouvement social*, no. 108 (1979): 89–112.

waves of immigrants quickly populated the nation.) In general, in seventeenth- and eighteenth-century France, urbanization did not profoundly alter the nature or rhythms of life. There were two different situations: first, the cities in quasi-stagnation—Dijon, for example, but also Toulouse, Rouen, Lille, and many middle-sized towns as well as the small provincial capitals such as Moulins and Grenoble. Second, we have the cities undergoing rapid growth and change: Paris, Bordeaux, other large port cities, and eighteenth-century Lyons. Whether their cities were afflicted by stagnation or instead experienced dynamic growth, individuals and families had a number of potential responses to their situations. Let me attempt to group them by type.

In a stable (or stagnating) town, there was a tendency to maintain the same number of artisans, or even to diminish their number somewhat, in order to better their social position. In the case where craftsmen sought to make their craft less accessible, certain practices became the rule: strict professional endogamy, intermarriage between families of equal status, and inheritance of masterships, which were usually reserved for the advantage of one child in the family.

When the craft seemed in irreversible decline, the inverse process occurred. Why bequeath a son an enterprise unlikely to survive? But one asks the same question when the prospect was not failure but success beyond the normal expectations of corporate reality. Take, for example, a butcher who estimated that he had accumulated enough profit and rank that there was no higher place in the craft, either for himself or for his offspring. He might well have a tendency to steer his children toward other pursuits, such as livestock trading, for which the knowledge of the butcher's craft would constitute an indispensable advantage.

These three types of situations, of course, are modified by other factors, whether general economic conditions or the number of heirs in a particular family. Since geographical mobility further complicates our understanding, even in towns that are relatively stable, we must follow the methods of demographic historians and persist with the patience of genealogists in our efforts to reconstitute individual families. If we accept the postulate that the conditions of access to a corporate craft in the Old Regime result in professional stability for the great majority of master craftsmen—an image well substantiated by the masters' "protocols," which listed the masters by seniority and established their access to guild offices—mobility ought not to be measured in terms of one individual, but rather over generations.

The Dijonnais example cited above implies a compelling internal hierarchy capable of provoking contradictory strategies. For example, the image of the wine merchant was probably so negative that one would not wish to transmit the shop to one's son. It was a trade, however, that garnered enough prestige on the outside that vine growers sought to take over failed retail wine shops. Jacques Rancière, whose essay appears later in this volume (chap. 11), finds in the low social and technical status of shoemakers and tailors one explanation of the small number of sons who wished to follow their fathers, as well as a reason for their political activism in the first half of the nineteenth century. As Rancière explains it, crafts like shoemaking and tailoring, which required little technical skill, earned little respect, and would soon be displaced by industrial technology, left their artisans time to pursue other modes of social formation and action.

To substantiate these working hypotheses, we must try to multiply genealogies of artisan families through several generations. We must no longer separate the small shopkeepers of the nineteenth century from their forebears of the Old Regime. I call your attention to an investigation currently under way in Lyons. In 1818, among the ninety-one active butchers in Lyons one finds only fifty-six different last names. Thirteen of these names, all of which can be traced to Old Regime butcher families, account for more than half this universe (forty-six shopkeepers). When we think of the astounding fertility of this professional group during the course of the Old Regime, it is not surprising to see the trade incorporate several sons, sons-in-law, or nephews. At the same time the growing wealth of the trade allowed some former butchers or their widows to live on annuities, and there began a process of diversification that permitted families of butchers to invest in related activities such as pork butchering, but also to take control of larger commercial operations, including upstream suppliers, with the goal of becoming livestock dealers or leather merchants.

But the strong population growth in Lyons after 1820 produced a total inversion of this general trend. In 1844 there were 197 butchers in the city, but they shared 172 surnames, among which only 21 names on the 1818 list survived. During this quarter of a century, then, there was a profound mutation in the trade, much more pronounced than that produced during the Revolution or the empire. Where did these new butchers come from? Or even more important, what became of their predecessors and their families? In the earlier period a small, cohesive community of butchers who were bound together through alliances and intermarriage carefully controlled recruitment in the trade so as to guarantee a place for the members of their large families either in the butcher business or in some related profession. In the later era we see a double phenomenon of escape and dispersion: the butcher trade retained few of its own; fathers no longer raised sons to succeed them. We must seek other sources to learn if competition caused the impoverishment of the old butcher families or, on the contrary, if urban expansion, by increasing consumption, brought rapid new wealth, allowing butchers and their children to leave their craft and, through education, to enter other tertiary activities or even large-scale wholesale trade.

This example, specific to the food trades, ought not to be extended to the totality of artisanal crafts, which moved much more rapidly toward large-scale industrialization. But the butchers are not a completely isolated example, and the questions posed are so many potential directions for research, as we attempt to comprehend the transformation of regulations, skills, and the role of the artisan in urban society throughout the nineteenth century—a phenomenon that perhaps reflects upon the resurgence of the artisan and the permanence of certain of his values today.

The colloquium at Cornell underlines the importance of a history of representations. The rare examples of worker autobiography, two of which are analyzed in this volume (Ménétra for the eighteenth century and Truquin for the nineteenth) contrast sharply with the dry, serial documents to which the historian must return when he tries to understand the social organization of these urban worker populations, still rather unaccustomed to expressing themselves through the written word.

But even without being able to reconstruct in all its vivacity the mental universe or the vision of the world of a Menocchio as Carlo Ginzburg has done in *Cheese and Worms*, historians researching the "monde du travail" ought to proceed with that goal in mind.[6] Our research into this world necessarily includes an interest in the history of techniques and gestures, and in apprenticeship, both as ethnohistory and as a history of the transmission and evolution of technical knowledge. In addition we must integrate into our efforts two other fundamental and complementary dimensions: the role of the family and the formation of a culture proper to each craft. Too often these two aspects have been obscured by the opacity of the corporate organization and by the idea of a political philosophy proper to the artisanal world, directly issued from the organization itself. If we begin to turn our attention toward the family, its networks, and its complementarities, if we begin to see children as something other than apprentices, and women as more than simple auxiliaries, we may comprehend another culture, with a moral and social aspect as well as a domestic and professional side. We might also gain another understanding of the intersections of stability and rupture over

[6]Carlo Ginzburg, *The Cheese and the Worms: The Cosmos of a Sixteenth-Century Miller*, trans. John Tedeschi and Anne Tedeschi (New York, 1980).

the long term. Today sociologists try to apply such methods to their studies of social mobility. The "monde du travail" needs a similar type of analysis, whatever difficulties hinder its implementation for the earlier periods.[7]

Translated by Cynthia J. Koepp

[7] See, for example, Claude Thelot, *Tel père, tel fils* (Paris, 1982), and Patrice Bourdelais, "L'industrialisation et ses mobilités (1836–1936)," *Annales E.S.C.* 39, no. 5 (September/October 1984): 1009–19.

10

A Nineteenth-Century Work Experience as Related in a Worker's Autobiography: Norbert Truquin

MICHELLE PERROT

Workers' autobiographies were relatively rare in France in the nineteenth century. Proletarians were hesitant about writing their memoirs and even more hesitant about publishing them.[1] Proudhon said it plainly: "The facts of my life are less than nothing. . . . It is inappropriate for the liberty and honor of a people for citizens to put their private lives before the public and thus treat each other as servants in a comedy or as saltimbanques."[2] There were many reasons for such reservations: cultural ones (Anglo-saxon travelers are, it seems to me, extensive writers) and existential ones. On the one hand, the sense of secrecy protects one from the intrusions of power: speaking openly is self-exposure. On the other hand, a certain feeling of class respectability tends to repress the inner self or at least renders one wary of making it public. Many texts of this kind, like the private diaries of women, undoubtedly have been destroyed or have been buried away in archives.[3] Those texts that have

---

[1] Norbert Truquin, *Mémoires et aventures d'un prolétaire à travers la révolution: L'Algérie, la république Argentine et le Paraguay* (Paris, 1888). The work was published by the Librairie des deux-mondes, Bibliothèque internationale, F. Bouriand, Librarie éditeur. This bookshop, at 17 rue de Loos, stated that it "specialized in socialist publications, social and political economy, natural sciences, philosophy and history." It published a journal, *La tribune des peuples: Revue internationale du mouvement social dans les cinq parties du monde*, of libertarian tendency. Numerous networks of this kind existed in the nineteenth century.

[2] Pierre-Joseph Proudhon, *Mémoires sur ma vie*, ed. Bernard Voyenne (Paris, 1983), p. 6.

[3] Jacques Rancière discovered and published the papers belonging to a Saint-Simonian worker, Louis Gabriel Gauny, a *parqueteur* who installed inlaid wooden floors. See his *La*

been published by their authors are filled with admonitions and seek self-justification by proclaiming their exemplary status.

If Norbert Truquin, in his fifties, made an "autobiographical pact"[4] to produce his memoirs, it was perhaps because, as an individualist, he did not feel tied to any model of worker action to which he would have had to conform. Undoubtedly he felt that he had led a full and exemplary life, the recollection of which filled his "sleepless nights." He wanted to transmit his experience, a desire he considered all the more important since he believed personal commitment was the key to social change. For example, Truquin writes: "It is urgent for all those who work and suffer from the ills of social organization to rely only on themselves in order to cope and to create, through solidarity, a better present and future. It is therefore important that each and every one contribute to the common task by publishing his notes, notebooks, memoirs, in short, all documents that can help to destroy the evils of the old world and to hasten the advent of social revolution" (p. 451). Self-taught and a latecomer to writing, Truquin believed in the power of the written word. His memoirs are more than testimony: they are a message. Truquin urges his fellow workers to take risks, not to remain in the closed world of the factories or offices, but rather to go out into the world as he has done, and especially to break new ground.

For Truquin, rooted as he is in the nineteenth-century European agrarian associative tradition, the salvation of the proletariat and of humanity would come about through the conquest of new land by socialist communities. Thus, as the title and subtitle indicate, this book is both a picturesque narrative of the "adventures of a proletarian throughout the Revolution" and the story of an exploration of virgin lands through pioneer action: "Algeria, the republic of Argentina, and Paraguay." Written in 1887, Truquin's book was printed in 1888 by the same Paris publisher-bookseller who published *La tribune des peuples: Revue internationale du mouvement social dans les cinq parties due monde.* Espousing libertarian values, Truquin's book relates a half-century of public and private life, with its struggles and its history. Let us review briefly the major stages of his life.

Norbert Truquin was born in 1833 in Rozières (the Somme) in what was then Picardy. He was the fourth child and only son of a ruined entrepreneur and inveterate gambler. His father, after becoming a widower, sent him at the age of seven to serve as an apprentice to a wool carder in Amiens. Thus began his life of work and wandering between

---

nuit des prolétaires: Archives du rêve ouvrier (Paris, 1981), and *Louis Gabriel Gauny: Le philosophe plébéien,* compiled by Jacques Rancière (Paris, 1983).

[4]Phillippe Lejeune, *Le pacte autobiographique* (Paris, 1974), and *Je est un autre* (Paris, 1980) has analyzed the complexity of social attitudes with regard to the practice of autobiography.

Picardy and Champagne, interrupted only briefly by a return visit to his native village in search of the family he never forgot and constantly sought. In 1847, for example, Norbert "went up" to Paris to seek out his father, who had remarried; there he was hired as a wool carder and learned about life in the capital as he roamed the streets and avidly visited museums. He also experienced the revolution of 1848 as a "*gamin*" and participated in the June Days. Truquin writes of that time: "I had just turned fifteen on 7 June and was precocious for my age. I couldn't resist going everywhere to help put up the barricades" (p. 112).

In 1851, disgusted by the reaction in France and attracted by the prospects opened up by the colonization of Algeria, to which many revolutionary workers had been deported, Truquin convinced his father, whom he had finally found, to emigrate. But these four years of life in Algeria (1851–55) did not bring him much satisfaction. Instead of working on the land, he became a domestic servant to army officers, a profoundly humiliating experience. He was forced into practicing religion (confession, taking communion), which he had despised since breaking off all contact with the church as an adolescent. He tried in vain to run away. Finally, upon coming of age, he freed himself from the tyranny of his father, whom he could no longer bear.

In 1855, then, he broke away from his family, returned to France, and took up a number of dead-end jobs such as digging wells. Finally he settled in Lyons and, in search of a real profession, decided to become a silk weaver, a *canut*. Following a classic entry into the trade, he married a young silk weaver, the daughter of a peasant family from the department of the Ain, set himself up with her and two looms, and became sufficiently integrated into groups of workers in small workshops to become their leader on several occasions. He was imprisoned as a result of his participation in the Lyons Commune in 1871.

This event was decisive in persuading Truquin to emigrate, especially since, like other Lyons workers, he was already adversely affected by a profound economic crisis in the silk industry.[5] When attempts to depart with a community failed, he took a first exploratory voyage to Argentina in 1873 on his own. In 1878 he left Lyons in the company of his oldest son, intending never to return. His wife, at first hesitant, joined him in South America nine months later. In 1881 the whole family settled in Paraguay near Villa Encarnacion, in Independencia, where he wrote his memoirs.[6]

Truquin's book follows a chronological thread but emphasizes first his

[5]Yves Lequin, *Les ouvriers de la région lyonnaise, 1848–1914*, 2 vols. (Lyons, 1977).

[6]There is little biographical material about Truquin elsewhere. He is not included in the *Dictionnaire biographique du mouvement ouvrier français*, ed. Jean Maitron (Paris, 1965); see Victor Advielle, *Le socialiste picard Norbert Truquin* (Paris, 1895).

childhood and youth (190 pages) and later the Latin American period (120 pages). The period in Lyons, though it lasted seventeen years (1855–73), is dealt with more briefly. It is as if this pause, the only stable period of his life, was a parenthesis in a lifetime obviously devoted to movement and committed to the belief that the rootedness of the working class is a cause of its misfortunes. He uses a reporter's style: concrete and precise, with circumstantial details to create the feeling—perhaps the illusion—of authenticity. He retells whole conversations and uses a few tales or fables to draw moral lessons. Although the narrative largely overshadows the expression of ideas or feelings, underlying the book is a moral vision and a goal that unify the whole. The author develops his philosophy and social criticism by setting off key phrases, sentences, and moral lessons in italics.

It is not my purpose here to criticize this text, which, like all autobiography, is first of all language, a self-styled effort, a stereotype—both the product of a culture and an expression of it. I intend to use Truquin's text as a document and, if possible, to try to understand its private vision, that subjective inward look that, even though reconstructed, makes us step through the looking glass or at least cross to the actor's side of the stage. Truquin's autobiography is sufficiently rare to merit this attention. His text can be subjected to several "readings," depending upon whether one wants to understand private life in *milieux populaires*, family relationships, gender relationships, religious and political representations, or cultural practice, specifically in their relation to reading and writing. All these subjects are richly documented here.

However, what does Truquin have to say about work practice and ideology?

An Account of Apprenticeship

First of all, Truquin gives us an account of his vagabond childhood. During the first half of the nineteenth century wandering was a rather common experience for young people and was considered relatively normal. There was as yet no specified status for youth under the law, even if there were some indications in the penal notion of "the age of understanding."[7] There was no legislation concerning intervention. The law of 1841, limiting children's working hours in the manufactories, although a very important symptom of change, had very limited effects. Administrative surveillance was weak: a police *commissaire* who found

[7]M. Perrot, "Sur la ségrégation de l'enfance au 19e siècle," *Psychiatrie de l'enfant* 25, no. 1 (1982) p. 180.

Truquin wandering about inquired about his parents, gave him some pocket money, and let him go.

Note that Truquin's wanderings are geographically circumscribed to a radius of sixty kilometers around his village. During his youth he never completely broke away from his family, which constituted an anchor. In the absence of a place or a home, the family network remained for all nineteenth-century migrants the basic form of sociability. Outside his home, Truquin was rarely alone, but almost always in the company of an adult who "protected" him in exchange for his services.

Within these limited parameters, however, where town and country-side were closely connected by networks of exchange, what mobility he had! After the death of his first master in 1843, Truquin, then ten years old, survived by small-scale trading with other orphans like himself. He was then taken in by prostitutes who bathed and clothed him, employing him as an errand boy, especially to fetch water, which they needed in great quantities. This child came to know the relative luxury and comforts of the brothels.

When the brothel was closed down, Truquin once again found himself in the street. He became in succession a ragman's helper, a peddler's helper, a slaughterhouse hand, a welldigger, a brickmaker, a grape-harvester, a *rattacheur* (machine tender) in a woolen mill in Amiens, and once again a peddler, this time of fashionable plaster figurines for an Italian who often employed children in his area. It is thanks to him that Truquin came to Paris. During the years 1840 to 1847 he held a dozen or more jobs and had as many masters, not counting the intervals when he was marauding as a petty thief with gangs of children whom he distrusted. Truquin recollects: "I struck up acquaintance with a half a dozen kids of my age who lived by petty theft; they ran away with grocers' shop food, carrying off everything they could get their hands on, figs, grapes, and such, which they shared with me, encouraging me to do the same. I felt an overwhelming repugnance for this job" (p. 26). Truquin had no taste for being marginal.

In all his work experience there was nothing that resembled apprenticeship in a trade. Truquin was not born into that technical heritage that survived the death of the corporations and maintained professional and family traditions long into the nineteenth century.[8] He bears no resemblance to the *compagnon-vitrier* (glazier) Ménétra with whom it is so interesting to compare him.[9] Norbert's father, a petty bourgeois on

[8]William H. Sewell, *Work and Revolution in France: The Language of Labor from the Old Regime to 1848* (Cambridge, 1980); Yves Lequin, *Ouvriers*, vol. 1, chap. 5, "La naissance et le métier."

[9]Daniel Roche, ed., *Journal de ma vie: Jacques-Louis Ménétra, compagnon vitrier au 18e siècle* (Paris, 1982).

his way to becoming a proletarian, did not hand down to him any knowledge, any secrets, or any social standing. When he apprenticed Norbert to the old wool carder of Amiens, Auguste, he recommended that his son be disciplined and that he be made to say his prayers every day. This particular apprenticeship, in fact, had only two elements: beating and, to a lesser extent, religion; artisanal instruction was totally absent.

Young Norbert was often beaten as a child. His first master slapped him at will and beat him with a broomstick or, more often, with a "doubled rope" until his face and back bled; this man forced him to undress or kneel in order to humiliate him, repeating constantly: "I'll get you yet; I've mastered others before you."[10] This former quartermaster, who was also a fencer, no doubt applied disciplinary measures used in the navy before the revolution of 1848, which outlawed flogging. However, the Belgian brickmakers followed the same practice with their children. Truquin states: "When the children did not behave according to their father's liking, he fell upon them like a demon and beat them. The other workers watched the punishment without flinching as if this was natural. I said to myself: in Belgium it seems to be a habit to treat children like beasts of burden."[11] Here Truquin's reflection intimates that children were treated differently in France. As for Truquin's father, he punished his son only rarely, but when he decided to impose his paternal authority by punishing the seventeen-year-old Norbert for running away from home, the consequences were serious. After this incident Truquin decided to break away and leave his father, a sign that he had reached his limits of tolerance. As an adolescent he no longer was willing to be treated like a child. His honor upon reaching manhood no longer allowed him to accept the treatment given children and women.[12]

The history of corporal punishment, linked to the image of the body and to that of childhood, is an important chapter in the history of education. In France there was a clear decline in the use of beating among the dominant classes. Could this be because such practices recall feudal times? Perhaps so, if one judges by the increase in the number of revolts against such harassment among lycée students after 1830. Contrary to what was happening in England, beating gradually disappeared from secondary colleges in France, where the reigning pedagogy required erect posture and submissive spirits, and where punishment was inflicted by other means.[13] But among the lower classes, relations to authority,

[10]Truquin, *Mémoires*, pp. 13, 17, 22–23, 34.

[11]Ibid. p. 57. On the condition of young Belgian workers, see E. Ducpetiaux, *De la condition physique et moral des jeunes ouvriers et des moyens de l'améliorer*, 2 vols. (Brussels, 1843), vol. 1, p. 423.

[12]Many other libertarian or socialist militants derived their revolt from confrontation with paternal authority or from the physical brutality connected with apprenticeship.

[13]In this respect see G. Vigarello, *Le corps redressé: Histoire d'un pouvoir pédagogique* (Paris,

both within the family and at school, remained much more direct and physical. Children tended to be thought of as potential rebels to be tamed. Take, for example, the brutality of apprenticeship in professions such as the iron industry.[14] The "apprenticeship of life and virility," that cornerstone of popular morals, included beating. Once this rite of passage was passed, one could brag about it: to be a man was to have been beaten. In theory there was no fixed limit on the family's right to discipline, a right then delegated to masters of apprentices. It was not until 1898 that a law provided for legislative intervention in the case of ill treatment. More generally, the notion of a child's interest, of "children's rights," emerged imperceptibly,[15] although we do find signs of it in liberal thought—with its concern for individual rights—in thinkers like de Tocqueville.

Religion was the other mode of education. "Don't forget to have him say his four prayers every day," Norbert's father reminds the wool carder. "If he's no good at anything else, I feel it's important that he at least be a good Christian."[16] Such instructions help us to measure how tradition is carried on, and they are corroborated by much popular testimony. Throughout the second half of the nineteenth century the child's first celebration of Communion remained the unrivaled rite of passage from childhood to adolescence. The free thought movement managed to establish a secular practice of marriage and particularly civil burials, but it never succeeded in replacing the first Communion, which persisted even in the anticlerical milieu of the working class.[17]

The wool carder never missed the chance to have little Norbert go to the cathedral "to take some blessed water, make the sign of the cross, and recite the Credo."[18] Norbert took pleasure in the beauty of the cathedrals, especially the paintings and the filtered light of stained-glass

---

1978); and the unpublished doctorat d'état by Michel Bouillé, "Lieux et corps pédagogiques du 17e au 19e siècle" (University of Paris VIII, 1984). Regulations throughout the nineteenth century outlawed corporal punishment. For example, the regulations concerning infant schools (*salles d'asile*) in 1834: "Children must never be struck"; article 29 of the primary school regulations of 1834, renewed in 1851. A regulation dating from 6 January 1881 is firmer still: "It is absolutely forbidden to inflict any form of corporal punishment." In practice, there were exceptions even in secondary schools, as Baudelaire relates in his *Correspondance* concerning the lycée in Lyons in 1833.

[14]Some examples: Gilland, *Les conteurs ouvriers* (Paris, 1849); "Les aventures du petit Guillaume du Mont-Cel" (an autobiographical account of an apprenticeship and a revolt); and J. B. Dumay, *Mémoires d'un militant ouvrier du Creusot (1841–1905)* (Paris, 1976), pp. 85–88 (the account of apprenticeship in various metalworking factories in the Grenelle quarter of Paris).

[15]M. Perrot, "La notion d'intérêt de l'enfant et son émergence au 19e siècle," *Actes: Cahiers d'action juridique* 37 (June 1982), 43–45.

[16]Truquin, *Mémoires*, p. 18.

[17]See P. Pierrard, *L'église et les ouvriers en France (1840–1940)* (Paris, 1984).

[18]Truquin, *Mémoires*, p. 13.

windows, and stopped on his travels to visit them.[19] However, this aesthetic appreciation did not prevent him from turning away from religion
early on. Truquin was critical of the Picardy workers' credulity, those
for whom "the priest's word was ... gospel" (p. 64). He broke away from
his family because he believed his only true salvation was his own individualistic work ethic, not a faith in providence urged by his devout aunt.
He took his first Communion only because the paternalistic director of
the wool-spinning mill in Amiens sent him to catechism as a matter of
course and gave him new shoes and a suit of clothes, the usual gifts to
those who take their Communion for the first time. Truquin made good
use of the suit and shoes for a long time, reserving them for special
occasions such as looking for work. In fact, he broke off completely from
the church. Truquin really agonized when he had to please his in-laws
by getting married in church: as peasants from Bugey, they attached
importance to Catholic ritual.[20] While it is not my purpose here to trace
Truquin's spiritual journey, it is important to see that religion formed
part of his apprenticeship and became an element in the construction
of his worldview.

Schooling, however, was totally absent from Truquin's childhood.
Mothers often instructed their children in reading and writing, but Truquin's mother's premature death denied him that early opportunity, and
his wanderings in a rural countryside far from literate culture offered
him little incentive to become literate. Much later, when over forty years
old and residing in Latin America, he finally learned these skills. At
several intervals he mentions his difficulties as an illiterate, moments of
feeling dependent upon those who could understand the printed page.
"As I didn't know how to read, I had a painful time learning catechism,"
he wrote at the time of his first Communion. "I begged the other workers
to help me a bit, but they were not always ready to do so" (p. 68). Twenty-
five years later while a prisoner in Lyons in 1870, he was strongly vexed
at not being able to read the books on Mexican history the prison chaplain
had borrowed for him: "As I had already great difficulty in reading by
myself, I begged my companions to read it together, but none of them
wanted to undertake it. . . . Deloche came up to my bunk to tell me that
he would have been willing to read as I requested, but he hesitated in
face of the distrust borne him by the others; he then offered to let me
read his defense. I had to confess to him that I didn't know how to read
handwriting; he could not believe it, and I was forced to assert it repeatedly" (pp. 294–95). We have here a moving testimony about the

[19]Ibid., pp. 22 and 76, his spontaneous visit to the cathedral in Beauvais.
[20]Ibid., p. 236: what most shocks Truquin is the obligation to confess.

need for instruction once such norms have been established in a population.[21]

Hence we see the importance of the oral tradition for Truquin. It represents his principal form of cultural acquisition and communication, and it accounts for the significance in his life of such cultural and historical "mediators" as the former soldiers of the imperial army, or half-pay soldiers, the real transmitters of revolutionary memory; the aristocrats who have lost their social position; and the self-taught workers, such as Constant at the Amiens spinning mill, a disciple of Cabet who initiated him into socialism. From this standpoint Norbert Truquin "lagged behind" those Saint-Simonian proletarians, practitioners of the written word (described by Jacques Rancière), and even behind a Ménétra. Truquin's lack of development, however, can probably be attributed less to the cultural backwardness of industrial northern France than to his unique personal itinerary.

The kind of work Truquin undertook is marked by his station in life. As a person with neither trade nor status, he was reduced to auxiliary jobs, stopgap or odd jobs—menial labor dependent upon the body—like women workers and other laborers without tools.[22] While working for Auguste, he was a *nacteur*: his job was to finish cleaning carded wool fibers of their last impurities. Holding them firmly with both hands, he had to scrape them with his teeth. He "could not spit out the impurities but rather had to let them run down in drips on each side of his mouth" as he worked from four in the morning until ten at night. "It is easy to imagine," he writes, "how unhealthy this work is for children. These poor little ones who are called nacteurs, are, for the most part, wizened, worn, and physically spent."[23] At the spinning mill he was a rattacheur. In other places he helped a ragman and a peddler and worked as a grape harvester. He often worked directly with another man to whom he was subordinate; his degree of exploitation depended upon his master's psychological sense, since there was no official limit to what could be demanded. This type of personal dependency makes children's work comparable to that of domestics. In fact, three types of activity were required of Truquin (he is here a good example of a well-known situation): personal service and housework, commonly women's occupations,

---

[21]On this subject, see J. Ozouf, "Le peuple et l'école: Note sur la demande populaire d'instruction au 19e siècle," *Mélanges d'histoire sociale offerts à Jean Maitron* (Paris, 1976).

[22]For a reflection on women's work in this regard see Paola Tabet, "Les mains, les outils, les armes," *L'homme: Revue française d'anthropologie* 19, nos. 3–4 (July–December 1979): 5–64; and N. Z. Davis, "Women in the Arts Mecaniques in 16th Century Lyon," in *Mélanges offerts à Gascon*, (Lyons, 1980).

[23]Truquin, *Mémoires*, p. 16.

which as an adolescent he found intolerable;[24] small trades (*les petits métiers*) of itinerant commerce, where children's mobility makes them ideal peddlers; and recovery activities essential to the economy of the poor, where waste, leftovers, and refuse are constantly recycled. Like a "scavenger" (which is what they were called), Truquin searched in gutters and in gaps between paving stones to recover old metal: "After a thaw, we set out to forage the brooks in search of pins and old nails, which we resold for a *sou* a pound; with this money we bought bread" (p. 25). "We also scoured the gutters in public urinals for excrement, which a druggist bought from us for four to five sous" (p. 26). He collected bones for a bone-black *fabrique*: "I went the rounds of bourgeois homes where they ate meat. I paid two half-farthings for a pound of bones; with my twelve sous I bought twenty-four pounds, which I brought to the workshop. What I earned from this sale allowed me to buy forty-eight pounds, and thus I continued my small commerce" (p. 61). In an attempt to set himself up in the trade, he bought an old mule to solve the crucial problem of transport. Similarly, children played a major role in town life as *tireurs de chassis* (hand-cart transporters). The use of children, valued for their mobility and agility, underpinned a whole marginal economy in which small trades had a useful function well beyond the picturesque, as a recent thesis has shown.[25] Such trades filled the gaps in urban commerce, where exchanges remained relatively unorganized.

Thus Truquin experienced highly varied workplaces: cottage industry, slaugherhouses, excavation or construction sites, manufactories, even a house of prostitution, and finally the open road, where he spent his greatest moments. "This freedom to walk, the open air, the flowers gave me a feeling of inexpressible happiness that made me forget all the past misery," he wrote about a moment he spent as a helper to an old peddler, a half-pay soldier of the *Grande Armée*.[26]

The most interesting part of Truquin's memoirs describes his impressions of the wool-spinning mill near Amiens. He suffered from the discipline imposed by work schedules. He had "to get up in the very early morning to be able to enter the fabrique as the bell rang quarter to five. The slightest lateness meant a fine and after the third infraction one was fired with a bad certificate, meaning that it would be impossible to find work elsewhere in the region" (p. 70). On the other hand, he appreciated the cleanliness of the workrooms, the rather relaxed atmosphere that reigned there, and especially the existence of a com-

---

[24]Three cases, in fact: in the brothel, *Mémoires*, p. 30; at the home of a day laborer from a construction site, ibid., pp. 45–46; and at the officers' quarters in Algeria, ibid., p. 135.

[25]Jean Michel Baruch-Gourdan, "Les petits métiers à Paris au 19e siècle: L'example des marchands de quatre saisons" (doctoral thesis, 3d cycle, University of Paris VII, 1983).

[26]Truquin, *Mémoires*, p. 40.

munity, more social than ideological. This rare testimony about a factory viewed from within is worth quoting:

> In the fabriques ... the workrooms are heated, sufficiently aired and lighted; order and cleanliness prevail; the worker finds himself in a social community. At this time the foremen were less demanding about quantity than about quality. One earned ten francs a week, sometimes twenty francs; the rate agreed upon was paid without any observations. When the foremen were absent we told stories and plays; jokers used to set up a pulpit and have fun preaching; we passed the time in gaiety (p. 70).

In sum, once within the walls, the factory space was as yet fairly unregulated, and this lack of defined space allowed for the possibility of freedom. This informality was something totally different from the industrial *bagne* or prison that was the epicenter of worker exploitation and consciousness. Moreover, the directors forestalled the slightest movement in that direction: "We never heard the slightest expression of political or social opinions; if by chance it was learned that a worker had sown some ideas of this sort, the directors arranged among themselves for him to be refused work" (p. 71). It is here, however, that Truquin met Constant, Cabet's fervent disciple, who initiated him into socialism. Misunderstood by his comrades, who mocked him ("Let's cut him up, let's halve him," they said), persecuted by the directors, who eventually fired him, Constant characterizes the strong militant who emerged from the "night of the proletarians," militants of the caliber to which Saint-Simonism and Cabetism give birth.[27]

At the end of this apprenticeship Truquin was acquainted with a number of occupations, but he did not identify with any of them. He felt a greater affinity with the woolen industry, but it was more likely a geographical affinity (Picardy) than a professional one. The only reason he was hired at a woolcarder's in Paris (rue Saint Maur) was because he knew the foreman there, a relative from his village. In this case neighborly relations played a stronger part than professional ones.[28]

The Diversity of Work Space and Practice

The absence of an apprenticeship and the lack of roots in a trade in part explain Norbert Truquin's extreme geographical mobility, his lack

[27]Ibid., pp. 71–74; an unknown figure, Constant does not appear in Maitron's biographical dictionary. The Saint-Simonian "networks" have been treated by Jacques Rancière in *Nuit des prolétaires*, and Cabetism, as a first form of workers' "party," by Christopher Johnson in *Utopian Communism in France: Cabet and Icarians, 1839–1851* (Ithaca, 1974).

[28]About this episode, very interesting as we seek to understand hiring practices, see Truquin, *Mémoires*, pp. 77 ff. The work involved is in a mechanized wool-carding workshop, equipped with modern machines, where he is an "operative" along with other children.

of professional definition, and the diversity of his work space and practice until his more stable period as a weaver.

Work was above all for him a means of existence, indispensable for living and often difficult to find. Truquin's adventures were, in a certain sense, a perpetual search for work, that is to say, subsistence. There were several kinds of obstacles, not just economic ones. The syncopated rhythms of the economy, the importance of off-seasons, the sensitivity of the Lyons silk fabrique to the dictates of fashion, and the periodic crises (such as the one in 1846–47, which led to reduced work hours at the wool-spinning mill and subsequent layoffs) all converged to produce frequent unemployment within an astonishingly elastic labor market.

Truquin's occupational fluidity was not necessarily an unhappy experience, since it had its compensations in the ease with which he was hired, given his willingness to accept any job. In fact, there were a great number of unskilled jobs in a labor-intensive economy that functioned with day laborers. Workers, once they had adapted to this situation, used the idle moments to do whatever they liked. "On the days we were idle, I took fencing lessons," Truquin relates, attracted, like all young people of the popular classes, to the aristocratic practice of arms.[29] Some laborers even chose to work intermittently. Those whom Norbert calls "the jokers" stopped working, at least while they were still single, when they felt they had earned enough.[30] There was still a widespread practice of "Saint Monday" (and even Tuesday), deplored by economists and industrial employers, which the Second Empire almost succeeded in overcoming.[31] We find a mixture of economic determinism and existential choice combined in this perpetual activity, this incessant mobility that the system of daily wages also fostered. There was job insecurity, it is true, but also a certain freedom. It is obvious that we are dealing here with another type of labor market regulation, another type of industrial society.

What counted in getting hired for work was one's physical appear-

[29]Ibid., p. 74. There is a strong attraction in the popular classes for the practice of arms. J. B. Dumay reports the same thing in his memoirs, relating that his father, who was nearly the same age as Truquin, was regarded with esteem because he was a fencer. Here we find an aristocratic trait asserted by diverse social groups (young bourgeois learn to fence and challenge each other to duels), which shows how strong the noble model remains in the area of custom. This point tends to strengthen Arno Mayer's thesis in *La persistance de l'ancien régime: L'Europe de 1848 à la grande guerre* (Paris, 1983; English ed., New York, 1981).

[30]Truquin, *Mémoires*, p. 209, gives us the portrait of an old soldier, a "half-pay" pensioner, an "old joker": "He was endowed with Herculean strength, which earned him the boss's esteem, but at the utmost he hardly worked three months a year." Working intermittently of one's own accord is very important during the nineteenth century.

[31]Compare Jeffry Kaplow, "La fin de la Saint-Lundi: Etude sur le Paris ouvrier au 19e siècle," *Temps Libre*, summer 1981; and the unpublished work of Alain Cailleaux, "Vie et mort de la Saint-Lundi en France au 19e siècle" (master's thesis, University of Paris VII, 1977).

ance—no need of a test to size up muscles; a glance would do. Clothes were also important: one had to be cleanly dressed to get hired in a workshop.[32] Norbert reserved his precious Communion suit for the moments when he had to present himself for hire. He had an obsession about owning shoes; not having any was humiliating: "The soles of the shoes my grandfather had bought me were worn through; the only ones left were those from my first Communion, which I cherished. I foresaw that in Paris it would not be easy to go barefoot to find work."[33]

In a society in which the social hierarchy was still inscribed in visualized codes, clothing was the sign of status, and even a profession. In any case, it was a mark of respectability. Moreover, work, at least of a certain kind, was not distributed according to criteria of "capacity" or need, but rather went to people presumed to be respectable. Employers were extremely distrustful of vagabonds, abandoned children, and convicts. So-and-so, because he had spent eighteen months in prison, was not hired: "As soon as it was learned that he had been convicted, he found all doors closed to him" (p. 29). That one had just come out of a reformatory was "a bad certificate to get work" (p. 31). Employers were suspicious of someone without family: "As I had stated that I didn't have any family, I was turned away on the pretext that there was no work for vagabonds" (p. 33). At this time little Norbert was forced to "forage in gutters," for "no one wanted to give me work" (p. 35).

Work then was considered a reward for honorability and virtue. Not everyone had a right to a job; one had to be worthy. Sometimes a rare commodity, work was a gift or a privilege that workers in a trade attempted to hand down to their children, hence their opposition to hiring apprentices outside their own families. Fabriques and trades thus tended to appear as self-contained and protected territory, not always easily accessible. Family economy and status segmented the labor market, which still functioned according to the norms of the *ancien regime*. When considered in this context, the importance of the debate in 1848 is understandable: the demands for "a right to work" as neither a group privilege, nor an act of charity but an individual right recognized by all.[34]

There were two outlets offered to those rejected by the labor market: small trades, whose economic utility I have already described, and navvy

---

[32]Truquin, *Mémoires*, p. 32: "As I was rather cleanly dressed, I presented myself in fabriques in order to get work."

[33]Ibid., p. 74; see also p. 68: "I feared being reduced to walking barefoot in town, which would have been a supreme humiliation."

[34]*Le droit au travail à l'Assemblée nationale: Recueil complet de tous les discours prononcés dans cette mémorable discussion par . . . , suivis de l'opinion de MM. Marrast. Proudhon, L. Blanc, Ed. Laboulaye et Cormenin, avec des observations inédites par MM. Léon Faucher, Wolowski, F. Bastiat, de Parieu et une introduction et des notes par M. Joseph Garnier* (Paris, 1848) (a "liberal" commentary on a fascinating collection of documents that is important for this subject).

work on public and private construction sites. Such work attracted all kinds of people—peasants in need of extra income, workers in difficulty, foreigners, and even women and children provided they had the required endurance.[35] Navvying—hard work, socially scorned, and exploited by middlemen who took advantage of the simpleminded character of the labor force—would be worthy of study on its own, given the place it held in the economy of large-scale construction during the nineteenth century.

Truquin's account is filled with characters engaged in these kinds of activities. He describes the harsh working conditions of Belgian laborers digging the Marne canal (p. 43), the even worse conditions endured by laborers on a railroad tunnel near Lyons (p. 203), and further, the work on the Parc de la Tête d'Or in 1857, which attracted nearly three thousand idle silk weavers.[36] In Truquin's view these jobs were the worst possible, particularly for one's health: rude piecework, housing in ice-cold huts, mediocre salary, insufficient nourishment, and the risk of accidents for inexperienced workers. Of the Belgians he writes, "few workers are over fifty, most of them die of pleurisy between the ages of thirty-five and forty–five" (p. 45). The Lyonnais weavers were unable to keep going: "Already more than five hundred of them had to be hospitalized; most of them had been hurt or had hernias caused by their sliding on silt-covered plateau land" (p. 208).

As for Truquin, he could not endure the accumulation of sickness and accidents. Moreover, in his testimony the image of a sickly body brings him to idealize and affirm his physical sense of self. Truquin confides the pain of having to share his straw mattress with a fellow laborer whose physical contact he loathed: "He used to drink spirits before going to bed and exhaled a strong odor of brandy and tobacco that used to suffocate me; but what I loathed most was to feel the contact of another man. For the first time I found myself in the position of having to share a bed with a man. In Algeria I used to sleep on the ground, it is true, but at least I slept alone. In France the climate does not allow one to do this."[37] To have a bed of his own was, from this moment on, a minimum requirement.

In Truquin's experience work, when reduced to its primary and subsistence functions, was not an object of personal investment. It was an

[35]There is frequent testimony about the presence of women on construction sites during the nineteenth century. Le Play mentions it. Here, Truquin, *Mémoires*, pp. 45–46, talks about the Belgians who were employed to dig the canal: "The numerous women among them were subjected to the same conditions as the men."

[36]Ibid., p. 208.

[37]Ibid., p. 204. Alain Corbin used this rather exceptional testimony about the memory of odors: see *Le miasme et la jonquille* (Paris, 1982).

abstract act of exchanging one's labor power for a wage.[38] Truquin often mentions his salary (more than twenty-five references), with astonishingly precise figures considering the time elapsed. One wonders whether he kept written notes on this subject. Similarly, he gives information about his budget—receipts and expenses, housing costs, the price of certain objects, his debts, and possible savings, the last so precarious and quickly spent (one entry includes loans that were never repaid). In his accounting Truquin has an excellent memory for money.[39] For him, earning money was the inescapable basis of freedom: "I considered that freedom did not exist for someone without money and in order to earn some, I counted on the risks of fortune" (p. 72). Women, who represented the savings bank of popular culture, gave him a semblance of luck. His mother's inheritance, which he had to claim, and his wife's dowry (was this calculated?) on two occasions provided him with the means to establish himself.

It was his dream to put together enough capital, one way or another, to set himself up in business: "To create for myself an independent position and to be able to live off my work" (p. 181). This was Truquin's explicit ambition, very similar to that expressed by most nineteenth-century workers who sought to preserve or acquire their autonomy through a domestic economy[40] or, better still, by creating a small commercial or industrial enterprise—an ideal that had remained attractive from time immemorial.[41] Truquin's originality is his predilection for the land and for breaking new ground—I will return to this aspect. But he also tried his hand at industry. After the failure of his Algerian experience, he hoped upon reaching manhood "to learn a trade" (p. 190). While traveling from Marseilles to the Nord, he considered stopping in Paris, the first big city he had experienced and liked, but a lack of resources forced him instead to stop in Lyons, where he became a canut.

Truquin provides us with a great deal of information concerning this work experience, information that has been put to good use in research on the Lyonnais region.[42] We learn about the working conditions of young women in the *ateliers*—women whom he characterizes as "victims

---

[38]These observations converge with those of Jacques Rancière in *Nuit des prolétaires*.

[39]I studied this problem of workers' relation to their budget in *Les ouvriers en grève* (Paris, 1974), 1:127ff., using as my major source the replies to the 1884 survey, and established a rather different picture; most of the workers who replied said that they never had a budget and did not keep accounts. This was not Truquin's case.

[40]L. Tilly and J. Scott, *Women, Work and Family* (New York, 1978).

[41]On this subject see the work done by Philippe Vigier's research team, and the issues of the *Mouvement social*, no. 108, *L'atelier et la boutique*, and no. 114, *Petite entreprise et politique*.

[42]See the studies done by Maurice Garden, *Lyon et les Lyonnais au 18e siècle* (Paris, 1960); Yves Lequin, *Les ouvriers de la région lyonnaise, 1848–1914*; by Laura Struminginger, *Women and the Making of the Working Class: Lyon, 1830–1870* (St. Alban's, Vt., 1979); and recently, Claire Auzias and Annick Houel, *La grève des ovalistes: Lyon, 1869* (Paris, 1982).

of premeditated assassination."[43] We learn about the social hierarchy of workers' jobs. Weavers of fancy articles were the aristocrats of the profession and distinguished themselves—by their clothes, by the things they purchased, by their life rituals, and by their opinions—from the weavers of plain goods, who were more conservative.[44] We read about the cultural forms of classes steeped in tradition, in historical memory, and yet at the same time tempted by all kinds of fads, such as spiritualism.[45] As an informed observer, Truquin provides an analysis that sharpens the picture of this special ethnic group, although it is not my intention to explore these topics here.

However, two things must be said about Truquin's attempt to set himself up in the trade. It is interesting to note the ease with which Truquin learned the trade. He began by weaving velvet: "I began to be good at it quickly" (p. 207). He went on to fancy items: "I started working on a piece that I had no idea how to weave, and nevertheless I succeeded at first try" (p. 211). By going from one atelier to another, from one article to another, by this turnover that still today so often substitutes for an apprenticeship, he became "by the end of a year a tolerable worker" (p. 212). He improved his theoretical knowledge of silk production with a teacher who made samples but was also especially enamored of history. This passage suggests the need for reflection on the question of skill: How relative is our concept of skill, and how often is it a problem of status as well as of sophisticated learning?

Truquin chose the classic way of setting himself up in the trade. He married a silk weaver, a daughter of peasants from the department of the Ain, who was lodged by her employer and therefore "respectable."[46]

She had accumulated some savings: "Two hundred francs put away at the savings bank" (p. 237). Despite Truquin's reluctance they were married in a religious ceremony—in this autobiography, as in many others, women appear as the pillars of the church—and settled in his small lodgings, where there was room for two looms. The cost of this operation was six hundred francs, financed partly by a loan, though its repayment was complicated by a six-month recession. These financial difficulties caused the couple some hardship. For example, Truquin's

---

[43]Truquin, *Mémoires*, pp. 212–15. Truquin is at the same time very misogynous (women are a bit behind the times ideologically, according to him) and very attentive to the damaging working conditions for women in industry; he gives accounts of these on several occasions.

[44]Ibid., pp. 216–17, an interesting description of the distinctive signs adopted by different categories of workers.

[45]Ibid., pp. 227–31. At the same period, the Lyonnais workers proclaim themselves to be "positivists," which shows the richness of ideological trends of thought in Lyons.

[46]Ibid., p. 234: "There are two categories of women silk workers, those who have their own rooms and those who live in lodgings furnished by their employers; the latter pass for more respectable."

wife was compelled to give birth not at home, but in the hospital, the place of poverty and death.[47] The couple's daily lot was that of the trade, with difficulties linked to nonpayment for finished samples, to the whims of fashion, and to the anguish of meeting rent payments (*le terme*).

Deteriorating working conditions, in part a result of the development of rural workshops condemned by Truquin, led to labor unrest. Norbert was one of the leaders of the coalition that succeeded in obtaining a 20 percent raise in rates. It was perhaps in this way that he was able to raise the money for his first trip to America. The structural crisis of the Lyonnais silk industry, the collapse of the canuts—the milieu in which he was active[48]—and finally the political events of the Commune and the subsequent repression, all contributed to Norbert's decision to strike out for virgin land and for the frontier that seemed to offer salvation.

Representations of Work: Salvation through the Land

Thus Truquin did not succeed in becoming a canut. His experience of being naturalized in the trade was a failure, perhaps because the profession was disbanded. Metalwork or machines would have afforded a more secure identification, but Truquin was undoubtedly not a reader of *Les merveilles de l'industrie*.

His failure strengthened his pragmatic and instrumental attitude toward work as a necessary, if not sufficient, way to ensure his individual independence. Truquin denied the notion of providential power, whether of God or of the state. He refused charity in the same terms as relief. A worker had to rely on himself alone. The way he broke with his family's religious practice over the question of work was consistent with this belief. A pious aunt who was shocked by his ignorance of prayers—in this case grace before meals—sermonized to him: "She told me that it was a great sin not to know how to pray, not to thank God for the good things he heaped upon us, for the food he gave us to eat, and so on." "My aunt," I replied, "God put mankind on earth, but if man didn't work, he wouldn't eat; it's not God, but work that provides us with food to eat" (p. 54). And like the rich young man in the Gospel, he "left his faith for good."

More than a guarantee of individual independence, work was also the basis of workers' strength. On this point Truquin embraced those ideologies that valorized the "producers" as agents of human progress and as social revolutionaries. His discourse was one of utility and therefore condemnation of social parasites. In theory he adopted the motto of

[47]On this history of the hospital system in Lyons, see Olivier Faure, *Genèse de l'hôpital moderne: Les hospices civils de Lyon de 1802 à 1845* (Lyons, 1982).
[48]On this subject, see Lequin, *Ouvriers*, 1:186ff.

L'Atelier: "He who does not work, shall not eat." "Socialism," he writes, "will bring everyone well-being by getting rid of idlers and by distributing work among all young and able-bodied persons, a large number of whom do useless or prejudicial things" (p. 307). Among the unproductive, Truquin classed priests who "run away from work to lead the good life" (p. 145), military men or at least officers,[49] who think only of their mistresses, and the bourgeoisie, who with their sumptuary spending mimicked the Old Regime, Jews, and civil servants. Truquin was party to popular anti-Semitism, which has almost always existed in France and for which Proudhon was a particularly virulent spokesman. While visiting museums in Paris, Truquin writes, "I noticed that those who had a full beard and a straight nose rarely refused to give me information, while I was unable to obtain anything from those whose nose was widespread or in the form of a parrot's beak" (p. 87). In 1848 "the Jesuits connived with the Jews, the consequence of which was the moral corruption of France and Europe. The future will tell the results of this agreement" (p. 103). He saw evidence of this Jesuit-Jewish coalition everywhere, notably in North Africa. The Jews brought their support to a feudal system that still existed.[50]

But Truquin's supreme loathing was directed against civil servants, whom he considered a breed of drones and sluggards who constituted both a social power and a moral threat for the working class—the threat of seduction for those workers who sought bureaucratic jobs for their children. Truquin complained that "the idea of a civil service career is so rooted in France that a great number of workers who have comfortable means (*even among the socialists of all persuasions*) think only in terms of educating their favored children for this career alone. A young man brought up with this educational background is unable to pick up a hammer or a file again; if he is a peasant's son, he can't stand the odor of manure, a substance that is the basis of fertility" (p. 423). In Truquin's view the seeds of corruption, the castraters of energy, were to be found in the sedentary life, in the reluctance to take risks, and in the avoidance of manual work.

Truquin's economic vision was resolutely antiurban and opposed to luxury. He was an advocate, although less explicit, of the ascetic, austere economy so forcefully proposed by Louis Gabriel Gauny, who wrote, "one less thing you need represents one more strength. Living with little is a great means of defense." He denounced "the concealed middleman who stands between the product and the consumer as an enemy, lying and obsequious, a deceiver who is never unmasked."[51] Like Gauny, Tru-

---

[49]Truquin, *Mémoires*, pp. 135–36.
[50]See Mayer, *Persistance de L'ancien régime*.
[51]*Louis Gabriel Gauny*, pp. 99 and 108.

quin considered commerce robbery and waste, even though he himself had benefited from it. A strain of physiocratic thought persists in the French working classes, as it does also in the theoretician of direct-action unionism, Fernand Pelloutier.[52]

Contrary to Saint-Simon, Truquin did not "bet in favor of industry."[53] He joined forces with the anti-industrial currents of thought that were so very strong in the first half of the nineteenth century and that undoubtedly restrained industrial investment. Truquin deplored the vicissitudes of the artisan: "since the Revolution, the artisanal trades have continued to be degraded" (p. 94). In his view, the fundamental source of wealth remained the land—the inexhaustible, abundant land. In opposition to Malthus, never named but present nonetheless,[54] Truquin believed that the world was not finished and that colonization could extend the limits of the civilized world. The way to escape slavery and to save the world was to clear the land. Many reformers, whether of socialist persuasion or not, were alarmed by urban migration and by the army of unemployed, and they advocated a return to the land. Such was the case of Huerne de Pommeuse,[55] who took up Henri IV's motto: "The government rules well when there are no men idle or fields fallow." Or take Ledru-Rollin, who declared in 1848 during the National Assembly debate on the right to work: "France is above all an agricultural country; therein lies her major strength; such has been the belief of all her great statesmen. Industry is secondary and must be an auxiliary but not a fundamental axis, as the navy would be to your military strength. What I am asking for is the return to agriculture, for the sake of protection, for the enobling of this art, for the great number of workers who swarm into our towns and become degenerate."[56]

However, Truquin did not advocate colonization for individual or national goals. In the promise of the New World he saw the possibility of establishing agrarian communities that would become model societies. In this sense he followed in the footsteps of Owen, Fourier, Considérant, and Cabet, for whom the diffusion and the attraction of these exemplary societies remained the best way to change the world—not by seizing power, but by the strength of their example. At several points in his book Truquin describes projects for socialist colonies, particularly in the "Story of Father Jack" (pp. 147–69), a kind of fable that takes place in an agrarian community where there are equal rewards for all. Here any

[52]Jacques Julliard, *Fernand Pelloutier et le syndicalisme d'action directe* (Paris, 1971).

[53]Cahiers de l'ISEA, under the direction of F. Perroux and P. M. Schuhl, *Saint-Simonisme et pari pour l'industrie, 19–20e siècles*, 4 vols., 1970 (April–June) and 1973 (January).

[54]*Malthus Past and Present*, ed. J. Dupaquier and A. Fauve-Chamoux (London and New York, 1983); see especially M. Perrot, "Malthusianism and Socialism."

[55]L. F. Huerne de Pommeuse, *Des colonies agricoles et de leurs avantages* (Paris, 1832).

[56]*Droit au travail*, pp. 119–20.

surplus is consumed at festivals, thereby implying a stationary state of the economy. The community is administered only by male veterans, over forty-five years old, who take turns governing. Although Truquin had been reluctant in his youth to follow Cabet's doctrine, which he considered too authoritarian, he constructed, in fact, his own *Icarie*.

The nineteenth century—this "time of prophets"[57]—overflowed with planners and creators of utopias. Truquin's originality lies in his carrying out his ideas (though there was no lack of attempts at agricultural co-operatives) and further still, in his choice of Latin America. First in Argentina, then in Paraguay, Truquin attempted the experience of stock farming rather than cultivation. There is no doubt that the Italian influence, so strong in Lyons (a Piedmont town), was decisive in this respect. He refers explicitly to this tradition at several points: "This is what the Italians do," he says to his Lyonnais comrades, who hesitate to contribute to a preliminary fund (p. 304). In the Lyons prison he showed interest in Latin American history, borrowing books on Mexican history from the chaplain. When considered from this viewpoint, Truquin's experience is one more example of the libertarian movements of southern Europe, so rich in imagination and trials.

Once on the other side of the Atlantic, wrestling with problems of ticks and the lack of tools, Truquin looked pessimistically upon the world he had left behind. He was dismayed by proletarianization and by the concentration of power engendered by industrial civilization, where technical progress served the power of a minority. He writes: "The more mechanization is improved, the easier it will be for a few clever people to keep the masses under their control" (p. 144). Already "France has become nothing more than a vast central prison inhabited by judges, jailkeepers, and enslaved men" (p. 423).

The working class could, of its own will, arrest and reverse this movement. Truquin directed his remarks to the members of his own class, exhorting them to take risks, to break the infernal circle of consumption. But he feared that their desire for roots and for social protection would push them to seek a job rather than real work. In all lucidity, he feared that the inordinate growth of the state would come about with the consent of its subjects. His contradictory vision of the future shares both the terrors of the romantic age, whence he came, and the dark forecast of George Orwell. Thus Truquin was neither an analyst nor a theoretician. As far as experience and reflection on work are considered, it is his adventures and his wanderings that interest us.

Translated by Helen H. Chenut
and Cynthia J. Koepp

---

[57] Paul Bénichou, *Le temps des prophètes: Doctrines de l'age romantique* (Paris, 1977).

11

The Myth of the Artisan:
Critical Reflections on a Category of Social History

JACQUES RANCIÈRE

Most historians concerned with labor and socialist movements in France have accepted practically without question the connection between professional qualification (skill) and militant consciousness (militancy): that is, that these movements developed as the expression of a working-class culture and were based on the actions and attitudes of the most highly skilled workers. Accordingly, they assert that technical ability and pride in work created the basis for early labor militancy—a militancy that ended only when the Taylorist revolution massively reorganized labor processes, which in turn led to the creation of a new working population lacking professional skills, collective traditions, and interest in their work.

I would like to show that such a view is highly debatable if one strictly analyzes militant practice and its basis in the trades. This supposed first axiom of labor militancy is most likely a belated interpretation born of political necessity in some sections of the labor movement that, in order to fend off new and competing militant forces, harked back to a largely imaginary tradition of "authentic" worker socialism.

The Illusion of the Elite Trades:
Tailors, Shoemakers, and Others

It is important that we go back to the period of the "first" worker socialism, which, through the strikes and associations of the 1830s and through the republican organizations, utopian groups, workers' literature and press of the 1840s, led to the workers' eruption of 1848. Indeed, we are accustomed to seeing the worker of 1848 as the typical representative of artisanal culture (whether it be, like Marx, to deprecate this culture or to revalorize it in opposition to Marxism).

Nevertheless, the facts relating to the trades most prominently represented in the republican associations, utopian groups, or simple street demonstrations seriously challenge this equation. The overrepresentation of certain trades and the predominance in particular of two of them—the tailors and the shoemakers—has been duly noted,[1] and the conclusion has generally been that these two groups were propelled to the front lines of combat by two factors: the consciousness of their own professional worth and the threat of professional deskilling linked to the invasion of ready-made clothing.

When considering the merits of such an interpretation we must, it seems to me, beware of our own tendency to project onto artisanal practice the image of bourgeois luxury, which is its end product. For example, we project the prestige of Parisian fashion onto the activities of the professionals of the clothing industries. In consequence, we misapprehend not only the reality of their working conditions but also the perceived value of their work, according to handicraft workers' own scale of values. Certain crafts that seem prestigious to us were in fact contemptible within the workers' tradition. The occupations of tailor and typographer, for example, seem noble to us because they touch upon fashion and intellectual life. Yet in the 1840s, the newspaper *L'Atelier* felt obliged to "prove to a gathering of workers of all crafts that a tailor handling his needle or a typographer aligning his letters of lead was just as worthy of the respectable title of 'ouvrier' as a baker, a cabinetmaker, or a tanner."[2] Traditionally, workers had regarded typography and tailoring as contemptible, since they required little strength, skill, or technical knowledge.

Within the world of work, however, one trade consistently symbolized the lowest of the low from the standpoint of the strong and skillful: that of the shoemaker. To understand the depth of the contempt associated with this trade, one might turn to the songs of the *compagnonnage*, including that of "conciliatory" tanner Piron, which stigmatized the shoemakers as "vile and abject" in their ridiculous oversized smocks, with their clumsy muffs and stinking pitch.[3] Shoemaking was scorned not

---

[1]This is particularly stressed by Christopher H. Johnson in *Utopian Communism in France: Cabet and the Icarians, 1839–1851* (Ithaca, 1974) as well as in his contribution to Price et al., *Revolution and Reaction: 1848 and the Second French Republic* (London, 1975).
[2]H. Leneveux, *Le travail manuel en France* (Paris, n.d.), p. 166.
[3]Jean-Francois Piron, "La fête des braves," in *Le Chansonnier du tour de France* (Paris, 1840). See, in the same collection, "Les braves" and "Reception d'un compagnon cordonnier."

only from within the crafts, but also from a larger cultural or ideological point of view: Ashaverus, the Wandering Jew, was a shoemaker. And since tradition taught that shoemakers fraudulently initiated each other into the secrets of the compagnonnage, it was recommended that shoemakers bearing emblems of the compagnonnage be killed.

This custom, of course, tended to fall into disuse among the compagnonnages, yet some shoemakers were still being murdered at midcentury. And the curse continued in another realm: shoemaking was condemned as the last of the crafts. Or rather, it was not really a craft at all: it was the occupation of concierges trying to supplement their incomes, or the apprenticeship for orphans and the unfortunate, the craft most often taught in charitable institutions. Or it was chosen out of necessity or bad luck, as in the case of the young haberdasher's apprentice who lost first his parents, then his tutor: this young man "remained alone after this second loss, and his health had suffered too much for him to continue in his preferred occupation. What could be done? An occasion presented itself for him to become a shoemaker, a trade he didn't like. He had to become a shoemaker."[4] Clearly then, it was not professional pride that fueled the militant ideas of the shoemakers. If the trade produced so many activists and dreamers, it is more likely because there was much forced leisure time and because the material and symbolic rewards of the trade were so very insignificant.

The tailor's craft did not suffer from the same contempt, yet it was also something of a refuge. Apprenticeship was relatively short—two to three years, and in general it required no payment by the apprentice's parents to the master.[5] In tailoring, then, one tended to find young men of very modest backgrounds as well as youngest sons on whom little expense was lavished. The tailor Constant Hilbey, for instance, originally hoped to be a turner's apprentice, but "the turner demanded more money than Hilbey's father was able to provide. The father then declared that he could only afford to have his son trained as a tailor."[6] Similarly, the leader of the tailors' strike, André Troncin, was condemned to take a tailor's apprenticeship after the death of his mother and the remarriage of his father, a wood seller in Besançon. When his stepmother took a dislike to the children of the first marriage, only his older brother received professional training, and André was shunted off to a poor man's apprenticeship.[7]

---

[4]Alphonse Viollet, *Les poètes du peuple au XIXe siècle* (Paris, 1846), p. 87. The reference is to the poet and shoemaker from Reims, Gonzalle.

[5]See the report of the tailor Deluc from Bordeaux that accompanies his project for an association (Archives nationales, F¹² 4631).

[6]Viollet, *Poètes du peuple*, p. 3.

[7]J. P. Gilland, "Biographie des hommes obscurs, André Troncin," *La feuille du village*, 28 November 1850.

Nevertheless, André Troncin was to have considerable professional success. He became a cutter and shop foreman while at the same time pursuing, through study and the company of students, his education in militancy. Hilbey, on the other hand, anxious to avoid taxing his mind and body with onerous travail, chose to make children's clothes because that specialty "required less attention and intelligence."[8] Generally speaking, however, the work activities in shops where workers were squeezed against one another, all bent over a too-narrow workbench with their legs crossed, the needlework accomplished "with a regularity approaching that of machines,"[9] offered little that could have contributed to strong professional pride. And the supposed contrast between the quality work of the professional tailors and the poor work of the clothing-industry workers is very dubious: tailors were the same workers who, when the shops were in their off-season, worked in the clothing manufactories.[10] In addition, corporate tradition and the collective consciousness were very feeble, thanks to the great mobility of the workers. A correspondent from *La Fashion* stressed the weakness of collective professional links, in contrast to the tradition of mutual aid among the compagnonnages; he wrote, "Nary a fraternal link uniting them. They see one another: Hello. They leave one another: Goodbye, and all is said. Another cause of their ruin is the brevity of their stay in each workshop. A term of three months is the longest."[11]

For the tailors and shoemakers alike, then, mobilization came not from professional links or from pride in their work, but rather from the particular "disponibilité" (freedom or detachment) of the workers. This basic detachment stemmed from the character of the trade itself: as a refuge for the needy, as overcrowded, as punctuated by off-seasons that meant a worker's identity included being unemployed; and it spawned an intellectual detachment or freedom, a result of the small intellectual and moral investment required to practice the craft. Indeed, this detachment or availability was a constant concern of bourgeois observers, who feared that certain working-class occupations were not interesting or challenging enough to occupy the mind as well as the body, thereby leaving the workers' minds idle and leading them to seek fulfillment elsewhere.[12] The shoemakers and tailors are a particularly clear example, and what is true for the common workers applies all the more to their leaders. These "easy" trades were those where one was most likely to

---

[8]Constant Hilbey, *Réponse à tous mes critiques* (Paris, 1846), p. 51.

[9] Pierre Vinçard, "Les ouvriers tailleurs," *Le travail affranchi*, 7 January 1849.

[10]See the analyses of the master tailor Canneva in his newspaper *La Fashion*.

[11]*La Fashion*, 20 April 1842.

[12]Monneret, *Hygiène des tailleurs*, published as a supplement in Augustin Canneva, *Livre du tailleur* (Paris, 1838).

find men whose intellectual capacities and human aspirations were neither required nor satisfied in the workplace.

The relationship between these two "disponibilités" allows us to conceive of the mobilization of a trade as the capacity of its workers to rally around values external, and even opposed, to those of the trade, whether political (i.e., republican) or ideological (i.e., utopian), and to follow leaders who are not so much representatives of the rank and file as the intellectuals of the craft. A man like Troncin, for example, who earned 2,400 francs a year—three times the average—and who, as shop foreman, enjoyed the confidence of his employers, had no financial motive to become a leader of corporate strikes. If he was always chosen to lead the movement it was because of his intellectual and political prestige and because of the authority he had acquired as a propagandist, less concerned with the specific details of wages and working conditions than with the "education" of his peers and the ways to make them partners equal in dignity to their masters.

If one were to multiply the case studies, one might well be led to a complete reversal of the prevailing opinion and come to assert that militant activity is perhaps inversely proportional to the organic cohesion of the trade, the strength of the organization, and the ideology of the group. Workers in what was considered the king of trades, carpentry (for carpenters were the direct descendants of the legendary builders of the temple of Solomon), were more than satisfied by their organization and by their awareness of professional superiority. When they became engaged in a collective struggle in the great strike of 1845, they were careful to select a royalist attorney in order to avoid any ideological or political overflow from their corporate struggle. Likewise the curriers, very advanced in terms of solidarity, were little heard from beyond their own circle.[13] In contrast, the highest level of militancy existed among the poor relations, those trades that were a crossroads or a catchall: for instance, among the tailors but not the hatters; among the shoemakers but not the curriers; among the joiners but not the carpenters; among the typographers, who, in their relation to the intellectual world, were outcasts as well. A strong militant identity among workers in a craft seems to imply a weak collective professional identity and vice versa. In this light the structure of the Saint-Simonian workers' groups is significant. The most active of these groups—the one in the twelfth arrondissement of Paris—included not a single representative of the leading industry in that area, that of the curriers, tawers, and tanners. Nor did it include any members of the next two most important trades in that

---

[13]On the forms of mutual aid among the curriers, see Office du travail, *Les associations professionnelles ouvrières* (Paris, 1900), 2:193.

neighborhood, metal casters and pottery workers. The militant worker population sat on the margins of the world of organic and united professional collectivities.[14]

The Ambiguities of "Love of Work"

It is also likely that militant worker ideology was characterized to some extent by rejection of the concept of "love of work." Nothing shows this denial better than the contrast between the ideas of the Saint–Simonian "priests" and those of the workers they recruited. The former sought to engage "robust" workers in the great epic of an "industrial army" that was to build the foundations of the future while preaching their gospel. The workers, however, were attracted for opposite reasons: as the worker and songster Vinçard tells us in his *Mémoires*, "There were many who, disgusted with their lives as wage earners, embraced Saint-Simonian ideas only because they hoped to bid an eternal farewell to the past."[15] The less sophisticated workers sought in Saint-Simonism a kind of mutual aid society that for the poorest among them would function as a welfare office, and for the others would provide a kind of social security system. The most enlightened workers were seeking intellectual growth, an escape from the worker's world.

The lives of these workers whose trajectories came to intersect those of utopian propaganda bring us to seriously reconsider our ideas about the artisan and his attitude toward work. The term "artisan" evokes for us a certain stability, a certain identification of an individual with a function. Yet identities are often misleading. We find, for example, that there are two haberdashers among the Saint-Simonian workers. But we discover on closer examination that they are "haberdashers" only because they had a chance to purchase some material at a low price, thus enabling them to try their luck at the "craft," which they might just as well have done in a different field. One of the two men, Maire, was a sailor who had recently left the service. The other, Voinier, was an obviously educated proletarian. Out of money, he was willing to accept a position as a servant with the Saint-Simonians, yet the following year he was working as a secretary for the Society for the Rights of Man. Later, upon being arrested by the police, he was identified as a wine merchant, and upon a subsequent arrest he was described as an accounting clerk. There is nothing exceptional about his case: the professional identities under

---

[14]On the groups of Saint-Simonian workers, see the archives of the Arsenal (*Fonds enfantin*, especially dossiers 7815 and 7816) and the second part of my book, *La nuit des prolétaires* (Paris, 1981).

[15]Louis Vinçard, *Mémoires épisodiques d'un vieux chansonnier saint-simonien* (Paris, 1879).

which militants are known to their colleagues, to "bourgeois" militants, or to the police are often only temporary stages in an otherwise rocky career. The same individual can be found self-employed in one trade, salaried in another, or hired as a clerk or peddler in a third. With the gaps caused by unemployment or the off-seasons, with their businesses crumbling as soon as they are set up, their bills and loan payments going unpaid, their feverish wait for provincial inheritances, their continual trips to the pawn shops, their hopes and disillusionments, these artisans often led a life quite similar to the one we associate with the "marginal" workers of today. And often they were no more committed to their work than are today's workers. Few Saint-Simonian artisans resisted the attractions of a job such as doorman, office boy, or railway guard. On the other hand, only the greatest need would lead them to work on the tracks or in the workshops. Reading their job applications, one gets a very "unartisanal" sense of work as an abstraction. Take, for example, a letter to Michel Chevalier from a bookseller who says that he is not put off by any kind of work and that he can just as easily "wear a smock, jacket, and cap as, if need be, put on a suit of fine cloth."[16]

Work as abstraction: what an ambiguous notion. One can get a sense of this ambiguity from two seemingly contrasting cases. The first is that of the archetypal militant artisan, Agricol Perdiguier, author of the *Livre du compagnonnage* and the *Mémoires d'un compagnon*. In the context of our labor history, he seems to represent a perfect example of a worker bringing into the political struggle his consciousness of himself as a proud and able worker. Yet his life story is puzzling: how could this joiner, who claims to have created dazzling work during his *Tour de France*, have wound up with such an undistinguished career? He apparently lived in poverty in a slum of the faubourg Saint-Antoine. And rather than making spiral staircases or other masterpieces of artistry, he made little dressing tables whose price was to diminish, in a few years' time, from twelve to seven francs apiece.[17] This simple work could have been done by the children of the German workers who populated the faubourg. To supplement his income he took in boarders, and his remarks during the crisis of 1846, which emptied the workshops, suggest that he was much more concerned about his boarders than his work and thus that they constituted his principal source of support. Similarly, his self-proclaimed title of "professor of architecture" hides the more modest economic reality: that he started to give lessons in order to boost his income. Nor does this proud artisan hesitate to badger George Sand into giving his wife some sewing work. We must there-

---

[16]Letter from Ruffin to Michel Chevalier, *Fonds enfantin*, MS 7606.
[17]On all that follows, see Agricol Perdiguier, *Biographie de l'auteur du Livre du compagnonnage* (Paris, 1846).

fore ask ourselves the following question: If he takes up his pen to sing the glories of the work of the compagnons and to rebuke them for their quarrels, is it not also in order to escape this "glorious" work himself? One is tempted to say yes, especially in light of his *Biographie de l'auteur du Livre du compagnonnage*, which is rather like the dark side of his two famous books. In it, the methodical accounting he presents of the splinters that have entered his body, the falling wood that has injured him, the lung disease caused by breathing sawdust, and finally his suicidal thoughts—all allow us to see the hatred he felt for this work, whose hero and eulogist he has come to be in the eyes of posterity.

Once again we are tempted to propose a law of inverse proportionality, to say that the men who sing the glory of "work" the most loudly are those who have most intensely experienced its degradation. This consciousness of disgrace is expressed with a naked force in some Saint-Simonian documents, and especially in the despairing letters of the joiner Gauny, whose hallucinatory descriptions tell of a life "imprisoned" by the "trap" of the proletariat, torn to shreds by the "frenzy of tyrannical activity of time."[18] But we also see it crop up in those newspapers of the 1840s that aspire to be the voice of the working people: in the anecdotes of *La Fraternité* or *La Ruche Populaire*, or in the editorials of *L'Atelier* that argued against any weakness in meeting one's obligations toward work. Such editorializing becomes even more significant when we see that one of the principal editors of *L'Atelier*, the locksmith Gilland, wrote in *Les Conteurs Ouvriers* of the hellish experience of apprenticeship and of the feeling of despair that accompanied his entry into working life. And then we see, twenty years later, the soul of that newspaper, the typographer and sculptor Corbon, apologize for and recognize the virtues of indifference toward work, as in Parisian workers whose indifference helped preserve their hopes for a better society.[19] One may object that these ambiguous attitudes are not those of the silent majority. But it is precisely those who are satisfied with their work who have no need to sing hymns to it.

One must nonetheless be careful not simply to turn the standard interpretation upside down. For hatred of work, like "love" of it, is ambiguous. Take, for instance, the case of the Saint-Simonian tailor Delas, who appears to be the complete opposite of Perdiguier. Vinçard, in his *Mémoires*, described this missionary worker as "a weak compagnon, working little and poorly, as a result of earning almost nothing and barely subsisting, having no concern for his future; if one asked

[18]The manuscripts of the joiner Gauny, a unique account of a worker's life, are preserved in the Bibliothèque Municipale de Saint Denis. I have collected the most significant of these texts in *Louis Gabriel Gauny: Le philosophe plébéien* (Paris, 1983).

[19]Anthime Corbon, *Le secret du peuple de Paris* (Paris, 1863).

him about his situation, he would reply: Who cares! This won't last; do you think I'm the sort to spend my life sewing petit point?"[20] From his vantage point forty years later, Vinçard sketched an exemplary portrait. And he conveniently forgot what might complicate it: that Delas, having chosen the missionary route to escape the workshop, wound up taking a certain interest in his craft. At the end of the 1830s he invented a machine to take measurements that revolutionized the industry. And in 1847 he was again a pioneer in creating an association between managers and employees in the clothing trade, where he played a leadership role. His lack of interest in "petit point" is not hard to reconcile with his passion for social innovation and for inventions that gave an "intellectual" dignity to the profession. During this entire period, the "geometric cut" was a great topic of discussion among tailors. It was generally favored by men of "progress"—the republican Canneva or the Fouriérist Barde—and even by men of "disorder" like Suireau, who joined Troncin in leading the strikers of 1840. The "geometric cut," scoffed at by political and sartorial conservatives,[21] was one of those inventions that, like a commitment to politics or literature, compensated for the baseness of one's work and broadened the career options of those with inquisitive and independent minds.

In the same way that the hymns to "work" purposely concealed disillusionment, so too indifference and even hatred of the servitude of work can lead to an adjustment, a series of compensations that turn everything around. In his occasional work as a floor layer, no longer under the gaze of his masters or in the presence of his companions in servitude or subject to the work bell, the joiner Gauny created for himself a relationship to his work that was both playful and ascetic, and thus he fashioned a basis for a philosophy of emancipation.[22] The ambiguity of labor is also seen in the workers' poetry, which combined a number of themes: the suffering of an existence that is lived far from its dream, the ascetic joy to be derived from the tour de force of successfully living two lives at once, and an image of work as an ambiguous activity that mediates between several worlds. Thus, in the verses of the stonemason Poncey, the virtue of work is identified with that of traveling between conditions of life:

> I have built poor little cottages
> And rich palaces with lofty domes;

[20]Vinçard, *Mémoires épisodiques*, p. 95.

[21]For more on the scoffers, see Couanon, *Journal des Marchands Tailleurs* (1835–47), and his *Le parfait tailleur* (Paris, 1852).

[22]Cf. Louis Cabriel Gauny, "Le travail à la tache," in *Philosophe plébéien*, pp. 44–49.

My hammers have chipped away at gothic
  convents
Whose walls of dust have flown off to the winds
A nomadic pariah, I have carried my trowel
Into brilliant boudoirs perfumed with love,
Into more than one tavern aspark with joy,
Where cups flow with generous wine
In smoke-filled garrets.[23]

The Ruse of Numbers and the Ruse of Words

These contradictory images and practices should encourage us to be systematically cautious whenever we wish to establish links between professional situations, militant practices, and ideological statements. Typically, historians make use of horizontal controls: accumulating, cross-checking, verifying certain kinds of data: economic statistics, descriptions of conditions, acts of repression, literature, and so forth. Their vigilance is generally much more lax when it is a matter of placing heterogeneous kinds of data and archives into a vertical relationship, or relating a worker's discourse to a material situation, or deducing a given type of militant practice from a given type of industrial organization. Between the different kinds of knowledge, the different kinds of data we use to piece together a picture of the militant worker, there are enormous gaps, lacunae that go unnoticed. And the historian who carefully verifies each level of data can all too easily underestimate these gaps and fill them in with ideas that seem so obvious that they hardly require verification. This inclination has indeed been the case for a whole series of representations of workers as a group in terms of their solidarity, their values regarding work, and the relation between their conditions and their forms of expression. Between the fumes of the factories and the grime of the slums, between the assaults of poverty and the fury of the struggle, between the brilliance of luxury and the conditions of the artisans, between the artisan's end product and the confidence of his hymn to "work," between the rumblings of the crowd and the voices of its representatives, an entire series of inferences impose themselves almost naturally and end up blinding us to the ruses of numbers and the ruses of words and the ruses of their relationships. I would like to consider only two examples of ruses that have helped form our image of the worker of 1848.

[23]Charles Poncy, "A Béranger," in *Le chantier* (Paris, 1844). See also my article "Ronds de fumée: Les poétes ouvriers dans la France de Louis-Phillippe," *Revue des sciences humaines* 190 (April/June 1983): 31–47. In his book *Work and Revolution in France* (Cambridge, 1980) William H. Sewell also analyzes Poncy's poetry, but from a rather different standpoint.

The first example concerns the *Statistique de l'industrie à Paris* [Statistical survey of industry in Paris], published during the revolution of 1848 by the Paris chamber of commerce. It describes the population of artisans as highly skilled, well paid, working as regularly as their trades allow, and possessing a solid education. This portrait confirms our image of the worker of 1848 as a skilled artisan, educated and relatively well-off, except during periods of economic and political crisis. The problem is that the survey was all too obviously conducted to produce just such an image. Without even discussing the wages quoted in the report (which were disputed at the time), how could one seriously believe statistics that assure us that 90 percent of the workers were able to read and write, when the letters and petitions we have examined elsewhere show that even the workers selected to do the writing had difficulty expressing themselves? Looking at these inflated figures, one must bear in mind that this survey is above all a countersurvey. Planned in 1847, it was accelerated in 1848 so as to appear before another survey commissioned by the Comité du travail of the Assembly. Conducted by employers who obtained their information from other employers, the report was intended to prove that "in normal and ordinary times, the working population of Paris leads a satisfactory existence in all respects."[24] Yet even the coordinator of the survey allowed that there might be some doubt about the authenticity of some information provided by employers out to prove their own conciliatory position, so as to "bring about the much-desired recovery in business and employment." In order to put the blame on political agitators, who theoretically worked alone and from the outside to upset industrial harmony, the employers did not hesitate to paint a more flattering picture of the workers' education and mores than the one they had in front of their eyes.

We find other distortions if we move from "bourgeois" statistics to "workers' discourse." While the former embellished the world of the artisan, the latter artificially joined the collectivity of workers to its "spokesmen." Whenever workers speak in the name of work, affirm its rights or glorify its greatness, we run the risk of inferring a false picture of the collectivity they represent or of the realities that underlie their speech, unless we determine very precisely who is speaking, who is being addressed, and what the stakes are. The presentation of the anthology *La parole ouvrière*—on which I collaborated with Alain Faure—now seems to me to give excessive credit to the idea of a workers' discourse collectively addressed to the bourgeoisie, to oversimplify the experience of collective struggle in the face of an opposing group.[25] Such an emphasis

---

[24]*Statistique de l'industrie à Paris, 1847–48* (Paris, 1851), p. 61.
[25]*La parole ouvrière, 1830–1851*, texts assembled and presented by Alain Faure and Jacques Rancière (Paris, 1976).

does not take into account two fundamental characteristics of these workers' publications: first, that they were polemical texts addressed to other factions of worker intelligentsia; and second, that they reflected political and ideological stakes of the "bourgeois" world. In my analysis of the principal workers' newspaper of the time, *L'Atelier*, I have attempted to show the complexity of these positions: the glorification of work that one finds in *L'Atelier* is neither the expression of a more or less diffuse "class consciousness" nor the view of an elite group of skilled workers.[26] *L'Atelier* did not stress the view of work as creative: it stressed the view of work as duty and *condemnation* in opposition to Saint-Simonian, Fouriérist, or communist utopias. On the one hand this conception, which was that of the neo-Catholic workers inspired by Buchez, provided a "realistic" way of dealing with feelings of helplessness in those increasingly marginal beings, the intellectual workers. On the other hand it was the instrument of a political struggle that sought to unite the forces of the intellectual and militant worker elite around a specific political force, that of the moderate republicans. The discourse on work or worker unity in *L'Atelier* is precisely the means by which it sought, paradoxically, to integrate the forces of the worker elite into an external political force. In the case of *L'Atelier*, the specifically political elements are quite visible. Yet very often, political conflicts were hidden behind the facade of collective discourse. From this point of view one might well reconsider the question of the "worker press" in 1848. In the anthology mentioned earlier I gave an important place to the *Journal des Travailleurs*, published in June 1848 by the "central committee" of the workers' corporations, an offshoot of the Commission du Luxembourg brought together by Louis Blanc. I presented this publication as an example of a kind of systematization of the experience of the corporations, as the crystallization of a united class ideology.[27] It now seems to me that one must take into greater account the ambiguity of this "avant-garde" of delegates to the Commission du Luxembourg who expressed themselves in the *Journal*. This self-proclaimed central committee is in fact largely dominated by representatives of specific political forces, and not by a collective of worker corporations. Although its most influential member, Pierre Vinçard, had the title "jewelry engraver," we have good reason to suspect that he spent very little of his life engraving jewelry. In 1848 he was already a journalist specialized in workers' issues—not a corporate representative. And it was Louis Blanc, not the jewelry engravers, who

---

[26]Rancière, *Nuit des prolétaires*, chap. 10.

[27]Faure and Rancière, *Parole ouvrière*, p. 287. On this question one must of course consult the fascinating analyses of Remi Gossez in *Les ouvriers de Paris* (La Roch-sur-Yon, 1967) while avoiding the temptation to see in the worker organization that he presents a foreshadowing of revolutionary syndicalism.

placed him on the commission. His former colleague from *La Fraternité*, the metal caster Malarmet, was an authentic worker, yet he too was elected not by his peers but by Louis Blanc. The sculptor Jules Salmson, author of an editorial in the *Journal des Travailleurs*, was most likely brought in by Louis Blanc as well, for he belonged to the same artistic circle as Louis's brother Charles Blanc. Although the *Journal des Travailleurs* appeared to be the collective organ of the workers' corporations, it was in fact a weapon in the conflict between the "avant-garde" and large sections of the rank and file. Accused by the latter of having been too preoccupied with the elections and having acted as satellites of the clubs, the editors counterattacked on economic grounds by proposing a territorial organization of links between producers and consumers that would counterbalance the separatist and apolitical tendencies of the corporation.

The Fabrication of Images: Methodological and Political Issues

The preceding examples focus our attention once again on an issue filled with complexities and contradictions: the relations between the labor movement per se and "outside" influences of a political and ideological nature. In many cases, we have a tendency to interpret as collective practice or class "ethos" political statements that are in fact highly individualized. We attach too much importance to the collectivity of workers and not enough to its divisions; we look too much at worker culture and not enough at its encounters with other cultures.

This tendency may well represent the other side of the coin of a certain number of good methodological principles. We have all followed the lead of the ethnologists who warned us of the dangers of ethnocentrism, who taught us not to project our reasons onto the practice of others. Most of us have learned elsewhere to beware of the political structures and ideologies proposed to the working class from above. Methodological considerations and political wariness thus work together to focus our attention on those aspects of the workers' struggle and discourse that can be explained exclusively in terms of their own practices and experiences. Thus we dutifully seek to place the origins of their words within the context of their trades, and we presume their representatives to be solidly anchored within the collectivity they represent. But in doing so we are perhaps avoiding one form of "intellectual racism" only to fall into another—one that consists of overstressing the *difference of identity*. By considering the joiner Perdiguier, the tailor Troncin, the locksmith Gilland, and the engraver Vinçard to be representative of the population of skilled artisans, we are not perceiving them for what they really are: They constitute a marginal group at the frontier of encounters with the bourgeoisie, characterized by the same migrations and instabilities, the same ambiguities and contradictions, that define the working class; but they are also *a particular category of intellectuals*, more intellectual in a sense than we are, for their intellectuality is a victory over their condition. With the good intention of limiting ourselves solely to the professional experience of the workers, we thus run the risk of reconfirming the old philosophical adage that recommends that workers not concern themselves with anything besides their work. We imagine a carpenter turning his phrases as he turns wood, seeing the world through his tools. Thinking we can define his militancy on the basis of his trade, we wind up defining it from the standpoint of our own functionalist preconceptions. And at the same time, we are ready to give credence to certain descriptions of workers' practices that transform political biases into ethnological traits.

I am thinking especially here of some descriptions of Denis Poulot's in *Le sublime* and the validation they received in labor historiography through the work of Georges Duveau.[28] Alain Cottereau has recently described the practices of worker resistance that Poulot denounced as a form of "cheating." But there is something else we must take into account. Denis Poulot was primarily a manager who accused workers. He was first of all a Gambettist political militant who wanted to discredit the militants of the Internationale and the working-class orators of the public meetings. Certain of his descriptions do not refer to any practices of the workers; rather, they are pure political mythologizing. Take, for example, his portrait of a group of worker leaders that he calls the "Sons of God": his discussion with them is filled with contradictions, to the point that one's image of them becomes completely inconsistent. They are but a political caricature, fleshed out by an imaginary anthropology. But the historian's gaze followed, and the polemical caricature was then validated as a form of anthropology that explained workers' behavior.[29]

We thus reach the heart of the paradox, which brings us back to our initial consideration: that the idea of "skilled workers' socialism" is a politically motivated concept. And those who have been the most intent upon showing the labor movement as an outgrowth of the workers' own culture and professional milieu have most often done so in order to subordinate this movement to a particular political point of view.

[28]Denis Poulot, *Le sublime, ou Le travailleur comme il est en 1870 et ce qu'il peut être*, reedited and with an introduction by Alain Cottereau (Paris, 1980); and Georges Duveau, *La vie ouvrière en France sous le Second Empire* (Paris, 1946).

[29]On this point, see Alain Cottereau's introduction and the debate caused by that introduction in *Les révoltes logiques* 12 (Summer 1980): 31–45.

We must also consider, then, the historiography of the labor movements in France, which has in effect developed essentially as an indirect form of political discourse. Those investigators of worker history for the most part were not historians but researchers, sociologists, or jurists, associated with weakening factions of the labor movement. The first major labor historians of the nineteenth century, Joseph Barberet and Isidore Finance, were political and trade-unionist militants, one linked to cooperatism, the other to the positivist school. Having been defeated and eliminated from the militant labor scene by the victory of the "collectivists" in the Workers' party, they became civil servants specializing in labor matters. There they delved into the history of trades, their tradition of struggle and trade associations. The result was that they presented, in contrast to the noisy scene of the socialist and revolutionary trade-unionist movement, the image of a more profound and authentic workers' movement, rooted in the traditions of the professions and in the solidarity of the corporate struggles. Generating its own forms of unionist or cooperative organization, the "authentic" movement would be ready to collaborate with the republican state in instituting an "industrial democracy" based on professional competence, the education of the masses, and social cooperations.[30] Such a notion would unite, despite their differences, those sectors of the labor movement threatened by the rise of Marxist socialism and revolutionary unionism: the world of the cooperatives and the mutual-aid societies, unionist factions influenced by positivism, institutions of popular education, and the "experimental" tradition of utopian socialism (claimed by Goden and his nephew Prudhommeaux). Outside the labor movement, this concept found support in the ideology of "solidarity" of radical politicans such as Léon Bourgeois, and in those circles where a new social science was being developed for the young republic, especially that groundbreaking edge of social science that was sociology. Indeed, it was the sociologist Célestin Bouglé who, far more than his colleagues in history, shaped the careers of the young researchers in labor history. On this fringe of the labor movement and the university, then, a new form of social history was founded, one that sought to counter socialist and Marxist "demagoguery" with a true national tradition of socialist humanism of the worker elite.

This new worker humanism, first linked to the rise of the radical republic, was then taken up by the Section française de l'internationale ouvrière (SFIO) and the reformist Confederation générale du travail (CGT) during the crisis of revolutionary syndicalism and the split in the

---

[30]See Joseph Barberet, *Le travail en France: Monographies professionnelles* (Paris, 1886–90), and Office du travail, *Les associations professionnelles ouvrières* (Paris, 1899–1904).

socialist movement. The SFIO and the CGT appropriated as their own the same vision proposed by the "reformist" militants of the previous generation. They then contrasted their labor movement, presented as that of the labor elites, to the communist movement, which they described as merely the expression of new unskilled workers, cut off from cultural and organizational traditions of the working class. This transformation occurred in two stages. It had its beginnings in the prewar years, as a way of explaining the crisis in revolutionary syndicalism. When this crisis made clear the enormous gap that existed between the humanistic, pacifist utopias of Pelloutier, Monatte, Albert Thierry, and others and the far less glorious reality of corporatist practices and sectarianism, a militant like Merrheim closed the gap in his own way by proposing a sociological interpretation of the situation. He asserted that with new ways of organizing labor processes (such as Taylorism) intelligence had been "driven out of the workshops."[31] Workers who had been masters of their work and of their own minds were now subjected to the laws of mindless, unskilled labor.

After the war the same interpretation was called upon to explain the failure of syndicalist-revolutionary "pacifism," the acquiescence of the working masses in contributing to wartime industry, and their sympathy for the Bolshevik revolution. Faced with the "revolution of the hungry," Merrheim adopted the theory of "industrial democracy" as his own and succeeded in imposing his very questionable sociological explanation. In fact, there was something in it for everybody: the socialist family was happy to take on a great tradition of the socialism of the professional elites; the communist family, ordered by Moscow to "change its class base," found that it was very much to its advantage to have others help them appear to be something they had never succeeded in being: the voice of the assembly-line workers.

From that point on socialist historiography, supported by intellectuals linked to the corporative movement and to socialist cultural organizations (like the "Centre confédéral d'études ouvrières" of the CGT and the "Institut supérier ouvrier" headed by Georges LeFranc), claimed for itself this "coutume ouvrière," a term that stands as the title of the best example of this tendency, *La coutume ouvrière* by the jurist Maxime Leroy. Leroy pursued this search for a "true" labor movement as an alternative to the cacophony of revolutionary demagoguery and in turn exaggerated the tradition of working-class humanism and "artisanal socialism." We know that one of the branches of this search led to the appropriation of the worker tradition for Pétain's new order.[32] The other branch had

[31]*Vie ouvrière*, 5 March 1913.
[32]Cf. J. Rancière, "De Pelloutier à Hitler: Syndicalisme et collaboration," *Les révoltes logiques* 4 (Winter 1977):23–61.

its swan song after the war, in works such as Michel Collinet's *L'ouvrier français: Esprit du syndicalisme*, which develops Merrheim's vision on the basis of dying hopes for revolutionary unionism. But there are political swan songs that echo in the realm of theory. Collinet's vision was revived and amplified by a double echo: that of the philosopher (Sartre) who imposed it on the politicans, and that of the sociologist (Alain Touraine) who reconfirmed it for the historian.[33] We know that those who are defeated on the battleground often get their revenge by imposing their views on historians. The reason is simple: it is they who, by impassioning history, make it interesting.

The Aims of the Analysis

It will perhaps be of use to specify what is at stake in these observations. I do not intend to deny the existence of that "worker humanism" expressed in the hopes of the nineteenth century and in the nostalgia of the twentieth. Rather, it is a matter of questioning its internal coherence and the dominant role attributed in it to work-related values.

Nor do I wish to deny the existence or the importance of these values. I have not claimed that apprenticeship was unimportant or that profession and professional competence did not play their role. I have meant to show the complexities involved in any definition of the working man and the values that are attributed to him. In *La nuit des prolétaires* I attempted to demonstrate the discontinuity that existed in the 1840s between the mentality of the worker that expresses itself in poems and workers' newspapers and that which sees itself living in the everyday context of the workshop. Between these two mental states there is a symbolic rupture that is constituted by the entry into writing, that is, into the domain of the literate. The locksmith Gilland or the typographer Corbon could be perfectly sincere about their workers' ideal. And they could, on occasion, experience equally sincere satisfactions in the exercise of their trades. Nonetheless, to put themselves in the position of writing "We, the workers" they first had to have felt very deeply the rage of the mistreated apprentice or the disgust of the autodidact at the attitudes and values of the workshop braggart. The representation of the worker

---

[33]Michel Collinet's influence is clear in the Sartrean analysis of anarchosyndicalism. See Jean-Paul Sartre, *Les communistes et la paix* (Paris, 1969), and his *Critique de la raison dialectique* (Paris, 1960); see also the writings of André Groz. Bernard H. Moss stresses his indebtedness to the analyses of Michel Collinet and Alain Touraine in *The Origins of the French Labor Movement: The Socialism of Skilled Workers* (Berkeley, 1976). See Alain Touraine, *L'evolution du travail ouvrier aux usines Renault* (Paris, 1955), and Michel Collinet, *L'ouvrier français: Esprit du syndicalisme* (Paris, 1952).

that they describe in the press and in politics is the fallout of an impossible effort to escape the "culture" of their everyday working lives.

Revolutionary unionism also attempted to unite, in its valorization of worker humanism and of the revoulation of the producers, a number of heterogeneous elements. Internationalism, pacifism, and the auto-didactic ideal of such men as Pelloutier, Monatte, and Péricat are much closer to the moral and intellectual vision of militant schoolteachers than to the corporate traditions of apprenticeship and hiring or the physical violence practiced by syndicalist gangs. But it was necessary, in the face of parliamentary socialism and Marxist dogmatism, to weld one to the other artificially in a concept of workers' self-emancipation that drew its values from the workplace.

If this bid for power has generally been validated by social historians, it is most likely because cultural models have imposed themselves. In attempting to reconstruct workers' attitudes against the simplifications of Marxist economism and political hagiography, historians naturally turned to the analysis of cultural anthropology. But in doing so they endorsed a problematic axiom: that of the homogeneity of so-called cultural practices, of a single meaning expressed through eating habits or learned discourses, through the products of work and those of leisure. In a conflictual universe where the barrier of leisure—the barrier sepa-rating the necessity of work and the luxury of thought—constitutes an essential stake, this undifferentiated sense of culture is likely to miss the originality of the representations in or at play in workers' discourse and politics. It would thus be advisable to rethink the relationship that links the identifications and symbolizations of the workingman with the prac-tices of his work and his material conditions as a worker, to rethink it apart from any axioms of cultural homogeneity. The remarks presented here have sought to go in that direction. "It is necessary," wrote Marcel Mauss, "that the sociologist (and the politician) not remain on a level of intellectual simplicity, but that he truly, like the psychologist and the doctor, come to realize that men can desire, think and feel contradictory things, be they at the same time or in successive moments.[34] The same goes for the historian.

Translated by David H. Lake
and Cynthia J. Koepp

[34]Marcel Mauss, "La nation," in *Oeuvres* (Paris, 1968), 3:579.

12

Statistical Representations of Work:
The Politics of the Chamber of Commerce's
Statistique de l'Industrie à Paris, 1847–48

JOAN W. SCOTT

L'examen qui place les individus dans un champ de surveillance
les situe également dans un réseau d'écriture; il les engage dans
toute une épaisseur de documents qui les captent et les fixent.
                              Michel Foucault, *Surveiller et punir*

Statistical reports were weapons in the debate on the "social question"
that preoccupied French domestic politics under the July Monarchy.
Private and public inquiries (*enquêtes*) were undertaken with increasing
frequency during the years 1830–48 as conservatives and social reformers alike collected evidence to support their positions. Analyses of social
problems and programs for reform (relating above all to the situation
of workers in cities and new industrial centers) rested on claims to scientific truth displayed and categorized in numerical tables. This approach, of course, looked to Enlightenment ideas about the power of
objective science and drew on methods of data collection and analysis
developed in the late eighteenth century.[1] Even as debates about how
to gather information and how to use it revealed the problematic and

The idea of undertaking an analysis of the *Statistique* came from a lecture by Dominick
LaCapra I heard in April 1984, on what he called "documentary history." I am grateful
to Donald Scott and Elizabeth Weed for their critical advice.

[1] Keith Michael Baker, *Condorcet: From Natural Philosophy to Social Mathematics* (Chicago,
1975).

ideological nature of such statistical truth, the parties to the debates nonetheless shared a belief in its objectivity and authority. The discourse of social reform in early nineteenth-century France was organized around the collection, presentation, and interpretation of supposedly incontrovertible statistical facts.

Statistics established an unprecedented sense of certitude and so legitimized the claims of bourgeois ideologists and their aristocratic and working-class critics; rarely was its status as objective science called into question. When the administrator of the prefecture of police, Louis Frégier, wrote in 1840 about Paris's dangerous classes, he offered statistics that he expected would correct exaggeration and error and "put enlightened minds on the road to truth."[2] Alexandre Parent-Duchâtelet, author of a massive study of prostitution published in 1836, insisted on expressing his findings numerically: "In collecting and editing all material I have made the greatest effort to present numerical results for every point I have treated, because at present a judicious mind cannot be satisfied with expressions such as many, often, sometimes, very often, etc. . . . especially in circumstances when it is a question . . . of serious determinations and grave consequences."[3]

When asked for advice about how best to promote reform, the novelist Eugène Sue urged the founders of the working man's paper *La Rûche Populaire* to "expose the situation of the working classes by facts and incontestable figures."[4] And the editors of another workers' newspaper, *L'Atelier*, sought to refute the "false allegations" of a member of the legislature by compiling information on wages, hours, and the cost of living in various trades. Facts and figures were a kind self-evident truth. "Our figures," they warned the erring politician, "will certainly be well worth your consideration."[5]

The legacy of all this investigation is volumes of statistical information on various aspects of economic and social life. Historians have found them invaluable sources for reconstructing the world of work and the lives of workers—the irrefutable quantitative evidence that leads to the revision of old and the formulation of new interpretations. In a sense we have accepted at face value and perpetuated the terms of the nineteenth-century debate according to which numbers are somehow purer

[2]Louis Frégier, *Des classes dangereuses* (Paris, 1840), 1:59, cited in Michelle Perrot, *Enquête sur la condition ouvrière en France au XIXe siècle* (Paris, 1972), p. 26. See also the classic discussion of these issues in Louis Chevalier, *Classes laborieuses et classes dangereuses à Paris pendant la première moitié du XIXe siècle* (Paris, 1958).

[3]Alexandre J. B. Parent-Duchâtelet, *De la prostitution* (Paris, 1836), 1:22, cited in Perrot, *Enquête*, p. 31.

[4]Cited in Gérard Leclerc, *L'observation de l'homme: Une histoire des enquêtes sociales* (Paris, 1979), p. 184.

[5]*L'Atelier* 2 (October 1840): 13.

and less susceptible to subjective influences than other sources of information. Even though the language of some social historians, with its hierarchical oppositions between quantitative and qualitative sources, numerical data and literary evidence, scientific and impressionistic analyses, hard and soft documentation, is less compelling than it was several years ago, there remains the tendency to treat numbers as significantly different from words. Accounts by French doctors who detailed the miseries of workers in new industrial centers are assumed to contain presuppositions, opinions, and political positions that must be decoded and explicated, whereas the figures they cite—wages, family size, number of employees per establishment—are accepted as essentially unproblematic (except perhaps from the technical points of view of accuracy, thoroughness, methods of calculation, etc.). This is even more true for statistical reports. Even when their purposes and specific contexts are duly noted, these are rarely considered part of the interest of the source. Instead we have plucked out the numbers without questioning the categories into which they are arranged, and we accept as equally objective the explanations that accompany the tables, rarely feeling the need to establish an identity for the anonymous reporters who were, after all, the authors of these texts.[6] This procedure has at least three results: it presumes to divide an indivisible or integral problem, that of the nature of reality and its representation; it denies the inherently political aspects of representation; and it simply underutilizes the sources.

It is not my intention here to dispute the utility of statistical reports that detail the growth of populations, the size of households, or the gender of a labor force. Rather, I want to argue against a simple positivist use of them and for a fuller and more complicated conceptualization of the reality they represent; for a reading of statistical reports that problematizes and contextualizes their categories and conclusions; for an end, in other words, to the separation of statistical reports from other kinds of historical texts.

Statistical reports are neither totally neutral collections of "fact" nor simply ideological impositions. At least since the eighteenth century, they have been compiled to provide information that can test (and thus refine or change) particular understandings of social organization and political

---

[6]I could list many examples, but perhaps it is best to make this an exercise in self-criticism. In most of my work and notably in *The Glassworkers of Carmaux: French Craftsmen and Political Action in a Nineteenth Century City* (Cambridge, Mass., 1974), *Women, Work and Family*, coauthored with Louise Tilly (New York, 1978), and most recently, "Men and Women in the Parisian Garment Trades: Discussions of Family and Work in the 1830's and 40's," in *The Power of the Past: Essays for Eric Hobsbawm*, ed. P. Thane, G. Crossick, and R. Floud (Cambridge, 1984), pp. 67–93, I have followed this procedure, harvesting "facts" from statistical sources whose categories, intentions, and politics I have rarely examined critically.

relationships.[7] In Gérard Leclerc's formulation, those in power attempt to control events by gathering information that permits constant revision of established models of the social structure. (Such information can also be used to create competing models that challenge those in power.) In Leclerc's terms, knowledge (*le savoir*) is organized ideologically, but it is constantly created and revised in dialectical relation to information (*l'information*). Information in turn is organized and categorized in terms of established models, though it is perceived as somehow independent of them.[8] Thus collecting population statistics according to households (rather than, say, villages or places of work) reveals and constructs (while it may also call into question) a certain vision of social organization based on a particular idea of the family. At the same time, of course, it does tell us how many people inhabited a town, city, or state. To take the numbers as the only reality of those statistics, however, denies the role that classification and interpretation play in the construction of reality— the reality contemporaries experienced as well as the different reality we may want to impute to their lives. To take another example, the world of work and workers was not merely reflected in the statistical inquiries of the 1830s and 1840s, but was defined and given meaning by them. Who would represent workers and in what terms was an issue of considerable political contest. Representation was not only a matter of the franchise or the delegation of civic rights; it was a question of the power to define reality itself—hence the proliferation of debates about the contents and methodologies of statistical inquiries and the articulation in any particular enquête of meanings in opposition to other definitions.[9]

Statistical reports exemplify the process by which visions of reality, models of social structure, were elaborated and revised. The reports embody the dialectical relation between le savoir and l'information, the

[7]For the history of these statistical inquiries see Bernard Gille, *Les sources statistiques de l'histoire de France: Des enquêtes du XVIIe siècle à 1890* (Paris, 1964). See also Perrot, *Enquêtes*, and her preface to the new edition of Léon Bonneff and Maurice Bonneff, *La vie tragique des travailleurs* (Paris, 1984); and T. Markovitch, "Statistiques industrielles et systèmes politiques," in Institut National de la Statistique et des études économiques, *Pour une histoire de la statistique* (Paris, 1977), pp. 318–21. For an original treatment see Marie-Noëlle Bourguet, "Race et folklore: l'image officielle de la France en 1800," *Annales, E.S.C.* 31:4 (July-August 1976), pp. 802–23, and her impressive dissertation (University of Paris I), "Déchiffrer la France: La statistique départementale à l'époque napoleonienne."

[8]Leclerc, *Observation*, pp. 195–97. The articulation of this purpose can be found in government demands for information. In 1831, for example, the commissioner of commerce asked for information about the state of the economy and explained his purpose this way: "The institution in the name of which I have the honor to consult you has as its essential purpose to reflect on facts and to form by continuity of observation the customary science of political economy..." Archives nationales (hereafter AN), F12 2713, dossier 6, Commission du commerce et des colonies, circular dated 19 February 1831.

[9]Hilde Rigaudis-Weiss, *Les enquêtes ouvrières en France entre 1830 et 1848* (Paris, 1936).

means by which certain representations of social, economic, and political life were constructed. If, in its final form, a statistical volume seems fixed and absolute—somehow true—its contents in fact suggest questioning and flexibility. Implicit in its pages are a series of debates and discussions on which its authors seek to have the final say. The fascinating aspect of reading these reports lies, in fact, in their method of argumentation, for statistical reports are constituted as, and in, political discourse. As such they provide valuable insight into the processes by which relationships of power are established, exemplified, challenged, and enforced.

My focus in this paper is on one such report, the *Statistique de l'industrie à Paris, 1847–48*, prepared by the Paris chamber of commerce and published in 1851.[10] The figures presented in it have permitted historians to gauge the size and describe the organization of a range of trades on the eve of the revolution of 1848. What has not been explored is how the document represents the world of workers and their work. My purpose here is to pursue that exploration, and I have attempted to analyze not only the contents of the *Statistique* but the form of its presentation and the rhetorical structure of its argument. I begin by placing it in its historical and political perspective, as part of an ongoing debate about the condition of workers in the 1830s and 1840s. Then I examine the categories of classification employed in the presentation of data and show how these drew on current theories of political economy and how they invoked the authority of science to make their case. Finally, I analyze how the authors of the report, by literal and metaphoric uses of sexual references, attempted to persuade readers of the necessity of accepting their interpretations. I conclude that the *Statistique* was designed to function not as objective science, but as a form of political argument and that a careful reading reveals that intention. The exercise, then, is less about what the *Statistique* says, for the terms of its argument will be familiar to students of nineteenth-century French history, than it is about *how* it operates as political discourse.

Part One

> Il faut aujourd'hui arracher les populations ouvrières à ses idées fausses et les ramener dans le cercle des réalités.
> *Le Moniteur Industriel* 2 July 1848

The Paris chamber of commerce was an elite group of businessmen, manufacturers, and economists. It was founded in 1803 when the prefect

---

[10]Chambre de Commerce de Paris, *Statistique de l'industrie à Paris, 1847–48* (Paris, 1851). (The *Statistique* was published in one volume but had two separately numbered sections. I will hereafter cite the volume as CCP and refer to part 1 or 2.)

of the Seine established an assembly of sixty businessmen to elect fifteen of their number to watch over economic matters in the capital city. Thereafter, the membership varied (between fifteen and twenty); new members were recruited by those on the board, and each year one-third of the group was replaced or reappointed. The chamber was a semiautonomous body, responsible ultimately to the minister of interior. It represented and permitted close collaboration between business and government during the period we are concerned with, the first half of the nineteenth century.[11]

The chamber of commerce began work on the *Statistique de l'industrie* in the second half of 1848, in an atmosphere charged with social tension. Although the introduction to the volume offers no explanation for the timing of the inquiry, it seems to have been the chamber of commerce's contribution to the "reestablishment of moral order, so profoundly troubled in our country."[12] There had been a revolution in February 1848 whose leaders wrestled with the establishment of a republic. In June an insurrection had revealed to the nation's leaders the extent of the danger of social revolution: "family, property, nation—all were struck to the core; the very civilization of the nineteenth century was menaced by the blows of these new barbarians."[13]

The "new barbarians" were the Parisian workers who had taken to the streets to protest the closing of government-sponsored national workshops, organizations designed to provide relief to the unemployed. In the eyes of the protestors the closing of the workshops signaled the government's betrayal of the principles of the revolution they had helped make in February, a revolution that replaced a monarchy with a republic. The government considered the protests a threat to the republic and sent troops, under the direction of General Louis Eugène Cavaignac, to restore order.

In the weeks that followed his quelling of the uprising, General Cavaignac, now head of the government and equipped with emergency powers, sought the aid of businessmen, politicians, and social scientists in the permanent restoration of order. He met with manufacturers in the various arrondissements of Paris and had them submit their analyses of the causes of the June Days[14]; he asked the government committee on labor to look into ways of stimulating economic recovery and to propose plans for relief of the unemployed[15]; and he requested coop-

---

[11]Chambre de Commerce de Paris, *Centenaire de la Chambre de Commerce de Paris, 1803–1903* (Paris, 1903), p. 48.

[12]Adolphe Blanqui, cited in Perrot, *Enquêtes*, p. 16.

[13]*Le Moniteur Industriel*, 2 July 1848.

[14]AN, F12 2337, Notes remises par les industriels des 8e et 9e arrondissements après une conference avec le Général Cavaignac, July 1848.

[15]AN, C926, "Procès verbaux des séances du Comité du commerce et de l'industrie."

eration from the Académie des sciences morales et politiques, the semi-official body of learned men who studied social questions and made policy recommendations.[16] These groups all recognized that the material conditions of workers had to be improved, but they also stressed the importance of ideology. In the words of *Le Moniteur Industriel*, a newspaper representing commercial and manufacturing interests, there had to be a concerted attack on the "false ideas" that had stimulated "uncontrolled ambitions," on the "thirst for reform so imprudently excited" by the extravagant promises of certain socialists, formerly members of the government. If the image of workers was of besotted, deluded savages whose passions had been stimulated beyond control, there was nonetheless the possibility of imposing discipline. An exposure to "reality" would restore the lost sense of balance. Workers had to be shown that their condition was not lamentable, that industry had not inevitably engendered poverty—indeed, that the personal efforts of the "intelligent" and "laborious" resulted in individual progress and collective improvement: "It is time to return to a more decorous language and a healthier estimation. Our society, thank God, does not merit all the curses it has received. Without doubt, it still has a way to go in ameliorating [social conditions] and it will do that . . . what has to be fortified today, however, is the sentiment of duty and the dominion of conscience."[17]

In the *Statistique de l'industrie* the chamber of commerce offered a blueprint for the "reality" of Parisian economic organization. The title word *statistique* identified the report with official compilations of information regularly prepared for administrative use and distinguished it from the highly politicized enquête of May 1848.[18] The authors placed the report in historical context explicitly to establish its superiority to earlier efforts; implicitly, they evoked the range of highly charged questions previously addressed.[19] This permitted them to speak to these issues, to offer opinions and answers, without having to acknowledge that an argument about causality and a set of political positions informed their own research. Under the guise of objectivity, the *Statistique* sought to have the last word in a long-standing series of political debates about how to evaluate the impact of industrial capitalism on the lives of French workers.

The debate involved at least three groups in French society. The first consisted of private social investigators, the most famous of whom were doctors attached to the Académie des sciences morales et politiques,

[16]See references in Perrot, *Enquêtes*, p. 16, and in Leclerc, *Observation*, pp. 202–3. See also F. de Luna, *The French Republic under Cavaignac, 1848* (Princeton, 1969).
[17]*Le Moniteur Industriel*, 2 July 1848.
[18]On this history see Gille, *Sources*, pp. 151–211.
[19]CCP, 1:11–15.

whose practiced scientific eyes assessed and recorded the details of the moral and physical degeneration of industrial workers. They attributed the crime, vice, and ill health they found in industrial centers to specific kinds of working conditions and employer practices. Thus Dr. Louis Villermé, in an 1840 study, cited three "pernicious practices" as fundamental causes of social disorder. These were the mixing of the sexes in factories, which led to the corruption of morals; the long day for child workers, which destroyed their health; and the practice of certain employers of advancing wages as loans to their workers, which led to improvidence and misery.[20] The point of most of these treatises was to argue for reform—philanthropy, savings banks, education, sanitary housing—or protective legislation—the child labor law of 1841, for example, which limited to ten the working hours of children in large factories. But while they insisted, often successfully, on the need for reform, the social investigators writing in the 1830s and 1840s also developed a powerful image of the working class: morally vulnerable, socially dependent, easily drawn to corruption and vice. Various influences were said to separate the dependable laboring classes from the dangerous classes; these were particularly geographic stability and intact family or familylike structures—at home and in the workplace.

The second group consisted of representatives of workers, who began through their newspapers in the 1830s to demand that the facts of working class immiserization be exposed by those who experienced them firsthand. The details of working-class life could not be understood by outside observers. Instead, they argued, accurate information and interpretation had to come in the form of testimonies by those who lived the experience. This group attacked the concentration of capital as the source of the deterioration of skilled trades, increased competition among wage laborers, and lower wages and greater suffering for families. Not moral failure, they insisted, but capitalism had degraded the work and lives of skilled craftsmen. From the columns of *L'Atelier* and *Le Populaire*, from the pages of Flora Tristan's *Union ouvrière* and Louis Blanc's *Organisation*

---

[20]Louis R. Villermé, *Tableau de l'état physique et moral des ouvriers employés dans les manufactures de coton, de laine et de soie*, 2 vols. (Paris, 1840), 2:93 and 358, cited in Rigaudis-Weiss, *Enquêtes*, p. 111. For an interesting discussion of Villermé, see William Sewell, *Work and Revolution in France* (New York, 1980), pp. 223–32. See also William Coleman, *Death Is a Social Disease: Public Health and Political Economy in Early Industrial France* (Madison, Wisc., 1981); B.-P. Lécuyer, "Démographie, statistique et hygiène publique sous la monarchie censitaire," *Annales de démograhie historique 1977*, pp. 215–45; idem, "Médecins et observateurs sociaux: Les annales d'hygiène publique et de médecine légale, 1820–1850," in *Pour une histoire de la statistique*, pp. 445–76; and Jan Goldstein, "Foucault among the Sociologists: The 'Disciplines' and the History of the Professions," *History and Theory* 23 (1984): 170–92.

du travail, came the call for government attention to these problems and political representation for the interests of labor.[21]

The third party in the debate about the "social question" was made up of government investigators who tried to collect statistics (usually from employers or chambers of commerce) on patterns of industrial growth, wages, and employment. Their stated concern was to keep track of economic activity because it established national prosperity. In this endeavor the condition of workers was not a primary concern; indeed, it was assumed that everyone ultimately benefited from economic growth. In the 1820s, information on workers was gathered as part of the computation of costs of production (the "price of manpower" headed columns of figures that would later be designated "wages").[22] The ambitious *enquête industrielle* conducted fitfully and imperfectly by the minister of commerce over the period 1839–47 planned to count all enterprises, document numbers of workers and their wages, and provide a comprehensive view of the state of the economy—presumably, at least in part, as a way of evaluating and responding to the cries for economic reorganization or reform.[23] Still, the concentration on industry denied the centrality of the problems of workers and the organization of labor.

That problem seemed to grow in significance during the 1840s, as reports on the misery or danger of the working classes were published and as strikes increased in size and frequency. In the political campaigns for reform that intensified during this period, advocates of republicanism took up the cry for government attention to labor. They denounced the bias or ignorance of existing economic and social data and called for official recognition of workers' problems in the form of a government inquiry into work and working conditions. "The enquête will not be the *how* of social reform, but the *why* of political reform."[24] Republican and socialist spokesmen likened the enquête to the *cahiers de doléances*, the lists of grievances articulated by various social groups on the eve of the French Revolution of 1789.[25] And they insisted on the self-evident truth contained in such documentation: it would dispel the image of a morally depraved working class and establish the case for recognizing the connections between workers' economic and political rights.

---

[21]For details on this see Rigaudis-Weiss, *Enquêtes*. See also Jacques Rancière, *La nuit des prolétaires: Archives du rêve ouvrier* (Paris, 1981); and Alain Faure and Jacques Rancière, *La parole ouvrière, 1830–51* (Paris, 1976).

[22]*Recherches statistique de la ville de Paris*, 3 vols. (Paris, 1823–29).

[23]*Statistique de la France: Industrie*, 4 vols. (Paris, 1847–52). On the history of this effort see Gille, *Sources*, pp. 200–203.

[24]*Le Journal du Peuple*, 8 June 1841, cited in Rigaudis-Weiss, *Enquêtes*, p. 170.

[25]*Le Populaire*, November 1844, cited in Rigaudis-Weiss, *Enquêtes*, 173. See her extensive discussion of this, pp. 169–78.

The success of this appeal became apparent in February 1848, when crowds demanding the "right to work" helped overthrow the July Monarchy and bring in the Second Republic. For the leaders of the new government, however, universal manhood suffrage was enough of a reform, and they sought to limit rather than increase the influence of labor in the administration of the country. Argument turned especially on the inclusion in the government of a minister of labor, who would presumably have power to implement fundamental economic change. The majority consistently refused this demand, substituting largely symbolic gestures. Thus Albert, a worker, and socialist Louis Blanc were included in the first provisional government of the republic, and the "right to work" was proclaimed a fundamental principle. Louis Blanc was assigned to preside over the Luxembourg Commission, a body devoted to examining labor/management disputes but that had no legislative or budgetary powers. Another commission allotted funds to cooperative worker associations, while the minister of public works directed the national workshops, a stopgap measure to relieve the massive unemployment that followed the revolution.

The final gesture was made in May 1848. After a demonstration on 15 May that included thousands of dissatisfied members of the national workshops, Louis Blanc repeated the demand for a minister of labor. A cabinet member with information and power would deal positively with economic and social questions and fulfill the promise of the revolution, he argued. The conservative Constituent Assembly refused his request and instead voted to launch an enquête on agricultural and industrial labor. The inquiry into work—a radical demand under the July Monarchy—became in May 1848 a conservative ploy to deny government standing and thus political influence for the interests of workers. In addition, some thought it might provide information to refute the most extravagant of the workers' complaints.[26]

Still, the enquête was a political compromise, and as such it embodied divergent approaches and methods. Though it was designed to thwart the most radical of labor's political demands, its questions, categories, and plan of implementation nonetheless registered the existence of a definable working class whose interests conflicted with those of its employers. Its twenty-nine questions focused almost exclusively on the conditions of work and the lives of workers in 1848. There were no questions about the capital resources of manufacturers, the organization of production, the volume of trade, or the value of commercial activity. There were questions about how new jobs might be created, about whether convent and prison manufacturing competed unfairly with artisanal pro-

[26]Rigaudis-Weiss, *Enquêtes*, pp. 191–93; and Leclerc, *Observation*, pp. 197–204.

duction, and about what measures might be taken to ameliorate the lot of poor working families. More striking (especially when contrasted with the later chamber of commerce *Statistique*) was the absence of elaborate exercises in definition. It was assumed that anyone answering the questions about apprenticeship, earnings, cost of living, housing conditions, religious and moral education, and the like knew what a worker was. Similarly, the committee of inquiry's decision to consult local delegates elected separately by workers and employers recognized basic conflicts of interest between them. It also accepted the notion that different perceptions of "reality" all of which were somehow "true" would be advanced by each of these groups. If the enquête was meant ultimately to provide documentation for a particular outlook, it nonetheless did not question the shared categories of social perception (of class conflict) that had emerged in the course of the revolution of 1848.[27]

The committee charged with conducting the inquiry (the committee on labor) was acutely aware of the volatile nature of its work, and it sought to avoid disastrous political consequences. It deliberated carefully about how to choose local representatives from whom to gather information, and it seriously considered the warning of the mayor of Paris that if elections were held among workers the gatherings might become a pretext for more street demonstrations. Committee members listened to delegations of angry workers who perceived them as heading a forum for airing and resolving grievances rather than as a neutral body devoted to gather information. And they sought to influence the conduct of these workers by publicly praising the decorous and respectful and denouncing the hostile and impetuous. An enquête that recognized the potential bias of its sources was bound to be perceived as an instrument of political influence. For this reason the committee had moved slowly at first; after the June Days it stopped work on the enquête altogether. Instead it turned its attention to other matters—providing workers with clean housing and savings institutions; creating agricultural colonies for abandoned children, orphans, and delinquents; revising the child labor law of 1841 to increase the permissible hours of work—all measures designed not to deal with workers' demands but to offer alternative solutions in the form of moral tutelage and social control.[28]

This, then, was the historical and political context for the chamber of commerce's *Statistique*. Government-sponsored research on work and working conditions had acquired enormous political significance, indi-

[27]AN, C943, "Assemblée constituante, enquête sur le travail agriculture et industriel," law of 25 May 1848.

[28]AN, C925, "Procès verbaux du Comité du travail," 3 vols., May 1848–March 1849, is a remarkably detailed source on the work of the committee charged with carrying out the enquête launched in May 1848.

cating not simply a desire for information, but the intention of acting on labor's demands. The chamber was determined to repudiate this connection between information and politics, so it prepared what it deemed a neutral report on an objective situation that would stand outside all political disputes. Its schedule of questions differed from those developed in May 1848. Neutral, paid investigators visited factories, workshops, and households to collect data. They asked for no opinions about how things might be improved; they simply wanted descriptions. The focus of their questions was industry, not labor. Indeed, although the bulk of the information sought treated workers (three-fourths of the tabulated figures dealt with them), the structure of the *Statistique* seemed to subordinate them—to place them where they belonged—in the economy, which was the ostensible focus of concern.

Somewhat surprisingly and without real explanation, the chamber's committee decided to compile retrospective information for 1847. A report, designed in June 1848 and carried out over the next months, might have been aimed at gauging the effects of the revolution, but this seems not to have been its purpose. Indeed, there were only occasional comparisons offered in the text of the report between the data for 1847 presented in the tables and the actual state of employment in particular trades in 1848. Rather, the point seems to have been to capture a more normal situation to which things could be returned. From this perspective the *Statistique* offered a plan for economic reconstruction and a way of demonstrating to frightened investors that the turmoil of recent months was an aberration, uncharacteristic of the basic organization and relationships of the Parisian economy.

The format of the report conveyed a sense of stability and control. Indeed, the visual impression as one turns page after page is of precision and order. There were thirteen sections representing the different types of industry in Paris (clothing, food preparation, chemicals, construction, etc.). Within each section particular enterprises were described. Figures were given for the average value of businesses of different sizes, the number of "employers," the age, sex, and number of their workers, the location of work, and the average daily wages paid. Underneath the tables, text amplified the description. For each kind of enterprise the text was divided into informational sections beginning with a discussion of the technology and organization of work, followed by details about apprenticeship practices, average wages, and seasonal variations in employment. The final section dealt with the "morals and customs" of workers. This last section examined traits of character and patterns of behavior that explained the prosperity or lack of it of any particular group of workers. The tone of this final section had the same impartiality as the discussions of technology and wages. References to workers' improvidence and dissipation, although we might see them as interpretations, were presented as facts, identical to the various numerical facts.

The classificatory scheme of the *Statistique* arranged all information according to the kinds of manufactured goods produced or sold and the types of manual services performed (repairing shoes or laundering, for example). *Industrie* denoted entrepreneurial as well as productive activity. Indeed, the authors of the report carefully defined and justified their depiction of the world of work as a world of entrepreneurs. Listed as heads of "enterprises" were (1) all self-employed individuals; (2) all individuals making goods to order who employed one or more workers, whether or not these were family members and whether or not they were paid; (3) all individuals making goods to order for "bourgeois clientele" (this category included tailors, dressmakers, and even washerwomen); and (4) all individuals making goods to order and working for several different manufacturers. The authors of the report recognized that the last two categories particularly could also be deemed "simple home workers," but they argued that precise counting required the entrepreneurial designation. Whereas workers employed in a shop or at home by a single employer would be enumerated by their bosses, those working for more than one employer might be counted twice or perhaps not at all. The solution was to define them as heads of businesses, however small their businesses were.[29]

The effect of this categorization was to reduce significantly the number of people who had come to think of themselves as workers in the Parisian population. The *Statistique*'s definitions denied the class identification that had from February to June joined impoverished masters, independent craftsmen, and employees of large establishments—all calling themselves workers or proletarians—in clubs, demonstrations, and producer associations. By referring to both workers and bosses as *industriels*—industrial producers—the *Statistique* refused the socialist terminology that sharply distinguished workers and bosses; it moved the focus away from the relations of production to the simple fact of productive activity. In this way the neutral terms of classification presented a particular picture of economic organization; one, moreover, that was associated with a set of conservative political beliefs.[30]

---

[29]CCP, 1:18–19, 21.

[30]This kind of association between certain classifications of economic activity and conservative politics had long characterized the debates about France's economy. In 1841 the editors of the workers' newspaper *L'Atelier* bitterly rejected the conclusions of the Baron Charles Dupin this way:

"Further on, we see that there are today in France 1,416,000 heads of industry [chefs d'industrie]. Included in this number, of course, are a crowd of men who, as heads of workshops in Lyon have been reduced to a position like that of a worker, properly speaking. ... But, let us admire the skill of the baron. He estimates four people for each family of

Instead of the conflict depicted in the socialist rhetoric, a conflict that had been acted out in the June uprising, the report presented a seemingly neutral picture in which hierarchical relationships (of ownership, management, skill, sex, and age) were part of the order of production itself, the guarantee of high quality and efficient adaptation to the market. Conflict was absent from the descriptions. If referred to, it was depicted as an unnatural aspect of the arrangements; its causes were extraneous to the system. The economy of Paris was portrayed as a busy world of *petites entreprises*. With pride the authors pointed to the art, ingenuity, and skill of these *industriels*: "Their infinitely varied products are known the world over.... The manufacturers often guide, and follow in their turn, the caprices of fashion and taste of the elegant world. The lively and intelligent workers adjust with marvellous skill to all changes of design."[31]

The *Statistique* retrieved from 1847, and presented in carefully categorized and ennumerated form, the "reality" of Parisian economic life. Implicitly, it disputed the radical claims of socialist revolutionaries, showing them to be misapprehensions, if not dangerous fantasies. The *Statistique* served essentially as an instrument of ideology, constructing and justifying the model according to which economic, political, and moral order would be restored. In this effort it invoked the science of political economy as its methodological and theoretical guide, the guarantee of accuracy and of truth.

Part Two

> La statistique est une verification de l'économie politique par les faits.
>
> E. Buret, *De la misère*, 1840

To direct its research effort the chamber of commerce chose the leading spokesman for the science of political economy. By his name alone, Horace Emile Say (1794–1860) embodied the French liberal school. His father, Jean-Baptiste Say, introduced France to Adam Smith's theories and added his own interpretations of the role of markets in economic

---

landowners and the same number for the families of heads of industry. We thus find in France 24 million landowners and more than six million heads of industry. Conclusion: there remain in France 2 million of the helpless, lazy, undisciplined, and brawling, and these are the men who want to dictate laws to industry, raise the price of labor, and demand, without working for it, a part of the property of others. As you can see, reader, the bogey-man has come back!"

[31]CCP, 1:11.

development. Indeed, if there was one name in France that immediately denoted political economy, it was that of the scion of a leading Protestant family, Jean-Baptiste Say. Horace Say studied in Geneva and worked for a large commercial company for a number of years, traveling to the United States and Brazil. In 1831 he was appointed a judge on the commercial tribunal of the department of the Seine, and in 1834 he became a member of the Paris chamber of commerce. He served on the municipal council of Paris (1846) and in 1846 published a book on the department of the administration of the city of Paris. In 1848, he was secretary of the Chamber of Commerce. Identified with the liberal Parisian bourgeoisie, Say joined the Conseil d'etat in 1849 and left it after Napoleon III's coup d'état in 1851. His experience mingled business and administration, and he exemplified the close ties between commerce and politics that existed under the July Monarchy and persisted into the Second Republic.

Horace Say was committed to propagating the teachings of his father. In 1842 he founded the Society of Political Economy, and throughout the 1830s and 1840s he published numerous editions of his father's books, adding his own revisions and commentaries. Of his own publications, the *Statistique* was probably Horace Say's greatest accomplishment. It won the statistical prize of the Académie des sciences morales et politiques in 1853, which conferred on it enormous prestige at a moment when the economic policy of the empire was still being formulated, and which probably also contributed to Say's election to the academy in 1857.[32]

Assisting Horace Say was his son Jean-Baptiste Léon (1826–96). Léon Say served as an administrator for the railroads after attending the Collège Bourbon, and he too was an active proponent of his grandfather's theories. He worked on the *Dictionary of Political Economy* and wrote in defense of free trade and individual liberty. After February 1848 he joined the Paris national guard, and he participated in the suppression of the June insurrection. A loyal supporter of Cavaignac, he campaigned for the general's election to the presidency of the republic in December 1848 against the more reactionary forces supporting Bonaparte. Léon Say became prefect of the Seine in 1871 and a minister of finance during

[32]Chambre de commerce de Paris, *Centenaire de la Chambre de commerce*, p. 52, lists Horace Say as director of the inquiry and indicates he was assisted by Léon Say (see note 33 below) and Natalis Rondot. Rondot was an economist who specialized in textiles, editor of the *Journal des Économistes*, and member of various societies of political economists. For information on him see *Dictionnaire universel des contemporains* (Paris, 1861), p. 1512. For biographical information on Horace Say, see *Dictionnaire universel des contemporains*, p. 1573. See also Horace Say, *Rapport du Comité central d'instruction primaire* (Paris, 1845); idem, *Etudes sur l'administration de la ville de Paris* (Paris, 1846); and P. Piazza, *Etude historique et critique des tribunaux commerciaux en France* (Paris, 1918).

the 1890s. In those years a conservative republican, his policies continued to follow the family doctrine.[33] In a funeral address in 1878 for the liberal economist Frédéric Bastiat, Léon Say recalled the sense of ideological embattlement he had felt in 1848: "In 1847 all of political economy's efforts were directed against the system of protection; in 1848 it was obliged to confront new adversaries. It found itself struggling against the socialists.... [These were] serious battles; liberty of commerce, protectionism became incidents; the central doctrine was that of the liberty of the individual; we had to save the individual from the new pantheism that would have absorbed all humanity into the state."[34]

The *Statistique* was part of the struggle being waged against socialism. It was framed according to the terms of political economy, a doctrine that claimed the status of science, and thus a truth value that stood outside human construction or control. J.-B. Say had written: "The general laws of the political and moral sciences are beyond dispute.... They derive from the nature of things as surely as the laws of the physical world; one does not imagine them, one discovers them."[35]

His followers accepted this reasoning, finding in the certainty of their science the explanations they needed for otherwise contradictory or confusing detail. Indeed, their procedure in the *Statistique* was to examine information closely, discussing it even when it did not seem to fit the general scheme, and then to resolve any tensions between information and categories of explanation by invoking the principles or laws of the theory. This was the case for the informing concepts of the report: the definition of productive activity as industrie and the designation of various kinds of producers, including some workers, as entrepreneurs or *chefs d'industrie*.

The focus of the report on *industrie* followed directly from J.-B. Say's writings. In the *Traité d'économie politique* he explained that *travail*, or labor, was too restrained a concept for describing production. Labor denoted only manual work or physical force, without including the knowledge of nature and the economy and the implementation of that knowledge (organizing production and selling goods or services) that

[33]On Léon Say see G. Michel, *Leon Say* (Paris, 1899), and G. Picot, *Leon Say: Notice historique sur sa vie* (Paris, 1901).

[34]Léon Say, *Discours prononcé à Mugron, à l'inauguration du monument élevé à la mémoire de Frédéric Bastiat* (Paris, 1878), pp. 10–11.

[35]Jean-Baptiste Say, *Traité d'économie politique*, 6th ed., ed. Horace Say (Paris, 1841), p. 12. On the work of J.-B. Say, see E. Treilhac, *L'oeuvre économique de J-B Say* (Paris, 1927); Michelle Perrot, "Premières mesures des faits sociaux: Les débuts de la statistique criminelle en France, 1780–1830," in *Pour une histoire de la statistique*, p. 134; C. Menard, "Trois formes de résistance aux statistiques: Say, Cournot, Walras," in *Pour une historie de la statistique*, pp. 417–20. See also Horace Say, ed., *Edition nouveau de J-B Say, Cours complet de l'économie politique* (Paris, 1890).

were also required to create value.[36] Those engaged in industry were entrepreneurs, even if, like a tailor or shoemaker, a dressmaker or washerwoman, they performed manual labor and earned very little. Indeed, the training, talent, and skill required of craftsmen almost by definition meant they were self-employed or potentially so and that they engaged in the thinking and commercial activities that distinguished *industrie* from *travail*. For Say, entrepreneurs served a critical function at the center of networks of production and exchange. When "events seconded their skill" they profited handsomely, and many acquired large fortunes.[37] If upward mobility and the possibility of steady improvement were synonymous with being an entrepreneur, then the larger the number of entrepreneurs, the more valid the association of capitalism's promise with individual economic progress. In contrast, being a worker (*ouvrier*) meant inhabiting an essentially stagnant position. Those called workers were unskilled; they executed their tasks under the direction of others, and they forfeited their part of the profits yielded by production in exchange for a wage.[38] Although there might be collective improvement for workers as civilization advanced, individual mobility was not held out as a goal.

Using Say's terminology, the *Statistique* listed three categories of chefs d'industrie in its columns. There were those who employed more than ten workers; those employing between two and ten workers; and those employing one or no workers. The last category included as workers the family members who assisted the "head" of the enterprise. Husbands of washerwomen "working with their wives," children, relatives or wives of shoemakers or tailors, all were counted as ouvriers.[39] The family work unit, whether genuinely an independent business (as were bakeries, butcher shops, and dairy stores) or a collectivity of wage earners (as were shoemakers or garment workers paid by the piece) became in this account a petite-entreprise.

If the tables fixed an impression of small businesses, the accompanying text recognized the problems inherent in applying the concept to certain categories of enterprise. Again and again, usually in the section on wages, the authors conceded that the term "employer" or "head of the business" was not an accurate rendering of the situation of many tradesmen and tradeswomen. Although counted as employers, these self-employed individuals were—and the language used is the same over and over again—"really workers."

[36]J.-B. Say, *Traité*, p. 586.
[37]Ibid., p. 371.
[38]Ibid., p. 592.
[39]CCP, 2:206, 302, for examples.

The caners and upholsterers of chairs working by themselves are really workers.[40]

The "employers" who make custom-made shoes are themselves really workers.[41]

The "employer" dressmakers working alone are really workers.[42]

The manufacturers of shawls are really master workers.[43]

The case of seamstresses was so confusing that a separate count was established by a house-to-house visit, and the reporters gave up trying to separate workers and the self-employed, presenting instead a table headed *ouvrières lingères* (seamstresses).[44] For tailors, a series of footnotes in effect withdrew the "employer" categories for those tailors, piecers, and used-clothing dealers who worked alone, assimilating them into the worker category for the purposes of calculating wages. Thus the report counted piecers as heads of their own businesses in one section: "The piecers working at home alone or with their wives are listed in the tables as industriels and not as workers."[45] But for purposes of listing average wages, the report redefined their status: "Employer-piecers are really workers. The product of their labor is the best proof of it."[46]

The statistics on wages might have called into question the prosperity and the entrepreneurial nature of many small trades and disputed the charts that fixed the numbers of manufacturers and their workers. By the authors' own admission, worker was a more appropriate term for many of the impoverished craftsmen and craftswomen who, in effect, sold their labor and not the goods they produced. But since the terminology of classification was held to stand outside human definition, the "facts" had to be interpreted within the given theoretical framework of political economy. Any other approach—modifying the model in light of the facts, for example—would have compromised the utility of this science for establishing the indisputability of the *Statistique*'s claims. So the authors dealt with the ambiguity of the situation of some producers only as a problem of methodology for the calculation of wages and not as a major challenge to their vision of economic organization.

As it presented its information, the *Statistique* addressed, but without

[40]CCP, 1:152.
[41]CCP, 2:239.
[42]CCP, 2:251.
[43]CCP, 2:339.
[44]CCP, 2:260.
[45]CCP, 2:302.
[46]CCP, 2:302.

acknowledging them, a series of alternative interpretations of the plight of workers. These interpretations were dismissed by simply asserting the axioms of political economy. Thus, for example, one such interpretation suggested that hundreds of small producers had been driven into poverty by an unregulated economic system. The *Statistique*'s reply was that state and corporate regulation necessarily hindered prosperity. "Private interest," J.-B. Say had written, "is the most skillful of masters."[47] Another interpretation cited excessive subdivision in the organization of production, particularly the subcontracting practice associated with ready-made garment manufacture and building construction. Indeed, workers' groups in 1848 had successfully lobbied for laws outlawing subcontracting, so convinced were they that these practices undermined the structure of their trades.[48] The authors of the *Statistique* referred obliquely to the debates of 1848 when they invoked Say's theory of markets to reject the idea that the "distress" of certain groups of workers could be attributed to subcontracting. Say had argued that the multiplication of enterprises always happened in response to consumer demand and inevitably stimulated production and employment.[49] In similar terms the authors of the *Statistique* observed: "It is difficult to accept the idea that the condition of workers has really been worsened by the presence of new industrial enterpreneurs [who] have augmented the demand for labor and offered a new resource during periods of unemployment; without doubt we must attribute the distress of these workers to other causes."[50]

The "other causes" ultimately had to do with the family, the "natural" organization within which people lived and that determined such economic phenomena as the law of wages. Indeed, the *Statistique* explained that the "distress" of seamstresses followed not from subcontracting in the ready-made garment industry, but from the fact that the conditions of female employment violated the law of wages. J.-B. Say had explained the law of wages in the *Traité*, and he pointed out that there was a different calculus for women than for men. A man's wages had to maintain the worker and provide for the subsistence of his children as they accumulated the physical "capital" that would fit them to be the next generation of unskilled manual labor. For men, then, the costs of the reproduction of the labor force were included in the "price" paid for labor power. Women and children, in contrast, were "natural dependents" and so never had to be entirely self-supporting. Those women who

[47]J.-B. Say, *Traité*, p. 195, also pp. 190–94.
[48]The best examples of these arguments are in R. Gossez, *Les ouvriers de Paris: L'organisation, 1848–51* (Paris, 1967).
[49]J.-B. Say, *Traité*, pp. 86–89.
[50]CCP, 1:54.

for some reason had to be self-sufficient were always at a disadvantage, since they faced competition from other women who needed only to supplement a family's income. This was the permanent state, the "law" of the female labor market.[51]

Neither J.-B. Say nor the reporters for the *Statistique* found wage earning itself a contradiction of female status. Women engaged in those "occupations of which they are capable," and this might even include some tasks traditionally performed by men. (In the *Statistique* the authors noted that Parisian compositors prohibited women from working with them although this was "work that they appear capable of performing without fatigue and that is permitted them in other towns, at Senlis, for example.")[52] The problem was rather that too many women "had the misfortune" to live outside their "natural" setting—the family—which in fact was the only economically viable context for all workers, women as well as men.[53]

The family was critical to the *Statistique*'s analysis not only of wages, but of all economic and social life. The authors located in the family not only a model for organizing production, but the sources of individual moral development. The family was the natural environment that fostered those qualities of individual discipline and orderliness necessary for the health and prosperity of society. Drawing on Say, and even more on the writings of the reforming doctors of the 1840s, the authors of the *Statistique* used the family as the governing conception for all social relationships. The focus of their analysis, moreover, was the worker and the extent to which he or she was embedded in family structures. Indeed, if the stated subject of the report was *industrie*, the preoccupation of its authors was with the morality of workers. Morality or its absence, of course, had political as well as economic consequences; the discussion of morality then permitted the authors to allude to the politics of 1848 in the context of a purely objective economic report.

In the *Statistique* the words that established moral contrasts linked work discipline and personal comportment. Good workers were orderly, hard-working, assiduous, punctual, law-abiding, and thrifty. Bad workers were turbulent, difficult to govern, lazy, dissipated, and improvident, indulging a taste for pleasure and frivolous conduct. These qualities were developed in the interlocking worlds of family and work. The analysis offered by the *Statistique* played back and forth across the organization of work and the condition of family life, using one to explain the other. The more closely the structure of work resembled a family, the more enmeshed in families the workers, the better behaved was the work force.

[51]J.-B. Say, *Traité*, pp. 371–74.
[52]CCP, 2:194, 246, 277.
[53]CCP, 1:52, 54.

Thus, although a bad family could transmit the "original sin" that forever tainted the morality of a worker, families were also influenced by the nature of the work their members performed.[54] The small shop, headed by a benevolent and fatherly employer with a stable group of married skilled workers, practicing a trade they had acquired by formal apprenticeship, was the ideal workplace. Workers were inevitably well paid and well behaved, replicating in their private lives the orderly relationships of the shop. If the natural substances they worked with had the right qualities, the positive effects were further enhanced. Thus, of all those working with metals, the craftsmen who used precious metals were best off. Gold and silver somehow developed in jewelry workers a civilized taste for good things, as water stimulated in those who worked with it—washerwomen and tanners, for example—an unfortunate and excessive thirst for alcoholic drink.[55] These references established a clear equation between material substances and the family. All were "natural," and their effects could be studied in similar ways.

Jewelry workers provided the exemplary case for the authors of the *Statistique*. They offered an idealized account of the "experience" of these workers in the form of a descriptive life history:

> In general the jewelry workers, who earn good wages, like to be well dressed; the vulgar pleasures of the cabaret attract them less than those of the dance, the theater, a walk in the country. It thus comes about that they prefer the domestic life to a disorderly existence [*une existence de desordre*]. They marry the more willingly because they can find work for their wives to do at home, without abandoning the care of the household.... Later the wife can take on as apprentices one or two young girls; the [worker's] children can also be initiated early into tasks suitable for their ages; order and comfort characterize the home, and the worker's household is transformed into a small shop.[56]

This rendition dissolved the line between family and workplace; the orderliness of one constructed the order of the other and led to the (self) improvement of the worker and his emergence as an entrepreneur: "It is easy for those with intelligence to become manufacturers on their own account if they want to."[57] As if to underscore the influences that led to such success, the authors closed their account by returning the jewelry worker to his place, naturally subordinated to his employer: "Relations between employers and workers have always been rather good. Reciprocal relations of politeness were generally observed, at least until the

[54]Cited and commented on in Chevalier, *Classes laborieuses et classes dangereuses*, p. 394.
[55]CCP, 1:70–71, 141, 154, 170.
[56]CCP, 1:65.
[57]CCP, 1:65.

revolution of February; many employers even followed the practice of holding a joyous repast annually for their workers; and when a worker married, he invited his employer and his wife to sit at the banquet table."[58]

The authors of the *Statistique* emphasized the importance of the small shop by comparing it with other kinds of workplaces; the *chantiers* with constantly shifting labor forces (as in the building trades); factories with large numbers of workers and with no traditional boundaries of age and sex separating them; and individual rooms, where pieceworkers toiled in isolation, unsupervised and therefore subject to no codes of professional or moral conduct.[59]

According to the report, the great disadvantage of the chantiers was that hiring took place outside; workers presented themselves at certain spots—the Place de Grève for the building trades, the Cloître-Saint Jacques-l'Hôpital for washerwomen—and waited for an offer of employment. The line between lounging and looking for work was hard to maintain, and the sexual overtones (waiting in the street for a proposition) were impossible to avoid. For building workers "many occasions for mutual stimulation arise, and the hiring place is often the starting point for pleasure trips by men of irregular conduct."[60] Washerwomen often had to listen to "vulgar propositions" and face the temptations of prostitution.[61]

The report pointed out that in the large factories employers could not vigilantly supervise their workers and "penetrate benevolently into their intimate lives."[62] Instead of apprenticeship, young workers learned by example; the imitation of their elders respected no differences of age and status and therefore was "often harmful to their morality."[63] The "vie commune" of the factory, the mixing of the sexes in the same workroom, relaxed moral restraint so much that "energetic men in these conditions easily become turbulent."[64] Overstimulated (the sexual metaphor was unmistakable), they were now open to "unfortunate illusions," to ideas that inevitably disrupted industrial production and political order.

Finally, on the *Statistique*'s list of negative examples there were the isolated workers, living on their own in the furnished rooms of the city. These *logements garnis* were temporary quarters for Paris's itinerant and migrant populations, for those outside the order of family or workshop. Having neither vigilant employers nor parents to train and supervise

[58]CCP, 1:65.
[59]CCP, 1:62–66.
[60]CCP, 1:63.
[61]CCP, 1:63; 2:206.
[62]CCP, 1:64.
[63]CCP, 1:106.
[64]CCP, 1:64.

them, these workers, said the report, had a "tendency" to misconduct, promiscuity, and, if they were women, prostitution.[65]

Although according to the *Statistique* conditions at work were critical to engendering good morals, the authors also suggested that an orderly family life might act as a corrective to a dangerous kind of workplace. Here building workers, and particularly masons, were an example. They were itinerant workers, but the report pointed out that theirs was a tight craft organization and apprenticeship was still in force. Although masons lived in furnished rooms in Paris, these residences struck the investigators as decent places since they were organized by trade and supervised by elders. Although temporarily living outside families, the masons were closely bound by family ties: "They have a family residence in their villages to which they contribute all their savings."[66]

Similarly, the *Statistique* drew a distinction among home workers. Those living in their own residences, married, and owning some furniture were, however poor, described as upright and honorable. And the investigators assumed that even those in furnished rooms had "good conduct" when they were married or when lodging was somehow organized by trade. In the marginal world of the logements garnis, which had been for Frégier in 1840 the breeding ground of the "dangerous classes," the authors of the *Statistique* found four categories of workers: those with good, passable, bad, or very bad moral conduct.[67] The determining factor was family ties *or* a trade structure with some vestige of hierarchy or regulation among its members. Regulation, moreover, was expressed ultimately as sexual repression. In the orderly and thrifty workers praised in the *Statistique*, all "turbulence," lust, passion, and excitement had been disciplined.

The proponents of free trade and individual liberty thus made a case for discipline and regulation. But unlike the socialists, whom they attacked for wanting to regulate the economy, Horace Say and his collaborators did not seek to impose artificial laws on what they defined as natural phenomena. Instead, they attributed a natural regulatory function to the family, whose existence and well-being it was then the function of the state to promote. The role of moral science was to find ways to nurture and protect this natural, hierarchical, and repressive institution. If for political economy "protectionism" had been anathema as economic policy, as social policy it was the order of the day.[68]

[65]CCP, 2:277.
[66]CCP, 2:83, 110.
[67]CCP, 1:202.
[68]The next step was to look more closely at the "matrimonial status" of workers, which the minister of commerce sought to do in 1849. He asked for statistical information on the "état civil des ouvriers appartenant aux dix principaux établissements manufacturiers dans chaque département." Information was collected and sent to the statistical bureau

The analysis of the family and of morality served several functions in the *Statistique*. It permitted the authors to endorse small-scale artisanal forms of organization without seeming to call for intervention in the economy, and it moved the causal explanation for the revolution of 1848 away from the economic system and toward the working-class family. As such, it served the polemic purpose of a reply to the socialists, in the guise of a scientific report. The terms of its science were powerful and persuasive, presented as descriptions of the workings of natural phenomena—the family and the economy. The ordering of its information in numerical tables appealed to a general belief that quantitative evidence could resolve politically inspired disputes. From this perspective the *Statistique* worked as documentation of an externally existing reality; its format and mode of presentation made an eloquent case for its status as fact.

Part Three

La criminalité de la femme est plus dangereuse que celle de l'homme parce qu'elle est plus contagieuse.
C. Lucas, *De la réforme des prisons*, 1838

In addition to its scientific description, the *Statistique* offered a political argument, veiled in a discussion of sexual disorder. The argument rested on the invocation of a dangerous and disorderly "reality" that competed with and threatened the "reality" the authors endorsed. The introduction of the second and antithetical "reality" at once made clear the necessity for accepting the authors' economic blueprint *and* called into question its objective or natural existence.

The *Statistique* presented the world of work in terms of oppositions between good and bad, orderly and turbulent, domesticated and dissipated workers. Although there were precise accountings of the numbers of men and women in the work force and in every branch of manufacturing, the attributions of types of moral conduct were specific to neither sex. According to the report, men and women were to be found in both the good and bad categories, often sharing similar traits in the same trades. Yet in their portrayal of family and morality the authors played on themes of unregulated female sexuality, using the image of the prostitute to conjure up visions of a (working-class) world dangerously out of control.

---

during 1849–50 and is conserved in AN, F501. The records for the department of the Seine seem never to have been collected.

The report used women to refer to either limit of the possibilities of moral behavior. Naturally associated with the family, they embodied and transmitted all its virtues: "Good conduct is often hereditary, especially from a mother to her daughter."[69] Like a mother, a vigilant (female) employer kept her young employees in line, screening out those with reputations or habits of "easy virtue." At the head of an enterprise (sewing garments or selling food) that they conducted in a family setting, married women exhibited impressive managerial and commercial traits. As workers, they were also more reliable when married, having accepted in the power and protection of a husband "the natural law" of their own dependency.[70]

In the *Statistique* the situation of the married working woman represented that of the "good" working class in relation to its employers—in exchange for a certain dependency (on the intelligence and resources of a boss), the worker relinquished his right to profit and accepted a wage. His good behavior, like a wife's sexual fidelity, acknowledged his place in a system of subordination and domination. Accepting the rules meant channeling one's desire, obeying the law one had not written and could not alter.

Women who lived outside a family lived outside the law, and this had worse consequences for some than for others. Old women living alone were miserable; unable to provide for themselves because they had lost their supporters, they had no control over their lives. The victims of circumstance (and beyond sexual corruption), they could only be pitied for their fate.[71] In contrast, young women on their own were dangerous, and their condition was synonymous with unfettered sexuality. Thus, for example, among milliners everything depended on

> the condition in which the workers are placed. Thus almost all those who live with the milliners who employ them display upright, orderly conduct, they are accustomed to thrift and order.... It is not the same for those women working in rooms and for those who are free to do what they wish at the end of the day; it is among them that one finds dissipation and hardship. In general, paid by the day or the piece, they earn wages sufficient for subsistence; the difficult position into which they too often fall must be attributed to their lack of thrift and their disorderly conduct.[72]

The authors of the *Statistique* developed the association between women and sexual indulgence by pointing out that women living alone exhibited worse conduct than men. Among groups of tumultuous workers the

[69]CCP, 1:186.
[70]CCP, 1:52.
[71]CCP, 1:160.
[72]CCP, 2:277.

women were typically cited as being "even more" turbulent or dissipated.[73] Lacking internal correctives, young women indulged passion and vice, and prostitution was inevitably the result. Inherently repugnant because they accepted and exploited sexuality, prostitutes also developed a taste for luxury that further corrupted their behavior. (J.-B. Say had warned that while consumption was important for the economy, luxurious tastes distorted its smooth processes.)[74]

> One notices sometimes the traces of a well-being that their avowed occupation cannot justify.[75]

> A great number of workers exhibit a doubtful conduct and have wages insufficient to support the style of life they lead. They are part of the personnel of public balls and are rarely assiduous at their work.[76]

The word "doubtful" (*douteuse*) recurred in references to single working women's conduct. It conveyed not only a negative judgment about dubious behavior, but a sense of duplicity and deception as well. The investigators could never be sure what these women really did; appearances might not be accurate, self-designated occupational titles might be a ruse. The double check the investigation designed to count seamstresses (taking information from employers and visiting all households where seamstresses might be living) represented not only the genuine difficulty of counting the numbers of home workers in a trade open to any woman with rudimentary sewing skills, but the difficulty of knowing what the truth really was: "The method of doing a census of seamstresses in their homes appears a more certain one."[77]

In many cases this method meant two visits, because the seamstresses lived in lodging houses that received exhaustive and detailed treatment in a separate section of the *Statistique*.[78] The count of seamstresses also involved a more through attempt to ascertain information about their

---

[73]CCP, 1:163. On the representation of political threats as sexual threats and on the use of female figures to accomplish that, see Neil Hertz, "Medusa's Head: Male Hysteria under Political Pressure," *Representations* 4 (Fall 1983): 27–54. A suggestive and important discussion of the uses of female sexuality in political analysis is Therèse Moreau, *Le sang de l'histoire: Michelet, l'histoire et l'idée de la femme au XIXe siècle* (Paris, 1982).

[74]J.-B. Say, *Traité*, p. 446. In this outlook, as in many others, Say shared the views of physiocrats such as Quesnay.

[75]CCP, 2:252.

[76]CCP, 2:266.

[77]CCP, 2:260.

[78]CCP, 1:201–4. The details presented in the section on logements garnis are extraordinarily through, more so than for any other section of the report. There are house-by-house descriptions of what the inspectors saw in each place and accounts of the lives of individual inhabitants. Coming at the very end of the report, this section leaves the reader with a distinctly negative impression of the disordered lives of the workers of Paris.

moral conduct: "Information on the living conditions of these workers came from the impressions the census takers had, . . . from answers the workers themselves supplied, and from their neighbors."[79] Even then, "it was difficult to evaluate the conduct of these workers" or even to decide if they were workers: "For a certain number the occupation of seamstress is clearly only a means of concealing their real sources of income."[80]

These women subverted the precision of the *Statistique*'s count of Parisian workers; they called into question the ability of the objective observers to "see" the facts, and they refused to fit into the established categories. The uncertain character of these so-called workers suggested the larger problem of determining the status of any single woman who lived outside the normal contexts of family, work, economy, and exchange. The hint of prostitution conveyed this sense of irregularity and corruption. Workers but not workers, these women were marginal to, yet part of, the world of Parisian *industrie*. In their behavior lay the threat to moral order, the destruction not only of work discipline but of all social relationships. Lacking proper appreciation of their subordination to a parent or husband, these women lived as outlaws. The very ambiguity of their situation, the fact that they defied categorization, was the measure of their dangerousness.[81]

The prostitute represented sexuality—male as well as female—corrupted, inverted, or simply unregulated, out of control. Women, in their "natural" subordination and dependency, metaphorically represented the working class in relation to capital.[82] In the text, representations of class and sexuality were displaced onto one another; the figure of the single working woman carried both references. Thus, in the *Statistique*'s obsessive preoccupation with women of "doubtful" conduct one finds encoded a set of observations and warnings about another "reality"— the dark and dangerous side of the working class (indeed of the human personality), which must be known if only to be contained.[83] Indeed,

---

[79]CCP, 2:272.

[80]CCP, 1:11; 2:272.

[81]'On the importance of "seeing" for these scientific reports, see Perrot, *Enquêtes*, 11, 21, 26, 28; and on the significance of categories as modes of "discipline," Foucault, *Discipline and Punish* (New York, 1979), p. 189.

[82]That this sort of connection existed in the minds of contemporaries is indicated by Karl Marx's discussion of prostitution in the *Economic and Philosophic Manuscripts* of 1844: "Prostitution is only a *specific* expression of the *general* prostitution of the *laborer*, and since it is a relationship in which falls not the prostitute alone, but also the one who prostitutes— and the latter's abomination is still greater—the capitalist, etc., also comes under this head." Cited in Lisa Vogel, *Marxism and the Oppression of Women* (New Brunswick, N.J., 1984), p. 44.

[83]The references to sexuality seem to be part of a more complicated process of "class construction" in which definitions of the middle class involve notions of sexual self-control

this "reality" always lurked below the surface; it was the underside of the busy, artistic, prosperous world of work the authors had proudly extolled in the introduction to the volume. It was, as the insurrection of June 1848 had shown, a dangerous and chaotic universe in which ordinary rules of conduct and natural hierarchies were overturned, in which the fatherly surveillance of employers could no longer contain the "turbulence" of their sons. The only corrective to this situation, the only way to prevent its reemergence, was to reimpose the terms of patriarchal law.

The authors of the *Statistique* thus offered both a vision of "reality" and an argument about why it had to be accepted as a framework for economic life. In so doing, they revealed something about their own conception of reality: contingent rather than absolute, constructed rather than discovered, imposed for clear political ends rather than lived naturally or inevitably. As the numerical tables ordered a mass of information into categories of understanding that conveyed a certain model of social structure, so the law must impose and enforce—make real— the desired relationships of social and political life.

Conclusions

In the years that followed the design and publication of the *Statistique*, the Second Empire's tough censorship laws and vigilant police informers prevented the appearance of alternative versions of the reality of the world of work. The terms of the *Statistique*'s analysis thus maintained a certain official status. The chamber of commerce continued to employ the *Statistique*'s categories in subsequent studies; the investigation into *Industrie à Paris* in 1860 followed the same format used in 1848. Under the Third Republic new techniques of investigation and a far different political climate spawned new kinds of statistical inquiries with different constructions of the world of work.[84] The histories of those efforts cannot preoccupy us here; when they are written, however, they will surely uncover for us not simply the organization and structure of the world of work, but the extent to which its very depiction was a matter of intense debate and political contest.

It is from that perspective that we can finally assess the uses for historians of the *Statistique de l'industrie* of 1847–48. Written in the wake of

---

and those definitions depend on negative examples, or social "others." In this case the social "other" is the working class; its "otherness" is indicated by representing it as woman.

[84]On these developments see Perrot, *Enquêtes*, pp. 18–20, and her "Note sur le positivisme ouvrier," *Romantisme* 21–22 (January–March 1978): 201–4; and A. Savoye, "Les continuateurs de Le Play au tournant du siècle," *Revue française de sociologie* 22 (1981): 315–44.

1848, it was intended to dispute the revolution's most radical economic and political claims and to reassert a vision of economic organization that had been severely challenged, especially by socialist theorists. Encoded in the documentation was the analytic framework of political economy and an argument about what might happen if it was not accepted. The scientific claims of the investigators and the tabular presentations of their information fixed the report's meaning and reinforced its status as authoritative description. This, and the political climate of the period, which permitted no challenges to be heard, gave the authors the final word not only for the moment, but for posterity. When its administrative and polemic uses had long been outdated, historians searching for unimpeachable data took the *Statistique* at face value, incorporating its documentation without questioning its categories and interpretations.[85] This procedure perpetuates a certain vision of the economy and of statistical science as an entirely apolitical enterprise; it makes the historian an unwitting party to the politics of another age. An alternative approach situates any document in its context and reads it not as a reflection of some external reality, but as an integral part of that reality, as a contribution to the definition or elaboration of meaning, to the creation of social relationships, economic institutions, and political structures. Such an approach demands that the historian question the terms in which any document presents itself and thus ask how it contributes to constructing the "reality" of the past.

[85]Such questioning might throw additional light on various criticisms of Jacques Rancière's "Myth of the Artisan," *International Labor and Working Class History* 24 (Fall 1983): 1–16 and this volume, chap. 11. Rancière argues that the vision of coherent trade structure and of artisanal devotion to work was an idealization constructed for political ends by worker-intellectuals in the 1830s and 1840s. Those who have insisted on the "reality" of coherent structures have tended to rely for their facts on documents such as the *Statistique*. See, for example, Christopher Johnson's reply to Rancière in the same issue, pp. 21–25, and especially p. 22. For additional debate and Rancière's reply, see *ILWCH* 25 (Spring 1984).

13

The Moral Sense of Farce:
The Patois Literature of
Lille Factory Laborers, 1848–70

WILLIAM M. REDDY

Most of us, at one time or another, have heard spine-chilling descriptions of conditions in factory towns during the Industrial Revolution of the first half of the nineteenth century. Men, women, and children in great masses, confined within foul-smelling, overheated brick barns, toiled twelve, thirteen, even fifteen hours a day at the tedious job of tending ceaselessly revolving steam-powered machinery. Their living conditions were just as intolerable we are told. Coal soot blackened the jerry-built mill towns; there was never enough room for the swelling population; families crowded into unsanitary rented rooms; the streets ran with raw sewage; consumption and cholera ravaged young and old. But the worst was that the moral lives of this new species of human being seemed to observers as foul as the physical surroundings. Adults squandered their meager earnings on beer and gin, passing their precious leisure hours in unsavory bars and cafés. Even worse, they seemed to connive at the exploitation of their own children, bringing them to work at seven or even younger, hiring them out to acquaintances or even using them themselves to crawl under and behind running machines to clean away oil-soaked cotton dust. Finally, their sexual lives were disorderly in the extreme; promiscuity and even incest were the norm.

For a generation the sudden appearance of such factory towns seemed to challenge European consciousness, bringing the terrible message that humankind's moral being was as fragile as its physical existence, and that both were being undermined by the startling new forces of the industrial age. For two decades, from about 1830 to 1850, this matter stirred extensive research and debate in conservative circles in England, France, and Germany; and from this debate the young socialist movement culled its most powerful arguments against the new order. In 1844 Friedrich Engels's investigation of the factory population of Manchester, drawing on several earlier studies by conservative social investigators, created the earliest Marxist image of an industrial proletariat, differing from earlier studies principally in that Engels posited the necessary rise of an all-consuming hatred of his oppressors in the breast of the new proletarian, a hatred that would in the end sweep away the industrial order. Across the English Channel the famous French utopian socialist Louis Blanc combed through similar investigations of factory towns for evidence to buttress his own arguments in favor of a completely new organization of work.

After the failure of the revolutions of 1848, in the new political climate of repression and *Realpolitik* of the 1850s, lamentations over the fate of the industrial working class quickly went out of fashion. Yet the impact of the earlier debate was permanent; the image it had created proved indelible, its influence still traceable through hundreds of works of fiction, history, and theory down to our own day.

Research by social historians over the past twenty years has shown, however, that this image is profoundly wrong. Perhaps the first step in its undoing came with the realization in the late 1950s that child labor in the early mills might more rightly be construed as an element of continuity with the past, not a symptom of extreme degradation. Children had always worked with their parents in cottage and field; this was necessary for subsistence and had always been viewed as a morally salutary part of their upbringing. What was new was that the family unit as a whole had moved into centralized steam-powered shops. In the altered environment, social investigators of that time mistook the fixity of custom for social pathology. That the family unit was still working together they took to be proof of its destruction. Once this most glaring of abuses began to appear understandable to historians of our own day, many of the other alleged faults of the millhands lost their frightening edge. On closer examination there was nothing in the evidence to indicate, for example, that sexual behavior or alcohol consumption were any worse among them than what was accepted as normal among middle-class Europeans and Americans at any time since World War I. No longer sharing the Victorian standards of the observers, we easily lose sympathy with their over sensitive moral judgments.[1]

---

[1] See Neil Smelser, *Social Change and the Industrial Revolution* (Chicago, 1959), and Edward Thompson's evaluation of this work in *The Making of the English Working Class* (New York,

The aim here is not to suggest that any of the physical conditions of which there is evidence did not exist. The mills did indeed operate thirteen hours a day, their soot did indeed cling to every surface for miles around; there were no sewers, dwellings were decrepit and too small. But the moral consequences that were deemed to flow from these facts were the fabrications of theoretical presumption and class prejudice. For example, more recent research suggests that discipline was lax in the mills; that harsh-sounding written rules of conduct were little more than wishful thinking; that machines failed to operate up to 45 percent of the time inside these mills.[2] Adult male mill operatives were quite well paid by the standards of the day, a fact that has been long known but conveniently ignored. This is not to say that they were not poor or that privation and disease were unknown to them; but the truth is that the boom-and-bust economic environment of those early years was the principal cause of the laborers' physical insecurity, not their boom-season wages.

It is not possible here to document this argument in every detail; but it is necessary to have a sense for the atmosphere in which this erroneous image of proletarian life with all its weighty consequences was originally constructed. How could eyewitness observers have made such serious errors about the social reality they saw before them?

Empirical social inquiry was in its infancy when the ideas of Malthus and Ricardo burst upon Europe between 1800 and 1820; what these two thinkers seemed to have proved by a faultless logic was that the vast majority of humankind was doomed forever to live out their lives on the edge of existence. The law of free competition in the marketplace coupled with the law of natural increase condemned the laboring poor always to work for a bare subsistence wage; whenever wages went higher their number would increase, and the new competitors would force the price of labor back down. It was Ricardo who had concluded from this that whenever laborers indulged in "the delights of domestic society" they were forcing their own wages down. In other words, intemperance and poverty—that is, moral decay and physical deprivation—were intimately linked. This remarkable, distasteful proposition is what sparked interest in the new factory populations. Social investigators came already knowing what to look for; they were searching for human beings on the edge—physically on the edge of survival, morally on the edge of humanity. And they easily convinced themselves that they had found them.

1963), p. 338. See also the more recent Patrick Joyce, *Work, Society and Politics: The Culture of the Factory in Later Victorian England* (Brighton, 1980).

[2]Output figures have been compared with technical output potential in William M. Reddy, *The Rise of Market Culture: The Textile Trade and French Society, 1750–1900* (New York, 1984), 89-1:2.

We can see the gratuitous way these observers connected physical deprivation with moral degeneracy in a famous description by Louis Villermé of a cellar dwelling in Lille. Lille by the 1830s had a hundred or so steam-powered spinning mills whose laboring population was crammed into decaying neighborhoods inside the old town walls. Villermé was given a tour of one of these neighborhoods in 1835; there he found certain cellar dwellings to be the worst of all. Here is how he described them:

> Day arrives for them an hour later than for the others, and night an hour earlier.
> Their ordinary furnishings consist of, along with the tools of their trade, a sort of cupboard or plank of wood for storing food, a pot, a small terra-cotta cooker, a few dishes, a small table, two or three bad chairs, and a dirty pallet made up entirely of some straw and a covering in tatters. I would prefer to add nothing to this list of hideous things that reveals at first glance the profound misery of the unfortunate inhabitants; but I must say that, in many of the beds I was just speaking of, I saw lying together individuals of both sexes and of very different ages, most without shirts and repulsively dirty. Father, mother, the aged, children, adults press upon each other there, pile up there. I stop. . . . The reader will complete the picture himself. But I warn him that if he wishes to keep it faithful, his imagination must not recoil before any of the disgusting mysteries that are accomplished on these impure beds in the bosom of obscurity and drunkenness.[3]

It is easy to see in this passage that Villermé moves swiftly and uncritically from observing deprivation to inferring immorality. Moreover, it is possible to demonstrate that every feature of this physical description had clear literary precedent in earlier descriptions—the bad chairs, the miserable cupboard, the lack of light, the dirty bedding—by 1840 Villermé knew his audience expected to hear of exactly such things.[4] The rapidity with which such descriptions became standardized in this kind of literature is remarkable.

Occasionally it is possible to trace the transfer of such images from social investigators to politicians and novelists. In 1851, for example, Adolphe Blanqui, a disciple of Villermé, wrote to Victor Hugo urging him to come to Lille and view the slum neighborhoods: "I know the

---

[3]Louis R. Villermé, *Tableau de l'etat physique et moral des ouvriers employés dans les manufactures de coton, de laine, et de soie*, 2 vols. (Paris, 1840), 1:82–83.

[4]Compare this passage with questionnaire responses of the general council of the Seine-Inférieure department, the Société industrielle de Mulhouse, chamber of commerce of Lille, chamber of commerce of Reims, all in Archives nationales, F¹² 4704–5. Compare also Ange Guépin and E. Bonamy, *Nantes au XIXe siècle, statistique topographique industrielle et morale, faisant suite à l'histoire de Nantes* (Nantes, 1835), pp. 483–84. For more detail, see Reddy, *Market Culture*, pp. 138-84.

terrain by heart," wrote Blanqui, "and you will learn more in one day than you could in ten years."[5] Hugo did come and later related in turn what he had seen in the cellars of Lille—in a draft speech for the National Assembly and in his long and bitter poem, *Les châtiments*; and of course the impact of such pilgrimages into the slums of France can be found throughout his *Les misérables*. Poverty, all were agreed, is inherently corrosive of moral fiber: the poor are not human in the normal sense; they lack the minimum necessary for human life. They are lost souls. This is what the French term *misère* came to convey.

But evidence concerning the actual moral character of the factory laborers, evidence stemming from the expressions of their own community life, utterly belies this prevalent equation of physical deprivation with moral decay. The fact is that in this very same town of Lille the factory laborers engaged in a constant round of community ceremonies and activities, producing in the process an extensive dialect literature unknown to all but a few local experts until it was brought to more general attention by a French historian, Pierre Pierrard, in the 1960s.[6]

Pierrard, working exclusively on the two decades between 1850 and 1870, has cataloged over eight hundred songs and poems in the local dialect of Lille, most of them written by illiterate or semiliterate textile millworkers and printed on broadsides or in small booklets to be recited or sung at carnival time, on other popular holidays, or among members of intimate singing clubs that met in neighborhood cafés. The urgent questions that the social historian brings to this literature are: What can it reveal about the laboring community's moral orientation to its own grinding poverty? How was deprivation experienced? What communal identity emerged in the midst of it?

The laborers' literature is in fact extremely self-conscious in the sense that they wrote of almost nothing except themselves, their town, their customs and frustrations. Therefore there is a great deal of material that bears directly on the question at hand, and even the most superficial review of it shows that it could easily be used to undermine Villermé's view of working-class life in Lille. Before putting these songs and poems to any such use, however, we must confront a methodological problem.

How can one come to any conclusion about the life of a community or its moral orientation on the basis of songs and poems, works of art whose status does not necessarily give direct access to the intentions of

[5]See the letter reproduced in Victor Hugo, *Oeuvres complètes*, 42 vols. (Paris, 1909–50), vol. 38, *Actes et paroles I*, pp. 434–38, where the draft of a speech may also be found. Blanqui's descriptions of Lille were even more baroque than Villermé's; see *Des classes ouvrières en France pendant l'année 1848* (Paris, 1849), pp. 97, 99.

[6]Pierre Pierrard, *Les chansons en patois de Lille sous le Second Empire*, Société de la dialectologie picarde, 8 (Arras, 1965); and idem, *La vie ouvrière à Lille sous le Second Empire* (Paris, 1965).

the artist? The social historian's first impulse—one that this dialect literature easily abets—is to read the literature as simple reportage. If a song describes a spat between husband and wife, one wants to seize upon this and say, thus were marital relations among the working class. If a song describes a street scene on market day, one wants to say, thus were the streets on market days. But nothing could be more misguided than such an approach. Precious as is the dialect literature as evidence on working-class life, there is no reason to accept it at face value any more than the literature of social investigators.

The first step must be to proceed, by inference and guesswork, to discover what place, what function these songs and poems served in the life of factory workers. One must infer what underlying principles governed their choice and handling of subject matter. Of all the things they could have written about, why these? Of all the tones of voice they could have adopted, why this one? Once the historian has an idea of the way *their* lens was constructed and what blinders they wore when *they* looked at the world, he will have two kinds of evidence to work with. (1) The evidence of the rules of literary convention and tone may speak of the community's ethos and ideals. (2) Evidence of actual occurrences or patterns of behavior described in the literature—*corrected for* by knowledge of their rules of selection and literary alteration—gives us a limited kind of direct information about the structure of community life and human relationships, especially when such evidence is confirmed by other sources. From there we can triangulate, so to speak, on our object of inquiry: the community's "consciousness" or "culture."

The first thing one notices is that the characteristic themes of the literature changed drastically in the early nineteenth century. Before 1800 Lille had been a stronghold of guild monopoly and merchant privilege in a sea of free trade. Woolen and linen weaving guilds inside Lille saw their trade decay owing to the competition of cottage weavers in the surrounding countryside. In the eighteenth century the local dialect literature was concerned almost exclusively with glorifying the urbanity and sophistication of Lille inhabitants at the expense of the ridiculous and naive country bumpkins of the surrounding Flemish plain. Inhabitants of the village of nearby Tourcoing—where cottage woolen production thrived—were in particular the butt of a thousand jokes and satirical stories. After 1790, however, this theme quickly faded. In fact it appears that in the subsequent decades of revolution, war, and nascent industrial development local interest in the dialect literature reached a low ebb.[7]

[7]On the eighteenth century, see Fernand Carton's introduction to his critical edition of François Cottignies dit Brûle-Maison, *Chansons et pasquilles* (Arras, 1965). Carton disagrees

The revolution of 1848, however, that great victory of the sovereign people over tyranny, seems to have sparked a new interest in the dialect among its speakers. It was in this year that a great efflorescence of songs and poems began in which the theme of self-conscious celebration of local life and custom quickly came to predominate. For some reason the political events of 1848 led factory laborers in Lille to discover themselves as worthy objects of literary expression; and once this discovery was made, it was not lost sight of even in the years of repression and dictatorial government that followed.

One writer in particular was overwhelmingly influential in this shift in the literature—Alexandre Desrousseaux. Between 1849 and 1851 his own broadsides and booklets catapulted him to local fame and saved him from penury. By 1854 he had been given a job at the town hall in recognition of his fame and had moved his family out of the slums into a more fashionable part of town.

Judging purely on the grounds of literary merit, there can be no doubt that Desrousseaux's works far outweigh in quality and quantity those of any other writer of the period. But this raises a problem. Is literary quality a safe guide to the utility of a piece for answering a nonliterary question? If anything the opposite would be the case. Surely one ought to feel safer with the bungling and inept efforts of the more typical unlettered writers. Or perhaps this is also too simple an answer.

The problem is complicated because some of Desrousseaux's compositions are clearly aimed at a middle-class audience of local merchants, shopkeepers, and clerks who had learned the dialect in childhood and who could afford to buy nicely bound books of quaint dialect poetry. Typical of this kind of product is Desrousseaux's most famous song, the "Canchon dormoire" ("Lullabye"), which depicts a working mother singing her baby to sleep with promises of unreachable riches; she needs to put him to sleep so she can get back to work knitting lace.[8] The song invites us to pity and enhances our sympathy with motherly love by depicting it in the midst of impoverishment. It is a sentimentalized view of poverty, from the outside looking in.

One may contrast this with what I consider to be Desrousseaux's best work, the poem called "Casse-Bras," one of his earliest productions, from 1849, before all the hopes of the revolution had been snuffed out.[9] The difference in tone is immediately apparent; this is a view of poverty from the inside. Casse-Bras is the nickname of an old man, laid off from his factory job because of his age, who has decided to retire to the *hôpital*

---

with Pierrard's view that the literature died out between 1800 and 1848; nonetheless it seems to have left far fewer printed pieces for those years.

[8]Alexandre Desrousseaux, *Chansons et pasquilles lilloises*, 2 vols. (Lille, 1855), 2:45–93.

[9]Alexandre Desrousseaux, *Chansons et pasquilles lilloises*, 2 vols. (Lille, 1865), 1:167–72.

(an institution for the elderly poor) for his last days, since he cannot support himself any more. His relatives come to see him off; a good deal of coffee is drunk, much of it laced, as was the custom, with eau de vie. Casse-Bras decides he had better leave for the hôpital before everyone is too drunk to come along. He takes his wife by the arm and starts off; the others follow. Unwittingly they form a procession; one of them grabs an old soapbox and begins beating a martial rhythm on it. People run from all around to see what is going on.

> In s' dijant comm' cha l'un à l'aute
> "Ch'est-i des gins qui faitt'nt ribote?
> U bien, s'in vont-i pou' plinter
> Incore un arbre d'liberté?
> —Non, dijot l'aut', ch'est un mariache!
> —Bah! ch'est d's ouveriers sans ouvrache!
> —Ch'est peut-ête eun révolution?
> —Mais non, puis qu'i n'ont point d'baton!"
> Su'vingt raisons, n'y-avot personne
> In état d'mette l'nez su' l'bonne,
> Et nous aute', in cantan' un r'frain,
> Nous allîm's no' bon-homm' de q'min.

> Saying to each other something like this:
> "Are those guys all completely pissed?
> Or maybe we're going to see
> Them plant another liberty tree?
> "No, it's a marriage!" says another, annoyed.
> "Bah! It's workers who are unemployed!"
> "Maybe it's a revolution?"
> "But no, they have no sticks, not a one!"
> Out of twenty reasons, not a person
> Was able to put a finger on the right one.
> And us, we just kept up a song.
> And kept on marching right along.

Casse-Bras and his companions decide to stop for further refreshment along the way. They stop in at the bar known as the Cat-Barré, the "Cat Barred"—a pun on the word *cabaret*—which really existed in Lille, having on its sign a picture of a cat and a metal bar. After further libations Casse-Bras ("who had some schooling") stands up on his chair to make a speech. He complains of being laid off after working thirty years at the same mill and faithfully raising his family. "You cannot say that I was ruled by vice." But his virtue and fidelity carried no weight.

> Et v'là comme je m' trouv' su'l'pavé!

Ah! si dins l'temps qu' j'etos soldat
Un boulet m'avot cassé l'bras,
J'aros dro' à les *Invalides*!
Comm' mes gamb's sont incor solides,
Là, du moins, j'aros l'contint'mint
De m'in aller, avé m' viell' gra-mère,
Bras, d'sus et bras d'zous, a l' barrière,
Boir' du vin, quand j'aros queq's sous!
Bah! ch'bonheur n'est point fait pour nous!

And that's how I ended up on the streets!
Ah! If only when I was a soldier
A bullet had hit me in the shoulder,
Then I would have a right to the Invalides!*
Since my legs are still quite solid,
There at least I would have had the pleasure
Of taking my old woman out for a walk
Arm in arm to the gates of the city wall
To drink a little wine if we had the money!
Bah! For us this was not to be!

At this Casse-Bras's wife interrupts in anger: What, you a good Lillois would drink wine instead of beer? Leave Lille and your family? I wouldn't do it, not for my weight in gold, she exclaims. She tells Casse-Bras to take courage, reminds him of his good fortune in having a roof and a bed and a little food at the hôpital for his declining days. Soon she will join him there. At this he cries out what a good wife he has had through all the hard years. The party takes up its journey again. At the end of the poem they break into a song, *Lillos-Trompette*, another of Desrousseaux's pieces. (This is an obvious cue for those listening to begin singing the song themselves.)

By contrast with the "Canchon dormoire," this poem invites the reader to admire (not pity or sentimentalize) Casse-Bras and his wife for the way they face privation and resist the temptation to give in to bitterness and resentment. Drinking is celebrated with naive enthusiasm, and the meeting of men and women in bars is treated as utterly unobjectionable—quite the opposite of the views of middle-class investigators. Nor are those who pass the difficult moral test of working-class life—that is, by resisting the temptation to bitterness—seen as exceptional; these are just some of the good people of Saint-Sauveur, the very area that Villermé saw as most ridden with vice and degeneracy.

In addition, "Casse-Bras" derives a particular beauty for a student of

*[The Paris rest home for disabled veterans.]

this literature from the way it brings together a number of characteristic themes. There was great interest in describing the stages of life; "Casse-Bras" is one of many poems treating old men and women looking back on life. Lille-area songwriters were fascinated with the public places— the bars, squares, and shops—of their own town; several such spots are celebrated in "Casse-Bras." There was likewise a deep concern with getting by: with prices of food, clothes, and housing, an issue central to the predicament of Casse-Bras. Finally, spontaneity of feeling was highly admired; closely coupled to this was a love of lighthearted farce, of good-natured trickery, that was deemed the trademark of the whole community.

Desrousseaux's "Casse-Bras" is exceptionally revealing concerning this last theme, for the poem shows a link between this love of farce and the whole nature of working-class experience. Nothing could be more somber than the event depicted in this piece: an old man going to a rest home for the destitute that he regards as a prison. But once he starts on his way the event is transformed. Relatives and neighbors who have come to see him off form into a column, rather by accident, as they begin walking through the streets. Someone starts beating on a soapbox as if they were in a parade. Suddenly they are playing an amusing trick on the whole town. And there is rich irony in the observers' speculations: Is it a marriage? A march of the unemployed? A revolution? For the march is at once a rite of passage for the unemployed Casse-Bras and a kind of protest demonstration. It is in contrast to this spirit of farce, of spontaneity and good humor, that Casse-Bras's bitter protest at the Cat-Barré must be called to order by his wife. Yes, life is hard, but the answer is not to poison it with bitterness; the answer is to turn even the gloomiest of its occasions into a pretext for good fellowship and redeeming silliness. Even the revolution, the poem seems to hint, should come in the form of a good trick.

In "Casse-Bras" the spirit of farce, so characteristic of this dialect literature, is presented as rising out of a conscious moral response to the hardships of life. It is appreciated not as an escape, not as a mere relief from the prevailing drudgery and privation, but as a morally pure reply to these conditions, one that preserves the individual from the twin hazards of despair and hatred.

The comparison of "Casse-Bras" with the "Canchon dormoire" presents in a nutshell the difficulty of dealing with Desrousseaux. We must always wonder whom he is writing for, and with pieces like "Casse-Bras" we must ask whether this careful weaving together of themes represents a faithful reflection of the internal order of the community's view of life or only a personal statement of his own.

One way to approach this question is to examine Desrousseaux's work in the context of other pieces, frequently of far less literary merit, that are known to have been written by mill operatives.[10] It turns out to be particularly revealing to compare the treatment by Desrousseaux and others of the following kinds of subject matter: love relationships and women's lives; the town and its buildings; money, work, and getting by; and the spirit of farce.[11]

Songwriting was a male activity, carried out most often in bars and male singing clubs, the ideal context for airing complaints against the opposite sex. Desrousseaux, along with many others, wrote numerous songs on this theme.

In "L'homme marié," Desrousseaux rehearses the traditional catalog of complaints: my wife kept herself beautiful before our marriage, claims the married man, but now she never washes.[12] (She is so sticky you could glue her to the wall.) When she is working at her lace, she is irritable. I bring her food, I wait on her hand and foot, but then she stops for hours to talk to her neighbor, drinking coffee and getting nothing done. She gives me another baby every year. When we had twelve I prayed God to stop it there; the next year she had twins. And I am the one who ends up taking care of them when I come home from work at night, laments the married man. One or more of these figures appeared in every song of this genre: women are pretty before marriage but not after; they are idle; they ruin the family budget drinking coffee; they forget to make the soup for dinner; they dominate; they have too many babies.

It is probably no accident that the complaint about unmade soup is heard most frequently of all. These songs do more than reflect an ingrained male chauvinism (which is unmistakable); they also speak of the hardships of running a household on a very small income brought in at the cost of very long hours on the job. The working male envies his wife's idleness because of his own prolonged absences from the comforts of home. Repeatedly songs dwell on how women fritter away their time during the day. The crowning irony, then, arises when the wife's domestic enjoyments lead her to forget her husband's need for a share of the same. We cannot conclude from the frequency of this complaint that women were bad housekeepers—or that they were good ones. However, the popularity of the unmade-soup lament may derive from a concealed protest against the work routine of the factory. It is highly likely that this reflects a piece of genuine popular experience: the exhaustion and the high expectation of relaxation felt by men coming home from the

[10]On the identity of songwriters, see Pierrard, *Chansons*, p. 21.

[11]This procedure is suggested by, although it is not precisely identical to, Pierrard's categorization of themes; ibid.

[12]Desrousseaux, *Chansons* (1865), 1:139–44.

mill. Women who worked also felt it, as is indicated in a song glorifying coffee, "Le plaisir des femmes" ("Women's Pleasure"):[13]

> Les femm's qui vont in fabrique
> Et donn'nt leus infants à soigner
> L'soir sorties d'leus boutiques,
> I faitt'nt bien vit' du café

> Women who go to the mill
> And leave their kids with others,
> In the evening on leaving work
> Make that coffee right away.

They make it, the song implies, even before picking up their children.

It is indicative of the way normal experience was deformed to make it "literary" that this sense of exhaustion and desire must be displaced and expressed indirectly in stylized complaints against the woman at home and in fantasies about her idleness, or else in a song in praise of coffee—an equally conventional theme.

Such literary transfigurations of everyday experience were what these songs and poems were all about; for writers and listeners this was their principal charm. Briefly they could contemplate themselves as dressed-up inhabitants of the picturesque world of Lille. Desrousseaux was not so much qualitatively different in his treatment of this theme as simply more resourceful than the others. In the case of husbands' laments, he followed closely the conventions prevailing among unschooled and less self-conscious writers, improving on them rather than seeking forms from outside.

There was in this literature a great preoccupation with specific geographical features of Lille. Such interest was dictated by the special self-consciousness these songs were meant to engender. Expressions of local pride and descriptions of local color were necessary to maintain the sense of quaintness and originality the literature attempted to create. But this confronted the songwriter with a problem. The grimness of the working-class environment was too salient to escape commentary. Nor did it. Writers did not shrink from dealing with the ugliest features of the landscape; yet one senses that they struggled to maintain the innocent, admiring tone they felt was essential to their literary idiom. The result in most cases was a satirical rehearsal of woes. Even in the best of cases, admiration was tinged with irony.

Slum clearance and street construction projects, launched in imitation

[13]Jean-Baptiste Lefebvre, "Le plaisir des femmes" (Lille, 1861), in Bibliothèque Nationale (hereafter BN), Ye 7182 (519); also cited by Pierrard in *Chansons*, p. 229.

of Paris, were common in most French towns of any size during the 1850s and 1860s, and these became favorite topics of celebratory songs in which irony shone with full force. Desrousseaux constitutes a telling exception here. When a well known bell tower was slated for demolition in 1857, for example, Desrousseaux lamented its passing in a poem called "L'ascension au befroi" ("The Ascension of the Bell Tower"), which includes an account of all the things one can see from this vantage point.[14] As Desrousseaux's eyes roam, he recalls significant moments of his youth: there is the square where he first courted his wife; yonder in the distance is Saint-Sauveur church where he was an altar boy. The passage of a landmark provides another opportunity for evoking simple nostalgia— a major theme for Desrousseaux and therefore, one must imagine, for his audience.

But nostalgia plays no role whatever in most songs of the period that deal with the urban improvement projects. Instead there is a great outpouring of tongue-in-cheek admiration. Gustave Bizard's "Rue de la gare," for instance, was written in 1870 in honor of a new broad avenue that was pushed through a poor neighborhood in order to connect Lille's train station with the town's main square.[15] The song has two refrains that go in opposite directions. The first is admiring:

> Cheull' rue d' la Gare
> Vous pouvez m' croire
> S'ra l' p'us bielle rue
> Qu'on n'ara jamais vu:
> Lillo's mes frères,
> Soyons fiers,
> L'agrandich'mint
> Nous met au premier ring.

> That rue de la Gare
> You can believe me
> Will be the most beautiful street
> Anyone ever did see:
> Lillois, my brothers,
> Be proud.
> Our rebuilding project
> Puts us in the very first rank.

The second chorus is a cry of distress:

> Cheull' rue d' la Gare

[14]As cited in Pierrard, *Chansons*, pp. 120–21.
[15]BN, Ye 971 (22).

> Que désespoir
> Qu'elle va donner
> Aux vieux du temps passé
> A tort quand même
> Les hommes les femmes
> Toudis r'grett'rons
> Ch'vieux marqué au pichon.

> That rue de la Gare
> What despair
> It will give
> To old people of the good old days.
> Mistaken, even so,
> Men and women
> Always will regret
> That old fish market.*

As the translation suggests, this second refrain is unclear. Does Bizard mean that people ought not to regret the demolition project or that the demolition itself is a mistake? At any rate, the rest of the song puts the emphasis on regret and reveals that much more than nostalgia is involved. Bizard evokes the prospect of carts and worn-out furniture cluttering the old streets where people are moving out of condemned buildings: "Ch'étot l'pillage dins l'rue d'un bout à l'autre" (the street was a wreck from one end to the other). He says he saw clearance project officials trying to lead away an old woman who was in tears at having lost her cat: "Ch'est des graigniards, ch'est un métier pour ça" (they have permanent frowns; the job requires it). As for the fish market that was being destroyed:

> Ch'est malheureux pour chés vielles pichonières
> Dans leu's vieux jours qui faut quitter ch'létat
> Il'y-en-a gramint qui vont faire leu' affaire
> Pour euss' aller morir á l'hôpita.

> It's too bad for those old women fishmongers
> To have to leave that trade in their later years.
> A good many are arranging their affairs
> So they can go die at the hôpital.

Quite clearly, urban improvements were personal disasters for hundreds of working-class people, and no mention of these projects could help but bring this out, even though convention may have required the

---

*[Which was being torn down.]

expression of simple local pride. The solution adopted was to offer an equally simple, understated (but crushingly obvious) ironic treatment of the subject. Another song about the rue de la Gare (by Louis Longret) carries the same message. The grandness of the project is contrasted with the private sufferings of persons affected, especially the aged, who have lived there for many years and find leaving difficult.

Another group of songs in this same genre deal with living conditions in the working-class neighborhoods. The experience of moving holds a great place in these songs, just as in those dealing with rebuilding projects, but the reason is different. People moved frequently because it was so hard to find a place one could tolerate. As an anonymous song of 1859 puts it:[16]

> Les dimanches d'dins Lille
> On vot d' tous les cotés
> Des gins canger d'asile
> Et tout déménager;
> Dins les rues d' Saint-Sauveur,
> Ch'est cinne eun' procession,
> Car tout l'monde, d'un bon coeur
> Démenage de s'mason.

> Sundays in Lille
> One sees on every side
> People changing homes
> And moving everything out;
> In the streets of Saint-Sauveur
> It's like a procession
> One and all with a good heart
> Move right out of their houses.

Pests were highest on the long list of reasons for moving out: cockroaches, lice, mice, bedbugs. Usually songs on this subject took the form of a lighthearted recounting of successive frustrations. The first place I lived in had cockroaches, says a song of 1885; in the next I woke up in the middle of the night to find bedbugs parading across my nose. I moved again, but the fireplace did not work. My next place was sold by the landlord and I had to move.[17] Also frequently complained of were leaky roofs, mildew that ruined clothes, landlords who didn't like children, insufficient light.

The complaints are more circumstantial than the descriptions of dwellings found in the investigative literature and are also starkly different

[16]Anonymous, untitled (Lille, 1859), BN, Ye 971 (112).
[17]Edouard Prévost, untitled (Lille, 1858), BN, Ye 7182 (672).

in tone. Villermé imposes a moral calculus. From each feature a moral consequence flows. The single bed means incest; the dirt floor means a dirty life; the absence of furnishings means a spiritual deprivation. These songs reinforce our sense of the injustice of such a procedure. For the workers, the drawbacks of these places are experienced an annoyances and inconveniences. They are sorely tried by dirt, cold, dampness, and vermin, but their souls are not besmirched by these things; quite the opposite. They try to bear up; they write songs, and in doing so they create that same light ironic tone that characterized their descriptions of slum clearance. If anything, because their homes offer another occasion for them to display their tolerant cheerfulness before life, in their own view they gain morally rather than lose by being forced to live in such places. On the theme of the town and its buildings, therefore, Desrousseaux's interest diverges markedly from that of other Lille poets. Where he seems moved by nostalgia, they swell ironically on the inadequacies of their housing or else on the contradiction that improvements can be made only at the price of destruction. In other words, over against Desrousseaux, most of those who deal with this theme remain faithful to the vision of "Casse-Bras": retreating from anger and despair into humor and irony.

Money was an inexhaustible theme for these laborer-songwriters. Buying with it, selling to get it, borrowing it, getting by without it, earning and losing it: every kind of experience with it drew their attention. They felt a particular fascination for the market vendors and shopkeepers who provided their daily needs. Some were poor themselves and were the object of deep affection. In the songs we find them walking the streets, filling them with color and with the sound of their clever cries. One fishmonger calls out to all the women by profession; she has eels for all the "devideusses, ratacheusses, faigeusses de sariaux, fileusses, bobineusses, couseusses de piqieaux, modisses, soigneusses, eplugueusses, brodeusses au crochet, gazeusses, faigeusses de dint'let" (reelers, piecers, smock makers, spinners, bobbin winders, quilt sewers, dressmakers, machine tenders, cotton cleaners, needle knitters, gauze makers, and lace makers).[18] They all need her eels. The feeling of intimacy with the workers and affection for them implicit in this call reflected the simple fact that most street vendors had started as laborers themselves and that most laborers dreamed of becoming vendors and escaping the factory. A hundred francs or so was enough to get started; such trades were therefore a realistic alternative to the mill.

In the face of the real insecurity and drudgery of factory work, songwriters in all their compositions concerning money followed their usual

[18]Anonymous, untitled (Lille, 1841), BN, Ye 7812 (150).

strategy of indirection. Their songs were to be not vehicles for complaint, but a means of depicting themselves as colorful and stalwart, the simple yet knowing people they wished to be. Therefore, among other strategies, they turned their eye away from their own sufferings and toward the enchanting figure of the street vendor, concentrating on his produce, his cry, his routine, his worries. This stock figure in their literature, like the stock image of the wife whose soup is late, speaks, by implication again, of that experience that was almost never directly mentioned, the life of work at the shop.

For work itself was a taboo subject to these songwriters. All indications of feeling about factory work come from indirect references. There is a song about a military conscript who is happy to be eating more regularly than when he worked in the mill.[19] A lullabye laments that the little girl who is being rocked to sleep will end up as a bobbin winder sooner or later.[20] Mill work, in other words, is inevitable, a trap, a fate unavoidable for the poor.

Bonnart's "Le chômage du lundi" ("Taking Mondays Off") is a defiant celebration of Monday absenteeism. The first verse and refrain are particularly revealing:

> Mais quo vous etes acore à l'brunne
> Epu l'machine est arreté,
> Tous les lundis ché toudie l'même
> Vous n'avez jamais bu assez;
> Apré in fait carnage,
> Parce qu'i n'a pu d'argint,
> l'diable est d'vint l'minnage.
> Vous êtes des drôles de gins.
>
> *Refrain*:
> Mes amis acouté chi
> In boen consel que j'vous donne.
> Grêce! et pour l'amour de Di
> N'faites jamais pu l'Lundi.
>
> *Réponse des buveurs*:
> In acoute poent chin te di
> Nous ferons toudi l'Lundi
>
> But while you are still in twilight
> And the machines are still at rest,
> Every Monday it is the same

---

[19] Anonymous, "Les consolations d'un conscrit" (Roubaix, n.d.), BN, Ye 971 (44).
[20] Lille, n.d., BN, Ye 7182 (563).

A bit more to drink would be best.
Later you are in for it,
The money has run out,
The devil is at the door.
You are peculiar louts.

Refrain:
My friends listen here
I'm giving you good advice
Grace! and for the love of God
Don't do Monday anymore.

Response of the topers:
We won't listen to what you say
We will always do our Monday.[21]

The song depicts the laborers arriving at the mill before sunrise, waiting for light to work by, but giving into the call of the café before the machines can be started. What hurts them later is not the foreman's discipline (which is not even mentioned) but exhaustion of Saturday's pay before the week is out. This is just what we would expect on the basis of evidence from other sources about the laxness of discipline in the shops. At the same time the song is true to form; nothing is said about work or those elements of the work experience that made absenteeism so desirable. Instead the workers are ironically castigated for being "des drôles de gins."

Why was the work experience a taboo subject? The most likely answer is that it did not fit into the special spirit that the songs were meant to express. One could not directly complain; one must eschew carping bitterly against fate or against the political order. What could be more futile or demeaning? The songwriters in their handling of themes anticipated the objections voiced to Casse-Bras by his wife: How can you, a good Lillois, give into bitterness? Look on the bright side, count your blessings, redirect your unhappiness into farce and irony. Hence work itself could not be directly dealt with.

Desrousseaux's "Casse-Bras" emerges from these considerations not as a personal statement, then, but as a genuine key to understanding the spirit of this whole literature. Working-class suffering, often explicitly dealt with, is nonetheless handled through understated irony or indirection. The effort is made to find a bright, humorous, or incongruous aspect of the matter and to concentrate on it to the exclusion of all else. In cases where Desrousseaux's own work diverges from the general

[21]No place, n.d., BN, Ye 971 (36).

pattern, it is he, not his fellow songwriters, who emerges as unfaithful to the spirit of Casse-Bras, leaving irony aside in preference to a nostalgic or sentimentalized view of the life of the poor of old Lille. It is important to note that there is no hint of escapism in the prevailing ironic tone; all evidence points to the conclusion that laborers handled their sufferings in this way by conscious choice, believing that it was a superior mode of reflection on life. In discussion of living conditions, for example, where negative commentary was less dangerous politically than, say, discussion of work, the songwriters did not mince words, yet they maintained a humorous or light tone in every case, allowing irony to drive home the point. There is no turning away from the bleakness of life in these songs; instead, it is treated explicitly as farcical and ironic.

Occasionally the songs deal with situations in which the spirit of farce was expressed through public, collective enactments. What these references tell us is that the pervasive tone of irony in the literature was more than just a literary convention, because in these public rituals farce was celebrated as an integral part of the ethos of the community. Desrousseaux's "Casse-Bras" now appears as a key not just to the dialect poetry but to the very structure of working-class culture.

One such reference may be found in Desrousseaux's "Broquelet d'autrefois" ("The Lace-Needle Day of the Past"), which describes the traditional mode of celebrating Saint Nicolas's feast day (no longer followed by the 1850s): a great procession filed through town led by a man dressed up as the saint. The procession came to its end at a square next to the canal, and as the saint turned to begin preaching to the crowd, he was picked up by two attendants and thrown into the water, to the cheers of the assembled people.[22] Likewise in the song "Ro bot!" ("The King Drinks!"), Desrousseaux describes a traditional banquet on the feast of the Epiphany (celebrating the visit of the three kings to the newborn Savior).[23] In this song's account, a great deal of alcohol is consumed during the meal. Once the banquet is completed, a hat is passed with slips of paper in it; on one slip the word *sot* (fool) is written. The person who picks this slip out of the hat (keeping it a secret) is then required to *faire des farces*—to play tricks on the others and act the fool.

These songs of Desrousseaux suggest that the spirit of farce antedated considerably the period under consideration. It is obvious that irony and trickery abounded in the eighteenth-century popular literature of Lille. In Desrousseaux's whole corpus, as well, there are countless traces of it. In an appendix to the 1855 collection of songs, for example, he explains the meaning of the work ban as follows:

[22]Desrousseaux, *Chansons* (1865), 1:72–76.
[23]Alexandre Desrousseaux, *Chansons et pasquilles lilloises* (Lille, 1849), pp. 10–13.

Applaudissement en cadence imité d'une batterie militaire. Il est d'un usage général, mais à Lille on y a fait de nombreuses modifications. Nous avons le *ban simple*, le *ban de chats*, le *ban de canards*, c'est-à-dire qu'en battant on imite le cri de ces differents animaux. C'est un spectacle assex réjouissant de voire quel importance on attache à cet exercise. Celui qui commande a dans sa prestance, quelque chose d'un tambour-major, qu'il représent en effet. Tous les regards sont fixés sur le sien pour y lire le signal de la fermeture du ban. Alors, si, suivant les regles, toutes les mains ont frappé comme une seule main, il s'écrie triomphalement: *Bien, n'y a point de conscrits!* Mais s'il y a un conscrit la punition suit immediatement la faute. Le conscrit, ou le coupable, comme vous voudrez, monte sur la table, et là, on lui fait boire, très lentement un vere d'eau tandis que ses camarades chantent à l'unison:

> I va passer par l'trouglouglou
> De ma tanturlurette;
> I van passer par l'trouglouglou
> De ma tanturlourou.[24]

Applause in rhythm imitating a military drum. This is done everywhere. But in Lille we make many variations. There is the ban simple, the ban of cats, the ban of ducks; that is, while clapping one imitates the calls of these animals. It's quite a delightful spectacle to see how seriously this exercise is taken. The commander has in his demeanor something of a sergeant major, which he is, in effect. All eyes are on his to see the signal of the cessation of the ban. If all hands stop clapping in perfect unison according to the rule, then he announces triumphantly, "Okay, there are no conscripts!" But if there is a conscript, the punishment follows immediately. The conscript, or the convict if you like, climbs up on a table and must drink a glass of water very slowly while his friends sing in unison:

> He must pass through the trouglouglou
> Of my tanturlurette
> He must pass through the trouglouglou
> Of my tanturlourou.

There are plentiful indications, in short, that farce played a ritualized role in traditional celebrations and activities in Lille (as well as signs that Lille's neighbors followed the same pattern). Desrousseaux's archaic interests, however, require that we question the extent to which such practices survived to the mid-nineteenth century. Yet there is evidence that, even if these practices fell into neglect, they were relayed by others—

---

[24]Desrousseaux, *Chansons* (1855), 2:202–3.

evidence stemming not only from Desrousseaux, but from less prominent songwriters as well.

From several songs (and other sources) we learn that puppet theater
was popular with Lille laborers.[25] Puppet shows were put on occasionally
by laborers who had learned the skill. They rented a cellar or café,
charged a sou admission, and put on a puppet play chosen from among
a highly restricted repertoire. Not children but adults made up the audience, and they could buy beer and food to consume in their cramped
seats. Everyone knew the plays by heart, and the crowd heckled and
harassed the puppets all through the play. Making puns on the lines was
particularly popular, and everyone waited for their favorite moments to
start up the teasing. Here is a passage from Descottignies's 1858 song,
"Le théâtre de César" ("Caesar's Theater"), describing a performance
of *Joseph vendu par ses frères* (*Joseph Sold by His Brothers*)—the story of
Jacob's son Joseph from the Bible.[26] Included in the account is a description of the usual points at which the crowd intervened:

> L'rideau s'lève et pou qu'mincher
> Les garchons d'Jacob sont in route
> Et faitt'nt l'complot que pindint l'nuit
> On j'ttra Joseph dins l'fond d'un puits.
> A l'plache de l'tuer, fort heureus'mint,
> Ruben, l'ainé des frères, décide
> Qui fait l'vinde un bon prix d'argint.
> L'marchand arrive et dit tout d'suite:
> Combien ch'qu'on vind ch'petit capon?
> —Deux doupe', un spectateur répond.
> ... Au 2ᵉ aque, on vot ch'garchon
> Chez Putiphar tout prés de s'femme:
> Ell' li caressot sin minton;
> Mais ch'benêt l'repoussot quand même.
> Dins l'caf' tout l'monde in veyant cha
> Crie: "Ell' l'ara point... Ell' l'ara!"
> Pindant qu'Joseph chez Pharaon
> Est in train d'li conter ses rèfes
> On intind dir' par un garchon
> "Te trann', comm' si t'avos les fièfes!"
> Et crac, i jett' su s'tiete d'bos
> Eunn' poir' cuit' qui l'retint su l'dos.
> ... Au 4ᵃ aque, Benjamin
> Veut s'in aller s'trouver ses frères
> Et l'père Jacob, qui s'crot malin,
> Répond chez pérol's singulières:

[25] See Pierrard, *Chansons*, pp. 230–33.
[26] Cited in ibid., p. 232.

"Allons, mon fils, allons ver eux."
Là-dessus chacun crie: "Eh! véreux!"
...l'dernier aqu n'a point pu s'finir
Tell'mint quis s'faijot du tapache;
Veyant cha, César a dû v'nir
Pinsint l'calmer par sin partache.
Mais l'voix de Joseph qu'il a gardé
Est caus' que l'tapache a r'doublé.

The curtain goes up and there we find
Jacob's sons on the road;
They are plotting to throw Joseph
Into a well during the night.
Instead of killing him, thank goodness,
Reuben the eldest brother decides
To sell him at a good price.
The merchant arrives and asks at once:
"How much for that little squirt?"
"Two cents," a spectator replies.
...In the second act, we see the boy
At Potiphar's quite close to his wife
Who caresses his chin;
But that simpleton rejects her anyway.
In the café everyone, seeing this,
Cries out: "She won't get him...Yes she will!"
While Joseph is with the pharaoh
Trying to explain his dreams
We hear a boy who says
"You look as though you've got a fever!"
And pow, he throws on his wooden head
A cooked pear which sticks to his back.
...In the fourth act, Benjamin
Wants to go find his brothers
And father Jacob, who thinks he is clever,
Responds with these singular words:
"Let us go, my son; Let us go toward them."
Thereupon all cry out "Huh! Wormy!"*
...The last act is impossible to finish
So loud was the ruckus they made;
Seeing this, Caesar had to come out
Hoping to calm them down with an appearance.
But he still spoke with Joseph's voice
Which caused the noise to redouble.

There is another account of 1855 (not in song form) of a performance
of *Joseph vendu* in which, with slight variations, the same scenario of

*The pun is on *ver eux*, toward them, and *véreux*, wormy.

crowd interference unfolds, culminating in an appearance of the puppeteer from behind the stage when the animal noises and laughter have
become too loud for the play to continue.[27] In this case the audience
does not feign astonishment when he speaks with the same voice as
Joseph, but the puppeteer's mock harangue is deflected in an equally silly
direction when someone in the crowd cries out, "No smoking here!" The
puppeteer picks this up at once: "Yes, that's right, no smoking here, no
smoking, please!" Everyone busily puts out their pipes. But of course
there is no such rule. Then the puppeteer makes a long speech to the
crowd about their bad manners. (They are called, among other epithets,
"méchants bougres"—"dirty buggers.") Finally the play resumes.

Plays mentioned in other songs include *Robinson Crusoe*, *Richard sans
peur* (*Richard the Lion-Hearted*), *Jeanne d'Arc*, and *Phinard et Lydéric* (two
giants who lived in Flanders in a mythical past). Not only are audience
interventions integral to accounts of these other plays, but there are
indications that the puppeteers took considerable liberties with their
scripts, embellishing their stories with delightful and ridiculous asides
and puns.[28]

Farce, then, as an organized part of the community's life, was still very
much alive in the Second Empire, even though its form may have changed.
These collective, ritualized occasions of farce modeled in a pure form
the attitude toward life that pervades the whole dialect literature. It is
important not to make the mistake of seeing these puppet plays or the
throwing of Saint Nicolas into the canal or rhythmic applause with animal
noises as merely a number of amusing leisure-time customs of some
poorly educated workers. What must be held in mind is the organic
relationship between these kinds of collective practices and the pervasive
preference for lighthearted irony and indirection that laborer-songwriters displayed in dealing with the bleakest and most troubling elements
of their lives. Encoded in the farcical ritual was a profoundly moral
response to lives of deprivation and hardship, a response deemed better
than any of the alternatives.

Nor should it be supposed that this moral choice was apolitical in
nature, turning laborers away from direct efforts to remedy their political impotence. There is, first of all, evidence of at least one episode of
conflict that suggests laborers sometimes brought the spirit of farce into
the workplace and turned it on their employers. In the case in question,
laborers at several mills made repeated complaints that the work they
had been set was too hard. The piece rate would have to be raised. It
was during the boom of the early 1850s, and the laborers had some easy

[27]Louis Vermesse, *L'amusement d'un lillois* (Lille, 1855), pp. 16–24.
[28]See, for example, Desrousseaux, "Les marionnettes," in *Chansons* (1865), 1:127–31, or
Gustave Bizard, "Le théâtre impérial" (Lille, 1870), BN, Ye 971 (27).

successes. At one mill, laborers all pretended to go on strike and then returned, on two successive occasions. In another, half the laborers quit work and the other half stayed on; under the direction of one of their fellows they feigned a series of difficulties with the work, quitting in their turn, one at a time. In yet another mill, laborers played at lighting their pipes in air that was filled with explosive cotton dust. On two of these occasions they successfully provoked clerks and owners into giving them angry lectures on their behavior. How many other campaigns of this kind may have been waged in Lille-area mills is impossible to know; history knows of this one only because luck has preserved some fragmentary reports.[29]

When the empire was proclaimed in 1852, one songwriter recounts, the prefect mounted a stand in the square and read the news out "d'un bon coeur" (with a good heart); a banquet followed, described in the song as "un diner à l'fourchette" (a dinner with forks). The songwriter's judgment on this affair is summed up in a single phrase: "D'parler politique / L'saison est passée" (for talk of politics / The season has now ended).[30] Here was another understated irony that passed by the police censors unnoticed and speaks of a lively interest in political affairs.

Once the empire had fallen and freedom of speech was gradually reestablished under a republican government, politics in fact became a favorite topic for songwriters. The development of the literature is more difficult to follow after 1870 because no one has done for this period the searching and collating that Pierrard has carried out for the 1850s and 1860s. Nonetheless, one may trace the laborers as they test the waters, so to speak, to see if they are safe in the early 1870s. Their attitude toward the new republic was far from unreservedly positive, to judge from a number of songs that deal with the end of excise taxes in 1873. These taxes had been instituted on coffee, chickory, and other items of common consumption to help pay off the indemnity owed to the Prussians following the war. The lifting of these taxes was a cause of celebration, as explained in Louis Longret's "Le dègrèvement de la chicorèe" ("The Abolition of the Chickory Tax"):

> In buvant de l'bonne chique
> Assis au coin d'min fu
> J'crie: viv' la République!
> L'impot est disparu.

---

[29] William M. Reddy, "The Batteurs and the Informer's Eye: A Labor Dispute under the French Second Empire," *History Workshop Journal*, no. 7 (Spring 1979): 30–44.
[30] Anonymous, untitled (Lille, n.d.), BN, Ye 7182 (171).

Drinking good old chickory
Sitting in the corner by the fire
I yell, Long Live the Republic!
The tax has finally expired.[31]

Empire or no empire, the songwriters of Lille still prefer the light touch—
so light one wonders if it is really there.

After the consolidation of the republican government and the re-
pulsing of the monarchists late in the 1870s, the laborers' attitude became
for a time frankly positive—that is, if we may judge from an 1879 Tourcoing song called "La république." The decline of the monarchist parties
is openly applauded:

> T'cheu bonheur
> Pour ach'teur
> Pu d'bétisse
> Eu d'royalisse
> Ché compris
> Din l'esprit
> Qu'in s'ra Républit'chin sa vie.

> Happiness is here
> For as of now
> No more mischief
> No more monarchism
> It's understood
> In the minds of all
> We are republicans for life.

This song reveals particular appreciation for the free flow of information
and freedom of expression that the republic brought with it and calls
on workers to open their eyes to the world:

> In République, in a de l'chance
> Eu d'savoir chin qui s'pass in France
> Pour vir claire, y n'faut pu d'ékance...
> Eu j'vous d'mande à quo qu'cha sert
> Eu d'dormir eu d'su l'ouvrage
> Y vaut mi les zis ouverts...

> Under a republic, we have the chance
> To know what's going on in France
> To see clearly, you no longer need an écang*...

[31](Lille, n.d.), BN, Ye 971 (404).
*Tool for separating linen fiber from the stem of flax.

I ask you what good is it
To sleep, bent over your work
Better to keep your eyes open....[32]

But in the Lille area as elsewhere, the disillusionments of the 1880s and the failure of Boulangism led to a massive turn toward the socialist parties in the 1890s. This too is reflected in dialect songs. Indeed, the rise of socialism may be considered the most significant challenge the dialect songwriters had faced since the earlier outburst of enthusiasm for songwriting in 1848. For the first time socialism called on the laborers to forgo their removed, ironic stance and to speak openly of their sufferings, their political feelings, and their aspirations. This deserves a moment of attention, even though the material stemming from that period has not been sufficiently explored to warrant firm conclusions.

Review of some songs that have survived from the 1890s uncovers three significant developments. First of all, the Desrousseaux tradition was kept alive for the new generation by younger prominent songwriters, the best known of these being Jules Watteeux of Tourcoing, known as Le Broutteux.[33] His themes remained the classic ones—coffee, marriage troubles, memories of childhood. At the same time numerous anonymous writers carried on the carnival and café song tradition; the contrast between their style and Le Broutteux's remaining much the same as that between their predecessors and the most self-conscious archaizing of Desrousseaux. There were shifts in the tone of these songs, but it would be premature at this point to attempt to characterize them. Finally, a group of songwriters began composing on socialist-inspired themes. There can be no doubt that they had the hardest row to hoe. The tradition offered them no hint of how to proceed; subtle irony had little place in the tough, intransigent style of Jules Guesde, whose socialist Parti ouvrier français had won widespread support in the Nord's mill towns by the early 1890s. The very popularity of this blunt, passionate orator signals a significant shift in the laborers' outlook. His lieutenant, Gustave Delory, elected mayor of Lille in 1896, among his many other activities, operated the "Workers' Press," which printed a large proportion of the region's dialect songs. Among its products were numerous pieces on socialist themes. Many, perhaps most of them, dealt with current affairs—elections, poor relief, military service—and were therefore only of temporary interest. Several of these songs significantly are not in dialect at all, but are written in perfect French, such as "Pour la patrie" ("For the Fatherland"), an 1895 composition written about the plight of working-class

---

[32]Joseph Bonte (Tourcoing, 1879), BN, Ye 971 (433).
[33]Jules Watteeux, *Chansons, fables et pasquilles tourquennoises* (Tourcoing, 1883).

conscripts. "Tu dois partir . . . pour servir la France" (You must leave . . .
to serve France), the song remarks,

> Pendant ce temps ton père dans les fabriques
> Souffrant la faim, se meurt en travaillant
> En maudissant ces hommes politiques
> Qui lui ravirent son soutien, son enfant.

> During this time your father is in the factories
> Suffering from hunger, dies on the job
> While cursing those men of politics
> Who have stolen his support, his child.[34]

Socialist dialect songs never involve such combinations of sentiment and
political analysis as the French productions that sometimes came out of
Delory's press. When the same subject of military service was taken up
in a dialect song, for example, the treatment was more direct, based on
an uncomplicated moral egalitarianism, as in "L'actualité Roubaisienne"
("Now in Roubaix"):

> J'veurro bin connaite in patron
> Qui a été blessé à la d'jerre,
> O bin qui a perdu sin garchon
> Pindint sin service militaire,
> Dit's inne fo l'nom d'vos calotins
> Qui sont morts sur in champs d'bataille?
> Comme mi vous nin connichi nin
> Vous êt's inn' vrai bind' de canailles.

> I would like to know one boss
> Who's been wounded in a war,
> Or else who has lost his boy
> Doing his military service,
> Just for once tell me the names of you churchgoers
> Who have died on a field of battle.
> Like me, you can't think of one,
> You're nothing but a bunch of rascals.[35]

This is bitter in tone, and the dialect becomes more thick at just the
point where the bitterness is most extreme: "Comme mi vous nin con-
nichi nin" (like me, you can't think of one). But if we compare such a

---

[34]Note that the author of this song was a woman; Irenée Roumieux, "Pour la patrie"
(Tourcoing, 1895), BN, 4°, Ye pièce 483.
[35]Henri Therin, "L'actualité Roubaisienne" (Roubaix, 1895), BN, 4°, Ye pièce 545.

piece with the products of the repressive days of the Second Empire, we must also admit that the literature has paid a price in cutting itself loose from its disingenuous irony. Having lost those moorings, it had not by 1900 found new ones. This is not to say that the price was not worth paying. Yet the laborers had much to learn about dealing directly with their social status.

There are a number of songs from the 1890s without explicit political references, written to be sung in the cafés for fun, but that also strike a sharper note, as in the song "L'expulsion des locataires" ("The Eviction of the Tenants") in which a landlord is decried for evicting a family after its head had lost his job.[36] Songs like this, if common, would be evidence for a general alteration of the songwriters' approach to suffering.[37]

This Third Republic material shows the dialect tradition prepared, even eager to deal with political issues, to wrestle with the problems of working-class life in a political context (once a vocabulary had been provided for doing so), to reach out for a wider point of view once freedom of speech was restored. But doing so involved an attempt to rework the farcical wisdom of the past, an attempt that underscores that this brand of wisdom had nothing to do with escapism or willful blindness to the oppressive conditions of working-class life.

Privation and insecurity, especially by comparison with the rest of society, was a central element of personal experience. But the laborers constantly wrestled with this experience, seeing it as a moral challenge, as something to be surmounted. The danger that privation might succeed in placing its stamp on the laborers' self-image was precisely what concerned them; they resisted this with might and main, as an inglorious and unworthy fate. The dialect literature conceals a cry of protest against the enduring and pervasive deprivation of working-class life, but one couched in positive terms. Within the literature the laborers were not merely deprived or impoverished, they were colorful, plucky, ironic, resourceful people who—by the way—had little money. They struggled, through the literature, at once to deny the vision of themselves as demoralized proletarians that the larger society had constructed and to resist within their own lives the temptation to brood upon their lack of money. This struggle so deeply marks the literature that we must resist seeing the literature as a reflection in any direct way of the way of life of the time. Instead, these songs and poems represent an effort to transform (not reflect) their lives, to transcend poverty and to counter the demeaning gaze of the better-off. It is only in this deeper sense, as the

[36]Anonymous (Lille, 1895), BN, 4°, Ye pièce 506.
[37]Greater clarity on all these matters will now emerge with the publication of Laurent Marty's book, *Chanter pour survivre: Culture ouvrière, travail et techniques dans le textile Roubaix, 1850–1914* (Roubaix, 1982), which has just reached me.

battleground of this struggle, that the literature reveals anything directly about them.

One may reserve judgment on whether light irony is actually the best way of dealing with grinding poverty and political disfranchisement. But this is not really the issue here. One may question whether all the laborers of Lille were equally enthusiastic in their commitment to the ethos of the songs and the farcical ritual. Doubtless they were not. But there can be little question what that ethos was or why it crystallized in a period of political dictatorship and stunning industrial expansion. The self-confidence of the employers and the government in the 1850s and early 1860s was unchallengeable; the enjoyment of the simplest civil liberties seemed an impossible dream. The dialect and its farcical traditions lived on, in a vacuum of alternatives. There were no press, no literate middle-class leaders, no religious life, no theater, no novels, no public speaking, no organizational form of any kind left to this community except the song and the singing club. If life was to be made good (or even just bearable), if collective reflection was to continue at all, it would be through this literature as it had come down from the past. No wonder it was suddenly infused with such vibrant new energy and vivid new meanings. No wonder the old irony was put to such unexpected uses. The laborers took what came to hand and did their best to make whole human identities out of it. In this, how do they differ from any of us?

14

Reinterpreting Capitalist Industrialization: A Study of Nineteenth-Century France

RONALD AMINZADE

Proletarianization, Small-Scale Industry, and Capitalist Industrialization

Accounts of capitalist industrialization have often emphasized the way industrial growth helped to create a propertyless wage-labor force by increasingly dispossessing producers of the means of production. "The capitalist system," wrote Karl Marx, "presupposes the complete separation of the laborers from all property in the means by which they can realize their labor.... The process, therefore, that clears the way for the capitalist system, can be none other than the process which takes away from the laborer the possession of his means of production; a process that transforms, on the one hand, the social means of subsistence and of production into capital, on the other, the immediate producers into wage labourers."[1] According to most accounts, a key facet of this process of dispossession, or proletarianization, during the nineteenth century

Erik Olin Wright and Michael Burawoy were unrelenting in their efforts to correct errors contained in an earlier draft. This essay has also benefited from insightful comments by Janet Blackman, Stuart Blumin, Keith Neild, Christopher Johnson, Steven Kaplan, Richard Lachmann, Yves Lequin, Mary Jo Maynes, and Charles Tilly. This chapter is part of a larger research project on political protest and capitalist development in nineteenth-century France. I am grateful to the National Endowment for the Humanities and the University of Wisconsin–Madison Research Committee for providing funding for this research.

[1] Karl Marx, *Capital*, ed. Frederick Engles (New York, 1967), 1:714–15.

was the decline of small-scale household and handicraft production. Faced with growing competition from new forms of capitalist production, like the factory, increasing numbers of small-scale master artisans were forced to close up shop and, along with their journeymen and apprentices, join the growing ranks of the propertyless wage-labor force. The general assumption in the literature on industrialization has been that small-scale household and handicraft workshops were static traditional forms that rapidly gave way to more modern forms of capitalist industry.

Recent research by economic historians of nineteenth-century Europe has reassessed the role of small-scale artisanal workshops in the process of capitalist industrialization and challenged the view that such enterprises were inefficient units of production destined to be rapidly supplanted by more efficient, large-scale, centralized, mechanized units. "Capitalist growth," writes Raphael Samuels of nineteenth-century England, "was rooted in a subsoil of small-scale enterprise." After documenting the persistence of nonmechanized, small-scale, labor-intensive production in a wide variety of different industries, Samuels concludes that industrial production based on "the primacy of labor power" and on the "strength, skill, quickness, and sureness of touch of the individual worker rather than on the simultaneous and repetitive operations of the machine" was the "dominant pattern of growth" in Victorian England.[2] In his analysis of British industrialization, Gareth Stedman Jones challenged the classical Marxist assumption of a nearly automatic relationship between industrialization and increases in the scale of production and organic composition of capital. In nineteenth-century Britain, he writes, "because labor was plentiful and cheap and demand was fashion-prone, in addition to being seasonally and cyclically variable, increasing demand was met by the addition of new units of production rather than by economies of scale; and new technology was capital- rather than labor-saving."[3]

Historical studies of nineteenth-century French industrialization have also emphasized the persistence and vitality of small-scale units of artisanal production. Patrick O'Brien and Caglar Keyder have documented very high levels of labor productivity in many industrial sectors that remained dominated by small-scale nonmechanized artisanal enterprises.[4] T. J. Markovitch's quantitative study of nineteenth-century French

---

[2]Raphael Samuels, "Workshop of the World: Steam Power and Hand Technology in Mid-Victorian Britain," *History Workshop*, no. 3 (Spring 1977): 8.

[3]Gareth Stedman Jones, "The Mid-Century Crisis and the 1848 Revolutions," *Theory and Society* 12, no. 4 (July 1983): 505–19.

[4]O'Brien and Keyder explain the strength of small-scale labor-intensive industrial production in nineteenth-century France, relative to Britain, in terms of the slower rate of urbanization, the segmented nature of the French domestic market and low proportion of industrial output sold abroad, and the higher proportion of consumers with "middling

industrialization found that small-scale household and handicraft production together accounted for a majority of French industrial output (59.9 percent) and employed the majority of French workers engaged in industry (70–75 percent) during the middle decades of the nineteenth century.[5]

The vitality and persistence of small-scale artisanal production suggests that although proletarianization, or dispossession of the means of production, may have been a central feature of the overall process of capitalist development, it was not the only means by which labor became subordinated to capital during the course of nineteenth-century European industrial development.[6] Throughout this process of industrialization, many master artisans in household and handicraft production retained ownership of their small workshops, and journeymen still owned the small tools they needed to ply their trades. This chapter argues that an understanding of how capitalist industrialization transformed class relations and antagonisms during the course of the nineteenth century requires that we look not only at the dispossession of workers from the means of production, but also at various other strategies of capital accumulation, such as control over raw materials, credit, labor recruitment, work organization, and product markets.

This research analyzes internal changes in class relations within small-scale household and handicraft production in France. During the course of the nineteenth century, owners of capital and employers of labor in small-scale industry pursued a variety of different strategies of capital accumulation. These strategies, designed to enhance profitability, did not necessarily entail the complete dispossession of workers from the means of production. They did involve important changes in class relations between merchant capitalists, master artisans, and journeymen producers—changes that brought an increasing subordination of labor to capital.

Although historians have documented the tenacity of household and handicraft production, they have shown relatively little concern with how class relations within these older forms of production were changed by their ties to an emergent capitalist order.[7] The best case studies of

---

incomes" who cared about high quality and design. In other words, they emphasize market factors but fail to explore how the changing character of production relations within household and handicraft industry may have contributed to the vitality and persistence of small-scale production. Patrick O'Brien and Caglar Keyder, *Economic Growth in Britain and France, 1780–1914* (London, 1978), pp. 164–67.

[5]T. J. Markovitch, "Le revenu industriel et artisanal sous la monarchie de juillet et le second empire," in *Economies et sociétés*, AF-8 (Paris, 1967), pp. 79, 85, 87.

[6]The term industry refers to the manufacture of commodities, even when this took place in "nonindustrial" forms of work organization like household and handicraft production.

[7]Important efforts to explore this issue with respect to household production have been made by Pat Hudson, "Proto-industrialization: The Case of the West Riding Wool Textile

nineteenth-century French artisans have explored the consequences of the movement of artisans into factories during the latter decades of the century.[8] Rather than analyzing the movement of artisans from workshops or households into factories, my research examines the changes that took place within handicraft and household workshops during the middle decades of the nineteenth century. My central argument is that these older forms of production were not simply vestiges of a precapitalist past that were destined to be rapidly eliminated or superseded by capitalist factory production; rather, they were linked in new ways to an emergent capitalist system and were internally changed. These internal changes, including the growing power of merchant capitalist entrepreneurs and of nascent capitalist artisanal masters, were an important part of early capitalist industrialization.

I shall begin with a brief discussion of the dominant features of household and handicraft production in nineteenth-century France and the different class relations that characterized these two different forms of urban artisanal production. I shall then proceed to case studies of the silk ribbon household weavers of Saint-Etienne and the handicraft artisans of Toulouse. These two cases were selected because they represent the two most important forms of small-scale industry in nineteenth-century France—household and handicraft production. Each case study begins with a discussion of the character of each form of production at the beginning of the nineteenth century and then documents the major changes that took place during the course of the century. The final section discusses the theoretical implications of these two case studies.

Household and Handicraft Production
In Nineteenth-Century France

Recent research by economic historians has emphasized the important role of rural household production in European industrial development. "Before capital intensive manufacturing became dominant," writes Charles Tilly, "Europe underwent substantial industrialization through

Industry in the 18th and 19th Centuries," *History Workshop* 12 (Autumn 1981): 34–57, and Harriet Friedman, "World Market, State, and Family Farm: Social Bases of Household Production in the Era of Wage Labor," *Comparative Studies in Society and History* 20, no. 4 (1978): 545–86. For a brilliant analysis of the changing class relations of mid-nineteenth-century Parisian handicraft tailors, see Christopher Johnson, "Economic Change and Artisan Discontent: The Tailors' History, 1800–1848," in *Revolution and Reaction*, ed. Roger Price (New York, 1975), pp. 87–114.

[8]See Michael Hanagan, *The Logic of Solidarity* (Urbana, Ill., 1980), and Joan W. Scott, *The Glassworkers of Carmaux: French Craftsmen and Political Action in a Nineteenth Century City* (Cambridge, Mass., 1974).

the multiplication of small producing units and modest capital concentration over the territory of rural regions organized around merchantile cities."[9] This process, generally referred to as "protoindustrialization," has been carefully researched in recent years by a number of scholars.[10] The term "protoindustrialization" is a misnomer to the extent that it implies that rural household production was everywhere a prelude to modern industry. In some industries, like cotton textiles, rural household production served as a transitional stage on the road to modern industry, whereas in others, like mining and steel, there was no such connection, since these producer-goods industries were dependent upon the derived demand created by an earlier phase of industrial growth. In some areas of rural household production, like Languedoc, "devolutionary patterns" occurred, with protoindustrialization followed by deindustrialization.[11] Research in this field has emphasized the key role of dispersed rural household production in generating the propertyless wage-labor force that eventually provided the basis for full-blown industrial capitalist development and the role of protoindustrial merchant capitalists in the process of primitive capital accumulation.[12] Researchers on protoindustrialization have generally assumed that this was an exclusively rural form of production.[13] For example, Peter Kriedte defines protoindustrialization as "the development of rural regions in which a large part of the population lived entirely or to a considerable extent from industrial mass-production for interregional and international markets."[14] Because of the exclusive focus on rural production, there has been no effort to consider the applicability of insights derived from the protoindustrial model to groups of nineteenth-century urban household producers, like silk weavers, who played an important role in French working-class protest. The following case study of urban household silk weavers suggests that the central constraints and dynamics of capital accumula-

[9]Charles Tilly, "Flows of Capital and Forms of Industry in Europe, 1500–1900," *Theory and Society* 12 (1983): 11.

[10]The best review of this literature is provided by Peter Kriedtke, Hand Medick, and Jurgen Schlumbohn, *Industrialization before Industrialization*, trans. Beate Schempp (London, 1981).

[11]Charles Tilly, "Clio and Minerva," in *Theoretical Sociology*, ed. J. McKinney and E. Tiryakian (New York, 1970), pp. 433–66.

[12]Kriedte, Medick, and Schlumbohn, *Industrialization*; Tilly, "Flows of Capital."

[13]Charles Tilly offers a definition of protoindustrialization that explicitly allows for the existence of urban protoindustry. "Proto-industrialization," he writes, "is the increase in manufacturing activity by means of very small producing units and small to medium accumulations of capital." This definition, which focuses upon the deployment and accumulation of capital, is an improvement, but by emphasizing the size of production units rather than on the character of the capital/labor relationship, it prevents us from distinguishing between small-scale household, handicraft, and nonmechanized factory production; Tilly, "Flows of Capital," p. 8.

[14]Kriedte, Medick, and Schlumbohn, *Industrialization*, p. 6.

tion that have been documented for rural "protoindustry" were also features of urban household production.

Alongside rural and urban household production, the other major form of small-scale nonmechanized production in nineteenth-century France was the handicraft workshop. Although historians often combine these two forms of small-scale nonmechanized production under the label artisanal production, such a procedure tends to conflate distinctive forms of class relations. Nineteenth-century French artisans worked in diverse settings, ranging from nonmechanized factories to households to small workshops, each typically characterized by different class relations. The term artisan should be used to refer to skilled workers who exercised substantial control over recruitment into their trades and training, not to a particular form of production or a distinctive set of class relations. Artisanal masters in handicraft, household, and factory work teams all worked alongside the journeymen and apprentices they employed, but the internal organization of these different types of artisanal production differed, as did their connections to the emerging capitalist system.

Handicraft production, like urban household production, was based on artisanal labor, small accumulations of capital, hand tools, and the consumption of very small amounts of nonhuman power. In both forms of production, artisans worked intermittently, filling the workday with breaks, discussions, and singing. Despite a relatively limited division of labor and small dispersed units of production, both handicraft production and urban household production fostered strong occupational communities among workers, owing to the opportunity for extensive on-the-job interaction, a high level of skill that encouraged commitment to the trade, and an apprenticeship period that socialized workers in craft traditions and occupational subcultures.

Although handicraft production displayed a number of similarities to urban household production, there were important differences in the role of family members in production and in the character of class relations. Unlike household production, handicraft production was not based on the household or family. Skilled male workers engaged in production, and women and children typically provided auxiliary services, such as cleaning the shop, dealing with customers, or keeping the books. The role of merchant capital in the organization of production also differed significantly in handicraft industry. Although merchant capitalists made increasing inroads into handicraft production during the course of the nineteenth century, they were by no means close to attaining the important role played by merchant capitalists in urban household production. In most handicraft trades, the majority of masters sold their finished products to local consumers, although in those trades where production was geared to a wider regional or national market, the master artisan typically relied upon merchant capitalists for distribution. Those handicraft industries, like carriage making or construction, that required the assembling of diverse groups of workers with different skills and trade organizations often relied upon merchant capitalists for credit or raw materials or both. Other handicraft industries that produced for a local market and employed workers within only one trade typically utilized only the capital of small masters.

Urban handicraft and household production were not static traditional forms that simply disappeared in the face of competition from more efficient units of factory production. In both cases, capitalist development produced important internal changes in the character of class relations—between master weavers and merchants in urban household production and between journeymen and masters in handicraft industry. Both forms of production experienced important changes during the course of the nineteenth century that were not connected to proletarianization, mechanization, or the movement into factory settings. The following sections document these changes in the household silk ribbon industry of Saint-Etienne and the handicraft industries of Toulouse.

Industrial Capitalist Development and Household Production at Saint-Etienne

Saint-Etienne expanded from a small city of 24,342 inhabitants at the beginning of the nineteenth century[15] to the seventh largest city in France by 1872, with a population of 110,814. Unlike other major cities in France at that time, Saint-Etienne had not been an important center of commerce, administration, or handicraft industry before the nineteenth century. Situated in the Stéphanois basin, alongside the industrial towns of Rive-de-Gier and Saint-Chamond, Saint-Etienne became a major center of coal mining and steel production during the nineteenth century. The growth of the city, however, was less a product of the development of capital-intensive steam-powered heavy industries than of small-scale units of handicraft metal and arms production and, especially, of household silk ribbon production.

Labor-force statistics for the entire Stéphanois region reveal the continuing importance of the silk industry, despite the growth of mining and steel. Silk workers remained the largest segment of the region's

[15]This figure includes the four adjacent suburban communes of Valbenoite, Outre-Furens, Montaud, and Beaubrun, which were annexed to the city in 1855. The city itself had only 16,259 inhabitants in 1801. Etienne Fournial, *Saint-Etienne: Histoire de la ville et de ses habitants* (Roanne, 1976), p. 232.

working class by 1872, numbering 40,000 to 45,000 individuals, compared with 3,000 hardware producers (*quincailleurs*), 4,900 artisanal arms producers, 5,000 workers in the government arms factory, 16,700 coal miners, and 12,000 workers in heavy metallurgy.[16]

The predominance of silk workers was even greater in the city of Saint-Etienne, which contained a relatively small number of miners and steelworkers. Silk ribbon workers in the city and adjacent suburbs numbered approximately 12,500 in 1825–27 and nearly 20,000 by 1851,[17] while workers in the city's four other major industries—hardware, armaments, mining, and heavy metallurgy—numbered approximately 7,400 in 1828 and 13,716 by 1848–51.[18] In a letter of May 1833 to local silk ribbon merchants, the leaders of Saint-Etienne's master silk ribbon weaver's association estimated that their industry employed at least half of the city's labor force.[19] In August of 1839, the mayor of Saint-Etienne declared that the "ribbon industry employs two-thirds of our working-class population."[20]

The silk ribbon weavers of Saint-Etienne were engaged in urban household production. Work took place in the household, with family labor usually supplemented by several journeymen and/or apprentices.[21] Master ribbon weavers received silk thread from the merchant or his agent as well as cardboard patterns for the Jacquard looms. The master's wife or daughter typically wound thread on spools while a skilled journeyman threaded the warp and the master, along with another worker or family member, wove the ribbon. The master weaver owned the loom and paid the costs of production, including rent, heat, lighting, and maintenance, but he typically worked on raw materials belonging to the merchant capitalist.[22] The typical ribbon weaving household workshop

[16]J. Schnetzler, *Les industries et les hommes dans la région de St.-Etienne* (Saint-Etienne, 1975), p. 78. Yves Lequin, *Les ouvriers de la région lyonnaise (1848–1914)*, 2 vols. (Lyons, 1977), 1:33.
[17]Fournial, *Saint-Etienne*, p. 203; Lequin, *Ouvriers*, 1:36–37. Gonnard estimates their number at only 8,000 in 1833–34. These different estimates may depend on whether the authors included the four suburban communes in their calculations and on the sharp yearly fluctuations in the ribbon industry, which experienced boom and bust years. Philippe Gonnard, "Les passementiers de Saint-Etienne en 1833," *Revue d'historie de Lyon* (1907): 2.
[18]Lequin, *Ouvriers*, 1:33, 36–37, 40–41; Fournial, *Saint-Etienne*, pp. 198–204; L. J. Gras, *Historie économique de la metallurgie de la Loire* (Saint-Etienne, 1908), p. 232.
[19]Office du travail, *Les associations professionnelles ouvrières* (Paris, 1899), 1:342–43.
[20]Fournial, *Saint-Etienne*, p. 203.
[21]George Sheridan's study of household silk weaving at Lyons found that during the crisis of the 1860s many household producers managed to remain viable by shifting away from wage labor and increasing the employment of family labor. George J. Sheridan, "Household and Craft in an Industrializing Economy: The Case of the Silk Weavers of Lyons," in *Consciousness and Class Experience in Nineteenth Century Europe*, ed. John Merriman (New York, 1979), pp. 107–28.
[22]Maxime Perrin, *La région industrielle de Saint-Etienne* (Tours, 1937), pp. 275–80.

contained one to four looms; there the master, his family, and three or four hired helpers worked.[23] Wives, daughters, and sons played an important part in the production process.[24]

Master silk weavers owned their means of production—the looms— but were dependent upon merchant capitalists to provide raw materials and to sell their products on interregional and international markets. Ribbon merchants did not hire wage laborers directly, and the organization of the work process remained under the control of the household producer. Merchants did not own looms, except for the small looms used to create sample patterns and new designs, and they typically kept small inventories and produced on short order. If the demand for silk ribbons suddenly dropped, as often happened in this luxury goods industry, merchant capitalists did not have to bear the cost of fixed capital. Ribbon merchants required relatively small amounts of capital, since the time lag between the purchase of raw materials and the sale of ribbons was not great, and fixed capital costs were negligible. The main use of capital was as collateral for advances from silk merchants.

During the eighteenth century, Saint-Etienne's distance from Lyons, the center of the French silk industry, compared with other silk ribbon centers like Saint-Chamond, favored the growth of the ribbon industry by making the enforcement of guild regulations very difficult, thereby attracting workers and merchant capitalists.[25] Whereas the rural silk weavers of the Stéphanois region generally produced plain ribbons *(unis)*, Saint-Etienne's producers specialized in fancier patterned brocaded ribbons *(faconnés)* that required more highly skilled labor. The weaving of ribbons became increasingly concentrated in the city of Saint-Etienne during the course of the eighteenth century, while other branches of the production process, like the reeling, spinning, and dyeing of silk, remained dispersed throughout the surrounding countryside.

During the first half of the nineteenth century, Saint-Etienne's silk ribbon industry grew extremely rapidly, despite sharp year-to-year fluctuations and frequent crises—in 1829–31, 1834–37, and 1846–48. Household production at Saint-Etienne and handicraft production at

[23]Gonnard, "Passementiers," p. 2, estimates an average of four workers per ribbon master at Saint-Etienne in 1832–33.

[24]Bonnefous observed that at Saint-Etienne "one no longer finds any women who know how to sew, since most of them have been working since infancy at cutting ribbons, preparing spools and warps, reeling, and the thousands of details of this industry." Women also typically took the finished ribbons to the merchant capitalist's warehouse, where they negotiated prices with clerks while their husbands remained at the looms. The local labor arbitration board *(conseil des prud'hommes)* routinely accepted testimony from women in disputes between masters and merchants; Eugene Bonnefous, *Histoire de St.-Etienne et de ses environs* (Saint-Etienne, 1851), pp. 400, 428.

[25]L. J. Gras, *Historie de la rubanerie et des industries de la soie à St.-Etienne et dans la région stéphanoise* (Saint-Etienne, 1906), p. 53.

Toulouse both experienced rapid growth in output and in the numbers of workers employed during the early and middle decades of the nineteenth century. In both cases this growth was uneven and marked by frequent crises. Whereas the economic expansion of silk ribbon production at Saint-Etienne was tied to the growth of an international market, the expansion of handicraft production at Toulouse was a result of increasing local consumer demand for food, clothing, and housing owing to the city's rapid population growth. The rapid growth of silk ribbon production allowed Saint-Etienne's merchant capitalists to amass great fortunes in a relatively short time[26] and ribbon merchants became the wealthiest segment of the city's bourgeoisie. There were 115 merchant capitalists (*fabricants*) in the ribbon industry in 1816, 172 in 1830, 200 by 1835, 220 in May of 1839, and 350 during the prosperous year of 1856.[27]

Although urban household silk ribbon weaving at Saint-Etienne differed from rural household weaving in relying heavily upon journeymen and apprentice wage laborers working alongside family members, the constraints and dynamics of capital accumulation that characterized urban and rural household production were the same. The central contradiction within the silk ribbon industry of Saint-Etienne was common the "protoindustrial" organization of production in general. Merchant capital remained in the sphere of circulation, not production, and this inhibited the ability of merchants to prevent thefts of raw materials[28] and to increase production during periods of peak demand. Local ribbon merchants persistently complained about the theft of thread (*piquage d'once*) and the artificial weighting or stretching of thread by weavers. Raw materials were very expensive, accounting for approximately two-thirds of the cost of production.[29] There was a large underground market in stolen silk thread at Saint-Etienne despite harsh penalties[30] and persistent efforts by merchants and local police. There were scandals in 1819 and 1837 when prominent merchants were convicted for dealing in stolen silk thread. In 1844 and again in 1858, the city's ribbon mer-

---

[26]David Gordon, "Industrialization and Republican Politics: The Bourgeois of Reims and Saint-Etienne under the Second Empire," in *French Cities in the Nineteenth Century*, ed. John Merriman (New York, 1981), pp. 117–38.

[27]Fournial, *Saint-Etienne*, pp. 203–4.

[28]This phenomenon, argues Clawson, "must be understood in the context of workers' traditional rights to a part of the product of their labor." Dan Clawson, *Bureaucracy and the Labor Process* (New York, 1980), p. 45.

[29]Gras, *Histoire de la rubanerie*, p. 144, estimates the cost of production in 1784 at 66.5 percent for raw materials costs, 16.5 percent for labor, 2.5 percent for dyeing, and 14.5 percent for merchants' profits.

[30]During the eighteenth century these penalties were especially harsh. In 1769 a woman convicted of stealing silk thread was publicly whipped, branded, and imprisoned for life for her crime; Gras, *Histoire de la rubanerie*, p. 87.

chants formed an association to prevent silk theft.[31] During the years from 1858 to 1870, twenty-four persons were convicted of silk theft at Saint-Etienne.[32]

The other key obstacle to capital accumulation faced by ribbon merchants was the backward-sloping labor supply curve that characterized protoindustrial production. During periods of expansion, when changes in style often meant great profits for the supplier who could bring the new product to market first, merchants were unable to force weavers to work longer hours. Increasing the rates paid for finished products to stimulate greater production often led to a reduction in output, with workers responding by increasing their leisure and maintaining rather than increasing their incomes. Reducing the amount paid for finished products was not a feasible solution, since workers might move to other merchants at a time when high prices demanded maximum production. In October 1849 Saint-Etienne's police commissioner complained to the prefect that although the ribbon industry was very active, merchants are refusing many orders because "the workers refuse to allow anyone to work past 7:00 P.M.," even though "the prices paid to them for their ribbons are more than double what they received one year ago!"[33]

One way merchant capitalists might overcome these obstacles to capital accumulation was provided by the factory. The centralization of production into factories offered employers greater control over hours of work, greater supervision of the use of raw materials, and increased supervision of the labor process. The creation of silk-weaving factories, however, faced two problems. First, high fixed capital costs were an important impediment in industries like silk textiles, where a volatile market for luxury goods provided a great incentive to minimize them. The extreme volatility of the product market thus discouraged merchant capitalists from attempting to seize control of the labor process or to set up factories, despite the tremendous problems that their lack of control of the labor process posed during periods of peak demand. Investing in looms and factories would have shifted the cost of adjusting to frequent cyclical movements within the industry from the ribbon weavers to the merchants. Second, when merchant capitalists did attempt to set up silk-weaving factories, this generated intense worker resistance. In 1829 a factory using eighteen steam- and water-powered looms was established at Bourg-Argental by the merchant Chazelles. It closed down in 1831 amid reports that the workers engaged in "disputes and quarrels every day and insisted that it was not possible to achieve a gentle enough

[31]Ibid., p. 191.
[32]Ibid., p. 194.
[33]Archives départmentales de la Loire (hereafter ADL), 10M 31.

movement of the loom except by hand."[34] Another attempt by the ribbon merchant Hippolyte Royet to set up a ribbon-weaving factory at La Seauve in 1830 also failed. A number of ribbon merchants did business with the city's six convent workshops. Although these workshops used handlooms, they resembled a factory setting in terms of the scale of production and the strict work discipline imposed on poorly paid adolescent workers by the nuns who directed production.[35]

The one branch of the city's ribbon industry that did witness the early growth of nonmechanized factories was velvet ribbon weaving. Because the market for velvet ribbons was less subject to style changes and market fluctuations,[36] merchant capitalists were much less hesitant to make fixed capital investments in this sector of the industry. During the first three decades of the nineteenth century, velvet ribbon weaving became an established industry at Saint-Etienne, and by 1833–34 there were thirty velvet ribbon merchants who owned four hundred looms and employed three hundred workers.[37] These looms, which cost 1,000 to 1,200 francs each, were owned by wealthy merchants, with master weavers serving as workers/foremen in the small manufactories where velvet ribbon weaving took place.[38] By 1855 there were 3,000 velvet ribbon looms in the city and over two thousand velvet ribbon weavers. The development of this branch of the industry involved merchants' rather than master weavers ownership of the means of production.

Despite the growth of velvet-weaving factories, the vast majority of Saint-Etienne's silk ribbon weavers remained employed in households, working on handlooms owned by master weavers. Household production, however, underwent important changes during the nineteenth century, changes that altered the balance of class power between merchant

[34]Gras, *Histoire de la rubanerie*, p. 364. Schnetzler, *Industries*, p. 74.

[35]Dominque Vanoli, "Les couvents soyeux," *Révoltes logiques* 2 (1976): 19–39. The convent workshops were a constant source of complaints by the silk weavers of both Lyons and Saint-Etienne, and rumors of poor diets, dungeons, oppressive working conditions, and sexual perversion fueled the weavers' animosity. In the industrial survey (enquête) of 1848, Saint-Etienne's ribbon weavers denounced the workshops as submitting adolescent women to "the tortures of the Inquisition" and to the "most humiliating practices." See P. Guillaume, "La situation économique et sociale du département de la Loire d'après l'enquête sur le travail agricole et industriel de 25 Mai 1848," *Revue d'histoire moderne et contemporaine* 10 (1963): 19. In April 1848 crowds of workers attacked the workshops of Saint-Etienne and burned the convents' looms in large bonfires. Two weavers were shot dead by national guardsmen during these attacks, and many more were wounded. Archives nationales (hereafter AN), BB30 366; S. Bossakiewicz, *Histoire général de St.-Etienne* (Saint-Etienne, 1905), pp. 248–49.

[36]Gras, *Histoire de la rubanerie*, p. 844.

[37]Ibid., p. 596.

[38]Armand Audiganne, *Les populations ouvrières et les industries de la France* (New York, 1970), p. 89.

capitalists and master weavers. In particular, power tended to shift to-ward capitalists owing to the growing indebtedness of master weavers, increased merchant control over the preparatory and finishing stages of silk ribbon production, and the introduction of new nonmechanized handloom technologies. Let us examine each of these changes in turn.

The silk ribbon industry was dependent upon an international export market, subject to both seasonal fluctuations in demand and recurrent short-term crises. The irregularity of employment, which resulted from the succession of boom-and-bust periods, encouraged the growing in-debtedness of master weavers. During periods of prosperity, such as the years from 1818 to 1828 when many new arrivals from the countryside set themselves up as master weavers in Saint-Etienne, merchants often gave them a start by extending credit. This tied the master weaver to a particular merchant capitalist, a seemingly temporary dependence that could easily become permanent. Merchant capitalists often sought to expand their power by extending credit to small producers against un-finished products, thus obligating the master to sell to nobody else.

Merchants also increased their power by taking over the earlier stages of the ribbon production process, which had traditionally been the re-sponsibility of the master weaver. During the 1820s, the preparation of the warp (*l'ourdissage de la chaîne*) and the weft (*dividage des trames*) in-creasingly took place in the small workshops attached to merchants' warehouses.[39]

The introduction of new weaving technologies played an important role in the growing power of merchant capitalists. During the second half of the eighteenth century, the Zurich loom, or *métier à la barre*, was introduced from Switzerland. The new loom had a single wooden cross-bar that moved numerous shuttles loaded with thread, thus permitting the simultaneous production of sixteen to twenty-four ribbons.[40] The Swiss government prohibited export of the new looms under penalty of death, but they were nevertheless smuggled into France. The first Zurich looms were introduced into Saint-Etienne about 1769 by Swiss workers.[41] The high price of the new looms, which in 1788 cost 560 livres compared with only 5 livres for a single-ribbon loom, inhibited their adoption. In 1770, after a group of ribbon merchants from Saint-Etienne and Saint-Chamond complained to the finance minister about Swiss competition and requested government aid, the monarchy granted a subsidy of 560

---

[39]Gras, *Histoire de la rubanerie*, p. 420. The task of reeling the weft onto the bobbins (cannetage) remained the responsibility of the master weaver and was typically done by his wife.

[40]Schnetzler, *Industries*, p. 51.

[41]Gras, *Histoire de la rubanerie*, pp. 68–70, 847.

livres (70 livres a year for eight years) to encourage the introduction of the Zurich looms.[42] Initially the new looms could weave only plain silk ribbons (unis), not patterned ones, and this delayed their introduction into Saint-Etienne. At the end of the eighteenth century the Zurich loom was adapted to make patterned ribbons, and during the following decades the number of such looms in the Stéphanois region increased rapidly. By 1811 there were 2,600 Zurich looms in the region, accounting for 18.8 percent of all looms.[43] By 1828 the number of Zurich looms had increased to 5,000 or 21.4 percent of the region's looms. They accounted for a much larger percentage of the city's looms, since most of these multiribbon looms were set up there, not in the countryside.[44] During the following decades, the multiribbon métiers à barre completely replaced the single-ribbon looms, which disappeared entirely from the region by the early 1850s.[45]

The other major innovation in silk ribbon weaving was the development of the Jacquard loom, which produced designs automatically from a perforated cardboard pattern. This new handloom thus engendered an increased separation of conception and execution,[46] with merchant capitalists or, more typically, the skilled ribbon designers they employed creating designs that were punched into cardboard patterns that weavers simply followed. These new looms also made rapid design changes easier, thus allowing merchants to respond more quickly to market fluctuations. In 1815 the Jacquard loom was modified to produce brocade ribbons, and in 1818 it was altered to permit the simultaneous weaving of numerous ribbons.[47] Although most master weavers could not afford these new looms, which cost three to four times as much as the older looms, without becoming heavily indebted to merchant capitalists, the looms spread rapidly in the city after 1824. Masters were eager to acquire them because their lower labor costs and higher productivity enabled their owners to remain competitive. Those masters who continued to produce on the older single-ribbon looms were at a severe competitive disadvantage and were increasingly unable to continue producing at the lowered piece rates that merchants offered after the introduction of the new looms. In 1828 the number of Jacquard looms reached 1,225, or 5.2 percent of the region's 23,350 looms.[48] Since most of them were established in the city of Saint-Etienne, thereby producing an urbanization of household ribbon weaving, they accounted for a much larger per-

---

[42]Ibid., pp. 70–74.
[43]Ibid., p. 582.
[44]Ibid., p. 587.
[45]Audiganne, *Populations*, p. 90.
[46]Harry Braverman, *Labor and Monopoly Capital* (New York, 1974).
[47]Gras, *Histoire de la rubanerie*, pp. 293, 295.
[48]Fournial, *Saint-Etienne*, p. 206; Gras, *Histoire de la rubanerie*, p. 587.

centage of Saint-Etienne's looms. During the crisis years from 1829 to 1832, the number of Jacquard looms in the region nearly doubled, reaching 2,000, or 8.7 percent of all looms in the region, by 1832. By 1840 there were 5,000 Jacquard looms in the region, and by 1855 the 9,000 Jacquard looms accounted for 60 percent of the region's 15,500 looms.[49]

What were the main effects of these new looms? Because they were still powered by hand, not water or steam, their spread did not transform the household organization of silk ribbon weaving. Nor did it mean the displacement of men by women and children, because the new looms required great physical strength. Activating the Zurich loom required moving a large wooden crossbar weighing as much as 250 kilograms. The spread of the Zurich and Jacquard looms did vastly increase the productivity of silk ribbon weavers and generate a sharp drop in the piece rates merchants offered.[50] The Jacquard looms also produced a deskilling of the labor force as designing ribbons became the province of the merchants and their hired designers rather than of master weavers. Although the growth of the Zurich and Jacquard looms did not result in loss of ownership of the means of production by master weavers, it did produce growing indebtedness. The high cost of the Jacquard looms, which included paying for reinforced floors and ceilings, increased the financial dependence of household producers upon merchant capitalists. Contracts between masters and merchants regarding the purchase of new looms often included the provision that for a specified period the master would produce only for the merchant who financed the purchase of the loom. In the 1848 survey (*enquête*) of the city's silk ribbon industry, weavers contested the accuracy of the term fabricant, or producer, used to designate merchant capitalists. They denied any productive role for the industry's merchants and argued that their role was primarily a financial one, characterizing the ribbon merchant as "a man who has money or credit."[51]

The economic crisis of the Second Empire (1851–70) further altered the balance of power between labor and capital by fostering the development of factory-based silk weaving. During the years from 1830 to 1856 silk ribbon production at Saint-Etienne expanded rapidly, despite severe crises in 1829–32, 1834–37, and 1846–48. Beginning in 1857, however, the industry experienced a severe depression, owing to a silkworm disease that produced a sharp rise in the price of raw materials, the oversupply of the American market, the financial panic in the United States, which was soon felt in Europe, and the new fashions' abandon-

[49]Fournial, *Saint-Etienne*, p. 206; Lequin, *Ouvriers*, 1:33.
[50]Gras, *Histoire de la rubanerie*, p. 595.
[51]Guillaume, "Situation," p. 14.

ment of silk ribbons.[52] During the early 1860s, increasing competition from mechanized ribbon production in England and Switzerland, the loss of the United Stated market during the Civil War, and high tariffs on United States imports of ribbons after the war exacerbated the crisis.[53] "The ribbon industry is seriously threatened," wrote the city's highest-ranking judicial official (*procureur imperial*) in December 1859. "Foreign competition has made rapid progress and each day the situation at Saint-Etienne worsens. The fabricants are beginning to realize that this is no longer a case of a crisis that will pass but of a real displacement. Ten thousand workers have already left the city to seek work elsewhere."[54] As in the 1829–32 crisis, some employers responded to the crisis by introducing factory conditions and, in the case of velvet ribbon weaving, by mechanizing production. The intensified competitive pressures facing merchants provided a strong incentive to eliminate the cost of silk theft and increase productivity in these ways. The number of mechanized looms in the Stéphanois region increased from 600 in 1860 to 1,000 in 1872. A mechanized steam-powered ribbon factory (*l'usine Giron*) was established at Saint-Etienne during the 1860s.[55]

The preceding account of the development of silk ribbon production in Saint-Etienne reveals that urban household industry, despite its reliance upon both family and wage labor, shared similar contradictions and constraints on accumulation with rural "protoindustry." The account documents the persistence of the household form of production despite important changes in production techniques. It also points to important shifts in the balance of class power despite continuing ownership of the looms by master artisans and shows the importance of periods of economic crisis and working-class labor market vulnerability (e.g., 1828–32, 1857–70) for the implementation of new accumulation strategies in the ribbon industry.

Capitalist Industrialization and Handicraft Production at Toulouse

Toulouse, the sixth largest city in France in 1851, was an important administrative and commercial center for the entire southwest of France. Industry was less developed at Toulouse than at Saint-Etienne, with 32.5

---

[52]Arthur Dunham, *The Anglo-French Treaty of Commerce of 1860 and the Progress of the Industrial Revolution in France* (Ann Arbor, 1930), pp. 263–64.
[53]Gras, *Histoire de la rubanerie*, pp. 613–16; Fournial, *Saint-Etienne*, p. 213.
[54]AN, BB30 379.
[55]Lequin, *Ouvriers*, 1:70–71; Gras, *Histoire de la rubanerie*, p. 628.

percent of Toulouse's labor force engaged in industry in 1830 and 38 percent in 1872.[56] Most of these workers, 74 percent in 1830 and 65 percent in 1872, were handicraft artisans employed mainly in the production of food, clothing, and housing. The rapid growth of the city's population, from 60,350 in 1830 to 110,990 in 1872, created an expanded consumer demand for the products of local handicraft industry. In 1872, as in 1830, the ten largest trades at Toulouse were tailors, shoemakers, joiners, masons, metalsmiths, hatters, bakers, carriage makers, carpenters, and plasterers.[57] The construction, clothing, baking, carriage, and metal industries employed the vast majority of the city's handicraft artisans. All of these industries remained predominantly based upon small-scale units of handicraft production, although they all witnessed either the penetration of manufactures, the growth of urban putting-out production, or the development of merchant capitalist subcontracting during the middle decades of the nineteenth century.

Artisanal masters in handicraft industry usually possessed very small amounts of capital, owing to the small size of workshops and the elementary tools used. Although some trades, like baking and metalworking, required substantial capital, in most trades the capital necessary to carry on production was devoted primarily to paying for raw materials and wages, rather than tools, before payments for finished products were received. The master artisan was thus less an owner of the means of production (i.e., of fixed capital) than someone with enough circulating capital to buy raw materials and pay wages. Working alongside the few journeymen and apprentices he employed, the master artisan was a provider of funds who brought together the necessary components of production—including labor, raw materials, and larger tools and equipment—in his workshop. As individuals, handicraft producers exercised control over the use of raw materials, the budgeting of time, and the recruitment and training of fellow workers. Although these decisions were typically made by individual masters rather than through collective decision making by the journeymen and apprentices of a shop, skilled handicraft workers did enforce upon their masters an adherence to traditional regulations. As Sewell writes of the Old Regime: "Attempts to employ subcontractors, or to put work out to domestic workers, or to produce low-quality standardized goods, or to multiply the division of labor, or to introduce untrained workers into the trade were contrary to the statutes of the corporations and therefore illegal. This did not mean that these practices never occurred, but it did mean that they

---

[56]Archives municpales de Toulouse (hereafter AMT), recensements de 1830, 1872.
[57]Ibid.

tended to occur either on a small scale, out of sight of the *jurés* of the corporation, or outside the corporations' jurisdiction."[58]

These traditional regulations governing handicraft production were increasingly challenged by three developments that marked mid-nineteenth-century capitalist industrialization at Toulouse: the growth of relatively small nonmechanized factories (i.e., manufactories); the penetration of merchant capitalists into a number of handicraft areas, including the garment, shoe, and construction industries[59]; and the internal transformation of handicraft production.

Despite the continuing predominance of handicraft industry at Toulouse, factory production did develop during the middle decades of the nineteenth century. Factory workers accounted for a small but growing percentage of the city's working class, increasing from 4.1 percent in 1830 to 11.3 percent in 1872.[60] These factories remained relatively small in scale, developed in a number of different industries, and relied heavily upon artisanal labor. Edmond de Planet's 1865 industrial survey lists 797 factories at Toulouse employing 8,587 workers, for an average of fewer than 11 workers per factory, as well as four government-owned factories employing 1,434 workers. There were only thirty-five establishments in the city that employed more than twenty workers with a total of 2,401.[61] Many of the factories listed in various industrial surveys of the period employed mainly artisanal labor. In 1840 factory artisans were employed in two machine shops, two foundries, and two scythe and file factories. These six factories employed 48 percent of the city's factory labor force.[62] Despite their relatively small scale and their reliance upon artisanal labor, Toulouse's nonmechanized factories differed from handicraft workshops in that factory employers, unlike master artisans, did not work alongside those they employed. These factories emerged in a number of different industries. The de Planet survey (1865) lists factories producing a wide variety of different goods, including machinery, metal, cannons, scythes, hardware, building materials, carriages, and hats, while the municipal survey of 1865 lists factories producing files, cut marble, and bread that are not included in de Planet's industrial survey.[63]

[58]William H. Sewell, Jr., *Work and Revolution in France: The Language of Labor from the Old Regime to 1848* (New York, 1980), p. 159.

[59]Whereas merchant capital at Saint-Etienne was almost exclusively involved in the products of household industry, at Toulouse merchant capitalists were primarily involved in the regions' prosperous grain trade. See Ronald Aminzade, *Class, Politics, and Early Industrial Capitalism* (Albany, 1981), pp. 16–28.

[60]AMT, recensements de 1830, 1872.

[61]Edmond de Planet, *Statistique industrielle du département de la Haute-Garonne* (Toulouse, 1865).

[62]AMT, Secretariat général 137.

[63]Archives départementales de la Haute-Garonne (hereafter ADHG), 12M 34.

Most of Toulouse's factories existed within industries that remained predominantly handicraft in character. For example, although most of the city's hatters continued to labor in small handicraft workshops, by 1865 local hat factories employed 308 workers, or approximately 45 percent of the city's hatters. Most cabinetmakers also remained employed in small handicraft workshops, but by 1865 there were five cabinetmaking factories employing 146 workers.[64] Although joiners, masons, and carpenters—the three largest construction trades in the city—also remained employed mainly in small handicraft shops, by 1865 there was a building-joining factory employing 135 workers and four marble-cutting factories employing 92 workers, and in 1868 there was a mechanized sawmill employing 32 workers.[65] The joiners, printers, carriage makers, metalsmiths, hatters, cabinetmakers, marble masons, and bakers who found work in these manufactories faced foremen and factory discipline, which their counterparts in handicraft industry did not have to contend with. Although the growth of these factories entailed an increased scale and greater division of labor, they typically did not involve the use of steam power or the mechanization of production. Although they were wage laborers, artisans in these early factories, like their counterparts in handicraft production, typically owned the small tools they used in the factory.

A second aspect of capitalist industrialization at Toulouse was the penetration of merchant capital into the city's two largest consumer-goods industries—tailoring and shoemaking—and into the industry that employed the largest number of the city's artisans—construction. During the 1830s and 1840s, ready-made standardized shoes and clothing increasingly challenged the custom-made products of small handicraft workshops. At Toulouse shoe warehouses emerged as centers of organization for cutting leather and distributing leather pieces that were then assembled in the homes of local shoe stitchers. By 1858 this merchant-capitalist organization of shoe production yielded an annual estimated output of one million francs, and the Toulouse chamber of commerce reported that "incessant activity reigns in the factories engaged in ready-made production of shoes and among the homeworkers (*ouvriers en chambre*) who supply them."[66] The de Planet industrial survey of 1865 lists three such "factories" (which were really warehouses that distributed cut leather to household workers), employing three hundred workers, or approximately 15 percent of the entire trade. In the 1830 manuscript census, all workers in the local shoe industry listed their occupations simply as shoemakers, cobblers, or bootmakers. By 1872 21 percent of

[64]Ibid.
[65]Ibid.
[66]ADHG, 12M 32.

all shoe workers listed occupational titles that implied participation in urban household production (e.g., shoe stitcher, boot stitcher, boot edger), while 79 percent listed their occupations as shoemakers, cobblers, and bootmakers.[67]

Urban household production made even earlier and greater inroads in Toulouse's garment industry. In the 1830 manuscript census 69 percent of all garment workers listed occupational titles that reveal an advanced division of labor characteristic of urban household production (e.g., garment cutter, seamstress, stitcher), while only 31 percent listed the title of tailor.[68] City directories provide evidence of the growing role of merchant capital in the garment industry during the middle decades of the nineteenth century.[69] The city directories of 1840 and 1872 list three types of tailoring establishments: (1) small-scale master artisans (*tailleurs à façon*), shop owners with little capital who produced custom-made clothing from cloth provided by their customers; (2) artisanal tailors (*marchand tailleurs*) who had larger capital investments, including stocks of cloth that they usually bought in volume from suppliers on credit; and (3) large-scale merchant-capitalist producers of ready-made clothing (*maisons de confection*). The 1840 listing of Toulouse's tailoring enterprises includes forty-four small-scale master artisans, thirty-three larger-scale artisanal tailors, and eighteen ready-made producers. In the 1872 directory there were listings for forty-nine small tailors, ninety larger artisanal tailors, and twenty-seven ready-made producers. In other words, small-scale custom-made tailoring dropped from 46 percent to 30 percent of local enterprises while larger-scale artisanal tailoring and ready-made production organized by merchant capitalists grew to include a larger percentage of local firms.

In both tailoring and shoemaking, the incursion of merchant capital meant a transformation of the labor force as women and children household producers increasingly replaced male handicraft artisans. This movement from handicraft workshops to household production did not, however, increase the control employers exercised over the work process. As in Saint-Etienne's silk ribbon industry, the household organization of clothing production at Toulouse presented merchant capitalists with problems of labor control. On 12 April 1837 the police commissioner reported to the mayor of Toulouse that six local garment industry employers, dissatisfied with the quality of the work they were receiving under the household system, had established a plan to eliminate household production. The plan, according to police, was "to force the workers to labor in shops" rather than in their homes. These employers drew

[67]AMT, recensements de 1830, 1872.
[68]AMT, recensement de 1830.
[69]AMT, annuaires 1840, 1872.

up an agreement not to engage in household production with the provision that violators would be forced to pay a fine of two thousand francs.[70] The growth of urban household shoe and clothing production did mean a more intensified division of labor than was the case in the handicraft industry. It also involved an expansion of the scope of the market, since urban household industries, like local manufactories, produced for an international world market, exporting their products throughout Europe and overseas to the colonies.

Merchant capital also made important inroads, by other means, into the city's construction industry. During the 1840s entrepreneurs increasingly hired subcontractors to organize different stages of the production process and provided credit, raw materials, or both to the subcontractors they hired. The subcontractor (*marchandeur* or *tacheron*) hired workers who, with materials and larger tools provided by the merchant-capitalist entrepreneur, executed the work given to them. This system of subcontracting (*marchandage*) made the maintenance of uniform wage and working conditions extremely difficult and generated intense hostility on the part of masters and workers in the building trades. In February 1848 the new republican national government, in a concession to its working-class supporters, outlawed subcontracting as an exploitative form of work organization, but the practice continued.[71] In May 1848 small masters expressed their opposition to this disruption of standard hours of work within the industry. They sent a letter to the new city council seeking approval for a request to enforce standard hours for starting, meals, and finishing throughout the construction industry. The masters affirmed their solidarity with their journeymen against local construction entrepreneurs, stating that "as workers ourselves, we will never abandon the cause of our brother workers; like them we have spent most of our lives with the hammer, trowel, and saw in our hands."[72]

The third aspect of capitalist industrialization at Toulouse, the most important in terms of the number of workers affected, was the response of small-scale handicraft producers to the growth of newer forms of industrial production. Some artisanal masters, along with their workers, were deprived of their jobs because the custom-made products of small-scale units of production could not compete with the cheaper ready-made products of capitalist factory and household industry. Many other small handicraft masters responded to growing competition by enlarging

---

[70] AMT, 1I 60.

[71] For a discussion of subcontracting in nineteenth-century France see Bernard Mottez, *Systèmes de salaires et politiques patronales* (Paris, 1966); Arthur Fraysse, "Le marchandage dans l'industrie du bâtiment" (Paris, 1911); Robert Bezucha, "The French Revolution of 1848 and the Social History of Work," *Theory and Society* 12, no. 4 (1983); 469–83.

[72] AMT, 2F 5.

the scale of their workshops, intensifying the pace of work, and ignoring traditional practices governing the use of apprentices and the division of labor. Faced with competition from factories or urban household production, they became capitalist masters; that is, they continued working alongside their journeymen and apprentices but enlarged the scale of their operations and altered the character of the work setting. The term "master" may not be entirely appropriate to designate these artisanal employers, given their altered position within the production process. Although in structural terms they occupied a "contradictory," or transitional, class location,[73] they are referred to as masters in existing documents, by government officials, and by their journeymen workers. This perception of these employers as masters reflected in part their past connections to the trade community. They had typically gone through the established apprenticeship training process before becoming journeymen and masters. Workers apparently continued to think of them as members of this corporate community, despite their violation of trade community norms and their altered position within the process of production.

Small-scale handicraft production continued to exist in most artisanal trades, but these small handicraft workshops increasingly coexisted alongside handicraft shops owned by master artisans who had enlarged the scale of their operations as well as alongside larger-scale manufactories. This development is evident in the city directory statistics cited above on different types of enterprises in the garment industry. Other sources document this same trend in a variety of different trades. A city council commission report of Toulouse's baking industry in March 1848 noted that although most of the city's 250 masters owned only one or two ovens and hired only one or two workers, there were 20 masters who owned three ovens and 11 masters who owned more than three.[74] A similar situation of the coexistence of large- and small-scale enterprises existed in the city's cabinetmaking industry. In 1869 only 38 of the city's 100 masters regularly employed workers, but 6 employers hired 118 of the city's 343 workers.[75] Although shoemaking workshops also remained predominantly small in scale, by 1855 a number of masters, including Jean Guille, who employed 20 workers, and Jean Barbet, who employed 20 to 25, had greatly expanded the scale of their operations.[76] During the wheelwrights' strike of 1861, a local police report stated that the small masters in the industry were very jealous of the real carriage makers ("*veritable carrossiers*"), like Monsieur Mercier, a master carriage maker

[73]Erik Wright, *Class, Crisis and the State* (London, 1978), pp. 68–110.
[74]ADHG, 4M 60.
[75]ADHG, M196.
[76]ADHG, 223U 10.

who had centralized the diverse operations of carriage construction under one roof in his own larger workshop.[77]

Those master artisans who managed to stay in business were able to remain competitive by enlarging the scale of production, hiring apprentices to do work formerly done by qualified journeymen, increasing the number of workers they employed, and intensifying the division of labor; in other words, by more efficiently exploiting the artisanal labor they employed rather than by introducing new machinery. Although their disregard of traditional regulations that had previously governed their trades generated intense conflict between masters and journeymen,[78] it enabled them to maintain their relatively small workshops and to expand their production. This pattern was by no means unique to Toulouse. Markovitch's quantitative study of nineteenth-century French economic development found that, during the middle decades of the century, productivity increases were more a product of the increasing division of labor then of the growing use of machinery, and that small-scale artisanal production provided the major source of capital accumulation.[79] Industrial capitalist development at Toulouse and throughout France did not eliminate artisans; it transformed their work settings and altered class relations within handicraft industry.

Conclusion: Capitalist Development and Theories of Industrialization

During the middle decades of the nineteenth century, industrialization at Saint-Etienne and Toulouse altered class relations within both household and handicraft production. These changes involved the growing subordination of master artisans in handicraft production to merchant capitalists and of journeymen artisans to nascent capitalist masters, and the increased subordination of master weavers in household production to merchant capitalists. This subordination was not primarily a matter of dispossession of the means of production. Master weavers retained ownership of their looms, and journeymen in handicraft industry, even when employed in enlarged workshops characterized by an increased division of labor, typically still owned the small tools they needed to practice their trades.

Although they were wage laborers, artisans employed in subcontract-

[77]ADHG, WU 72.
[78]Ronald Aminzade, "French Strike Development and Class Struggle: The Development of the Strike in Mid-Nineteenth-Century Toulouse," *Social Science History* 4, no. 1 (1980): 57–80.
[79]T. J. Markovitch, "Revenu industriel et artisanal," pp. 86, 88.

ing arrangements typically owned part of their means of production. In the construction industry, for example, they typically owned the saws, trowels, and planes they used but not the scaffolding or the raw materials they worked on. Journeymen in handicraft industries generally owned their own small tools, but they could make use of these tools only by selling their labor power to a master who owned the workshop and the raw materials they worked on. Master artisans in handicraft industry typically owned their workshops, although in trades in which merchant-capitalist entrepreneurs were making inroads they often did not own the raw materials. In the case of urban household weavers, journeymen and apprentices were wage laborers who owned neither looms, workshops, nor raw materials. The masters typically owned the looms but were dependent upon merchant capitalists who owned the raw materials and, in the case of Jacquard looms, the cardboard patterns that controlled them. Master weavers could not use their looms outside of relations with merchant capitalists. The subordination of master weavers at Saint-Etienne involved various strategies of accumulation by merchant capital, extending from the merchants' early control of raw materials and finished products, to growing indebtedness that made many masters only nominal owners of their looms, to merchant ownership of the cardboard patterns necessary for use of the Jacquard looms.

These findings suggest that it was not changes in legal ownership of the means of production, but rather changes in effective power over persons and productive forces that were the central feature of capitalist industrialization in mid-nineteenth-century Toulouse and Saint-Etienne.[80] Only such a broad view of the process of capitalist development can account for the diverse strategies of accumulation and mechanisms of subordination of labor to capital that occurred in nineteenth-century France. The separation of workers from the means of production was indeed important in the overall process of capitalist development, but it is only part of a more general process of the subordination of labor to capital by various means.

"Sociology," writes Philip Abrams, "proceeds in its most typical forms by way of the typing of structural systems—for example, industrialism, feudalism, legal-rational authority.... Logically ordered contrasts between structural types have been treated, quite naively for the most part, as though they effectively indicated chronologically ordered transitions. ... On this basis, a sociological past has been worked up, a past which is linked to the present not by carefully observed and temporally located social interaction but by inferentially necessary connections between concepts.... The function of the sociologists' past ... has not been to provide

---

[80]Gerald A. Cohen, *Karl Marx's Theory of History: A Defense* (Princeton, 1978), p. 62.

a frame of reference for empirical studies of the mechanics of transition but instead to furnish a rationale for side-stepping such tedious historical chores."[81] Such an ahistorical treatment of the past is quite evident in the literature on the sociology of economic development. Conceptual polarities like particularism/universalism or ascription/achievement have been used to characterize the past and present and to derive tendencies of development from logical procedures rather than historical research.[82] Theories of economic development that rely upon ahistorical conceptual dichotomies to counterpose the past and present typically emphasize the rapid displacement of older "traditional" or "precapitalist" forms of production by newer "modern" or "capitalist" forms of industry. My research suggests that such theories fail to appreciate the importance of the reconstitution of older forms of industry in the process of socio-economic change. This process of reconstitution has often been overlooked by historians as well, perhaps because it typically left intact the outward form of production—the household and workshop—while transforming class relations internally. The central implication of this research is that in order to theorize and decipher the dynamics and tendencies of capitalist development, we need more historical case studies of the diverse local patterns of capital accumulation that marked different phases of the process of industrialization. Such studies should provide us with a better understanding of the various means, including but not limited to proletarianization, by which labor has been subordinated to capital.

[81]Philip Abrams, "The Sense of the Past and the Origins of Sociology," *Past and Present* 55 (1972): 18–32.

[82]See, for example, Bert F. Hoselitz, "Main Concepts in the Analysis of the Social Implications of Technical Change," in *Industrialization and Society*, ed. Bert Hoselitz and Wilbert E. Moore (New York, 1966).

15

Proletarian Families and Social Protest: Production and Reproduction as Issues of Social Conflict in Nineteenth-Century France

Michael P. Hanagan

At the founding meeting in 1844 of the Saint-Jean-François-Régis Society for the Marriage of the Poor and the Legitimation of Their Natural Children in the provincial industrial city of Saint-Etienne, well-dressed men maintain an attitude of sleepy, patient stoicism while a secretary reads a document bemoaning the plight of modern industrial society:

> More and more we see multiply in large cities, and chiefly in large industrial cities and among the working classes, those unions created by passion alone or by libertinage and maintained by culpable habit outside the law and the church. Religion sighs deeply over these corrupted morals, but it is not alone in grieving and deploring these unions. The social order is no less concerned with them. Society insofar as it has been created by Christianity rests almost entirely on the family, and the family on marriage, . . . It is difficult for those who have strayed from the path of good to stop on the bad road that they have taken . . . Ideas of order, love of property, the desire of acquiring and transmitting which motivates the efforts of the laborious worker, have no hold on their spirit.'

I thank, for their insightful comments, Ronald Aminzade, Steven Kaplan, David Kennett, Ben Kohl, Yves Lequin, Robert Moeller, Michelle Perrot, Joan Scott, Louise Tilly, and participants in the Columbia Doctoral Seminar on Social History.

'"Société charitable de Saint-Jean-François-Régis pour le mariage des pauvres et la légitimation de leurs enfants naturels," 1844, Archives départementales de la Loire (hereafter ADL), 28M 1.

A few months earlier in the same city, another group of middle-class men appears more intent. In a courtroom an eloquent and ambitious young lawyer is explaining to his audience why a group of several hundred working-class men and women threw rocks at a convoy of troops that had arrested striking miners: "The authorities should have avoided conveying [the prisoners] in open carts in broad daylight in the midst of crying mothers and wives, those poor workers that one knew in the bottom of one's heart to be in the right."[2] And only four years later when the conservative economist Adolphe Blanqui, brother of the famous revolutionary, tried to explain the united protests of Stéphanois workers, he could think of no better metaphor for collective solidarity than that of the family: "... the ribbon-weavers, the armorers, the forgers, the miners. They live together like a family, by groups organized in almost a military fashion, and as much disciplined for collective protest as they are little disciplined for work."[3]

In these brief passages middle-class speakers, addressing middle-class audiences, present very different images of working-class family life under industrial capitalism. For the men who belonged to the Saint-Jean-François-Régis Society, the strengthening of the working-class family was necessary to inculcate and ignite love of possession and work discipline among the working classes. For the lawyer, natural feelings of family solidarity seemed a readily comprehensible and justifiable explanation for violent working-class protest. And for Adolphe Blanqui the solidarity of protesting workers seemed uncomfortably similar to the self-sacrificing and benevolent affections attributed to family life.

Together, these contrasting images of working-class family life in a French industrial town that was feeling the full force of the Industrial Revolution pose some questions about the compatibility of industrial proletarian families and industrial capitalism. On the one hand there is the image of the patriarchal family with its conservative work ethic and mean spirit toward the world outside the privacy of the individual family. It is this image that scholars use when they picture both capitalism and familialism as sharing common privatistic and hierarchical values.[4] On the other hand there is the image of self-sacrifice and collective goods that unites men and women, young and old, and that can mobilize its members forcefully against those who threaten it. The family is seen as

[2] Archives nationales (hereafter AN), BB18 1420

[3] Adolphé Blanqui, *Des classes ouvrières en France pendant l'année 1848* (Paris, 1849), pp. 35–36.

[4] See Heidi Hartmann, "Capitalism, Patriarchy and Job Segregation by Sex," *Signs* 1, no. 3, pt. 2 (Spring 1976): 137–69; and Heidi Hartmann and Ann R. Markusson, "Contemporary Marxist Theory and Practice: A Feminist Critique," *Review of Radical Political Economics* 12, no. 2 (Summer 1980): 87–94. See also Michelle Barret and Mary McIntosh, *The Anti-Social Family* (London, 1982).

the most important preindustrial social organization to survive intact into the capitalist era and as a social organization capable of providing a critical alternative to the existence of the capitalist order. This is the image that scholars use when they picture the family as a bastion of communitarian ethics holding out against the onslaught of commercialism.[5]

Proletarian Families and Industrial Capitalism

In this essay I seek to explore the compatability of industrial capitalism and the proletarian family. I argue that to understand the outbreak of some large proletarian protest movements, it is necessary to understand changes in family structure, family employment patterns, and fertility strategies. I maintain that family issues were capable of reconciling capitalists with workers as well as of throwing them into conflict, and I try to make explicit some of the circumstances that determined when proletarian families and industrial capitalists might come into conflict.

The study of industrial proletarians and their families pertains especially to the nineteenth-century because the proletarian family was largely a nineteenth-century creation. The plight of the industrial proletarian family in the city intrigued Dickens, Gaskell, Hugo, and Zola, partly because it was such a recent problem. For centuries, unskilled or semiskilled laborers had existed as temporary labor or unmarried dependents; these workers often labored alongside artisans or highly skilled craft workers whom it is necessary to distinguish from unskilled or semiskilled proletarians.[6] In old industrial cities like Lyons, unskilled workers

[5]See Jane Humphries, "Class Struggle and the Persistence of the Working-Class Family," *Cambridge Journal of Economics* 1(1977): 241–58, and idem, "The Working-Class Family, Women's Liberation and Class Struggle: The Case of Nineteenth Century British History," *Review of Radical Political Economics* 9, no. 3 (Fall 1977): 25–41. See also Bruce Curtis, "Capital, the State and the Origins of the Working-Class Household," in *Hidden in the Household: Women's Domestic Labor under Capitalism* (Oshawa, Ont., 1980). For one important attempt at synthesis, see Ruth Milkman, "Redefining 'Women's Work': The Sexual Division of Labor in the Auto Industry during World War II," *Feminist Studies* 8 (Summer 1982): 337–72.

[6]Since proletarian workers lacked the ability to control entrance to their occupation and, at least after the earliest days of the Industrial Revolution, did not work together in family units, it is worth emphasizing the distinction between "artisanal" and "proletarian" workers. A useful definition of the term "proletarian" drawn from the work of Gary Cohen is that the "proletarian is the subordinate producer who must sell his labor power in order to obtain his means of life" (p. 73). See Gerald A. Cohen, *Karl Marx's Theory of History: A Defense* (Princeton, 1978). Applying this definition, "industrial proletarians" are those employed in industry. The present essay distinguishes between "proletarians" and "artisans." "Artisans" are those industrial workers who through formal or informal organizations exert substantial control over access to skilled positions in industry. Following Cohen's definition, artisanal workers are incompletely subordinate workers, and so they are not

who were not part of a skill hierarchy were usually single men or women working for a time in the city to accumulate money for a dowry or a farm. Older unskilled workers either were single people who had been incorporated into a household headed by a master or skilled artisan or were members of families personally dependent on an employer.

Industrial worker families had first developed among cottage laborers in the countryside, but even these usually earned a supplementary agricultural income from a plot of land or owned a cottage. One of the chief attractions of cottage industry for early and mid-nineteenth-century capitalism was that its workers did not have to be paid a subsistence wage, and many never were. In nineteenth-century Europe, hundreds of thousands and then millions of people were lured to cities and there persuaded that, on the basis of their future in industrial proletarian employment, they could start their own independent families. Such a development was almost unparalleled, and so were the resulting social problems.[7]

It is with the formation of the industrial proletarian family that the demand for a "family subsistence wage" really begins in industry; artisanal workers typically did not generate this type of demand. The industrial proletarians' new demand stemmed from their work situation. The industrial proletarian was completely at the mercy of the free market; unlike the artisan he was unable to influence his wage level by controlling access to his trade. Industrial proletarians did often exert some control over admission to industrial employment; typically employers drew recruits from among their workers' friends and relatives.[8] However, since they lacked any control over admission to skill hierarchies, industrial workers were unable to use their influence in labor recruitment to reorganize the world of industrial labor more to their liking. Deprived of these informal mechanisms for balancing family needs and work requirements, industrial proletarians had to reach a balance by other means; a "family subsistence wage" either had to be formally negotiated with employers with strike threats as their major coercive weapon or had to be obtained by political concessions from the state.

A "family subsistence wage" is defined as a wage adequate to minimally support a worker's family at standards set by custom and considered by

---

"proletarians." For a discussion of definitions of "artisanal" and "industrial" workers, see Michael Hanagan, "Industry, Workers," in *Historical Dictionary of the French Third Republic*, ed. Patrick Hutton (Westport, Conn., forthcoming).

[7]On proletarianization before the Industrial Revolution, see David Levine, *Family Formation in an Age of Nascent Capitalism* (New York, 1977); and C. Lis and J. Soly, *Poverty and Capitalism in Pre-Industrial Europe* (Atlantic Highlands, N.J., 1979).

[8]A good example of the services kin might provide in recruiting and assisting their relatives in industry is that of the textile workers of Amoskeag; see Tamara K. Hareven, *Family Time and Industrial Time* (Cambridge, 1982), pp. 85–101.

working-class communities to be acceptable during normal times; it also included sufficient additional wages or financial guarantees to provide, at least for a time, for the workers and for the spouses and young children of workers who were victims of accident, illness, death, or temporary unemployment. Since "minimum subsistence" was a category based on workers' own conceptions of customary sanctions, there was room for reshaping their meaning; but there is little reason to believe workers' conceptions changed substantially during the first half of the nineteenth century. Only during the second half of the century did popularly priced, consumer-goods industries undergo great expansion in England and France.[9] By themselves, the falling costs of textile products and garments made from them were unlikely to have greatly altered workers' living standards. Also, workers' demand for a "family subsistence wage" did not necessarily mean that the head of household was the family's sole wage earner. Rather, it meant that the ultimate responsibility for family subsistence devolved on the household head; that amid the goings and comings of employed family members in the household, the head's wage had to be sufficient to balance family needs against family income.

If proletarian families did not receive a subsistence wage, the usual result was not starvation but family dissolution or degradation and a search for alternative employment. The immediate response of working-class families when wages sank below the minimum was to seek outside supplements and aid. Women and children went to live with relatives, families threw themselves on private or public charity, or they went begging. Over the long term, the workers' response to wages that declined below the minimum was flight; working-class families simply looked elsewhere for work.

Industrial workers looked first to their employers for the guarantee of a "family subsistence wage." Of course, capitalist employers had a vital interest in the existence of a proletariat, but they were not a reliable source of support; capitalism often drove wages too low to support a family. Employers were then forced to rely on temporary migrants or members of urban families whose principal breadwinner was employed elsewhere. In industries where routinized production was important and where the costs of finding and retraining temporary workers were higher than the wages necessary to support a stable work force, most large

[9]Charles Wilson has emphasized the importance of consumer goods in late Victorian England in "Economy and Society in Late Victorian Britain," *Economic History Review*, ser. 2, 18 (August 1965): 183–98. Although it may have started somewhat earlier, the same phenomenon seems to have occurred in France during the Second Empire and the early Third Republic; see Michael B. Miller, *The Bon Marché: Bourgeois Culture and the Department Store, 1869–1920* (Princeton, 1981); Louis Bergeron, "Permanences et renouvellement du patronat," in *Histoire des Français, XIX–XX siècles*, 2 vols. ed. Yves Lequin (Paris, 1983), vol. 2, pp. 255–72.

companies sooner or later undertook some type of obligation to tide their workers over crises. In industries that benefited from a permanent work force and could afford to pay for one, the aim of employers was to pay a subsistence wage but not more. Yet since subsistence was determined by workers' traditions and their experience in agriculture and rural industry, minimum levels could be determined only by trial and error, and employers attempting to set a minimum family wage were seldom likely to err on the side of generosity. Also, in periods of generalized industrial crisis when workers most needed support, employers were often strapped, and any company guarantees could last only as long as the company that made them.

Still, for the greater part of the nineteenth century, French industrial workers looked first to their employers for guarantees of a survival wage, because the opportunity for government intervention in this area was so bleak. During the early years of the First French Republic, 1792–94, legislators had provided social welfare legislation, but the workers' hopes were quickly dashed by the republic's inability to carry out its enactments.[10] Under the July Monarchy and the Second Empire, workers' participation in politics was at a minimum. The state showed little interest in the welfare of the work force, and the working-class population scarcely had the political weight to exert significant pressure on the government.

Although nineteenth-century men and women disagreed about how the industrial proletarian family was to be kept together, churchmen, popular writers, and influential politicians were all agreed that industrial growth and family life were desirable ends that needed to be reconciled among the working classes. The legitimacy, even within the context of capitalist society, was exactly what made family issues so explosive. Capitalists believed in the sanctity of the family. The conservative economist Joseph Schumpeter believed that the desire to accumulate wealth to pass along to children was the fundamental moving force of competitive capitalism[11] The right of parents to seek sustenance for their children was far more universally acknowledged than most of the other rights asserted by the nineteenth-century workers' movement; in contrast, the workers' movement's assertion of a "right to work" and even of a "right to live" did not go unchallenged. More to the point, capitalists also recognized that without working-class families they would be dependent on agricultural conditions for their work force. Although this dependence had characterized one whole epoch of capitalist development, in the nineteenth century industrial capitalism began to break these chains.

[10]See Alan Forrest, *The French Revolution and the Poor* (New York, 1981). On workers' demands in 1848, see especially Remy Gossez, *Les ouvriers de Paris*, vol. 24 (Paris, 1967).
[11]Joseph Schumpeter, *Capitalism, Socialism, and Democracy*, 3d ed. (New York, 1950), pp. 157–60.

Workers' pleas that their families' welfare was at stake resonated beyond the world of industrial capitalism, and such pleas could have an effect on the very important sections of French society—the royalists and principally the Catholic church—that remained outside the domination of industrial capitalism. The church, too, condemned the hypocrisy of a new industrial order that often challenged religious dogmas, but above all else it counseled patience and quiescence. Yet the church styled itself a defender of the family, and its defense of family survival must have reinforced workers' own feelings in a region of France where Catholicism was still strong. In 1844 Cardinal de Bonald, the powerful conservative leader of the Lyonnais church, whose see included the department of the Loire, refused to condemn the miners' strike and wrote a letter to the curé of Notre Dame in Rive-de-Gier inquiring whether the families of those workers who were injured in the 5 April confrontation with the troops needed aid. A royalist newspaper in Lyons explained that the strike was a product of the "cupidity" of the coal company.[12]

The Region under Study: The Stéphanois

To understand some of the real issues behind early industrial workers' struggles, it is necessary to pay close attention to local industrial conflicts. This chapter focuses on one particular industrializing area of France, the Stéphanois region, the industrial basin that formed around the city of Saint-Etienne in the southeast of France, and on one particular occupational group, the coal miners. The Stéphanois region provides a particularly good vantage point from which to examine the processes of class formation. Between 1840 and 1880 it was one of the leading industrializing areas of France; it has been labeled the "cradle of the Industrial Revolution in France." In those years the Stéphanois coal miners were renowned throughout France for their industrial militancy. In 1844 and 1869 the miners had launched strikes that echoed throughout the country. In the period between 1844 and 1869 there were several other very important strikes, and in 1848 coal miners played a major role in local political upheavals.[13] In addition to the local tradition of militancy,

---

[12]Paul Droulers, "Le Cardinal de Bonald et la grève des mineurs de Rive-de-Gier en 1844," *Cahiers d'histoire* 6, no. 3 (1961): 265–85.

[13]On the course of industrialization in the Stéphanois region: Pierre Cayez, *Métiers jacquard et hauts fourneaux* (Lyons, 1978); Yves Lequin, *Le ouvriers de la région lyonnaise*, 2 vols. (Lyons, 1977); Maxime Perrin, *Sainte-Etienne et sa région économique* (Tours, 1937); and Jacques Schnetzler, *Les industries et les hommes dans la région stéphanoise* (Saint-Etienne, 1975). On the course of worker upheavals in the Stéphanois region: Petrus Faure, *Histoire du mouvement ouvrier dans le département de la Loire* (Saint-Etienne, 1956); Etienne Fournial,

coal miners are interesting because they were among the first large groups of semiskilled adult male workers to appear in emerging French industry. Coal after all was required to fuel the plants that would employ the rest of the French industrial work force in heavy industry.

The Stéphanois coal basin forms a narrow triangle with its eastern base at Rive-de-Gier, its western base at Firminy, and its apex a little above Saint-Etienne (see fig. 15.1). Coal can be mined almost anywhere in this triangle except in the area around Saint-Chamond in the east, where the presence of "pudding" rock makes the coal seam sterile. The coal comes closest to the surface on its eastern base, and there coal has been mined for centuries.[14] As the demand for coal increased during the nineteenth century and as new technologies lessened the cost of excavation, coal mining operations extended into the coalfield's center and its western edge. Since differences in mining operations and urban environment are substantial, particularly between eastern and western edges, and because the mining environment is likely to affect the growth of militancy, I shall focus on coal miners in two Stéphanois towns, each in a different wing of the basin. These two communities are Le Chambon–Feugerolles and Rive-de-Gier.

Family Survival: The Struggle for Subsistence, 1844–1851

In the first half of the nineteenth century, miner militancy was concentrated in the old established mines of the eastern face of the triangle, centered on the city of Rive-de-Gier. A look at the development of mining militancy in Rive-de-Gier shows how family concerns could both stimulate and hinder the outbreak of worker militancy. In 1844 concern for family issues caused miners and their families to unite to carry out militant strike action. In 1847, in contrast, family issues helped to prevent militant actions. Events in both years, however, underscore the importance of the relationship between family and mass protest.

In 1844 in the city of Rive-de-Gier the situation of coal miners and their families was particularly desperate, and the passion behind miners' protest and politics flows from the gravity of the threat to their family

---

Saint-Etienne: Histoire de la ville et de ses habitants (Roanne, 1976); P. Heritier et al., *150 ans de luttes ouvrières dans le bassin stéphanois* (Saint-Etienne, 1979); Fernand L'Huillier, *La lutte ouvrière è la fin du second empire* (Paris, 1957); and Lequin, *Ouvriers de la région lyonnaise*.
On Stéphanois coal mining: Pierre Guillaume, *La Compagnie des mines de la Loire, 1846–1854* (Paris, 1966); Louis Simonin, *La vie souterraine: Les mines et les mineurs* (Paris, 1867); and L. J. Gras, *Histoire économique générale des mines de la Loire*, 2 vols. (Saint-Etienne, 1922).

[14]M. Perrin, "Le bassin houiller de la Loire," *Annales de géographie* 39 (July 1930): 359–75.

Fig. 15.1. Administrative map of the Loire and the Stéphanois region. From Michael Hanagan, *The Logic of Solidarity: Artisans and Industrial Workers in Three French Towns, 1871–1914* (Urbana: University of Illinois Press, 1980)

life. The massive strike that brought two thousand workers out in April and May of 1844 was provoked chiefly by the last in a series of successive wage reductions. Between 1838 and 1845, by gradual steps, most of the collieries in the Stéphanois basin were consolidated into a single powerful cartel, the Compagnie des mines de la Loire: the company used it monopolistic power to ensure stable revenues. The "hungry forties" was an uncertain economic era, and the new company responded to fluctuating demand by cutting production, lowering wages, and so holding prices steady.[15]

The coal miners hardest hit by these wage reductions were those of Rive-de-Gier. Of all the regional cities, it provided the least female employment and thus the least opportunity for secondary income to supplement miners' wages. Unlike other cities and rural communities, no domestic industry flourished in Rive-de-Gier, and the other major industrial employer in the city, glassmaking, employed almost exclusively the children of glassworkers.[16] Also, the foothills that surround the city on two sides meant that far fewer Ripagérien miners owned or leased small farms than other miners in the region. A Ripagérien proverb, modeled on a saying about Paris, ran, "Rive-de-Gier is hell for horses, purgatory for men, and heaven for women."[17] Once the horses were lowered into the pits to haul coal, they rarely emerged alive; the miners spent half their lives underground; and women in Rive-de-Gier did not engage in industrial employment. When the proverb originated, it probably referred to the wives of the glassworkers, but later it was applied indiscriminately to the mining population, whose wives also were not engaged in industrial labor. For coal miners' wives, however, what might have seemed heavenly during years of prosperity became its own hell when times were hard.

Evidence suggests that the wage cuts finally provoked the miners to action when they threatened the men's ability to support their families. However, the strike was initiated not by imminent starvation but by the anticipation of hunger, by the imposition of a wage rate so low that normal fluctuations in the price of commodities would sooner or later have brought Ripagérien miners with families to the point of begging or relying on municipal assistance or private charity. Figure 15.2 shows that the 1844 strike broke out when real wages were at the highest point they were to reach during a whole decade of wage decline.[18] This increase in real wages, at a time when money wages were being reduced, was

[15]Guillaume, *Compagnie des mines de la Loire.*

[16]On the Ripagérien economy in the first half of the nineteenth century, see J. B. Chambeyron, *Recherches historiques sur la ville de Rive-de-Gier* (Rive-de-Gier, 1844); Felix Lardon, *Rive-de-Gier: Une ville précoce de la première révolution industrielle* (Rive-de-Gier, 1979); Guillaume, *Compagnie des mines de la Loire,* pp. 142–43; and "Enquête de 1848— Canton de Rive-de-Gier," AN, C956.

[17]A. Audiganne, *Les populations ouvrières et les industries de la France* (Paris, 1854), pp. 100–101. This same saying can be found in Louis-Sebastien Mercier, *Le tableau de Paris,* ed. Jeffry Kaplow (Paris, 1982), p. 31 (1781–88). Mercier is referring to survival rates of women, men, and horses in the urban environment of the capital.

[18]The real-wage index is based on the price of bread and meat, distributed in the proportions described in 1848 workers' budgets. The real-wage index was found in Service éducatif, *La mine et les mineurs* (Saint-Etienne, 1981).

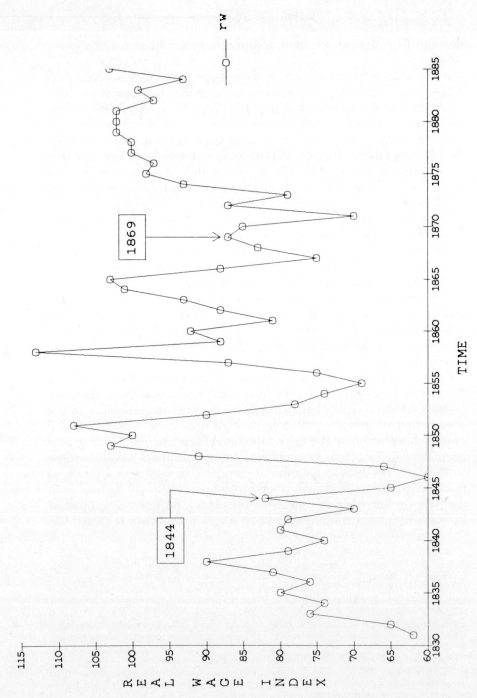

Fig. 15.2. Real wages of coal miners, 1831–85

chiefly caused by a fall in bread prices. But the price of bread fluctuated dramatically before 1870, and workers knew that sooner or later it must rise and reduce their real wages to very low levels. For the miners, 1844 was a relatively good time to strike; the wage reduction outraged and united all workers, while the low price of bread meant that miners had sufficient margin to at least contemplate going out on strike.[19] The periodic failure of the annual family wage that miners anticipated did not so much threaten starvation as force reliance on the uncertain support of private charity, of municipal assistance, or of kin employed elsewhere.[20] Not fear of starvation but fear for family security drove Ripagérien miners to strike.

Estimating minimum family wages is always difficult and frequently impossible, but a crude estimate is feasible in the Ripagérien case and lends credibility to workers' claims that the 1844 wage reductions threatened family survival. In 1848 delegations of workers and employers met to respond to a detailed government questionnaire, one part of which concerned family budgets. Workers' and employers' estimates diverged widely; the employers' assessment of a minimum family budget was half that of the workers. But even the company conceded that three kilograms of bread and a kilogram of meat were part of a minimum budget for a family of four. Yet according to the calculations of Pierre Guillaume, using the average wages imposed by the employers in the 1844 strike and the cost of meat and bread, a miner could not purchase these necessities in three of the eight years between 1847 and 1854[21] In much of the rest of the region, where family members could find employment in other industry or could work on their own land, this kind of calculation would not apply, but in Rive-de-Gier it most nearly describes the plight of young miners who were starting families and whose children were not yet of age to earn income.

The government of the July Monarchy resisted the strike firmly and actually tried to strengthen the will of some local coal owners who tried to negotiate with their workers. Several militant trade unions in Paris

[19]Ibid.

[20]To combat begging, midcentury middle-class reformers urged the establishment of a *dépôt de mendicité*, since the Stéphanois region did not possess one: see P.-L., "Du pauperisme et de la mendicité," *Bulletin de la société agricole et industrielle de l'arrondissement de Saint-Etienne* 18 (1841): 121–34. Victor Smith claimed to remember bands of beggars roaming the Stéphanois countryside in his youth during the 1840s: see Victor Smith, "Chants du pauvres en Forez et en Velay," *Romania* 2 (1873): 455. For an interesting discussion of the structure of welfare in the Lyonnais region during the first half of the nineteenth century, see Janet Ruth Potash, "The Foundling Problem in France, 1800–1869: Child Abandonment in Lille and Lyon" (Ph.D. diss., Yale University, 1979).

[21]Guillaume, *Compagnie des mines de la Loire*, pp. 141–42. Several missing data points in the graph of real wages were estimated by linear interpolation.

and members of secret societies in Lyons tried to give financial aid to the miners engaged in the illegal work stoppage, but it was the families of the miners that bore the brunt of the struggle.[22] As the strike wore on and the miners' slender resources collapsed, reports that their wives and children were begging in the countryside came to the prefect's attention.[23]

Family members not only bore the cost of the strike but participated in the struggle. The events of 5 April 1844, referred to in the beginning of this essay, have all the characteristics of an ambush planned and organized by an entire community. The ambush took place at La Grand-Croix, a coal-mining community strategically placed where the railway and the main road between Rive-de-Gier and Saint-Etienne converged. A convoy of troops passing through the town was attacked by a mass of three or four hundred men. According to the procureur général's report, a group of children between twelve and fourteen years old rushed ahead to seize the bridles of the horses. As the horsemen drew back and began forming a circle to repulse the attack, "the women from the top of the houses rained rocks down" on the troops. In the melee that followed an unmarried eighteen-year-old miner was killed and a sixteen-year-old boy was wounded. In opening his investigation, the procureur himself had ridden on horseback to the town the day after the attack, even though he was warned that the women were "still preparing to throw rocks at the soldiers from the roofs of their houses." He concluded that "the whole community had participated" in the attack.[24]

As the 1844 strike wore on, new demands arose among the miners, including a fixed wage schedule, a *conseil de prud'hommes* to settle industrial disputes, and an accident insurance fund administered by the workers.[25] This last was to become one of the central demands of miners in the nineteenth century. The accident insurance fund was a source of perpetual miner indignation. Existing funds were administered entirely by coal companies, although much of the money came from compulsory deductions from the miners' pay or from fines levied on workers for infractions of work rules. Although French law required mining companies to establish such a fund, the law did not regulate its administration. Companies were free to dip into the fund if they so desired. Should a mining company fail there was no protection for the fund, and it was likely to disappear with the company. To make matters worse, the fund

[22]Eugène Tarlé, "La grande coalition des mineurs de Rive-de-Gier en 1844," *Revue historique* 177 (1936): 249–78, esp. 270–71.

[23]Jean-Pierre Aguet, *Les grèves sous la monarchie de juillet (1830–1847)* (Geneva, 1954), p. 278.

[24]Report of the procureur général, 7 April 1844, AN, BB18 1420.

[25]Tarlé, "Grande coalition des mineurs," p. 262.

aided the worker only so long as he worked in the individual mine; a miner who found work in another mine lost the benefits accruing to him through his first employer. Also, company insurance funds did not become available to miners until after any litigation concerning the accident was settled; not infrequently company funds were used to blackmail injured workers to drop court cases.[26] For all these reasons, the company-administered funds did not provide workers' families with security in the event of the miners' injury or death.

The fight to achieve this kind of security was the one fixed point in nineteenth-century miners' struggles. This issue is particularly important in relating family interests to worker militancy, because sickness and accident insurance have a special significance as family issues. Once a family subsistence wage is attained, it is difficult to accumulate evidence about how the worker's income is distributed throughout the family. But sickness and accident insurance generally becomes relevant only during family crises, when expenditures for personal luxuries can be discounted. The ultimate example of workers' concern for social insurance as particularly benefiting their families is the issue of insurance coverage in the case of the household head's death. To be sure, miners' focus on this demand had considerable propagandistic value, since many community members were sympathetic to the dangerous conditions in the mines. But of all the issues concerned with social insurance the need for ample death insurance was most frequently raised.

Although the miners were forced back to work in 1844, employers found themselves compelled to mitigate some of the worst consequences of the wage reductions. Several mines lured their workers back by promising them various temporary gifts to tide them through financially difficult periods. Complete victory, after all, was not in the best interest of the mining companies. With the low wages already in force in the Ripagérien mining basin, the very existence of working-class families there would be threatened by the rising price of bread; in 1845 miners real wages dropped dramatically, and in 1846 they received the lowest real wages in the entire century between 1830 and 1930 (see fig. 15.2). A strike that broke out in April 1846 near Saint-Etienne quickly turned to violence, and six people were shot dead by soldiers.[27] The coal companies soon found it necessary to take action to preserve their work force intact.

In the beginning of 1847, with its legendary bad harvests and rising grain prices, the coal companies had to face the full consequences of their successful wage reductions. As the price of bread rose throughout

[26]The miners' descriptions of the company insurance funds in 1843, "Commissaire de police de Rive-de-Gier à M. le sous-préfet à Saint-Etienne—March 17, 1843," ADL, 28M/1, are very similar to those repeated in *L'Eclaireur* of 5 February 1870.

[27]On the 1846 miners' strike see Gras, *Histoire économique générale*, 1:314–16.

the Stéphanois region, the authorities became alarmed. In the first half of the nineteenth century, the working classes did not yet possess those reserves that later enabled them to sustain prolonged periods of price increase; the margin between the industrial working classes and the class of vagabonds and beggars was hardly as well established as it would be in the second half of the century. In October 1847 an alarmed prefect reported: "Already misery has begun to reach the majority of families. Jewelry, furniture, even looms have been sold to buy bread. Many have already spent everything they possess. Thus in order to procure the necessities some have resorted to begging during the day, but the greater part beg during the night."[28]

During the whole of 1847 the miners' situation was desperate; some of the younger miners who did not have families to support began to talk of striking; not only was the price of bread rising, but wages were falling as a result of the faltering market for coal. But early in 1847 the Compagnie des mines took action; it promised that it would subsidize the price of bread whenever it rose above 0.45 centimes. Since bread had already passed this price in late 1846, the company announcement really constituted a wage increase. The coal company issued tokens that coal miners and their families could present to bakers.[29]

The authorities concerned about the possibility of mass protest regarded this as a shrewd move. The procureur noted that the company's action divided single miners from those who were fathers of families.[30] The single workers earned enough to be sure of their bread, but declining mine production was lowering their wages and shrinking their overall income; the single men wanted to take action. Bread loomed much larger in the consumption of families, and its secure price counted for more to the family men. The procureur predicted that despite ferment among the miners, the strike would not materialize because "wives will be very opposed to a suspension of work that would leave them without resources and without hope of obtaining anything from public charity."[31] Whether or not married women articulated such sentiments, it seems clear that family interests were a stake in this dispute. Generally, periods of declining economic activity are bad times to strike, and there were doubtless other considerations that influenced miners' calculations. But in any case the procureur's predictions proved right; the ferment

[28]Préfet, 13 October 1847, AN, F12 4476B.
[29]Aguet, *Grèves sous la monarchie de juillet*, p. 352. On the 1844 strike, see also Droulers, "Cardinal de Bonald et la grève des mineurs," 265–85; and Pierre Guillaume, "Grèves et organisations ouvrières chez les mineurs de la Loire au milieu de XIXe siècle," *Mouvement social*, no. 43 (April–June 1963): 5–18.
[30]Procureur général, 15 February 1847, AN, BB18 1450.
[31]Procureur général, 19 February 1847, AN, BB18 1450.

in the coal fields in 1847 subsided, only to resurge after the revolution . of 1848.

For really the first time in the nineteenth century, the revolution of 1848 and the formation of the Second Republic gave Stéphanois miners a chance to voice their grievances publicly and to attempt to win reform through political means. Their appeals in 1848 reveal an appreciation of the force of family issues in appealing to a larger public as well as within the mining community. The workers' responses to the administration inquiry stressed their dilemma as family members and particularly as fathers. They pleaded for support "for the household where there are 4, 5, and 6 children who are not yet able to work.... These poor children are covered with rags and sometimes go barefoot for lack of money to buy shoes." The miners lamented that they were often forced to send their children to the mines at too tender an age; "education among the miners is totally neglected because the miners who are fathers of families are forced to make their children work because their own wages are insufficient to provide an education." And they deplored that "fathers of families are obliged to impose upon themselves rigorous privations that are yoked to the hardships of their work."[32]

Although workers realized that appeals to defend the family had a telling effect on middle-class opinion, their concern with family issues was more than rhetorical. The replies of Ripagérien miners to the government questionnaire revealed a full-fledged plan of mine reform that would have benefited local miners and their families at the expense of migrants. This scheme would have given miners' sons first chance at new mining jobs. Since miners lacked the scarce industrial skills that artisans used to enforce their rules, their plan depended on government enforcement for its success. To justify government intervention, the miners based their case on safety. The major cause of death and accidents within the mines, they argued, was the flood of inexperienced migrants from the agrarian countryside who were entering the mines. A compulsory apprenticeship program would make the mines safe, and it would slow down the influx of migrants by allowing their employment only after the needs of local workers had been met. The miners thought that such restrictions would also benefit agricultural production, which they believed was suffering because too many rural dwellers were swarming into the mining communities. Migrants dazzled by city ways (Rive-de-Gier had a population of almost twelve thousand in 1846) and unaccustomed to mining soon "wished they have never set foot in the mines."

The proposed apprenticeship program would be enforced by local miners elected from among their fellow workers; in addition, these min-

---

[32]"Enquête de 1848—mineurs de Rive-de-Gier," AN, C956.

ers' delegates would participate in much of the day-to-day decision making in the mines. Furthermore, the miners demanded a minimum wage for all miners and workers' control over the workers' pension and accident insurance fund currently administered by the company.[33] If companies could not live with such a program, a local newspaper announced, then perhaps the mines should be taken over by the government. The newspaper, *La Mercure Ségusien*, was tied to local middle-class groups hostile to a coal trust dominated by outsiders.[34]

Militant workers' concern with family welfare in 1848 is exhibited not only in their appeals and demands but in the actions of leading labor militants. The workers' response to the government inquiry was delivered by Anton Prugnat, a miner delegated to represent his fellow workers' demands. In December 1848, after the definitive failure of the hopes engendered by the revolution, Prugnat was a leading figure in the establishment of a mutual benefit fund to provide for coal miners and their families in the event of accident or death in the mines, a fund dissolved in the years of repression that followed the coup of 1851.[35]

Family Survival: The Struggle for Stability, 1851–69

Between February and June of 1848 the hopes of the Ripagérien miners collapsed as the provisional government gave way to the Executive Commission and then to the dictatorship of Cavaignac; the attempt at social reconciliation was abandoned. Nevertheless the demands of the workers in 1848 provided a benchmark for surveying the evolution of mine workers' protest in the Stéphanois region. After 1848 a new political realism set in—the broad assertion of the right to participate in everyday workplace decisions narrowed to a set list of very specific areas in which workers sought to obtain representation. Over the next forty years, miners' concerns with workers' control restricted themselves to having workers' representatives verify the weighing of the coal and to appointing workers' delegates to immediately investigate and report on accidents. Also, the great inflow of migrants into mining over the next decades meant that miners had to accept the presence of outsiders in the basin; their demands for the restriction of access to the trade also disappeared after 1848.

[33]"Enquête de 1848—mineurs de Rive-de-Gier," AN, C956. For a general survey of the results of the Stéphanois questionnaires, see Pierre Guillaume, "La situation économique du département de la Loire d'après l'enquête sur le travail agricole et industriel du 25 mai 1848," *Revue d'histoire moderne et contemporaine* 10 (January–March 1963): 5–34.

[34]*Le mercure ségusien*, 24 March 1848.

[35]Police reports on Prugnat, ADL, 10M 301, 16 January 1849, and ADL, 1J 440, 20 February 1853.

The idea that the workplace was responsible for providing for the workers' families survived. Indeed, the notion that employers should support sick, injured, and disabled workers and their families not only endured but was asserted with a new and single-minded determination. As real wages reached levels where family subsistence was ensured as long as the principal breadwinner was employed, the workers' movement could devote its attention to those uncertain but still routine circumstances when sickness or accident could reduce a coal miner's income below a family subsistence wage. But over time, as the structure of the Stéphanois economy changed, the "family subsistence wage" took on new significance. In 1844 Ripagérien miners had been particularly moved to militancy because the lack of employment for women in the city meant that men's wages were the sole support of young families. As domestic industry declined in the Stéphanois region, employment for women also declined, and in many cities in the area families became even more dependent on the male household heads' income. Thus one of the results of the logic of the "family subsistence wage" was that mining militancy could be provoked by changes in economic structure entirely unconnected with mining.

Before looking at the great wave of miners' militancy that erupted in 1869, however, let us look at the very important ways Stéphanois mining had changed between the end of the Second Republic and the last days of the Second Empire. The Ripagérien miners' plight was only partly ameliorated by the years of prosperity that followed in the 1850s. One of the reasons their employers refused to grant wage increases in 1844 may very well have been the declining profitability of the mines in this section of the coalfields. Although miners' wages shot up well past the family subsistence minimum in the 1850s and 1860s, the instability of employment in the Ripagérien mines and its growing financial difficulties led family-minded workers to seek employment elsewhere. Midcentury marks a real watershed in the development of Rive-de-Gier. Before 1851 the town exhibited far higher rates of natural increase than after. "Natural increase" refers to the number of births minus deaths in the intercensal period.[36] In the three census periods between 1836 and 1851 the average annual rate was 10.01 per thousand; for the five census periods between 1851 and 1876 the average rate of natural increase was about 1.01 per thousand. In Le Chambon–Feugerolles, the annual rate was about 8.66 per thousand between 1836 and 1851 and averaged 11.09 in the period between 1851 and 1876.

In the years after 1848 the eastern, Ripagérien wing of the coal basin

[36]The rate of "natural increase" represents the balance of births and deaths in the intercensal period with the earliest census period as the base: see George W. Barclay, *Techniques of Population Analysis* (New York, 1958), p. 35.

lost its position as the major center of militancy; gradually miner protest established a new stronghold in the western wing and in the center of the coalfield. In the newly militant regions, no single town such as Rive-de-Gier emerged as the generally recognized center of strike militancy; cities like La Ricamarie, Le Chambon–Feugerolles, and Saint-Etienne would all have been candidates for study. I chose Le Chambon–Feugerolles because I know more about its occupational structure and about the history of its political development.

In focusing on the coal mining community of Le Chambon–Feugerolles it is important not to lose sight of conditions among the miners of Rive-de-Gier. As the coal miners of Le Chambon became well known for their militancy, those of Rive-de-Gier became quiescent or passively followed the leadership of others. Factors that explain the new militancy of Chambonnaire miners may also cast light on Ripagérien quiescence. In addition, the availability of reasonably reliable statistical sources after midcentury further encourages systematic comparison.

Between the wave of worker militancy in 1844–48 and the great strike of 1869, many changes occurred in the coal mines and in the towns where miners lived. In 1851 Napoleon III divided the Compagnie des mines into four separate, autonomous companies. Although the monopoly was destroyed, a strongly oligopolistic situation remained; miners complained that militant workers were blacklisted throughout the basin.[37] But far more important than changes in industrial structure were the changes in the nature of the work force. Uninterrupted by the apprenticeship regulations that had been demanded in 1848, immigration from outside the coal-mining towns continued unabated. By 1856 marriage records in Rive-de-Gier show that under 30 percent of the grooms employed in mining were natives of Rive-de-Gier. Rive-de-Gier was a center of migrant labor, and though other industries such as metalworking and glassmaking also attracted migrants, they were more prevalent among miner grooms than among grooms of these other industries or among the whole population of grooms. In 1856 all the miner grooms in Le Chambon–Feugerolles were migrants, but in that year mining was not an important industry in Le Chambon, and the total number of mining grooms was small (seven).[38]

In the decade after 1848, amid the going and coming of temporary workers, a number of miners settled down and established families in the coal-mining communities. The very fact that, unlike other migrant groups, coal miners did marry where they worked indicates some attachment to their place of residence. Unlike those in such migratory

[37] Guillaume, *Compagnie des mines de la Loire*, pp. 186–224.
[38] Marriage records for Le Chambon–Feugerolles and Rive-de-Gier in 1856 were consulted at the Palais de justice in Saint-Etienne.

occupations as day laborers or construction workers, in 1856 miners contributed a substantially larger proportion of bridegrooms to the married population than their proportion in the labor force, and the age distribution of coal miners was not very different from that of day laborers and construction workers. Partly because families headed by coal miners were being formed in the city, the native population engaged in coal mining grew. Twenty years later in 1876 about 45 percent of the mining grooms were natives of Rive-de-Gier, and this was well above the average proportion of employed natives in the population; fewer than a third of all grooms were native. Among the rapidly growing mining population of Le Chambon–Feugerolles, miners were far better represented among the grooms than construction workers or day laborers.[39]

Probably the biggest single change in the fortunes of coal mining in the three decades after 1848 was the westward expansion of the mining industry. Between 1856 and 1876 the proportion of employed males engaged in Ripagérien mining dropped by half, from 15.32 percent to 7.88 percent. At the same time the population of Rive-de-Gier stagnated. Meanwhile, males employed in Chambonnaire mining as a percentage of the male work force increased almost three times, from 6.80 percent to 18.27 percent. The population of the town nearly doubled in the same period. Expanding opportunities in Chambonnaire coal mining created jobs for younger job seekers. In 1876 the average age of mine workers in Le Chambon was younger than that of those in Rive-de-Gier, and the younger miners in Le Chambon were disproportionately concentrated in the age categories between twenty and twenty-nine, the age groups in which most men married and their wives began to bear children. Figure 15.3 shows the age distribution of the coal mining population of the two towns in 1876, divided into five-year age groups beginning at age fifteen.[40]

After midcentury, not only did the coal-mining population of Rive-de-Gier decline, but the composition of the coal-mining work force changed. Even though the mining population of Le Chambon was younger than that of Rive-de-Gier, a far greater proportion of miners in Le Chambon were household heads. In the 1850s the Ripagérien coal-mining population was composed predominantly of miners who were

[39]Marriage records for Le Chambon–Feugerolles and Rive-de-Gier in 1876 were consulted at the Archives départementales de la Loire. All manuscript censuses were consulted at the Archives départementales de la Loire. Samples of different sizes were drawn from the manuscript censuses of the two cities. In 1856 a 50 percent sample was drawn from Le Chambon–Feugerolles and a 20 percent sample from Rive-de-Gier.

[40]Mining is an industrial classification, but the censuses of 1856 and 1876 are classified only by occupation. Occupations were therefore assigned industrial classifications based on a judgment about which industry they most typically belonged to.

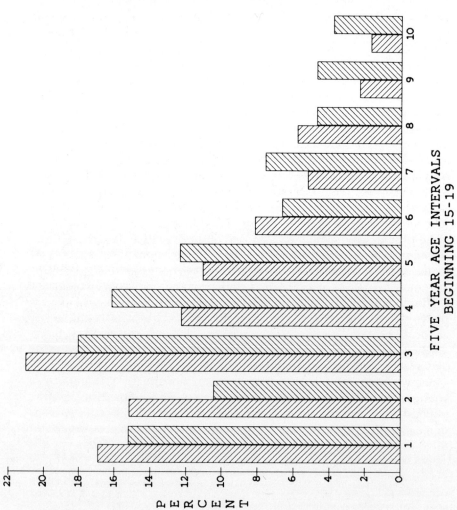

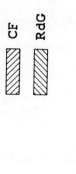

CF

RdG

FIVE YEAR AGE INTERVALS
BEGINNING 15-19

Fig. 15.3. Comparison of miners' age distributions, Le Chambon–Feugerolles and Rive-de-Gier, 1876

heads of households with spouses or children present; such household heads composed 59 percent of the mining work force in 1856; sons made up another 15 percent and unmarried boarders about 24 percent. By the mid-1870s, household heads composed only 39 percent of the mining work force: the proportion of sons had grown to 22 percent, and the proportion of unmarried boarders had grown most rapidly of all, to 31 percent. In 1876 Ripagérien miners were no longer starting families in the numbers they had in 1856. Although the proportion of native coal miners grew in Rive-de-Gier, the proportion of boarding, migrant coal miners also grew; More to the point, neither migrants nor young Ripagériens started families at the same rate as their peers in Le Chambon.

One of the results of these new employment opportunities in Le Chambon was an increase in the fertility in miners' wives. In part these opportunities promoted a low age of marriage among miners' wives and encouraged high fertility by lengthening their childbearing years. Although the number of miners marrying is small in any one year, a clear pattern can be detected. In 1856 in Le Chambon–Feugerolles the median age of the seven women who married miners was 24.5 years; in 1876 the median age of the twenty-one women who married miners there was 21. Rive-de-Gier, too, witnessed a drop in the median age of marriage of miners' wives. In 1856 the median age of the thirty-four women marrying miners was 23.5 years; in 1876 for the eighteen women marrying miners the median age was 23. Miners' median age of marriage did not change as substantially as that of their brides. The presence of many single male migrants in Stéphanois towns created a sexual imbalance that made it more difficult for miners to find partners and easier for local women. By itself the changing sex ratio is an insufficient explanation for changes in marriage age. Between 1856 and 1876 the proportion of male migrants to Rive-de-Gier had grown much faster and was much larger than those to Le Chambon, yet changes in marriage age were greater in Le Chambon.

A comparison of changes in the fertility of miners' wives in Rive-de-Gier and in Le Chambon–Fuegerolles using child/woman ratios shows that although the difference in median age of marriage helps explain a portion of the greater fertility of Chambonnaire miners' wives, important differences in fertility behavior occurred within marriage and were not caused by differences in age structure or age of marriage.[41] One likely explanation of the considerable differences in fertility between the same occupational groups in two towns scarcely twenty miles apart is based on families' expectations about the future of their occupations and their

[41]On the child/woman ratio and techniques of fertility estimation, see appendix 15.1.

towns. Between 1856 and 1876 coal mining entered a period of decline in Rive-de-Gier, and the other industries in the town were not expanding to provide secure alternative employment. In the same period in Le Chambon–Feugerolles, coal mining was expanding dramatically, as were the local metalworking industries, and the opportunities for the employment of adult males seemed secure. Figure 15.4 shows coal production of the mines of Firminy and of Rive-de-Gier; the Firminy mines were a large employer of Chambonnaire miners and provide a good indicator of production trends in the western wing of the coal basin. And for those adult men who possessed secure jobs in mining, living standards began to improve. Between 1856 and 1876, average miners' wages increased about 80 percent; the biggest increases came toward the end of the period, after 1870.[42] Still, the real wage increase was not steady but was subject to considerable fluctuation. In the Stéphanois region, mining production increased greatly over time, as did the price of coal. As a result, most other factors in mining, such as the number of workers employed in mining and money wage, are highly correlated with time. Real wages are the exception; the real wage trend between 1831 and 1885 was one of gradual increase, and it was only mildly correlated with time. The reasons for the mild correlation were the erratic fluctuations of bread and meat prices, which continually jeopardized workers' living standards until they were stabilized in the early years of the Third Republic.[43]

But at a time when the wages of miners were increasing, it is more difficult to generalize about family income; opportunities for the employment of family members besides the head of household followed different trends in the two towns. In Le Chambon–Fuegerolles, employment opportunities for women and children were contracting. In 1856 ribbon weaving had been an important domestic industry in Le Chambon and was a major employer of young women. In 1856, 7.80 percent of all spouses of household heads were employed, and 31.78 percent of all families had children who were employed, many in ribbon weaving. But the 1860s witnessed a decline in ribbon weaving that hit domestic weavers hardest, and when the industry did revive in the mid-1870s it remained confined to the large-scale workshops in Saint-Etienne. By 1876 ribbon weaving in Le Chambon–Feugerolles had disappeared, and the old domestic industry had not yet been replaced by any new

---

[42]F. Simiand, *Le salaire des ouvriers des mines de charbon en France* (Paris, 1907); see appendixes 15.2 and 15.3.

[43]The correlation of raw production with time is .960, of the value of coal production with time, .909, of the number of workers employed, .955, of money wages, .931. In contrast, the correlation of an index of bread prices with time is .502, and of real wages, .483.

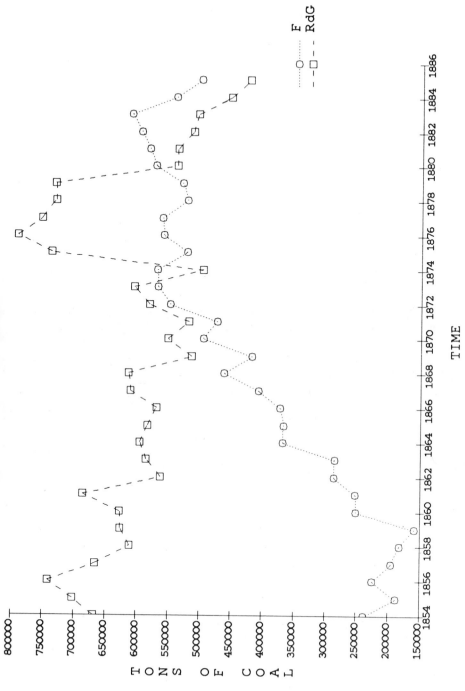

Fig. 15.4. Coal production: Firminy and Rive-de-Gier, 1854–85

one. By 1876, 6.33 percent of all spouses were employed, and 19.70 percent of families had children who were employed. In contrast, in Rive-de-Gier employment opportunities for children were increasing. Although spouse employment remained insignificant in both years, the number of families with children who were employed rose from 14.76 percent in 1856 to 22.27 percent in 1876. In two decades most of the growth in Ripagérien employment came from the expansion of unskilled and semiskilled jobs in metalworking and glass; many of these jobs were taken by younger male children of workers already employed in Ripagérien industry. For detailed analysis of changes in employment structure of the two cities between 1856 and 1876, see Appendix 15.2 and 15.3.

At first sight the differences in fertility behavior and employment opportunity in the two towns may seem puzzling. Chambonnaire miners' fertility was increasing at a time when employment opportunity for children was decreasing. Of course, the employment opportunities for children were partly a result of differences in age structure caused by patterns of fertility increase. But very substantial variations in the structure of employment show up if employment rates are standardized for age[44]; participation rates were dropping dramatically among the younger age groups of both sexes in Le Chambon–Feugerolles at the same time that they were increasing rather significantly in Rive-de-Gier.

Several factors help explain these differences. First of all, the difficult situation of Ripagérien miners' families should be noted. In the mid-1870s the Ripagérien mines began to increase their production, but this sudden large increase, which did not last long, had been preceded by nearly three decades of declining production. In 1864 the price of Ripagérien mining company stock dropped alarmingly amid newspaper rumors that the company was in a precarious financial state.[45] In contrast, the Chambonnaire mining area had rapidly increased its production since 1860, and the two major mining companies in the area, Roche-la-Molière and Montrambert, were among the largest and most profitable in all of the Stéphanois region. Chambonnaire miners did not have to fear bankruptcy or the sudden disappearance of their jobs. In addition,

---

[44]The standard used was an average of the age structures for three Stéphanois towns in 1856 and 1876. For Le Chambon–Feugerolles the age-standardized labor participation rate for males in 1856 was .9857, for females .3355. In 1876 it was .7756 for males and .1878 for females. In Rive-de-Gier the estimated age standardized labor-force participation rate for males in 1856 was .7715, for females .1519. In 1876 it was .8533 for males, .1583 for females. Labor-force participation was calculated on the basis of the population over age fifteen. For the decompositions of these rates between census years for individual towns, see appendixes. On the estimation of labor-force participation rates for the population of Rive-de-Gier in 1856, see appendix 15.3.

[45]See Gras, *Histoire économique générale*, 2:751.

the biggest single changes in labor participation in Le Chambon occurred among young girls who had formerly worked in domestic industry; they now had no remunerative employment. Once the head of household's income was secure, the presence of unemployed young girls in the household may have encouraged fertility by providing additional help in child rearing.

At all events, the families of Chambonnaire miners were becoming increasingly dependent on the head of household's wages for their income. The ratio of workers to consumers among families headed by miners drives this point home.[46] In 1856 the miners' ratio was the lowest of any major industrial group in the city, .4043, and by 1876 it had dropped to .3352, still the lowest in the city. The ratio of Ripagérien miners was .3596 in 1856, above that of most of the major industrial groups, and it rose to .3775 in 1876, still above that of most of the major industrial groups in the city. Between 1856 and 1876, Chambonnaire families of miners became much more exclusively dependent on the head's mining income than formerly, while Ripagérien families became somewhat less exclusively dependent.

The 1869 Miners' Strike and the Struggle for a Stable Family Subsistence Wage

In the late 1860s the foundations of Chambonnaire miners' families began to shake as miners' wages were subjected to new forces of instability. Save for the crisis of 1858–59, the expansion of coal output in the years between 1850 and 1870 had been largely sustained. The Stéphanois coal industry remained largely unaffected by the general economic slowdown of the 1860s because the basin was an important center of steel production and much of the steel used in converting the French railway from iron to steel was produced here. Whereas local metalworking expanded and with it the demand for coal, local coal companies found themselves unexpectedly hard pressed. In the 1860s coal from the new mines in the Nord and Pas-de-Calais began to appear on the French market in large quantities for the first time.[47] The distant northern and eastern markets for Stéphanois coal rapidly fell away, faced with this cheaper and better-quality competitor. But most alarmingly, northern

[46]The weights were .55 for children aged zero to four, .65 for children five to nine, and .75 for children ten to fourteen; above age fifteen equals 1. These weights came from Peter Lindert's work, found in Karen Oppenheim Mason, Maris Vinovskis, and Tamara Hareven, "Women's Work and the Life Course in Essex County, Massachusetts, 1880," in *Transitions: The Family and the Life Course in Historical Perspective*, ed. Tamara K. Hareven (New York, 1978), pp. 187–216.

[47]Jean Bouvier, *Le mouvement du profit en France au 19e siècle* (Paris, 1979), pp. 48–49.

coal began to appear in the Lyonnais, and, driven by competition, other coal basins began to drop their prices and seek markets even in the Stéphanois region itself. Here local coal producers began to dig in their heels. They were determined to remain the sole coal suppliers in the region, for they feared that once connections had been made between local manufacturers and alternative suppliers these connections might be hard to sever when local demand declined.[48]

The heightened competition that produced the increased demand added new elements of instability to the incomes of Stéphanois miners. All the miners' problems revolved around the system of wage payments.[49] Stéphanois miners were paid according to the weight of the coal they produced. The most highly paid men employed in mining were always those working at the coal face, and the most highly paid coal hewers were those who cut the most tons of coal. But competition and increased demand forced the local mines to expand production by opening new pits; the pressure to increase production also led to the more rapid exhaustion of the existing mines. Increasing construction diverted miners from high-paying coal cutting jobs to lower-paying construction jobs. Within every Stéphanois coal company, the wages of some miners increased as companies raised the wages they paid to those employed in construction, but the wages of former elite group of miners—those employed in cutting coal at the face—stagnated as the demand for their labor declined. Wage differentials between workers employed in construction and workers employed in coal cutting may have tended to even out, but real wages diminished during the period and greater equality came partly at the expense of the experienced adult workers employed in coal cutting. Miners suffered a wage reduction when they were transferred from coal cutting to construction, so many construction workers were bitter. Yet the wages of coal cutters declined relative to those of construction workers, and thus coal cutters also felt aggrieved.

In addition, the exhaustion of existing veins lowered production and brought a consequent reduction of wages; the most dramatic threat to the stability of miners' yearly income was the decline of productivity. Figure 15.5 shows the dilemma confronting Stéphanois coal producers. With powerful new competitors often producing a superior grade of coal, the cost of labor per ton of coal produced was rising in the Stéphanois mines while the price of coal at the pithead was declining or stagnating during almost the entire period of the 1860s. It is in the

[48]Journal de la Compagnie des mines de la Loire; company records are on deposit at the Archives départementales de la Loire; for 1867–69, ADL, 15J 860.
[49]On the radicalizing potential of this form of wage payment, see Rolande Trempé, *Les mineurs de Carmaux, 1848–1914*, 2 vols. (Paris, 1971). On the miners' grievances in the Stéphanois region connected with this form of payment, see *L'Eclaireur*, 12 June 1869.

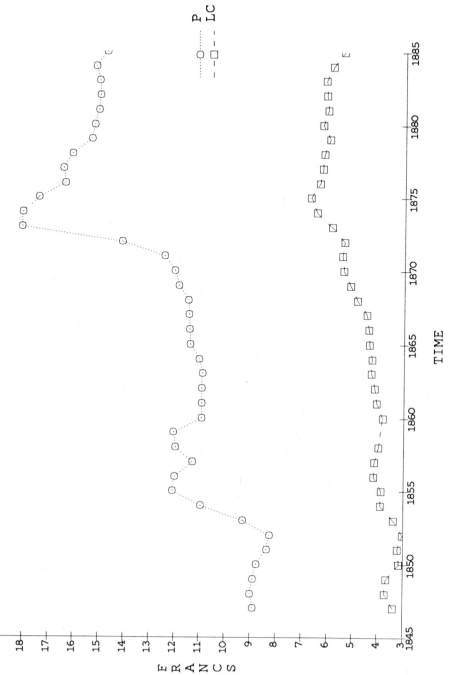

Fig. 15.5. Price and labor cost of a ton of coal, 1845–85

period between 1865 and 1869 that the two curves—cost of labor and price of coal—move most closely together, and this is precisely the period that saw the greatest pressure on the coal miners to increase their production.

As seams petered out and the proportion of rocks to coal increased, it became impossible for miners in some pits to maintain production levels, and hence the piecework pay of coal miners fell. Productivity as crudely measured by the proportion of wages per ton of coal produced had begun to decline slowly in the 1860s, but productivity dropped spectacularly in 1868.[50] In 1869, several months before the outbreak of the great strike, a mine manager reporting to the company executives in Paris lamented that "the examination of the table of sales shows the demonstrable differences of sales among our various pits. The Loire pits have sold only 28,745 tons; in the first trimester of 1868, it had sold 34,097 . . . I'm afraid that we will not be able to accumulate the stocks indispensable for the winter."[51] Perhaps even more important than a reduction in coal production was a reduction in the quality of the coal produced. Throughout 1868 and 1869 the manager's journal laments the poor quality of the coal and lists the local markets being lost because of it. This manager, whose pits were to be hard hit by the strike, also noted that "the scarcity of workers seems to put insurmountable obstacles in the face of production."

In addition to the fluctuations in income, accidents also loomed as a threat to family stability. The increasing dependence on the income of the head of household by Chambonnaire miners' families heightened the impact of mining accidents. Accidents fluctuated randomly over the period, but a number of patterns stand out.[52] First, there were many deaths and serious accidents in both the basin of Rive-de-Gier and the basin of Saint-Etienne—statistics were kept separately for the two wings of the coal basin until 1873. To pick a typical year, in 1867 over 2 percent of all miners in the Stéphanois basin were seriously injured or killed in work-related accidents, as were 1.1 percent of all the miners in the Ripagérien basin. In other words, a miner who spent twenty years in the Stéphanois mines had a 33 percent chance of being seriously injured or killed, while a Ripagérien miner ran a 20 percent risk. The example accurately represents the substantial difference in accident rates between the two basins. Perhaps because of the increase in construction, accidents

[50]Simiand, *Salaire des ouvriers des mines*, appendixes.

[51]Journal, ADL, 15J 860.

[52]Statistics on accidents came from the Ministère des travaux publics, *Statistique de l'industrie minérale* (Paris, 1865–72). On accidents in French mining, see Donald Reid, "The Role of Mine Safety in the Development of Working-Class Consciousness and Organization: The Case of the Aubin Coal Basin, 1867–1914," *French Historical Studies* 12, no. 1 (Spring 1981): 98–119.

were much more frequent in the newer western wing of the coalfield. Systematic reports are not available for each year, but a series can be drawn up for the eight years between 1865 and 1872. The base used is that of underground miners; the overwhelming proportion of accidents occurred underground. Between 1865 and 1872 1.44 percent of all miners were killed or injured each year in the Ripagérien basin; 0.47 percent were killed, and 0.97 percent were injured. For the same period, 2.00 percent of all miners were killed or injured each year in the Stéphanois basin; 0.80 percent were killed and 1.20 percent injured.

The serious risk of accident weighed on all miners, but it was worse in the western part of the coal basin, where the risk was greatest. It weighed most heavily of all in towns like Le Chambon, where families were most dependent on the head of household's income. Even an accident that disabled a worker for a few weeks could seriously upset the family's budget. The restrictions and limitations of the company welfare program continued to irk the workers, as they had in 1844 and 1848. They were perhaps even more concerned in 1869 than formerly, because in the late 1860s the rulings of the local judiciary were particularly sympathetic to the companies. In 1866 a local mine manager admitted in correspondence with his company executive that in cases of accident the settlements obtained recently by the company were "very fortunate ... thanks to the good spirit and benevolent disposition of the [judicial] tribunal."[53]

Coal miners and their families seem to have accepted the high accident rates in the Stéphanois mines as part of their job. But precisely because accidents were an occupational hazard, miners had strong feelings that compensation for injured workers and their families was part of the coal companies' responsibility. In 1860 a social reformer who lauded the medical and social services provided by the company was surprised by the miners' ingratitude: "Have the miners appreciated this assistance, these [charitable] establishments, these services? When one digs down in the bottom of their souls, when one looks for it in their casual conversations, in their intimate thoughts, do they show one sign of gratitude? No; they seem to believe it is a question of a pure and simple obligation."[54]

To provide against accidents in view of the inadequacy of the employers' benefit society, in 1866 miners in the western wing of the coalfields took the lead in organizing their own insurance society, the Société fraternelle. For a fee of one franc a year the society undertook to provide aid in case of sickness and accident and to contribute toward the funeral

[53]Journal, ADL, 15J 860.
[54]Audiganne, *Populations ouvrières*, 2:120–21.

expenses of departed members. Over the next couple of years the society was able to recruit five thousand members.[55]

The Fraternelle provided the leadership and the organizational structure for mobilizing workers in the great strike of 1869. Although the exact circumstances have never been precisely clarified, it seems that the leaders of the insurance society thought they had reached an understanding with the prefect of the Loire in May 1869; if the leadership of the society would support the imperial candidate in the approaching elections, the prefect would intervene with the company to win concessions for the society, concessions especially touching the question of workers' participation in the administration of the companies' insurance societies.[56] With the Fraternelle's support the imperial candidate squeaked by, but the miners' disillusionment was great when no concessions from the company were forthcoming. On 11 June 1869 bands of workers fanned out over the western and central mining regions and ordered miners going to work to return home. The coordination of these bands and the wide support they received show a degree of organization that could have come only from the leadership of the Fraternelle. Within sixteen hours the strike was general in the western and central coalfields, and ten thousand men were out on strike. In the next two or three days the strike spread to most of the eastern wing.[57]

Over the next several days committees were elected that claimed to speak for the striking miners. Most observers considered the committee supported by the Fraternelle to have the most popular support, and it was the only one to come up with a concrete list of demands. The committee's list contained three major points. First, the committee demanded the ten-hour day. Second, it asked that a minimum wage be established throughout the basin for each category of miner. Third, it asserted that the company insurance funds must be placed under the workers' control. Although the content of the workers' demands in 1869 changed somewhat from those of 1844, the problems they were trying to solve remained the same. Miners were still concerned to obtain a stable income and security against accidents that would enable them to ensure their families' survival. Although workers in 1869 stressed that the ten-hour day would give them more time at home with the family, it was the latter demands—the demands for a minimum wage and for worker-controlled insurance funds—that were crucial for family interests. A minimum wage would protect them against the dramatic shifts in income that were then going on in the mines. Worker-controlled

[55]Heritier et al., *150 ans de luttes ouvrières dans le bassin stéphanois*, pp. 87–89.
[56]Bernard Delabre, "La grève de 1869 dans le bassin minier stéphanois," *Etudes foréziennes* 4 (1971): 139–56.
[57]L'Huillier, *Lutte ouvrière à la fin du second empire*, pp. 25–28.

insurance funds would listen more sympathetically to the workers' grievances and ensure them adequate, uniform treatment no matter where
they worked or how often they switched jobs within the region.[58] Long
after the fall of the Second Empire, miners would seek to resolve these
and other problems through strikes and through participation in radical
and socialist political parties.

In 1869 as in 1844, industrial workers' demands that centered on
family concerns served to rally all family members around the struggles
of adult male workers. Nothing shows the extent of family solidarity
more clearly than the massacre of La Ricamarie, an event during the
1869 strike that echoed the actions of April 1844. On the morning of
16 June 1869 word spread throughout the western wing of the valley
that workers were coming from a nearby metalworks to load the coal
stockpiled at a local mine. Soon word came that workers trying to prevent
the loading had been arrested and were being escorted to Saint-Etienne
by cavalry. At Le Brûlé, between La Ricamarie and Le Chambon, bands
of workers converged on the infantry escort and demanded that the
soldiers release the prisoners. In the chaos that followed the commanding officer ordered his men to fire, and thirteen people were killed. The
officer claimed subsequently that "in the front ranks of this crowd were
twenty women whose frenzied cries and violent gestures increased the
excitement of the mass."[59] A journalist from the republican newspaper
L'Eclaireur, who interviewed those arrested after the massacre, also noted
that "all these men are in accord on this point. It was from the crowd,
overexcited by the women who provoked the cries, threats, and rocks
...that the first shots were fired."[60] Subsequent investigation did not
confirm the paper's assertion that the first shot came from the crowd.[61]
In any case such claims of "overexcited women" fit too neatly with nineteenth-century male stereotypes of female behavior to be accepted at
face value. But the roll call of the massacre confirms female participation.
Two women and a sixteen-month-old child were killed by the troops.

The strikers held out for weeks despite the massacre, but though the
miners won some concessions, their major objectives still eluded them.
They had won a slight wage increase but not a uniform wage schedule
or, more important, a minimum wage. They had obtained the establishment of a valley wide insurance program and worker participation in
its administration, but the companies still retained control over decision
making and basic administration. Finally, the miners won some reduction
in the length of the workday, but the extent of the reduction was not

[58]Delabre,"Grève de 1869," pp. 121–22.
[59]*L'éclaireur*, 18 June 1869.
[60]Ibid.
[61]Delabre, "Grève de 1869," pp. 126–28.

large, and it varied from mine to mine. The principal leaders of the strike were sentenced to prison, but most of them were granted amnesty by Napoleon III.[62] Although the strike of 1869 cannot be considered a success, it was not a total failure.

Conclusion

The analysis of the causes of the 1869 strike, as with that of 1844, can be sharpened and clarified by placing it in the context of family needs and circumstances. A look at mining unrest over almost thirty years shows that attention to family concerns consistently improves our understanding of the dynamics of worker protest. In some cases, such as in 1844 and 1869, family needs pushed workers to protest. In other cases, such as in 1846, family issues divided the working class and hindered worker militancy. Over the thirty-year period considered here, and given the limited nature of the available evidence, it seems that family concerns were more frequently a stimulus to protest than a retardant. Still, whenever a substantial number of unmarried workers, living outside their families of origin, work side by side with large numbers of family men there is a possibility of dividing the working class on family issues. What seems most important is that the families of those workers who contemplated strike militancy were not simply passive spectators whose interests were considered simply to reflect those of the individual worker; in almost all the important strike decisions, evidence suggests that family issues were squarely addressed, and that when militant action was taken, family members participated actively in that action.

Another conclusion suggested by my survey of miners militancy is the complexity of the "family subsistence wage" issue. The history of Stéphanois coal-mining struggles in 1844 and 1869 reveals the persistence of workers' demands that their employers recognize their right to a "family subsistence wage" and the steadfast refusal of employers to concede on this issue. The 1844 miners' strike in Rive-de-Gier shows the most direct and simple aspect of the issue. In 1844 miners' wages were reduced to levels that would inevitably push their income below the subsistence minimum. Although even in 1844 the difficulties of Ripagérien miners also sprang from the unusually poor opportunities for female employment in Rive-de-Gier, the struggle was mainly a response to changes in the wage levels of household heads.

The 1869 strike shows the more complicated aspects of the "subsist-

[62]For the general settlement, see L'Huillier, *Lutte ouvrière à la fin du second empire*, p. 332; for where the changes in company pension programs fit in with existing plans for reform, see Gras, *Histoire économique générale*, 2:535–38, and 756–72.

ence wage" issue. It illustrates that "family subsistence" was not simply a function of the level of wages paid to the household head; it also depended on family and household size, on opportunities for family employment, and on the stability of family income. The issues that united the coal miners in 1869 were only partly related to wages and to the work situation in the mines. The rise in miners' fertility that preceded the production crisis of Stéphanois coal and the decline in employment opportunities for females in ribbon weaving probably contributed as much to workers' decision to strike as their oscillating income and the increased accident rate.

What can the issue of the "family subsistence wage" tell us about the nature of nineteenth-century industrial workers' struggles? Its primary value may be the light it casts on the relation between proletarian families and industrial capitalism. Industrial capitalism and the industrial proletarian family were products of the nineteenth century; both survived that century, but neither survived it unchanged. In the course of the century, the traditional instability of proletarian industrial jobs gave way to relatively stable jobs that were occupied by adult male proletarians, and this in turn had its effect on the family.

Newly stable employment in male hands inevitably meant that those females still involved in unstable, traditional domestic industries would become "secondary" and "supplementary" workers whose jobs opportunities would be subordinated or sacrificed to those of adult males. But also, adult males' interpretation of the meaning of "stable employment" evolved as family employment patterns changed and as family income became increasingly dependent on their jobs. Increasingly, workers expected industrial employers to provide adequate protection when "supplementary" family workers were unemployed, when accident or sickness overtook workers and their families, and when workers' financial obligations grew owing to an increase in effective fertility.

Employers were generally unwilling to undertake a commitment to a family subsistence wage; the power to fire employees in bad times and to set wages based on productivity was felt to be integral to the capitalist regime of production. Still, the issue was not so intractable as it sometimes seemed. After all, large-scale employers wanted a stable, permanent proletariat. When large numbers of workers failed to earn a "family subsistence wage" the quality of the work force declined, and large employers usually intervened to protect their regular workers. Such employer intervention increased workers' conviction that employers were responsible for providing for their family subsistence and that this responsibility needed only to be routinized. Through force of circumstance and owing to self-interest, employers were recognizing workers' demands and so legitimizing their claims.

The conflict over the family subsistence wage brought about the slow beginning of reforms that provided government protection for workers and their families during the Third Republic. Already in the 1890s strongly organized working-class groups like the miners were able to win social-reform legislation that was not extended to the whole body of the French working class until the 1930s with the advent of the Popular Front. Even in the short run the struggles over the family subsistence wage were not completely fruitless; such struggles usually won concessions and enabled many endangered families to survive. But such struggles also used family values to mobilize workers against capitalism. Against the massive offensive of proletarianization and the widespread dissemination of the ethics of the free labor market and competitive individualism, it seemed to many workers that their most secure defense was to rally behind the family unit and family values. The industrial proletarian family played an important role in building an opposition that ultimately succeeded in moderating the full force of capitalist industrialism.

Appendix 15.1
Estimating Fertility

To estimate fertility, the "child/woman ratio" was used; this is the ratio of children aged zero to four years to married women aged twenty to forty-nine with husbands present in the household. Some students of fertility have questioned the reliability of the "child/woman ratio" in the French context because of the prevalence of wet-nursing in France. George D. Sussman's important study indicates that industrial workers were less likely than other sectors of the population to have recourse to wet-nursing and that it was relatively little used in cases where, as in Rive-de-Gier and in Le Chambon, there was little employment for adult women outside the home (see George D. Sussman, *Selling Mothers' Milk: The Wet Nursing Business in France, 1715–1914* [Urbana, Ill., 1982] pp. 170–74). Some standard demographic tests for undercounting were applied, but the rapid rates of migration in the Stéphanois region make these tests unreliable as indicators of "undercounting," though the results are interesting in another context. For example, when life-table survival rates were applied to five-year totals of birth figures based on vital statistics, they revealed as many cases of overcounting as undercounting, and in cases of both undercounting and overcounting, differences were correlated with the disproportionate presence or absence of married women in the age groups twenty to thirty-five. Since high rates of overcounting do not seem likely, these results, combined with the findings about married women, suggest the effect of migration on the population. The comparison of survival rates for yearly births with the presence of children aged zero to four in the census of population suggests, particularly for 1876, that families with young children were disproportionately moving *to* Le Chambon and *away* from Rive-de-Gier, which reinforces the general picture of change in these two towns.

To take into account differences in the age structure of the married female population, I used two types of standardization. First, the age of married females was distributed in five-year intervals to correspond to the actual age distribution of the married female population; this gives a measure of fertility as it must have seemed to contemporaries in the two towns. Second, the age distribution of married females was distributed by five-year intervals and apportioned to correspond with the age distribution of the Massachusetts population of 1885, the standard proposed by Hareven and Vinovskis. The Hareven-Vinovskis age distribution allows us to compare fertility as if the towns had had the same age structure of married women. For the Hareven-Vinovskis standard, see Tamara K. Hareven and Maris A. Vinovskis, "Patterns of Childbearing in Late Nineteenth Century America: The Determinants of Marital Fertility in 1880," in *Female Population in Nineteenth Century America* (Princeton, 1978), pp. 85–125; see p. 93 for standard distribution.

The results of the standardized child/woman ratio reveal that the higher fertility of Chambonnaire miners' wives compared with that of Ripagériens was a product both of the actual age distributions in Le Chambon and of higher marital fertility in this city. First, let us examine the actual age distributions. In 1856 the child/woman ratio of women married to miners in Le Chambon–Feugerolles, standardized for the actual age distribution of women married to miners, was 944.22 ($N = 36$), and in Rive-de-Gier it was 614.55 ($N = 75$); by 1876 the ratio in Le Chambon–Feugerolles was 1131.16 ($N = 81$), and in Rive-de-Gier it was 554.17 ($N = 29$). Although in 1856 the ratio already was higher in Le Chambon–Feugerolles than in Rive-de-Gier, the further increase in the Le Chambon ratio combined with the Ripagérien decrease brought the Chambonnaire ratio to almost 60 percent higher than the Ripagérien ratio in 1876. A look at the Hareven-Vinovskis ratio sheds some light on this difference. In 1856 the ratio for Le Chambon–Feugerolles was 941.56, for Rive-de-Gier, 546.03; in 1876 the ratio for Le Chambon was 1005.96, for Rive-de-Gier, 580.83. In both years the younger age of Chambonnaire married women than those of Rive-de-Gier helps explain the fertility differential, but age structure plays a larger role in explaining the differences between the two towns in 1856 than in 1876.

The same basic pattern remains if these own-children estimates are adjusted for the effects of child mortality. Life tables were calculated individually for the two towns, for 1854–58 and 1874–78 for Le Chambon–Feugerolles and for 1855–57 and 1875–77 for Rive-de-Gier. Using these life tables to compensate for the effect of mortality shows that miner fertility was fairly similar in both towns in 1856 but diverged greatly in 1876; in 1876 miner fertility in Le Chambon had increased substantially over that of 1856, while miner fertility in Rive-de-Gier had decreased substantially. A discussion of these results and the methods employed will be found in my manuscript "Industrial Workers: Proletarian Families: Family Formation and Class Formation in the Stéphanois Region of France during the Industrial Revolution, 1840–1880." On differences in miner fertility, see Michael Haines, *Fertility and Occupation: Population Patterns in Industrialization* (New York, 1979).

Appendix 15.2. Components of labor force change: Le Chambon–Feugerolles, 1856–76

Age	Effect of population change (%)	Effect of activity rate change (%)	Interaction effect (%)	Total change (%)
		Males		
10–14	55.50	−43.21	−23.97	−11.68
15–19	62.80	−31.81	−19.97	11.02
20–24	101.35	−26.28	−26.63	48.44
25–29	108.13	−9.99	−10.81	87.32
30–34	85.90	−4.17	−3.59	78.15
35–39	139.66	−3.16	−4.42	132.08
40–44	88.87	−1.32	−1.17	86.38
45–49	164.70	−7.30	−12.04	145.36
50–54	88.91	−5.08	−4.52	79.32
55–59	123.73	−6.98	−8.64	108.10
60–64	40.22	−13.34	−5.36	21.51
65–69	42.72	3.72	1.58	48.03
70–74	40.90	18.15	7.45	66.50
		Females		
10–14	96.64	−60.64	−58.61	−22.61
15–19	130.84	−46.20	−60.45	24.19
20–24	89.28	−45.23	−40.37	3.68
25–29	58.57	−58.00	−33.97	−33.40
30–34	70.63	−60.97	−43.03	33.37
35–39	73.75	−41.44	−30.56	1.75
40–44	107.33	−46.46	−49.88	11.00
45–49	123.29	−46.75	−57.61	18.93
50–54	66.50	−43.72	−29.09	−6.31
55–59	120.00	−2.71	−3.29	−114.00
60–64	126.42	−26.50	−33.42	66.50
65–69	88.75	32.50	28.75	150.00
70–74	90.25	−34.38	−31.00	24.88

Appendix 15.3. Components of labor-force change: Rive-de-Gier, 1856–76

Age	Effect of population change (%)	Effect of activity rate change (%)	Interaction effect (%)	Total change (%)
		Males		
10–14	−12.55	119.01	−14.96	91.49
15–19	−14.14	36.48	−5.16	17.17
20–24	−8.86	22.31	−1.98	−11.47
25–29	−14.20	−8.93	1.27	−21.86
30–34	−14.38	−0.49	−0.07	−14.94
35–39	−10.15	5.64	−0.58	−5.08
40–44	−6.25	0.45	−0.03	−5.83
45–49	24.36	6.13	1.50	31.99
50–54	−11.50	6.10	−0.71	−6.11
55–59	33.34	8.51	2.83	44.68
60–64	48.78	7.19	3.51	59.49
65–69	25.00	10.48	2.62	38.10
70–74	29.44	71.67	21.11	121.22
		Females		
10–14	−12.67	14.67	−2.00	0
15–19	0.80	−31.50	−0.26	−30.95
20–24	−10.18	53.21	−5.41	37.61
25–29	−22.40	−8.40	1.87	−28.93
30–34	−6.33	6.75	−0.42	0
35–39	15.07	4.27	0.67	20.00
40–44	25.63	39.25	10.13	75.00
45–49	8.50	−19.38	−1.63	−12.50
50–54	42.50	40.89	17.22	100.11
55–59	1.86	12.29	0.29	14.29
60–64	47.67	12.83	6.17	66.67
65–69	100.00	−25.00	−25.00	50.00
70–74	126.40	32.60	41.00	200.00

Note: Refined activity rates for Rive-de-Gier in 1856 are based on estimates.

Appendix 15.4
Estimating Employment Patterns, Rive-de-Gier, 1856

Child-employment patterns for roughly 25 percent of the Rive-de-Gier census of 1856 had to be estimated because this information was unaccountably missing from the manuscript census records. The process of estimation proceeded in two stages. Occupations of household heads, which are intact even in the incomplete portion of the census, were used as a basis for estimating the employment of male children of the household head, which are missing from a portion of the census. First of all, children of those household heads who belonged to occupational groups that were disproportionately represented in the missing material were estimated on the basis of the child employment patterns of children of household heads belonging to those occupational groups in the complete census. Second, children of those household heads belonging to other occupational groups were estimated on the basis of the child employment patterns of the children of household heads belonging to all the remaining occupations once the larger groups were ignored. Miners were disproportionately absent from the missing portion, and no possible values could be assigned to the miner employment patterns that would change their level substantially. In comparing rates for the complete portion of the population with rates for the total population, which includes the complete portion plus the estimated portion, the relative absence of children in the missing portion results in only a small change in the refined activity rate for men. The refined activity rates for men in 1856 were 0.8145 for the completed portion and 0.7715 for the total population. All figures for aggregate employment in Rive-de-Gier in 1856 are estimates.

–16–

Apprenticeship in Nineteenth-Century France: A Continuing Tradition or a Break with the Past?

YVES LEQUIN

Of all the subjects of study concerning the working class in nineteenth-century France, few enjoy as much consensus as the crisis that hit the apprenticeship system. That a crisis was felt is certain, if we only consider the plethora of laws and statutes applied to the various aspects of professional training. From the decree of March 1791 banning the attribution of masterships (*maîtrises*) and suppressing the guilds to the Astier law of July 1919 that attempted to treat the problem as a whole, no fewer than eighty-seven texts, laws, decrees, and circulars were drafted in an attempt to remedy the situation.[1]

And yet the apprenticeship system of the nineteenth century underwent a process not unlike the decline of the nobility that began at the close of the Middle Ages. It is hard to find words too strong in deploring the end of apprenticeship, but in fact, though on modest scale, the system perpetuated itself. How can one blame those enlightened spirits who observed only the incapacity of the system to adapt to a new world and sought other solutions? How could one not believe that without the institution of apprenticeship the working class would lose a certain measure of control over the working process? And can one really be unaware that, behind a somewhat nostalgic discourse that bathed itself in the myth of savoir-faire, a movement of resistance was taking shape?

[1] See, for general information pertinent to this essay, J. P. Guinot, *Formation professionnelle et travailleurs qualifiés depuis 1789* (Paris, 1946), and a more recent work by A. Prost, *L'enseignement en France, 1800–1967* (Paris, 1968), p. 305.

The backdrop of this drama, recognized by everyone, was the progressive replacement of the skilled craftsman by the unskilled worker, of manual dexterity by physical force. But must we accept this transformation as complete when recent historical research has shown how far the industrial forces in France managed to adapt themselves to the traditional mold? In this essay I have no other ambition than to ask, concerning apprenticeship, at what points one can observe the continuity of a tradition (or a break with the past) in "working class habits" (*la coutume ouvrière*). My question first of all concerns work practices that have at least in part escaped the eye of the most attentive observer.

The few objective sources available to us from the nineteenth century confirm that the discourse of the times reflected the facts. In 1848 a survey done by the Paris chamber of commerce revealed that for every seventeen skilled workers there was only one apprentice. A bit later, at the beginning of the Second Empire (1852–70), apprentices were estimated to number 20,000 out of 420,000 industrial workers, of whom some 120,000 were no doubt adolescents. In 1865 another more general survey of professional training programs concluded that apprenticeship, defined as receiving one's training in a trade workshop, was virtually nonexistent. These findings are corroborated by studies carried out on the occasion of the 1862, 1867, and 1878 world's fairs, all of which reveal a dropping off of individual workshop training. The same is observed by the Lyons Workers' Congress (Congrès ouvrier de Lyon) in 1894, and by 1906 it was no longer possible to distinguish apprenticeship from the other forms of technical training (professional training schools, courses offered by private associations, and generally mediocre municipal programs). Hardly more than 70,000 boys and girls attended any of these programs, although young people made up some 870,000 of the salaried work force in industry and commerce. This change was the result of a slow evolution, one long misunderstood by historians, who virtually restricted their study to Paris and the other large cities: by 1848 no apprentices could be found in the metropolitan factories or mills, any more than they could ten years later in the metallurgical industries, mining concerns, or textile mills in the rest of the country.

The apprenticeship crisis was not just a crisis of numbers; it affected equally the working conditions of those still within the apprenticeship system. The specifics of the law of 22 February 1851 that tried—to no avail—to right the situation, imply the kinds of problems that existed: the need for a written contract, for working hours to be specified, for the type of training in question to be clearly stated, and for the respective obligations of the apprentice and his master to be defined. The first problem was therefore the rapid disappearance of the written contract, backbone of the apprenticeship system under the *ancien régime* and doubtless the first contact most manual workers had with notarial practices. Out of 19,000 apprentices that the Paris chamber of commerce managed to identify in 1848, nearly 14,000, or three out of four, had no more than an oral agreement with their employers. In 1869 the percentage of those benefiting from a written contract was lower still, and by 1903 written contracts were a rare exception—only three percent of the cases known.

Concerning the length of the apprentices' working day, there seems to have been no set rule—or more exactly, their hours were fixed according to the regular legal working day of paid employees of the factory or workshop. The apprentice was nothing more than another young worker, indistinguishable from his fellows in the amount of time he worked and the tasks he performed. His duties were simply adapted to his strength or level of competence. "Today's apprentice is often confined to performing only the most menial of chores," someone declared at the Workers' Congress of 1894. Here we face the very "children of drudgery" (*enfants de peine*) that Corbon had spoken of so eloquently some fifty years before, little more than servants or, perhaps more appropriately, beasts of burden, as Denis Poulot often said. Here the apprentice was charged with making deliveries or running errands, there with cleaning the workshop at the end of the day, elsewhere with turning the wheel; but in any case he was a child-servant of all work, simply another manifestation of undifferentiated child labor that was the rule during the entire nineteenth century. Consider Norbert Truquin in the 1840s, who had to get up an hour early to light the fire in the wool-carding shop, then was off to get water and the daily provisions as well as act as nurse, nauseated and awkward, when his employer fell sick.[2] Or take the young glassworker Eugène Saulnier, three-quarters of a century later, who had to make ready the work of the older men, workers who "expected to be served."[3] Be this as it may, it is not certain that the laws governing the length of the working day in 1892 and 1900, or those covering accidents, as in 1898, were necessarily successful in protecting child laborers. Indeed, many of the young were simply pushed to work harder, since the social insurance contributions paid by their employers were the same as those for adults, but children, necessarily, were not as productive. In any case, from one end of the century to the other, it is clear that the status of the apprentice became assimilated to that of the industrial working class in general.

In the face of this evolution, a number of workers and workers' groups

[2]Norbert Truquin, *Mémoires et aventures d'un prolétaire à travers le révolution* (Paris, 1977), pp. 22–24.

[3]M. Chabot, *L'escarbille: Histoire d'Eugène Saulnier, ouvrier verrier* (Paris, 1978), p. 35.

resisted. From the Restoration to the turn of the century (the Belle Epoque), their efforts were unremitting. But might one not see in the very constancy of their struggle the proof of their ultimate failure? Here we are in 1820: the most dynamic French industrialists watch the rapid progress of English industry with consternation, trying to imagine ways to improve the technical ability of their own workers. The first "apprentice schools" are founded by the printer Chaix and by Teste, a pin manufacturer in Lyons. In 1827 we find the Ecole Saint-Nicolas of the Brotherhood of Christian Schools. Finally come the innumerable good-will societies, of which the most famous is the Oeuvre catholique des patrons de l'enfance (Catholic Society for the Protection of Children), which seeks to find "good bosses," tries to encourage them to train apprentices, and sees to it that proper contracts are drawn up. During the July Monarchy (1830–48) more of these "apprentice schools" are founded, like the Industrial Society of Nantes (1832), which organizes a two-part course, half at school and half in the workshop, encouraging competition by handing out awards for a final piece of work, submitted to a jury— an obvious throwback to the guild masterpiece. Some time later, in 1842, we find the Charitable Association for Apprentices (Oeuvre des apprentis), still in the tradition of Christian Brotherhood, overseeing the terms of contracts and through the establishment of ad hoc committees finding posts for apprentices approaching the end of their training.

Under the Second Empire these organizations became more specialized, addressing the needs of specific trades. Thus in 1861 we find names like the Goodwill Society for Children Employed in Flower and Feather Manufactories (Association patronale pour les enfants employés dans les fabriques de fleurs et plumes) and the Fraternity for the Protection of Children in the Cabinetmaking Trade (Société fraternelle pour le patronage des enfants de l'ébénisterie). At the same period, however, more all-encompassing organizations also were founded, such as Father Halluin's School (Ecole de l'Abbé Halluin) in Arras, the Catholic Workers' Societies (Cercles ouvriers catholiques), or the Société Saint-Vincent de Paul. But the most far-reaching, at least in intent, was the Society for the Protection of Apprentices and Children Employed in the Manufactories (Société de protection des apprentis et des enfants employés dans les manufactures), founded after the 1867 world's fair. This title clearly expresses the founders' preoccupations as well as their desire to try to adapt to the new industrial world.

Just as important, perhaps more so, are the efforts of the municipalities, particularly Paris. In 1842, and again in 1844, the Paris council created "apprenticeship prizes," given to the young workers who best fulfilled their indentures. This competition was renewed again in 1868 and 1869. Then, starting in 1875–80 under the Third Republic, more direct municipal participation was ensured by the establishment of apprenticeship schools geared to training young people in some of the more traditional trades of the capital, from the school on the boulevard de la Villette (1874)—later to become the Ecole Diderot—to the Ecole Dorian (1893). After schools specializing in cabinetmaking or printing (1882) came those for ironworking, ceramics, sculpture (1883), furnituremaking (1887), and so on. By 1889 there were a dozen such establishments for boys and girls that offered a three-year course as well as technical night courses.

Paris was by no means the first city to take this initiative, nor was it the only one. Beginning in 1867, the city of Le Havre began opening trade schools offering courses in carpentry, cabinetmaking, lock-smithing, machine fitting, ironworking, boilermaking, and so forth. I should also mention a public school of clockmaking in Besançon and schools in other professions adapted to local needs in Saint-Quentin and Douai, to name only a few.

In spite of these new opportunities, the results were disappointing. By the end of the July Monarchy, these various services had touched no more than five thousand apprentices, and in 1870 fewer than three thousand had benefited from the numerous possibilities offered in the city of Paris. If we look ahead to the twentieth century, when workers' unions began to take a hand in setting up training programs, we find that even then they had only twelve thousand students in five hundred courses offered throughout the entire country. Who is to blame for this state of affairs? Any diagnosis must be followed by an attempt to identify the cause of the illness.

The first of the guilty parties were undoubtedly the masters, or employers, themselves. The first objective of many of the apprentices' goodwill societies was to find "good bosses," not only people who desired to transmit their knowledge to others, but those with know-how worth transmitting. More and more often, however, the workshop foremen had only the barest modicum of formal training, if any at all; one can hardly be expected to pass on more than one knows or to train an apprentice if one has never been one. Ignorance is born of ignorance, and crisis feeds upon crisis. In 1889 the Fédération des travailleurs du livre (Federation of Workers in the Book Trade) reached an agreement with the corresponding goodwill society to establish the ground rules for apprentices' contracts. It was a unique effort, which served above all to point out the general lack of initiative in the other trades, and it happened in a profession that was already rather special. A survey conducted by the Statistique générale de la France in 1871 decried "bad bosses'" lack of commitment, echoing a complaint heard throughout the century criticizing the desire for profit on the part of employers who had no intention of wasting time—in other words money—and had no other goal than to fill their immediate wants.

Corresponding to the inability or refusal to transmit knowledge was the refusal to learn. The outcry against this came early, but the reasons for its existence are easy to explain. In the first place, a good apprenticeship cost a lot of money, and many parents simply could not afford it; with the growing lack of expertise, the period of training lasted four to five years, and the expense increased as well. But more than that, the utility of the apprenticeship program was not obvious to the young candidates; the constraints were more evident (the bonds formed in cramped working quarters are not necessarily the most cordial, as we shall see later), with no apparent advantages to outweigh them, or so it seemed to youngsters who could not really appreciate the value of what they would learn. Thus they were tempted to go to work directly in the factories, which, contrary to popular opinion, offered more freedom. The common complaint of the day was that breach of contract was the plague of the Second Empire, while large cities swallowed up the young, who lost themselves in the ever growing, ever changing, and anonymous working population. Speaking before one of the workers' investigation committees of 1867, the clockmaker Wilmot mentioned the "constant sidetracking of the young apprentices" that discouraged even the most well intentioned; and some time later Denis Poulot denounced the indifference of parents who "put their sons into apprenticeship in order to get rid of them."[4] In fact, all of them participated in one way or another in the "dérangement fréquent," the unceasing mobility during the nineteenth century of the working classes, who searched for opportunity, or wealth, in an economy of changing tempos, whether in different trades, cities, or workshops. By the end of the century, a certain settling had begun to take place, but there were other forces as well, all working in the same direction: during the Belle Epoque, an apprentice earned ten francs a month his first year, twenty his second, and thirty his third, all less than the monthly wage of an unskilled factory worker. Nothing short of changes in work itself contributed to diverting the young from apprenticeship; why waste one's time learning a trade when any idiot could do simple, repetitive work that required no training and paid more than a skilled professional could earn? So in 1946 Guinot's conclusions were little different from Poulot's, when he laid the blame on the "materialism of the parents."[5]

We have finally arrived, perhaps, at the crux of the matter: the behavior of the different actors in this drama is merely the reflection of

[4]Denis Poulot, *Le sublime, ou Le travailleur comme il est en 1870 et ce qu'il peut être,* reedited and with an introduction by Alain Cottereau (Paris, 1980), p. 315.
[5]Guinot, *Formation,* p. 171.

shifts in the economy and in the ways of working. Contemporary observers recognized the implications of these changes from the outset. Like Anthime Corbon, Pierre Joseph Proudhon incriminated large industry, especially factories designed—rightly enough—to bring together a certain number of basic techniques in the making of a whole, thereby obscuring any concept of the final product, a concept upon which apprenticeship and the attainment of mastership are built. Similarly, Augustin Cochin, who came from an entirely different orientation, also placed the blame on mechanization and the division of labor. "Work is becoming automatic," cried Corbon, foretelling the fragmentation of labor (*le travail en miettes*) of the twentieth century. The case was heard, and later historians would take up the same refrain. Thus there was nothing new in Guinot's analysis of the evolution of professional training in France, made just after World War II. He states his position clearly: the division of labor necessarily brings about the deskilling of the worker, since there is no place "for taking any initiative, or demonstrating any intelligence," and since this attitude which formed the basis of a certain type of working knowledge, was part of "an economic system that was out of date."[6] From that standpoint, what was the use of concerning oneself with a question that was of archaeological interest at best, that involved a handful of people—hangers-on of the compagnonnage ideal of the old trade guilds—in a system whose decline was a result of its inability to adapt to the times?

One must admit that all the attempts to restore the apprenticeship system in the nineteenth century were strangely out of step with economic reality. Nevertheless, certain of the most modern enterprises had their own schools of apprenticeship. Early on, this was the case of Boncourt in Guebwiller and of some concerns in Mulhouse and La Ciotat. Later would come more famous ones: Schneider in Le Creusot, Peugeot near Montbéliard, De Wendel, and well into the twentieth century, the larger automobile firms of Renault, Berliet, and Citroën. But one should not be misled by the similarity of terms, for these "apprenticeship schools" were set up to teach certain very precise techniques, limited to the particular factory in which they were to be used. They did not attempt to accomplish what the old system had done, namely, to teach a person a craft. J. B. Dumay, for instance, spent several long months as a Schneider apprentice in 1860. At the end of this training he knew little more than how to make a few very specialized types of bolts; beyond that, the choice of relevant jobs was extremely limited.[7]

[6] Ibid., p. 85.
[7] J. B. Dumay, *Mémoires d'un militant ouvrier du Creusot (1841–1905)* (Paris, 1976), p. 80.

There were other forms of apprenticeship in private businesses in which workshop training played an important role as part of a more general education. After a long period of gestation, this practice eventually led to the creation of a kind of "professional education," no longer within the confines of the factory but under the auspices of the state. This development was inspired by old Martin Nadaud (trained as an apprentice himself) and was promulgated by the law of 11 December 1880 that called for the establishment of "apprenticeship schools for the manual trades" (écoles manuelles d'apprentissage). The schools that grew out of this initiative at Vierzon (1881), Armentières and Voiron (1882), and Nantes (1898) were in fact forerunners of changes that would happen during the twentieth century rather than a product of tradition. On another front, evening courses were set up by workers' unions, more interested in gaining recognition for their institutions than in training people. In the end, the Parisian schools (Estienne, Dorian, and Boulle) catered only to a small elite, specialists in a few very marginal professions.

Notwithstanding the creation of these new schools, a few diehard organizations kept the flame of traditional apprenticeship burning, in spite of the changes in the economic climate. These groups, such as the Brotherhood of Christian Schools (Frères des écoles chrétiennes), the Charitable Association of Apprentices (Oeuvre des apprentis)—of which one of the guiding lights was the count of Melun—and the "Workers' Circles" (Cercles ouvriers) aimed at helping unhappy children and, more than that, at raising the moral standards of the working class while trying to rechristianize industrialized society. It is not just by chance that at the end of the July Monarchy and under the Second Empire we find Protestant organizations parallel to the Catholic effort and working in the same vein, such as the Committee for the Protections of Apprentices of the Reformed Church (Comité de patronage des apprentis de l'Eglise réformée). Obviously these endeavors were more concerned with a kind of social Christianity than with professional training and therefore belong only on the fringes of a history of the working class.

Thus it is not surprising that although working-class discourse expressed more or less the same diagnosis (whether directly or indirectly), it did so in different ways. Above all, one never heard the slightest sigh of regret. Where it still existed, the system of apprenticeship was seen less as a guardian of tradition than as a focus of decay, not the least of which was moral. "What a sorry sight," laments Anthime Corbon, referring to the apprentices who spent at least as much time drinking with their companions in cabarets, in spite of their youth, as they did working. In the workshop he found the situation hardly better, for he witnessed less instruction than "strange things to be heard and kept in mind."[8] In 1834–35, debauchery and sloth were named the irredeemable corruptors of young apprentices, inculcating in their minds "a spirit of impudence and depravity they will never lose."[9] "Their morals are shameful," declared the housepainters' delegate at the 1867 world's fair, but then, could one really expect anything else in a situation where vice, debauchery, and disrespect are commended, virtue is held up to ridicule, and vile language is the rule? Vice is what the child learns about in apprenticeship, and we know well the role attributed to it by D. Poulot in his classification of the Parisian working class at the end of the Second Empire.[10]

All this rhetoric led reformers to turn their backs on the restoration of apprenticeship in the workshop.[11] Etienne Cabet and the Icarians were left to dream on about a mythical education "at home"; they had no followers. Corbon and Poulot, on the other hand, agreed with many other less famous analysts: The learning of a profession had to be steered away from the workshop and ripped out of the hand of corruption that had taken hold of these fake fraternities. Was not the working class losing its soul there? One would guess so, judging by this strange admonition a father might give his twelve-year-old son as he entered the labor market, imagined by the housepainters' delegate at the 1867 fair: "Choose a craft, but not mine. It's too horrible. To make this choice damns one's own destiny." This plea was no less than a denial of a worker's own situation and of the pride—whether real or imaginary— in the working-class condition. In an indirect way, this warning reflects the way the crafts were changing to meet changes in the economic situation. Educational training was one way not only to shorten and simplify the work one did, but also to dominate the working situation as well, by breaking from a kind of occupational heritage, turned fate, and thus opening up the doors to new choices. The people grouped around *L'Atelier* believed that mechanics should know how to draw and be familiar with geometry, that workers in the building trades should know descriptive geometry and factory workers the basic principles of physics and chemistry. In 1859 Corbon proposed that everyone should be familiar with a number of different professions, an idea that was taken up in an 1879 poster that demanded that prospective workers be taught "the essential elements of one or two different manual professions."

"For real perfection, you have to be educated" was a song heard in

---

[8] Anthime Corbon, *De l'enseignement professionnel* (Paris, 1859) p. 25.
[9] Poulot, *Sublime*, p. 77.
[10] Ibid., pp. 315–19.
[11] G. Duveau, *La pensée ouvrière sur l'éducation pendant la seconde république et le second empire* (Paris, 1948), p. 356.

Lille in 1881,[12] but the people who sang did not have apprenticeship in mind. Poulot was of the opinion that workers' practical training should not be separated from their moral instruction, a feeling echoed by the people behind *L'Atelier*, who added that both types of education should be given only after one had basic familiarity with the craft through written texts. This is interesting in light of the basic conviction (especially on the part of Corbon) that the secrets of the traditional crafts could not be transmitted by the written word, an idea reinforced in the mystical rites and practices of the few trade corporations that were left.

In a word, the young had to be armed both morally and intellectually before entering apprenticeship. The workers themselves subscribed to this basic philosophy, and about 1848 they urged that instruction and knowledge, however elementary, be provided to everyone. These reforms were taken up not only by those who best expressed the working condition at the time (Joseph Benoît, Anthime Corbon, Agricol Perdiguier), but also by the Parisian delegates to the Geneva Conference of 1846. Nevertheless, the traditional strict separation of the roles of teacher and master craftsman was carefully observed. Poulot imagined professional schools for the young (but not too young) associated with the large factories. Like others, he felt that they should provide an "industrial education" with a mixed program: on the one hand, a general elementary education for everyone; on the other, an apprenticeship system in which future workers would work with professionals. Ideally, the entire operation would be run and overseen by workers' associations, at least in the eyes of some of the delegates to the London world's fair of 1862, who were perhaps not quite free of their own workshop memories. By the end of the Second Empire, the number of proposals for setting up "professional schools," organized by the workers themselves and founded on an ideal of mutual improvement and egalitarian dispersal of knowledge, had mushroomed. On another plane, the trade unionists of 1890–1900 dreamed of establishing organizations whose primary purpose would be to inform others of the working condition, in all its aspects.

The accent was no longer on the acquisition of professional training. Georges Duveau has pointed out to what an extent the working-class concept of education had changed; by the middle of the nineteenth century priority was given to guaranteeing a good general education.[13] In this case workers' education was no longer the domain of the workers themselves—the state would necessarily have to play a part. By the turn of the century, the education of the working classes had indeed been

[12]L. Marty, *Chanter pour survivre: Culture ouvrière, travail et techniques dans la textile, Roubaix, 1850–1914* (Lille, 1982), p. 22.
[13]Duveau, *Pensée ouvrière*, p. 99.

incorporated into a general educational system. Didn't the workers now risk losing their identity? This result was hardly what the first reformers of the 1840s had in mind, and the possible appearance of a sort of technological aristocracy, forgetful of its social origins, was strongly decried as a future source of working-class fragmentation, with consequences far worse than those deplored under the trade guilds and the apprenticeship system. But perhaps this is only a secondary issue.

Indeed, the positions of Corbon and Poulot are not wholly unambiguous. Although the former qualifies the level of knowledge and professional know-how gleaned from apprenticeship as "hardly above zero," he remarks that others defend it with aplomb and concedes that one learns many other worthwhile things that he simply considers less important, concluding, "It does wake the youngsters up a bit." Others observe that the worker who seems the most irresponsible in the workshop may appear to his family and the outside world in general as most serious and respectable. Later, taking his sources perhaps too literally, Guinot condemns the frequenting of wine sellers, which creates ties as strong as but less desirable than those of fellowship; I would observe that the two are not mutually exclusive, and that the former do not necessarily lead simply to debauchery and dissipation.[14] Still other observers at the turn of the century comment on the sketchy knowledge that provincial workers bring to Paris. This information could be interpreted either negatively or positively: as a condemnation of their low level of professional skill or as a recognition that they had at least some knowledge. For example, the limited knowledge and specialized skills of J. B. Dumay, mentioned earlier, do not seem to have hindered him when he left Le Creusot. In the next few months he managed to hold several different jobs, apparently adapting easily to his new surroundings each time, whether he was working in a small shop in a Burgundian village or for a large company in Grenelle or La Ciotat.[15] In fact, because of their own backgrounds, the nineteenth-century observers, followed by a certain type of twentieth-century historiography with a nostalgic view of artisanal life, limited their studies almost entirely to the small workshops in large cities, in professions that were becoming increasingly marginal. Overall, the apprenticeship crisis they describe is undoubtedly less concerned with problems of professional training than with the crisis of a social system inherited from the *ancien régime* in which the employed could no longer expect, in time, to become the employers. The industrialization of France made this system obsolete. But far from eliminating

[14]Guinot, *Formation*, p. 124.
[15]Dumay, *Mémoires*, p. 84.

the traditional apprenticeship system, factory life may very well have saved it, as becomes clear if we refrain from trying to fit it into a conceptual model created during the interwar years.[16]

First of all, we must make a distinction between the nineteenth-century factory and the type of integrated factory system we know today. For example, according to G. Noiriel, the construction of the Lorraine steelworks was, until a relatively late date, based on the juxtaposition of independent units grouped around the traditional forge, with the blast furnaces and steel manufacture upstream and the facilities for laminating, hardware, valves, and fittings downstream. He found the same pattern in glassworks, among the largest industries of the period; they expanded by simply adding new "ovens" (*fours*) and "shops" (*places*) next to the ones already in place.[17] This dispersal of the various activities reveals the nature of work in the new industrial situation, a sort of gathering together of the separate professional workshops of the old industries. It was not so much their function as their proximity that was new, for the traditional division of labor, work organization, and circulation of knowledge were kept largely intact.

Let us look more closely at the situation. If we place ourselves in the Lorraine iron mines of 1900, we see that their organization follows that outlined above.[18] The extraction of the iron ore depends on the coordination of different teams of workmen, each of which reproduces a workshop model with a piecework system of payment. What counts is the team, three men whose jobs were inseparable; the miner (*mineur*) who gives orders, his assistant (*aide-mineur*), and his wheeler (*rouleur*). Let us move on to the iron- and steelworks. We have already seen the spatial separation of the various branches; each one has its independent organization, not so different from that of the mines. If we look at what goes on in the blast furnaces, for instance, we see the "founders" (*fondeurs*) who must regulate the temperature, the "second founders" (*deuxième fondeurs*) who do the sow channel, and the "third founders" (*troisième fondeurs*) who spread the sand. The whole operation depends on teamwork in which every action, no matter how elementary, moves at the same rhythm: six arms fused together while moving the heavy steel bars, three bodies that move as one to avoid the flying sparks.[19] This basic

[16]Concerning the historical development of the factory, see Michelle Perrot, "De la manufacture à l'usine en miettes," *Mouvement Social* 125 (October–December 1983): 3–12.

[17]G. Noiriel, "Espace de production et luttes sociales: L'exemple des usines sidérurgiques lorraines (1880–1930)," *Mouvement Social* 125 (October–December 1983): 25. See also Michael P. Hanagan, *The Logic of Solidarity: Artisans and Industrial Workers in Three French Towns, 1871–1914* (Urbana, Ill., 1980), p. 93.

[18]G. Noiriel, "Les ouvriers sidérurgiques et les mineurs de fer dans les bassin de Longwy pendant l'entre-deux-guerres" (thesis of third cycle, University of Paris VIII, 1982), 1:81.

[19]Ibid., 1:93.

nineteenth-century model continued well into the twentieth century, as witnessed by Eugène Saulnier in his recollection of a 1920s glassworks. Under the direction of the "shop foreman" (*chef de place*), the "gatherer" (*gamin*), a young boy, gathered the glass from the furnace, the "big boy" (*grand garçon*) prepared the mold so that the "blower" (*souffleur*) could give the bottle the correct shape, and there were a multitude of "carriers" (*porteurs*) and the "basket weavers" (*tresseurs de paillon*) who made the straw cases for the bottles.[20] But perhaps the most surprising instance is that of the mechanized spinning mills of Lille in the 1880s and 1890s, basically organized similarly to a domestic industry. The "spinner" (*fileur*) who directed each "square" (*carré*) or work space reigned over a hierarchical world in which one's rank depended upon age and ability rather than the job performed; they ranged from the "*bâcleurs*," twelve to sixteen years old, to the "*rattacheurs*" and "*conducteurs*," who were older.[21]

"Spinning is a craft," said one of these workers, and we would do well to consider the weight of these words, for in many ways the "spinner" filled all the functions of the old-style master craftsman. He organized and evaluated the work and was in part responsible for choosing the boys who would be hired as bâcleurs, just as the miner or the shop foreman of the bottle works chose and trained his team, combining the ability to recognize talent with ties of family and friendship. The endurance of the piecework system of payment only makes the parallel between the workshop and the factory more evident: in the mines and glassworks, it was not uncommon for the foreman to redistribute the end price (*prix fait*) paid by the employer, dividing it up among his subordinates according to their ability and rank.

Contrary to Guinot's belief, the factory strategy was not yet that of trying to reduce everything to one job, even if evidence of that policy began to emerge with the creation of the skilled worker.[22] Rather, the aim was to take the maximum advantage of the workers' previous knowledge, the existence of which was never questioned. This basic premise is clearly that of the workers themselves, judging from their opinion as expressed by their representatives. The men of *L'Atelier* remembered with pride the role that certain artisans, like Jacquard or Watt, played in the Industrial Revolution. The artificial-leaf maker Pagnerre referred to "lost" trade secrets, whose existence he took for granted, and the technical vocabulary of which, though a late development, gave weight to a discourse of independence and resistance.[23]

---

[20]Chabot, *Escabille*, p. 10.
[21]Marty, *Chanter pour survivre*, p. 48.
[22]Guinot, *Formation*, p. 86. See also Michelle Perrot, *Les ouvriers en grève, France, 1871–1890* (Paris, 1974), 1:336.
[23]For examples, see Marty, *Chanter pour survivre*, p. 37.

For their part, the employers seem to assume the same expertise. The Foundry Commission (Comité des forges) recognized founders' "particular skills": for example, they instinctively sensed the instant when they must move back from the mouth of the blast furnace; and in the steelworks, a work inspector referred to a certain "physiological knowledge" that provided a kind of selective endurance in the face of the blast.[24] Even in the middle of the twentieth century, Michael Hanagan observes glassworks engineers' admiration for the skill of the "shop foreman" in knowing, empirically, when the molten glass is ready to be shaped, since the slightest mistake can make the difference between the success or failure of the finished piece.[25]

Indeed, everything we learn about daily life in a nineteenth century French factory confirms this reliance on human skill and knowledge. In the Lorraine, the choice of location for a mine, the angle of perforation, the way to crib a specific mine shaft—all depended upon expertise. In the iron- and steelworks, the founders' importance was based not only on their own physical force but also on a talent for judging the quality of ore samples that look alike but have different densities, for verifying the condition of the blast-furnace crucible, checking for faults in the molds and the position of the blast pipe, and so forth. Even though steel manufacturing was very new, it demanded great precision because of the speed and the violence of the process: one had to have an eye for the color of the flame, an ear for the quality of the sound, and expertise in regulating the air and gas flows in the new Martin convertors. Nevertheless, Noiriel notes with astonishment the incredible loyalty to simple tools, like the rabble, and the similarity between the movements, gestures, and body position of the steelmakers and those of the old-fashioned founders or laminators with relation to the blast.[26]

This apparently gradual change is not simply a result of technological inertia, and mechanization does not automatically lead to the deskilling of a craft—as Marty has demonstrated in his recent work on the Lillois textile industry.[27] I will not go into the fact that even the most sophisticated techniques incorporate certain manual tasks. More to the point is the case of sorting raw wool, a necessary task done well in advance of spinning or weaving. At the end of the nineteenth century, this process was entirely dependent upon the sorter's ability to ascertain the wool's quality by sight and touch. Only time could teach one how to do it, and the employers were forced to admit their inability to reduce the tech-

[24]Quoted by Noiriel, "Ouvriers sidérurgistes," 1:93, 114.
[25]Michael P. Hanagan, "Organisation du travail et action revendicative: Verriers et métallurgistes de Rive-de-Gier à la fin du XIX siècle," *Cahiers d'histoire* 26 (1981): 11–12.
[26]Noiriel, "Ouvriers sidérurgistes," 1:81, 93, 114.
[27]Marty, *Chanter pour survivre*, p. 31.

nique to a simple formula and thereby appropriate it for themselves. Again, the scientific evaluation of fibers and dyes was severely limited; only the spinners could correctly judge their optimum moisture and temperature. At the turn of the century, the incorporation of a laboratory in the Lorraine iron- and steelworks was not yet in sight, in spite of the growing number of engineers employed. Iron masters had to face the fact that a real working knowledge, whether individual or collective, was indispensable. In a word, nothing could replace a craft. Only by seeing how a sample cracked or by watching the color of the metal in fusion could the founders "make their analysis" or the steelworkers decide what should be added, just as the miners sensed the safety (or danger) of a gallery by the curve of the roof or the sound of the ore under the picks.[28]

Far from eliminating the need for skills, mechanization simply created a demand for new ones, as Marty has shown in his study of the Lillois textile mills. The "spinner" was responsible not only for the tasks I have already mentioned, but also for running sophisticated machinery, making constant adjustments as it ran—the fitter and repairman were rarely needed.[29] The Lorraine miners repaired their own tools; founders not only coordinated the actions of their team, they also repaired broken blast pipes; as for the laminators, they adjusted their mills with a mallet and changed the rollers when necessary. Until World War I, the iron and steel industry in the Lorraine still depended upon the multiplicity of separate jobs, and the Foundry Commission praised a certain economic rationality of this system. Because of the growing complexity of the machines, their upkeep was becoming more and more difficult to separate from the production process and turn over to the maintenance service.[30] Even as late as the 1920s, the metalworkers of Fives-Lille, in Givors, affirmed that each machine had a personality of its own, and that the only person who could repair it when it broke down was the man who used it. The large factory had not yet brought about the fragmentation of labor, and industry relied on a certain versatility on the part of the workers. Professional skill was still sorely needed at the turn of the century, although it was a skill of another kind: the day of the carpenter and blacksmith had passed on to the machine mechanics and fitters.

From a purely formalistic point of view, then, the apprenticeship system did not reestablish itself. Witness Norbert Truquin, who, in the middle of the nineteenth century, took only a few weeks to become competent in weaving silk cloth. With a mechanical wool-carding machine, in 1880, "a guy with a little common sense learns how to card in three days." In the Lille cotton mills, "for the first day or two, the ap-

---

[28]Noiriel, "Ouvriers sidérurgistes," 1:81, 93.
[29]Marty, *Chanter pour survivre*, p. 40.
[30]Noiriel, "Ouvriers sidérurgistes," 1:81, 108–9.

prentice learns how to make knots. The second and third days, how to start the loom running. Then how to set the quill and charge it without twisting the thread. Finally, he begins to weave."[31] In 1902 the Labor Commission concluded that as much could be learned in two weeks in a factory as in four years of apprenticeship. Differences notwithstanding, however, the factory atmosphere was as brutal as the workshop had been up through the Second Empire: to "teach" Norbert Truquin how to card, he was whipped with a rope; J. B. Dumay was showered with threats on his way to becoming an assistant puddler in Grenelle; and as a young boy in the glassworks, Eugène Saulnier had to "watch the seat of [his] pants" at the beginning of the twentieth century. Nevertheless, Saulnier's experiences were not all bad, and it is worth considering them in more detail here.

Although there were "drunken brutes," Saulnier also met "old man Pilon," patient, anxious to share what he knew with others, one who did not hesitate to help his fellow workers out of a fix, though it was not part of his job. When a blower took a little time off, the young "gatherer" could take up the blowpipe; if he did not do it on his own, he would be invited to try, perhaps during the time-out, and old man Pilon would coach him, correcting his clumsy attempts and "showing the correct gestures, how to do it." Slowly, over the course of months if necessary, the techniques were learned under the watchful eyes of the "old-timers," who demonstrated, judged, and rewarded the youngsters for their accomplishments.[32] The tricks of the trade were learned through observation on the job, limited in the beginning to knowing when to open and close the furnace, signaled by the sound of the shoe hitting the bottle as it was being molded. It was not through the instruction of one teacher that the apprentice learned the profession, but with the help of the entire team. Here we have, once again, the old idea of sharing knowledge and the unveiling of trade secrets that others, like those grouped around *L'Atelier*, had dreamed about a half-century before, in their attempt to transform professional training and the apprenticeship system. But whereas Martin Nadaud or Agricol Perdiguier gave night courses on building techniques after the day's work, here was their heir, old man Pilon, teaching in the factory itself.

A technological revolution had brought about these changes, whose overall effects the early planners could not have foreseen. The wool spinner in Lille was also a teacher, and it was he who chose, among the sixteen- and seventeen-year-olds, who would be a "rattacheur" and who a "conducteur." By watching the founder or the steelworker, one could

---

[31]Marty, *Chanter pour survivre*, pp. 31, 60.
[32]Chabot, *Escabille*, pp. 28–30, 43–44.

eventually become his equal. In the Lorraine steelworks, although the foreman's first responsibility was to organize the manufacture of the steel—making sure that the sand was ready, that the molding boxes and patterns were in good shape, that the molds were correctly filled—he was also there to help, "by his personal experience, any time a worker was unsure of himself." In the mines, the foreman supervised the work of those under him, to be sure, but he also showed them the proper way to do things. "You always learned something," recollected a weaver in a Lillois cotton mill who had learned how to weave in little more than one week. Of course he still had a lot to learn—the most important part of his trade, no doubt—the adjustments that had to be made for the different kinds of fiber and cloth, or how to maintain and repair the machines he worked with. "By watching the foreman, I learned something about the mechanics of the loom, and managed to adjust mine myself," says another weaver.[33] And so the factory, in time, with its division of labor and diversity of jobs, became a kind of apprentices' textbook, such as a certain tradition had only dreamed of.

Learning the job was not the only thing that was taught in the textile mills of Lille. When a young "bâcleur" was hired, he was taken to a corner of the factory, undressed, and masturbated, "to see if he's a man." Doubtless in 1848 this was seen as another proof of the moral depravity of the workshops. Today one might be more inclined to consider such practices a kind of admission ceremony or initiation rite and to see entry to the workshop and the working world as part of the worker's *apprenticeship*, within the framework of an anthropological history of the working class that has barely been launched. For the moment, anecdotal accounts prompt us to reconsider the question of apprenticeship from a more limited point of view, since, if we consider the literary reflections of those such as Corbon or Poulot, we discover that by the beginning of the twentieth century professional training was simply another arm of public education, run by the state, a far cry from the dreams of 1840, even if those dreams gradually become accustomed to the state's role.

During this period of change, the traditional type of apprenticeship did not disappear with the arrival of the mechanized factory, it simply shifted gears—although this adaptation seems to have passed unnoticed by even the most careful observers. Apprenticeship had remained faithful to those principles that had given it value in the first place: an initiation into a working knowledge that could be successfully transmitted only by demonstration (for it was difficult to explain otherwise) and daily practical training that implied equality in the distribution of knowledge

[33] Noiriel, "Ouvriers sidérurgistes," 1:81, 165. See also Marty, *Chanter pour survivre*, p. 61.

and lent strength to the workers as a group. It was not apprenticeship that had changed but the industrial world to which it gave access and in which the integrated, hierarchical working group had taken the place of the master craftsman's workshop. The workshop was a crucible of social advancement, or at least exposed one to it, whereas the factory locked one into the working condition, even if there was a ranking based on criteria other than advancement on the road toward mastership. Throughout this essay I have attempted to point out the continuity of concrete practices, though the demonstration has been limited to the acquisition of certain techniques. Quite obviously, apprenticeship is far more than that: it is also an initiation into a certain social condition. I refer you to Alain Cottereau's well-known inverted reading of Poulot's descriptions of working-class mores under the Second Empire, in which vice is turned into virtue.

At the end of the century apprenticeship remained, above all, an integral part of a community, even though the nature of that community had changed. What is astonishing is that apprenticeship had managed to adapt itself to the new environment and still keep its basic character. One has only to rid oneself of the nostalgic image of the mythical workshop in order to see this. There will have to be other revolutions to break the "working-class habit," and the apprenticeship crisis is yet to come.

Translated by Mary Hyman

$-17-$

The European Science of Work: The Economy of the Body at the End of the Nineteenth Century

ANSON RABINBACH

In the three decades before World War I, European scientists produced an extensive literature on the physiology, psychology, and practical aspects of industrial work. Unlike the perception of labor found in earlier doctrines of moral or political economy, this literature centered not on the "worker" in a social sense, nor on the economics of wage labor, but on the body of the worker, whose movements and rhythms were subjected to the most detailed investigation. Although they were similar in reducing work to the worker's measurable physical movements, there were also significant differences between the new "science of work" (*science du travail, Arbeitswissenschaft*) and its more successful American counterpart, the Taylor system or "Scientific Management."[1]

I thank Patrick Fridenson, Steven Kaplan, Mary Nolan, and Jacques Rancière for their helpful suggestions.

[1] The literature on Taylorism is extensive. The most important general discussions are Daniel Nelson, *Frederick W. Taylor and the Rise of Scientific Management* (Madison, 1980); Harry Braverman, *Labor and Monopoly Capital: The Degradation of Work in the Twentieth Century* (New York and London, 1974); Sudhir Kakar, *Frederick Taylor: A Study in Personality and Innovation* (Cambridge, Mass., 1970); *Technology, the Labor Process, and the Working Class*, special issue of *Monthly Review* (July/August 1976); Michael Burawoy, "Toward a Marxist Theory of the Labor Process: Braverman and Beyond," *Politics and Society* 8, no. 4 (1978): 247–312; Georges Friedmann, *Industrial Society: The Emergence of the Human Problems of Automation* (Glencoe, Ill., 1955), esp. chap. 1; E. J. Hobsbawm, "Custom, Wages and Work Load in Nineteenth-Century Industry," in *Workers in the Industrial Revolution*, ed. Peter N. Stearns and Daniel Walkowitz (New Brunswick, N. J., 1974), pp. 138–76; and most recently Judith A. Merkle, *Management and Ideology: The Legacy of the International Scientific Management Movement* (Berkeley and Los Angeles, 1980).

Characterized by a greater remove from the imperatives of industry or factory discipline, the European science of work had its origins not on the shop floor but in the laboratory. It found its greatest resonance not among engineers and managers, but among scientists, doctors, hygienists, and social reformers. Whereas Taylorism placed the interests of management in the forefront to ensure labor passivity and higher productivity, the science of labor wanted to mediate social conflict by transforming work in the interests of both labor and management. Whereas Taylorism was predicated on the transfer of knowledge from the discretion of the individual worker to the control of management, the European science of labor was based on the physiological and psychological rationalization of the laboring body—on the elimination of fatigue, overwork, and wasteful motion. Taylorism's appeal was directly to managers and owners of large firms, offering greater productivity, increased tempo, and greater profit. The European science of labor appealed to the state for increased surveillance and control over the excesses of management and labor in the interest of providing the nation with healthier and more productive workers. For these reasons the European science of labor saw American scientific management as a threat, and it rose to the challenge when, on the eve of the war, the American system began to achieve its first successes in the Old World.

MAN = MACHINE

To understand the origins of the European science of labor it is necessary first to explore in general terms two profound changes that occurred in the perception of the body and the nature of work in the second half of the nineteenth century. First, the moral model of behavior as motivated by ethical and cultural imperatives was increasingly replaced by a medical model that stressed the natural sources of activity in biology, physiology, or psychology. In France, for example, such concepts as "degeneration" and "hysteria" provided the perception of behavior with a medical vocabulary weighted with strong social overtones.[2] In Germany, too, the rise of mechanical materialism and "psychophysics" brought a utilitarian and scientific language to social consciousness, often with

[2]On Degeneration see Robert A. Nye, "Degeneration and the Medical Model of Cultural Crisis in the French *Belle Epoque*," in *Political Symbolism in Modern Europe: Essays in Honor of George L. Mosse*, ed. S. Drescher, D. Sabean, and A. Sharlin (New Brunswick, N. J., 1982), pp. 19–41; on hysteria see Jan Goldstein, "The Hysteria Diagnosis and the Politics of Anticlericalism in Late Nineteenth Century France," *Journal of Modern History*, 54, no. 2 (June 1982): 209–39.

an underlying emphasis on power or force.[3] Second, and perhaps more important, the theory of energy conservation and "thermodynamics" provided scientists and popular writers with a new image of the body as a reservoir of energy awaiting conversion to work.[4] Semantically, this meant that the word "work" was universalized to include all activities of all "motors," animate as well as inanimate; culturally, it signified the triumph of the idea of energy as the transcendental force basic to all reality.

The idea that the human organism resembles a machine has ancient roots and was a central motif of seventeenth- and eighteenth century science and philosophy. Leibniz noted that "living bodies are from their smallest parts ad infinitum machines," and La Mettrie gave the mechanical analogy its classical formulation in his *L'homme machine* (1748), which compared the human organism to the mechanism of a highly complex clock. For La Mettrie, "the human body is a machine that winds its own springs; a living image of perpetual motion."[5] For these early rationalists descended from Descartes, "the thinking machine" was conceived by nature in its own image; the great natural machine produced the human machine as the mirror of its mechanical body. Drawing on this metaphor, physiologists such as Giovanni Borelli produced a substantial corpus of literature on the mechanics of the body, its laws of motion, and the physical properties of the human machine.[6]

[3]On scientific materialism in Germany see Frederick Gregory, *Scientific Materialism in Nineteenth Century Germany* (Boston, 1977); John Theodore Merz, *A History of European Thought in the Nineteenth Century*, 2 vols. (New York, 1965); Everett Mendelsohn, *Heat and Life: The Development of the Theory of Animal Heat* (Cambridge, Mass., 1964); idem, "Physical Models and Physiological Concepts: Explanation in Nineteenth Century Biology," *British Journal for the History of Science* 2 (1965): 201–19; Oswei Temkin, "Materialism in French and German Physiology of the Early 19th Century," *Bulletin of the History of Medicine* 20 (1946): 322–27; George Canguilhem, "What Is Psychology?" *Ideology and Consciousness* 7 (Autumn 1980): 37–50.

[4]For the significance of energy conservation see Yehuda Elkana, *The Discovery of the Conservation of Energy* (Cambridge, Mass., 1974); Thomas S. Kuhn, "Energy Conservation as an Example of Simultaneous Discovery," in *The Essential Tension: Selected Studies in Scientific Tradition and Change* (Chicago and London, 1977), pp. 66–104; P. M. Harman, *Energy, Force, and Matter: The Conceptual Development of Nineteenth Century Physics* (Cambridge, 1982); Dolf Sternberger, "Natural/Artificial," in *Panorama of the Nineteenth Century*, trans. Joachim Neugroschel (New York, 1977), pp. 17–38.

[5]There is an extensive literature on the philosophical analogy of man and machine. See, for example, Leibniz, "Monadologie," in *Philosophische Schriften*, vol. 1, *Kleine Schriften zur Metaphysik*, ed. Hans Heinz Holz (Darmstadt, 1965), p. 469; Julien Offray de La Mettrie, *L'homme machine* (Paris, 1748); Arno Baruzzi, *Mensch und Maschine: Das Denken sub specie machinae* (Munich, 1973), pp. 63, 81; Arno Baruzzi, ed., Aufklärung und Materialismus im Frankreich des 18. Jahrhunderts (Munich, 1968), pp. 21–62; J. E. Poretzky, *Julien Offray de La Mettrie* (Berlin, 1900); J. Kirkinen, *Les origines de la conception moderne de l'homme-machine* (Helsinki, 1960); E. J. Dijksterhuis, *Die Mechanisierung des Weltbildes* (Berlin, Göttingen, and Heidelberg, 1956) Aram Vartanian, ed., *La Mettrie's L'Homme Machine: A Study in the Origins of an Idea* (Princeton, 1960).

[6]The historical background of these controversies is given in Martin Sheldon Staum,

By the end of the eighteenth century the mechanical metaphor began to appear in more practical guises. The French scientist-philosopher C. A. Coloumb investigated the maximum work that could be done without injury to the health of the worker in the most arduous occupations, and Charles Dupin, the remarkable savant of the polytechnical school of Metz (which included Claude-Lucien Bergery, the founder of the science of industrial management in France), used studies of soldiers and artisans as early as the 1820s "to examine the means available for use in order to increase the absolute force the human being can employ in industrial work."[7] Although there were opponents of the mechanical view of the body—the vitalists often appeared triumphant in the first half of the nineteenth century—the mechanical metaphor remained firmly entrenched as the dominant scientific paradigm for investigating the properties of the human body at work. Corporal mechanics attested to the persistence of a fascination with the idea of the equivalence of man and machine.[8]

By midcentury, however, the analogy of man and machine began to undergo a profound transformation. Not only were the views of the older generation of mechanists found wanting in theoretical rigor, but the image of the machine itself began to change. The anthropomorphics of the machine, until that time, had remained relatively uncomplicated, reflecting the idea intended by the creators of the original seventeenth-century "automata" that had inspired Descartes and Hobbes, that the mechanical functions were analogous—for example in Vaucanson's famous "flute player"—to those of human functions. But the power of the machine remained external to it and when compared with the "perpetuum mobile" that was so ardently sought after in that epoch, largely inadequate. With the discovery of modern steam power, which by 1851 was anthropomorphized in the popular imagination, this older concep-

---

Cabanis: Enlightenment and Medical Philosophy in the French Revolution (Princeton, 1980), pp. 49–71; A. Doyon and L. Liagre, "Méthodologie comparée du biomécanisme et de la mécanique comparée," *Dialectica* 10, no. 4 (1956): 292–335; Bernard Balan, "Premières recherches sur l'origine et la formation du concept d'économie animale," *Revue d'histoire des sciences et d leurs applications* 28 (1975): 289–326.

[7]C. A. Coulomb, "Mémoire sur la force des hommes," presented at the Académie royale des sciences, 24 February 1798; idem, *Théorie des machines* (Bachelier, 1821); Charles Dupin, *Géometrie et mécanique des arts et métiers et les beaux arts* (Paris, 1826), p. 105, and the inaugural lecture of Charles Dupin at the Conservatoire nationale des arts et métiers (discourse of 25 January 1829); on Bergery and Dupin see Michelle Perrot, "Travailler et produire: Claude-Lucien Bergery et les débuts du management en France," in *Mélanges d'histoire social offerts à Jean Maitron* (Paris, 1976), pp. 177–90.

[8]Doyen and Liagre, "Méthodologie comparée"; Georges Canguilhem, "The Role of Analogies and Models in Biological Discovery," in *Scientific Change: Historical Studies in the Intellectual, Social and Technical Conditions for Scientific Discovery and Technical Invention from Antiquity to the Present*, ed. A. C. Crombie, Symposium on the History of Science, Oxford University, 9–15 July 1961 (New York, 1963), pp. 507–20.

tion of the machine was found wanting. In the popular scientific reviews, such as *La nature* or *Le magasin pittoresque* in France, or in the writings of Samuel Butler in England, reverence was combined with more than a touch of demonology: "How many human beings today already live in complete dependence on the machine? How many spend their whole lives, from the cradle to the grave, to serve it day and night? Is it not clear that it is already taking ground from us, if we think about the growing number of those who serve it as slaves, and those who devote their souls to the progress of the kingdom of the mechanical?"[9] But apart from this image of the omnivorous power machine, it is the quality of the machine as a producer of energy that is completely new. What disappears is the classical conception of the mechanical as a system of interrelated parts and movements, whose energy source or motion lies outside of it—the passive machine. What arrives in its place is the energumen, the creator of movement or energy—the motor.[10] This change is at the heart of the new metaphor, articulated by Hermann von Helmholtz, who in 1854 proclaimed that the human machine more accurately resembles a power machine, which transforms matter into "work energy."[11]

Corporal Thermodynamics

Beginning in the 1850s and 1860s, the old mechanical image of the body with its mysterious forces or movements of liquids and solids began to be superseded by an image of the body predicated on a new kind of nature, constituted by the indissoluble unity of matter and motion. No longer were the forces powering the machine external to it, and no longer was nature viewed in strictly mechanical terms with myriad forces distributed throughout. Under the influence of Helmholtz and the discovery of "conservation of energy" those diverse forces were "united" into a single force present in all matter and capable of conversion into a variety of forms. Taking as their starting point Helmholtz's view that nature was a vast cistern of protean energy awaiting conversion to work, German and French physiologists began to adopt a series of concepts that transposed corporal physics onto the functions of "life," deposing the corporal mechanics of the classical period. For Helmholtz's followers, as Carl

[9]Samuel Butler, *Erewhon, or Over the Range*, cited in Günther Metkin, "De L'homme-machine à la machine-homme: Anthropomorphie de la machine au XIXe siècle," in *Junggesellen Maschinen/Les Machines célibataires*, ed. Michel Carrouges (Paris, 1975), p. 58.

[10]Michel Serres, "C'était avant l'exposition (Universelle)," in ibid., p. 65.

[11]Hermann von Helmholtz, "Über die Wechselwirkung der Naturkräfte: Ein populärwissenschaftlicher Vortrag," in *Populäre wissenschaftliche Vorträge*, 2d ed. (Braunschweig, 1876), 1:101–31.

Ludwig declared to Emile Du Bois-Reymond as early as 1848, physiology had to be "founded on the physics and the chemistry of the organism."[12] What distinguished the Helmholtzian paradigm from that of the mechanists was the universality of energy in all manifestations of nature. In short, all of the forces "of nature, heretofore differentiated into *'puissance motorice,' 'Spannkraft,' 'Arbeitskraft,' 'vis viva,'* etc.... are integrated into the concept of *énergie*."[13]

Energy became the highest principle of nature, the source of knowledge of the world and "a means that satisfied the philosophical need for an overview of nature and insight into its major interconnections."[14] In the words of Etienne-Jules Marey, whose work thoroughly assimilated Helmholtzian ideas into French physiology, "only the present day" was capable of comprehending the "bearing and justice" of the analogy between living beings and machines. For Marey, the concept of energy "changed the face of science."[15] The discovery of the properties of heat, electricity, and steam power as different *forms* of the same transcendental energy ended forever the dualism of matter and motion: "all of the forces of nature are reduced to only one. Force may assume any appearance."[16] The new emphasis on the immutable quantity of energy in

---

[12]Georges Canguilhem, *Etudes D'histoire et de philosophie des sciences* (Paris, 1968), p. 251.

[13]Elkana, *Discovery of the Conservation of Energy*, p. 161.

[14]Georg Helm, *Die Lehre von der Energie: Historisch-kritisch Entwickelt* (Leipzig, 1887), p. 32. The shift from the mechanical standpoint, which sees energy as external to matter, to one that places energy at the center of all physical reality as an explanatory principle extended far beyond physics and chemistry to include the life sciences and social sciences as well. This development is detailed in Helm, *Lehre von der Energie*, pp. 71–76, and in Wilhelm Ostwald, *Energetische Grundlagen der Kulturwissenschaft* (Leipzig, 1909), and is subjected to a penetrating critique by Max Weber in his "Energetische Kulturtheorien," in *Gesammelte Aufsätze zur Wissenschaftslehre*, ed. Johannes Winckelmann (Tubingen, 1968), pp. 400–426. Weber identified the value-laden assumptions of the new energetics and denounced what he called the "intemperate arrogance" of the attempt to lend normative significance to the categories of the natural sciences and apply them to social and cultural issues. This criticism could be expanded. In moving from science to discourse, the conceptual structure of the epistemological system is universalized, constructing and circumscribing reality within its system of referents. The universalization of the invisible concept of energy to all areas of life, the shift to a "conceptual architecture" that is hidden, that dissolves the distinction between the organic and inorganic, and that assigns transhistorical value to such concepts as force, conservation, and entropy had deep social implications. Above all it assumed a similar normative arrangement in the natural and social worlds; the theory of energy conservation gives primacy to the laws of the efficient transformation of one form of energy to another. In short, it guides the natural and human sciences toward production and efficiency. For a discussion of the profound cultural implications of the conceptual structure of the "organic"—which performs a similar function in the eighteenth century—see Michel Foucault, *The Order of Things: An Archaeology of the Human Sciences* (New York, 1970), pp. 226–32.

[15]Etienne-Jules Marey, *Animal Mechanism: A Treatise on Terrestrial and Aerial Locomotion* (New York, 1874), p. 6, translation of his *La machine animale: Locomotion terrestre et aérienne* (Paris, 1873).

[16]Ibid.

each sphere had far-reaching consequences for the perception of the physical laws of the body. The capacity for energy production became the leitmotif of a body seen as a system of economies of force with quantifiable rules. As André Liesse, one of the first to summarize the principles of the new science of the working body, wrote in 1899, "the animal organism is not simply composed of levers, gears, and presses; it is a thermodynamic machine that augments, transforms, and distributes force according to the needs of the organism."[17]

The new science of labor made possible the search for the precise laws of the muscles, the nerves, and the deployment of energy within the human organism. It permitted the discovery of the most suitable external conditions for the efficient utilization of those forces in labor. In short, it imposed the idea of the efficient expenditure of energy on the body itself. The working body became a "human motor" rather than a machine.[18]

Social Helmholtzianism

Social Helmholtzianism thus offered the promise of a labor force that did not have to be inculcated with eternal truths about the importance of will, the sin of idleness, or the value of work. Moral exhortations, the idealization of the "sublime" worker, and even the reflections of the political economists on the worker's "system of needs" began to appear obsolete. In their place emerged a scientific and medicalized discourse on labor—corporal physics instead of appeals to conscience. The old forms of industrial discipline characteristic of the first half of the nineteenth century (paternalism, familialism, surveillance) began to take second place to questions of wages and hours, and to the discipline of production itself. The "new factory" was rapidly deskilling the work force while increasing the tempo of production; unions were challenging management on the question of work norms and the right to determine them. In short, in an era when the nature of work was measured in terms of "time and motion" rather than in terms of desire or the will, the prospect of a purely technical solution to what Michelle Perrot has called the "crisis of discipline" was particularly welcome.[19]

[17]André Liesse, *Le travail aux points de vue scientifique industriel et social* (Paris, 1899), p. 18.

[18]For an interesting discussion of this distinction in nineteenth-century science and literature see Serres, "C'était avant l'exposition (Universelle)," pp. 64–74.

[19]Michelle Perrot, "The Three Ages of Industrial Discipline in Nineteenth-Century France," in *Consciousness and Class Experience in Nineteenth Century Europe*, ed. John M. Merriman (New York and London, 1979), pp. 160–63. For a description of the idealized worker see Denis Poulot, *Question sociale: Le sublime, ou Le travailleur comme il est en 1870 et ce qu'il peut être* (Paris, 1980).

We can distinguish three phases in the development of the European science of labor: (1) a period of theoretical development in the study of the economies of energy, heat, motion, and fatigue governing the working body (1867–95); (2) the growth of a scientific study of labor, the emergence of laboratories for the social application of new discoveries, and the collection of survey data (1895–1910); and (3) the first interventions in the actual workplace and the challenge of the Taylor system on the eve of World War I (1910–14). In the first phase the problem that emerged as the most salient feature of the new thermodynamics of the "human motor" was the production of heat. This problem, as historians of science have pointed out, provided the most fertile ground for the application of energy conservation to physiology, a point of contact between the animal machine and the laws of inorganic nature. As noted by Adolf Fick, German physiologist and pioneer of the new science, the comparison between the action of the muscle and the steam engine was "apt and instructive," since "in both cases we are concerned with the effects of chemical forces, through which the motion of certain masses and also heat are created."[20] By distinguishing between the inner forces (muscle tension, electrical current, heat oscillation) and "the surface appearance of the ... moving body," the German Helmholtzians attempted to demonstrate the relevance of energy conservation, noting that the course of inner transformation of the muscles always remained the same despite varying external conditions of load.[21] Like the theory of energy conservation, studying the work of the muscles revealed that "the sum of potential and moving energy of the system is always of constant size, which cannot be altered by any positive or negative work of any force within the system."[22]

In France, the theory of animal heat also underwent an intensive development in the same period, above all as a result of the work of Marey and his associate Auguste Chauveau. In his 1867 lectures at the Collège de France, Marey argued that the body was ultimately comprehensible in terms of simple physical laws, challenging Claude Bernard's view that physiological processes were not reducible to the nonorganic model of German mechanism. The physiologist, Marey countered, "ultimately recognizes that the chemical actions that take place in the organism are the cause of the production of heat in animals," and consequently "the animal organism is no different from our machines

[20]Adolf Fick, *Mechanische Arbeit und Wärmeentwicklung bei der Muskelthätigkeit* (Leipzig, 1882), p. 153.

[21]Adolf Fick, *Untersuchungen über Muskel-Arbeit* (Basel, 1867), pp. 15–18.

[22]Fick, *Mechanische Arbeit und Wärmeentwicklung*, p. 33.

except by its more advantageous efficiency."[23] The reduction of work to the transformation of heat into energy, and by definition, to the analogy of the animal machine, was even more pronounced in the work of Chauveau.[24] But as Chauveau also recognized, the persistent difference between the organic and the inorganic was a stumbling block to the development of a theory of the human motor. The distinctions between mechanical work and the work of the body could no longer be ignored in "muscular thermodynamics."[25] These distinctions had to guide further research, which for Marey and Chauveau concentrated on the specific aspects of human—or animal—work: (1) the problem of converting heat into energy; (2) the "physiological time" involved in the impulse sent from the nerves to the muscles; (3) the elasticity of the muscles and shock; (4) the problem of fatigue and reparation; (5) the analysis of time and motion.

For Chauveau, "one grand physical fact ... dominates all theories ... of the internal mechanism of muscle contraction: the contracted muscle is a result of a special and absolutely perfect elasticity of the muscles ... adapted to the functional purpose envisaged and anticipated by muscular work."[26] Whereas mechanical motion was simply the conversion of energy into work, the unique feature of the "animal motor" was that it was not limited to either passive or active work, but always maintained a level of energy even when no work was performed. For Chauveau, the "solution to the problem of muscular thermodynamics rested on the determination of the relationship that exists between the elasticity contained in the muscle and the energy that the design of that elasticity sets into motion."[27] For Marey too, what distinguishes the human motor is above all the suppression of shock, the transformation of forces of varying

---

[23]Etienne-Jules Marey, *Du mouvement dans les fonctions de la vie: Leçons faites au Collège de France* (Paris, 1868), p. 69.

[24]Cf. August Chauveau, *Le travail musculaire et l'énergie qu'il représente* (Paris, 1891); idem, *La vie et l'énergie chez l'animal: Introduction à l'étude des sources et des transformations de la force mise en oeuvre dan le travail physiologique* (Paris, 1894); and the sketch of his life in F. A. Lesbro, *Notice sur la vie et les travaux de J. B. A. Chauveau* (Paris, 1919). Chauveau is credited with discovering the laws of muscular energy and with establishing the principle of equivalence that governs all transformations of energy in the body. His experiments on the flexors of the forearm demonstrated that in human work the principle of the conservation of the internal energy of the muscles manifests itself in "the unconscious but constant effort to reduce the total expenditure of energy to a minimum and the voluntary realization of mechanical conditions corresponding to this minimum of expenditure." See Josefa Ioteyko, *The Science of Labour and Its Organization* (London, 1919), pp. 18, 19. Chauveau was in fact a crucial link between the energeticist principles established by German physiology and the more practical directions of the French science of work.

[25]Chauveau, *Travail musculaire*, p. 4.

[26]Ibid., p. 10.

[27]Ibid., p. 4, x.

intensity and irregularity into a durable, steady force, capable of use. From the standpoint of the efficiency of the body, therefore, the elasticity of the muscles demonstrates the principles of economy: "this elasticity is not only purposeful for creating movement, it creates a great economy of work as well."[28]

Fatigue and the Economy of Energy

Helmholtzian physics not only provided a way of investigating the precise economies of labor power, it also identified fatigue—as opposed to the moral scourge of idleness—as the central mode of the body's resistance to work. The change is striking. Whereas before 1870 there were hardly any studies of fatigue, and none from a scientific point of view, treatises on work and idleness continued to be published extensively. But by the 1880s the literature on idleness had begun to dry up, while the floodgates of fatigue research released a vast outpouring of literature on all aspects of fatigue.[29] The long tradition of industrial edification—in which the "power of the will" and the moral, intellectual, and spiritual benefits of work are opposed to the debilitating effects of sloth, indolence, and the endemic laziness of barbaric peoples—began to lose its discursive power.[30] This tradition, which sees in work the properties of moral as well as economic emancipation—as opposed to drudgery and pain—derived its legitimacy from the idealization of the artisan and the attempt to impose that image on industrial work. With the social decline of the artisan, idleness lost its capacity to conjure up the moral terror of the workless state. Instead, it was excessive, irregular, and poorly organized work that produced fatigue and defeated the body.

[28]Etienne-Jules Marey, "L'économie de travail et l'élasticité," *Revue des idées* 1, no. 4 (1904): 161.
[29]For a more detailed discussion of fatigue research and the meaning of fatigue in nineteenth-century culture see Anson Rabinbach, "The Body without Fatigue: A Nineteenth-Century Utopia," in *Political Symbolism in Modern Europe: Essays in Honor of George L. Mosse*, ed. Seymour Drescher, David Sabean, and Allan Sharlin (New Brunswick, N. J., 1982), pp. 42–62.
[30]This change is noted by Georges Ribeill in his comments on the French (expanded) version of my above-cited paper: see Georges Ribeill, "De L'oisiveté au surmenage: Les figures critique du travail au XIXe siècle," *VRBI: Arts, histoire, ethnologie des villes* 2 (December 1979): xlix–lvi; and in Perrot, "Three Ages of Industrial Discipline," pp. 160–65. The influence of the ideology of artisanal labor on social theory, as well as on contemporary historians of nineteenth-century labor, is mercilessly investigated in Jacques Rancière, "The Myth of the Artisan: Critical Reflections on a Category of Social History," chapter 11 of this volume. The shift from the moral critique of idleness to the medical assault on fatigue is also indicative of the broader displacement of the terrain of industrial conflict to the shop floor from the wider "milieu" of the working class—a result of both the creation of the new factory and the politics of trade unionism that occluded the familial, domestic, and personal from its purview.

As early as 1867, Marey identified the central role of fatigue in his law of human effort: "a muscle is subordinate to two influences—one reparative: nutrition; the other exhausting: its motor function. The body's capacity to produce motion varies according to the one or the other influence affecting it."[31] A few years later, Hugo Kronecker, experimenting with the muscular characteristics of the frog, determined that fatigue had its own dynamic laws and that the intensity of muscle contractions—like other manifestations of energy—diminishes with *regularity* until the organism can no longer perform work.[32] The classical text of fatigue science was, however, a product not of Germany or France, but of the liberal Italian physiologist Angelo Mosso of Turin. His *La fatica* (1891), the result of a decade of laboratory investigation, placed the study of fatigue firmly within the canon of modern science. Drawing on the mechanical inscription devices pioneered by Helmholtz and Marey (to whom he was indebted), Mosso invented the first technologically efficient and accurate measure of fatigue, the *ergograph*, which inscribed on a rotating drum a record of the fatigue of the middle finger that occurs while lifting a weight (fig. 17.1). Mosso's ergograph permitted all types of fatigue to be subjected to intense observation and quantification. These studies, he argued, proved that "the intimate and most characteristic feature of our individuality—the manner in which we fatigue" was still subordinate to the laws of nature: "If, every day at the same hours we were to make a series of contractions with the same weight and in the same rhythm, we should obtain tracings which all had the same outline, and thus we should convince ourselves of the constancy of individual fatigue."[33] Mosso claimed two decisive discoveries: first, that fatigue is an objective phenomenon and the laws of fatigue are analogous to the laws of energy in general; second, that fatigue demonstrates a consistent "diminution of muscular force" that can be graphically represented and measured.[34]

Mosso's breakthrough resonated far beyond his Turin laboratory. If fatigue could be reproduced and studied under controlled conditions, it was entirely possible that "the conservation of the internal energy of the muscles" could be "enhanced."[35] As the French physiologist and aesthetic theorist Charles Henry noted in his laudatory review of the French translation of Mosso's work, the discovery of the "curves of exhaustion of different animated motors" was a "new chapter of animal

---

[31]Marey, *Du mouvement dans les fonctions de la vie*, p. 72.
[32]Angelo Mosso, *Fatigue*, trans. M. Drummond and W. B. Drummond (London, 1906), p. 82.
[33]Ibid., p. 92.
[34]Ibid., p. 154.
[35]Ibid.

Fig. 17.1. Mosso's ergograph during a fatigue tracing (1891). From Angelo Mosso, *Fatigue*, trans. M. Drummond and W. B. Drummond (London, 1906), p. 88

mechanics, and from all points of view, its most interesting."[36] According to Henry, along with Mosso's discoveries, the accumulation of complementary statistics on the movements of the body "on the march, on the track, and so forth, would make it possible to transform these speeds of work into units of time and consequently to calculate the curves of exhaustion."[37] Henry's prescient remarks foretold how the study of the "excellence of the animal motor," and the discovery of its precise laws of motion, would result in the practical application of laboratory research to actual situations.

E. J. Marey: Corporal Dynamics

The goal of discovering the laws of human and animal motion, "to give to the subtle and fugitive phenomena of life a permanent and true expression," was the task set out by Etienne-Jules Marey in his Paris laboratories from the early 1860s until his death in 1904.[38] For Marey

[36]Charles Henry, "A travers les sciences et l'industrie": *La fatigue intellectuelle et physique* d'après M. Mosso," *Revue blanche* 4 (1894):170.
[37]Ibid., p. 177.
[38]"Discours de M. Marey," in *Institut Marey: Hommage à M. Marey* (Paris, 1902), p. 14.

Fig. 17.2. Marey's odeograph and track at the physiological station, Paris (1882). From Etienne-Jules Marey, *Le mouvement* (Paris, 1894), p. 72

the body was a theater of motion that could best be understood through the analogy of the machine. His version of Helmholtzian physiology was oriented toward those physical phenomena most receptive to the mechanical interpretation: heat, elasticity, optics, acoustics, and above all locomotion (flight, gait, aquatics). Marey believed he had discovered, along with his German predecessors, the key to the problem of corporal dynamics, which had eluded his contemporaries. His method was to discover the *"langue inconnue"* of the body's forces through the apparatus of measurement and mechanical inscription, to which he brought his considerable skill as a craftsman and inventor. This explains his fascination with the instruments of notation, capable of reading the body's most invisible signs, of registering its most elusive movements. These inscriptors, including his myograph (for the muscles) and his odeograph (for measuring the velocity of runners, horses, carts, and such), created a new scientific language "without words, irrefutable and constant, of a striking semantic superiority (fig. 17.2)."[39] The graphic method not only augments the insufficiencies of the senses, it overcomes the limits of language: it permits us to "study forces in their dynamic state."[40] Even

[39]L. Campan, "Marey et la capture des temps physiologiques," *Agressologie* 19, no. 4 (1978): 236.
[40]Etienne-Jules Marey, *La méthode graphique dans les sciences expérimentales et principalement en physiologie et en médecine,* 3d ed. (Paris, 1885), p. iii.

more important, the graphic method makes it possible for the physiologist to grasp the nature of duration within the space of the body, to give its movements a chronology: "the graphic method translates all the changes in the activity of forces into a form we might call the language of the phenomena themselves, so much superior to all other modes of expression."[41] Like his contemporary Proust in literature and like Bergson, his colleague in philosophy at the Collège, Marey was concerned with those dimensions of time and motion that were not directly accessible to language and consciousness.

Armed with these inscription devices, the physiologist could now investigate "the most rapid and the weakest movements" without missing the slightest variations in energy. For Marey, all movement "is the product of two factors: time and space; to know the movement of a body is to know the series of positions that it occupies in space in a series of successive instants. The inscriptive devices trace in a regular manner that relation of space and time that is the essence of movement."[42] Marey summarized his motion studies in *La machine animale* (1873), in which he subjected diverse forms of locomotion to scientific examination with graphic notation. Marey's interests were unique in their microphysiological orientation, in his singular focus on the forms of motion and the position of bodies in time and space. Yet he remained acutely aware throughout of the utilitarian issues his research addressed: "if we knew under what conditions the maximum of speed, force or labour which the living being can furnish might be obtained," he wrote, "it would put an end to much discussion."[43]

Chronophotography

In 1881 the municipality of Paris and the Chamber of Deputies conceded to Marey's requests for support, providing the financing for a new outdoor laboratory in the Parc de Prince in Paris, Marey's new physiological station coincided with a new turn in his research: motion photography. Influenced by the Anglo-American Eadweard Muybridge, whose instantaneous photographs of the horse caused a great sensation when Marey introduced him to Parisian artistic and scientific circles in

[41]Ibid., p. iv; also see Etienne-Jules Marey, *Le mouvement* (Paris, 1894): English trans. E. Pritchard, *Movement* (New York, 1895), pp. 4–7; René Quinton, "E. J. Marey," *Revue des idées* 1 (1904): 481–83: "Marey was and remains, par excellence, a man of graphics, of the visual image. Others represent or measure phenomena in terms of numbers; Marey grasped nature and represented it by images."

[42]Etienne-Jules Marey, "Travail de l'homme dans les professions manuelles," *Revue de la Société scientifique d'hygiène alimentaire* 1 (1904): 194.

[43]Marey, *Animal mechanism*, p. 3.

the fall of 1881, Marey was determined to use photography in the study of motion. But whereas Muybridge, using multiple cameras with trip-wire electrical shutters, had succeeded in decomposing motion into space, his "frozen images" fell short of what Marey wanted to achieve: the decomposition of motion into time. To achieve this goal, the precise intervals between the exposures had to be included, necessitating a single objective camera, which Marey invented in 1881, first with the "photo-graphic rifle" and shortly thereafter with a single fixed plate and a sta-tionary camera capable of multiple exposures at precisely equal intervals. Marey dressed his subject in a white suit in order to reflect the sunlight and provide a sharp contrast with the black background. As the man in white moves across the screen, the rotating glass disk records his move-ment without confusing the image with the previous one. These first motion photographs were published in July 1882. Marey soon added a device (chronometer) that was to become his signature: a clocklike ap-paratus with a luminous dial that provided an image of the equidistant intervals of time in the photograph itself (fig. 17.3). With chronopho-tography, as Marey called it, motion could be read as time.[44]

Marey clearly saw the implications for the study of the body in work: "Chronophotography ... provides us with precise knowledge of the speed of the different parts of the body, the scale permits us to measure the mass in movement, and we can thus establish, with sufficient accuracy, the work utilized in the different acts of locomotion."[45]

The New Science of Labor (1895–1910)

The first direct applications of chronophotography to the study of physical labor were undertaken in Marey's laboratory in 1894 by a me-tallurgist, Charles Fremont, and were published in the popular Paris *Le monde moderne* in February 1895. Fremont provided an interesting con-trast between his chronophotographs and the representation of work in Diderot's *Encyclopédie*, to demonstrate how "in all those drawings, the attitudes are never exact, the movements are false."[46] Using Marey's

[44]Etienne-Jules Marey, "La photographie du mouvement," *Nature*, 22 July 1882, pp. 115, 116; and see his own account in *Le développement de la méthode graphique par la photo-graphie* (Paris, 1885), p. 23; *La chronophotographie* (Paris, 1899), pp. 6–40; and "The History of Chronophotography," Smithsonian Institution Annual Report, 1901 (Washington, D.C., 1902), pp. 317–40.

[45]Etienne-Jules Marey, "Etude de la locomotion animale par la chrono-photographie," in *Association française pour l'avancement des sciences, compte rendu de la 15e session* (Nancy, 1886), p. 67.

[46]Charles Fremont, "Les mouvements de l'ouvrier dan le travail professionnel," *Monde moderne* 1 (February 1895): 189.

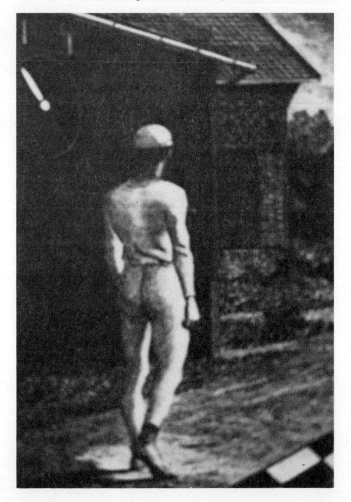

Fig. 17.3. Runner in white in front of dark screen with
chronometer (1882). From E. J. Marey, *Développement de la
méthode graphique par l'emploi de la photographie* (Paris, 1885),
p. 23

facilities, Fremont depicted two workers (sometimes one) striking a red-
hot iron on an anvil with a hammer. Unlike even the highly aestheticized
and sanitized preindustrial milieu in Diderot's forge, Fremont's forgers
perform before a dark field with only a chronometer visible in the foreground (fig. 17.4). In these images the body of the man is also blurred,
and only the hammer is shown in its successive phases in order to capture
the successive positions of the handle and the hands: "the position of

Fig. 17.4. Charles Fremont's chronophotographic motion study of forgers (1894). From *Le monde moderne*, February 1895, p. 192

the worker is ignored."[47] Fremont then translated the chronophotographs into mathematical line drawings to show the "instinctual" economy of force practiced by the workers "with the least amount of fatigue."[48]

With Fremont's studies the science of work moved from theory to practice; his is a qualitatively new *image* of work completely cleansed of all social and cultural relevance, reduced to pure, quantitative "performance."[49] The new science of work presents an impression of work deprived of all normative significance—it is no longer emancipatory, morally satisfying, contextually embedded, or *"tätige Last"* in the religious sense. The practical consequences were nonetheless immediate.

[47]Ibid., p. 192.

[48]Ibid., p. 193.

[49]This change in the perception of work is discussed in terms of sociological theory by Axel Honneth, "Work and Instrumental Action," *New German Critique*, no. 26 (Spring/ Summer 1982): 38. Honneth notes that "the history of sociology provides an outstanding example of this gradual "cleansing" [Reinigung] of traditional normative contents from the concept of work . . . in the social scientific theory of the work process . . . which is now investigated exclusively from the viewpoint of insuring increased productivity." This is precisely what Fremont's studies do. Honneth's argument is wrong only when he attributes this development solely to the "Taylorization of industrial work," which postdated the European science of labor. The perceptual revolution, in short, antedated the social and organizational transformation.

By 1900 laboratories devoted to the experimental science of the "human motor" had been established in almost all continental countries. Mosso's laboratory in Turin, for example, conducted extensive research on the conditions governing the optimum of work, intervals necessary for rest, mental fatigue, and so on.[50] Marey and his associates, especially the gymnastics expert Georges Demeny and the equestrian expert Emil Duhousset, published prodigiously on all aspects of motion, especially the military drill, which Marey already had treated in the early 1880s.[51]

After 1900 this research spawned a second generation of field and laboratory researchers—for example, Jules Amar and Armand Imbert in France, whose work on fatigue and respiration in specific trades constituted the first full-scale efforts at establishing a European laboratory science of work (fig. 17.5).[52]

In Belgium Ernest Solvay established an institute in 1900 for the purpose of applying the physiological studies of Marey and Mosso to a wider range of phenomena. Solvay wanted to combine physiological research with the psychological studies of intelligence and mental fatigue pioneered by Alfred Binet to create a new social science, based entirely on the new Helmholtzian idea. Solvay was motivated by the conviction that "all the factors that directly or indirectly intervene in the organic phenomena relevant to the human being living in society have a physioenergetic value that can be determined by means of the same unit," a belief he translated into the search for the improvement of "social

[50]Review of A. Mosso, *La fatica*, by Théodule Ribot, *Revue philosophique* 32 (1891): 415, 416; Francesco S. Nitti, *Le travail humain et ses lois*, trans. N. Politis (Paris, 1895), pp. 15–29; Ioteyko, *Science of Labour*, p. 12.

[51]Etienne-Jules Marey, "Etudes sur la marche de l'homme," *Revue militaire de médecine et de chirurgie* 1 (1881): 244–46. A good discussion of the influence of the science of work on French military training is Alain Ehrenberg, *Le corps militaire: Politique et pédagogie en démocratie* (Paris, 1983), pp. 113–18. For a survey of the science of labor in France see Georges Ribeill, "Les débuts de l'ergonomie en France à la veille de la première guerre mondiale," *Mouvement social* 113 (October–December 1980): 3–36. More technical aspects are discussed in Dragolioub Yovanovitch, *Le rendement optimum de travail ouvrier: Etude sur les stimulants moderne de l'activité ouvrière* (Paris, 1923), pp. 231–62, and in Ioteyko, *Science of Labor*. Also see Charles Fremont, *Etude experimentale du rivetage: Memoires, Société d'encouragement pour l'industrie nationale* (Paris, 1906); idem, *Evolution de la fonderie de cuivre* (Paris, 1903); idem, *Le balancier à vis pour estampagne* (Paris, 1916); Georges Demeny, *Les bases scientifiques de l'éducation physique* (Paris, 1893); idem, *Méchanisme et éducation des mouvement* (Paris, 1904).

[52]On Jules Amar and Armand Imbert see Ribeill, "Débuts de l'ergonomie," pp. 14–18, 24–27; Jules Amar, *Le rendement de la machine humaine* (Paris, 1909); idem, *Le moteur humain et les bases scientifiques du travail professionnel* (Paris, 1914); idem, *L'organisation physiologigue du travail et le système Taylor* (Paris, 1917); Armand Imbert, "Mode de fonctionnement économique de l'organisme," *Scientia* (May, 1902); idem, "L'etude scientifique expérimentale du travail professionnel," *Année psychologique*, 1906; idem, "Les méthodes de laboratoire appliques à l'étude directe et pratique des questions ouvrières," *Revue genéral des sciences*, 30 June 1911, pp. 478–86.

Fig. 17.5. Study of apprentice using file with respirator (ca. 1913). From Jules Amar, *The Human Motor, or The Scientific Foundations of Labor and Industry* (London: George Routledge, 1920), p. 407

efficiency" through the expansion of the energies deployed in the social totality.[53]

Among the voluminous publications of the Solvay Institute devoted to fatigue in military, educational, and other institutions was Charles Henry's remarkable study of "the measurement of intellectual and energetic nature" according to the laws of statistical probability.[54] Henry's

[53]Ernest Solvay, *Note sure des formules d'introduction à l'énergétique physio- et psycho-sociologique*, Institut Solvay, Travaux de l'Institut de sociologie, Notes et mémoires (Brussels and Leipzig, 1902), p. 14. Also see idem, *Considérations sur l'énergétique des organismes au point de vue de définition, de la genèse et de l'evolution de l'être vivant*, Travaux de laboratoire de l'Institut Solvay (Brussels, 1901); and his programmatic *Principes d'orientation sociale* (Brussels, 1904).

[54]Charles Henry, *Mesure des capacités intellectuelle et energétique*, Institut Solvay, Travaux de l'Institut de sociologie, Notes et mémoires (Brussels and Leipzig, 1906). Also see Alfred Binet and Charles Henry, *La fatigue intellectuelle* (Paris, 1897).

subsequent studies, as well as those of the Belgian fatigue expert Josefa Ioteyko (who tried to prove her feminist views on the equality of men and women through fatigue science), dealt with what they called "the law of the diminution of effort" and the changes in fatigue curves under different conditions.[55] What motivated their search for the "laws of ergonomy" was the firm belief that "it is not impossible, within the impassable limits of the law of the conservation of energy, to communicate an activity to the human motor which will favor the liberation of one form of energy rather than another."[56] Fatigue was the "psychic factor which regulates the expenditure of energy of the human motor, so as to ensure its most economical working, the factor which guides the animal machine to adaptation to the best conditions for work."[57]

In Germany two distinct tendencies in the science of work emerged in the mid-1890s: the physiological school of Otto Fischer, Christian Wilhelm Braune, Nathan Zuntz, and Max Rubner; and the psychophysical research of Emil Kräpelin and Hugo Münsterberg. Following Marey (and to some extent Mosso), in 1895 Fischer published his pioneering work *Der Gang des Menschen*, which employed chronophotography to provide a detailed study of the asymmetrical bodily movements of a German regiment (Eighth Royal Regiment Prinz Johann Georg) at drill.[58] Some six years earlier, Fischer and Braune had experimented with cadavers to determine "the center of gravity of frozen cadaver parts and whole bodies." Their work was followed by a proliferation of studies and manuals on the physical economy of drill and other aspects of military training.[59] Georg Kolb's work on sports, and the textbook of the Bavarian staff military doctor Anton Leitenstorfer, *Das militärische Training*, which provided extensive data on the fatigue and exhaustion of recruits, were important examples of the practical works that derived from this tradition.[60] But the most important work of this genre, Nathan

[55]These efforts are summarized in Josefa Ioteyko, "Les lois de l'ergographie," *Bulletin de l'Académie royale de Belgique* no. 5 (May 1904), extract.

[56]Ioteyko, *Science of Labour*, p. 4.

[57]Ibid., pp. 20, 21.

[58]Otto Fischer, *Der Gang des Menschen: Abhandlungen der sächsischen Gesellschaft der Wissenschaft* (Leipzig, 1895), 21, part 1:153–322.

[59]Christian Wilhelm Braune and Otto Fischer, *Über den Schwerpunkt des menschlichen Körpers* (Leipzig, 1889). Other important studies of movement include their: *Das Gesetz der Bewegungen an der Basis der mittleren Finger und in Handgelenk des Menschen* (Leipzig, 1887); and their *Bestimmung der Trägheitsmomente des menschlichen Körpers und seine Glieder* (Leipzig, 1892).

[60]Georg Kolb, *Physiology of Sports: Contributions towards the Physiology of a Maximum of Physical Exertion*, trans., 2d ed. (London, 1893); Anton Leitenstorfer, *Das militärische Training auf physiologischer und praktischer Grundlage* (Stuttgart, 1897).

Zuntz and Wilhelm Schumburg's *Studien zu einer Physiologie des Marsches* (1901), undertook an extensive survey of all aspects of drill: the function of clothing, nutrition, the length and speed of the march, the influence of rest, and above all the "pathology of the march" and march-related illnesses (e.g., heatstroke).[61] Max Rubner's important studies of nutrition and his work at the Institut für Arbeitsphysiologie, which he founded in Berlin in 1913, were further examples of the transformation of the theory of energy conservation into a politically oriented social program.[62]

In contrast to the military and political orientation (often from opposed viewpoints) of the physiological camp, Emil Kräpelin's *Zur Hygiene der Arbeit* (1896), the first German scientific study of labor, took as its starting point the psychophysics of Ernst Heinrich Weber and Gustav Theodor Fechner in analyzing the relation between psychology and physiology in all aspects of the work process.[63] Kräpelin's work, and the subsequent research done in his laboratory at Munich, was almost exclusively concerned with the problem of intellectual and industrial fatigue. Kräpelin saw as "the central goal of this young science the struggle against fatigue. In fatigue lies the curse, the danger of labor."[64] If, as he believed, a measure could be found for the "quantity of work performance" within a given time, it would be possible to calculate the changes that occur under the most different conditions of everyday life.[65] The effects of fatigue were directly evident in the "progressive fall of work performance," so that under the influence of fatigue "the bodily movements lose not only energy, but also safety and subtlety."

Although Kräpelin acknowledged that the feeling of tiredness (*Müdigkeit*) acted as a kind of protective mechanism, his theory rested on the all-important distinction between tiredness and fatigue. For him these were "two totally different states." There are people "for whom the warning signal of tiredness persists to their great detriment, despite fatigue," while there are others for whom fatigue is not accompanied by such manifestations at all.[66] In the struggle against fatigue, therefore, it is necessary to distinguish between those "weapons" that only attack the appearance of fatigue, such as effort of will and mood, "without raising the lowered supply of energy," and the "effective means of struggle" such as rest or work pauses. In sum, the subjective, moral, or psychic aspects of what is experienced as fatigue had to be eliminated from the

---

[61]Nathan Zuntz and Wilhelm Schumburg, *Studien zu einer Physiologie des Marsches* (Berlin, 1901), pp. 13–19.

[62]Richard Kremer, "From Stoffwechsel to Kraftwechsel: Voit, Rubner and the Study of Nutrition in the 1880s," History of Science Society paper, October 1983.

[63]Emil Kräpelin, *Zur Hygiene der Arbeit* (Jena, 1896).

[64]Ibid., p. 8.

[65]Ibid., p. 7.

[66]Ibid., pp. 10, 13.

real—that is, scientifically demonstrable—effect of fatigue on "work performance."[67]

Between 1896 and 1910 Kräpelin and his students energetically pursued the struggle against fatigue, since, as he put it, "sword and powder alone do not determine the fate of a people."[68] Their psychophysical credo was the elimination of such ephemeral qualities as tiredness, attitude, and "*Arbeitsfreude*," or motivation, from the "objective qualities of fatigue" that determined performance and efficiency. In hundreds of microstudies and experiments, Kräpelin and his assistants demonstrated the considerable discrepancy between the two states, concluding that "control over the economy of forces, and with it the organic self-regulation of work" could indeed be measured.

In contrast to Mosso, who was criticized by the Germans for concentrating on the work of only one muscle, Kräpelin's "work curve" measured the expenditure of energy of the entire body in concrete situations. His solution to the problem of fatigue was to stress the uniqueness of each individual's rhythm and tempo in work and modify these through "training" or "practice" (*Übung*), while also adjusting the rhythm of the work to the individual's capacity. Such concerns underscore the links between the new science of work and modern industrial processes, as opposed to artisanal or skilled labor. In Kräpelin's view the "mechanization of work" made it imperative that individuals be brought into harmony with the nature of the work process. Since the "muscle is the most highly perfected dynamic machine," this could easily be achieved, and the training of a new generation of workers would result in a "constant improvement in the relationship between physiological work performance and physical energy performance."[69]

Kräpelin, like Hugo Münsterberg, whose work in Berlin and at Harvard University made him the best-known of the psychophysically oriented psychologists, saw an intimate connection between the development of modern technology and the "unnatural" character of the industrial work process. In this idealized vision of preindustrial work as "natural" and rhythmic—influenced no doubt by Karl Bücher's extensive ethnological work on the natural rhythms of savage work habits—they contrasted the economies of the body in the modern workplace with those of a romanticized past.[70] Technology, according to Kräpelin and Münsterberg,

---

[67]Ibid., p. 20.

[68]Ibid., p. 30.

[69]Emil Kräpelin, *Psychologische Arbeiten* (Leipzig, 1897), 2:399; *Die Arbeitskurve* (Leipzig, 1902).

[70]Bücher's work, which deserves more detailed treatment then this essay permits, completely revised the stereotypical image of primitive work habits as characterized by laziness and lack of time sense. Instead he posited the central role of music and song in determining

necessarily imposed a rigid economy of force on the actions of the body, constraining movement and reducing activity to those muscles directly engaged in the process. Like Marey and Fremont, they too placed the entire emphasis on the corporal dynamics of work, though unlike the French they explicitly saw this *reduction* as a consequence of modern technological work. For Kräpelin this truth constituted no less than a special law of work, which he identified as the "principle of the smallest muscle." The steady displacement of force from the larger masses of muscles to the smaller was the historical teleology of modern work. As a result of this progressive dematerialization of labor power, energy could be more efficiently deployed (since brute strength was obsolete) and exercises could be designed to apply strategically to the affected area, permitting a slower rate of decline and a lessening of fatigue in the work curve.[71]

The highly abstract character of the German *Arbeitswissenschaft* (science of work) and its remoteness from the real world of production and labor soon produced dissatisfaction with its results. By 1910 critics both inside and outside the research community began to view Kräpelin's theories with considerable skepticism. The concept of fatigue as a measurable quality—distinct, of course, from tiredness—appeared more opaque and less "homogeneous" than he assumed. Second, the dichotomy between subjective weariness and objective fatigue was not, as other experimenters noted, even borne out by Kräpelin's own data.[72] These points underscored the suspicion that there was no relation between the "abstract psychology of work" and "real work," as Max Weber put it in a lengthy review of the achievements and failures of the psychophysical school of industrial work research, published in 1909. For Weber, as for the disappointed researchers in Kräpelin's own laboratory, experimental psychology had a negligible effect on actual performance in the workplace. Weber concluded by noting that it was a sad truth that such criticisms had "wholly and completely destroyed the initial and most cherished hopes of the Kräpelin school."[73]

French Physiology versus German Psychology

These problems notwithstanding, by the turn of the century the science of labor had established firm communities of advocates in France,

work rhythms and documented his research through ethnological studies. See Karl Bücher, *Arbeit und Rhythmus* (Leipzig, 1897).

[71]Cited in Max Weber, "Zur Psychophysik der industriellen Arbeit," in *Gesammelte Aufsätze zur Soziologie und Sozialpolitik* (Tübingen, 1924), pp. 77–82.

[72]Wladimir Eliasberg, "Arbeit und Psychologie," *Archiv für Sozialwissenschaft und Sozialpolitik* 50 (1922): 86–127.

[73]Weber, "Psychophysik der industriellen Arbeit," p. 110.

Belgium, Germany, and Italy, with outposts in America and even Japan. But we should not neglect the important national differences in the style and social background of the science of work. Clearly the prodigious French were in the forefront, largely under the aegis of medically oriented specialists (with the exception of Fremont) who were themselves on the margins of the major schools of French physiology. This is hardly surprising in late nineteenth century France, where technical inferiority was compensated for by medical sophistication. In Germany the leading figures came from the ranks of the *Gewerbehygieniker* (occupational health specialists) or from neurology and psychiatry, like Kräpelin.[74] These differences account for the largely physiological orientation of the French as opposed to the more "*geisteswissenschaftlich*" psychological and sociological trends across the Rhine. Whereas the French were advocates of political and social reform and wanted to extend the science of work to large groups outside the laboratory, the German psychologists tended to be politically conservative, and with few exceptions remained confined to experimental work under closely controlled conditions.[75] The German proponents of Arbeitswissenschaft advocated an "energetic labor law" (*energetisches Arbeitsrecht*), which saw the human being as a "labor factor" and proposed rest pauses, training programs, and state intervention only so long as these served the "energy economy." For them the subjective aspects of labor were "in no way decisive for the cultural importance of work," which was seen in terms of national energy supply.[76] German sociologists, however, were far more liberal and reform oriented and did carry out investigations of "real work," though without the assistance of the sophisticated physiological methods developed by the French.

In all countries, the optimism of the science of work was based on the belief that greater productivity could lead directly to social happiness—and not, as in Taylorism or later in Fordism, on the view that unhappiness had to be compensated for through external, non-work-related

---

[74]Giese, "Die Eigenart der französischen Arbeitswissenschaft," in *Annalen der Betriebswirtschaft* (Berlin, 1927), 1:405.

[75]Ibid., pp. 108–10; Fritz Giese, *Philosophie der Arbeit* (Halle, 1932), pp. 76–69. On the German "Arbeitswissenschaft" see R. W. Hoffman, "Die systematischen und historischen Voraussetzungen der Arbeitswissenschaften," in *Analyse der Arbeit: Möglichkeiten einer interdisziplinären Erforschung industrialisierter Arbeitsvollzüge*, ed. Konrad Thomas, *Göttinger Abhandlungen zur Soziologie*, vol. 16 (Stuttgart, 1969), pp. 102–10; "Arbeitswissenschaft," in *Handwörterbuch der Arbeitswissenschaft*, ed. Fritz Giese (Halle, 1930), pp. 418–20; Fritz Giese, "Die Eigenart der französischen Arbeitswissenschaft," pp. 403–16; Eliasberg, "Arbeit und Psychologie," pp. 86–127; Wladimir Eliasberg, "Richtungen und Entwicklungstendenzen in der Arbeitswissenschaft," *Archiv für Sozialwissenschaft und Sozialpolitik* 56 (1926): 66–101, 687–732; Adolf Weber, *Der Kampf zwischen Kapital und Arbeit* (Tübingen, 1910), pp. 84–91.

[76]"Arbeitsrecht, energetisch," in *Handwörterbuch der Arbeitswissenschaft*, ed. Fritz Giese (Halle, 1930), pp. 406–9.

material rewards.[77] To the European practitioners of the science of labor the American Taylorists and their British disciples appeared hopelessly regressive,"grotesquely childish," and, worse, uneducated in the scientific skills necessary to fully comprehend the problem from an untendentious standpoint. Other distinctions might also be noted: the French tended to concentrate on measuring respiration in the "human motor," while the Germans, again influenced by questions of "*Gewerbehygiene*," debated questions of nutrition—the most interesting, the famous Kartoffel versus Brot debate of the 1880s—in the constitution of the workers' good health.[78]

Despite these differences, by the turn of the century links were established among an international community of doctors, scientists, and hygienists engaged in the common pursuit of the "laws of ergography." Initially there were two broad tendencies. "The human motor," as Ioteyko noted, "may be studied from two very different points of view": first by laboratory researches "having for their chief object the verification of the laws governing the transformation of energy in the living being," and second, by "submitting the working of the bodily organs to experimental tests with a view to discover their best working conditions, to detect fatigue, and to lay down a scientific basis for industrial work."[79] Results were transmitted internationally by thorough reporting in physiology and psychology journals, quick translations, and frequent personal contacts among the major figures of the movement. In this regard the International Congresses of Hygiene and Demography (Paris, 1900; Brussels, 1903; Budapest, 1904; Berlin, 1907; Washington, D.C., 1912), all of which dealt with "fatigue in industrial work," played an indispensable role. The congresses raised the problem of fatigue to international significance, providing statistical results and comparative data, but even more important, they mobilized the medical and physiological concern with fatigue toward more practical social and political involvement. The Brussels and Berlin congresses represented the vanguard of liberal "social medicine," already well established in such areas as alcoholism, housing, and tuberculosis, and applied it for the first time to the "organization of work."[80]

[77]Eliasberg, "Richtungen und Entwicklungstenzen," p. 80.

[78]Carl von Voit, for example, argued that based on the comparative figures on worker's nutrition, German workers should not receive more than seventy percent of their necessary carbohydrates in the form of bread, with the additional 30 percent supplied by potatoes and vegetables. See "Ernährung," *Real-encyclopädie der gesamten Heilkünde: Medizinisch-chirurgisches Handwörterbuch für praktische Ärtze,* ed. Albert Eulenburg (Vienna and Leipzig, 1881), 5:77. Also see Franz Joseph König, *Chemie der menschlichen nährungs und Genussmittel* (Berlin, 1879–80), p. 123

[79]Ioteyko, *Science of Labour,* p. 4.

[80]R. Lépine, "L'Évolution de la médecine à la fin du XIXe siècle," *Revue de mois,* no. 12 (1906): 705–15; *XIIIe Congrès international d'hygiène et de démographie, Compte rendu du congrès,*

Fatigue, Science and the Social Question

After 1900 there is a clear trend toward the politicization of the science of work in all countries, especially evident in such areas as occupational health and safety and in its growing attraction to progressive social reform as the vehicle for realizing its aims. The "etiology of occupational fatigue in the social problems of labor" could no longer be ignored, and it became a matter of faith that the results of any "branch of human knowledge" had implications for "some social problem."[81] For the advocates of the science of labor, the cooperation of the state became indispensable to achieving acceptance as a mediator of social conflict. At the Brussels Congress, for example, there was a consensus that the central problem for the science of work was to determine the policies and arguments that the physiological and medical sciences could or might recommend to government "in favor of specific methods for the organization of labor."[82] At Brussels, proposals also included government support for the creation of permanent laboratories for the experimental study of work. Yet the requirements were not limited to financing. Even more essential was the basic belief that there was an elective affinity between scientific knowledge as a neutral field of discourse and the state as the appointed arbiter of social conflict. This alliance of science and the state had far-reaching implications. At the most fundamental level it meant an increasing dependence of science on state agencies concerned with collecting data about work, such as the French Office du Travail, established in 1891 for the purpose of "research and publication that concerns the state and the development of production, the remuneration of work, and its relations with capital and the conditions of the workers."[83] Of even greater significance was the extensive collection, throughout Europe, of data on workers' mortality, health, and accidents after 1890 (although it began somewhat earlier in Germany). Only when these data were used as evidence for the pathological effects of fatigue and overwork, and utilized in support of concrete proposals for reform, did fatigue research begin to outgrow the confines of the laboratory and enter the terrain of politics.

---

vol. 5 (Brussels, 1903); *Bericht über den XIV. Internationalen Kongress für Hygiene und Demographie*, vol. 2, Berlin, 23–29 September 1907 (Berlin, 1908).

[81] Armand Imbert, "Le surmenage par suite du travail professionnel au XIVe Congrès international d'hygiène et de démographie (Berlin, Septembre 1907)," *Année psychologique*, 14 (1908): 242.

[82] *XIIIe Congrès international d'hygiène et de démographie*, 5:76,77.

[83] Paul Louis, *L'ouvrier devant l'état: Histoire comparée des lois travail dans les deux mondes* (Paris, 1904), p. 40.

The growing social concern of the science of work after 1900 also coincided with the first highly informal attempts to collect actual data on fatigue from those most directly affected, through questionnaire surveys. In 1903 the French physiologist A. M. Bloch simply asked Parisian artisans: "When you have been busy, where do you feel fatigue?" receiving the response that fatigue predominates in the groups of muscles that become immobile when contracted, a phenomenon he named "static fatigue."[84] Even more extensive was the survey conducted by the German Adolf Levenstein to consider "the social-psychological side of the modern large factory and its 'psychophysical' effects on the worker."[85] Levenstein's famous *Arbeiterfrage* (1912) contains an extraordinary wealth of information not only on fatigue, but also on cultural questions such as books read, hopes and expectations, and the like, among the miners, textile workers and machinists he queried. Levenstein polled 2,086 miners about their experience of fatigue, with the not very astonishing result that only 81 responded that they were not tired, while 2,005 reported fatigue and 216 said they were "permanently" tired.[86] Even more fascinating is the depth and subtlety of many of the individual responses. One metalworker, who had spent his life on the land and only two years in a factory, noted: "After the weekend and two hours before the end of the shift I am already tired. But it is a different tiredness. Not tired like at home, when you work the whole day with a scythe or walk behind the plow. Here my limbs always tremble. And also, in the country after work there was so much laughing. Here you see only sullen faces."[87] These early studies were followed by the more comprehensive enquiries of the Verein für sozialpolitik, and the sociological investigation of specific plants, like the Siemens-Halske works in Berlin—which demonstrated the efficacy of introducing plant canteens to reduce alcohol consumption and control the timing of the breaks.[88] There were also extensive studies of "neurasthenia in workers' circles" on the basis of

[84]A. M. Bloch, "Enquête sur la fatigue musculaire professionnel," *Bulletin de la Société de biologie* 66 (1903): 548.

[85]Adolf Levenstein, *Aus der Tiefe* (Berlin, 1909); idem, *Die Arbeiterfrage* (Munich, 1912; reprinted New York, 1975).

[86]Ibid., p. 88.

[87]Ibid., p. 77.

[88]M. Bernays, *Auslese und Anpassung der Arbeiterschaft der geschlossenen Grossindustrie: Schriften des Vereins für Sozialpolitik*, vol. 133 (Leipzig, 1910); Ernst Bernhard, *Arbeitsintensität und Arbeitszeit, Schmollers Forschungen*, no. 138 (Leipzig, 1909); Stanislaw von Bienkowski, *Untersuchungen über Arbeitseignung und Leistungsfähigkeit der Arbeiterschaft eines grossindustriellen Betriebes* (Berlin, 1910); Fritz Schumacher, *Auslese und Anpassung der Arbeiterschaft in der Automobilindustrie und einer Wiener Maschinenfabrik* (Leipzig, 1911); Alfred Weber, "Das Berufsschicksal des Industriearbeiters," *Archiv für Sozialwissenschaften und Sozialpolitik* 34 (1912): 377–405; Emmanuel Roth, "Ermüdung durch Berufsarbeit," in *Bericht über den XIV. Internationalen Kongress für Hygiene und Demographie*, 2:593–625.

figures culled from medical insurance statistics and with the aid of German sanatoriums.[89]

In the atmosphere of heated controversy about the length of the working day, methods of remuneration, working conditions, and above all industrial accidents, the science of work began to take an active role in seeking an objective solution to the labor question. From the outset there was an agreement between the agencies of government dedicated to reform and the proponents of social medicine that "the methods and techniques of the laboratory, applied to the study of the worker question, are in many ways capable of furnishing the perhaps indispensable data to establish the most equitable solution to the conflict between labor and capital."[90]

One of the first applications of the science of labor for resolving a social issue was a study conducted for the French Office du Travail by Imbert and Mestre on the relative merits of the *cabrouet* (hand truck) versus the *brouette* (wheelbarrow) in a brickyard. Though it resulted in legislation on the maximum loads adolescents of both sexes could be allowed to carry, the study was ironically completely ignored in the 1908 law that prohibited the cabrouet in those cases where it was markedly inferior to the brouette, but in another case, prohibited the brouette where it proved superior.[91] In Belgium the campaign for a shorter working day was advanced by an attempt by the Solvay Institute, in collaboration with the Office du Travail, to promote the success of a model chemical factory that introduced three eight-hour shifts, demonstrating increased productivity over the previous twelve-hour shifts.[92]

Although some, like Kräpelin, cautioned that the science of labor should not take a position of the length of the working day, and warned that the fatigue study should not reduce productivity, most of its promoters were reform oriented. Apart from the French, scientists from diverse countries, such as Ioteyko (Belgium), Tréves (Italy), and Roth and Münsterberg (Germany), agreed that shortening the working day and introducing rest pauses or even a rest day (*repos hebdomadaire*) in midweek would result in greater productivity. The efficiency achieved by eliminating overwork would be more than a sufficient compensation

---

[89]P. Leubuscher and W. Bibrowicz, "Die Neurasthenie in Arbeiterkreisen," *Deutsche medizinischer Wochenschrift*, no. 21 (1905): 820–24; M. Schönhals, *Über die Uraschen der Neurasthenie und Hysterie bei Arbeitern* (Berlin, 1906).

[90]Imbert, "Méthodes de laboratoire et questions ouvrières," p. 481.

[91]Armand Imbert and Mestre, "Recherches sur la manoeuvre du cabrouet et la fatigue qui en résulte," *Bulletin de l'inspection du travail*, no. 5 (1905); Armand Imbert, "Etude experimentale du travail de transport de charges avec une bronette," *Bulletin de l'inspectation du travail*, no. 1, 2 (1909); idem, "Exemples d'étude physiologique directe du travail professionnel ouvrier," *Revue d'hygiène et de police sanitaire* 31 (1909): 750–70.

[92]L. G. Fromont, *Une expérience industrielle de réduction de la journée de travail* (Brussels, 1906), p. 2

for reform, they argued, since their claims were based not on "a utopian conception but [on] precisely known facts."[93] Speaking at the Berlin Congress in 1907, Roth explained that any reduction of the working day was desirable from a "hygienic standpoint," as long as the gain in recouping the day's energy (*Kräfteersatz*) from the longer rest period, or from the more efficient movement of the worker, was greater than the energy consumed by "the intensification of the tempo of work."[94]

In contrast to those who "quite wrongly" regarded such controversies over the length of the working day and the conditions of work as purely economic issues, the science of labor believed that the interests of society as a whole could be served by the new economy of force. It was as applicable to society as to the single muscle: "the human motor deteriorates, which causes injury to the worker . . . and the efficiency of that motor diminishes, which causes injury to the entrepreneur who employs it, independent of the social costs that must later be borne by that deterioration."[95] For this reason, they believed, "experimental science is called upon to play the role of finding a truly equitable solution to these contests through research."[96]

The Politics of Industrial Accidents

The most important opportunity for such a role was provided by the debates, especially, but not exclusively in France, on the law proposed to provide indemnity for workers' accidents incurred in most occupations. Even more than the length of the working day, the issue of industrial accidents provided a striking example of the place of social medicine in the struggle between capital and labor. With the passage of social legislation against industrial accidents, in Germany in 1884 and in France in 1898, responsibility shifted from the worker, who in the past had to prove the negligence of the employer, to the latter, who was now held liable unless the victim could be proved at fault.[97] In France, the long decade of debate on the law, first proposed in 1888 and finally passed in April 1898, provided an arena of combat, of rhetorical swordplay, where the claims of the science of work could be tested against one of the burning questions of the day. On the one side were those defenders of the old order who believed that "*risque professionnel*" was an

[93]Imbert, "Surmenage par suite du travail," p. 247.
[94]Roth, "Ermüdung," p. 595.
[95]Armand Imbert, "Le surmenage par suite du travail professionnel," in *Bericht über den XIV. Internationalen Kongress*, 2:635.
[96]Ibid., p. 637.
[97]See Louis, *Ouvrier devant l'état*, pp. 292–353, for an extensive discussion of the importance of this legislation.

ancient threat in all aspects of life and not a responsibility of government: "le grand risque professionnel de l'humanité, c'est que tout être humain est mortel et peut perdre ses facultés physiques et mentales."[98] On the other side were those who argued for the "modernity" of risk in the modern factory with its new technology.

In the debate on the origins of the accidents, which persisted after the passage of the law, the political implications of fatigue research became apparent. Contractual relations between worker and employer took on a new dimension with the mandatory collection of data on all industrial and occupational accidents and with the high indemnities paid by the quasi-public insurance companies.[99] By 1900, when the first reported statistics revealed an increase of 36,000 accidents over the previous year, there was a public outcry from the *patronat* and from certain conservative sectors of the medical profession against what was called "the epidemic of simulations," against the "professionals" of industrial accidents, and against the fraudulent misuse of the law by those who took advantage of naive medical practitioners not trained in "suspicious medicine."[100] Treatises on the simulation of accidental injury abounded, and one doctor, the author of several studies of a similar problem in the military, noted that the new law was "a clear menace for the laboring Frenchman," who, "upon entering the hospital or the bedchamber as a result of an occupational accident, dreams of only one thing—not of departing cured, but of departing with an income."[101] At the same time, the socialists also attacked the law as far too limited in its definition of an "accident," excluding, as it did, exhaustion or long-term occupational illness.[102]

For the science of labor the statistical data on industrial accidents provided an incomparable source of evidence supporting the claim that it was not simulation or greed, but the progressively debilitating effects of fatigue that accounted for the vast majority of incidents. The explosion of accidents demonstrated that fatigue was a scourge not only for the

[98]Léon Say, Sénat séance du 12.3.1889, in *Histoire des accidents de travail*, no. 10 (1981), special issue on the law of 9 April 1898 by Yvon Le Gall, p. 45.

[99]See Patrick Fridenson, "France–Etats-Unis: Genèse de l'usine nouvelle," *Recherches* 32/33 (September 1978): 375–88.

[100]Hubert Coustan, *De la simulation et de l'évaluation des infirmités dans les accidents du travail* (Montpellier, 1902), p. 9.

[101]Ibid., p. 7.

[102]Louis, *Ouvrier devant l'état*, p. 353. Similar criticisms can be found in Victor Griffuelhes and Louis Niel, *Les objectifs de nos luttes de classes* (Paris, 1909), p. 19. The definition of an accident as *"un evénement soudain, et la maladie qui est, au contraire, un état continu et durable"* is Léon Bourgeois's. State officials also tried to interpret the law to exclude all "conséquences lointaines des fatigues ou des insalubrités de métier." See Coustan, *Simulation*, p. 16. For the debates on fatigue in the Chamber of Deputies see Séance de la chambre, 28 October 1897, in the *Journal officiel*; for a more balanced medical view see P. Chavigny, *Diagnostic des maladies simulées dans les accidents du travail* (Paris, 1906), p. 211.

worker, but for the expenditure of energy in the nation as a whole. Criticizing the insurance companies for their lack of interest in the "way the human organism functions," Imbert, with the inspecteur du travail of the department of Hérault, Mestre, undertook a series of detailed investigations of the 2,065 accident victims in that department in 1903.[103] Since the 1898 law made mandatory the reporting of all accidents in each department, with a description of the time, day, and nature of the incident, a close study of the distribution of accidents during the day and the week could, they believed, yield significant results. They speculated that there was a correlation between fatigue and the occurrence of accidents, evident in their distribution. Imbert and Mestre found that the accidents climbed progressively in the period before midday break, following the same pattern even more acutely during the afternoon, with the highest proportion of accidents falling in the last hours of work. Their research proved the "influence of the fatigue of workers on the production of accidents."[104]

Moreover, in his direct observations of the dockworkers of Sète, Imbert disputed the claims of the insurance companies that the disproportionate number of accidents in that city, as opposed to other ports, indicated the likelihood of organized fraud and premeditation on the part of the workers. In reality, he argued, fatigue was much more marked at Sète as a result of the greater tonnage of merchandise handled, so that "the larger number of accidents thus appears as a physiological consequence of the particularities of the work, independent of the struggle between workers and the bosses."[105] Similar statistics collected in other departments, as well as in Germany and Sweden, also showed that "industrial accidents stand in a definite relationship to the hours of the day."[106]

In the German case, however, the fact that more accidents fell on Mondays than on Saturdays showed that "besides work itself, the conduct of life is of decisive importance for safety and for the question of fatigue."[107] In other words, reports of the disappearance of *"blaue Montag"*

[103]Armand Imbert and Mestre, "Statistique d'accidents du travail," *Revue scientifique*, 24 September 1904, pp. 385–90; also see Armand Imbert, "Les accidents de travail et les compagnies d'assurance," *Revue scientifique*, 4 June 1904, pp. 711–19; Armand Imbert and Mestre, "Nouvelles statistiques d'accidents du travail," *Revue scientifique*, 21 October 1905, pp. 520–26; and the *Congrès international médical des accidents de travail, Liège, 1905: Rapports et communications* (Brussels, 1905).

[104]Imbert and Mestre, "Statistiques d'accident du travail," p. 386.

[105]Imbert, "Surmenage par suite du travail professionnel," 2:386.

[106]Roth, "Ermüdung," p. 618; Weber, *Psychophysik der industriellen Arbeit*, p. 138; H. Bille-Top, "Die Verteilung der Unglücksfälle der Arbeiter auf die Wochentage nach Tagesstunden," *Zentralblatt für allgemeine Gesundheitspflege* 27 (1908): 197. Hugo Münsterberg, *Grundzüge der Psychotechnik* (Leipzig, 1914), p. 394.

[107]Roth, "Ermüdung," p. 606.

in the twentieth century were premature. Yet there were other interesting and unexpected results from these investigations. As Roth declared at the 1907 Berlin congress, the "progressive rise in general
accidents stands in a certain causal relationship to the reduction of labor
time and to some extent represents its reverse side."[108] If the reduction
of labor time produced still greater fatigue and more accidents as a
result of the intensification of work, then exclusive emphasis on the
shorter working day was misplaced. Fatigue was a product of work time
and not the absolute length of the working day. It was becoming increasingly clear that the real issue was no longer simply wages and hours,
but control over the speed of work—over time and motion. This fundamental shift in the nature of work was reflected in the most fundamental
concerns of the science of labor, though researchers were somewhat late
in recognizing its centrality. Although it was already evident to the trade
unions that the reduction of labor time "provoked a new speedup of the
machinery on the part of the bosses," for the science of labor the struggle
over production norms brought the belated acknowledgment that even
the most progressive reforms and the application of scientific methods
might not always yield neutral or desired results.[109] By 1908 it was becoming obvious "that the question of fatigue of the working class could
not simply be limited to the hours of work, or even the question of
organization of work and the workplace from a more or less advanced
technical point of view, but [involved] a large number of other questions
of a social, economic, personal and psychological nature."[110]

The New Science and the New Factory

Despite its origins in the physiological laboratories of the Helmholtzian
revolution, the European science of labor was forced to come to terms
with the transformation of the work process and the birth of the "new
factory" at the end of the nineteenth century.[111] Concern with fatigue,

[108]Ibid., p. 619.
[109]Fridenson, "France–Etats-Unis," p. 382.
[110]Z. Tréves, "Le surmenage par suite du travail professionnel," in *Bericht über den XIV.
Internationalen Kongress für Hygiene und Demographie* 2:626.
[111]At another level the science of labor was certainly not, like Taylorism, simply an
ideology of management, as Harry Braverman and Judith Merkle have implied. Rather,
it represented a "third stage" in the political struggle over the working body. The first
represented the creation of a disciplined work force; the second was characterized by the
struggle over the duration and value of labor time. The science of labor represented a
struggle over the intensity of labor power within a fixed duration of labor time and in the
context of mechanization and factory organization. It was a struggle over energy and
fatigue rather than time and money.

time, and motion reflected deep social changes in the nature of the factory and the emergence of a work force that no longer had to be subjected to the moral economy of industrial discipline outside the workplace. Instead, workers had to be taught to internalize the regularity imposed by machine technology and adapt to newly intensified work norms. Fatigue was its most immediate and universal consequence, its corporal embodiment. "Chronic fatigue," noted one of the resolutions adopted in 1907, "or exhaustion [is] observed in all the factories where the intensity of labor is regulated by the machine."[112] This transformation in the nature of work demanded a redefinition of its scientific conceptualization. As Imbert defined it; "instead of taking into account the conditions of existence of the worker outside the hours spent in occupational work, instead of regarding the animated motor solely to determine its proper nature and discover its general laws of functioning, it is a question of moving to the direct, experimental, microscopic study of occupational work itself."[113]

The science of labor was predicated on the idea that neither capital nor labor could accurately perceive that the determination of the maximum efficient expenditure of energy transcended ideology. If capital had to be taught to see labor not as a socially hostile corpus, labor had to understand that the work of the body had to conform to the laws of energy rather than the imperatives of politics. As opposed to what they considered to be the "colossal illusions" of the socialists, the central principle of the science of labor was "productivism," the "social equivalent of energeticism."[114]

It is entirely understandable, therefore, that the initial response of both labor and capital was suspicion and mistrust. In Germany, the first extensive survey of a large-scale enterprise indicated a deep skepticism by the workers in regard to concepts such as "pleasure in work," or efficiency, concluding that, alas, "money was the only bond that tied them to their activity."[115] Imbert's work on the dockers and Gautier's research on the wine and spirit storehouse workers of the south were greeted by the "hostile indifference" of the local labor organizations.[116] Nevertheless, Imbert persisted in his desire to see workmen take part in scientific congresses, eventually securing the cooperation of some Confédération générale du travail (CGT) representatives at the First International Medical Congress of Occupational Accidents in May 1905.[117]

---

[112]Imbert, "Surmenage par suite du travail professionnel," p. 243.
[113]Imbert, "Exemples d'étude physiologique," p. 750.
[114]Solvay, *Principes d'orientation sociale*, p. 33.
[115]Bernays, *Auslese und Anpassung der Arbeiterschaft*, p. 189.
[116]Ioteyko, *Science of Labour*, p. 35.
[117]A. Imbert, "Congrès ouvriers et congrès scientifiques," *Revue scientifique*, 13 May 1905,

Even more significant in promoting the science of labor among the French trade unions was the formation of the Association ouvrière pour l'hygiène des travailleurs et des ateliers de Paris in 1904. Organized by the leaders of a variety of labor organizations the association wanted to bring, from the workers' standpoint, *"un sens pratique"* to the inspection of working conditions, which in their view, despite good legislation, was practically nonexistent.[118]

Employers were also less than enthusiastic about opening their doors to physiologists or worker-inspectors as the association demanded. In a report published by the French Ministry of Commerce (Millerand) in 1903, the socialist minister complained that "the majority of leaders of industry are less than struck by the primordial necessity of measures involving hygiene...and have made the work of the inspectors particularly difficult."[119]

More revealing was the survey conducted by the chief engineer of the Berlin municipal waterworks, W. Eisner, which provoked a storm of indignation from his fellow delegates when he presented it at the 1907 Berlin Congress. Eisner undertook the defense of the unjustly "rejected" entrepreneur by demonstrating that fatigue, "the condition in which the worker, despite a well-intentioned attempt on the part of his mental functions and his body's limbs, is no longer master," could not be shown to exist in reality. Eisner's method was to distribute a questionnaire to the managers (*Betriebsleiter*) of fifty firms, asking if fatigue was noticeable before the normal close of the shift, either in the general appearance of the workers or from a decline in performance. The vast majority indicated that such fatigue was unusual, particularly since, as one respondent noted: "if we have an after-work party for our people we observe that they cheerfully dance until the early morning hours. People who are too fatigued would not do this."[120] Eisner concluded that fatigue "is so rarely found that it is useless for our purposes" and the "relationship between 'fatigue' and work could hardly be demonstrated by experiments and generalizations." Although Eisner's conclusions were countered by Roth, among others, who cited a number of Berlin sanatoriums in which overwork was endemic among working-class patients, Eisner's questionnaire is a good indicator of the attitude of German

---

pp. 588–90; "Rôle des ouvriers dans certains congrès scientifiques," *Grande revue*, 10 April 1909, pp. 574–78. Also see Ribeill, "Débuts de l'ergonomie," p. 27.

[118]*Bericht über den XIV. Internationalen Kongress für Hygiene und Demographie* 4:267–304; *Premier congrès de l'hygiène des travailleurs et des ateliers*, October 1904 (Paris, 1905).

[119]Cited in Louis, *l'Ouvrier devant l'état*, p. 292.

[120]W. Eisner, "Die Ermüdung durch Berufsarbeit," in *Bericht über den XIV. Internationalen Kongress für Hygiene und Demographie*, 2:583.

managers toward the concerns of the science of labor.[121] Imbert and the other French scientists also complained of the dearth of information or cooperation from the entrepreneurs.[122]

Productivism, the Social Equivalent of Energeticism

If the efficient deployment of the energies of society could not be realized in the atmosphere of class antagonism, it fell to the state to provide the necessary surveillance to ensure "a permanent medical supervision of all manufacturing institutions."[123] Since the state was slow to respond to such appeals from science and medicine, a stronger authority, the military, provided an even more appropriate model for the reorganization of work in the interests of production. For Imbert, the science of labor "envisages a vast organization capable of individual surveillance of all workers... the creation for industry of an institution comparable to the army health service corps [*Service du santé*]."[124] Only such an authoritarian solution could overcome the "fears and inhibitions" of the entrepreneurs, who could not be made to understand that individual concerns should "not be confused with the general interest."[125] The trade unions too had to be educated to see that the scientific training of the working class, the cultivation of proper habits through physiological medicine, and the intervention of a "science of aptitudes" would result in the most efficient deployment of labor and "augment the ease, the speed, the accuracy, and the uniformity of an act."[126] "For better or worse," Imbert sadly declared, "this militarization of the working population is no longer characteristic of our epoch. But in the case of the army, as in industry, it is now desirable to utilize, for each unit, worker or soldier, all the capacities and resistances compatible with a vigorous state of health."[127] Such radical prescriptions naturally provoked skepticism about the practicality of the science of labor. As Hector Depasse, a member of the Conseil supérieur du travail, remarked as early as 1895: "it is possible, to a certain extent, to supervise the employment of time, but how do you supervise the employment of energy?"[128]

[121]Ibid., pp. 586–92.
[122]Imbert, "Surmenage par suite du travail professionnel," p. 232.
[123]Ibid., p. 243.
[124]Ibid.
[125]Ibid., p. 232.
[126]Omer Buyse, "Le problème psychophysique de l'apprentissage," *Revue psychologique* 3 (1910): 377–99.
[127]Imbert, "Surmenage par suite du travail professionnel," p. 238.
[128]Hector Depasse, *Du travail et de ses conditions (Chambres et conseils du travail)* (Paris, 1895), pp. 52, 53.

The Challenge of Taylorism

The introduction of Taylorism in France and Germany in the years just before World War I brought about the most profound crisis of the science of labor. For the physiological and energetic approach, the rapid diffusion of Taylor's ideas in Europe, and their adoption in some of the most important French and German plants, such as Renault and Borsig, presented a challenge of major proportions.[129] In the context of the existing efforts of management to regulate the "time and motion" of workers and to control the production process to a heretofore unthinkable degree, the introduction of "scientific management" was greeted with unmitigated hostility by the workers' representatives. It was apparent to them that in marked contrast to the science of labor, the desirability of the new American system lay in its one-sided devotion to output and profit, and in its callous disregard of the worker. As Alphonse Merrheim, the French trade union leader, declared: "personality, intelligence, the very desires of the workers are eliminated, annihilated, banished from the workshops and factories."[130] Emile Pouget, a labor leader, denounced the system as "the organization of exhaustion," and even the conservative journal of the Verein deutscher Ingenieure remarked in 1913 that the workers of recently Taylorized Borsig plant in Berlin-Tegel, despite their traditional submission to the modes of work imposed on them, received the new system "very badly."[131]

For the science of labor, Taylorism represented a total regression to prescientific attitudes toward work, a "superproductivism" without constraints. Jules Amar, for example, judged Taylor's methods insufficient because they were incapable of measuring fatigue and the expenditure of energy resulting from the intensification of work.[132] For Ioteyko too,

[129]On the introduction of Taylorism in France see Aimée Moutet, "Les origines du système de Taylor en France: Le point du vue patronal (1907-1914)," *Mouvement social* 93 October–December 1975): 15–49; for Germany see H. Homburg, "Anänge des Taylor-Systems in Deutschland," *Geschichte und Gesellschaft* 4 (1978): 170–94; for Renault see Patrick Fridenson, *Histoire des usines Renault*, vol. 1; *Naissance de la grande enterprise, 1898–1939* (Paris, 1972), pp. 70–79; Patrick Fridenson, "Die Arbeiter der französichen Automobilindustrie 1890 bis 1914," in *Wahrnehmungsformen und Protestverhalten: Studien zur Lage der Unterschichten im 18. und 19. Jahrhundert*, ed. Detlev Puls (Frankfurt am Main, 1979), pp. 228–64.

[130]See the article by Alphonse Merrheim in *Vie ouvrière*, 20 February 1913, pp. 214, 215. An early German critic is Dr. Sachs, "Ein System zur Auspressung der Menschenkraft," *Frankfurter Zeitung*, 2 February 1913.

[131]Emile Pouget, *L'organisation du surmenage* (Paris, 1914); *Zeitschrift des Vereines deutscher Ingenieure*, 8 March 1913.

[132]See Jules Amar, *Le moteur humain et les bases scientifiques du travail professionnel* (Paris, 1914), pp. 609–15. Ribeill points out that Amar was the most ambivalent of the critics of Taylorism in the camp of the science of labor in France. The most extreme negative position was taken by Jean-Marie Lahy in his *Le système Taylor et la physiologie du travail*

Taylor's system ignored the fact that "fatigue intervenes in the action of the human motor," permitting the worker only "the freedom of the individual to overwork."[133] Münsterberg also criticized the Taylor school, though less harshly than the French, for its lack of interest in experimental psychology.[134] Most critical was Jean-Marie Lahy's comprehensive *Le système Taylor et la physiologie du travail professionnel*, which denounced the system because "the worker is not considered anything but one of the pieces of the grand checkerboard that forms the factory."[135] Completely partisan in its emphasis on output, ruthless in its "carrot and stick" methods of wage premiums, and devoted to giving management full control over the labor process, the Taylor system ensured the absolute hegemony of the manager in the new factory: "Neither the participation of the worker nor the control of the public power can modify it given the current state of legislation," Lahy concluded.

Taylorism threatened to eclipse the most central concerns of the science of labor: the rational determination of the point of optimal efficiency for both labor and capital, the regulation of the expenditure of energy, and the determination of the laws of fatigue. In opposition to the American system, the European science of labor maintained that "only the cooperation of a man of the laboratory, disengaged from partisan interests, is capable of establishing rules of work adapted to the physical limitations of the workers. But as a result of persistent prejudice, the industrialists attempt to rob the men of science of their initiatives."[136]

The interest of European management in American "scientific management" as opposed to the science of work cannot simply be attributed to the technical superiority of the Taylor system over the experimental determination of ergographic laws. Its appeal also lay in the practical and political nature of its precepts and in its purely instrumental reliance on engineers as opposed to esoteric—and often marginal—European doctors and physiologists with a limited knowledge of real work environments. Taylorism grew out of the needs of management rather than the universal aims of scientific discourse. But even more important, the

---

professionnel (Paris, 1921), which is a summary of his prewar articles. See Ribeill, "Débuts de l'ergonomie," p. 32.

[133]Ioteyko, *Science of Labour*, pp. 85–87.

[134]Hugo Münsterberg, *Psychology and Industrial Efficiency* (Boston and New York, 1913), pp. 308–9. This should not be taken as evidence of Münsterberg's lack of sympathy with the project of scientific management, "den Mechanismus dem ökonomischen Verlangen nach rhythmischer Muskeltätigkeit anzupassen." See his *Psychotechnik*, p. 382. In fact, he reaches a height of lyricism when he proclaims that "the heightening of the individual's joy in the work and of the personal satisfaction in one's total life development belongs among the most important indirect agencies of the new scheme" (*Psychology and Industrial Efficiency*, p. 51).

[135]Lahy, *Système Taylor*, p. 141.

[136]Ibid.

science of labor had to concede to Taylorism its most essential point: that it had proved that workers could become "twice, three times, or even four times as productive as they originally were," demonstrating "that there was no hard-and-fast relation between labor of whatever kind and fatigue."[137]

In two fundamental ways the science of labor and Taylorism had the same goals: a belief in productivism, and a focus on both aptitude and the elimination of "slow and useless" movements.[138] Both schools took as a starting point the reduction of labor to a series of abstract relations: fatigue, time and motion, units of work, and so forth. For both it was the body that constituted the horizon of labor power in industrial society, not the social relations of work or its intrinsic meaning. In both, the rationalization of production was predicated on the rationalization of the body. And even the trade union leaders who opposed Taylorism accepted its credo that the reward of work was not to be found it the production process, but outside it, in leisure and consumption.

By the end of World War I there was, in both camps, a growing recognition that the two methods were not irreconcilable, and that a rapprochement would permit an even greater perfectibility of the system.[139] This is in fact what occurred during the war when aspects of both Taylorism and the science of work were adapted to the exigencies of combat and the home-front imperatives of production. Indeed, by the 1920s and 1930s many of the ideas of the science of labor and of Taylorism were absorbed by the more sophisticated European science of rationalization of that generation. Often this amalgamation was at the expense of the early utopian reformism of the science of labor, though with some concession of the crudeness of Taylor's initial prescriptions. One commentator complained in 1927 that in Germany the "*Amerikapsychose*" of the postwar period had caused the French and German science of labor to be "unjustly forgotten" because of the exaggerated influence of the American school.[140]

Conclusion

The science of labor emerged from the convergence of three developments in the last decades of the nineteenth century: the appearance

[137]Ibid., pp. 141, 142.
[138]Ioteyko, *Science of Labour*, pp. 54, 55.
[139]Ibid., p. 88. Also see the rapprochement suggested by Henri Le Chatelier, who brought Taylor's ideas to France and remained his greatest advocate, in his preface to Jules Amar's *Organisation physiologique du travail*. Le Chatelier argues for the perfectibility of the system with the aid of the physiologists.
[140]Giese, "Eigenart der französischen Arbeitswissenschaft," p. 403.

of a scientific discourse founded on an analogy between the conservation of energy in the universe and the laws of energy in the body; the rise of a "new factory" and new technologies that demanded the integration of the human organism into highly specialized and—as a result of labor conflict—intensified work processes; and the development of a state sector, however weak, to mediate the conflict between labor and capital. The science of labor is a reflection, therefore, of a new relationship between knowledge and work in a period when the total deployment of the labor power of society and the social organization of production took precedence over the old conflicts about the distribution of goods and the creation of a disciplined work force. Standing above the contending social forces, the science of labor was suspect for its very lack of partisanship. From the standpoint of capital, its advocacy of a shorter working day, rest pauses, employee protection, and rational work norms appeared to contradict the imperatives of profit and the hegemony of management. From the standpoint of labor, its emphasis on the rationalization of the most minute motions of the body, the study of fatigue, and state surveillance threatened to deprive the working class of its most important source of autonomy, the power of collective action. The greatest weakness of the science of labor lay in its most compelling assumption: that scientific objectivity and productivism were socially neutral discourses and that labor power was subject to its own objective laws of economy that could be located, measured, and determined. The crisis of the science of labor was a consequence of the inadequacies of its central metaphor, which perceived the body, the factory, and society as extensions of the "human motor."

−18−

Automobile Workers in France and Their Work, 1914–83

PATRICK FRIDENSON

Early automobile workers in France, from 1890 to 1914, did not draw the attention of many scholars or writers.[1] The same, however, does not hold true for their successors, who seem to typify the second Industrial Revolution. They have become the subject of popular histories and films,[2] and even sociologists have paid them much attention.[3]

In these circumstances, can the historian still say something new? First, he must be careful not to fall into the same traps as his predecessors: technological determinism, generalizations from global to particular, or a reductionism that equates thought with daily experience. By avoiding these mistakes the historian will be more conscious of the divisions among autoworkers, of the alliances among their different groups, and of the goals and results of their struggles.[4] In addition, the historian must carefully describe the specific elements of this peculiar trade in com-

---

[1] Patrick Fridenson, "Les premiers ouvriers français de l'automobile (1890–1914)," *Sociologie du travail* 21 (July–September 1979): 297–325.

[2] Most of them deal with Citroën. Among novelized narratives: Ilya Ehrenburg, *The Life of the Automobile* (New York, 1976; originally published in French, 1929); Georges Navel, *Travaux* (Paris, 1945); Claire Etcherelli, *Elise, ou La vraie vie* (Paris, 1967); Robert Linhart, *The Assembly Line* (Amherst, Mass., 1980). Among films: Louis Malle, *Humain, trop humain,* 1974.

[3] In chronological order of original publication: Georges Friedmann, *Industrial Society* (Glencoe, Ill., 1955); Michel Collinet, *L'ouvrier français: Essai sur la condition ouvrière* (Paris, 1951); Alain Touraine, *L'évolution du travail ouvrier aux usines Renault* (Paris, 1955); Pierre Naville et al., *L'etat entrepreneur: Le cas de la régie Renault* (Paris, 1971); Michel Freyssenet, *La division capitaliste du travail* (Paris, 1977).

[4] Charles F. Sabel, *Work and Politics: The Division of Labor in Industry* (Cambridge, Mass., 1982), pp. 4–10.

Table 18.1. The labor force in the French automobile industry

1913	36,000	1956	125,000
1920	75,000	1975	260,745
1929	109,000	1981	240,000

parison with other branches and other forms of contemporary industrial work.[5] Finally, he must examine the major stages in the evolution of these workers, for these previous stages still mark the industry today, even though collective memory continually modifies their representation.

The period under study, 1914–83, has an undeniable unity. Its focus is on the introduction, expansion, and crisis of Fordism à la française. The product manufactured by the automakers remains the same: "Great as have been the engineering advances since 1920, we have today basically the same kind of machine that was created in the first twenty years of the century," wrote General Motors' former president in 1963.[6] Yet the historian shares the sociologist's basic question: "But is it still the same industry and the same worker?"[7] The working population has increased and changed; so has the type of work. We may therefore suppose that the attitudes of autoworkers in France toward their work did change—given certain inevitable continuities. These attitudinal shifts cannot be reduced to a simple reaction to further losses of workers' autonomy—losses that began with Taylorism before 1914. On the contrary, these attitudes relate to the appearance of new strategies by workers and to new kinds of struggle.

Establishing Fordism (1914–45)

A number of French automakers introduced certain Fordist production methods quite early. In the course of World War I the space of the factory was reorganized, work on-line was started, semiskilled workers were massively hired (especially women and foreigners), and welfare programs were developed in order to modify the workers' way of life. There was only one French exception to the original rules of Fordism: this renewed labor force in most cases did not receive hourly wages but remained under the incentive of the piecework and bonus systems. The same was true of most other European automakers. After the war, wel-

[5]Michel Verret, *L'ouvrier français*, vol. 2, *Le travail ouvrier* (Paris, 1982), pp. 10–12.
[6]Alfred P. Sloan, Jr., *My Years with General Motors* (Garden City, N.Y., 1964), p. 219.
[7]Verret, *Ouvrier*, p. 17.

fare programs rapidly declined—only to reappear in the 1930s and 1940s.[8] Other aspects of Fordism were implemented on a large scale inside factories during the 1920s, and even the 1930s, but they progressed slowly, as in the rest of Europe, and with marked differences between firms.[9] How did autoworkers experience and adapt to this switch to mass production?

The Expectations of Workers' Groups

The major attraction of auto work was the same as in prewar times: the pay was good, higher than in most other activities requiring equivalent skills. Unlike employees in many other industrial sectors, autoworkers gained another substantial advantage in the 1920s: the establishment of the eight-hour day.[10]

Women held similarly positive views about auto work. For them, too, money was the primary motivation, even though women's wages were lower than men's by at least 25 percent. A women working in a test workshop for new gears at Renault in March 1920 observed: "Here, nothing. No other goal than the earning of one's daily living." She mentioned the inducement of piece rates in a large factory that was offered to one of her neighbors. This woman, who had made shells at Renault during the war, had married a Renault worker and had just returned to auto work: "My husband and I will earn sixty to sixty-five francs, so

[8]André Citroën, "L'organisation du travail, les règles de l'hygiène et du repos dans une usine moderne," *Science et la vie*, 8 (December 1917–January 1918): 61–70; Sylvie Schweitzer, *Des engrenages à la chaîne: Les usines Citroën, 1915–1935* (Lyons, 1982), pp. 56, 101–6; Yves Cohen, "Ernest Mattern, les automobiles Peugeot et le pays de Montbéliard industriel avant et pendant la guerre de 1914–1918" (thesis, University of Besançon, 1981), pp. 189–380; Cohen, "L'espace de l'organisateur: Ernest Mattern, 1906–1939," *Mouvement social* 24 (October–December 1983): 80–93; Gilbert Hatry, *Renault usine de guerre, 1914–1918* (Paris, 1978), pp. 93–145; Alain Pinol, "Travail, travailleurs et production aux usines Berliet (1912–1947)" (mémoire de maîtrise, University of Lyons II, 1980), pp. 36–74; Annie Fourcaut, *Femmes à l'usine: Ouvrières et surintendantes dans les entreprises françaises de l'entre-deux-guerres* (Paris, 1982), pp. 200–204; Aimée Moutet, "Patrons de progrès ou patrons de combat? La politique de rationalisation de l'industrie française au lendemain de la première guerre mondiale," *Recherches* 13 (September 1978): 452–54, 463–64, 466, 471, 478–83; Wayne Lewchuck, "Fordism and British Motor Car Employers, 1896–1932," in *Managerial Strategies and Industrial Relations*, ed. Howard F. Gospel and Craig R. Littler (London, 1983), pp. 84–89.

[9]Patrick Fridenson, "The Coming of the Assembly Line to Europe," *Sociology of the Sciences* 2 (1978): 159–78; Aimée Moutet, "Introduction de la production à la chaîne en France du début du XXe siècle à la grande crise en 1930," *Histoire, économie et société* 2 (January–March 1983): 63–82; Lewchuck, "Fordism," pp. 89–107; Jean-Paul Depretto and Sylvie Schweitzer, *Le communisme à l'usine: Vie ouvrière et mouvement ouvrier chez Renault, 1920–1939* (Roubaix, 1984), pp. 73–75.

[10]Pierre-Jean Lavirotte, *L'évolution des salaires en France depuis la guerre: Etude statistique* (Langres, 1939); Fourcaut, *Femmes à l'usine*, p. 99; Depretto and Schweitzer, *Communisme*, pp. 15–19.

Fig. 18.1. Peugeot rear-axle assembly line at Sochaux in 1931, showing conveyance system of the chain. Notice female as well as male workers. Service photographique, Peugeot (Sochaux), kindly supplied by Yves Cohen

we will drink champagne every day."[11] Again, at Renault in March 1920, a peasant woman who was afraid of the factory finally made up her mind to work there because of high wages: "I am glad to have found good people here. I had been told that a factory attracted only rabble." She was employed in the tempering workshop. There she met a shopgirl whose boyfriend had threatened to leave her. Alone, with only the wages of a clerk, the shopgirl could not have met her needs. Hence her move to Renault. Thus the automobile factory continued to draw part of its labor force from other economic sectors—just as it had done during the war. The great attraction for both women and their employers was that auto work required little or no training time.[12]

However, for a minority of women auto work offered even more

[11]Fourcaut, *Femmes à l'usine*, pp. 62, 124, 169–70.
[12]Ibid., pp. 154–55.

complex benefits. It gave them a more varied social life and a comparative emancipation, unlike the usual practice in small enterprises. Such was the impression conveyed by young women workers of the Panhard factory in Paris in 1928:

> Their work gave them a certain amount of independence toward their husbands. Spouses treated each other as good comrades. They both took their share of domestic tasks. The first to come home would prepare dinner or wash up dishes. Their life was more comfortable and less meek than others. They wanted either few children or none, because parenthood would mean either the renunciation of work or a harried life combining factory work and child rearing. These women liked the easy life. They had little to do at home, and factory life with all its gossip, incidents, and sociability pleased them and turned their thoughts in other directions.[13]

Similarly, the married woman worker at Renault in March 1920 whom I mentioned earlier had come back to work despite the "big money" her husband made "because she liked factory work" and also because "occupying a furnished flat, she was bored at home." Women made up about 10 percent of the labor force in the French auto industry of the 1920s.[14]

In the same way, some men wanted to join the large auto company to escape the risks of working in a small enterprise. When interviewed recently, a semiskilled worker born in the Isère department emphasized one advantage of a large-scale factory: everything is provided for, nothing is left to chance. "I asked to come back to Berliet because it was big business, things were correctly done, no need to wait till the sister of the chap who . . . made up her mind to pay out the wages." Another semiskilled worker, born in Paris, recalled that after having worked in a small jewelry shop as an apprentice he wanted to be hired at the Renault factory in 1933 because he thought that "in a large-scale enterprise it would be easier to earn one's living." In June 1936 a skilled moroccoleather dresser of Paris was hired at Renault as a semiskilled worker because he was attracted by the life of "the large factory."[15]

Last, a small group of skilled workers who had been trained in the automakers' own schools of apprenticeship were positively motivated. As a former worker pointed out: "whereas masses of men became mass-production robots, a minority of machine adjusters and toolmakers constantly had to raise their level of ability to answer the demands of modern

[13]Ibid., p. 103.
[14]Ibid., p. 170; Schweitzer, *Des engrenages*, p. 57.
[15]Pinol, "Travail," p. 143; Georges Choquenot, "Mon témoignage," *De Renault frères constructeurs d'automobiles à Renault Régie nationale* 1 (December 1971): 91; Robert Francotte, *Une vie de militant communiste* (Paris, 1973), pp. 124–27.

Fig. 18.2. Peugeot assembly plant at Sochaux in 1931: line of boring machines on engine blocks supplied by nonmechanical conveyor on rollers. Service photographique, Peugeot (Sochaux), kindly supplied by Yves Cohen

work."[16] The Berliet Company had had a school since 1906. After 1919 Citroën trained young people, most of whom were workers' sons, but soon this was not enough. In 1927 the company set up training workshops in its Javel Embankment factory, and more specialized schools were promptly added in its other factories. In 1919 Renault too created its school of apprenticeship. At its 1920 awards ceremony winning apprentices received pocket cases of mathematical instruments, slide rules, and technical books. By 1937 this school numbered 915 apprentices under age eighteen. In 1919 Peugeot also equipped its works with a

[16]Navel, *Travaux*, p. 83.

school.[17] The alumni of these schools still insist on the contrast between the school and the factory: "at school one must learn how to do well, at the workshop one must know how to do quickly." These schools did not succeed in completely suppressing the traditional oral transmission of technical knowledge in the workshop by the senior workers, whose practice was both domination and exchange of knowledge: "We, the young ones, wanted to work; the old journeymen liked us and [they were] proud to teach us their tricks of the trade on condition that we played the game and that at the outset we became to some extent their servants.... But as soon as [there] was an interesting piece of work, [the senior worker] showed me how to do it, [he] helped me."[18]

Therefore auto work bears the stamp (in Pierre Bourdieu's terminology) of the adjustment between workers endowed with different ethos and various segments of the labor market.

Workers' Strategies

Autoworkers' attitudes toward their work depended not only on their expectations, but also on their integration in the firm, their skills, their jobs, and their strategies, whether individual or collective.

Their integration was uneven. The major cleavage was between stable and transient workers. Let us consider a sample of former Berliet workers. Transient or short-term workers on an average stayed in a factory for two or three years, sometimes working at several jobs. Stable workers were all employed for more than twenty years, but their employment was not permanent either. Often it was interrupted by temporary resignations. Stable workers seem not to have had a clear understanding of the changes in the labor process, partly because it was a gradual evolution and partly because of their own stability. On the contrary, transient workers had a full awareness of these modifications and of the spread of Fordism, probably because they had worked in numerous factories. Most stable workers were skilled; they would quit whenever the factory's business declined and either join a small engineering firm or even, as in the nineteenth century, set up on their own. Transient workers were mostly unskilled or semiskilled people with little seniority, engaged in toilsome labor or unskilled tasks that characterized Fordist rationalization.[19] The Chinese leader Chou En-lai, when he worked in

[17]Pinol, "Travail," pp. 25, 138–39; Schweitzer, *Des engrenages*, pp. 93–95; Gilbert Hatry, *Louis Renault patron absolu* (Paris, 1982), pp. 180–81, 267; Ernest Mattern, *Création, organisation et direction des usines* (Paris, 1926), pp. 304–7; Mattern, "Apprentissage," *Bulletin des usines Peugeot* 1 (17 February 1919): 65–67.

[18]Pinol, "Travail," pp. 138–39, 157–58.

[19]Ibid., pp. 116, 133, 142–43.

a Parisian auto factory, remained there only nine months, explaining: "It was too inhuman."[20]

The nature of the job also influenced workers' perceptions. Let us go back to the Berliet case, which is now well known, thanks to a variety of master's theses.[21] First, Berliet had two factories that were completely different. From the mid–1920s onward, the Lyons-Monplaisir factory concentrated all the services focusing on the design of new models, repairs, and workshops producing on a small scale—in short, the operations that required a skilled labor force and technical know-how. The Vénissieux factory was left for all other operations. Thus Vénissieux factory workers nicknamed Monplaisir "the old-age home." Second, in Vénissieux itself one workshop was not as demanding as another. Workers learned to spot hard workshops—here the forge, the foundry, the small presses, the screw-cutting area—and those considered less laborious, such as repair shops and maintenance, where discipline was not so strict and semiskilled or unskilled workers were allowed to move about. Third, even within a workshop one job never was exactly the equivalent of another. On some very onerous tasks, a worker could not stay more than a week or two: these were jobs of passage. Finally, even in such a rationalized factory, the allocation of the jobs resulted not only from people's aptitudes, but also from personal contacts and from tacit agreements between workers and their chiefs. A worker appreciated the foreman who transferred him near the forges and foundries in winter, thus allowing him to enjoy the diffused heat without undergoing the dirtiness and roughness of these workshops. The recognition of good workshops and good posts was nothing new. It was a tradition among French metalworkers.[22]

Skill levels also shaped relations to work. Women, who mostly were semiskilled or unskilled, pointed out the boredom, the lack of interest, and the fatigue brought on by most tasks. At Renault in 1919 and in 1920, just as at Panhard in 1928, they deeply felt and resented the prohibition on moving about and talking, the loudness of the noises, the obligation to

[20]James Leung, "The Chinese Work-Study Movement: The Social and Political Experience of Chinese Students and Student-Workers in France, 1915–1925" (Ph.D. diss. Brown University, 1982).

[21]Pinol, "Travail"; Gérard Declas, "Recherches sur les usines Berliet (1914–1949)" (University of Paris I, 1977); Elisabeth Chahinian, Sylvie Murgia, and Marie-Noëlle Pichon, "La vie quotidienne de vingt-cinq ouvriers chez Berliet entre 1919 et 1939" (University of Lyons II, 1979); Philippe Cohen and Elisabeth Convert, "La crèche et la bobine—Berliet: Huit itinéraires de vies" (University of Lyons II, 1980); Nicole Tredant, "La qualité de la vie des familles ouvrières chez Berliet pendant l'entre-deux-guerres" (University of Lyons II, 1980).

[22]Alain Pinol, "Travaux ouvriers et témoignages oraux: L'exemple des usines Berliet pendant l'entre-deux-guerres," in *Mémoire vivante: Dires et savoirs populaires*, ed. Jean-Baptiste Martin (Lyons, 1982), pp. 212–24; Hyacinthe Dubreuil, *J'ai fini ma journée* (Paris, 1971), p. 61.

remain standing, and the dirtiness of the shops.[23] On the other hand, recent historians insist that early Fordism still allowed French skilled workers a certain amount of latitude. Their work became much more specialized, and in some cases even repetitive. However, at least in the 1920s, quality remained their categorical imperative, and they continued to use tools that they themselves had made during their apprenticeship.

Some skilled trades declined or disappeared, yet new machines created new tasks. Confronted with the new division of labor, skilled workers in the auto industry tried to find their place in it rather than see these changes as threatening. A significant incident happened in spring 1917 at Berliet. The assembly line had been introduced, but the technical system of production did not adapt well to the conveyor, and poorly standardized parts had to be disassembled, filed down and scraped, and reassembled. Here deskilled assemblers became fitters again for some time, thus recovering the know-how against which the assembly line was aimed. Except for assembly (where the transition from stationary on-line work to the moving assembly line was gradually achieved), it was probably not an exaggeration to write that at this time "the power relationship is still favorable to the skilled workers."[24]

The splitting of the labor force, its growth and constant renewal, and the complexity of the changes in the auto industry, as well as the relatively high level of pay, all explain why the workers' actions were characterized less by collective organization than by individual strategies.

Concerning collective action, the prewar period had left an unfavorable legacy of minority trade unions, divided in outlook and in interests, with a record of continual defeats.[25] The war had seemed to alter that trend. In almost every auto factory it had generated an active nucleus of conscripted skilled workers, who were instrumental from 1917 onward in the coming of mass unionism and in the institution of shop stewards, both of which brought collective workers' control as a counterpart to the beginnings of Fordism. But official suppression of the May 1918 strikes, the difficulties of industrial reconversion, the failure of major strikes in spring 1919 and 1920, and finally the scission of the national unions in 1921 led to the suppression of the shop stewards after the Armistice and to the sharp decline of unions.[26] An effective strategy of repression

[23]Fourcaut, *Femmes à l'usine*, pp. 96–99, 100–101, 124.
[24]Schweitzer, *Des engrenages*, pp. 60–62, 70, 89–90; Pinol, "Travail," pp. 152, 154–57.
[25]Fridenson, "Premiers ouvriers," pp. 301–2, 321–23.
[26]Edmond Pelé, "Le mouvement ouvrier lyonnais pendant la première guerre mondiale, 1914–1918" (mémoire de maîtrise, University of Lyons II, 1970), pp. 176–227; Bertrand Abhervé, "Les origines de la grève des métallurgistes parisiens, juin 1919," *Mouvement social* 16 (October–December 1975): 75–85; Depretto and Schweitzer, *Communisme à l'usine*, pp. 54–63, 78–80; Hatry, *Renault usine de guerre*, pp. 113–45; Hatry, *Louis Renault*, pp. 130–44, 190, 284–85; Declas, "Recherches," pp. 123–25; Mattern, *Création*, p. 291; Cohen,

staged by employers did not make it necessary, as in the United States, to implant more than a handful of house unions, even though Citroën's house organ, the *Bulletin Citroën*, sang their praises once or twice. As for the introduction of politics into the factory, the Bolshevization of the French Communist party was slow to bear fruit.[27]

Individual strategies other than a more-or-less meek acceptance of Fordism fell into two categories. One was flight from work, by absenteeism or voluntary departure. As in the United States, automakers quickly became attentive to the problem. Absenteeism was a traditional refuge for French workers. During the era of rationalization they also resorted to it often. Given the current state of my research, however, it is difficult to distinguish layoffs, illnesses, and voluntary departures, and the statistical data at my disposal do not allow many historical comparisons. Nevertheless I may cite two examples of this rapid turnover. The Renault works at Billancourt hired 135,925 individuals during the course of World War I and yet (because of departures and absenteeism) had an actual labor force of only 22,500 in 1918.[28] In 1928, at Citroën's forge factory of Clichy, management had to hire 4,600 workers to keep a constant level of 3,300. Its archives give some explanations. In November 1928, out of 333 workers who left the factory, 235 had resigned. One historian comments: "Fifty-four felt that their working conditions were impossible. Thirty had found a better paid job. Twenty criticized wages as inadequate. Twenty went to serve with the colors. Four could not stand discipline. Thus the harshness of working conditions, heightened by rationalization . . . , ranked first. On the other hand, the elimination of idle periods, which can be assimilated to discipline, was not perceived as such."[29] Turnover also existed in the provinces, and it has been described as "a Brownian motion of the workers' population." Yet the tempo of departures was lower in the provinces than in the Parisian area, according to Ernest Mattern, who was a manager first at Peugeot's Lille factory, then at Peugeot's Audincourt factory, and from 1922 to January 1928 at Citroën in Paris and thus in a good position to compare.[30]

The other strategy, on the contrary, focused on the job. Semiskilled

---

"Quand les masses viennent au syndicat (moralisation et représentativité)," *Révoltes logiques* 4 (Summer 1979): 28–51.

[27]Schweitzer, *Des engrenages*, pp. 112–13; Schweitzer, "Regards sur la bolchevisation: Le cas de la cellule 410 de l'usine Citroën (1924–1925)," *Cahiers d'histoire de l'Institut de recherches marxistes* 2 (April–June 1981): 75–93; Depretto, "Les problèmes posés par l'étude de l'implantation du P.C.F. à l'entreprise (1920–1936): Renault," in *Sur l'implantation du P.C.F. dans l'entre-deux-guerres*, ed. Jacques Girault (Paris, 1977), pp. 205–33.

[28]Mattern, *Création*, p. 150; Hatry, *Renault usine de guerre*, pp. 113–15.

[29]Schweitzer, *Des engrenages*, pp. 80–82.

[30]Pinol, "Travail," pp. 140–46; Schweitzer, *Des engrenages*, p. 71; Cohen, "Espace de l'organisateur," p. 90.

workers tried to challenge Fordist dictates concerning discipline and production methods by orally transmitting resistance practices among themselves—even though Fordist rationalization aimed in particular at eliminating this type of transmission. The channels for this communication were outside the workshop: in locker rooms, mass transportation, canteens, cafés. A woman worker at Panhard in 1928 explained: "In the locker rooms, in the lunchroom, in front of the factory's gate or in the tramway I found it possible to chat with my fellow workers. I found them more obliging than at the dye-works [where she was previously an employee] and ready to lend me a helping hand: none of them ever was reluctant to leave her machine to pull me through a difficulty. [At the lunchroon they] talked as much as they ate. The conversation was fed by gossip, narratives of news items, workshop stories."[31] This communication of experiences was fostered by unions and political parties but watched over or thwarted by employers.

Workers might offer resistance to disciplinary rules (some of which were not new). At work it was forbidden to sit down, move about, eat, smoke, speak, or read a newspaper.[32] Both archival documents and oral history interviews give evidence of successful transgressions of these interdictions. Most took place on the sly; a few happened openly. In some cases they gave rise to conflict; for example, drinking wine on assembly line number six at Berliet-Vénissieux in 1939. Or they were aided by connivance or tolerance: at Panhard in 1928 women workers might sit down for one minute from time to time in front of an indulgent work-team leader, who told them: "I will close my eyes this time, but try not to get caught by the foreman."[33] During the depression of the 1930s these violations of discipline were fought more vigorously, in the Paris area as well as in the provinces,[34] because employers were less and less willing to tolerate interruptions in the work process.

Workers might also offer resistance to the labor process itself. They used two methods. In the course of rationalization, some semiskilled workers empirically gained a technological know-how and found tricks and dodges enabling them to cut down the time necessary for machining,

[31]Fourcaut, *Femmes à l'usine*, pp. 101–2.

[32]This list of forbidden actions comes from Georges Floris, "Le règlement général de 1919," *De Renault frères* 1 (December 1971): 92–93, and "Le règlement général de 1923," *De Renault frères* 4 (June 1973): 235; and Fourcaut, *Femmes à l'usine*, pp. 98–99, 100, 124. The lists given by Pinol, "Travail," pp. 191–93, and Depretto and Schweitzer, *Communisme*, pp. 38–39, are incomplete. Examples of transgressed prohibitions are to be found in Navel, *Travaux*, p. 90; Pinol, "Travail," pp. 191–93, 228; Fourcaut, *Femmes à l'usine*, p. 100; and Schweitzer, *Des engrenages*, p. 147.

[33]Depretto and Schweitzer, *Communisme*, pp. 13, 41–43, 76–98; Pinol, "Travail," pp. 183–85.

[34]Patrick Fridenson, *Histoire des usines Renault* (Paris, 1972), 1:208–9; Pinol, "Travail," p. 166.

for painting small parts, and so on. Another method, which did not call for any know-how, was not executing a task fully: for instance, omitting a designated treatment. Management was alert to this emergence of technical knowledge among semiskilled workers. The institution of suggestion boxes in the Renault and Berliet factories, probably on the American pattern, gives proof of this. The consequences of these resistances differed from one type of job to another. When the pace of work was set by the machine, they allowed workers to gain spare time, and or to go to sleep, or to earn more money. When time-and-motion studies determined the pace, they allowed workers either to save time by a technical trick or to sustain the level of their wages. As soon as they understood the motions of Taylorism, it became easy to limit production.[35] Restriction of output was often observed, and management repeatedly opposed it. At Renault in March 1920, the women of the workshop that tests new gears "rapidly learn that if they produce more, piece rates will be lowered after a time clocker's visit. They soon find it an advantage not to exhaust themselves, and they stint on their work. ... Indeed, women who seem neither to organize nor to unite in the factory have almost only this *vis inertiae* or these silent struggles to defend their interests and to check the trend toward a decline in women's wages." At Citroën's forges and foundry in Clichy, management writes in 1928: "Every worker [who receives individual efficiency wages] limits his output, more often than not because he places no reliance on the stability of the rates."[36]

Automakers believed they had found a solution to this problem when, from 1927 onward, they simultaneously introduced a new method of remuneration (the collective bonus) and widened the responsibility of lower management over day-to-day production and working conditions.[37] Such incentives to collective responsibility of workers can be interpreted as a managerial acknowledgment that, far from annihilating workers' spirit of mutual understanding in the workshop, Fordism might give rise to a new kind of control of productive norms.

This control was encouraged by the atomization of tasks, which often brought about a greater dependence on other workers. Let me give some examples. In 1919, at the Renault workshop where valves were ground, a woman who resumed her work after a power outage (then a frequent occurrence) did so "with such eagerness that my neighbors, men and

---

[35]Pinol, "Travail," pp. 185–89; Schweitzer, *Des engrenages*, pp. 146–49; Fourcaut, *Femmes à l'usine*, p. 198; Moutet, "Introduction," p. 81.

[36]Fourcaut, *Femmes à l'usine*, p. 125; Schweitzer, *Des engrenages*, pp. 83, 147–49.

[37]Moutet, "Introduction," pp. 80–82; Daniel Henri, "La Société anonyme des automobiles Peugeot de 1918 à 1930" (mémoire de maîtrise, University of Paris I, 1983), pp. 131–32; Pinol, "Travail," pp. 172–73.

women, were terrified and told me: 'Don't work so much! It's too much of a hurry! If you are too quick, you will make them lower the job rate.'" She answered: "But I don't produce too much. I stop so often that I have not reached my two francs per hour." In such a case, "they do not care any more, they nod approvingly and go back to their work."

Another stance was the retention of information and of empirical knowledge. At Renault in March 1920, the test workshop for new gears "is not tuned up," says a young worker who previously worked in Canada. "I have plenty of ideas on what their problems are because I saw how it was done overseas. But there is no chance that I will express my views. The foreman would take them for himself." At Berliet's machining workshops and in particular at screw cutting, workers agreed to follow the pace of the slowest worker, especially when they were timed. Those who infringed these norms were blacklisted and in some cases were physically assaulted.[38]

If workers thus gradually resorted to individual resistance methods, more or less concerted, it was partly because opposition to Fordism by unions and parties had become less clear. As for "confederate" unions (which followed the reformist-socialist line of the "majoritarian" Confédération générale du travail (CGT), "la vieille maison"), the bringing out in 1929 of *Standards*, a book by Hyacinthe Dubreuil, a metalworker and a trade unionist, epitomized the new sensibility vis-à-vis American methods of mass production. The "unitary" unions (which followed the "communist and revolutionary" minority that had seceded from the CGT in 1921) and the Communist party went through three successive stages. Up to 1924, indifference prevailed. When they were required to take a position, it was screened by the distinction between good and bad rationalization. The Metalworkers Federation of the CGT had asserted on 18 April 1919: "workers must sympathetically adjust themselves to the development of mechanization and to the rational working methods." Its "unitary" successors initially remained on the same wavelength. From 1924 to 1927, under the influence of syndicalist leaders and also of an increased rationalization, trade unionists shifted to a criticism of rationalization, focusing on a denunciation of deskilling and of the lowering of piece rates. However, from 1927 onward, partly because of unemployment and of new payment systems, "unitary" trade unionists did not question the new methods any more and cared only about remedies for their consequences, especially for a shorter working day or week.[39] Such

[38]Fourcaut, *Femmes à l'usine*, pp. 95, 97; Pinol, "Travail," pp. 190–91, 226–27; Navel, *Travaux*, pp. 110–11.

[39]Dubreuil, *J'ai fini*, pp. 92–126; Pierre Saint-Germain, "La chaîne et le parapluie: Face à la rationalisation (1919–1935)," *Révoltes logiques* 1 (Spring–Summer 1976): 87–124; Fridenson, "Coming," pp. 168–72; Schweitzer, *Des engrenages*, pp. 126–30; Pinol, "Travail,"

were workers' possible attitudes to changes in work that favored new qualities among workers: dexterity, diligence, regularity, quick reactions, strong nerves, and endurance.

I have not yet mentioned strikes. Indeed, they were unusual in this period. After 1920 only the Citroën factories experienced three total strikes that paralyzed operations (1924, 1927, 1933); Berliet had none, and Peugeot and Renault had one each. As for strikes limited to one craft or to one workshop or two, they also rarely occurred. Strikes, then, meant that tensions had erupted and the breaking point had been reached, even though the official demands of labor often hinged on wages.[40]

The Backlash

Why then did these tensions germinate from 1934 onward and lead to many more open conflicts, especially more strikes from 1936 to 1938 and, from 1940 to 1944, to growing insubordination? Of course one may put forward motives that lie outside the relationship between autoworkers and their job. These include, among others, the new strategy followed by Communists and "unitary" trade unionists, probably from 1932, the rise of Nazism, and the coming of the Popular Front and, later, of the National Resistance. It appears that this new environment unleashed workers' energies and allowed a brief encounter—but how explosive!—between autoworkers and organizations, whether parties or unions.[41]

But the auto industry itself also proved propitious terrain for the development of such conflicts. The rationalization policies that the auto companies implemented in the early 1930s to fight the depression seriously modified the working conditions of most skilled workers and clashed strongly with their corporate traditions. By simultaneously lowering wages, the automakers sowed discontent among the unskilled and further aroused the skilled workers.

From 1933 onward, however, the skilled workers found themselves in a stronger position to challenge their employers because of a growing shortage of skilled labor and because of the critical role that skilled labor played in specific production strategies elaborated by the automakers to

---

pp. 169–73; Bernard Doray, *Le Taylorisme: Une folie rationnelle?* (Paris, 1981), pp. 137–39, 142–44, 152–57; Depretto and Schweitzer, *Communisme*, pp. 20–21, 24–28.

[40]Annick Castellani, "Les grèves dans l'industrie automobile de la Seine, 1921–1930" (mémoire de maîtrise, University of Paris VII, 1974); Depretto, "Une grève générale à l'usine Renault de Billancourt (mai 1926)," *Cahiers d'histoire de l'Institut Maurice Thorez* 12 (January–March 1978): 47–68; Eugène Hug and Pierre Rigoulot, *Le croque-rave libertaire* (Paris, 1980), pp. 83–87.

[41]Bertrand Badie, *Stratégie de la grève* (Paris, 1976), pp. 55–60; Francotte, *Vie de militant communiste*, pp. 125–37.

combat the depression. Thus a contradiction emerged, fraught with danger for the employers.[42] At the same time, the labor force became more homogeneous: many immigrant workers had been dismissed by the companies in the early 1930s.[43] I should add that the combination of a majority of semiskilled workers without union traditions and a minority of skilled workers lacks the quality of social stability that French automakers ascribed to the work force for many years. Indeed, this mixture is unstable and at certain junctures it is inflammable.

It has often been argued that the discipline of sit-down strikes in 1936, then the quick growth of mass unions and parties, meant that autoworkers had finally accepted the rules and constraints of Fordist factories and adapted themselves to Fordist methods of work in part by delegating their powers to left-wing organizations. It is so sure? First, workers at Renault and probably at other Parisian auto factories took the occasion of the Popular Front's victory to keep their pace of production stable or even to diminish it, from June 1936 to November 1938. Similarly, it may be observed that in the United States, when Ford recognized the United Auto Workers in 1941, "production standards were everywhere cut back."[44] Second, the available documents issued by employers and law courts show that sabotage and destruction of property were actually perpetrated during and after the sit-down strikes. At the end of 1936, in 1937, and in 1938 a good deal of physical conflict often took place in Renault involving unionized workers and foremen or workers who refused to restrict their output, to unionize, or to strike. Punctuality and discipline also greatly decreased.[45] The same strained relations prevailed at Citroën, at Simca, and at other Paris auto factories in the last months of 1937 and the first six months of 1938.[46] By 1936 a number of Citroën's workers and even foremen had already been forced to join the CGT union; from that moment, part of the labor force experienced the union

[42]Bertrand Badie, "Les grèves du Front populaire aux usines Renault," *Mouvement social* 12 (October–December 1972): 72, 74, 78–79; Pinol, "Travail," pp. 176–77; Doray, *Taylorisme*, pp. 156–57; Schweitzer, *Des engrenages*, pp. 55–57; Hug and Rigoulot, *Croque-rave*, pp. 150–51; Hatry, *Louis Renault*, pp. 283–84; Declas, "Recherches," p. 130.

[43]Fridenson, *Histoire*, p. 207; Depretto and Schweitzer, *Communisme*, p. 70.

[44]Fridenson, *Histoire*, pp. 270–71; Depretto and Schweitzer, *Communisme*, pp. 209, 244, 256; Nelson Lichtenstein, "Life at the Rouge: A Cycle of Shop Floor Power, 1941–1960," to appear in *Mouvement social*.

[45]Francotte, *Vie de militant communiste*, p. 130; Michael Seidman, "The Birth of the Weekend and the Revolts against Work: The Workers of the Paris Region during the Popular Front (1936–1938)," *French Historical Studies* 12 (Fall 1981): 256–61, 264, 270–73; Depretto and Schweitzer, *Communisme*, pp. 191, 254–57.

[46]Author's interview with Robert Doury, former secretary general of the CGT's metalworkers' union of the Paris area, 16 June 1976; Guy Bourdé, *La défaite du Front populaire* (Paris, 1977), pp. 33–37; Francotte, *Vie de militant communiste*, p. 133; Henri Jourdain, *Comprendre pour accomplir* (Paris, 1982), p. 29.

as one more constraint.[47] When a sit-down strike broke out at Renault on 24 November 1938 to protest against a longer workweek, it gave rise to violence and to costly damage.[48]

In short, these years saw a backlash against Fordism. All these events lead me to believe that the adaptation of French autoworkers to the Fordist factory was incomplete and partial—hence their interest in holidays with pay and the five-day, forty-hour week with the weekend free. Though productivism had become the common creed for every left-wing organization, it thus appears that a large proportion of autoworkers, especially semiskilled workers, did not concur in this view. This is all the more striking because the mechanization of work considerably increased in the auto factories during the years 1936–38. Thus, both employers and the public powers drew the logical conclusion at the end of 1938: the workers' adaptation to the modern factory would require much greater coercion. In the Renault strike of 24 November and in the nationwide general strike of 30 November the government used the police against the autoworkers. After the strikes and the ensuing lockouts, several thousand autoworkers were laid off, most of them union or party activists. The law courts sentenced union leaders to fines and even in some cases to jail. At the entrances of Renault's factory, turnstiles were brought into use again and Renault workers' productivity soared, by 10 to 25 percent. In the whole French auto industry, the influence of the CGT union and the Communist and Socialist parties was reduced, though not extinguished.[49]

Hardly had the breaches in the Fordist order been closed when, from 1940 to 1944, because of World War II, they reappeared. This time insubordination had the aura of patriotism. But engineers and managers of the auto companies were not mistaken about its meaning. Autoworkers' practices of absenteeism, turnover, lack of discipline, and resistance (including even a few strikes) had a conspicuous likeness to those of the prewar period.

Since automakers had profited by the war and occupation years by intensifying the rationalization of work, workers' actions were aimed not only at the Germans, but at the Fordist style of management. To be sure,

[47] Schweitzer, *Des engrenages*, p. 120.

[48] Robert Durand, *La lutte des travailleurs de chez Renault racontée par eux-mêmes (1912–1944)* (Paris, 1971), pp. 78–81; Francotte, *Vie de militant communiste*, pp. 135–37; Hatry, *Louis Renault*, pp. 293–95; Depretto and Schweitzer, *Communisme*, pp. 264–71; Bourdé, *Défaite*, pp. 143–49.

[49] Declas, "Recherches," p. 133; Bourdé, *Défaite*, pp. 189, 214–15, 224–25, 227, 229, 240–42, 248, 322, 325–29; Fridenson, "Le patronat français," in *La France et les Français en 1938–1939*, ed. René Rémond and Janine Bourdin (Paris, 1978), pp. 145–48; Seidman, "Birth," pp. 249, 272–76; Depretto and Schweitzer, *Communisme*, pp. 267–79, 285.

not every worker took part in this process of insubordination, and not all categories of workers used the resistance methods to the same degree. Yet in August 1943 a Renault engineer noted in his private diary: "At present there is no more discipline. . . . The times for production are no longer complied with." The investigations carried out after the liberation in 1944 by British and American intelligence teams confirm that beyond food privation and specific material shortages, this resistance to work discipline accounted for a large part of the decline into productivity of the French auto industry.[50] Only when the French state had been restored in 1944 and order reestablished in French society could work in the auto factories regain its legitimacy.

The General Mechanization of Work (1945–70)

These years were distinguished by the widespread use of specialized machines and by the introduction of automatic machines, which changed the nature of factory work. They brought with them a redistribution of skilled labor from fabrication to toolmaking and maintenance and the massive hiring of untrained labor, rural or foreign workers, who were assigned to repetitive tasks, often in decentralized production units. The automakers merely compensated for all the disadvantages at work by offering wages relatively higher than elsewhere.[51] Faced with this reorganization of labor and with the narrow scope of jobs, the renewed workers' population either retained or rediscovered a good many attitudes or practices that autoworkers had embraced in the beginnings of Fordism. Accounts by such workers as Daniel Mothé for the 1950s and 1960s, Georges Douart for the early 1960s, and Robert Linhart for the

[50]National Archives, Washington, D.C., Record Group 243, U.S. Strategic Bombing Survey, Renault files, 1944–45; Imperial War Museum, London, A series, box 1, Combined Intelligence Objectives Subcommittee (CIOS), "Vehicle Targets in France and Belgium Visited September–November 1944," reports by A. Pershouse and J. P. Den Hartog, 4–5 December 1944, pp. 3, 4, 12, 17; box 2, CIOS, "The Peugeot Organisation," report by Arthur R. Stella, 14 December 1944, p. 23; Durand, *Lutte*, pp. 103, 105–15, 117–25, 129–37, 149–60, 164–71; Fernand Picard, *L'épopée de Renault* (Paris, 1976), pp. 122–23, 126, 143, 176, 198, 208, 218, 222; Declas, "Recherches," pp. 119–20, 133–35, 199–201; Marcel Peyrenet, *Nous prendrons les usines* (Geneva, 1980), pp. 12, 17–19; Hug and Rigoulot, *Croquerave*, pp. 179–84; Fridenson, "Die Auswirkungen des zweiten Weltkriegs auf die französische Arbeiterschaft," in *Zweiter Weltkrieg und sozialer Wandel*, ed. Waclaw Dlugoborski (Göttingen, 1981), pp. 202–6; Hatry, *Louis Renault*, p. 292; Jourdain, *Comprendre*, pp. 44–47, 60; Jean-Louis Loubet, "La Société anonyme André Citroën (1924–1968)" (thesis, University of Paris X–Nanterre, 1979), pp. 342, 344, 352–53; Claude Poperen, *Renault, regards de l'intérieur* (Paris, 1983), pp. 34–39.

[51]Bardou, "Labor and Industrial Relations since 1945," in *The Automobile Revolution*, ed. Jean-Pierre Bardou et al. (Chapel Hill, N.C., 1982), pp. 233–49.

late 1960s stand as cases in point.[52] Thus it appears there was a constancy in the relationship of the autoworkers to their work, in the depths of consciousness. Still some aspects of this relationship changed as time went by: after an attempt to rehabilitate work, the new industrial organization produced two effects, either rejection of the job and the company or submission.

The Failure of the Rehabilitation of Work

At first the unions greeted with enthusiasm the new wave of mechanization. "We think that Renault should aim for modern, well-equipped factories, with high productivity, in order to be equal to the best American and Soviet companies," the head of the CGT's union of Parisian metalworkers declared in October 1944. Thus their old, deep-seated desire for productivity reached its climax. Moreover, the unions and the Communist party in the automobile industry undertook a true rehabilitation of work and of productivity. Nowhere was this action carried as far as in the two firms that were then under state control: Renault and Berliet. At Berliet the Communist manager, in keeping with the CGT locals, declared his will to bring out "a new worker" who would be reconciled with the machine and the factory. Communist activists wrote in praise of Stakhanov. The company's monthly newsletter also held Stakhanov up as an example and cited the names and deeds of the most productive workers while pillorying by name those who could not keep up the pace or were conspicuous by their absenteeism; the company's Communist journal did the same. Several buildings committees and a works committee advised management on production, productivity, and the arrangement of workshops. In December 1945 the unions also accepted the creation of a productivity bonus. At Renault the CGT demanded and finally obtained the establishment in each department of a mixed production committee that offered rewards for workers' suggestions concerning higher production and technical improvements. In April 1946 the CGT asked for a "progressive productivity bonus...to stimulate each worker's effort."[53] Of course this shift in the policy of the

---

[52]Daniel Mothé, "Les grèves chez Renault," *Socialisme ou barbarie* 9 (January–February 1958): 48–71; idem, *Journal d'un ouvrier (1956–1958)* (Paris, 1959); idem, *Militant chez Renault* (Paris, 1965); idem, *Les O.S.* (Paris, 1972). Mothé is the pseudonym of Jacques Gautrat, who during these years operated a milling machine in Renault's Billancourt works. Georges Douart, *L'usine et l'homme* (Paris, 1967), pp. 131–87, 236, 256–57, 281–82, 287; Douart was then an electrical worker, mostly in Berliet's Vénissieux factory. Linhart, *The Assembly Line*; Linhart worked at Citroën and Panhard as a semiskilled worker.

[53]"Les usines Renault," *La Vie ouvrière* 35 (5 October 1944). On Berliet see M. G., "Stakanovistes," *Le Mécano* 1 (February 1945); "Les ouvriers russes," *Contact* 2 (1 March 1945); Félix Besson, "Rapport de la section syndicale ouvrière C.G.T.," *Contact* 2 (8 October 1945); Marcel Mosnier, "Un travailleur nouveau," *Contact* 3 (March 1946); Mosnier, "Soyons

CGT and the Communist party was not specific to the auto industry—
it happened everywhere. The two organizations thus did their share in
the reconstruction of France and showed their will to preserve national
independence. Simultaneously they now appeared as administrators of
the labor force, proving, as Berliet workers were told on 3 February
1946, the workers' ability to manage the companies themselves.[54]

From September 1944 to 1946, most French autoworkers approved
this policy. Productivity increased, absenteeism declined, and turnover
and other forms of workers' action remained within reasonable limits
given the difficulties of living in postwar France. In return work rules
were liberalized. But this new relationship to work finally broke down.
In 1946 a brief strike for better working conditions at Renault's Le Mans
factory and a toolmakers' strike at Berliet were early indications of growing worker dissatisfaction. In 1947 autoworkers left the "battle of production." First, strikes by sector or category broke out at Renault from
January onward, then a strike broke out at Citroën in mid-April. Contrary to the advice of the CGT and the Communist party, a major strike
was generalized throughout Renault's workshops from 25 April to 16
May. There followed a six-week strike at Citroën and, in late August
and early September, major strikes at Peugeot-Sochaux and Renault–
Le Mans. In November and December, the massive participation of
autoworkers in the nationwide general strike led by the CGT definitively
confirmed that the support for productivism had been broken. Historians have often insisted on the economic (uncertain food supply and
inflation) and political (the beginnings of cold war) causes of these strikes
and of this rupture of the productivist consensus. However, they were
also triggered by the new mechanization and shop management that
employers had developed since the liberation. In every strike of 1947
autoworkers criticized the increase in the pace of production and efficiency wages. At Renault in spring 1947, the strike was particularly strong
in the most modernized departments, where the proportion of semiskilled workers in the labor force kept growing, while the toolmaking

vigilants," and "Au pilori," *Contact* 3 (May 1946); "Règlement de la prime de production
et de gestion," *Contact* 3 (December 1946); and three historical studies: Declas, " 'Berliet
sans Berliet' (1944–1949): Une expérience autogestionnaire?" *Recherches et travaux de l'Institut d'histoire économique et sociale de l'Université de Paris I* 5 (December 1978): 71–105; Pinol,
"Travail," pp. 194–204; Peyrenet, *Nous prendrons les usines*, pp. 41–49, 51–57, 65, 70–92,
96–102. On Renault: Pierre Donnatau, "La Régie Renault devant la concurrence et les
tentatives de planification," *Economie et humanisme* 13 (September–October 1953): 70–81;
Anne-Sophie Perriaux, "La création du Comité d'établissement de Renault-Billancourt,
1945–1952" (mémoire de maîtrise, University of Paris I, 1983), pp. 23–98; Poperen, *Renault*, pp. 42, 45–51.
[54]Ambroise Croizat, *Discours*, Notes et études documentaires, no. 83 (Paris, 1946); Annie
Lacroix-Riz, *La C.G.T. de la Libération à la scission de 1944–1947* (Paris, 1983), pp. 18–70,
75–78.

departments where skilled workers were still in the majority stuck to the productivist attitude of the CGT. This cleavage originated in the discontent created among semiskilled workers by the move to mechanized mass production of a new model (the 4CV). The semiskilled were affected by transfers from one workshop to another, specialization, compulsory overtime, and, for some, deskilling. Skilled workers were less affected and on the whole had comparatively profited by this period. But semiskilled workers were now the majority of the labor force, while the new shop management depended on growing numbers of white-collar workers to prepare and control work. Significantly, two of the November strikes (at Citroën and Berliet) were distinguished by the antagonism between workers and executives or foremen. Nor could the productivist alliance between workers and white-collar employees stay the emergence of a new world of work.[55]

The New World of Work

The automakers kept the initiative during the years that followed the CGT's defeat of 1947. They carried on the technical integration of production, namely, the construction of simple systems allowing the transfer of parts from one work station to the next and the coordination of machines with each other. But they now added a two-pronged organizational readjustment: decentralization and job evaluation. Decentralization began in 1952, with the opening of a Renault factory at Flins. It meant transferring to the provinces the most deskilled and repetitive tasks (i.e., assembly and the making of certain parts). The decentralized production units became the focus of a concentration of semiskilled labor (just as in Berliet's Vénissieux factory in the 1920s). Moreover, whereas the proportion of semiskilled workers in the labor force of the parent factories remained stable, in the decentralized factories it grew—by 10 percent in the Renault group between 1953 and 1969.

The new factories were built to attract people who were new to industrial work: mostly peasants, a few women, and later, foreign immi-

---

[55]On Citroën: Pierre Bercot, *Mes années aux usines Citroën* (Paris, 1977), p. 24; Loubet, *Société anonyme*, pp. 376–77. On Renault: French National Archives, 91AQ2, RNUR yearly reports for 1945, 1946, 1947; Philippe Fallachon, "Les grèves de la Régie Renault en 1947," *Mouvement social* 13 (October–December 1972): 111–42; Edmond Le Garrec, "37 années aux usines Renault," *De Renault Frères* 5 (December 1974): 82, 85–86; Paul Pommier, "Le département 76," *De Renault Frères* 6 (December 1975): 194; Michel Freyssenet, *Division du travail et mobilisation quotidienne de la main-d'oeuvre: Les cas Renault et Fiat* (Paris, 1979), pp. 76–79; Poperen, *Renault*, pp. 52–57. On Unic: Dominique Dubarry, *Unic passe avant tout* (Paris, 1982), p. 73. On Berliet: Declas, " 'Berliet sans Berliet,' " pp. 93–101; Pinol, "Travail," pp. 208–15; Peyrenet, *Nous prendrons les usines*, pp. 125–36, 162–89. On several auto companies: Jourdain, *Comprendre*, pp. 72–73; Lacroix-Riz, *C.G.T.*, pp. 222–25, 247–48, 278, 290–93, 331–32, 336–37.

grants. The working and living conditions in the factories were better than in Paris or Sochaux, and most workers either resided near the factory in workmen's garden cities or lodgings for young workers or lived in rural villages from which they were brought every day by company buses (this was also the case for Peugeot-Sochaux). It is interesting to quote the comments of Citroën's chairman about the workers of his factory in Rennes: "The nature of the work they did appeared different from work in the Paris area: less active because men did not wish to hurry in order to save twenty to thirty minutes per day; regular production, of good quality; manufacturing costs kept at the expected level."[56] Accompanying this decentralization was a move toward further subcontracting for those parts that required highly specialized skills no longer found in auto factories.[57] Most skilled activities (especially maintenance and toolmaking) remained concentrated in the areas of Paris or Sochaux. As a result, the autoworkers were able to "avoid a frontal conflict with the traditional working class," since skilled workers could protect their jobs and since the machines they used left them some elements of initiative.[58]

Job evaluation, inspired by American specialists, now set the rate of pay for semiskilled workers not by the quality of their work but by the posts they occupied. It also meant that a shift from one job to another might entail a drop in pay. By determining classification and wages independent of the skills of the individual worker and by tying them to work posts, this arrangement destroyed any possibility for the semiskilled worker to acquire a personal sense of identification with his work. Job evaluation was introduced in the early 1950s, first by Renault, then by Simca. Significantly, Renault tested it in its first decentralized fac-

[56]National Archives, Washington, D.C., Diplomatic Papers, 851.659/4–449, "Observations of public affairs officer, Lyons, while visiting Peugeot plant," 4 April 1949 (by Horatio Mooers, American consul); James C. Nwafor, "L'évolution de l'industrie automobile en France: Une étude de géographie industrielle et d'aménagement du territoire" (doctoral thesis, University of Paris I, 1974), pp. 110–254; Bercot, *Mes années,* pp. 58–63; Jean Chardonnet, "La contribution de l'industrie automobile à l'aménagement du territoire en France," *Géographie et recherche* 8 (February 1977): 53–64; Olivier Bertrand and Alain Bonnet, *L'évolution des emplois et la main-d'oeuvre dans l'industrie automobile* (Paris, 1978), pp. 43–48, 60–64; Michel Mesaize, "Renault, Flins, Aubergenville et les Mureaux: Une implantation industrielle de l'après-guerre et ses retombées locales (1950–1980)," *Bulletin du Centre d'histoire de la France contemporaine* 2 (October 1982): 98–103; Fridenson, "L'usine Renault de Flins," *Monuments historiques* 13 (August–September 1984): 7–14; Mesaize, "Renault-Flins et l'ancien canton de Meulan" (thesis of 3d cycle, University of Paris X, 1984).

[57]Bruno Vennin, "Pratique et signification de la sous-traitance dans l'industrie automobile en France," *Revue économique* 26 (March 1975): 280–306.

[58]Bernard Dézert, *La croissance industrielle et urbaine de la porte d'Alsace* (Paris, 1969), pp. 277–81; Freyssenet, *Division,* p. 55.

tory, Flins, in 1952. One of its executives declared: "This system calls for men who act like oxen."[59]

Employers were conscious that these technical and organizational readjustments would change the relationship of the various categories of autoworkers to their work. They used several methods to prevent workers' resistance. Certain companies preferred to avoid all unionism within the firm as in the 1920s and early 1930s or else to keep a house union. After the failure of a major strike in 1950 at the large Ford factory at Poissy, most union leaders were dismissed in 1951, and trade unionism was emasculated for thirty years. At Citroën, where unions influenced one-third of the work force, unions were constantly harried and were rendered leaderless at regular intervals. In the Simca factory at Nanterre, the company developed two house unions that were joined by more then 50 percent of wage earners.[60]

The other companies, Renault and Peugeot, developed departments of human relations and, as a response to numerous actions by workers, introduced collective bargaining, American style. The wage agreements they signed (first Renault, then Peugeot) incorporated two major innovations that compensated for the changes in work. An extra week of vacation with pay was granted from 1955 onward and another was added in 1962–63. A supplemental pension, financed by a retirement fund, was also introduced in 1955. The result of this new strategy was a reduction in the number of total strikes. The most frequent channel for discontent became short work stoppages limited to a workshop, a department, a category of workers, or a plant. It generally focused on the pace of production. Unions became institutionalized,[61] but shop stewards who demanded direct control of the job at the level of the shops and

---

[59]Alexandre Chabert, *Les salaires dans l'industrie française (la métallurgie)* (Paris, 1955), p. 151; Solomon Barkin, ed., *Automatisation, progrès technique et main-d'oeuvre* (Paris, 1966), pp. 42–44; Doray, *Taylorisme*, pp. 95–96; Poperen, *Renault*, pp. 183–88.

[60]National Archives, Washington, D.C., Diplomatic Papers, Department of State, Office of Intelligence Research, "The position of labor in the French automobile industry," 26 February 1952, pp. 12–13; Bercot, *Mes années*, pp. 24–26. Author's interview with François Lehideux, former chairman of Ford-France, 12 December 1978.

[61]On Peugeot: Dézert, "Quelques aspects géographiques de la grève des usines de la S.A. Peugeot en avril–juin 1965," *Bulletin de l'Association des géographes français* 56 (January–February 1966): 20–36; Georges Minazzi, *En marche* (Paris, 1978), pp. 22, 40–42, 46–60, 71–74. On Renault: Jacques Commaille, "Les élections professionnelles," *Mouvement social* 6 (April–June 1966): 93–106; Jean-Luc Bodiguel, *La réduction du temps de travail enjeu de la lutte sociale* (Paris, 1969), pp. 100–128, 146–89; Joëlle Créau and Claude Fontan, "Le mouvement des débrayages à l'usine Renault de Billancourt de 1950 à 1967" (mémoire de maîtrise, University of Paris I, 1970); Roger Deliat, *Vingt ans O.S. chez Renault* (Paris, 1973), pp. 34–68, 97–105; Pierre Dreyfus, *Une nationalisation réussie: Renault* (Paris, 1981), chap. 2.

production lines were kept at arm's length. The situation was similar at Berliet.[62]

Employers had still other means at their disposal. Company periodicals—at Peugeot, Berliet, and Simca—kept bombarding workers with optimistic views of work. They extolled self-discipline of body and mind. They emphasized temperateness: *Berliet Information* in July–August 1952 praised "the eagerness to use leisure hours moderately before returning to work." They presented factory work as a fair exchange: "Let us repay [the company] for its advantages with devotion to work," *Simca Information* said in October 1952. They tried to develop the workers' sense of belonging to the company, and they characterized the firm as a dynamic and pragmatic community in order to counterbalance the intensification of work. They invoked the workers' moral values. According to *Berliet Information*, in August 1954, work was "an inexhaustible source of joy and happiness." *Notre Usine-Peugeot* of January 1948 justified good work: "Work hard, the quality of your product will reward you for all your labor." This press glorified the consent to work.[63] More subtle and innovative was the automakers' appeal to the social sciences, which owed its inspiration to the earliest productivity missions to the United States. Renault again led the way, creating a social-science section in the personnel department (1952) and also financing specific research by academics. Their observations resulted in an ergonomic approach to working conditions and, later, in actions against occupational pathology.[64]

The rise of real wages and of various allowances, full employment, and job security became the rule; shutting down factories or layoffs became the exception. These were the obvious counterparts of the new world of work. In addition to the labor policy of the automakers, they contributed to the relative submission of the autoworkers. However, beyond the various types of strikes I have just mentioned, other practices of resistance did persist, just as in the interwar and war years. In the face of growing mechanization, some workers responded by slowing down their output and by deliberately bad workmanship, both of which pointed to the continued rejection of repetitive work by at least part of the renewed labor force. In the face of organizational readjustment, absenteeism and turnover increased during the 1960s and indicated a growing indifference to the job. The reduction of working time reappeared as a major theme of workers' demands.[65] But can we go so far as to speak of a revolt against work?

[62]Douart, *Usine*, pp. 143, 151, 163–64, 166–67; Bodiguel, *Réduction*, p. 207; René Caille, *La boîte* (Monaco, 1978).

[63]Doray, *Taylorisme*, pp. 136–37, 145–51; Serge Paganelli and Martine Jacquin, *Peugeot, la dynastie s'accroche* (Paris, 1975), pp. 82–101.

[64]Alain Drouard, ed., *Le développement des sciences sociales en France au tournant des années soixante* (Paris, 1983), pp. 104–5, 124–28.

[65]Paul Froidevaux, "L'absentéisme: Le cas Berliet," *Hommes et commerce* 18 (April 1973):

The Specific Attitudes of Semiskilled Workers

As a matter of fact, during these years semiskilled autoworkers were characterized both by the ambivalence of their attitudes to work and by the fluctuation of their practices over time. Whereas most skilled workers continued to consider work "a central value that regulates their life," semiskilled workers did not identify with their production. This difference was a consequence of the technical changes and of the organizational readjustments. Yet a survey of the Saviem truck factory at Caen in the late 1960s shows that at the same time these semiskilled autoworkers had developed an ideology of work (and of skill). They did not reject work as a whole, but they criticized the work they had to do. Some of them found a way out through deviance that could easily be construed as resistance: taking tranquilizers and sleeping pills, "drifting," alcoholism. Others dreamed about another type of work they could identify with and consequently led struggles at regular intervals against "scientific management." If they wanted to be promoted to skilled workers, it was mostly not to earn more money but to do "more interesting work" so as to prove their individual capacities. Thus those who questioned most the deskilling of work and those who attached the greatest importance to work were the same semiskilled workers. At this stage their vision of work became contradictory.[66] These ambivalent features were true of men but not of women, and they could also be found in other factories such as Berliet, Peugeot, or Renault.[67]

These ambivalent attitudes toward work resulted in unsettled work practices. The mobilization of semiskilled workers against foremen or employers tended to ebb and flow. Its instability can be explained not only by the frequent changes in the national and international environment, but also by the heterogeneity of the semiskilled workers' group itself. Their geographic origins, educational levels, jobs, and dwellings had indeed become extremely diverse; the contrasts between a majority of young workers and a minority of old ones, a majority of men and a rising proportion of women increased this diversity, which in turn created in the group an unceasing effervescence.[68] In the Saviem truck

18–25; Jean-Louis Rigal, *L'absentéisme aux usines Renault de Billancourt depuis 1962* (Paris, 1979); Minazzi, *En marche*, pp. 71–74; Bardou, "Labor," pp. 242–43.

[66]Danièle Kergoat, *La combativité ouvrière dans une entreprise de camions: L'entrée en lutte des ouvriers spécialisés* (Paris, 1977), pp. 215–17, 275–80, 390–402; idem, *Les pratiques revendicatives ouvrières* (Paris, 1978), pp. 23–50. A comparison might be made with the drug addicts in United States auto plants: see B. J. Widick, ed., *Auto Work and Its Discontents* (Baltimore, 1976), pp. 14–15.

[67]Douart, *Usine*, pp. 134–35, 147, 151; Minazzi, *En marche*, pp. 48–59; Deliat, *Vingt ans*, pp. 57–58.

[68]Roger Biard, "La répartition géographique du personnel de la Régie Renault dans la région parisienne," *Bulletin de l'Association des géographes français* 41 (May–June 1971): 117–

factory in Caen in the late 1960s three patterns of behavior were visible: integration, passivity, and pugnacity (with two alternative options: revolt or radicalization). The unstable relationship between these categories of workers gave an unpredictability to working life and to the recurrent labor conflicts that punctuated it, as workers shifted between two poles: either competition between individuals and groups or collective dynamics of solidarity in the face of the conditions and nature of work.[69]

If we take another criterion—geographic origins—it becomes necessary to distinguish four types of semiskilled workers. Workers from rural areas who migrated to the towns suffered both from the mechanized factory and its extreme division of labor and from a segregated social life in the cities. So they played a leading part in labor struggles. This was precisely the case of a good many autoworkers at the Saviem factory in Caen. By contrast, those peasant workers who remained on their land and maintained a reduced agricultural activity (for instance at Citroën's factory in Rennes, Berliet-Vénissieux, or Peugeot-Sochaux) depended less directly on their factory work and often considered it "a promotion, with a regular schedule, higher earnings, and weekends." They took a much smaller part in collective action. In similar fashion, the foreign workers who had come to France to make money for a brief period and then return to their homeland would not readily join other workers in labor conflicts that threatened their pay. But the foreigners who integrated themselves into the French society were very active in the struggles over work because they looked forward to lasting improvements in working conditions.[70]

Finally, this massive hiring of rural and immigrant workers accelerated after 1965, gradually undermining the submission to mechanized and reorganized work as it produced groups of workers who could no longer bear its tight restraints. Hence came repeated strike movements in the auto industry: strong participation in the nationwide generalized strike of May–June 1968 in most auto and truck factories, with numerous total or partial strikes at Renault, Berliet, and, on a smaller scale, Peugeot. As in 1936 and 1947, this challenge to industrial work coexisted with other motivations, either economic or political, whose importance must

---

24; Jeanne Dufour, "L'influence de l'usine Renault du Mans sur la vie rurale du département de la Sarthe," *Norois* 8 (October–December 1961): 452–57; Douart, *Usine*, pp. 134, 139, 142, 149, 185; Dézert, *Croissance*, pp. 239, 248–50, 255–79; Bercot, *Mes années*, p. 60; Kergoat, *Combativité*, pp. 96–110; Freyssenet, *Division*, pp. 279–312, 347–52; Mesaize, *Renault–Flins*, pp. 97–101, 134–40, 218–348.

[69]Kergoat, *Combativité*, pp. 239–60.

[70]Douart, *Usine*, pp. 134, 147, 148, 149; Dézert, *Croissance*, pp. 300–312; Jacques Frémontier, *La forteresse ouvrière: Renault* (Paris, 1971), pp. 84–112, 125–44; Bercot, *Mes années*, p. 60; Bertrand and Bonnet, *Evolution*, pp. 143–51.

not be minimized. But work was nonetheless the underlying theme of all these struggles.[71]

The growth of workers' actions in the late 1960s was made possible by alliances between the various groups and networks of semiskilled workers in the French auto factories. These alliances were sometimes conflictual and occasionally extended to skilled workers. Their impact was strong enough to contribute to major changes in technology and industrial relations.

Toward the Automation of Work (1970–83)

From 1960 to 1970 French auto production per worker had increased by 6.1 percent each year, a rate higher than that of the global French economy, which was 5.3 percent.[72] These improvements in productivity were quite satisfactory for the automakers. But the sharpening of worldwide competition required a shift to a further stage in the division of labor: automation. This change also had a social dimension. Leading engineers who had been worried since the early 1950s by the impression that the productivity drive in France "almost entirely resulted from workers' efforts, at the expense of their health" now could openly advocate automation as an efficient way either to solve what was then called "the problem of semiskilled workers" by putting an end to toilsome or de-skilled tasks or to skirt workers' practices of resistance.[73]

Indeed, France's growth of 124 percent in units produced per hour worked from 1970 to 1980 exceeded the growth in all other auto industries except Japan's.[74] However, it soon became obvious that the march to automation did not eliminate the workers' own know-how, which held good or revived, or labor conflicts, which came back to the forefront at the end of this period.

[71]Kergoat, *Combativité*, pp. 5–45; Louis Géhin and Jean-Claude Poitou, *Des voitures et des hommes: Les vingt ans de Renault-Sandouville* (Paris, 1984); Paganelli and Jacquin, *Peugeot*, pp. 110–17; Minazzi, *En Marche*, pp. 89–110; Claude Angeli and Nicolas Brimo, *Une milice patronale: Peugeot* (Paris, 1975), pp. 15–19, 24–25; Poperen, *Renault*, pp. 161–72, 186–90; Frémontier, *Forteresse*, pp. 343–74.

[72]François Caron, "L'industrie: Secteurs et régions," in *Histoire économique et sociale de la France*, ed. Fernand Braudel and Ernest Labrousse, vol. 4, part 3, *Années 1950 à nos jours* (Paris, 1982), p. 1290.

[73]Archives of the Section d'histoire des usines Renault, Billancourt, Debos papers, file 81, report by Paul Pommier on his mission to the United States, February 1954. Pierre Debos, "L'automatisation, seule solution à long terme au problème capital de la main d'oeuvre non qualifiée (O.S.)," *Arts et métiers* 23 (June/July 1973); Antoine Héron, "Le Taylorisme hier et demain," *Temps modernes* 31 (August–September 1975): 270–78.

[74]Alan Altshuler et al., *The Future of the Automobile* (London, 1984), p. 203.

The Remaking of Work

Employers gradually modified working conditions, adapting their labor policies to the new economic environment and to the workers' actions. The earliest changes dealt with working schedules and methods of payment. Up to the late 1960s, the custom in French auto plants, unlike their Italian counterparts, was one shift in the daytime. To cope with the rising demand for cars, French automakers not only hired many semiskilled workers, but persuaded the trade unions to agree to two shifts a day. Workers worked one week in the morning, the next one in the afternoon. The "two-by-eights" were introduced at Renault-Flins and Billancourt from January 1969 onward. They often brought about an influx of foreign workers, given the shortage of French rural, semiskilled workers during this time in the region surrounding Paris. A large part of these foreigners stayed in workingmen's homes within close range of the factories. Thus the "two-by-eights" reinforced the ethnic divisions within the labor force. They also "broke up the groups of pals" that had formed.[75] The other important reform was the gradual generalization of the monthly payment of wages that workers had demanded for many years. This change met the needs of auto managers, who now wanted to stabilize their manpower. And with this reform they finally implemented one of the original components of Fordism that French (and English) automakers had hitherto refused most of their wage earners: time payment. Monthly payments at Renault were initiated in 1952 and applied to 22 percent of the labor force. By 1969 they extended to 35 percent, and in 1969 the whole French industry accepted the government's suggestion to generalize them. In 1974 every worker in the French auto companies was paid by the month.[76]

Then, in response to labor unrest or instability, the automakers conducted various experiments to redesign jobs. Such ventures were undertaken either in existing shops or in newly decentralized plants. They juxtaposed or combined the enlargement and the enrichment of jobs. But as they spread, they aimed less and less at "fulfilling the new expectations of men at work" (as Renault's deputy chairman had declared on 12 February 1973) and more and more at introducing a flexibility that would correct the rigidities of Fordist plants and thus help auto producers better serve a more differentiated market. The economic crisis

[75]Nicolas Dubost, *Flins sans fin...* (Paris, 1979), p. 49; Freyssenet, *Division*, pp. 12, 43–45, 163; Mesaize, "Renault-Flins," pp. 404–19. But for a new hiring of rural workers see Paul Larivière, "La zone de recrutement de main-d'oeuvre de l'usine Citroën de Chartres-de-Bretagne," *Norois* 28 (July–September 1981), 389–94.

[76]Fridenson, "Les usines Renault de 1898 à nos jours," in *La terre, l'usine et l'homme au XXe siècle* (Paris, 1974), pp. 43–44; Freyssenet, *Division*, pp. 136–37; Jean Bunel, *La mensualisation, une réforme tranquille?* (Paris, 1972); Chabert, *Salaires*, p. 159.

beginning in 1973 especially contributed to this new significance of job redesign, a shift also achieved by other European and American automakers committed to similar programs.[77] In plants where efforts were devoted to such a reorganization, workers' absenteeism and grievances clearly declined. But productivity did not improve in every case.

Shortly after, semiskilled workers' actions led to a recasting of the workers' classifications. In 1972–73, job evaluation was abolished at Renault. Workers were henceforward rated with regard to both their personal skills and their job level; this also meant for them a minimum-wage guarantee if they were shifted to another job. Moreover, just as in 1944–47, the wage scale was modified and promotions were granted by "giving the highest classification of the former wage scale to the category of workers who, after deskilling, found themselves the most skilled of all."[78]

Last, automating production was given priority over job redesign. Accelerating from the mid–1970s onward, automation was applied to the production of mechanical components and later to all assembly operations except the final assembly. Automation resulted in a profound change in the composition of the labor force. It put an end to many jobs for standard semiskilled workers and created instead a smaller number of overseers, that is, semiskilled workers who no longer would be needed for their specialized training but would be limited to carrying out a few orders drawn up by the production methods departments. Automation also attacked the last citadel of skilled workers under Fordism: the sectors of tooling and maintenance. Automation required more mobility of workers between different jobs.

When confronted with automation, workers reacted in two ways. Production workers (mostly semiskilled ones) experienced great difficulty in adjusting to new conditions. Maintenance workers (mostly skilled), on the contrary, quickly adapted themselves and even modified the new shop management by enlarging their range of work. The first type of workers had problems because their former experience of work was narrow and specialized. The second type were already familiar with complex tasks and could mobilize their practical knowledge against the parceling of work under automation because this new manufacturing system required greater coordination across work groups. Automation

[77]Renault Archives, statement by Christian Beullac; Robert Weil, "Formes nouvelles d'organisation du travail dans l'industrie automobile européenne," *Sociologie du travail* 18 (January–March 1976): 15–35; Bertrand and Bonnet, *Évolution*, pp. 92–99; Benjamin Coriat, *L'atelier et le chronomètre* (Paris, 1982), pp. 243–61.

[78]Jacques Vincent, "Les problèmes de personnel dans l'industrie automobile à l'heure du VIe plan," *Mouvement social* 13 (October–December 1972): 148–50; Freyssenet, *Division*, pp. 35, 58, 167–69; Bardou, "Labor," p. 260; anon., "La forteresse ouvrière," *Gazette ouvrière* 2 (May–June 1975): 21–39.

had another consequence: it often made traditional Fordist work in nonautomated areas more difficult to bear.[79]

In the short run these changes in employers' strategy scored significant results: absenteeism, conflicts, turnover, and the number of retouches declined, especially after 1975. Of course other causes played their part in this trend. Industrial relations became tougher, more strained. In some firms (Peugeot, Citroën, Chrysler-France) industrialists had recourse to strong action, with company police, special recruitment activity, and further support for house unions.[80] At a more general level, the gloomy prospects of the world economic crisis after 1973 and of rising unemployment made collective action more risky. Yet all the efforts of the automakers could not erase workers' autonomy, which took new forms.

The Persistence of Workers' Know-how

By the 1960s engineers, on the one hand, and sociologists, on the other, had already established that in the decentralized auto factories workers were able to maintain some degree of autonomy and a specific knowledge—even semiskilled workers, who officially were denied any kind of ability. In these highly mechanized plants the proportion of white-collar executives and technical specialists had been reduced to a minimum. But machines very often failed to work: breakdowns, errors, and deviations of tuning or timing happened every day. Middle managers who were employed in such plants were not able to cope with these mishaps, since the whole production process had been designed at the company headquarters. In the Saviem truck factory at Caen, as in other plants, it soon became clear that workers (and particularly semiskilled ones) constantly intervened not only to correct these repeated defects, but even to enforce the standard pace of production.[81] The same features

[79]Automobiles Citroën, *Bienvenue à Aulnay* (Paris, 1979), pp. 5–27; Géraldine de Bonnafos, "L'adaptation des travailleurs au changement technologique: L'introduction des robots à la Régie Renault" (thesis of 3d cycle, University of Paris I, 1982); Pierre Bézier, "Petite histoire d'une idée bizarre," *De Renault frères* 13 (June 1982): 256–68 and 13 (December 1982): 319–31; Daniel Richter, "L'automatisation à la Régie Renault," *Cahiers français* 38 (January–March 1983), notice 3; Géraldine de Bonnafos, Jean–Jacques Chanaron, and Laurent de Mautort, *L'industrie automobile* (Paris, 1983), pp. 61–80; Dominique Anquetil, "Automatisation et organisation du travail dans l'automobile," *Critiques de l'économie politique* 6 (January–March 1983): 63–83; Jean-Pierre Durand, Joyce Durand, Jean Lojkine, and Christian Mahieu, *Formation et informatisation de la production: Le cas de l'industrie automobile* (Vitry, 1984), pp. 145–312; Poperen, *Renault*, pp. 210–13.

[80]Angeli and Brimo, *Milice patronale*, pp. 59–102; Daniel Bouvet, *L'usine de la peur* (Paris, 1973); Minazzi, *En route*; Freyssenet, *Division*, p. 226; Poperen, *Renault*, p. 199; Henri Rollin, *Militant chez Simca-Chrysler* (Paris, 1977).

[81]Kergoat, *Combativité*, pp. 149–51, 218–19, 269–71.

were observed by sociologists in the early 1970s, even in the parent factories of Paris or Lyons.[82]

In 1977–79 another survey, conducted at the request of Renault in four assembly workshops (three in Billancourt, one in Le Mans), showed that the numerous refinements of Fordist methods of shop management introduced since the 1950s were frustrated in two ways. They still could not analyze group activities in the workshop: the exchange of information, combinations of motions, and collective regulations, all of which gave work an important part of its efficiency. They also did not really take into account the growing uncertainties of automobile production: more diversified products, unsteady level of production, and workers' unstable level of absenteeism. So both foremen and workers (and not the central methods departments) became the daily managers of these uncertainties.[83]

Let us now look at one of the Berliet truck factories near Lyons in 1982. An economist worked there in an assembly shop.[84] Even in an age of automation, he noticed that semiskilled workers succeeded in achieving cycles of operations in a shorter time than had been allocated by the methods departments. Thus they increased their periods of time without work. How was it possible? First, they executed their tasks faster than required. They "doubled up." Secondly, they found tricks and dodges that they handed on to their comrades, ploys that attested to the genuine technological culture of semiskilled workers. Some of these tricks dealt with the transformation of materials: simplification of some operations, suppression of others, changing the set of tools. Some workers deliberately recombined the cycles of operations, as workers specialized the jobs and modified their repetitiveness and their separation. The semiskilled workers under observation also managed to get into a tempo of production different from the pace of the assembly line. This was not necessarily the tempo they desired, or even a tempo that would break the monotony of work. It meant that workers at some stages worked ahead of schedule, went up the line, more and more above their official working post and put parts into stocks. Their goal was the "release" moments when it would be possible either to slow down or to stop completely in order to have a snack, to talk, to read newspapers, and es-

---

[82]Philippe Bernoux, Dominique Motte, and Jean Saglio, *Trois ateliers d'O.S.* (Paris, 1973).

[83]Christophe Midler, "L'organisation du travail et ses déterminants: Enjeux économiques et organisationnels des problèmes de restructuration des tâches dans le montage automobile" (thesis of 3d cycle, University of Paris I, 1980), pp. 76–157, 177–97; Denis Bayart and Christophe Midler, "Systèmes de gestion et innovation organisationnelle," *Communiquer* 2 (July–September 1983): 6–10.

[84]Jean-Marc Bidaux, "Le cycle et la chaîne: Les ouvriers manient le dérailleur," *Economie et humanisme* 43 (January–February 1983): 8–13.

pecially, to leave the line early, before mealtime or before the end of the shift.

This workers' know-how is partly the heritage of their predecessors in the early Fordist period and partly the fruit of their own innovations: "results reached in the past, information piled up day after day on the place of production, assimilation and transformation of the formal knowledge transmitted by education."[85] Their various strategies stand as further proof that semiskilled workers had not entirely lost their command of the tempo of production, contrary to the statements made by the promoters of job redesign. While workers realized that this command was not enough to break the monotony of their work, employers realized that it might be useful for the industry. For example, the recent introduction of quality-control circles, inspired by Japanese auto companies' methods, was clearly aimed at picking up and exploiting semiskilled workers' own wisdom.

The New Wave of Conflicts

In most factories that were in the process of automation, however, French automakers did not depend on workers' know-how or did not allow them enough opportunities to exercise initiative and independent judgment concerning their work. This was in part the outcome of conflicting views between the departments of production methods and of industrial relations. But after some five years of relative lethargy in the labor force, a wave of strikes broke out in September 1981 and hit one auto factory after the other. It ended only in January 1984. Certain observers have explained this movement in political terms: workers consciously attempting to take advantage of the rise to power of the French Left to improve their position, just as in 1936–38. Others invoked religious reasons: the spread of Islam among migrant semiskilled workers, giving them a feeling of strength.[86] Both arguments have merit, but I suggest that there also was a backlash effect, of the kind I mentioned for 1936–38, 1947, and 1968. In the 1970s and early 1980s workers'

[85]Christian Le Bas and Christian Mercier, "Les savoir-faire ouvriers, enjeu des changements techniques," *Economie et humanisme* 43 (January–February 1983): 4–5.

[86]Marc Anvers, "Grèves dans l'automobile: Les stratégies, les enjeux," *Regards sur l'actualité* 9 (June 1983): 35–39. On Citroën, two contradictory books: Floriane Benoit, *Le printemps de la dignité* (Paris, 1982), and "Ewald" (pseud.), *L'école des esclaves* (Paris, 1983). On Talbot: Gabriel Ducray, ed., *Travail et formation des ouvriers de fabrication de l'industrie automobile* (Paris, 1983); Confédération Française Démocratique du Travail, *L'effet Talbot* (Paris, 1984). On Renault: Alfredo Peña-Vega, "Première contestation ouvrière et conflit social après le 10 mai 1981 chez Renault-Billancourt" (mémoire de maîtrise, University of Paris VII, 1983); Poperen, *Renault*, pp. 205–6. General surveys: Daniel Richter and Fabienne Lauret, "Dix-huit mois de conflits à la chaîne," *Travail* 1 (June 1983): 8–34; Giancarlo Santilli, "Auto e crisi in Francia," *Primo maggio* 12 (Spring 1984): 12–18.

productivity and pace of production had increased, often causing read-justments of shop organization. Directly linked to automation, these changes allowed the firms to gradually reduce the number of their wage earners from 1977 onward. This labor force was thus no longer regularly renewed. It grew older and older (the average age at Talbot-Poissy in 1983 was thirty-nine). Simultaneously, its average seniority increased. This new situation transformed most workers' goals. They now wanted steady jobs, a career, and real training, unlike a number of their pred-ecessors, who had resorted to frequent turnover. Both the aging of the labor force and the coming of automation made the parceling of work more difficult to accept. Anxieties about workers' employment and their ability to adapt increased.[87] Shared by many skilled workers, anxiety about automation and the desire for a stable position in the same firm were the two new features of these strikes, which otherwise focused on shop management just like the conflicts of the late 1960s and early 1970s.[88] A major exception to these movements was the decentralized Renault factory at Douai. A new management combined automation, reorgani-zation of work, and employee participation in gradual transformation of work processes. Another exception was Renault–Le Mans, where sim-ilar programs were conducted as a result of the strike of 1975.[89] Clearly, a new managerial strategy was under way, trying, as in other industrial countries, to accommodate autoworkers to the constraints of cost re-duction, rapid technological change, improvements in product quality, and employment shrinkage.

Conclusion

I have sketched the long history of French automobile workers' shop-floor responses to the technological revolutions in twentieth-century in-dustrial production. Yet this is not the full picture. I have concentrated on the workplace. Further research should examine how far new forms of sociability were created in the world outside the factory, based on

[87]François Cochet, "Quelle robotique industrielle pour la France?" *Critiques de l'économie politique* 6 (January–March 1983): 34; Robin Foot, "Cadences: La valse du temps," *Travail* 1 (June 1983): 35–40; Martine Blanc, "Les O.S. derrière la grille," *Travail* 1 (June 1983): 41–44; de Bonnafos, Chanaron, and de Mautort, *Industrie automobile*, pp. 59–60.

[88]Christophe Boulay, "Les robots chez Peugeot-Mulhouse," *La Croix* 101 (15–16 May 1983): 11; Bruno Dethomas, "Industrie automobile: Des robots ou des hommes?" *Monde* 40 (19 November 1983): 19–20; Catherine Salès, "O.S. à Poissy: No future," *Matin de Paris* 8 (6 January 1984): 5.

[89]Christian Mahieu, "Les enjeux de la formation professionnelle, de l'organisation du travail et de la gestion dans un atelier robotisé," in *Formation et informatisation*, ed. Durand et al., pp. 215–312; Alain Machefer, "Renault–Le Mans: Une meilleure expression des salariés est aussi source de gains de productivité," *Monde* 40 (19 July 1983): 13.

such factors as kinship networks, national or geographic origins, culture or the practice of leisure, and how new patterns of community life also contributed to frame workers' representations of auto work.[90]

The key points to the present study are clear. The continued existence of Fordism covered (and sometimes obscured) unremitting changes in work, technologies, shop management, labor supply, wage systems, and a renewal of the working class. But there was an overall continuity to the struggle of large groups of workers against Fordism and for auton-omy, which management was never fully able to contain in spite of the specialization of tasks and of the improvement of its control of the workplace.

A number of workers maintained or re-created a specific know-how and practices of resistance. Periodically, workers were able to restore some sort of unity. Then collective action became possible and broke out; it secured changes in work for a while, soon followed by an erosion of workers' cohesion. Trade unions, though quite important at some stages, were not a necessary vehicle in some struggles, which, in fact, often went on without a union's presence or in the face of union discouragement.[91]

After 1944 the rehabilitation of work, which Communist-led organi-zations tried to promote, did not last long. Yet it met the expectations of most skilled workers of the French auto industry, whose ethics re-mained work centered, and it is still shared by many activists: "a good activist is above all a good skilled worker," a skilled worker of the Saviem truck factory at Caen declared in 1969.[92] But there was a major shift away from skilled-worker views and values to a framework in which the militance of the ordinary line workers emerged. Semiskilled workers thus wavered between resigned submission and various kinds of oppo-sition to the content and methods of work, between a relative stability and frequent turnover, as they all reacted to the physical and nervous demands of a job that was not yet the work they kept dreaming of.[93] Automation suppressed the direct relationship between workers and

[90]See already Jean-Claude Backe and Hubert Faure, "Enquête sur les loisirs et mode de vie du personnel de la Régie nationale des usines Renault," *Consommation* 17 (April–June 1971): 3–35 and 18 (January–March 1972): 3–40.
[91]Annie Doña Gimenez, "Travailleur collectif, autonomie ouvrière et crise du procès de travail: Le cas du collectif de travail à la Régie Renault" (thesis of 3d cycle, University of Grenoble II, 1978), pp. 143–217; Jacques Freyssinet, *La politique d'emploi des grands groupes industriels* (Grenoble, 1982).
[92]Kergoat, *Pratiques*, p. 31; Dubost, *Flins sans fin*, pp. 69–77, 138–40.
[93]Mark Fuller, "Note on the World Auto Industry in Transition," Harvard Business School, Case Study 9–382–122, Cambridge, 1982, p. 22, writes of the French auto industry: "Labor relations were generally peaceful, except at Renault, where politically motivated strikes were common during the 1970s." This analysis is inadequate, and I hope readers will be convinced that it does not fit the reality.

their products, but the actual volume of production still strongly depended on workers.[94] Therefore, even if better-educated and younger workers are expected in the late 1980s, their motivation to work will become a central issue for the future of the automobile.

[94]De Bonnafos, "L'automatisation dans l'industrie automobile et le devenir des ouvriers de fabrication," *Bref* 2 (January–February 1984): 3.

Afterword

CHRISTOPHER H. JOHNSON

This volume amply demonstrates the richness and sophistication of the study of work in recent French historiography. Although it may not be apparent at first glance, these essays have a unity of focus rare in such a collection. From a wide variety of angles, they all probe a fundamental historical question: To what extent are work, the division of labor, and the general terrain of the social relations of production molded by impersonal market forces, and to what extent do the struggles (and the compromises) that characterize these social phenomena act back upon such forces to reshape them?

Current social science debate over work process, division of labor, and labor market segmentation, most of which uses a vocabulary established by Marxist theory even though many of the protagonists are pointedly anti- Marxist, has largely fallen between two poles, one rigidly economic-determinist, the other what might be labeled "culturalist." The clearest representations of these positions are Harry Braverman's *Labor and Monopoly Capital*, which poses a lockstep causal sequence from market competition to scientific management and Fordism to a new division of labor that created a new framework of subordination but simultaneous homogenization of the twentieth-century proletariat, and Charles Sabel's *Work and Politics*, which argues that economic activity (division of labor, the use of technology, the structure of the labor market, and presumably the product market itself) and the nature of work are shaped by "ideas about the world, political conceptions in the broadest sense" and how such views clash or harmonize in the arena of the social relations of production. Both titles do indeed sum up each perspective, with the second element dominating the first. And the use of words is obviously important: for Braverman "labor," an economic abstraction; for Sabel "work," a "human," cultural phenomenon.[1]

Pressures toward polarization have been exerted on both sides by people who, ironically, seem to agree on what the Marxian theory of history is. The anti-Marxist culturalists, who like Sabel are influenced strongly by the cultural anthropology of Clifford Geertz and the sociology of Max Weber, view all analysis that operates within the Marxist paradigm as essentially akin to Braverman's mechanistic perspective. In effect, they make the erroneous assumption (or deliberate misrepresentation) that Marxist theory views the *social* sphere as merely derivative, that the character of social life, whether one speaks of class formation or class conflict, is inevitably structured by extrinsic economic forces and, in the direct line of causation, by the consequent division of labor. Thus if they can demonstrate, as does Sabel, (1) that people occupying the same place in the division of labor (e.g., "peasant workers" from southern Italy and more savvy "would-be craftsmen" in low-skill production jobs) have quite divergent career expectations and reveal modes of behavior vis-à-vis the boss that vary according to specific historical circumstances, or (2) that skilled workers possess a "career-at-work" profile that can make them revolutionary at one point and conservative at another, or (3) that production worker splits and skilled/unskilled dichotomies can be and are overcome not by any dramatic change in the division of labor but by the workings of politics and of new ideological commitment, or (4) (and above all) that the struggle itself reshapes the division of labor and significantly alters the expected march of capitalism without overthrowing it, then "Marxist" theory is incorrect.

On the other hand, there is indeed an important strand of Marxist thought stressing that capitalism, impelled forward by its own laws—laws that also endowed the ruling class with political power and cultural hegemony—has turned out to be an amazingly adaptable and resilient system, beside which instances of worker resistance pale in significance. As Lawrence McDonnell put it in a recent review essay against Herbert Gutman and David Montgomery, the central question is not why labor "survived," either by cultural maintenance or by active workplace struggle, but "why capitalism triumphed." McDonnell (with Perry Anderson) banishes E. P. Thompson, Gutman, and other historians of working-class culture to the misty marshes of liberalism and thus tends to agree with anti-Marxist Sabel. (Sabel is happy to have them, of course.) Montgomery remains "in," but his "economism" blinds him to the importance

---

[1]Harry Braverman, *Labor and Monopoly Capital: The Degradation of Work in the Twentieth Century* (New York, 1974); Charles Sabel, *Work and Politics: The Division of Labor in Industry* (Cambridge, 1982), esp. p. 227.

of politics—in this case, the necessity of having a workers' party whose function it is to shape the critical struggles at the workplace into a simultaneous assault on the capitalist state, the ultimate mechanism by which the power of capitalism is maintained.[2] What is galling about both positions (for I happen to agree with most of what each has to say) is their determination to declare ideological war, the one to attack a narrowly conceived Marxism, the other to defend it.[3]

The fact is, of course, that the exercise of state power and the "role of the revolutionary party" themselves are subjects to be included in the analysis of social relations, as are, more obviously, workplace relationships among workers and within production hierarchies, labor market control and manipulation, the cultural structures of social differentiation and accord, and the multiple manifestations of social conflict itself. Although social relations must not be regarded as an autonomous force, "it is," as Richard Price remarked in an important recent essay, "in the *historical* dynamic of these social relations, rather than any exogenous technical or market forces, that one can see the *agency* of (labor process) formation," that is, the changing structure of work, the division of labor under capitalism.[4] His plea, and mine, is certainly not to ignore the limits imposed by those exogenous forces, but to explore the vast arena of human interaction within them and assess the impact of these histories on the boundaries of basic economic structures.

The theoretical stakes of such analysis are high. Sabel, for instance, posits that a particular set of historical circumstances rooted in disparate political decisions of groups with divergent world views created the possibility of a new form of division of labor under advanced capitalism. Decentralized, independent, high-tech cottage industry ruled by artisanal petty capitalists in an increasingly specialized product market (mainly numerically controlled machine-tool products) now occupies a significant niche in Italian capitalism and will continue to flourish and stimulate the economy despite the fears of the large-scale, traditional corporate enterprises. It is economically viable and can multiply, although its survival

[2]Lawrence T. McDonnell, " 'You Are Too Sentimental': Problems and Suggestions for a New Labor History," *Journal of Social History* 17, no. 4 (Summer 1984): 629–54.

[3]Sabel goes out of his way to attack "radicals" Noble, Gordon, Reich, and Edwards for a technological determinism none of them profess. See, above all, Richard Edwards, *Contested Terrain: The Transformation of the Workplace in the Twentieth Century* (New York, 1979); David Gordon, Richard Edwards, and Michael Reich, *Segmented Work, Divided Workers: The Historical Transformation of Labor in the United States* (Cambridge, 1982); and David Noble, *Forces of Production: A Social History of Industrial Automation* (New York, 1984). McDonnell, for his part, ignores the iconoclastic Marxists of *History Workshop*, no doubt because they do not fit handily into his categories.

[4]My emphasis. Richard Price, "Theories of Labour Process Formation," *Journal of Social History* 18, no. 1 (Fall 1984): 91–110, quotation from p. 107. This review article has had an important influence on my thinking in this essay.

depends on *will*, he says, as well: the will of the skilled-worker types who run it to retain their worldview emphasizing problem-solving and creativity and the will of the Italian Left (particularly the Emilian Communist Party) to continue to support it with special privileges and incentives until it gets well established. Sabel's petty-capitalist utopia unfortunately fares poorly in light of historical experience—or so it appears in view of the boundaries of capitalism past. Many innovative activities within developing industries began as small, high-risk experiments that coexisted with low-quality, low-technology segments as the unstable sector of the market providing boom-time goods. Once they proved their value, however, they either expanded to challenge the industry giants or were absorbed by them. Time, as they say, will tell. But time past has already had something to tell.[5]

There is perhaps no more fascinating arena for examining changing social relations of production than the long and convoluted history of industrial capitalism's emergence against and within the household and artisanal modes of production. The latter served as pillars of the society of orders but clearly did not go away when the legal framework of that society fell with the Revolution. All the chapters except Rabinbach's and Fridenson's in one way or another deal with the phenomenon on either side of the revolutionary divide, although, unfortunately, none examines the significance of the French Revolution itself. They look at these modes of production, as it were, from the inside and outside—as work experienced and work formally represented, work as it figured in ideological constructs either defending or promoting the transformation of the existing social structure.

To begin with the latter, Koepp and Sewell explore capitalist visions of rationalized market structures and work processes, bourgeois utopias unencumbered by the sociolegal and cultural constraints of the ancien régime. Such visions did not come out of thin air. What they did come out of, however, appears to be a matter of debate, and the structure of the collection creates a probably unintended idealist bias. Quite obviously, the drive for market rationalization and technical proficiency

---

[5]Sabel argues that demand in advanced capitalist economies is rapidly diversifying. No longer satisfied with the standardized goods of the era of Fordism, consumers want more and more specialty products. This is one of the reasons small-scale enterprise has a good chance. One of the examples he repeatedly uses, the American baking industry, is supposedly splintering under the impact of specialty products beyond (and replacing) basic white bread. If Samuel A. Matz is correct, however, Sabel is misinformed about trends in this industry. See Matz, "Modern Baking Technology," *Scientific American* 251, no. 5 (November 1984): 122–37. Subtitled "This \$30-billion-a-year industry relies on mass production to meet demand for its varied product," the article points to the reabsorption of the market by the large manufacturers using expensive, flexible, high-technology machinery.

had been going on for rather a long time as European commercial capitalism expanded its influence within the land-based economy of medieval and early modern Europe. Many merchants and financiers had long been aware that those with the fullest knowledge of market conditions and those who organized their operations with the greatest precision were the most successful. Although the rationalization of industrial production lagged behind, there were pockets of the economy with deep experience in large-scale, elaborately subdivided, and technically sophisticated industrial organization in Europe itself, especially in mining, metallurgy (above all as it related to the military), and shipbuilding. More important, where work took place at the point of a gun and the crack of a whip, highly elaborated divisions of labor were experimented with (although success was hardly guaranteed, given that perverse human will to resist oppression) not by *philosophes*, but by planters. Nothing reminds one so much of the regimented, faceless, technology-dominant depictions of work in the *Encyclopédie* as the illustrations of sugar production facilities in the Caribbean dating back to the sixteenth century. Moreover, skill knowledge, tool design, and other craft secrets had been falling into the hands of nonguildsmen (often merchant-entrepreneur interlopers in the trade) and published for the world to see for a good century before 1750 in England, and to no avail did guildsmen seek legal redress.[6] Certainly, this phenomenon was among the "English ideas" known to Enlightenment thinkers.

Above all, of course, Europe—France clearly included—was witnessing a process of industrialization in textiles in which merchant-manufacturers bypassed the guilds by going into the countryside for labor and simultaneously manipulated labor markets and won legal support to develop their domination over the guilds of urban carders, weavers, and croppers. Rural and urban outworking and subcontracting producing for an international market and impelled by merchant capital was an industrial capitalist phenomenon, whose first major reverberations in fact were agitating French public discourse at the very moment that the *Encyclopédie* was being conceived. Following a decade of industrial strife in which wool weavers and croppers from Carcassonne to Sedan and silk weavers in Lyons rose in rebellion against assorted *fabricants*, a two-pronged attack by the law, one side prohibiting "compagnons et ouvriers" from "caballing" against their masters, the other denying weavers' and croppers' guilds the capacity to contravene the fabricants' right to hire nonguild workers, was turned on the producers. The struggle between transforming merchant capital (the very word "merchant-manu-

[6] The most recent and interesting study is Mary Robishon, "Scientific Instrument Makers in London during the Seventeenth and Eighteenth Centuries" (Ph. D. diss., University of Michigan, 1983).

facturer" captures the essence of the process occurring) and the producers' corporations—masters and journeymen alike—is obviously a major chapter in the history of social relations under nascent industrial capitalism and one that clearly demonstrates the contradictions under which the French eighteenth-century state labored.[7] As Kaplan shows so well, Turgot represents an existing reality, the desire of capitalist entrepreneurs for industrial liberty, but the great majority of frightened guildsmen represented an equally powerful reality: the privileged and hierarchical society of orders that provided the social cement maintaining the regime. To survive, the state needed both the wealth generated by the first and the stability fostered by the second. It could not (and in the end did not) have it both ways. Capitalism, I would argue, was a good deal more than a "cultural construct" in eighteenth-century France. Changes were occurring in the structure of the economy, within the corporate world and beyond it, changes that—despite resistance and concessions—were reshaping the structure and nature of work.

And the stability of the social system suffered because of it. Truant's Lyons and Nantes on one hand and Shephard's Dijon on the other illustrate what was happening. The latter, an important administrative center, saw the maintenance of open access to mastership in its craft guilds down to the Revolution. Here the Old Regime worked, as the sons of guildsmen often moved on to professions associated with the city's functions and new men, in a tight labor market, moved in to replace them. Lyons and Nantes experienced massive economic change under the impetus of the intertwining workings of both commercial and industrial capitalism, leading to urban protoindustrialization, petty capitalist behavior in the traditional crafts pressuring small masters, and widespread "illegal," extracorporate hiring as job-seeking poor from the countryside poured into the cities. Master/journeyman conflict was endemic and, she concludes, journeyman power, manifested through their associations (especially the *compagnonnage*), contributed to the breakdown of the Old Regime. In Dijon, the compagnonnage was also powerful, but here, Shephard notes, it served, along with the masters' *corporations* (despite considerable conflict between the two), to buttress the Old Regime. It seems to me that it is incorrect to say (as Truant does) that the compagnonnage and its tradition of "liberty," insubordination,

---

[7]See Maurice Garden, *Lyon et les lyonnais au XVIIIe siècle* (Paris, 1970), esp. pp. 582–92; Gerard Gayot, "Dispersion et concentration de la draperie sedanaise au XVIIIe siècle," *Revue du Nord* 51 (January–March 1979): 127–48; Serge Chassagne, "La diffusion rurale de l'industrie cotonnière en France (1750–1850)," *Revue du Nord* (January–March): 97–114; Gerard Gayot, "La longue insolence des tondeurs de draps dans la manufacture de Sedan au XVIIIe siècle," *Revue du Nord* 63 (January–March 1981): 105–34. The key documents relating to the woolens industry are located in Archives nationales (hereafter AN), F12 753–90 (corporations), 1344–94 (draperie), and 2301–2 (armée).

and so on, is the source of change, for in one town it served to maintain the Old Regime and in the other two it undermined it. Same tradition, different results. The cause of change was the complex restructuring of the social relations of production accompanying the growth of capitalist practices in industry.

Michael Sonenscher develops one of the most interesting insights in the entire book, for he challenges the very notion of "tradition," arguing instead that in the "traditional" "artisan" craft of tailoring—one assumes that unlike Paris but like most provincial cities tailoring in Rouen was not significantly influenced by capitalist practices in the period he examines—workshop harmony was invented, an "artifice" to deal with a most vexing problem: massive turnover. Regularized recruitment procedures were critical, and the master had to be nice if he was to get any work done. The experience of Ménétra the glazier corroborates this. What Sonenscher is saying, of course, is that there is nothing inherently harmonious about precapitalist social relations of production, but that the circumstances of producing at all seriously affected the way those relations sorted themselves out. This raises a troubling issue for modernization stage theorists.

At the same time it raises questions about Soboul's vision of the *sans-culottes*, for he perhaps too easily accepted as reality, in their expressions of workshop harmony and the unity of the small, what may indeed be a fiction devised to deal with specific circumstances that no longer obtained in 1793, after the abolition of the guilds. Or maybe the reasons for expressing such fictions had become all the more pressing. Essays in this book confirm that Paris was different. Ménétra stresses the unpleasantness of the Parisian masters even in his little trade, but once he becomes one, though he remembers the lot of the journeyman, he nevertheless seeks what advantages the economic conditions might allow. He breaks the code, starts another shop, and rails against the guild's *jurés*, who try to forestall enterprise. The point is that Parisian trades of all sorts were undergoing the birth pangs of capitalist practices *and* had a glutted labor market well suited for entrepreneurial development. If Paris masters were bad apples (Elophe must have been positively awful), many had the luxury of easily finding replacements for the uppity likes of Ménétra.[8]

Given this situation, the likelihood of an explosion of entrepreneurial initiative accompanying the abolition of the guilds was great (it is little studied, however); but the economic circumstances, which went from bad to worse in 1792 and 1793, meant—despite the attempt to restore

---

[8]It is also true that the labor market for many others, the *ébenistes*, for example, remained tight.

some "order" in the labor market with the Le Chapelier law of 1791—that the need for a pliant work force was all the more necessary. Unquestionably there were plenty of small masters (like the Rouen tailors of the later 1770s) who only wanted to go on doing their small work and really wanted cooperation. But "big masters" obviously needed the fiction as well. And who ran the sans-culotte ideology mill? All evidence—and that of Richard Andrews is the best and should be published in full despite his maniacal determination to destroy Soboul—points to the fact that relatively well-off people who were lesser professionals or had "artisan" titles but entrepreneurial backgrounds or aspirations were the key leaders. Morris Slavin, who certainly would never want to hurt Soboul, has found the same types leading the sans-culottes of the Section droits de l'homme, and so have I in looking at Lodève.[9] What for Sonenscher's tailors was a *functional* ideology, a means of dealing with the tricky labor market/production problem, and no doubt remained so for many small masters and their journeymen in the revolutionary era, may well have been a kind of paternalist rhetoric for large segments of a new petty-capitalist subclass who used it to palliate their worker-followers. The artisan world was splintering, "tradition" being rent asunder, but as is perhaps always the case, words—that many contemporaries and plenty of historians believed—sought to hold it together. We are in Sonenscher's debt for forcing us to think about the "production" of social relationships and the rhetoric that surrounds it.

The fracturing and transformation of artisan industry remains one of the most fruitful areas for historical research, especially in France. Kaplan stresses the need for detailed study of master/journeyman relations after the trauma of 1776 and points to the possibility of an "aristocratic reaction" among frightened masters. Largely untapped source materials such as those utilized by Shephard, Sonenscher, and Truant will allow deep study of corporate relations. Just as important is the need to understand the divergent paths of master artisans. Although in general the harbingers of industrial capitalism came from the world of exchange—cloth merchants become fabricants, for example—by the later eighteenth century thousands of industrial guild masters were breaking the codes of their own corporations, raiding the territory of others, seeking profit for reinvestment to expand operations—in short, acting like capitalist entrepreneurs. For the most part, because their access to

[9] Richard Andrews, "Politics and Social Structure in Revolutionary Paris"(paper presented at Duke University, Consortium on Revolutionary Europe, 16 February 1984); Morris Slavin, *The French Revolution in Miniature* (Princeton, 1984); and Christopher Johnson, "Artisans vs. Fabricants: Urban Proto-industrialization and the Evolution of Work Culture in Lodève and Bédarieux, 1740–1830" (paper presented at the Colloquium on Work and Family in Pre-industrial Europe, 1–2 October, 1984, European University Institute, Florence, published as a "working paper" of the institute, 1984), pp. 20–35.

capital resources was much more limited than that of the *négociants*, their activities remained small scale. But some, indeed, made their way. And unquestionably the abolition of the guilds (and the opportunities afforded by revolutionary politics) opened, or seemed to open, vast new opportunities.

My favorite example is Michel Causse, *fils*, born to a shepherd's family in the causse de Larzac. During the American Revolution he and his father migrated to Lodève, the booming center of military cloth production, and set themselves up, in rented quarters, as independent weavers, thus bucking the trend then occurring toward wage-work weaving in large *ateliers* owned by the fabricants. It is not known whether they were members of the weavers' corporation (which was much weakened in any case because of the burgeoning authority of the fabricants in this protoindustrial setting), but they may well have been because there was a corporative tradition in the villages of the upper Sorgue valley whence they came. In any case, they did well, working largely for a major manufacturer (and a leader of Lodève's municipal revolution in 1789), Pierre Fabreguettes. Both experienced difficulties in the hard years of 1787–91, although the Causses, expert and hardworking weavers, apparently got work from others and even (illegally) made cloth on their own, which they sold in the commercial market. With the abolition of the guilds, they declared themselves manufacturers, profiting from the huge demand for army cloth that came with the growing threat of war in early 1792. But young Michel also mixed in politics, and by the summer of 1793 had emerged as the town's leading Jacobin and a recognized voice of the sans-culottes and as its eighth-largest cloth manufacturer. We are ignorant about the precise details of how they interconnected, but these facts undoubtedly had something to do with each other. Causse survived Thermidor with the help and protection of Fabreguettes and Joseph Rouaud, a radical dyer-fabricant who had also done well by doing good but was less politically compromised than Causse. The latter's saga went on, though he continued to irritate the town's old manufacturing elite by becoming the arch-advocate of textile machinery promoted by the Napoleonic regime. They all but cheered when his pioneering efforts of 1809 failed, but, undaunted, he moved his business (wisely) to Bédarieux and became one of the leaders of its industrial revolution.[10]

But for every successful Causse, there were ten like him who failed and fifty others who never tried at all. Still, there are those who tried. Although corporate patterns and modes of behavior obviously outlasted

---

[10]The Causse story is drawn from a wide variety of local archival sources (see Johnson, "Artisans," nn. 39–56), but especially important was the vitriolic attack on him by a conservative manufacturer in Cincinnatus, "Mémoire" (sent to post-Thermidor officials in Montpellier and relayed to Paris sometime in 1795); AN, F7 3678².

the corporations defined as legal entities, many masters and men broke with the tradition and journeyed along the entrepreneurial pathways of industrial capitalism. We know very little about this process, but to understand this entrepreneurial drive (as both a reality and an "idiom") is certainly as important as to understand the ongoing significance of the corporate tradition. Most did not fully succeed. The Horatio Algers were rare, or so existing studies of the *grande bourgeoisie industrielle* indicate, but modest success there certainly was as small enterprises proliferated during the nineteenth century, filling important sectors in the product market. Although pressures on them could be immense, they found a place within the new industrial system, and many survived. Simultaneously, many of the workers within such industries retained at least partial ownership of the means of production.

Aminzade's analysis of these kinds of industries (perhaps we should use the word "handicraft" rather than "artisan," given the ideologically loaded character of the latter) carries us far beyond the single examples—such as mine on Parisian tailors—that we have so far. What is important, of course, is that these are not "backward," "traditional," or aberrant elements in the industrial capitalist system, but an integral part of its development. While they do tend to employ a decreasing proportion of the working population as the era of mass production emerges, they hardly disappear. In some cases social cost, not cost price, was the main reason for their decline—I have in mind the sweatshops of the garment trades. But as Tessie Liu has shown, cottage industry often revives in the wake of factory-industry decline and continues to serve what Sabel and others define as the unstable sector of the product market.[11] And clearly as well, high-risk but often technologically sophisticated industry can profit, on a small-scale basis at least, until it proves itself.

In the era of the nineteenth-century Industrial Revolution, however—and this is my main point here—small-scale handicraft industry was a major component in the industrial capitalist mix, and many of the workers in it also sensed the entrepreneurial possibilities that its development evinced. But there was always the pressure of competition that only economies of scale could meet. The niches in the product market could quickly disappear as new products won allegiance. Household production, such as that at Saint-Etienne, became precarious, a situation producing bitter class conflict. Sometimes, as Robert Liebman has shown for the master silk weavers of Lyons, the household producers could work out a *modus vivendi* with the merchant-manufacturers, structuring the

[11]Tessie Liu, "From De-industrialization to Cottage Industry: The Southern Anjou Linen Industry, 1880–1914" (paper presented at the North American Labor History Conference, Wayne State University, 19 October 1984).

labor market to the advantage of both,[12] but the normal process was a heightening of class tensions in the small-enterprise sector as pressures mounted. Small entrepreneurs went under. They and their workers faced unemployment and displacement. Theirs was a resentment against capitalism born not of its violation of their traditions, corporate or otherwise, but of its failed promise.

Norbert Truquin was a son of that milieu. It is interesting that though he was a proletarian in the full sense of the term—a man without a profession who worked to live and little more—he also possessed a spirit of risk taking and adventure no doubt shared by his father. But whereas his father lived by his wits on the edge of the criminal world of Paris, Norbert quickly made his way to socialism—communism in fact—as he learned his first lessons from an Icarian. Cooperation and trade socialism were not for him—but neither was industrial civilization. Truquin's complete rejection of industrial capitalism was born of bitter experience. The popularity of O'Connor's land scheme with Chartists and Raspail's communalism with French workers shows the appeal of such agrarian socialism. Truquin thought there was a distinct, rural alternative. For millions of other workers like him, however, such an alternative was unimaginable. What they did imagine was a civilization without capitalism in their own backyard.

Poverty, deprivation, meanness, disillusionment, and an absence of a work culture marked Norbert Truquin's formative years. Jacques Rancière asks us to remember that for tens of thousands of "artisans"—those supposedly in the corporate world of skill and professional pride—life was not much different. And their protest generally went well beyond a mere defense of craft interests, to which more corporate, closed crafts such as carpenters, limited their action. He challenges the very notion of skill when applied to the kind of work most tailors and shoemakers did.[13] More important, however, Rancière (he could be thinking of Truquin) questions just how important the actual work one does, one's *precise* place in the division of labor, in fact is. Changing jobs or having trouble getting the job you were trained for (à la Perdiguier) is pretty normal. Clearly Truquin knew he was in the working class—he lived the life of a proletarian. But it was that life lived in all of its ramifications that made him say no to capitalism.

For Michael Hanagan, the moment of protest is when the family in-

[12]Robert Liebman, "Restructuring the Fabrique: Employer Policy after the Second Republic," (paper presented at the Social Science History Association Meeting, Toronto, 28 October 1984).

[13]For an interesting discussion of "skill" under the ancien régime see Michael Sonenscher, "The Meaning of Skill in Eighteenth-Century France" (paper presented at the Colloquium on Work and Family in Pre-industrial Europe, 1–2 October, 1984, European University Institute, Florence).

come can be stretched no further. Family formation and development were an integral part of working-class survival strategies, and the family value system among industrial workers was a force superior to values and traditions relating to their work. On the other hand, he does point out that for a small proportion of workers skill made an enormous difference—but they were also the ones who had sufficient income from the skilled man's wage alone. Rancière thus makes a fundamental point that finds considerable support in other essays here: the meaning of work varies substantially from one group of workers to another. Those we call "artisans" divide on this question. Indeed, as I have tried to argue throughout, artisan is a social category being splintered by the economic forces of the age: there are capitalist artisans, failed capitalist artisans, proletarianizing artisans, highly skilled "corporate" artisans, and not-so-skilled and less-corporate artisans. And running through it all are people in the same alleged category who fall on different sides of the wage bargain (although that is certainly not always as clear as it seems from today's vantage point).[14]

What we get back to, then, are conditions of life, not simply work, and how they change. Poverty and degradation deeply influence how workers—even skilled workers—react. The timing of the emerging tool-and-die makers' militance in Detroit, a movement that served as a catalyst for the rise of the production workers' drive to organize the United Auto Workers, is intriguing. Not only had a larger percentage of them been permanently laid off than was the case among production workers, but the take-home pay of those who remained employed was 30 percent in 1932 of what it had been in 1929, slashes much greater than those experienced by the average factory worker. Their life situation, in fact, was becoming very much like that of production workers in all respects *except* the way they worked. Such facts, not skill dilution (though some of that was going on as well), were critical as bases for their electrifying strikes in 1933.[15]

The similarity of life situation was not the only factor that united these workers—supposedly labor aristocrats—with production workers, however. Another was ideology, working-class ideology.

During the twenties, tool-and-die men emerged as a new elite, replacing the skilled molders, trimmers, and finishers whose jobs the machines and dies they fashioned were meant to eliminate. They were

---

[14]On the complexity of wage structures and relationships in the early Industrial Revolution see William Reddy, "Modes de paiement et contrôle du travail dans les filatures de coton en France, 1750–1850," *Revue du Nord*, 63 (January–March 1981): 135–46; and his *The Rise of Market Culture* (Cambridge, 1984).

[15]See Steve Babson, "The Rise of the Tool and Die Maker, 1899–1937" (unpublished paper, Wayne State University, April 1984): Walter P. Reuther Library of Labor and Urban Affairs, Maurice Sugar Collection, box 41.

glorified as capitalist heroes of labor, and competition for their services was keen among companies and jobbers. Such capitalist ideology sought to underscore their "aristocratic" character. But prominent among them were men who had left Britain in the twenties, men with experience in the Shop Stewards' Movement or the General Strike and well armed with Socialist, Communist, or Independent Labour Party ideologies of class conflict. They did not swallow the capitalist line of the twenties and were prepared in the thirties to fight for general industrial unionism. Although it can be argued that "skilled worker" values reinvaded the union after 1945 as it sought security and privilege for its lucky, organized members in a way similar to the "new model" unions of mid-Victorian England, it was not until those old ideologies were squelched or neutralized, smothered in the end by American capitalism's astonishing world conquest of power, that this occurred.

We are talking, of course, about politics, the politics of class relations. The four essays that I have not yet touched upon present subtle insights into how capitalist hegemony and working-class resistance work. Joan Scott presents the *Statistique* of Parisian industry of 1848 as a carefully articulated liberal-positivist instrument of class defense that seeks to show how stable, "in reality" (Gradgrind's reality), the world of Parisian work was. All this noise out there, Say implies, must be the work of evil "agitators." There are threats to this stability, such as single women, and they must be addressed by the law. The much larger national inquiry on agricultural and industrial work, ordered by the National Assembly, suffers from many of the same disabilities and must be studied with similar care. Its entries tended to be more transparently class biased because the local justice of the peace for each canton generally chose the representatives. Even though there were supposed to be an equal number of *patrons* and *ouvriers* elected by each branch of economic activity, this rarely occurred. Normally, bourgeois cronies of the justice of the peace wrote the document. Where workers were strong enough to fight for their right to representation, there were frightful struggles. In Paris and three cantons in Lyons, the study was never completed because workers demanded that *their* statistics and *their* evaluations have equal (or greater) weight. In one industrial town, Lodève, a workers' version was submitted because their representatives took over the enquête. The justice of the peace apologized, remarking that the results were "prejudiced."[16] That some workers understood the importance of controlling the terms of scientific inquiry as early as 1848 is fascinating. That bourgeois would fight so hard to keep them from doing so (the Parisian study

[16]AN, C 943–69; C. H. Johnson, "The *Enquête sur le travail agricole et industriel* of 1848 in the Hérault: An Internal Analysis"(unpublished paper, Wayne State University, 1972).

was discussed by workers as a *response* to Say's *Statistique*) shows that they knew well what the class struggle was about on this level.

Anson Rabinbach's engrossing study takes us into the more rarefied and sophisticated atmosphere of late nineteenth-century science. Should one say "bourgeois science"? Obviously the science of work was not a conscious instrument of class defense in the manner of the 1848 document analyzed by Scott. It was the product of dedicated, ideologically neutral research and was promoted by social reformers. Its disdain for Taylorism and concern for workers' health and safety seems to exonerate it from an anti-working-class bias. Moreover, while it did not necessarily think that a reduced workday was the answer, the heart of its analysis focused on fatigue. But the trade-union movement in France greeted it with "hostile indifference." Why? Was it because they instinctively knew that a set of ideas that totally depersonalized work and objectified the worker was to be feared? Or because, despite the rhetoric proclaiming the goal of harmony between capital and labor, union people understood that the ultimate objective was increased productivity within the capitalist mode of production? Finally, could it not be seen that the science of work fit rather nicely with a variety of programs then being promoted by republican reformers and supported by "progressive" capitalists— profit sharing, company insurance programs, credit unions, worker housing schemes, and a host of educational training programs—all for workers' benefit, but designed to keep workers workers?[17] That the science of work finally reconciled its differences with Taylorism after the war (when it counted, for only then did Taylorism begin to have an impact in France) indicates that like so many of the Progressive reforms in the West of the early twentieth century, it ultimately functioned to contain the class struggle without ending bourgeois dominance.

Sentiments and day-to-day modes of worker resistance occupy Reddy's and Fridenson's attention. Reddy's essay is a gem. His close analysis of artistic evidence, its sources and purposes, shows that he is fully aware of the interpretive pitfalls, noted by Rancière, in working with such material. Reddy captures a quality in working-class experience that far transcends his Lillois. The joke, the ironical twist—taking grim circumstances and turning them on their head in the form of farce—appear again and again in the records documenting working-class life in the modern world. Tricking the foreman, insulting the policeman, mocking the rich should be added to the wry humor about the uncertainties of daily life that these songs depict. Reddy caught glimpses of such farce-in-action in another article, and anyone who has gone into the rich documentation of social conflict in nineteenth-century France knows about

[17]See especially Sanford Elwitt, *Order and Progress* (Baton Rouge, forthcoming).

the place of humor in the class struggle. But this essay deals with more subtle forms of irony. It ultimately faces the issue of whether such songs imply a kind of withdrawal behind the protection of humor or indeed must be interpreted as a bitter cry against oppression. Reddy comes down on the side of the latter with his final two paragraphs, which offer remarkable insight into the working-class experience. The fact is, of course, that any literature of this sort will depict both resignation and resistance. Reddy has sorted through the complexities of the problem and has come to a nuanced conclusion that thoroughly undermines both the Meacham "life apart" and the Brecher spontaneity interpretations of the working-class mind set.[18]

Fridenson sketches the long and twisting history of automobile workers' shop-floor responses to the technological revolutions in twentieth-century industrial production. As the reigning expert on the history of French autoworkers, he has a sure grasp of the entire process, and his analysis, drawing together economic and political trends in a brilliant manner, provides an overview of worker adaptation and resistance. The key points are clear: (1) there was an overall continuity to the struggle against Fordism that management was never fully able to contain; (2) trade unions were not a necessary vehicle in the struggle, which in fact often went on without a union's presence or in the face of union discouragement; and (3) after 1945 there was a major shift away from skilled-worker leadership in the battles over job control to a framework in which they became an impediment to the emerging militance of the ordinary line workers. Fridenson's essay provides a perfect capstone to the collection. It summarizes many of the main themes of the entire book while simultaneously demonstrating the profoundly new directions that work and the conflict surrounding it have taken in the twentieth century.

Both essays therefore stress that the political battle is a daily one and that most workers, particularly in the great mass of the less-skilled, carry with them an anticapitalist bundle of sentiments that can be readily kindled. *How* it was kindled and what happened when it was, what forms of organization grew or collapsed, who won or lost and why—such questions are not broached in this book. Although the entire book is about the social relations of production, the impact of capitalism upon them, and the significance of resistance in redefining, if not breaching, its boundaries, the actual fights are rarely glimpsed. Moreover, with the exception of the compagnonnage and the masters' corporations and occasional references to the state, the institutions through which the

[18]Standish Meacham, *A Life Apart: The English Working Class, 1890–1914* (Cambridge, Mass., 1977), and Jeremy Brecher, *Strike!* (Boston, 1972).

social relations of production are filtered and by which organized struggle is realized are absent from view. Revolutions, riots, strikes, the law, police forces, movements, parties, unions—is their study old-fashioned? Of course none of the authors believes it. And all no doubt would agree that we must readdress the history of all these phenomena and institutions in light of the kind of sociocultural or structural history represented here. But I think there is another reason that the actual fights and the institutions are left out. This book is the fruit of a conference about work and its representations. It is not the case that we conceptualize "work" in cultural terms and infuse it with moral content, indeed tend to sanctify it? Does this not unconsciously draw us to study it as structures, balances, and harmonies with "deeper" meanings? It really is rather a shock (and refreshing) when, in chapter 10, we get to Norbert Truquin and he starts bouncing around from job to job, hardly giving a thought to what he is doing in them. Yet he is clearly a worker and long led a working-class life. Perhaps excessive preoccupation with work inadvertently leads us away from the study of that life in all its complexity.

NOTES ON CONTRIBUTORS

RONALD AMINZADE is Assistant Professor of Sociology at the University of Minnesota. He is the author of *Class, Politics, and Early Industrial Capitalism* (1981) and of "Social Mobility in a Nineteenth Century French City" (*American Sociological Review*, August 1982). He is currently working on a comparative urban study of republican party formation in mid-nineteenth-century Toulouse, Rouen, and Saint-Etienne.

PATRICK FRIDENSON is Maître-Assistant of Contemporary History at the University of Paris X–Nanterre and the editor of *Le mouvement social*. He is the author of *Histoire des usines Renault*, vol. 1, *1898–1939* (1972) and the coauthor of *La France et la Grande Bretagne devant les problèmes aériens, 1935–1940* (1976) and of *The Automobile Revolution* (1982). He is completing the second volume of the *Histoire des usines Renault*, covering the years 1939 to 1975.

MAURICE GARDEN is Professor of Modern History at the University of Lyons II, where he formerly directed the Centre Pierre Léon. *Lyon et les Lyonnais au XVIIIe siècle* (1970) is his most influential work. His major current interest is the demographic history of France, particularly in urban locus, from the eighteenth century to the present.

MICHAEL P. HANAGAN is Assistant Professor of History at Columbia University. He is the author of *The Logic of Solidarity: Artisans and Industrial Workers in Three French Towns, 1871–1914* (1980). He is engaged in research on the history of working-class families, labor-force formation, and worker militancy in nineteenth-century France.

CHRISTOPHER H. JOHNSON is Professor of History at Wayne State University. He is the author of *Utopian Communism in France: Cabet and the*

Icarians, 1839–1851 (1974) and several articles on aspects of French economic and social history. He is currently writing a book on regional deindustrialization, *The Life and Death of Industrial Languedoc, 1700–1920*.

STEVEN LAURENCE KAPLAN, Professor of European History at Cornell University, recently published *Provisioning Paris: Merchants and Millers in the Grain and Flour Trade during the Eighteenth Century* (1984). He is also the author of *Bread, Politics and Political Economy in the Reign of Louis XV*, 2 vols. (1976), *La Bagarre: Galiani's "Lost" Parody* (1979), and *Le complot de famine: Histoire d'une rumeur* (1982). His latest project deals with the end of the corporations in France.

CYNTHIA J. KOEPP is a Ph.D. candidate in the Department of History at Cornell University and Visiting Instructor of History at Cornell College in Mount Vernon, Iowa. She is completing a dissertation on the idea of work in eighteenth- and early nineteenth-century France.

YVES LEQUIN is Professor of Contemporary History and director of the Centre Pierre Léon at the University of Lyons 2. He is the author of *Les ouvriers de la région lyonnaise (1848–1914)*. Under his editorial aegis, the first volume of *Histoire des français, XIX–XXe siècles* appeared in 1983.

MICHELLE PERROT is Professor of Contemporary History at the University of Paris VII. Her special interests include the history of the world of work, of crime and punishment, and of women. She is the author of *Les ouvriers en grève, 1871–90* (1974), *L'histoire des femmes est-elle possible?* (1985), a critical edition of Tocqueville's *Ecrits pénitentiaires* (1985), and *Histoire de la vie privée au dix-neuvième siècle* (in progress).

ANSON RABINBACH is Assistant Professor of History at the Cooper Union and a member of the Institute for Advanced Study, Princeton, 1983–84. He is the author of *The Crisis of Austrian Socialism: From Red Vienna to Civil War, 1927–1934* (1983) and of "The Aesthetics of Production in the Third Reich," *Journal of Contemporary History* (1976). He is completing a study of the perception of work and the working body in the late nineteenth century.

JACQUES RANCIERE is Maître-Assistant of Philosophy at the University of Paris VIII. He is the author of *La nuit des prolétaires* (1981) and *Le philosophe et ses pauvres* (1983) and the coauthor of *La parole ouvrière, 1830–1851* (1976). He is now at work on the history of social science and social representations.

WILLIAM M. REDDY is Associate Professor in the Department of History, Duke University. He is author of *The Rise of Market Culture: The Textile Trade and French Society, 1750–1900* (1984). He is working on a second book entitled *Money and Liberty in Modern Europe: A Critique of Historical Understanding.*

DANIEL ROCHE is chairman of the History Department of the University of Paris I. Among his best-known studies are *Le siècle des lumières en province: Académies et académiciens provinciaux, 1680–1789* (1978) and *Le peuple de Paris* (1981). Taking special responsibility for the cultural dimension, he has just completed, with Pierre Goubert, a two-volume portrait of the ancien régime, *Les français et l'ancien régime* (1984).

JOAN W. SCOTT is Professor in the School of Social Science of the Institute for Advanced Study, Princeton. Author of *The Glassworkers of Carmaux* (1974), she also wrote, with Louise Tilly, *Women, Work and Family* (1978). She is now at work on a book on gender and class formation in nineteenth-century France.

WILLIAM H. SEWELL, JR., is Professor of History and Sociology at the University of Michigan. He is the author of *Work and Revolution in France: The Language of Labor from the Old Regime to 1848* (1980) and of *Structure and Mobility: The Men and Women of Marseille, 1820–1870* (1985). He is writing a history of the working class of nineteenth-century Marseilles and conducting research on the cultural history of the French Revolution.

EDWARD J. SHEPHARD, JR., is a Ph.D. candidate in French history at Johns Hopkins University. He is currently employed at the Glenn G. Bartle Library, State University of New York at Binghamton.

MICHAEL SONENSCHER teaches history at the Middlesex Polytechnic in London and is a member of the editorial board of *Social History*. He is currently working on a study of workshop organization, wage systems, and artisanal culture in eighteenth-century France.

CYNTHIA M. TRUANT is Visiting Assistant Professor of French Civilization at the University of California at Riverside. She has recently been awarded the Monticello College Foundation Fellowship by the Newberry Library to complete her manuscript on the journeymen's associations known as compagnonnage in the period from the mid-seventeenth to the mid-nineteenth centuries.

INDEX

Library of Congress Cataloging-in-Publication Data

Main entry under title:

Work in France.

Selection of essays first presented at Cornell University on 28–30 April 1983 as part of a conference entitled Representations of Work in France.

Includes index.

1. Labor and laboring classes—France—History—Congresses. 2. Work—History—Congresses. I. Kaplan, Steven L. II. Koepp, Cynthia J.

HD8428.W67   1986   331'.0944   85-22352

ISBN 0-8014-1697-3 (alk. paper)